CANINE COLORADO

THIRD EDITION

WHERE TO GO
AND WHAT TO DO
WITH YOUR DOG

Cindy Hirschfeld

FULCRUM
GOLDEN, COLORADO

To Clover:
May you always bark softly
and carry a big stick.

This publication is provided for informational and educational purposes. The information herein contained
is true and complete to the best of our knowledge.

Library of Congress Cataloging-in-Publication Data

Hirschfeld, Cindy.
 Canine Colorado : where to go and what to do with your dog / Cindy
Hirschfeld. -- 3rd ed.
  p. cm.
 Includes index.
 ISBN 978-1-55591-710-4 (pbk.)
 1. Travel with dogs--Colorado--Guidebooks. 2. Colorado--Guidebooks.
I. Title.
 SF427.4574.C6H56 2009
 917.8804'34--dc22

                    2009030657

Printed on Sustainable Forestry Initiative–approved paper in the United States of America by Malloy, Inc.
0 9 8 7 6 5 4 3 2 1

Cover and design by Jack Lenzo/Rudy Ramos
Cartography by Marge Mueller, Gray Mouse Graphics
Interior illustrations: © Shutterstock I dulebskii
Cover images (clockwise from top left): © Shutterstock I Maksym Gorpenyu, © Shutterstock, © Shutterstock
I Susan McKenzie, © Shutterstock I Denis Babenko

CATHY (p. 6) © Cathy Guisewite. Reprinted with permission of UNIVERSAL PRESS SYNDICATE. All
rights reserved.

Fulcrum Publishing
4690 Table Mountain Drive, Suite 100
Golden, Colorado 80403
(800) 992-2908 • (303) 277-1623
www.fulcrumbooks.com

Contents

Acknowledgments, iv

Introduction, 2

Denver Metro Area, 15
  1. Denver and Vicinity, 16
  2. Boulder and Vicinity, 79
  3. Central City, Clear Creek County, and Vicinity, 102

Northeast Colorado, 109
  4. Fort Collins and Vicinity, 110
  5. Greeley and Northeastern Plains, 125
  6. Estes Park, 133

Northwest Colorado, 147
  7. Winter Park, Grand Lake, and Granby, 148
  8. Steamboat Springs and North Park, 160
  9. Summit County, 171
 10. Vail, Leadville, and Vicinity, 183
 11. Aspen, 198
 12. Glenwood Springs and Vicinity, 210
 13. Northwestern Colorado, 222
 14. Grand Junction and Vicinity, 228

Southwest Colorado, 241
 15. Black Canyon Area, 242
 16. Gunnison, Crested Butte, and Lake City, 249
 17. Telluride, Ouray, and Silverton, 265
 18. Mesa Verde and Vicinity, 278
 19. Durango and Vicinity, 289

Southeast Colorado, 302
 20. San Luis Valley and Vicinity, 304
 21. Arkansas River Valley and Vicinity, 315
 22. Pueblo and Points Southeast, 330
 23. Colorado Springs and Vicinity, 342

Appendix A: Fourteener Dogs, 366
Appendix B: Gearhound, 368
Index, 374
About the Author, 380

Acknowledgments

This book was made a reality with the support and encouragement of so many people. A special thank-you goes to my husband, Todd Hartley, for pitching in with hours of phone calls during this third-edition update and for accompanying me on numerous research outings to hotels, hiking trails, and dog parks. Thank you to everyone at Fulcrum Publishing who helped shepherd this book through its various stages, especially editor Carolyn Sobczak, for so amiably sticking with me through many deadline extensions and for her careful copyediting. And, of course, thank you to Clover, my ever-faithful golden retriever, who is now 16; she's not only been with me in this endeavor every step of the way, but she's trained Tansy, our three-year-old mutt, in the ways of the world and the ways of dog research (though I still refer to Tansy as "the intern").

The scores of hotel owners, forest service rangers, national park representatives, Bureau of Land Management staffers, state park personnel, animal control officers, city park planners, and others with whom I spoke during the course of my research provided essential information.

A special acknowledgment to all the readers who gave me feedback on the first two editions, whether by letter or e-mail, or at one of the many book signings Clover and I did.

Of course, thanks go to the rest of my family, especially my mother, who continued to keep up Clover's and Tansy's energy level during research with home-baked dog biscuits. And finally, thanks to my cat, Blue, who is beyond sick of all this dog stuff, for accepting the fact that there will still be no *Feline Colorado*.

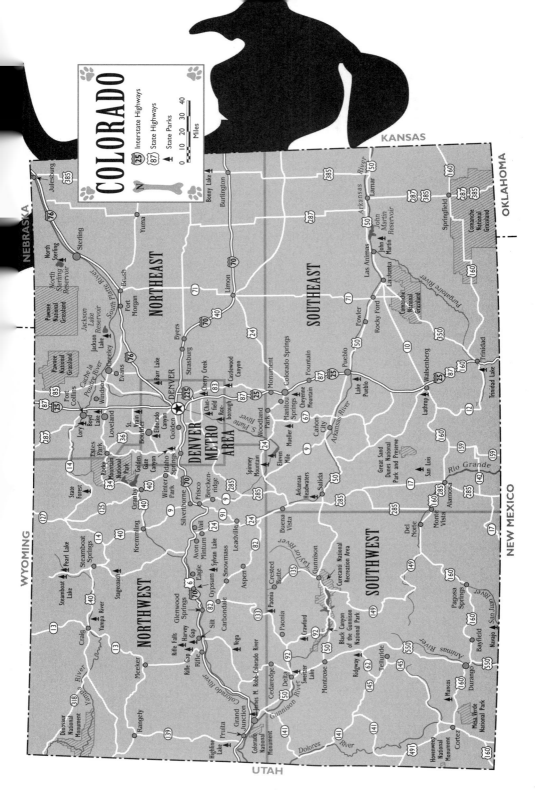

COLORADO

Interstate Highways 75

State Highways 87

State Parks ▲

Miles
0 10 20 30 40

N

KANSAS

NEBRASKA

WYOMING

UTAH

NEW MEXICO

OKLAHOMA

NORTHEAST

SOUTHEAST

NORTHWEST

SOUTHWEST

DENVER METRO AREA

# Introduction

A 2004 survey by the American Animal Hospital Association (AAHA) shows that 67 percent of dog owners in the United States and Canada have brought along their pets when they travel. This proves something that you and I have known for a long time: Dogs are part of the family—if not your primary family—and vacations can be a lot more fun when shared with a furry, four-legged companion. Traveling with Rover in tow, however, requires a bit of prep work because, believe it or not, not everyone loves our dogs as much as we do! To this end, my faithful research assistants, Clover and Tansy, and I have scoured the state searching out dog-friendly activities and accommodations. We hope the results of our research will help you and your dog discover that Colorado is a great place for canines!

In this introduction, you'll find some of the headings that are used throughout the book, with explanations of what each section contains, the criteria for selection, and other tips that will help you and your dog make informed travel decisions.

The information in this book is accurate as of summer 2009. *Please keep in mind that policies, prices, or regulations are always subject to change. Just because you read it here doesn't mean a detail is set in stone. It's best to call ahead, especially for lodging, to confirm that Rover is indeed still welcome.* Traveling with a dog can be like traveling with kids: the keys to success are to be flexible and have some alternate plans to fall back on, if necessary.

The maps in this book are for general reference purposes only. You'll need to consult a topographic map for specifics on the trails described herein.

THE MUCH-MALIGNED DOG

Allow me to mount my soapbox for a minute in defense of dogs. During the course of researching this book, I encountered many people who visibly flinched at the mere mention of the word *dog*. People like these don't want dogs to be able to hike on trails, stay at hotels, or participate

Don't let your dog do the driving.

in a whole range of day-to-day activities with their owners. As a result of such attitudes, dogs have acquired a strange status: not quite human, not quite animal. They're not allowed in most public places because they're, well, dogs, yet many people believe dogs should be restricted in the natural world as well. One woman at a forest service office, who will remain unidentified, patiently explained to me that dogs must be kept leashed in designated wilderness areas so that they won't harass wildlife. As she spoke, my eyes were drawn to a hunting guide prominently displayed on the counter. I mentioned that it seemed ironic that hunting is allowed in these areas, yet dogs are required to be restrained; the woman responded with a blank look. "Well," she finally said, "all those animals would just starve to death otherwise." Oh.

I firmly believe that dogs—and humans, too—are a part of nature, not apart from it. We should all do our best to reasonably minimize our impact. Yet dogs have the same right to be outside, to run in the grass, to follow a scent, to play in the snow as any other animal. Those who would scowl at a dog are missing out on one of life's greatest opportunities to share and to bond with another living creature.

Okay, it's time to dismount and get on with the nitty-gritty.

TAIL-RATED TRAILS

Clover, Tansy, and I have "sacrificed" many hours to hike most of the trails (and visit most of the dog parks) described in this book and determine their dog suitability. We considered several factors that seem to make a trail particularly enjoyable for dogs: whether or not they can be off leash, if water is readily available for a drink or for swimming, and if other dogs (and their owners) frequent the trail. For your sake, I've also taken the scenic component into account.

Four tail wags

Drooping tail

Trails are rated on a scale of one to four tail wags, with four signifying the hikes that were our favorites. Also included are trails or areas where dogs are not allowed—indicated by a drooping-tail symbol—so you'll know ahead of time to leave your dog at home. Naturally there are many more dog-suitable trails than I've been able to describe in this book. When making the final selection, I deferred to my faithful companions. Consider our recommendations either a jumping-off point or a foolproof list if you have limited time to spend in an area.

Land-Use Policies

Following are general guidelines for the different types of land you may encounter on your excursions. For more specifics, refer to the descriptions of the individual trails and parks in each chapter.

National Parks and Monuments

First, the bad news: in general, dogs are not allowed on any of the trails in Colorado's national parks and monuments. And you cannot leave your dog unattended anywhere, be it at a campsite, at a trailhead, or in your car. The good news is that they're not banned entirely. As long as you keep your dog on a leash no longer than six feet, you can bring him (or her) to the campgrounds and picnic areas. And you can take a walk with your leashed dog on closed roads (i.e., during the winter, when they're not plowed), though your dog must not venture more than 100 feet from the roadside or parking area. So if you're planning to center your trip on hiking or backpacking in a national park or monument, Rover will need to stay home.

Tansy slacks off from work with a sneaker.

As with most rules, however, a few exceptions exist. Leashed dogs are allowed to hike in parts of the Great Sand Dunes National Park and Preserve near Alamosa, and they're permitted on a few short trails in the Black Canyon of the Gunnison National Park. You can also bring your dog to visit Bent's Old Fort in eastern Colorado and Hovenweep National Monument, which straddles the Colorado-Utah border. And, finally, dogs are allowed on the trails at Curecanti National Recreation Area, which is

TRAVEL TIPS

• In March 2000, Congress approved regulations that require airlines to disclose how many animals were killed or injured on flights. In response, many airlines changed their pet-travel policies. Continental, for example, no longer allows dogs to travel as checked baggage. Small dogs can still travel in the cabin; otherwise, you'll have to send Fido separately through the airline's PetSafe cargo service. Southwest permits small dogs (and cats) in the cabin only. Frontier, on the other hand, only allows dogs as checked baggage and not in the cabin. From May 15 to September 15, Delta will only transport pets as cargo; the rest of the year they can travel as checked baggage. Other airlines will allow dogs to travel in plane cargo holds only within certain outside temperature ranges.

If Fido does get the go-ahead to travel in the baggage compartment, he'll have to ride in an airline-approved cage, labeled Live Animal. Feed and water him within four hours of the flight's departure. Provide a dish of fresh water in his cage; consider freezing the water first so it won't spill during transport but will melt in time for a midflight drink. Ten days or less before your flight, bring Rover to his vet to undergo an exam and get a current health certificate and proof of rabies

vaccination, which you'll often need to present at the airport. Tranquilizing your dog before travel is controversial. Many animal experts advise against it—dogs who have a bad reaction to sedatives or who receive too large a dose can die. If you have a particularly hyperactive dog, talk to your vet about alternatives to sedation. Your airline may have additional requirements, which you should inquire about when making your reservation.

• When traveling by car, avoid feeding your dog for at least three hours before you leave to help prevent carsickness.

• Make sure your dog's vaccinations are up-to-date. Bring along copies of his rabies certificate and proof of other vaccinations in case you need to day-board him while traveling.

• Be sure to have your cell-phone number on your dog's tag so that if you and he become separated while on the road, the person who (hopefully) finds him will be able to actually get in touch with you rather than just your voicemail. PetSmart stores offer a nifty option for IDing your pet: in-store machines that produce customized tags in just a few minutes.

managed by the National Park Service, outside Gunnison.

An entry fee is required at all national parks and monuments.

National Forest and National Forest Wilderness Areas

Here's a "secret": dogs are not required to be leashed on most national forest land unless it is a designated wilderness area (though the forest service often advises that they be on a leash). I call this a secret because, unfortunately, many of the forest service employees with whom I spoke are not familiar with their own agency's policy. If you ask about dogs on trails at a ranger district office, chances are the person behind the desk will insist that dogs have to be leashed everywhere. In actuality, leash laws apply only in the following situations: (1) you are in what's considered a "developed recreation site," such as a campground or picnic area; or (2) the forest service supervisor in a particular district has issued an order specifying that dogs be leashed on a particular trail (some of the more heavily used trails have leash regulations and should be signed as such at the trailhead).

Dogs are required to be leashed, however, within most designated wilderness areas. You and your dog will know you're entering a wilderness area from signs either at the trailhead or on the trail if a wilderness boundary lies along your route. (Note that mountain bikes are not allowed in designated wilderness areas.) Wilderness boundaries are also clearly indicated on topographic maps. And a handful of wilderness areas in Colorado actually don't have a leash requirement (another little-known fact). Refer to individual chapters for more information.

State Parks

In general, you must keep your dog on a leash no longer than six feet in all state parks. The exceptions are the couple of state parks that have off-leash dog areas: Cherry Creek and Chatfield. And some parks don't allow any dogs whatsoever: Roxborough, Harvey Gap, Cheyenne Mountain, and Mueller (dogs can stay at Mueller's and Cheyenne Mountain's campgrounds). Keep in mind that dogs are not permitted in any swim or water-ski beach areas in any of the state parks.

An entry fee is required at all state parks. If you're a frequent visitor, you'll save a bundle by getting a season pass, which is good at all of the parks.

Bureau of Land Management (BLM) Land

The BLM, more than any land overseer in Colorado, has the most liberal policies regarding dogs. Dogs are not required to be leashed anywhere on BLM land, even in wilderness study areas. Of course, much BLM land is undeveloped, meaning there aren't nearly as many trails as on national forest land. The flipside is, because these areas can be remote, you're less likely to encounter other people who may be bothered by your dog.

Hunting Season

When fall comes, so comes hunting season in Colorado. And that means that from about mid-September to the beginning of November, you should take extra care when hiking with your dog in national forest (including wilderness) areas. This

Tansy joined Clover on the Canine Colorado *team as an intern in April 2006.*

is definitely not the time to let your dog run around wearing those fake antlers you bought him last Christmas. One of my friends went to her local Walmart and bought a bright orange hunting vest—for her dog to wear. Ruffwear offers the Track Jacket, a water-resistant safety vest made of fluorescent orange nylon with reflective trim (see the Gearhound appendix for contact information). You can take a precaution as simple as tying bright orange tape to your dog's collar. The point is to avoid having your dog wind up like Tripod, a dog we met near Aspen who had been shot in the leg by a hunter's errant bullet. For information about specific hunting seasons, contact the Colorado Division of Wildlife office in Denver at 303-297-1192 or go to www.wildlife.state.co.us.

TRAIL ETIQUETTE
The Leash

I'm lucky in that Clover is well behaved on trails (Tansy, meanwhile, is still learning): she doesn't stray, she doesn't chase deer or elk, she waits for me to catch up if she gets too far ahead, and she goes off the trail to poop. Nevertheless, I always carry her leash, just in case. If your dog can be an unruly hiker, keep him leashed on heavily used trails; your outing will be more pleasant without the glares of other hikers. And if your dog is a wildlife chaser, definitely keep his leash at the ready. According to Colorado state law, dogs can be shot for harassing livestock or wildlife. Some people claim that you can never control a dog in time to keep him from taking off after a deer. I disagree, simply because I've seen otherwise. If you pay attention to your dog and your surroundings, you can nab him and put him on his leash before he dashes. But you know your dog the best. If you feel you can't control him or don't want to stay on the alert during a hike, keep him leashed.

Ask Before He Sniffs

You and your dog will win many friends if you train him not to approach other people or dogs uninvited. When your off-leash dog encounters an on-leash dog, communication is especially important. That dog may be leashed for reasons other than simple owner control: he may be sick, skittish around other dogs, or even downright unfriendly.

The Clean-up Routine

Those plastic bags that your newspaper comes in serve double duty as handy pooper scoopers. Many forward-thinking towns also provide dispensers of pet-pick-up baggies, or receptacles for donated plastic bags, at popular parks and trailheads.

If you're on a trail in a national forest or other more remote location, I think it's perfectly acceptable to train your dog to poop off trail; or you can fling the poop

off the trail into the woods with a stick. After all, no one's cleaning up after all those other animals that use the outdoors as their restroom!

CYCLING FOR CANINES

As an added activity bonus, we have scoped out places where your dog and your mountain bike can travel in tandem. For the fit dog, nothing beats a run beside one's pedaling owner for exercise efficiency. But—and this is an important but—you must approach biking with your dog differently than a solo ride. This should be a shared activity; if you're a hardcore rider, for example, don't expect your dog to keep up while you try to ride faster than your friends—the results could be fatal! And cycling with your dog is not the time to engage in screaming descents; in fact, you should stop often, allowing your dog plenty of time to catch up with you and to rest. The bottom line is that your dog, not you, should dictate the pace of the ride. If your primary purpose in riding is to get an intense cardiovascular workout, leave Fido at home.

Your dog should be in good condition before you ask him to keep up with you when you're biking. (Though if you're on a very technical trail, he may well outrun you!) You are the best judge of your dog's physical fitness; if he gets regular exercise and is generally healthy, he's probably able to accompany you on a short bike ride. The fact that you're reading this book is a good sign that you keep your dog fairly active. Just remember that your dog can't tell you that he's too tired to keep running. Make sure that he will have access to water and bring extra for rides in dry areas. And save those 30-mile cycles for a time when your dog is at home resting.

The rides listed range from easy to moderately technical in terms of terrain and are generally under 10 round-trip miles in length (keep the distance under 10 miles for the few rides described that have slightly higher mileage). I've only included areas where dogs can safely be off leash. Unfortunately, this leaves out a lot of good biking terrain. If you've figured out how to ride on singletrack or otherwise technical trails with your dog on a leash, more power to you! None of the rides involve traveling on paved roads, even for a short segment. Traffic and dogs just don't mix. And, as a final caveat, I've steered away from some of the more heavily trafficked biking trails, popular as they may be, because I know you'd hate to have your pooch mowed down by one too many kamikaze cyclists.

POWDERHOUNDS

Most dogs I know love the snow, so what better way to enjoy the winter together than to take your dog along skiing or snowshoeing? Most chapters include a few suggestions on where you can do this. Plowing through snow when you have four legs and are only a foot or so off the ground takes a lot of effort and can even result in injury. Trails or roads that have been packed down by other skiers or snowshoers are the most canine friendly. If Rover is lagging behind or is otherwise obviously tired, shorten your outing so he'll still be able to accompany you on the next one. It's also a good idea to invest in some booties to protect your dog's paws from painful snow and ice buildup; dogs with webbed feet are especially prone to this. See the Gearhound appendix for more information.

As this book is by no means intended to be a backcountry ski guide, I've only included trails that have minimal avalanche danger and are fairly straightforward. In addition, you'll see that several Nordic ski areas have some trails set aside for dogs and their owners, ideal for the type of short ski outings that will keep your dog healthy and happy.

CREATURE COMFORTS

Before I began researching accommodations that accept dogs, I envisioned quaint bed-and-breakfasts (B&Bs) that would welcome canine guests with open arms, presenting them with freshly baked dog biscuits and perhaps even a resident play companion. Clover and I would spend the day frolicking in a beautiful mountainside setting and then return to a charmingly furnished room. Well, I quickly discovered that such was not the case. Many hotels, motels, and, alas, B&Bs in Colorado want nothing to do with four-legged visitors. (Some proprietors, however, admitted regret at not being able to put out the canine welcome mat; said one innkeeper, "If it makes you feel any better, we don't accept children, either!") Diligent research, however, turned up many places that do accept pets, with a broad range of prices and lodging styles from rustic to ultraluxurious. You may be pleasantly surprised at how many accommodations will welcome you and your dog.

Unfortunately, some accommodations have changed their pet policy, and dogs are no longer welcome. Even more unfortunately, this is due in large part to inconsiderate owners who allowed their canines to wreak havoc. Just a couple of bad experiences can be enough to persuade a lodging owner that accepting pets is not worth the potential hassle. *I cannot emphasize enough how important it is to ensure that your dog is well mannered before you allow him to be a travel companion.*

The good news is that there are more places than ever where you can stay with your dog, including many of Colorado's nicest hotels. In addition, most places that used to restrict dogs and their owners to smoking rooms have broadened their policy to include a choice of nonsmoking rooms, too (or, in some cases, the entire property has become nonsmoking). I certainly appreciate the recognition that smokers and dog owners are hardly one and the same.

I've included any and every place I could track down that accepts pets. (By the way, tourism brochures, while helpful, were by no means always accurate or comprehensive.) This means not every accommodation listed is a place you, let alone your dog, would choose to spend the night. But sometimes the need to find somewhere to stay (especially one that's within your budget) outranks preference. A few places will accept pets on a case-by-case basis, depending on who else is staying there, the dog's temperament, and so on, but they didn't want to be listed in this book. If you have your heart set on a particular hotel, it doesn't hurt to ask if they'll take your dog, too.

Here's a brief rundown of what you can expect to find in the lodging listings:

Exceptionally dog friendly

Some lodgings don't merely allow dogs, they actively welcome them, through attitude and with treats at check-in and perhaps the use of a bed and/or food and water bowls during their stay. These are also good places to choose because they're used to accommodating dogs and often have more liberal policies than other hotels; your furry traveler will often find like company at these places, too.

Price symbols: Because rates are often in flux, I've devised a simple scale to guide your expectations rather than give specific prices. Rates are based on a standard room for two people per night, unless otherwise indicated:

$ = up to $49
$$ = $50–$99
$$$ = $100–$149
$$$$ = $150 and up

You'll notice that many lodgings straddle price categories.

Name, address, phone number, website: Many of the toll-free phone numbers listed for chain hotels and motels go to a national reservations center. Although you can find out rates and room availability through these centers, contact the individual lodging directly to notify the management that you'll be bringing your dog and to confirm the pet policy.

Brief description: For places other than chain accommodations or standard motels, I've provided a summary of the lodging setup and amenities.

Dog policy: A frequent response to the question "Do you allow dogs?" was, "Yes, if they're well behaved and housebroken." Because it should almost go without saying that you should not impose your dog on any hotel, motel, or other accommodation if he doesn't match that description, I didn't mention it repeatedly in every lodging write-up. But I'll say it here: *Please, for the sake of the rest of our dogs, leave your dog at home until you've trained him to be a courteous guest. I have heard earfuls of stories from disillusioned lodging owners who used to allow pets but stopped doing so because they had too many bad experiences.*

When inquiring about dog policy, I asked if a fee or deposit is required; about any guidelines that dictate the size, type, or number of dogs in a room; and whether a dog can be left unattended in the room. As you'll notice, the answers varied among lodging providers. I've noted which places request a fee or deposit, and how much; if a listing doesn't include either, you can assume your pet is gratis, though it's always a good idea to double-check. As for deposits, the most common way to put one down is with a credit-card imprint; you won't actually be charged unless Fido does damage. Some places will put up you and your dog in a smoking room only—good news if your dog is a smoker (though personally I don't think that dog breath is anywhere near as foul-smelling as stale smoke!). Some managers I spoke with were adamant that guests not leave their dogs unattended in the rooms, while others didn't have a problem with it as long as the housekeeping staff is notified—presumably so that a housekeeper won't be licked to death while trying to change your sheets! If a listing has no specific information on dog policy, it means that no fee or deposit is charged, you and your dog can stay in any room, and you cannot leave your dog unattended inside.

Some experts advise against leaving a dog unattended in a hotel room. If your lodging choice allows this, I feel it's a useful option to have as long as you're confident that your dog can stay on his best behavior. Although I don't recommend leaving Fido for more than a couple of hours, it's a far better alternative than leaving him in a car in warm weather if you're headed into "absolutely no dogs" territory (e.g., a restaurant). Of the lodging operators who permit this, many rationalized that a dog's owner is the one who will best know if the dog can be left alone. All emphasized that dogs on their own must be quiet and nondestructive. Many of the places that allow you to leave Rover unattended require that he be in a travel kennel—an item you might consider bringing along just for that purpose. If you're staying at a place where your dog cannot be left unattended, please don't jeopardize the pet policy for the rest of us by ignoring the rules.

Following each chapter's listing of accommodations is a selection of nearby campgrounds, in case your dog decides he'd rather "ruff" it for the night.

WORTH A PAWS

This is a catch-all category. I've included out-of-the-ordinary dog activities, ranging from benefit events in which you can participate with your four-legged friend to Frisbee competitions and self-service dog washes. Not only are these diversions fun for the pooch (well, except for the dog washes, maybe), they allow you to mingle with other dog owners who may be just as nuts about their canines as you are about yours.

CLOVER AND TANSY'S PACKING LIST

dog-specific travel bag	
portable food and water bowls	Optional: dog bed or blanket
leashes	medication
dog food/biscuits	booties (in winter)
pick-up baggies	doggie backpack
towels	(for backpacking)
brush	travel kennel or
toys/tennis balls	crate

DOGGIE DAYCARE

Despite your best intentions, you may want to do or attend something while traveling that your dog just can't join in on (e.g., a day at a national park, a hike up a challenging fourteener, or that fancy-dress family reunion party). Although I don't think road-tripping with your canine friend should entail stashing him in a kennel on a regular basis (after all, you could have just left the dog at home), it's handy to know there are places that will welcome your dog for a day or even for just a few hours. Most daycare providers require reservations a few days in advance, as well as proof that your dog is up-to-date with his vaccinations, including rabies, distemper, and bordatella (kennel cough). Some require

initial screening visits or interviews, too, so would be most suitable if you're looking for longer-term daycare. Moreover, if your dog is not a Colorado resident, he's technically supposed to have a health certificate from his hometown veterinarian in order to cross state lines. While only a few of the kennels included here actually require this, it wouldn't hurt to procure a certificate before leaving home if you think you might need to board Rover.

PET PROVISIONS

You've run out of Wellness halfway through your trip, and your dog only turns up his nose at supermarket dog food. I've included selected lists of where to restock. Note that for ethical reasons, I've tried to avoid listing pet stores that market puppies and kittens along with supplies. If you're far from the nearest pet emporium, remember that most vets and many dog daycare facilities also carry specialty dog foods and other supplies. Look under Doggie Daycare and Canine ER for locations of the nearest kennels and veterinarians in each region.

CANINE ER

One of the worst potential travel scenarios for your dog would be to get sick or injured while on the road, far from your friendly hometown vet. The veterinarians and clinics listed throughout the book offer either 24-hour or on-call emergency service. I used a few methods to narrow down the listing of veterinarians within each area. If a region has veterinary clinics that are open 24 hours a day—generally in cities such as Boulder, Denver, Colorado Springs, and Fort Collins—I've listed only these clinics, since they'll be able to serve all your dog's needs at any time. In areas that have no 24-hour clinics but still offer a wide range of veterinary services, I honed the list to include just those veterinary hospitals that are certified by the American

FIRST AID FOR FIDO

Can my dog be affected by the altitude?
Dogs who already have some sort of heart or respiratory illness at sea level may have trouble at higher altitude. But, in general, healthy, active dogs should have no problems. Chances are good that if you're doing okay at a higher altitude, your dog definitely is.

Will my dog get giardia from drinking out of streams?
Just like humans, dogs can get giardia, a single-cell parasite that often causes cramps and diarrhea, from drinking untreated water. Many dogs who have been exposed to it, however, never show any symptoms. Or your dog might get the runs for just a few days. Bottom line: when you're out hiking with your dog, it's going to be difficult to prevent him from slurping out of streams. And he'll probably be fine. If you prefer to take precautions, ask your vet about a giardia vaccine. Of course, if your dog has persistent diarrhea or other gastrointestinal problems, bring him to a vet to be treated with antibiotics.

Can my dog get dehydrated?
Yes! Remember that your dog is probably working harder than you during most physical activities. Dogs seem to cover about twice the mileage of their owners, running back and forth on the trail. And they have those fur coats to deal with. Sticky gums are a sign of dehydration. Make sure that your dog always has an ample water supply, whether you're carrying it (along with something he can drink out of) or from streams or ponds in the area you'll be hiking, running, or biking through.

What should I do if my dog gets heatstroke?
Difficulty breathing or rapid breathing, vomiting, high body temperature, or out-and-out collapse are all signs of heatstroke. Submerge your dog briefly in cool (not ice) water. Keep him wet and cool—wrap him in a wet towel if you have one—and encourage but don't force him to drink water. Follow up immediately with a visit to the vet.

What should I do if my dog gets hypothermia?
Low body temperature, a decreased breathing rate, and shivering are all signs of excessive chilling or hypothermia. Move your dog to a sheltered area or, ideally, inside, and wrap him up in a sleeping bag or multiple blankets. Gently rub him to help rewarming. Never put an electric heating pad against your dog—it can easily burn him.

What should I do if my dog is bitten by a snake?
Restrain and calm him so that the venom won't spread further. Apply a flat tourniquet if he's been bitten on the leg. Encourage the wound to bleed and wash the bite area with soap and water. Apply a cold compress, if possible. Take Fido to the vet ASAP.

For more information on helping your dog if he's injured, refer to *First Aid for Dogs: What to Do When Emergencies Happen*, by Bruce Fogle, DVM.; *Field Guide: First Aid Emergency Care for the Hunting, Working, and Outdoor Dog*, by Randy Acker, DVM.; or *Dog First Aid*, put out by the American National Red Cross.

Animal Hospital Association; you'll see *AAHA certified* in parentheses after the hospital's name. The AAHA has stringent standards that a hospital must meet in order to be certified, including complete diagnostic and pharmacy facilities, sanitary conditions, proper anesthetic procedures, modern surgical facilities, nursing care, dental service, medical records for each patient, and emergency service. Although my method of selection undoubtedly omits many caring and qualified veterinarians, relying on the AAHA certification allowed me to point your pet in the right direction without actually evaluating each vet. And, finally, in areas that have neither 24-hour clinics nor AAHA-certified hospitals, I've listed all the veterinarians that provide on-call emergency service. Hopefully you and your dog will never need to use any of this information.

RESOURCES

Here you'll find addresses and phone numbers of tourist information centers, chambers of commerce, and land-use agencies that can provide additional information for your travels.

WHY YOU WON'T FIND PLACES TO EAT WITH YOUR DOG IN THIS BOOK

It's often nicer to have your best friend at your feet during mealtime than stashed in a room or a car (assuming, of course, that Rover is not up for membership in Beggers Anonymous). Unfortunately, Colorado law prohibits dogs from being in any area where food is served, even if it's an outdoor patio. Of course, this doesn't mean that you won't see dogs and their owners enjoying a bite to eat together at outside dining venues. But I didn't want to get any of these accommodating restaurants in trouble by letting the dog out of the bag, so to speak. Your best bet is to scope out places that offer dining alfresco and then ask if Rover can join you.

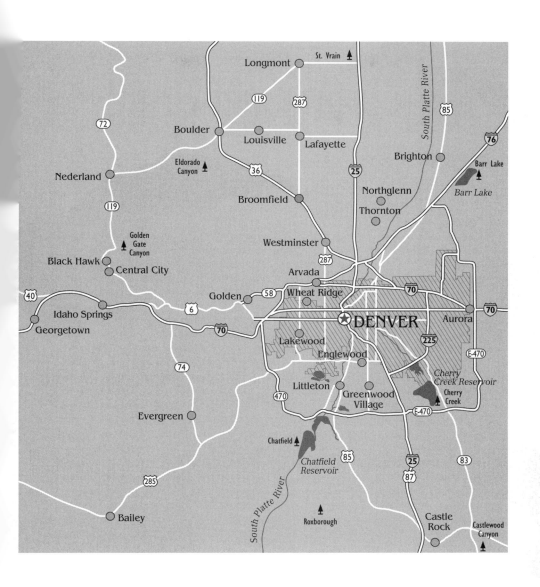

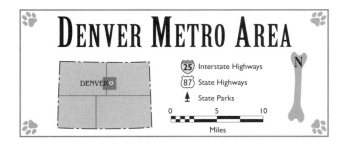

One
Denver and Vicinity

THE BIG SCOOP

For a city, Denver's a pretty good place in which to be a dog. Lots of hotels and motels welcome four-legged travelers, and there's plenty to do out of doors. The mile-long 16th Street pedestrian mall in the heart of Denver's downtown is the perfect place for the urban dog to catch up on his people watching. Chic dogs will want to stroll with their owners through Cherry Creek, the city's toniest shopping district. Or they might want to visit trendy LoDo, which includes Coors Field; though normally not allowed inside the baseball stadium, dogs can gaze longingly at the exterior and imagine all the balls that could be chased down inside.

Within the City and County of Denver, as well as in surrounding towns in the Denver metro area, dogs must be leashed when not on private property. Resident dogs must be neutered/spayed and vaccinated annually against rabies once they're six months old, and dogs are required to wear a city license tag within thirty days of moving to the city (Denver Animal Control, 303-698-0076, www.denvergov.org). Moreover, if your Fifi happens to be a pit bull, her options in Denver, both city and county, are very limited: she can ride through in a car but can't legally go outside for so much as a pee break. And taking up residency in the Mile High City is verboten. Jefferson, Adams, and Douglas Counties (west of Denver, northeast of Denver, and south of Denver, respectively) have leash laws as well. Dogs may be walked under voice command, however, in the unincorporated parts of Arapahoe County (including the City of Centennial).

TAIL-RATED TRAILS

As might be expected in a city that is home to an active population, it's not difficult to find a great selection of easily accessible hiking trails near Denver. You and your dog will have to travel to the outskirts of the city and beyond to reach many of the trails that will allow you to enjoy a less-developed hiking experience. Denver and its surrounding communities, however, have an extensive network of paved bike paths and trails, often known as greenways or greenbelts, that your dog will enjoy exploring. Some extend for several miles, others for just a few blocks.

You'll find some of the best hiking opportunities in the Jefferson County Open Space parks, many of which are described in this section. Not all of these parks, however, are necessarily suitable for dog hikes, due to heavy mountain-bike use. If you don't want to worry about Fido and his leash having a too-close encounter with spokes (or don't want to put up with the exasperated looks of riders who think you didn't get out of their way quickly enough), take your dog somewhere other than White Ranch (north of Golden), Apex (on Golden's western side), and Matthews Winters (next to Red Rocks) parks. Of course, when the trails are snowy or especially muddy, you and your dog will encounter relative solitude in these latter parks—just make sure to bring a large towel for after-hiking paw and leg cleanup. Several parks also have some hiker-only trails, including all of Mount Galbraith Park (note that dogs are *not* allowed, however, on the two hiker-only trails at the Lookout Mountain Nature Center and Preserve).

A more recent, and particularly welcome, addition, to the Denver dog scene is off-leash dog parks. The City of Denver oversees six dog parks, and more off-leash areas are being proposed as part of a master plan. And a group billing themselves as the Railyard Dogs has been working for several years to build a state-of-the-art dog park in downtown Denver at 19th and Basset Sts., in the Riverfront Park neighborhood development (to learn more or make a donation, go to www.railyarddogs.typepad.com). Many other communities in the metro Denver area have also built dog parks; see the listings in this section for specifics. Refer to the chapters on Boulder, Fort Collins, and Colorado Springs for details on other Front Range dog parks.

For more information on hiking trails west of Denver, refer to *Foothills to Mount Evans: West-of-Denver Trail Guide, Seventh Edition*, by Linda McComb Rathbun and Linda Wells Ringrose. For information on other trails in the Denver area, look at the 12 Short Hikes series, by Tracy Salcedo (two volumes cover the Denver foothills). The Pike National Forest southwest of Denver, including the Lost Creek Wilderness Area, has an extensive trail system. The South Platte Ranger District (see Resources) provides informative, detailed written descriptions of a wide range of hikes in this area.

Denver

There are more than 200 city-maintained parks throughout Denver. Four of the most popular are described here, as well as six off-leash dog areas, but there are plenty more for your dog to explore. To download a map or find more information on a particular park, go to www.denvergov.org/parks.

Denver Dog Parks

Regulations: All dogs must have rabies tags and, for Denver residents, a local dog license; dogs must be spayed/neutered or, if a Denver resident, have a Denver intact permit; no pit bulls, aggressive dogs, females in heat, or sick dogs; owners must supervise their dogs and pick up after them; dogs must be supervised by someone 18 or older; children ages 12 to 17 must be accompanied by an adult; no children under 12 in the park; human food is not allowed.

Dogs can be off leash.

One of the most popular of the off-leash dog areas is in the northwest corner of **Berkeley Lake Park** (from Sheridan Blvd., immediately south of I-70, turn east at the traffic light onto 46th St.; the park entrance and parking lot are just ahead on the left). When we visited it on a sunny Friday afternoon, there were big dogs, little dogs, Labs, poodles, border collies, mutts—all having a great time running around the park's 2 fenced acres. The dog looking for a peaceful getaway won't find it here; highway noise is a constant background. And the large roller coaster across the street at Lakeside Amusement Park is a reminder that lots of people, too, play in this area. There's no access to Berkeley Lake from the dog park, but when you exit the park you can walk over to the almost mile-long paved path that encircles the lake for a pre– or post–dog park stroll. Bring your own water.

The **Barnum Dog Park** is adjacent to Hwy. 6, but it's much nicer than you might expect for a park right off a major roadway. Drive over Hwy. 6 on Knox St., then turn left (east) onto 5th Ave.; go for two blocks to a cul-de-sac at the park's edge, where there are parking spots. A chain-link fence sections off the park from the highway; the rest of it is unfenced (though sections of split-rail fence mark the boundaries). Dogs have a nice, grassy expanse of 3 acres to romp on, with mature shade trees around the perimeter. There aren't any benches or picnic tables, but the grass was nice enough when we visited that, if it's held up, you could put out a blanket in the park when it's not crowded. Barnum Lake is at the bottom of a hillside that falls away from the dog park, but it's not accessible for canine paddling. There's no water here.

Fuller Dog Park, at the intersection of Franklin and E. 29th St., next to Manual High School, is the most urban of the dog parks. The 1-acre fenced area has a packed-dirt surface, and there's no water on-site. When Rover wants a break, he can amuse himself by watching a pick-up game of hoops on the adjacent basketball court.

The 3-acre **Kennedy Dog Park** is in the Kennedy Soccer Complex (from Hampden Ave., east of I-25, turn south on Dayton St., then turn left at the sign for the soccer complex; parking is just ahead). The unfenced dog area has a dirt surface and, as a backdrop, Cherry Creek Dam looming in the distance. The dog park's boundaries are defined by short segments of split-rail fence at the corners. There's one bench for owners. Bring water.

Stapleton Dog Park is part of Greenway Park at the former Stapleton Airport site, which has been completely redeveloped into what could be a town of its own. Take Quebec south from I-70 to MLK Jr. Blvd. and turn left. Turn right on Syracuse and drive south to 24th St., where you'll turn left. Park at the end of the block on the right, on the street. This 3-acre dog park—it has three entrances—has proven so popular that part of it was partitioned off for reseeding when we visited. Since then, the surface has been changed to a more durable mix of sand and soil. Three (nonfunctioning) fire hydrants immediately attract canine leg-lifters, and picnic tables and funky shaded benches give owners ample opportunities to socialize, too. While the pooches are running

around, they can also have fun running up and down several grassy, man-made mounds in the park—the landscape design was inspired by the idea of a bouncing ball. Three water fountains for dogs and people keep everyone hydrated.

If you and your dog are touring the housing developments near Denver International Airport, the **Green Valley Ranch East Dog Park** would be worth a stop. From Tower Rd., take 48th Ave. 1.2 miles east to Jebel St. Make a right on Jebel; parking is just ahead on the right. The park was redesigned in 2009 and now features 1.5 fenced acres (the former park was unfenced). Inside the park, several benches under a shade structure and a water fountain were added.

Washington Park

Access: The park is bordered by Virginia Ave., Franklin St., Louisiana Ave., and Downing St.

Dogs must be leashed.

Denver dogs in the know come to Wash Park to participate in one of the city's best canine social scenes. The 154-acre park is also one of Denver's largest, with two small lakes, colorful flower gardens (one a duplicate of George Washington's gardens at Mount Vernon), an indoor recreation center, playground, lawn-bowling court, soccer field, and lighted tennis courts. You and your dog have several strolling options: a 2.35-mile crushed-gravel trail goes around the park's outer edges, while a paved inner trail makes two loops within the park, each about 1 mile in length.

Commons Park

Access: The park is at the intersection of 15th and Little Raven Sts.

Dogs must be leashed.

Another active canine social scene takes place at Commons Park, a 19-acre expanse of green bordering the South Platte River that's a poster child for new urbanism, adjacent to recently built lofts and apartments, hip stores, coffee shops, and a huge REI store down the street. This spot is also considered the birthplace of Denver—gold was discovered in the vicinity in 1858. Confluence Park, where the South Platte and Cherry Creek meet, is just across 15th St., and the Riverfront Park neighborhood, with its distinctive, shiplike Millennium Bridge, is on the other side of Little Raven. Dogs will likely be most interested in sniffing out the paved Platte River Trail, which runs in paw-dipping range of the river. And if the need for a canine shopping break arises, stores like Colorado Petfitters and Zen Dog are nearby.

Cheesman Park

Access: Close to Capitol Hill, the park is between 13th and 8th Aves., Humboldt and Race Sts.

Dogs must be leashed.

At 82 acres, Cheesman Park is a pleasant oasis, with gardens, a pavilion, and a view west to the mountains. Make sure your dog takes time to sniff the flowers here, as he's not permitted in the adjoining Denver Botanic Gardens. Two main walkways wind around the park: a gravel-surfaced one that's 1.6 miles long, and a paved one at 1.4 miles.

City Park

Access: The park is located north of 17th Ave., between York St. and Colorado Blvd.

Dogs must be leashed.

Denver's largest park, at 314 acres, City Park is also the site of the Denver Museum of Nature & Science, the Denver Zoo, and a public golf course. Dogs will have to content themselves with a saunter around the park's two lakes and its gardens. A .84-mile paved trail encircles City Park Lake, and a 3-mile natural surface trail tours the park's perimeter. You'll also find playing fields, a band shell, playgrounds, picnicking spots, and lighted tennis courts on park grounds.

North of Denver

Westminster Dog Parks

Regulations: Dogs who are residents of Westminster must be licensed; all dogs must be vaccinated and spayed/neutered; dogs who are aggressive, sick, in heat, too young to get a rabies vaccine, or not under voice command are not allowed; dogs can't chase or harass wildlife or other dogs; owners must be with their dogs, have a leash for each one, and pick up after them; owners must assume all legal responsibility for their dogs' actions.

Dogs can be off leash.

Much more than your typical dog park, the 420 acres known simply as the **Westminster Hills Dog Park** includes huge swaths of meadow where dogs can run until they're tuckered out and connects to a couple of hiking trails in the Westminster Hills (formerly known as Colorado Hills) Open Space, where dogs can also be off leash. Clover and Tansy gave it a very enthusiastic four wags. Follow 108th Ave. west until it ends in Simms St. Turn left and park in the large lot on the west side of Simms, across from 105th Dr. (For a smile, be sure to check out Advice from a Dog, posted on the signboard at the entrance.) A split-rail fence runs along the parking area and delineates the boundary line with the neighborhood on the north, but that is the extent of the park's fencing, so Rover should be proficient at voice command. If your dog is looking to socialize, he's bound to see other dogs in the area's most parklike section, near the entrance. There's a bench under a shade structure not too far from the parking lot if all you want to do is sit and watch Fido play. A small, easily accessible pond that's fed by the Dry Creek Valley irrigation ditch is just west of this area, with two big cottonwoods for shade and a bench where you can relax while your dog cools off. If you want to explore farther, head west from the parking area on the **Westminster Hills Trail**, which ends 1.9 miles later at the wonderfully secluded Mower Reservoir. Along the way, you'll top out on a plateau with all-encompassing views of Standley Lake to the south, and the foothills and Indian Peaks out to the west. For a shorter hike, take the 1.9-mile **Westminster Hills Loop Trail**: hike west from the parking area and at the trail intersection, go left. After about .5 mile, you'll meet up with the Westminster Hills Trail. Turn right to return to the trailhead. As you and your dog explore this area, keep an eye out for rattlesnakes.

The dog park at **Big Dry Creek Park** (128th Ave. and Zuni), which opened in 2008, consists of 2 fenced acres of irrigated turf (that's showing the wear and tear of active paws). Enter Big Dry Creek Park via 128th St., just east of Zuni. The dog park is on the left just after the main entrance, and parking is available adjacent to it. Amenities include a few benches inside the park and a water fountain and dog bowls. A small grove of young trees at the center will eventually provide shade. Just outside the park is a bilevel human/canine water fountain.

West Arvada Dog Park
Access: From Hwy. 93, turn east on W. 64th Pkwy. The dog park is about .5 mile from the highway on the left (north) side of the road.
Regulations: Dogs must have current rabies and ID tags; dogs who are aggressive, sick, too young to have a rabies vaccine, or who haven't been spayed or neutered

Madison and Tamra Hoppes take a break after visiting the West Arvada Dog Park.

are not allowed; owners must be present at all times, oversee no more than three dogs at once, and pick up after their dogs; pinch or spike collars must be taken off before a dog enters the park; dogs must be supervised by someone 18 or older, and anyone younger than 18 must be supervised by an adult.
Dogs can be off leash.

If your dog can't run off his energy in this 5-acre fenced park, something's wrong. And another 15 acres of off-leash terrain will eventually be added. The first section of the park, near the entrance, is somewhat bowl-like in shape; a short, steep section leads downhill, and dogs tend to congregate at the bottom. If you have a tennis-ball addict, throwing the ball back uphill should help tucker him out. The park's surface is a combination of natural grasses and gravel, and several nonnative features that look suspiciously like fire hydrants may bring a smile to your dog's face. Smaller or shy dogs, meanwhile, can take refuge in a separately fenced area within the park. A wide dirt path circles the park's perimeter, and a couple of laps around it with Fido could almost constitute a hike. Three benches are placed along the path, in case you want to take a break and enjoy the nice views of the foothills to the west, especially close to sunset. One thing the park lacks is shade. And you'll need to bring your own water. Lots of bag dispensers have been placed around the park, so there's no excuse not to pick up after your dog!

Firestone Dog Parks

Regulations: Dogs must have ID tags, licenses, and vaccinations, and must be spayed or neutered; puppies under four months and aggressive dogs are not permitted; owners/custodians are legally responsible for any damage, disease, or injury caused to other people or dogs; no more than three dogs per person; owners must carry a leash and remain in the park with their dog(s); children under five are not permitted in the park, and children under 14 should be supervised by an adult; owners must clean up after their dogs.

Dogs can be off leash.

This burgeoning community east of I-25 has two parks where dogs can play off leash. To reach **Settlers Park**, in the Oak Meadows subdivision, take Exit 240 off I-25 and drive east on Firestone Blvd. Make a left on Colorado Blvd., then take the first right, on Oak Meadows. Take the first left, Deerfield, and follow the road around to the park. This .64-acre fenced dog park includes a small pavilion with a picnic table—so at least you can get some shade while your dog frolics in the sun. There's also a water fountain with both human and dog levels.

Aisik's Meadow is named in honor of Firestone's first police dog. From Firestone Blvd., turn right on CR 15 and drive for .6 mile to St. Vrain Ranch Blvd. Turn right into the Ridge Crest subdivision, then make an immediate left on Foxfire. This grassy, fenced 1.2-acre park serves up great views of Longs Peak and the Indian Peaks to the far west. It's divided into large and small dog sections. Here, too, are a pavilion-shaded picnic table and a dual-level water fountain.

Canine Corral Dog Park, Frederick

Access: The park is on the west side of Colorado Blvd. (CR 13), just north of Godding Hollow Pkwy. (CR 18).

Regulations: No aggressive dogs; clean up after your dog.

Dogs can be off leash.

A little more than an acre in size, this fenced park includes some agility-course-type jumps and tunnels, benches for owners, and a water fountain with human and canine levels. Pick-up bags and trash cans are also provided. Milavec Lake, a popular fishing spot, is right next to the park; a 1-mile, gravel-surfaced trail encircles the lake, where you and your leashed dog can take a leisurely stroll and view the variety of waterfowl.

Bill Goodspeed Happy Tails Dog Park, Northglenn

Access: From E. 10th Ave., drive north on Irma Dr. for almost two blocks, past Jaycee Park. The dog park, and parking, is on the right.

Regulations: Dogs must be vaccinated; no aggressive dogs, females in heat, or puppies under six months; owners must have a leash for each dog, stay in the park, and bring no more than four dogs at one time; owners must also clean up after their dogs; no glass, bikes, or motorized equipment can be brought into the park; children must be under adult supervision; only bite-sized dog treats are allowed.

Dogs can be off leash.

The park's namesake, the late Bill Goodspeed, was a Northglenn councilman who spearheaded the establishment of a town off-leash area. So make sure your dog gives a tail wag in his honor. The park covers about 1 fenced acre and has lots of shaded seating—benches under a wooden shelter and three canopied picnic tables under the Siberian elm tree near the entrance. A bilevel water fountain is usually turned on from May through September.

Golden Gate Canyon State Park

Access: The main access from the eastern side, which will bring you by the park's visitor center, is via Golden Gate Canyon Rd., a signed turnoff from Hwy. 93 just north of Golden. The drive to the park is 13 miles from the turnoff. Entry fee is $6 per vehicle.

Dogs must be leashed.

Located 16 miles northwest of Golden, this 12,000-acre mountainous park offers 35 miles of trails, all with animal names, that you and your dog can enjoy together. One particularly nice hike follows the **Horseshoe Trail**, a 3.6-mile round-trip route from the Frazer Meadow trailhead to Frazer Meadow and back. To reach the trailhead, turn right at the T-intersection just after the visitor center, pass the Ralston Roost trailhead on the left, then pull into the next trailhead parking area on the left. You'll ascend a moderate uphill alongside a creek for most of the hike, then reach a large meadow flanked by stands of aspen. Head right for a few minutes on the intersecting **Mule Deer Trail** to view the old homestead in the meadow. Other park trails that follow streams for a good portion of their length include the 2.5-mile **Raccoon Trail**, which makes a loop from the Reverend's Ridge Campground in the park's northwestern corner; the **Mountain Lion Trail**, which forms a 6.7-mile loop

that begins and ends at the Nott Creek trailhead in the northeastern corner of the park; the 2.4-mile round-trip **Buffalo Trail**, which goes from the Rifleman Phillips Group Campground in the northern part of the park to Forgotten Valley; and the 2.5-mile **Beaver Trail**, which follows a loop beginning and ending at the visitor center and includes a short detour to Slough Pond. 303-582-3707, parks.state .co.us/parks/goldengatecanyon

Happy Tails Dog Park, Brighton

Access: From I-76, head west on Bromley Ln. Make a left on Judicial Center Dr. and drive about 1 mile to the Brighton Sports Complex, on the right. Take the second entrance, which will lead to parking spaces closest to the dog park, on the complex's southern end.

Regulations: Owners must be present at all times; no aggressive or sick dogs, and no females in heat or dogs too young to have rabies vaccinations; no children younger than six; owners must assume all legal responsibility for their dogs' actions; dogs must be picked up after.

Dogs can be off leash.

This approximately 4-acre fenced park is fairly basic and has no shade, but your dog is unlikely to mind as long as he can run around. And if he hits the park at the right time (usually in spring), a depression in the park's middle fills up with water and morphs into a temporary pond for swimming and wading. There's a human/dog water fountain on-site and a picnic table.

Broomfield County Commons Dog Park

Access: From the intersection of 13th Ave. and Sheridan Blvd., head east into the large Broomfield County Commons Park. Drive to the roundabout and exit north to reach a large parking lot. The dog park is on the left.

Regulations: Dogs must be current on vaccinations and have ID tags; no female dogs in heat or puppies under four months; halters and choke or link collars should be removed from dogs; owners must be present at all times, clean up after their dogs, and supervise no more than three dogs at a time.

Dogs can be off leash.

The dog park is billed as temporary, though it's unlikely to disappear or be relocated within the next several years. Within its 3.5 fenced acres, you and your dog will find separate areas for large and small dogs, some fire hydrants and a couple of agility obstacles, a water trough that's kept filled via an automatic system, and two benches under shade structures.

Barr Lake State Park

Access: Take I-76 northeast from Denver for about 20 miles to the Bromley Ln. exit. Turn right on Bromley, then right on Picadilly Rd. Look for the well-signed park entrance on your right. Entry fee is $6 per vehicle.

Dogs must be leashed.

Barr Lake, a day-use park, provides an easily accessible refuge for the dog who wants to get out of the city. He'll get a panaromic view of the Front Range foothills and the snowcapped peaks beyond. The lake itself is ringed by shady cottonwood trees, a habitat that attracts more than 300 bird species. An 8.8-mile gravel and natural-surface trail loops around the lake—the canine caveat is that dogs are not allowed on the southern part of the trail, about a 4-mile section, because it is in the park's wildlife refuge. Dogs are usually permitted, however, to accompany their owners in viewing the exhibits at the indoor nature center at park headquarters. A nice, semiloop hike of several miles is to head north from

the parking area on the lakeside trail and walk on top of the dam at the lake's northeast end; return via the trail below the dam. 303-659-6005, parks.state.co.us/parks/barrlake

Crown Hill Park

Access: From Lakewood, take Kipling Ave. north to W. 26th Ave. and make a right. Two parking areas for the park are on the lefthand side of the block.

Dogs must be leashed.

This 242-acre Jefferson County Open Space park is a perfect spot for an after-work stroll with Rover. The most obvious route to take is the 1.2-mile **Lake Loop Trail,** a paved path that encircles Crown Hill Lake and its resident ducks; just keep your dog on a short leash so that he doesn't have any entangling encounters with a bicyclist or in-line skater. The **Outer Loop Trail** takes you around the park's perimeter, but you won't be near the water. A number of unnamed horse trails, on which dogs are allowed, too, wind through the park. There's also a 1-mile fitness course near the lake that includes access for disabled exercisers. Note that dogs are not allowed on the nature trail that loops around Kestral Pond in the northwest part of the park—the area is designated as a wildlife sanctuary.

Van Bibber Park

Access: Located in Arvada, the park has two main access areas with parking lots: off Indiana St. and off Ward Rd., both just south of W. 58th Ave.

Dogs must be leashed.

From either side of the park, you'll start out on the paved **Van Bibber Creek Trail,** which is 1.5 miles from end to end. You'll soon reach a small network of natural-surface trails that meander through the 130-acre Jefferson County

Open Space park. Van Bibber Creek, which runs through the park's northern section, is often dry midsummer but has water at other times of the year. As you and your dog walk (or jog—this is a good venue for a run), you'll glimpse the somewhat odd combination of farmland and suburban palaces that's becoming common to the metro area. If you're starting out at the eastern side of the park, you'll reach the middle before leaving behind the rush of traffic on busy Ward Rd. No dogs are allowed on the Jimmy Go Trail, which leads to an observation deck in the wetlands section of the park; if your dog wants to walk a large loop, you and he will need to briefly exit, then reenter the park.

 Two Ponds National Wildlife Refuge. Dogs are not permitted at this 72-acre urban wildlife sanctuary in Arvada.

East of Denver

 Aurora Dog Parks
Regulations: Restricted breeds (pit bulls, American bulldogs, American Staffordshire terriers, Dogo Argentinos, Japanese Tosas, Canary dogs, Brazilian mastiffs, Staffordshire bull terriers, Cane Corsos, and Presa Mallorquins) must be muzzled, remain on leash, and be under the care of someone 21 or older; no puppies younger than four months, females in heat, or dogs that bark excessively; owners must stay present in the park and cannot have more than three dogs at a time; children under 12 must be accompanied by an adult; no alcohol or human food can be brought into the park. *Dogs can be off leash.*

Grandview Dog Park, by Quincy Reservoir, is off E. Quincy Ave., about .25 mile east of the intersection with S. Buckley Rd. Though there is a fee to access the reservoir (and dogs aren't allowed at it

anyway), there's no fee for the dog park. Suburban dogs can get some breathing room here from the houses and backyards that have sprouted seemingly everywhere in this area, and the 5.6 fenced acres provide lots of space for the large dog who needs to run. Located on a slight hill, the park includes a separately enclosed small-dog area; a permanent agility course with five obstacles to go through, over, or under; and several picnic tables. A water spigot operates during the summer.

Aurora's newest off-leash area, the **Jewell Dog Park**, opened in 2009. Take Jewell Ave. east from Tower Rd., past the Great Plains Park; parking for the dog park is just past Great Plains, on the left. At 8.9 acres, the fenced park can accommodate lots of dogs, with plenty of room for all. Right now, the park's size is its main draw (the only real amenity is a seasonal water spigot in summer). There's also an entertainment element—watching the jets take off from nearby Buckley Air Force Base. Once the budget allows, however, this park could become one of the Denver area's premier dog parks; plans call for a separate enclosure for small dogs, a shaded shelter for owners, some trees, canine obstacle courses, and a crushed-surface trail inside the park's perimeter.

Though it doesn't warrant a special trip, if you happen to be in the vicinity of Genoa St. and 58th Dr. in northeast Aurora (by Denver International Airport),

Tansy takes five in the shade.

there's a small **off-leash area** in the neighborhood of **Singletree Park**. The area is less than an acre, but it is fenced. You'll need to bring water.

Bluff Lake Nature Center. Because it's a wildlife refuge, dogs are not permitted at this area within the Sand Creek Regional Greenway system.

West of Denver

Forsberg Iron Spring Dog Park, Lakewood
Access: From the three-way intersection of W. Jewell Ave., Bear Creek Blvd., and Alameda Pkwy., drive .4 mile west. The park entrance is on the left. You can either park in the main lot inside the park or in the temporary parking lot that's been erected on the south side of Alameda, near the dog park entrance. The dog park is on the eastern end of the main park.
Regulations: Dogs who are residents of Jefferson County must have a local license; owners must clean up after their dogs and not leave behind any type of water container.
Dogs can be off leash.

When we visited this very popular park on a windy fall Saturday, not too long after it had opened, about three dozen dogs of all shapes, sizes, and breeds were chasing each other around, their tongues all lolling happily. The 4-acre park is laid out along a south-facing slope, and the terrain encompasses several smaller hills that dogs enjoy running over and around. A crushed-gravel path loops around the perimeter, for dogs who prefer to hike rather than play free form. Picnic tables and benches have been set throughout the park on flattened areas, and a bilevel water fountain at the entrance is turned on during the summer. Currently, there's no shade, though trees have been planted. And if your dog still

has energy left, Green Mountain Park, which has a good network of hiking trails, is on the other side of Alameda.

Elk Meadow Park/ Off-Leash Dog Area
Access: From Denver, take I-70 west to Exit 252, then head toward Evergreen on Hwy. 74 east. At 5.3 miles from the first traffic light after crossing over I-70, turn right (west) on Stagecoach Blvd. Drive 1.25 miles to the off-leash park parking area on the left. Parking is also available in the main Elk Meadow lot on the right if the dog area lot is full.
Regulations: Dogs must have current rabies tags and licenses; no aggressive, sick, or injured dogs; female dogs in heat are not allowed; children under 12 must be accompanied by an adult; clean up after your dog.
Dogs must be leashed, except in the dog park.

This Jefferson County Open Space park, on 1,385 acres, has 13.1 miles of trails, including a 3.7-mile (one-way) ascent of 9,600-foot Bergen Peak, which will give you a panoramic view of the Continental Divide. Your dog might be most interested, however, in sniffing out the off-leash area. From the parking area, a handicap-accessible trail leads straight to the easternmost of the fenced dog park's five entrance gates. Three of the other gates are opened on a rotating basis to reduce the impact of everyone entering and exiting by the same route. Once inside the park, your dog will have 5 acres of native-grass meadow in which to retrieve a stick or ball, run in circles, or play with other four-legged friends. About 1 acre of the park is separately fenced, for smaller dogs or dogs who may need to be watched more closely, and the gate to this section is always open. When your dog needs to pause for a drink, water is often available from a natural spring outside the park's western fence. The land immediately surrounding the fenced park is also designated off leash. Eventually, a 1- to 1.5-mile loop trail will be constructed next to the park's eastern boundary, where dogs will be able to hike off leash with their owners. Right now, if Rover wants to do a bit of off-leash exploring, take him on the distinct but unmaintained footpath that parallels the dog park to the south and then runs up the east side; it also provides access to an irrigation ditch. Just keep an eye out for a sign that indicates you're leaving the park and entering private property, a route you'd want to avoid.

Beaver Ranch Bark Park, Conifer

Access: From Hwy. 285 south, exit onto Kennedy Gulch/Foxton Rd. (just past the Safeway). Turn left, and go under the highway. Make a left on Foxton and drive .25 mile to the park entrance on the right. Once you're in the park, drive another .6 mile, following the signs to the Bark Park. There's a small parking area right by the dog park.

Regulations: Sick or aggressive dogs, or dogs in heat are not allowed; no more than two dogs per person; all dogs who get in a fight must leave the park immediately; dogs can't dig or otherwise disturb the park; no children under age six; clean up after your dog.

Dogs can be off leash in the dog park; they must be leashed elsewhere in the park.

As you might expect in a town named Conifer, the 2-acre fenced dog park is graced with many lodgepole pines, providing shade and giving the park a woodsy feel. It's divided into sections for big and small dogs, and the wood-chip surface is gentle on paws. A water tank with a spigot inside the park provides hydration year-round. A picnic table rounds out the amenities. The surrounding

446-acre Conifer Community Park at Beaver Ranch, a former kids' camp that is now owned by Jefferson County Open Space, has about 6 miles of trails as well as two lodges, cabins, camping, and an outdoor chapel.

Golden Dog Parks

Regulations: Owners must pick up after their dogs. *Dogs can be off leash.*

The **Tony Grampsas Dog Park** is a little oasis within the Tony Grampsas Memorial Sports Complex at W. 44th St. and Salvia (44th St. parallels Hwy. 58, north of the highway). To reach the dog park, walk your leashed dog up a concrete path to the right of the main parking lot, past the playground and softball and archery fields. The 2.5-acre fenced dog area has ample shade, thanks to clusters of large cottonwood trees, and, occasionally, water: an irrigation ditch by the entrance runs periodically, and a storm ditch through the middle of the park runs after heavy rain. That said, the ground can get muddy in places, so you might want to pack a towel for Fido. Some benches and picnic tables provide spots for owners to socialize or just relax, enjoying the peaceful, natural setting.

The smaller **Homer's Run Dog Park** at Ulysses Ball Park (off Ulysses Ave. and 10th Ave.) consists of about three-quarters of an acre and is also fenced. Park in the lot on 10th Ave., then walk toward the first baseball field; the dog park is west of the field. One picnic table is in the park, along with a few small trees.

Maxwell Falls Trail

Distance: 4 miles round-trip
Elevation gain: 1,000 feet
Trailhead: From the stoplight on Hwy. 74 in downtown Evergreen, head south on Hwy. 73 for about 1 mile. Make a right on Brook Forest Road Dr. for 3.6 miles to the lower

trailhead parking in a small fenced area on the left side of the road.

Dogs must be leashed.

Oh, my, there has been a lot of barking (among humans) over leash laws on this trail in the past several years. Maxwell Falls was listed as an off-leash venue in previous editions of *Canine Colorado,* based on the information I received from the US Forest Service. However, Jefferson County animal control officers started to routinely patrol the trail as Denver dogs eager for a leash-free romp flocked to it. The county believed that its leash law superceded the policy of the national forest, where dogs can often be under voice control outside of designated wilderness and developed areas, such as campgrounds and picnic areas. Well, unfortunately, it turns out the county is right (which was news at the time to the Clear Creek Ranger District, which oversees the trail too). Rather than delete this trail entirely (which is tempting, given the amount of rancor that resulted from its inclusion in this book), I've decided to keep it in, as it's one of the closest national forest trails to Denver and features plenty of access to water, lots of trees to sniff, and a brief scenic vista. But for everyone's sake, keep your dog leashed!

Begin by heading up the path marked by the brown carsonite post in the southwest corner of the parking area. (Did I mention that your dog should be on a leash?) You'll make a moderate ascent through a forest of fir, pine, and aspen, contouring southwest across a hillside and following the route of an unnamed creek. The trail eventually fords the creek and switchbacks up to a clearing on a small saddle (this is where you'll get the view). Cross an old dirt road and follow the trail down the other side of the saddle. From here the trail stays fairly level as it goes into the Maxwell Creek drainage. After crossing the creek, head left (upstream); the falls themselves are about .25 mile ahead.

After viewing the falls, you can either return the way you came or, if your leashed dog is up for a longer hike, follow a loop that adds about 1.25 miles to the total distance. To access the loop, backtrack from the falls a few hundred yards to an intersection. Follow the intersecting trail as it switchbacks uphill and then runs above the creek. In about .3 of a mile, this trail ends at the upper trailhead for Maxwell Falls, at an unmarked parking pullout off of Black Mountain Rd. Before reaching trail's end, however, ford the creek and head left on a wide dirt path that doubles back along the creek. This path, which is actually the old dirt road that you crossed earlier in the hike, starts to head away from the creek. After about 1 mile, you'll come out on the same saddle that you traversed earlier. Look for the intersection with the Maxwell Falls Trail (unmarked) and go right to return to the lower trailhead parking area (in case you're still wondering, yes, your dog has to be on a leash).

Pine Valley Ranch Park

Access: Head south on Hwy. 285, going through Morrison, Aspen Park, and Conifer. In Pine Junction, make a left at the traffic light onto Pine Valley Rd. Head southeast on Pine Valley Rd. for about 6 miles, until you come to a hairpin turn in the road. Go right on Crystal Lake Rd. and follow the signs to Pine Valley Ranch.

Dogs must be leashed.

Pine Valley Ranch Park, on 820 acres, has a beautiful, wide-open feel. And though somewhat removed from the madding crowd, it's still a Jefferson County Open Space property. In the middle lies small, scenic Pine Lake, and the North Fork of the South Platte River runs across the park. As a bonus, the park's southern boundary abuts Pike National Forest. To hike along the rushing waters of the South Platte, take the 2-mile **Narrow Gauge Trail** in either direction from the parking area; the trail follows the route used by the Colorado and Southern Railroad in the early part of the century. A .6-mile, hiker-only trail loops around **Pine Lake**. To head into the national forest, follow the **Buck Gulch Trail** for 1 mile to the park boundary; the trail then continues for another 2.2 miles as a forest service trail. It's possible to do a long loop (5.3 miles) by combining the **Buck Gulch**, **Skipper**, and **Strawberry Jack Trails**; note that these are also popular mountain-biking trails.

Deer Creek Canyon Park
Access: Take the Kipling Rd. exit off I-70 and drive south on Kipling. Make a right on W. Ute Ave., then another right on Deer Creek Canyon Rd. Turn left on Grizzly Dr. and look for the parking area .25 mile ahead on the right. *Dogs must be leashed.*

This Jefferson County Open Space park, which encompasses 1,881 acres, feels more remote than South Valley Park, which abuts it on the north. Three hiker-only trails allow you and your dog to avoid mountain-biking traffic somewhat, though you will have to take some potentially busy multiuse trails to reach two of them. A portion of a fourth hiker-only trail, Black Bear, starts in the park and leads outside the boundaries for another .7 mile. For a good, fast workout, catch the 3.2-mile round-trip **Meadowlark Trail** from the parking area. This hiker-only route climbs at a steady pace and soon affords great vistas of the forested and sandstone-studded surroundings. In its last third, the trail descends to a bridge crossing Plymouth Creek—where your dog should be able to find a drink even when it's not running at full capacity—and the **Plymouth Creek Trail**, popular with bikers. You can take this trail for 1.1

miles back to the parking area if you prefer a loop to retracing your steps on the Meadowlark Trail. If you and your dog want to hike farther, turn right and begin ascending again, at times steeply, on the Plymouth Creek Trail. Within 15 to 20 minutes, you'll come to the intersection with the hiker-only **Homesteader Trail**, which traces the north rim of a canyon. This trail leads to the **Scenic View Trail**, which delivers on its name by leading to the top of Plymouth Mountain. The other hiker-only trail, **Golden Eagle**, is in the middle of the park and also affords a scenic view from a lower summit.

Lair o' the Bear Park
Access: From Morrison, take Hwy. 74 west toward Evergreen. After going through Idledale (don't blink), look for the signed park entrance on the left. *Dogs must be leashed.*

Tucked into the side of Bear Creek Canyon, this 319-acre Jefferson County Open Space park offers a healthy-sized stream with easy access for dog dips as well as 4.3 miles of trails. And because the park is relatively small, you're not likely to encounter as many of the mountain bikers who frequent other Jeffco Open Space areas. The **Bear Creek Trail** parallels Bear Creek for 1.7 miles (and continues through three adjacent Denver Mountain parks—Corwina, O'Fallon, and Pence—for a total of 6.3 miles). From the parking area, head toward the creek and pick up the .3-mile **Creekside Trail** going in either direction. Heading right (west) brings you to the Bear Creek Trail (note that dogs are not allowed on the Creekside Loop Trail, a short diversion off the main trail a little farther west). If you go left (east), you'll eventually cross the Ouzel Bridge—keep an eye out for these small gray birds plunging into the water—and meet up with the easternmost segment of the Bear Creek Trail, which ends at Denver Mountain Parks' Little Park, primarily a picnic spot, about .25 mile to the east. Or hike west from the bridge along the **Bruin Bluff Trail**, which then loops for 1.3 miles through the forest above the creek's south side.

Alderfer/
Three Sisters Park

Access: From Evergreen, drive south on Hwy. 73. Turn right (west) on Buffalo Park Rd. Drive for about 1 mile to the parking area on the right. Another parking area is .5 mile farther west, also off of Buffalo Park Rd.

Dogs must be leashed.

Named in part for a distinctive trio of rock formations, this Jefferson County Open Space property serves up 12.5 miles of hiking trails that crisscross 770 acres close to "downtown" Evergreen. Clover spent much of her hiking time here wagging her tail because of the ready abundance of great sticks, thanks to the dense ponderosa forest that blankets much of the park. From **Brother's Lookout**, a little more than .5 mile from the parking area off Buffalo Park Rd., you and your dog can take in a panoramic view of Evergreen just below and Mts. Evans and Bierstadt farther west. The only water comes from Wilmot Creek, an intermittent stream that crosses the **Evergreen Mountain East Trail** in the park's southern section.

Lookout Mountain and
Beaver Brook Trails

Distance: 9.5 miles one way
Elevation gain: 1,000 feet
Trailhead: This hike starts across from the Lookout Mountain Nature Center, which you can reach in one of two ways: from Hwy. 6, coming from Golden or Lakewood, turn west on 19th St., which becomes Lookout Mountain Rd., and follow the switchbacks up, past Buffalo Bill's grave, to Boettcher Man-

sion and the nature center. From I-70 west from Denver, take Exit 256, make a right at the stop sign, and follow the brown signs along Paradise and Charros Rds. to Lookout Mountain Rd., where you'll turn right to head up to the nature center. Either way, look for the parking pullout on the other side of the road from the nature center main entrance.

Dogs must be leashed (and note that dogs are not allowed on the Forest Loop and Meadow Loop Trails in the Lookout Mountain Nature Preserve).

This well-established but not necessarily well-known trail was built in 1917 by Colorado Mountain Club volunteers. Denver hikers would travel by trolley and train to the trailhead near Lookout Mountain Park, then hike the trail to Genesee Park and overnight at the Chief Hosa Lodge before returning by train and trolley to the city. It's not for the dog, or human, who's a tenderfoot on the trail, as parts involve crossing talus and clambering over rocks. But the reward for those who do venture out are great views and relative solitude for a hike that's so close to Denver. The Lookout Mountain Trail drops down a hillside in the cool shade of lodgepole pine for 1 mile before intersecting with the Beaver Brook Trail. Take a left at the trail intersection; the right ends at a busy trailhead on Lookout Mountain Rd. known as Windy Saddle. As you hike, you and your dog can take in a bird's-eye view of Clear Creek Canyon below and the Front Range's northern foothills—as well as of the gamblers speeding toward Black Hawk and Central City on curvy Hwy. 6. Shortly after joining up with the Beaver Brook Trail (there's no brook along this part), you'll encounter two short talus fields, which may test your pooch's—and perhaps your—rock-hopping skills. The next section of trail includes a few places where you'll have to scramble up and over some rocks; the trail then mellows out again as it continues to wind along the south side of the canyon, interrupted by some small creek crossings. At about 4.5 miles, if you've chosen to go this far, you'll pass the Gudy Gaskill Trail, which makes a 2.5-mile loop off the main trail. If you and your dog are particularly ambitious, or if you've arranged a car shuttle, you can hike for a total of about 9.5 miles from the Lookout Mountain trailhead to the Beaver Brook Trail's western terminus in Genesee Mountain Park (Exit 253 off I-70).

Meyer Ranch Park

Access: Head south on Hwy. 285 from Denver. Before you reach the town of Aspen Park, you'll see a turnoff for South Turkey Creek Rd. and a sign for the park on the left. From South Turkey Creek Rd., the parking area is almost immediately on the right.
Dogs must be leashed.

This 397-acre Jefferson County Open Space park has about 4 miles of trails that wind through the forested hillside to the south. This is a particularly nice place to hike in September when the aspen change color. The trails are wide and well graded, with benches conveniently placed along them if you or your dog need to stop for a breather. In the early 1940s, a small ski area was located on the southern end of the property, now overgrown with aspen. The **Old Ski Run Trail** (1.4 miles from the parking area) takes you to this spot, though you probably won't be able to recognize the formerly skiable terrain. There's no water along any of the trails, just a small creek near the parking lot.

Mount Falcon Park

Access: From Morrison, head west on Hwy. 74 (Bear Creek Canyon Rd.) to Hwy. 8. Drive south on Hwy. 8 to Forest Ave., shortly past Morrison Town Park on the right. Turn right on Forest, then right on Vine.
Dogs must be leashed.

This park, another Jefferson County Open Space property, features 11.1 miles of trails spread over 2,248 acres. It's located on land formerly owned by John Brisben Walker, a wealthy gent who lived here at the turn of the century until his house burned down in 1918 (you can visit the remains). The trails here receive a lot of mountain-bike use, so you and your dog may want to stick to the 3.4-mile out-and-back **Turkey Trot Trail**, which is for hikers only. Though you can access the trails in the park's western side by hiking across on the **Castle Trail**, it's quicker to reach them by driving to the west parking lot, via Parmalee Gulch Rd. off Hwy. 285 south. A nice 3-plus-mile loop involves taking the **Castle Trail** from the western trailhead, passing by the castlelike Walker Home Ruins, to the steep but short **Two-Dog Trail**, which ends at a lookout with a view of Denver and Lakewood, Red Rocks Amphitheatre, and the plains to the east. Return via the **Meadow Trail**, which branches off the Castle Trail, then hooks into it again .4 mile from the parking area. There's no water along this route.

South Valley Park

Access: From C-470 south, take the Ken Caryl Ave. exit and head west. Turn left on South Valley Rd. and follow it to the parking area.
Dogs must be leashed.

This 909-acre Jefferson County Open Space property includes expansive, rolling fields and distinctive red and yellowish sandstone formations. It's bordered by the large Ken Caryl subdivision on one side and Lockheed Martin headquarters on the other (which includes the large silver building you'll see), so you and your dog won't feel like you've completely escaped suburbia. Among the almost 7 miles of trails is the hiker-only **Swallow Trail**, which makes a good canine destination. Combine the Swallow Trail with the **Coyote Song Trail** for a 2.2-mile loop that highlights the park's varied scenery. There's little shade along the trails, so keep that in mind when planning a summer hike. An intermittent stream runs alongside the Swallow Trail, so your dog may find some water in the spring. You can link up to the trails in adjacent Deer Creek Canyon Park via the Rattlesnake Gulch Trail off the Grazing Elk Trail, in South Valley's southern section. That area is closed seasonally during elk migration, however.

O'Fallon Park

Access: Part of Denver's Mountain Parks system, O'Fallon is located just east of Kittredge off Hwy. 74. If you're coming from Denver, look for a large, three-sided chimney/fireplace structure after passing Corwina Park—this is your cue that the entrance to O'Fallon is coming up on the left. Follow the road from the entrance as it goes left, until it ends in a parking area.

Dogs must be leashed.

Though there are some picnic sites near the park entrance, O'Fallon, like most other Denver Mountain Parks, is in the process of getting a more developed, mapped-out trail system. There are currently almost 4.5 miles of hiker-only trails within the park, as well as a portion of the 6.3-mile multiuse Bear Creek Trail, which runs from adjacent Pence Park through Lair o' the Bear Park (part of the Jefferson County Open Space system). From the parking area, cross the bridge over Bear Creek and and follow the **Meadow View Loop Trail** as it ascends amid stands of caramel-scented ponderosa pine along an intermittent stream. Stay right at the fork .4 mile in; you'll intersect the **Bear Creek Trail** soon after. For a shorter hike (a little more than 1.5 miles total), turn left on the Bear Creek Trail. Pass the Meadow View Loop Trail as it comes in from the right and briefly joins the trail you're on, then follow Meadow View Loop to the left shortly after and return to the parking area. For a slightly longer hike (about 2.5 miles), turn right on the Bear Creek Trail when you first intersect it. Follow it for .4 mile until it meets up with another portion of the Meadow View Loop Trail and turn left. Hike Meadow View Loop to your car.

South of Denver

Englewood Dog Parks

Regulations: For parks that allow dogs off leash—owners must carry a leash, pick up after their dogs, and keep dogs out of playground and shelter areas. For Canine Corral—dogs must be vaccinated and licensed; no females in heat or puppies under four months old; dogs must be accompanied by someone 16 or older; children must be under adult supervision; owners should have a leash on hand for each dog and clean up after them.

Dogs can be off leash.

Englewood has an active dog-lovers community, with four neighborhood parks where dogs can be off leash throughout plus one fenced dog park, and an advocacy group, Englewood Unleashed (www.englewoodunleashed .org), which works to maintain local off-leash dog privileges and educate owners. Before you bring your dog to one of the neighborhood parks, make sure he's completely schooled in voice command so that he doesn't become a nuisance to other park users.

At 37 acres, **Centennial Park** is the largest of Englewood's parks that permit off-leash canines. The facilities include three picnic pavilions, a playground, ball fields, and a basketball court. There's also a lake and a trail. To reach it from S. Federal Blvd., drive east on W. Union Ave., then turn left (north) on S. Decatur.

Duncan Park's 4 acres include a playground and picnic area. There's some nice, paw-cooling grass for your dog to run on here. From S. Broadway, head east on E. Layton Ave. to S. Pennsylvania St. Turn left.

The 8-acre **Jason Park** has a picnic pavilion, playground, basketball court, and soccer and softball fields. Be sure your dog stays away from picnickers and kids in the playground and that he doesn't interfere with any ball games going on in the field (you might think it's cute if Fido runs off with the softball—the players, not so much). To reach the park from S. Broadway, head west on W. Quincy Ave. to S. Jason St. and turn right.

Northwest Greenbelt has a picnic area, playground, trail, and stream on its 11 acres. This narrow park runs east from Zuni St. to Pecos. Parking is available on Vassar Ave., between Zuni and Tejon Sts.

The newest—and the first dog-dedicated—park is the **Englewood Canine Corral**, in the western part of Belleview Park. The park was spearheaded by Englewood Unleashed, which also raised most of the funds to build it. From the intersection with S. Santa Fe Dr., drive east on Belleview to Windermere St. Turn left. The park is about .5 mile ahead on the right. The 1.5-acre fenced dog park has benches and some shaded spots. You'll need to bring water for your dog.

Highlands Ranch Dog Parks

Regulations: Dogs must be vaccinated; no aggressive dogs or females in heat; owners must pick up after their dogs, carry a leash at all times, and remain in the park with their pets; dogs must be under voice control at all times; children must be supervised by an adult. *Dogs can be off leash.*

Highlands Ranch looks after its dogs well, with four dog parks that give canines some much-needed roaming space in this hyperdeveloped area. **Fido's Field at Foothills Park** (1042 Riddlewood Dr.) is off the beaten path but worth finding. From County Line Rd., drive south on Broadway for 1.8 miles. Turn right on Lucent Blvd., then take the first left, onto Timbervale Tr. Go .5 mile to Riddlewood Rd. and turn left into the park. You'll see the dog park down below from the parking lot. From the lot, walk right of the playground on a paved path. After the Potato Patch community garden, turn right on the path and follow it up and around to the dog park. The 2-acre Fido's Field is shaped like a lollipop and offers nice views of the Front Range foothills. In addition to romping in the mix of natural grasses and shrubs that surface the park, your dog can walk along Fido's Footpath (six laps equal 1 mile, for the dog in training). He can also taunt the metal sculpture of a cat on a fence post in the middle of the park. A pump-activated watering hole dispenses needed refreshment in warmer months.

Digger's at Dad Clark Park (3385 Asterbrook Cir.) comprises 2 acres that contour around the side of a gentle slope, with several picnic tables placed throughout. It, too, has a pump-activated watering hole in summer (and part of spring and fall). From County Line Rd., head south on University Blvd. for about 1.8 miles to Highlands Ranch Pkwy. and make a right. When you reach the second traffic light, turn left on Fairview Pkwy. and drive for .8 mile to Summit View Pkwy.; turn right. Take the second right onto Asterbrook Wy., then a right on Asterbrook Cir.

To reach **Hound Hill**, take C-470 south to the Quebec St. exit. Head south, going through the intersection with University Blvd. Just after the entrance to Highland Heritage Park, make a right on Dutch Creek St. and go left into the large parking area. Don't be deterred by the signs stating that no dogs are allowed in Highland Heritage Park; Hound Hill takes exactly the opposite approach. Dogs have ample room to romp in the dog park's 3-acre fenced area, which is adjacent to Quebec St. The small hill provides a venue for uphill canine sprints. A water pump provides necessary refreshment in the summer (it's shut down in winter).

Rover's Run is part of Redstone Park. To reach it, take the Lucent Blvd. exit off C-470 south and make a right on Town Center Dr. Look for Foothills Canyon Blvd. on the left after about 1 mile. Parking is available in a lot on the right; the park itself is on the left. Once your dog enters the park's 3 acres, he'll probably want to make a beeline for the fire hydrant in the middle to make his mark (the hydrant is purely for "aesthetic" purposes). Then you can relax at one of the picnic tables while Rover runs. Water is available during the summer.

Chatfield State Park

Access: The park is southwest of Denver, via C-470 east or Wadsworth Blvd. south. If you're coming from C-470, take the Wadsworth Blvd. exit and drive south for 1 mile to the park entrance on the left. Entrance is $7 per vehicle.

Dogs must be leashed, except in the dog training area.

Like Cherry Creek State Park, Chatfield is best known for its reservoir and the water recreation it provides, but dogs will be much more interested in the off-leash area set aside for them. What began as a training area for sporting dogs has become one of the most popular off-leash dog sites in the Denver metro area. So, for starters, if your dog doesn't enjoy

lots of company, don't bring him here. Located in the northeast corner of the park, the **dog-training and exercise area**, as it's officially known, encompasses almost 80 acres. There's even two adjacent ponds (though the water level in one varies), where several dogs were practicing their ball-in-the-water retrieval skills when we visited. To reach the site, turn left (north) at the T-intersection after going through the park entrance station. Follow the road up and around the top of the dam to the Stevens Grove picnic area, where parking is available (if the lot is full, try the nearby Owl Glen or Cottonwood Grove picnic areas). From there, a trail leads around the ponds. You and your dog can also head east on the trail (away from the ponds), but Fido will have to leash up when crossing the marked dog area boundary; you'll connect with the paved **Centennial Trail**, which runs along C-470. The dog training area also extends on the other side of the road from Stevens Grove as well as from the next picnic area, Cottonwood Grove; your dog can either follow some small social trails here or explore among the trees—just keep an eye out for the boundary markers. For the best meet-and-greet opportunities, however, the pond's the place. Technically, dogs are not supposed to have access to the South Platte River, which borders part of the off-leash area's east side, but the signs delineating no-dog's land keep disappearing.

The park has some paved trails that run along the west and south sides of the reservoir. And the **Highline Canal Trail** is just outside the park's south and east boundaries. 303-791-7275, parks.state.co.us/parks/chatfield

Cherry Creek State Park

Access: The park, located in Aurora, has two main entrance gates: The east entrance station is off of

Parker Rd., 1.5 miles south of I-225; the west entrance station is reached via Yosemite St., south of I-225, and Union Ave. Currently, if you walk (or bike) into the park from one of the several trail accesses (pick up a park map for locations), you don't need to pay an entrance fee. Entrance is $8 per vehicle.

Dogs must be leashed, except in the dog training area.

Though known primarily for its reservoir, Cherry Creek State Park rates high among the canine set because of the **off-leash dog area** at the southern end of the park. To reach this section, which is designated on the park map only as the 12 Mile Multiuse Area and covers about 125 acres, drive south on the main park road from the east entrance station and park in the lower parking lot for the 12 Mile House group picnic site. You'll need to keep your dog leashed for about the first 500 yards, until you pass the dog area boundary sign. You can also access the off-leash area by heading west on Orchard Ave., off Parker Rd., for about a half block to a parking area (there's a self-service fee station). The multiuse area consists mainly of open grassland crisscrossed by several wide gravel trails; water-loving hounds will seek out Cherry Creek. There's plenty of room for your dog to get a good workout, play with a friend, or chase down a ball. Because the area is not just for dogs, be aware that you may encounter hikers, bikers, and horseback riders, so your dog should be good at responding to voice commands.

If he tires of the scenery, put him back on his leash and bring him to explore the rest of the park, which has about 12 miles of paved trails and various gravel trails. The park is still in the process of mapping out and improving the signage on its trails, so you and your dog should expect to do some exploring rather than following a set route. The paved **Cherry Creek Trail** runs through the park from north to south; north of the dam, outside the park boundary, a portion connects to the **Highline Canal Trail**. The **Perimeter Trail**, also paved, goes along the southern end of the reservoir, from the marina area east to the Shop Creek area. Dogs (along with bikes and horses) are not permitted on the Wetlands Trail in the park's wetlands preserve, which bounds the reservoir's southeastern end. From the Shop Creek trailhead, which is off the main park road south of the east entrance station, dogs can hike the .3-mile **Shop Creek Trail** and access the Perimeter Trail. Dogs are not allowed at the reservoir's swim beach or at the White Tail group picnic area. 303-690-1166, www.parks .state.co.us/parks/cherrycreek.

Devon's Dog Park at Greenland Open Space

Access: From Larkspur, take I-25 south to Exit 167 (Greenland). Drive west on the gravel road for .25 mile, then turn left and go another .5 mile to the Greenland Open Space trailhead. Drive east from the main parking lot to reach the separately fenced parking area for the dog park.

Regulations: Dogs must be current on vaccinations; no sick or aggressive dogs, females in heat, or dogs too young to be vaccinated against rabies; no food is allowed inside the park; owners must pick up after their dogs and maintain voice control of them; children must be supervised by an adult.

Dogs can be off leash.

Douglas County Girl Scout Devon Theune deserves a big paws-up for not only initiating this 16.5-acre dog park in an unincorporated area of the county, but also raising the money to fence it. The park incorporates the natural grasses of the surrounding open space; amenities are limited to pick-up bags and a trash can. Look southwest, and you'll be able to see the top of Pikes Peak looming over the foothills.

In addition to wide-open vistas, a visit here also has historical interest. Greenland was established in 1875 as a small town and shipping point on the Denver & Rio Grande Railroad, with two train stations. By the 1930s, the town had essentially disappeared, but a couple of vestiges remain, like the former schoolhouse. Before or after playing at the park, you and Fido (on his leash) can hike on all or part of the **Greenland Trail**, which includes an 8.5-mile loop from the trailhead.

Dog Park at Glendale Farm Open Space

Access: Take I-25 south from its intersection with C-470 to exit 190 (Surrey Ridge). Turn left at the end of the exit ramp and cross under the highway. The open space area is on the right.

Regulations: Dogs must be current on vaccinations; no sick or aggressive dogs, females in heat, or dogs too young to be vaccinated against rabies; no food is allowed inside the park; owners must pick up after their dogs and maintain voice control of them; children must be supervised by an adult.

Dogs can be off leash.

Located between Lone Tree and Castle Rock, the 17-acre fenced dog park has become a popular area for Douglas County pooches to play. But the easy access also means you'll never escape the background noise from the interstate. The gently sloping terrain of the dog park is peppered with native grasses. Adjacent is the **Glendale Farm Trail**, which makes a 1.6-mile loop through open space (Fido must be leashed). There's no water here, so you'll have to bring your own.

Dog Park in Bayou Gulch Regional Park

Access: From Parker, take Hwy. 83 south to Bayou Gulch Rd. Turn left and go for 1 mile to Fox Sparrow Rd. Make another left. Drive past the middle school; the dog park is at the top of the hill, on the right.

Regulations: Dogs must be current on vaccinations; no sick or aggressive dogs, females in heat, or dogs too young to be vaccinated against rabies; no food is allowed inside the park; owners must pick up after their dogs and maintain voice control of them; children must be supervised by an adult.

Dogs can be off leash.

This 2-plus-acre fenced park in one of Douglas County's regional parks gives dogs about an acre of room for play at any given time. The dog park is split in half, and only one half is open at a time, giving the irrigated turf in the other half a chance to recover from the wear and tear of busy paws. The two sections rotate opening every month or so. There's a bench inside the park, but no water; you'll have to bring in your own (water is available elsewhere in the larger park). Your dog may want to check out (or mark) one of the park "pets"—a large plastic dog and cat—that serve not only as decorative elements but to draw dogs away from the heavily trafficked entrance area and into the park. Two gravel trails comprising a total of about 4 miles wind around the overall park, so you and your dog can take a leisurely (leashed) stroll after a dog-park visit.

Dog Park in Fairgrounds Regional Park

Access: Take I-25 to Exit 181 and head east on Plum Creek Blvd. for .8 mile to the third park entrance, on the left (you'll pass a first entrance on Plum Creek Pkwy. and a second one along the way). After entering the main park, turn right to reach the upper parking lot. The dog park is there.

Regulations: Dogs must be current on vaccinations; no sick or aggressive dogs, females in heat, or dogs too young to be vaccinated against rabies; no food is allowed inside the park; owners must pick up after their dogs and maintain voice control of them; children must be supervised by an adult.

Dogs can be off leash.

Part of the larger Fairgrounds Regional Park in Castle Rock (the site of the Douglas County Fair, rodeo events, and dog shows, among other things), the dog park consists of a little more than 2 fenced acres on a distinct slope. Just outside the entrance are a shaded picnic pavilion and a water fountain with human and canine levels. Inside, the park is divided in two, with one half at a time open so the irrigated turf in the other half can grow back. There are a few benches and two park "pets"—plastic sculptures of a dog and a cat to attract dogs, and people, away from the sometimes-busy entrance area, where the park's turf gets the most beat up (concrete pavers by the entry also help handle the traffic).

Wynetka Ponds Bark Park

Access: From the intersection of W. Bowles Ave. and S. Lowell Blvd. in Littleton, go north on Lowell and turn at the second left into Wynetka Ponds Park. The dog park is just south of the parking lot; look for the pick-up-bag dispenser at the beginning of the short trail that leads to it.

Regulations: Dogs must be licensed and have current vaccinations; no aggressive dogs, females in heat, or puppies younger than four months; no more than three dogs per person; owners must have a leash on hand, watch their dogs at all times, and clean up after them; children must be supervised by an adult.

Dogs can be off leash.

The 3-acre park is divided into two rotating parcels so that the turf can regenerate, so 1.5 acres is actually open at any

given time. Each side has benches and picnic tables and a bilevel water fountain for you and your pooch. There's also a fire hydrant in each half so canines can make their mark. For a cool-down after playing, take your leashed dog on one of the main park's two crusher-fine-surfaced trails: one goes most of the way around the perimeter, the other loops around the pond (despite the park's name, there's currently only one pond here).

Bark Park at David A. Lorenz Regional Park

Access: Take E. County Line Rd. about .5 mile east of Colorado Blvd. Note that you can't reach the dog park from the regional park's main entrance off Colorado Blvd.

Regulations: Dogs must be licensed and have current vaccinations; no aggressive dogs, females in heat, or puppies younger than four months; no more than three dogs per person; owners must have a leash on hand, watch their dogs at all times, and clean up after them; children must be supervised by an adult.

Dogs can be off leash.

About a quarter of this 2-acre fenced dog park in unincorporated Douglas County consists of a gently sloping hill, making the terrain a little more interesting than at the average pancake-flat dog park. (And if your dog is training for a race, he can get in some fartleks on the hill for extra conditioning.) The park is divided into two sections, which are opened on a rotating basis to allow the grass in each side to regenerate. Each half of the park contains picnic tables, and a water spigot is in one section.

Castlewood Canyon State Park

Access: From Denver, take either Hwy. 83 (S. Parker Rd.) south or I-25 south to

Castle Rock, then Hwy. 86 east 6 miles to the intersection with Hwy. 83. The main park entrance (and visitor center) is 5 miles south of this intersection, on the right. There's also a west entrance, reached via Castlewood Canyon Rd. off Hwy. 86 from Castle Rock. Entrance is $6 per vehicle. *Dogs must be leashed.*

Castlewood Canyon, a day-use park in Franktown, seems something of an anomaly, a small canyon set near the edge of the eastern plains. The park provides a nice alternative to a mountain hike; you and your dog will be surrounded by farmland yet can still view the peaks of the Front Range in the distance, including Pikes Peak. A pleasant short hike (about 2 miles) combines the **Lake Gulch** and **Inner Canyon Trails**. From the parking area, the Lake Gulch Trail (there is no lake) begins as a paved path before changing to gravel surface. You'll hike among ponderosa pine and juniper before descending to Cherry Creek and its riparian habitat. After crossing the creek, go right to pick up the Inner Canyon Trail. You may want to make a short detour to the left, however, to view the ruins of the dam, which collapsed in 1933. The Inner Canyon Trail follows the course of the creek before crossing it and switchbacking up to the parking area. If your dog is interested in a much longer hike, you can add on a loop of the **Creek Bottom** and **Rim Rock Trails** (about 3.8 miles), which cover the park's western section. Dogs are not allowed on the East Canyon Trail, which runs for 4 miles in the park's easternmost section, a preservation area that's managed for minimal disturbance (other than human hikers, that is). Castlewood Canyon is also popular with rock climbers, so your dog shouldn't be alarmed if he spots a gear-laden human spider. 303-688-5242, www.parks.state.co.us/parks/castlewoodcanyon.

Roxborough State Park. Dogs are not permitted in this day-use state park southwest of Denver.

Waterton Canyon. You'll have to leave your dog at home if you want to hike or bike the 6.5-mile trail that winds through this scenic canyon along the South Platte River to Strontia Springs Dam. The northern terminus of the Colorado Trail, which traverses the state for 469 miles, is at the end of the canyon. You will need to bypass the first part of the trail and pick it up at CR 96 (S. Platte River Rd.) if you're planning a cross-state hike with Rover.

CYCLING FOR CANINES

Since dogs cannot be off leash in Jefferson County, none of the national forest trails that are popular for mountain biking (e.g., Buffalo Creek, southwest of Denver) are suitable for riding with your dog. The only place your dog can accompany you on a ride is at the **Westminster Hills Open Space** in Westminster (see the entry for Westminster dog parks in Tail-Rated Trails). Refer to Chapters 2 (Boulder and Vicinity) and 3 (Central City et al.) for more options.

POWDERHOUNDS

See Chapters 2 (Boulder and Vicinity) and 3 (Central City et al.) for some of the nearest canine-suitable skiing and snowshoeing trails.

CREATURE COMFORTS

Unless otherwise stated, dogs should not be left unattended in the room or cabin.

Aurora

$–$$ Crossland Economy Studios Aurora, 3705 N. Chambers Rd., 303-307-1088, www.extendedstayhotels.com. All the studios have refrigerators, microwaves, and cooktops. The pet fee is $25 per night, with a maximum fee per visit of $150. You can leave your dog unattended in the room, but unless he's in a travel kennel, you won't get housekeeping service.

$–$$ Homestead Studio Suites Aurora, 13941 E. Harvard Ave., 303-750-9116, www.extendedstayhotels.com. All the studios have refrigerators, microwaves, and cooktops. The pet fee is $25 per night, with a maximum fee per visit of $150. The hotel prefers that you not leave your dog unattended in the room, but if you absolutely have to, for a short period of time, you must leave a contact number at the front desk.

$–$$ Motel 6, 14031 E. Iliff Ave., 303-873-0286, 800-466-8356 (national number), www.motel6.com. One medium-sized dog per room (with some flexibility in actual weight) is permitted.

$$ Extended Stay Deluxe Aurora, 14095 E. Evans Ave., 303-337-7000, www.extendedstayhotels.com. The large studios contain full kitchens. The pet fee is $25 per night, with a maximum fee per visit of $150. There's no stated policy on whether or not your dog can be unattended in the room, but housekeeping won't enter unless he's in a travel kennel.

$$ La Quinta Inn Denver Aurora, 1011 S. Abilene, 303-337-0206, 800-753-3757 (national number), www.lq.com.

$$ Super 8 Aurora, 14200 E. 6th Ave., 303-366-7333, 800-800-8000 (national number), www.super8.com. Dogs must be under 25 pounds; there's a $20 one-time fee for each.

$$–$$$ Aloft Denver International Airport, 16470 E. 40th Cir., 303-371-9500, www.starwoodhotels.com/alofthotels. The trendy new Aloft chain, part of the Starwood hotel group, welcomes dogs up to 40 pounds with biscuits and a tennis ball, and use of a dog bed and food and water bowls during their stay. You can leave Fido in the room unattended if he's in a travel kennel.

$$–$$$ Best Western Gateway Inn and Suites, 800 S. Abilene St., 720-748-4800, 866-748-4800, www.bestwesterncolorado .com. There's a nightly fee of $15 per pet. You can leave your dog unattended in the room if he's in a travel kennel.

$$–$$$ Comfort Inn Airport, 16921 E. 32nd Ave., 303-367-5000, 800-424-2464 (national number), www.comfortinn.com. Dogs are permitted for $10 extra per night, per pet and can be left unattended in your room if in a travel kennel. The motel is 7 miles from DIA.

$$–$$$ Comfort Inn Southeast, 14071 E. Iliff Ave., 303-755-8000, 800-424-6423 (national number), www.comfortinn.com. Dogs must be 30 pounds or under. The motel charges $15 nightly per dog, plus a $50 deposit, and there's a limit of two dogs per room.

$$–$$$ Sleep Inn Denver International Airport, 15900 E. 40th Ave., 303-373-1616, 800-SLEEP-IN (national number), www.sleepinn.com. Dogs pay $10 extra per night, as well as a $25 deposit. There's a limit of two dogs per room. The motel is 6 miles from DIA.

 $$$–$$$$ Red Lion Denver Southeast, 3200 S. Parker Rd., 303-695-1700, 800-RED-LION (national number), www.redlion.rdln.com. There's a $20 one-time fee to stay with your dog (or free if you're a Red Lion R&R Club member), with a limit of two dogs per room. Cherry Creek State Park, which has an off-leash dog area (see Tail-Rated Trails) is across the street (though you'd probably want to drive to the off-leash area—it's a big park).

Brighton

$$ Super 8 Brighton, 15040 Brighton Rd., 303-659-6063, 800-800-8000 (national number), www.super8.com. The motel has designated pet rooms and charges $10 for one dog, and $5 for each additional dog, with a limit of three dogs per room. You can leave your dog unattended only if he's secured in a travel kennel.

Broomfield

$$–$$$ Aloft Broomfield Denver, 8300 Arista Pl., 303-635-2000, www.star woodhotels.com/alofthotels. Part of the Starwood hotel group's trendy new Aloft chain, the Broomfield branch welcomes dogs up to 40 pounds with a small package of treats and use of a dog bed and food and water bowls during their stay. You can leave Fido in the room unattended.

$$$–$$$$ Omni Interlocken, 500 Interlocken Blvd., 303-438-6600, www.omni hotels.com. This large resort, despite its location in the Interlocken business park, includes a 27-hole golf course, restaurant, spa, two outdoor heated pools, and almost 400 rooms. Though the official pet policy is that dogs should be less than 25 pounds, the hotel is often flexible about size. There's a $50 one-time fee. You can leave your dog unattended inside the room as long as you let the front desk staffers know so they can alert housekeeping.

Castle Rock

$$ Castle Rock Motel, 125 S. Wilcox, 303-688-9728. Dogs are welcome in some of the motel's rooms for $10 additional per night.

$$ Days Inn and Suites Castle Rock, 4691 Castleton Wy. (off I-25), 303-814-5825,
800-329-7466, www.daysinn.com. Dogs are generally put in first-floor rooms, with a $10 nightly fee.

$$ Super 8 Motel, 1020 Park St., 303-688-0880, 800-800-8000 (national number), www.super8.com.

$$–$$$ Comfort Suites, 4755 Castleton Wy., 303-814-9999, 800-424-6423 (national number), www.comfortsuites. com. For $10 per night, dogs can stay in any of the suites, though they'll likely be put in a first-floor room. They can be left unattended inside, but housekeeping won't come in during that time.

$$–$$$ Hampton Inn, 4830 Castleton Wy., 303-660-9800, www.hamptoninn.com. There's a $25 fee for the first night of your stay and $5 for each night after. The pet agreement you'll be asked to sign includes a notice that additional charges, starting at $50, will be assessed if professional pet cleaning is required after your stay.

$$–$$$ Holiday Inn Express, 884 Park St., 303-660-9733, www.hiexpress.com. Dogs usually stay in first-floor rooms. You can leave your dog unattended inside the room for a short time only.

$$–$$$ Quality Inn, 200 Wolfensberger Rd., 303-660-2222, 800-228-5151 (national number), www.qualityinn.com. Dogs are allowed for $10 extra per night, per pet.

$$–$$$$ Best Western Inn and Suites Castle Rock, 595 Genoa Wy., 303-814-8800, 888-386-2927, www.bestwestern castlerock.com. It's second-floor rooms only for dogs, with a $15 nightly fee per pet.

Centennial

$$–$$$ Candlewood Suites, 6780 S. Galena St., 303-792-5393, www.candle

woodsuites.com. All of the suites here are dog friendly, and all are studios with full kitchens. Dogs must be 50 pounds or less, and no more than two can stay per unit. For stays of one to six nights, there's a $75 one-time fee; for stays of seven nights and longer, the fee is $150. A dog-walking area is in back of the hotel.

$$$ Staybridge Suites Denver Tech Center, 7150 S. Clinton St., 303-858-9990, www.staybridge.com. Dogs up to 150 pounds (which should cover most of them, unless you're trying to disguise your pony as a dog) can stay in these extended-stay, studio to one-bedroom suites for $20 per night for up to six nights. For stays of seven nights or longer, there's a $150 one-time fee. A dog can be unattended inside only if he's in a travel kennel.

Denver—Downtown

$–$$ Motel 6 Central, 3050 W. 49th Ave., 303-455-8888, 800-466-8356 (national number), www.motel6.com. There's a limit of one well-behaved dog per room.

$$ Econo Lodge Downtown, 930 E. Colfax Ave., 303-813-8000, www.econolodge .com. It's $25 a night per pet, with a limit of two dogs per room. You can leave your dog unattended in the room, but he needs to be in a travel kennel if housekeeping is going to come in. Music fans will appreciate the fact that the motel is across the street from the Ogden Theatre and one block from the Fillmore.

$$ Knights Inn Denver, 2601 Zuni B St., 303-433-8586, www.knightsinn.com. Under the same management as the Ramada Denver Midtown next door, the motel allows dogs for a $25 one-time fee in designated rooms. You can leave your dog unattended inside only if he is in a travel kennel.

$$–$$$ Comfort Inn Central, 401 E. 58th Ave., 303-297-1717, 800-424-6423 (national number), www.comfortinn .com. There's a $10 one-time fee per pet, and you'll be asked to sign a waiver stating that you'll take care of your dog. He can be left unattended in the room as long as he stays in a travel kennel.

$$–$$$ The Holiday Chalet, A Victorian Bed and Breakfast, 1820 E. Colfax Ave. (18 blocks east of downtown), 303-437-8245, www.holidaychalet.net. "We're puppy-dog friendly," says the owner of this small, homey B&B in a restored 1896 former private residence, "but they have to be well mannered." For $5 extra per night, your dog can stay with you in one of the ten rooms, each with Victorian-style or wicker furnishings and a fully equipped kitchen with cool vintage appliances. He can be unattended in the room as long as he's in a travel kennel; if you don't have one, you can borrow one from the B&B. And for $20 per day, owner Crystal Sharp and her black Lab, Clementine, can even dogsit, which includes taking your pooch on a 1.5-mile walk. Plus, Cheesman Park (see Tail-Rated Trails) is only two blocks away.

$$–$$$ Hotel VQ, 1975 Mile High Stadium Cir., 303-433-8331, 800-388-5381, www .hotelvq.com. Dogs who love the Broncos will want to stay at this hotel within barking distance of Invesco Field. There's a $20 nightly fee and a doggie weight limit of 120 pounds, and you can leave your dog unattended in the room. At check-in, you'll be asked to sign a pet liability form.

$$–$$$ La Quinta Inn Denver Central, 3500 Park Ave., 303-458-1222, 800-531-5900 (national number), www.lq.com. You can leave your dog unattended in the room as long as you hang the Do Not Disturb sign on the door.

$$-$$$ Ramada Inn Denver Midtown, 2601 Zuni St., 303-433-6677, www .ramada.com. The motel accepts pets in one of its two buildings, for a $25 one-time fee.

$$-$$$ Ramada Inn Downtown Denver, 1150 E. Colfax Ave., 303-831-7700, www.ramadadenverdowntown.com. Dogs are permitted in all rooms with a $100 deposit. They can be left unattended inside as long as they don't disturb other guests.

$$$ Holiday Inn Denver Central, 4849 Bannock St., 303-292-9500, www.holi dayinn.com. Most rooms are dog friendly for a $50 one-time fee.

$$$-$$$$ Comfort Inn Downtown, 401 17th St., 303-296-0400, 800-237-7431, www.denvercomfortinn.com. The hotel, which is indeed in the heart of downtown Denver, is a notch (or two) above the typical Comfort Inn, in terms of amenities and, well, comfort. Under the same management as the historic Brown Palace across the street, the hotel is connected to the former by an elevated walkway, so you and your dog will have easy access to many of the Palace's amenities, including room service. Canine guests must pay a $50 one-time fee, and there's a maximum of two dogs per room. You can leave your dog unattended in your room, as long as you hang out the Pet in Room sign and leave a cell-phone number with the front desk staff.

$$$-$$$$ The Curtis Hotel, 1405 Curtis St., 303-571-0300, 800-525-6651, www .thecurtis.com. Billed as a "fun boutique hotel," the Curtis sounded like it could either be quirkily amusing or really annoying when we reserved a room there. Luckily, we found it more on the amusing side. Each floor has a different pop-culture theme—e.g., one-hit wonders,

big hair, chick flick—and modern decor, retro childhood games and images, and details like wake-up calls that feature Elvis's voice define the hotel's light-hearted approach. Dogs shouldn't take it personally that they're all put on the sci-fi-themed eighth floor—they're really not regarded as aliens. They are charged $15 extra per night, per pet, with two dogs maximum in each room. There's also a 40-pound weight limit, which is flexible for well-behaved pets. You can leave your dog unattended inside, but housekeeping won't service your room during that time. The staff can provide complimentary dog-walking service, and if Fido runs out of biscuits during his stay, stock up on more in the 5 & Dime off the lobby.

$$$-$$$$ Gregory Inn, 2500 Arapahoe, 303-295-6570, 800-925-6570, www .gregoryinn.com. This bed-and-breakfast comprises two completely renovated twin homes that were originally the wings of a larger house built in 1884; they're on the National Register of Historic Places, and the surrounding Curtis Park neighborhood also contains many historic homes. Small- to medium-sized dogs are allowed in the nine timelessly elegant guest rooms, all with private baths and all but one with gas fireplaces. Larger dogs may stay in the Carriage House, which includes a full kitchen (there's a two-night minimum stay here). "I want people to be very responsible with them, but I love dogs," says owner Steven Gregory. If your dog is unattended in your room, he must be in a travel kennel. Your dog can also play in the large, fenced yard, under your supervision, or just relax on the front veranda and bask under the ceiling fans.

$$$-$$$$ Residence Inn by Marriott Denver City Center, 1725 Champa St., 303-296-3444, 800-593-2809 (national number), www.marriott.com. Dogs pay a $75 one-time fee to stay in the eighth-floor studio to two-bedroom suites, all with full kitchens. Your dog can be unattended inside, but housekeeping will only come in if he is in a travel kennel. On the sixth floor is an outdoor pet-relief area, with wood chips and a fake fire hydrant, making Fido's bathroom breaks more convenient. A hot breakfast buffet is included in the room rates, as is a cocktail hour with appetizers Monday through Thursday.

$$$–$$$$ Residence Inn by Marriott Denver Downtown, 2777 Zuni St., 303-458-5318, 800-331-3131 (national number), www.residenceinndenverdowntown .com. The Residence Inn offers studio or penthouse loft luxury suites, both with fully equipped kitchens. There's a $75 one-time fee to stay with your dog, and you can leave him unattended in the suite, though housekeeping won't service your room during that time. A hot breakfast buffet is included in the room rates, as is a cocktail hour with appetizers Monday through Thursday.

$$$–$$$$ Sheraton Denver Downtown Hotel, 1550 Court Pl., 303-893-3333, www.sheratondenverhotel.com. Dogs who like to be in the heart of the action will enjoy a stay at the Sheraton, which is on the 16th St. pedestrian mall. The hotel has undergone a $70 million renovation to give it a more modern, yet not totally trendy, look from its former incarnation as the Adam's Mark. Your dog need only ask that you sign the hotel's pet waiver (which reiterates that your dog cannot be in the room without you) and, perhaps, request the pet package for him, which includes a Sweet Sleeper dog bed (based on the Sheraton's signature Sweet Sleeper bed), food and water bowls, and a packet of treats and pick-up bags.

$$$–$$$$ TownePlace Suites by Marriott Denver Downtown, 685 Speer Blvd., 303-722-2322, www.marriott.com. In a change from the usual suburban-style buildings that house extended-stay hotels, this one is located in the former headquarters of the A.B. Hirschfeld Press (no relation to me, unfortunately), built in 1947 and featuring a distinctive rounded facade that's a landmark on Speer Blvd. Dogs can stay in designated suites, ranging from studios to two bedrooms and all with full kitchens, for a $100 one-time fee. Your dog can be unattended inside your room.

$$$–$$$$ Warwick Denver Hotel, 1776 Grant St., 303-861-2000, 800-525-2888, www.warwickdenverhotel.com. The recently renovated Warwick, near Capitol Hill, has large, elegantly appointed rooms. Dogs under 50 pounds are welcome in the hotel's third-floor rooms with a $50 one-time fee per dog, and a maximum of two dogs per room. You can leave Fido unattended inside as long as you provide contact info for the front desk staff. Amenities include a restaurant and bar, fitness center, and rooftop heated swimming pool that's open year-round. The hotel is a few blocks from downtown, which means some grassy areas and parks for dog walks are nearby.

$$$$ The Brown Palace, 321 17th St., 303-297-3111, 800-321-2599, www.brown palace.com. Dogs can get a keen sense of Denver's history with a stay at the city's most storied hotel. The Brown Palace opened in 1892 and has operated ever since. Guests have included every US president (except Calvin Coolidge), The Beatles, and present-day celebs like U2 and the Rolling Stones (the hotel has even put together an iPod mix of songs by all the musicians who have stayed there). Rooms are plushly appointed in either Victorian-era style or, more interestingly, art deco; there are also three over-the-top presidential suites. The hotel includes six restaurants and a full-service spa. Canine guests

Clover checks out the eight-story atrium at the dog-friendly Brown Palace Hotel in Denver.

are welcomed with a trio of biscuits baked at the hotel and Brown Palace–logoed bowls and a bed for use during their stay. There's a $75 one-time fee for dogs and a maximum of two dogs per room. Unfortunately, your dog won't be able to join you for daily afternoon tea—a century-old Denver tradition—in the hotel's awesome atrium lobby, but you can leave him in your room unattended, as long as you hang the Pet in Room sign and leave a cellphone number at the front desk.

$$$$ The Burnsley Hotel, 1000 Grant St., 303-830-1000, 800-231-3915, www .burnsley.com. This apartment-style suite hotel near Capitol Hill accepts dogs on one of its floors, for $25 extra per night, per pet. All of the units on the pet-friendly floor are "Denver suites"; each is a generous 700 square feet and includes a bedroom with king-size bed, full kitchen, separate living and dining areas, and a balcony. You can leave your dog unat-

tended inside if you give the front desk your contact info. The hotel has a restaurant and—an especially nice touch—parking is included in the room rates.

 $$$$ Hotel Monaco, 1717 Champa St., 303-296-1717, 800-990-1330, www.monaco-denver.com. Part of the Kimpton group of hip boutique hotels, the Monaco takes pride in its pet friendliness. Not only can you bring your dog, but if you want extra company, a companion goldfish can be brought to your room for the length of your stay. The hotel is housed in two renovated historic buildings near the 16th St. Mall; rooms are large with vividly colored furnishings and decor. Complimentary wine is served each evening in the fancifully ceilinged lobby, and your pooch is welcome to accompany you. During our stay, a therapist from the Aveda Renaissance Spa off the lobby was giving free chair massages during happy hour, and Clover was delighted to find that the woman had just completed a course in canine massage. The pet agreement you'll sign at check-in states that dogs are not to be left unattended in the room, but you may find the hotel flexible on this policy. Dog-dedicated amenities include food and water bowls, a fleecy mat for restful snoozing, bone-shaped biscuits embossed with "Monaco," and a card that details nearby grassy spots where Fido can do his business. A special pet package that you can book in advance also includes a larger welcome package from a local pet boutique and four hours of petsitting arranged through the concierge. And all dogs are welcomed by name on a special dog-shaped sign by the front desk.

 $$$$ Hotel Teatro, 1100 14th St., 303-228-1100, 888-727-1200, www.hotelteatro.com. The Teatro scores extrahigh on the dog welcome meter; Clover rates it as one of her favorite hotels in Colorado. The hotel resides in what was once the home of the Denver Tramway Company, built in 1911. Later, the building housed the University of Colorado at Denver before sitting empty for almost a decade. It's now been beautifully restored into the Teatro, which pampers its human guests with sleek furnishings, luxurious marble baths, Frette linens, and impeccable service. As for canine amenities, at check-in dogs receive Milkbones, a toy, a welcome card detailing the nearest parks, and a Pet in Room sign to alert housekeepers. And waiting for them in the room are personally labeled food and water bowls on bone-shaped placemats, and bottles of Fiji water. If you upgrade to the Pets in the City package, your pooch will also receive a special gift bag with an assortment of treats and toys, a personalized ID tag with the hotel's info on it, pick-up bags, and a copy of *Colorado Dog* magazine. Plus the hotel donates $5 to the Denver Dumb Friends League, the local animal welfare society. You can leave your dog unattended in the room, perhaps while you catch a performance at the Denver Center for the Performing Arts, across the street, and the concierge will walk him on request. Guests, including dogs, can also catch a complimentary ride anywhere in town in the hotel's Cadillac Escalade.

 $$$$ JW Marriott, 150 Clayton, 303-316-2700, 800-372-0064, www.jwmarriott denver.com. Dogs with a yen for shopping will love the JW Marriott's location in the heart of Cherry Creek, home to Denver's chicest boutiques. And the hotel makes a point of welcoming canine guests, with amenities like a personalized biscuit from the nearby Three Dog Bakery, elevated food and water bowls, and a faux-sheepskin bed in the room. Rooms and suites are colorfully furnished in a style you might term modern

traditional. The hotel also has a full-service spa and restaurant. Though you're technically not supposed to leave your dog unattended in your room, the staff might make an exception if you have an especially quiet dog—we recommend asking. Otherwise, dogsitting and walking can be arranged through the concierge.

$$$$ Lumber Baron Inn & Gardens, 2555 W. 37th Ave., 303-477-8205, www.lum berbaron.com. Originally built by a Scottish lumber baron in 1890, and painstakingly restored by the current owners after they came across the by-then abandoned house in 1991, the B&B frequently hosts weddings and murder mystery nights—and dogs. Located in the eclectic Highlands neighborhood, the Queen Anne Victorian house has three richly detailed guest rooms, all with private baths and Jacuzzis, and large-screen TVs. If you leave your dog unattended in your room, he must be in a travel kennel. When you both need a rest after checking out the hip clothing and home accessories boutiques lining 32nd Ave., your dog is welcome to hang with you in the B&B's gardens. "It's practically our own off-leash dog park," says owner Walter Keller, who has two dogs of his own.

$$$$ Oxford Hotel, 1600 17th St., 303-628-540, 800-228-5838, www.the oxfordhotel.com. Best known for its authentically art deco Cruise Room bar, which opened in 1933, the historic Oxford is also quietly very dog friendly. Located in vibrant Lodo, the hotel opened in 1891 and was designed by the same architect who built Denver's Brown Palace hotel. Most of the individually decorated rooms, which range from Victorian and French inspired to art deco, accommodate pets. Visiting dogs get yogurt-covered, bone-shaped biscuits with the Oxord logo at check-in and, in the room, dog dishes on a special mat and bottles of water. A stash of treats is kept in the lobby, and dog walking by the staff is available if things aren't too busy. You can leave your dog unattended in your room while you sip a martini in the Cruise Room or sample oysters at McCormick's Fish House in the hotel.

$$$$ Ritz-Carlton, 1881 Curtis St., 303-312-3800, 800-542-8680 (national number), www.ritzcarlton.com. Pampered Fidos and Fifis (though only one per room) will lack for nothing at the Ritz, which has, as you might expect, huge rooms (starting at 550 square feet) with tastefully neutral, classic furnishings, high-tech entertainment systems, and Frette linens. The hotel asks that you place the Pet in Room sign when your dog is inside, whether attended or not, as housekeeping will only come in if a dog is leashed or in a travel kennel. And if your dog is lucky, the Ritz's chef may whip up a batch of his secret-recipe dog biscuits before arrival. Even canine luxury has its price, of course: an extra $125 per stay.

 $$$$ The Westin Hotel Tabor Center Denver, 1672 Lawrence St., 303-572-9100, 800-228-3000 (national number), www.westintaborcenterdenver .com. The sleekly appointed Westin has a dog-loving management that accepts canines with nothing more than your signature on the hotel's pet waiver. Four-legged guests receive packages with treats and pick-up bags and can request to use a Heavenly dog bed (derived from the Westin's signature Heavenly Bed for humans). As long as your pup behaves quietly, you can leave him unattended in the room while you peruse the shops downstairs in the Tabor Center, perhaps, or visit the on-site spa. And if it's not too busy, the concierge may be able to provide dog-walking outings.

Denver—East

$-$$ Motel 6 Denver East, 12020 E. 39th Ave., 303-371-1980, 800-466-8356 (national number), www.motel6.com. One dog per room is allowed.

$$ Days Inn Denver Business Place, 7030 Tower Rd. 303-373-1500, wwwdaysinn .com. Similar to its sister hotel next door, the Ramada Limited, there's a $35 one-time fee, per pet, with a maximum of two dogs per room (though dogs can't be left unattended here, even if they're in a travel kennel).

$$ Hotel 3737, 3737 Quebec St., 303-388-6161. The hotel is across the street from the old Stapleton Airport and is slated to become a Best Western at some point, but should remain pet friendly. Dogs are allowed in designated rooms with a $15 one-time fee per pet. You can leave your dog unattended in the room if he is in a travel kennel.

$$ Microtel Inn, 18600 E. 63rd Ave., 303-371-8300, 800-771-7171 (national number), www.microtelinn.com. The motel has just two pet-friendly rooms for $10 extra per night, per dog. You can leave your dog unattended as long as you also leave a cell-phone number at the front desk.

$$ Quality Inn Denver East , 3975 Peoria Wy. (12 miles from DIA), 303-371-5640, www.qualityinn.com. Dogs are allowed only in smoking rooms for $10 extra per night.

$$ Super 8 Denver Stapleton, 7201 E. 36th Ave., 303-393-7666, 800-800-8000 (national number), www.super8.com. Dogs are permitted in all rooms for a $15 one-time fee per pet. And your dog can stay unattended in the room.

$$-$$$ Drury Inn Denver, 4400 Peoria St., 303-373-1983, 800-325-8300 (national number), wwwdruryhotels.com. All rooms are dog friendly.

$$–$$$ La Quinta Inn & Suites Denver Airport DIA, 6801 Tower Rd. (6 miles from DIA), 303-371-0888, 800-531-5900 (national number), www.lq.com. You can leave your dog unattended inside the room as long as you leave a contact number at the front desk.

$$–$$$ Quality Inn and Suites, 6890 Tower Rd. (8 miles from DIA), 303-371-5300, www.qualityinn.com. Dogs can stay only in smoking rooms with a $25 one-time fee.

$$–$$$ Ramada Limited Inn and Suites Denver International Airport, 7020 Tower Rd., 303-373-1600. www.ramada.com. Dogs usually stay in third-floor rooms, for a $35 one-time fee per pet. If you leave your dog unattended in the room, he must be in a travel kennel.

$$–$$$ Red Lion Denver Central, 4040 Quebec, 303-321-6666, 800-RED-LION (national number), www.redlion.rdln.com. Dogs stay free if you're a Red Lion R&R Club member; otherwise, it's $20 per stay. There's a limit of two dogs per room. The full-service hotel has a restaurant, fitness center, and pool.

$$$ Embassy Suites Denver-Aurora, 4444 N. Havana St. (12 miles from DIA), 303-375-0400, 800-EMBASSY (national number), www.embassysuites.hilton.com. The two-room units are equipped with refrigerator, microwave, and coffeemaker. You can leave your dog unattended in the room but housekeeping won't come in.

$$$ Hampton Inn DIA, 6290 Tower Rd. 303-371-0200, www.hamptoninn.com. Dogs 25 pounds and under are permitted in first-floor rooms.

$$$ Staybridge Suites DIA, 6951 Tower Rd. (7 miles from DIA), 303-574-0888, www.staydia.com. The nicely appointed studio to two-bedroom suites at this extended-stay hotel all have full kitchens. There's a $75 one-time fee to stay with your dog. You can leave Fido unattended in the room; just put up the Pet in Suite sign you'll get at check-in.

$$$–$$$$ Crowne Plaza, Denver International Airport, 15500 40th Ave. (10 miles from DIA), www.cpdenverairport.com. Dogs pay a $25 one-time fee. There's a fitness center, indoor pool, and restaurant on-site.

$$$–$$$$ Doubletree Denver Hotel, 3203 Quebec St., 303-321-3333, 800-222-TREE (national number), www.doubletree.com. Located across from the former Stapleton Airport, the hotel permits dogs 30 pounds and under in all rooms with a $75 one-time fee, so a single night stay would be on the pricey side. It's okay to leave Fido unattended in the room. The hotel has a restaurant, fitness center, and Olympic-size indoor pool.

$$$–$$$$ Homewood Suites Denver International Airport, 4210 Airport Wy. (13 miles from DIA), 303-371-4555, www.homewoodsuites.hilton.com. For up to six nights, there's a $75 one-time fee to bring your dog along to this extended-stay hotel, where units range from studios to two bedrooms, with full kitchens. The fee is $150 for stays of seven nights and longer. You can leave your dog unattended inside.

$$$–$$$$ Radisson Hotel Denver Stapleton Plaza, 3333 Quebec St., 303-321-3500, 888-201-1718, www.radisson.com. The hotel charges a one-time fee of $50 per pet, with a limit of two dogs per room. Dogs must also weigh less than 70 pounds.

$$$–$$$$ Renaissance Denver Hotel, 3801 Quebec St., 303-399-7500, www .denverrenaissance.com. At this large, full-service hotel, run by Marriott, dogs usually stay with their owners in fourth-floor rooms. There's a $35 one-time fee and a limit of two dogs per room. At check-in, four-legged guests receive small, portable water dishes and a bag of treats from Denver's Three Dog Bakery. A dog can be unattended in the room if he has a travel kennel to stay in.

$$$–$$$$ The Timbers Hotel, 4411 Peoria St., 303-373-1444, 800-844-9404, www.timbersdenver.com. At this all-suite hotel, the one-bedroom and executive units have kitchens, while regular studios have refrigerators and microwaves. Up to two dogs per suite are permitted in designated units for a $50 one-time fee. If your dog is in a travel kennel he can stay unattended in the room.

Denver—North

$ Valli-Hi Motor Hotel, 7320 Pecos Ave. (off Hwy. 36), 303-429-3551, www.val lihimotel.com. There's a $3 fee per night, per dog.

$ Western Motor Inn, 4757 Vasquez Blvd., 303-296-6000. Dogs are welcome for $5 extra per night each.

$$ Howard Johnson Inn Denver, 4765 Federal Blvd., 303-433-8441, 800-I-GOHOJO, www.hojo.com. Dogs are allowed in one of the motel's three buildings for a $25 one-time fee per dog. You can leave your dog unattended as long as you put out the Do Not Disturb sign.

$$ Super 8, 5888 N. Broadway, 303-296-3100, 800-800-8000 (national number), www.super8.com. Dogs under 20 pounds can stay at no extra charge. Larger dogs must pay a $25 one-time fee per visit, per pet. You can leave your dog unattended

inside for short periods of time.

$$–$$$ Quality Inn Central, 200 W. 48th Ave., 303-296-4000, www.qualityinn .com. There's a limit of two dogs per room, and each dog pays a $30 one-time fee.

Denver—South

$–$$ Crossland Economy Studios Denver-Cherry Creek, 4850 Leetsdale Dr., 303-333-2545, www.extendedstayhotels.com. All of the studios have refrigerators, microwaves, and cooktops. The pet fee is $25 per night, with a maximum fee per visit of $150. You can leave your dog unattended in the room if he's in a travel kennel.

$–$$ Homestead Studio Suites Denver Tech Center North, 4885 S. Quebec St., 303-689-9443, www.extendedstayhotels .com. All of the studios have refrigerators, microwaves, and cooktops. The pet fee is $25 per night, with a maximum fee per visit of $150. You can leave your dog unattended inside, though on cleaning day he'll need to be in a travel kennel.

$$ Cameron Motel, 4500 E. Evans, 303-757-2100. Small dogs are allowed in five of the smoking rooms for $5 extra per night, per pet.

$$ Homestead Studio Suites Denver-Cherry Creek, 4444 Leetsdale Dr., 303-388-3880, www.extendedstayhotels.com. All of the studios have refrigerators, microwaves, and cooktops. The pet fee is $25 per night, per pet, with a maximum fee per visit of $150 per pet. You can leave your dog unattended in the room if he's in a travel kennel.

$$–$$$ Boston Commons Executive Hotel and Suites, 6380 S. Boston, 303-290-1100, 866-413-4437, www.bostoncom mons.com. The hotel offers standard guest rooms as well as one- to three-bedroom apartment-style suites with fully outfitted kitchens, gas fireplaces, and washers and dryers. For nightly stays, there's a $25 fee per night, per dog; for stays of a week or more, there's a $75 one-time fee (or $150 for two dogs). You can leave your dog unattended inside as long as you let the front desk know so that arrangements can be made for housekeeping.

$$–$$$ Drury Inn and Suites Tech Center, 9445 E. Dry Creek Rd., 303-694-3400, 800-325-8300 (national number), www .druryhotels.com. The suites have separate bedroom and living areas. Generally, two dogs are allowed per room. You can leave your dog unattended for up to 30 minutes inside, as long as you leave a cell-phone number at the front desk.

$$–$$$ La Quinta Inn Denver Cherry Creek, 1975 S. Colorado Blvd., 303-758-8886, 800-753-3757 (national number), www.lq.com. Dogs are allowed in any of the rooms here.

$$–$$$ TownePlace Suites by Marriott Denver Southeast, 3699 S. Monaco, 303 759-9393, 800-257-3000 (national number), www.marriott.com. There's a $100 one-time fee for your dog to join you at this extended-stay hotel. Dogs can be left unattended inside the suites, which range from studios to two bedrooms, with full kitchens.

$$–$$$$ Embassy Suites Denver-Southeast, 7525 E. Hampden Ave., 303-696-6644, 800-EMBASSY (national number), www.embassysuites.hilton.com. Dogs 35 pounds and under can stay in designated rooms for $35 per night. You can leave your dog unattended inside, but if he's not in a travel kennel, the housekeepers won't enter to service your room.

$$–$$$$ Hampton Inn and Suites, 5001 S. Ulster St., 303-804-9900, www.hampton

inn.com. All rooms are pet friendly. Your quiet dog can be left unattended inside, but housekeeping won't enter during that time.

 $$–$$$$ Loews Denver Hotel, 4150 E. Mississippi Ave., 303-782-9300, 800-345-9172 (national number), www.loewshotels.com. Thanks to its enlightened former general manager Matthew Kryjak and his dog, Blondie, this particular hotel spearheaded the now-nationwide Loews Loves Pets program. For a $25 one-time fee, dogs are welcomed in the fairly luxe rooms on floors two through six. On check-in, Fido receives his own pawprint bag full of complimentary treats and toys and an ID tag, as well as a personal welcome note from the GM that includes a list of nearby walking routes to sniff out (such as the Cherry Creek bike path, two blocks away), veterinary info, locations of pet shops and groomers, pet-sitters, and pet-friendly restaurants. The hotel also offers a special room-service menu for pets, which includes grilled lamb or chicken with rice and "bowwow tenderloin" (and grilled liver or salmon with rice for visiting cats). The recipes were developed with a veterinarian and are designed to help your dog deal with any travel stress, including jet lag or altitude adjustment. If you don't want your dog to get too used to specially cooked meals, you can also order him up some regular old dry or canned dog food. Regardless of choice, he can then nosh in style with hotel-provided food and water bowls on a special pet placemat. And for canines who turn up their noses at mere tap water, bottled water is available. Once he's happily sated, Fido can take a long snooze on the in-room dog bed (available on request), and you can even put out a special Do Not Disturb sign when you head out for your own gourmet meal. The hotel asks that you leave a cell-phone number if you do leave your dog unattended; if he makes a nuisance of himself, the staff may remove him from the room and bring him downstairs—as well as contact you. Pet videos are available if Fido wants something to be entertained by while you're gone. And when he is ready to go out and explore the city, the hotel will loan him a leash or collar if he forgot to pack his (travel kennels are also available for loan). For short outings, bring him to the hotel's own enclosed backyard, where Fido can romp off leash if he's a good listener and pick-up bags are provided for easy cleanup.

$$$ Fairfield Inn and Suites, 1680 S. Colorado Blvd., 303-691-2223, 800-690-9799, www.fairfieldinn.com. The hotel has eight designated pet rooms available with a $50 one-time fee. You can leave Rover unattended in the room as long as he doesn't cause anyone to complain about excessive barking.

$$$–$$$$ Four Points by Sheraton Denver Southeast, 6363 E. Hampden Ave., 303-758-7000, www.fourpointsdenver southeast.com. This large, full-service hotel only asks for a credit card as a deposit to stay with your dog, and pets are usually placed in lower-level rooms for easier outdoor access. Rover can be unattended inside the room, but unless he's kenneled, housekeeping won't come in during that time.

Denver—West

$$ Days Inn Central, 620 Federal Blvd., 303-571-1715, 800-DAYS-INN (national number), www.daysinn.com. Dogs can stay in one of the hotel's designated pet-friendly rooms for a $25 one-time fee, per pet. Also, your stay with your dog can't exceed five nights.

$$ Howard Johnson Inn, 4765 Federal Blvd., 303-433-8441, 800-I-GOHOJO (national number), www.hojo.com. There's

a $25 one-time fee for dogs, and it's okay for them to be unattended in the room.

Englewood

$–$$ Homestead Studio Suites Denver Tech Center South, 9650 E. Geddes Ave., 303-708-8888, www.extendedstayhotels .com. All of the studios have refrigerators, microwaves, and cooktops. The pet fee is $25 per night, per pet, with a maximum fee per visit of $150 per pet. You can leave your dog unattended inside as long as he's in a travel kennel.

$$ Days Inn Englewood Denver Tech Center, 9719 E. Geddes, 303-768-9400, 800-DAYS-INN (national number), www .daysinn.com. Dogs are allowed for a $25 one-time fee, but they can't stay longer than three nights.

$$ Extended Stay Deluxe Denver Tech Center South, 9604 E. Easter Ave., 303-858-0292, www.extendedstayhotels.com. All of the large studios have full kitchens. The pet fee is $25 per night, per pet, with a maximum fee per visit of $150 per pet. You can leave your dog unattended inside, but housekeeping will only service your unit if he's in a travel kennel.

$$–$$$ Candlewood Suites, 10535 El Diente Ct. (Meridian Business Park), 303-858-9900, www.candlewoodsuites.com. There's a fairly steep $75 one-time fee for dogs if you stay one to three nights, and a $150 fee for longer stays. Only studio and one-bedroom suites are pet friendly, and dogs must be less than 80 pounds.

$$–$$$ Holiday Inn Express Hotel and Suites, 7380 S. Clinton St., 303-662-0777, www.hiexpress.com. The dog fee is $50 per stay.

$$–$$$ Hotel Gold Crown, 7770 S. Peoria St., 303-790-7770. The hotel, formerly a Holiday Inn, requires only a credit card as deposit to stay with your pet, and usually there's a maximum of two dogs per room. You can leave Fido unattended in the room at your discretion.

$$–$$$$ Homewood Suites by Hilton Denver Tech Center, 199 Inverness Drive West, 303-706-0102, www.homewoodsuites.hilton.com. The one- and two-bedroom suites all have full kitchens, and rates include breakfast and a reception Monday to Thursday that includes a light meal. But not only is the pet charge a $100 one-time fee, but that's per dog (with a maximum of two dogs). Even for a long-term stay, that's pricey.

$$–$$$$ Hyatt Summerfield Suites, 9280 E. Costilla Ave., 303-706-1945, www.summerfieldsuites.hyatt.com. You'll find one- and two-bedroom suites here with lots of amenities as well as fully equipped kitchens. But there's a whopping $150 one-time pet fee for a one-bedroom suite, $200 for a two bedroom. You can leave your dog unattended inside, preferably in a travel kennel; if your dog isn't kenneled, housekeeping won't enter during that time.

$$$ Residence Inn by Marriott Denver Tech Center, 6565 S. Yosemite, 303-740-7177, www.residenceinndenver.com. You and your dog can stay in either studio or penthouse suites, both with fully equipped kitchens, but it won't be cheap for a short-term stay. There's a $75 one-time pet fee, per dog, with a maximum of two dogs per room. You can leave Rover unattended inside as long as you put out the Pet in Room sign; housekeeping will only come in, however, if he's in a travel kennel.

$$$–$$$$ Embassy Suites Denver Tech Center, 10250 E. Costilla Ave., 303-792-0433, 800-EMBASSY (national number), www.embassydenvertech.com. All of the two-room suites are pet friendly, with no restrictions.

Golden

$–$$ Golden Motel, 510 24th St., 303-279-5581. For stays of one or two nights, there's a $10 one-time fee per dog; if you're staying three or more nights, the fee is $20 per dog. Some units have kitchens. You can leave your dog unattended in the room for a short time.

$$ La Quinta Inn Denver Golden, 3301 Youngfield Service Rd., 303-279-5565, 800-753-3757 (national number), www.lq.com. Dogs are welcome in all rooms, and you can leave yours unattended inside.

$$–$$$ Comfort Suites Denver West, 11909 W. 6th Ave., 303-231-9929, www.comfortsuites.com. Dogs may stay in designated rooms for $10 per night, per pet, and there's a pet agreement you'll be asked to sign at check-in. Your dog can be unattended in the room as long as you leave a contact number at the front desk.

$$–$$$ Holiday Inn Denver West, 14707 W. Colfax Ave., 303-279-7611, 800-HOLIDAY (national number). You can leave your dog unattended inside the room, but housekeeping won't enter during that time.

$$–$$$ A Touch of Heaven/Talmar Bed and Breakfast, 16720 W. 63rd Pl., 303-279-4133, www.coloradovacation.com/bed/talmar. This B&B offers several elaborately decorated rooms, including the Royal Suite, which features a sunken bathroom with waterfall, Jacuzzi, and sauna as well as a sitting room with marble fireplace and a white baby-grand piano. Dogs are welcome for $20 extra per night, and "we try to give them some special treatment," notes owner Kathy Bury. Bury may be able to do some dog-sitting if you have to leave your pooch behind. The B&B is home to a pair of Arabian stallions who like to interact with guests.

$$$–$$$$ Candlewood Suites, 895 Tabor St., 303-232-7171, www.candlewood suites.com. Dogs under 80 pounds, up to two per unit, are allowed in the studio and one-bedroom suites. There's a $75 one-time fee for stays of one to six nights, and a $150 fee for stays of seven nights and up. You can leave your dog unattended inside as long as you put the Pet in Suite magnet on your door, but you'll have to take your dog with you when housecleaning is scheduled.

$$$–$$$$ Quality Suites, 29300 Hwy. 40 (at Evergreen Pkwy.), 303-526-2000, www.qualityinn.com. Though it has a Golden address, the hotel is actually at the Evergreen exit off I-70. Dogs can stay in patio rooms, which have easy outdoor access, with a $50 deposit. They can be unattended in the room only if in a travel kennel. The historic El Rancho restaurant is next door.

$$$–$$$$ Residence Inn Denver West/ Golden, 14600 W. 6th Ave., 303-271-0909, 800-283-1084 (national number), www.marriott.com/dengo. Unlike some other extended-stay hotels, this one differentiates between short-term and longer dog visits. For a stay of up to three nights, there's a $25 one-time fee to stay in one of the pet-designated suites. For stays of four nights or more, the one-time pet charge is $100. You can leave your dog unattended in the room, but housekeeping won't come in during that time.

 $$$$ The Golden Hotel, 800 11th St., 303-279-0100, 800-233-7214, www.the goldenhotel.com. This comfortably appointed boutique hotel within walking distance of everything in downtown Golden offers four-legged guests a nice change from nearby chain hotels along with a warm welcome. Canine guests up to 75 pounds each (with a limit

of two per room) pay an extra charge of $15 per night, per dog, to stay in designated rooms and must put down a deposit of $100. They get treats and a bandanna at check-in and can request bowls to use during their stay. The paved Clear Creek bike path, right next to the hotel, is convenient and scenic for dog walking. And the hotel has info on other nearby hiking trails and dog parks, as well as veterinarians, groomers, and dogsitters.

$$$$ Table Mountain Inn, 1310 Washington Ave., 303-277-9898, 800-762-9898, www.tablemountaininn.com. This southwestern-style hotel in downtown Golden allows dogs (by advance reservation only) in its traditional king and double queen rooms, in the hotel's original section, which dates to 1925 (the rooms are thoroughly updated). There's a $10 nightly fee, with a maximum of two dogs per room. You can leave your dog unattended in your room if he's in a travel kennel, perhaps while you enjoy a margarita and chile rellenos at the popular southwestern restaurant off the lobby.

Glendale

$$–$$$$ Staybridge Suites, 4220 E. Virginia Ave., 303-321-5757, www.stay bridge.com. Up to two dogs per unit are welcome in the suites, which range from studios to two bedrooms. For stays of one or two nights, there's a $25 nightly fee. If you and your dog stay from three to six nights, the charge switches to a $75 one-time fee. After that, the one-time fee is $100 for a seven-night stay, $125 for eight nights, and $150 for stays of nine nights and longer. If your dog has a travel kennel to be in, he can remain unattended in the room.

Greenwood Village

$–$$ Homestead Studio Suites Denver Tech Center South-Greenwood Village, 9253 E. Costilla Ave., 303-858-1669,

51

www.extendedstayhotels.com. All of the studios have refrigerators, microwaves, and cooktops. The pet fee is $25 per night, per pet, with a maximum fee per visit of $150 per pet. You can leave your dog unattended inside, but housekeeping won't enter while he's there alone.

$–$$ Motel 6, 9201 E. Arapahoe Rd., 303-790-8220, 800-466-8356 (national number), www.motel6.com. If you're staying with one dog, there's no extra charge. If you've got two, there's a $5 one-time fee.

$$ Extended StayAmerica Denver Tech Center North, 5200 S. Quebec St., 303-220-8448, www.extendedstayhotels.com. All rooms are studios with full kitchens. The pet fee is $25 per night overall, with a maximum fee per visit of $150. It's okay for your dog to be unattended in the room.

$$ Ramada Inn Denver Tech Center, 5150 S. Quebec, 303-721-1144, www.ramada .com. Dogs are allowed in most of the motel's rooms with a $25 one-time fee.

$$–$$$ Hampton Inn, 9231 E. Arapahoe Rd., 303-792-9999, www.hamptoninn .com. Two dogs per room are allowed; they can be left unattended only if they're in a travel kennel.

$$–$$$ La Quinta Inn and Suites Denver Tech Center, 7077 S. Clinton St., 303-649-9969, 800-753-3757 (national number), www.lq.com. Dogs are allowed in all rooms.

$$–$$$ La Quinta Inn and Suites Denver Englewood Tech Center, 9009 E. Arapahoe Rd., 303-799-4555, 800-753-3757 (national number), www.lq.com. The suites range from studios to one bedrooms, some with kitchens that include a stove but no oven, some with minifridge and microwave only. You can leave your dog unattended inside as long as you leave a phone number at the front desk.

Henderson
$$ Super 8 Henderson, 9051 I-76 (at 88th Ave.), 303-287-8888, 800-800-8000 (national number), www.super8.com. Dogs are permitted in certain rooms for a $15 one-time fee.

$$–$$$ Holiday Inn Express, 9041 Brighton Rd., 303-301-1050, www.hiexpress .com. Dogs usually stay in first-floor rooms, for a $15 one-time fee per pet and a credit-card deposit. They can be unattended in the room if they're in a travel kennel.

Highlands Ranch
$$–$$$ Comfort Suites Denver South, 7060 E. County Line Rd., 303-770-5400, www.comfortsuites.com. One dog who weighs 50 pounds or less is permitted per room with a $15 nightly fee. In addition, a $50 deposit is required.

$$–$$$$ Residence Inn by Marriott–Highlands Ranch, 93 W. Centennial Blvd. 303-683-5500, www.marriott.com. The apartment-style suites range from studios to one and two bedrooms. All have fully equipped kitchens, and the two-bedroom units have gas fireplaces, too. There's a $100 one-time fee for a dog, and he can be left unattended inside. You'll want to let the front desk know if your dog's alone so they can alert housekeeping.

Lakewood
$–$$ Extended StayAmerica Lakewood South, 7393 W. Jefferson Ave., 303-986-8300, www.extendedstayhotels.com. The studios have full kitchens. The pet fee is $25 per night, per pet, with a maximum fee per visit of $150 per pet. Your dog can be unattended in the room as long as you post the Pet in Room sign you'll receive at check-in.

$–$$ Motel 6, 480 Wadsworth Blvd., 303-232-4924, 800-466-8356 (national number), www.motel6.com. Dogs up to 30 pounds, one per room, get the nod here.

$$ Extended StayAmerica Lakewood West, 715 Kipling St., 303-275-0840, www.extendedstayhotels.com. The studios have full kitchens. The pet fee is $25 per night, per pet, with a maximum fee per visit of $150 per pet. You can leave Fido unattended inside if he's in a travel kennel.

$$–$$$ Best Western Denver Southwest, 3440 S. Vance St., 303-989-5500, 800-707-5188, www.bestwesterndenver.com. The motel has designated pet rooms and two dog-walking areas, one on each side of the building.

$$–$$$ Comfort Suites Southwest, 7260 W. Jefferson , 303-988-8600, www.comfortsuites.com. The pet charge is $15 per night, per dog. All of the suites have two rooms and include microwaves, refrigerators, and coffeemakers.

$$–$$$ Holiday Inn, 7390 W. Hampden (at Wadsworth), 303-980-9200, www.holidayinn.com. Canines 30 pounds and under are permitted, usually in second-floor rooms, for a $50 one-time fee. They can be left unattended in the room as long as the front desk is notified.

$$–$$$ La Quinta Inn and Suites Denver Southwest Lakewood, 7190 W. Hampden Ave., 303-969-9700, 800-753-3757 (national number), www.lq.com. Your dog can be unattended in the room if you leave a contact number with the front desk staff.

$$–$$$ TownePlace Suites by Marriott, 800 Tabor St., 303-232-7790, 800-257-3000 (national number), www.marriott.com. There's a $100 one-time fee to stay with your dog at these studio to two-bedroom suites with kitchens, so an extended stay would make the most sense. You can leave your dog unattended inside.

$$–$$$$ Sheraton Denver West, 360 Union Blvd., 303-987-2000, www.sheraton.com. Dogs 80 pounds or under can stay here, and they receive a small package of treats and pick-up bags for their owners at check-in. The only thing you'll need to do is sign the hotel's pet waiver.

Littleton

$$–$$$ Holiday Inn Express, 12683 W. Indore Pl., 720-981-1000, www.hiexpress.com. First-floor rooms are dog friendly for $20 per night extra and with a maximum of three dogs per room. You can leave your dog unattended inside if he's in a travel kennel and you leave a cell-phone number at the front desk.

$$–$$$ Homewood Suites, 7630 Shaffer Pkwy., 720-981-4763, www.homewoodsuites.hilton.com. These studio to two-bedroom suites have full kitchens, and rates include breakfast and a reception with a light meal Monday to Thursday. Unlike most extended-stay hotels, this one differentiates a bit in its pet fee, depending on the length of your stay. For visits of less than ten nights, you'll pay a $50 one-time fee for your dog, plus a $10 nightly charge. For stays of more than ten nights, there's a $150 one-time fee. You can leave your dog unattended if he's in a travel kennel.

Lone Tree

$–$$ Extended StayAmerica Denver–Park Meadows, 8752 S. Yosemite St., 303-662-1511, www.extendedstayhotels.com. All rooms are studios with full kitchens. The hotel prefers dogs under 30 pounds, with a limit of two per room. The pet fee is $25 per night, per dog, with a maximum fee per visit of $150 per dog. You can leave your dog unattended inside the room.

$$$–$$$$ Staybridge Suites Denver South–Park Meadows, 7820 Park Meadows Dr., 303-649-1010, www.staybridge .com. The dog fee is more reasonable for these studio to one-bedroom suites than at many other extended-stay hotels. It's a $20 nightly fee, with a max of $100 per stay, even if you're there longer than five nights. You can leave your dog unattended in the room, preferably in a travel kennel. And there's a dog-walking area on the south side of the building.

Northglenn

$$–$$$ La Quinta Inn Denver Northglenn, 345 W. 120th Ave., 303-252-9800, 800-753-3757 (national number). The hotel is popular among dog-show competitors. Dogs are allowed in all of the rooms and can be left unattended inside (you'll be asked to sign a pet agreement at check-in that if you do leave your dog unattended, he won't disturb other guests).

$$–$$$ Ramada Plaza Denver North, 10 E. 120th Ave., 303-452-4100, www .ramada.com. Dogs under 30 pounds are allowed, with a $25 one-time fee and a maximum of two dogs per room. Your dog can be in the room unattended if he's in a travel kennel.

Parker

$$ Super 8 Parker, 6230 E. Pine Ln., 720-851-2644, 800-800-8000 (national number), www.super8.com. Dogs are put in a pet-friendly wing of the motel, with a $25 one-time fee per pet. If your dog stays in a travel kennel, he can be left unattended in the room.

$$$–$$$$ Holiday Inn Select, 19308 Cottonwood Dr., 303-248-2147, www .hiselect.com. If you're really stuck for a place to stay with your dog in Parker, you might consider this Holiday Inn, which charges a $75 nightly fee if your dog is contained within a travel kennel, and a

$150 nightly fee if he doesn't have a travel kennel. Your dog can be unattended in the room if he's in his kennel. The on-site restaurant is a steak house (if you have any money left over).

Thornton

$–$$ Crossland Economy Studios, 8750 Grant St., 303-430-4474, www.extended stayhotels.com. All the studios have refrigerators, microwaves, and cooktops. The pet fee is $25 per night, per pet, with a maximum fee per visit of $150 per pet. You can leave your dog unattended in the room, but unless he's in a travel kennel, you won't get housekeeping service.

$–$$ Motel 6, 6 W. 83rd Pl., 303-429-1550, 800-466-8356 (national number), www.motel6.com. Though the motel prefers small dogs (15 pounds), you probably won't be turned away if your pooch weighs in on the larger side.

$$ Sleep Inn, 12101 N. Grant St., 303-280-9818, www.sleepinn.com. There's a $10 one-time fee per dog.

Westminster

$$ Extended StayAmerica Denver– Westminster, 1291 W. 120th Ave., 303-280-0111,www.extendedstayhotels.com. All rooms are studios with full kitchens. The pet fee is $25 per night, per dog, with a maximum fee per visit of $150 per dog. The hotel prefers that your dog not be unattended in the room, but if you do have to leave him for a short while, you must leave a contact number with the front desk staff.

$$ Super 8 Westminster Denver North, 12055 Melody Dr., 303-451-7200, 800-800-8000 (national number), www .super8.com. The motel permits dogs in pet-designated rooms for $5.50 per night, per dog. They can be left unattended inside if they're in a travel kennel.

$$–$$$ Comfort Inn Northwest, 8500 Turnpike Dr., 303-428-3333, www.com fortinn.com. Dogs are permitted in the rooms only, not the suites, for $10 extra per night, per pet, with a maximum of two dogs per room. It's okay to leave your dog unattended inside.

$$–$$$ Comfort Suites, 12085 Delaware St., 303-429-5500, www.comfortsuites .com. Dogs are permitted in designated units for a $15 one-time fee per pet. All of the suites have two rooms, with refrigerators, microwaves, and coffeemakers. Your dog can be unattended inside as long as you put out the Do Not Disturb sign.

$$–$$$ La Quinta Inn and Suites Westminster Promenade, 10179 Church Ranch Wy., 303-438-5800, 800-753-3757 (national number), www.lq.com. Dogs 35 pounds and under are allowed in all of the rooms; you can leave yours unattended but housekeeping won't come in during that time.

$$–$$$ La Quinta Inn Denver Westminster Mall, 8701 Turnpike Dr., 303-425-9099, 800-753-3757 (national number). Dogs are allowed in all of the rooms. You can leave your dog unattended inside if you let the front desk staff know.

$$–$$$$ Doubletree Hotel Denver–North, 8773 Yates Dr., 303-427-4000, www .doubletree.com. Most rooms here are dog friendly with a $25 one-time fee. Your dog can stay unattended in the room. The hotel has an indoor pool, sundeck, fitness center, and Cajun-style restaurant.

$$–$$$$ Residence Inn Westminster, 5010 W. 88th Pl., 303-427-9500, www.marriott .com. There's a $75 one-time fee for dogs to stay in any of the suites, which range from studios to two bedrooms. You can leave your dog unattended in the room.

 $$$–$$$$ Westin Hotel Westminster, 10600 Westminster Blvd., 303-410-5000, www.westindenver boulder.com. Though the official policy states that guest dogs must be 30 pounds or under, larger dogs do often stay at the hotel. Four-legged visitors get to use a Heavenly dog bed (based on the hotel's signature Heavenly people bed) and food and water bowls during their stay, and a welcome package includes biscuits. If your dog forgot to pack his leash and/or collar, he can request new ones from the hotel. You can leave your dog unattended in the room; the pet waiver you'll sign at check-in requests a contact number so you can be reached in case there's any problem. This Westin has two restaurants, an indoor pool, workout room, and sauna, as well as a large conference center. Grassy areas for dog walking are nearby.

Wheat Ridge

$–$$ Motel 6, 9920 W. 49th Ave., 303-424-0658, 800-466-8356 (national number), www.motel6.com. One dog per room is permitted.

$$ Ramada Denver West, 4700 Kipling, 303-423-4000, www.ramada.com. Dogs are welcome with a $25 one-time fee and you can leave yours unattended in the room, as long as you leave a contact number at the front desk.

$$–$$$ Howard Johnson Inn Denver West, 12100 W. 44th Ave. (Exit 266 off I-70), 303-467-2400, 800-I-GOHOJO (national number), www.hojo.com. It's $10 a night for your dog to stay at HoJo's.

$$$ Holiday Inn Express, 10101 S. I-70 Service Rd., 303-424-8300, www.hi express.com. One dog per room, who weighs less than 10 pounds, can stay for a $25 one-time fee.

MOUNTAIN COMMUNITIES SOUTHWEST OF DENVER
Bailey

$$–$$$ Glen-Isle Resort, 573 Old Stage Coach Rd., 303-838-5461, www.colo radodirectory.com/glenisleresort. This longtime family-owned resort is situated on the South Platte River. The lodge building, which dates from 1900, is on the National Register of Historic Places. Dogs are permitted in the resort's fifteen cabins, almost all with fireplaces and some with kitchens, for $5 extra per night, per dog. In addition to the scenic setting, there's a large gift and antique shop here. The resort is in full operation from Memorial Day through Labor Day. During the winter, only a few of the cabins remain open.

Evergreen

$$–$$$ Bear Creek Cabins, 27400 Hwy. 74, 303-674-3442, www.bearcreekcab insco.com. Built in 1947, these eight studio log cabins have been renovated and include kitchens and wood-burning fireplaces. Up to two dogs each are allowed in most of them for a $20 one-time fee (and another $10 if you have a second dog). Your dog must promise not to jump up or sleep on the furniture. The property's 3 acres, which Bear Creek runs through, include open meadows for walking your pooch on a leash, as well as grills and picnic tables for dining alfresco. Catch-and-release fly-fishing is available on the creek, too.

$$$ Bauer's Spruce Island Chalets, 5937 S. Brook Forest Rd., 303-674-4757, www.bsichalets.com. Located on 16 acres with a pond, these seven units range from studios to four bedrooms. The studios come with microwave and refrigerator; others have full kitchens, and some have fireplaces. The three- and four-bedroom chalets are each separate houses. All are furnished in what you could call vintage country style. For dogs, there's a $30 nightly fee per pet. You can leave Rover unattended inside the three individual chalets as long as he's in a travel kennel; he cannot be left unattended inside the other four units, which are all in one building. The pet agreement you'll sign at check-in spells out all the stipulations (e.g., no jumping up on the furniture). Be sure to keep your dog leashed at all times when outside. Note that minimum-stay requirements apply.

$$$–$$$$ Alpen Way Chalet Inn, 4980 Hwy. 73, 303-674-7467, www.alpen waychalet.net. The inn has two units where dogs 20 pounds and under are allowed: one suite in the main lodge and one cabin. The fee is $20 per night, per pet. You'll be able to exercise Fido, on his leash, on the surrounding acre of mountain property, the site of a former estate from the 1930s.

Pine

$$$–$$$$ Meadow Creek B&B Inn, 13438 Berry Hill Lane, 303-838-4167, www.meadowcreekbb.com. Located on 34 acres, this well-kept B&B consists of a large stone house, built in 1929 by an Italian prince for his Colorado-born wife, and a separate cabin. Of the seven rooms, four are dog friendly (including the cabin), and all of these have private entrances. The pet fee is $25 per night, and whether the fee is charged per pet or not (if you're traveling with a pair of dogs) depends on the size and type of dogs you have. All rooms have private baths, and three of the dog-friendly ones also have fireplaces, kitchenettes, and interior hot tubs. If you leave your dog alone in the room, he should be in a travel kennel. Kelly, a mixed breed, is the resident four-legged greeter. The inn frequently hosts weddings on summer weekends, something to keep in mind when booking.

CAMPGROUNDS

Bear Creek Lake Park. This City of Lakewood–run park is off Morrison Rd., .25 mile east of C-470 (47 sites).

Chatfield State Park. 1 mile from the intersection of C-470 and Wadsworth Blvd., southwest of Denver (197 sites).

Cherry Creek State Park. 1.5 miles south of I-225, off Parker Rd. in Aurora (125 sites).

WORTH A PAWS

Furry Scurry. The first weekend in May, dogs from all over the metro area and their owners convene in Denver's Washington Park to participate in this walk/run, which raises money for the Denver Dumb Friends League, which celebrates its 100th birthday in 2010. The 2-mile course circles one of the park's lakes. After the "race," dogs can check out the booths purveying pet products and information, enjoy a variety of treat samples, or enter competitions such as best trick or closest owner/dog look-alike. Owners can fuel up on bagels and other snacks and model their Furry Scurry T-shirts. It's the canine social event of the year! You can register in advance or on race day; in addition to the registration fee, funds are raised through pledge donations that you can collect. For more information, contact the Dumb Friends League at 303-751-5772 or go to www.ddfl.org.

Wag 'n Trail. Held at the Glendale Farm Open Space in Douglas County the third Saturday of September, this hike for dogs and their people covers the 1.6-mile trail that winds around the open space. There's no entry fee, but you're encouraged to raise money through pledges, which will benefit the Dumb Friends League Buddy Center, an animal shelter in Castle Rock. If you raise at least $75, you'll get a T-shirt, a photo of you and your pooch hiking, and ice cream for both of you. After the hike, you and Rover can browse pet-friendly products for sale, watch demos by groups like the Douglas County K-9 unit or the Team RUFF flyball dogs, or listen to the live music. For more information, contact the Dumb Friends League at 303-751-5772 or go to www.ddfl.org.

MaxFund Lucky Mutt Strut. Since 1988, the MaxFund Animal Adoption Center, a nonprofit no-kill shelter, has helped injured animals who are ownerless. The 2-mile Lucky Mutt Strut (a run/walk) for dogs and people is held in late August at Denver's Washington Park, and registration fees and pledges raised benefit MaxFund. After the strut, stick around for canine demos and pet-related exhibits. Dogs should be at least six months old to participate, and one dog per runner or walker is allowed. Each human participant gets a Mutt Strut T-shirt, and each dog gets a goody bag. Register in advance or on race day, either as an individual or as a team of people and dogs. Call 303-595-4917 for details or go to www.max fund.org.

Intermountain Humane Society Dog Walk. This early summer event (late June to mid-July) brings together dogs and owners from the mountain communities southwest of Denver, and visitors, for a day of hiking and fun at the private Meyer/Motorhead Ranch in Conifer. The centerpiece event is a 2-mile-loop hike around the historic ranch property, with informational placards along the trail put up for the day by the Conifer Historical Society. Or opt for the half-mile family stroll around the ranch's pond. For both, the rule is one leashed dog per person. Donuts and coffee are served before the hike; afterward are pet-themed exhibits; trolley rides to the ranch's historic main house; a low-cost microchip clinic; flyball, agility, and dog water-rescue demos; live music; food booths; and even the chance to buy a take-home DNA test so you can figure out once and for all what kind of mutt you have. Register in advance online or at the event; entry fees benefit the humane society's animal shelter, located in Pine, and participants get a T-shirt and pet goody bag. For more information, contact the Intermountain Humane Society at 303-838-2668 or go to www.imhs.org.

Colorado Flyball/Team RUFF. Flyball is a fast-paced canine sport that's as fun to watch (for humans) as it is to play (for dogs). Developed in California in the 1970s by a dog trainer, flyball involves a relay race between two teams of four dogs each. The dogs run down a course with four hurdles, release a tennis ball from a spring-loaded box, catch the ball, then run back over the hurdles to tag their next teammate. Top teams can complete the course in less than 16 seconds (all four dogs).

At least a dozen flyball teams now exist around Colorado. Team RUFF was Colorado's first club, formed in 2000; its athletes give demos at various events (even Nuggets and Broncos games) and the team sponsors four tournaments a year in the Denver area. And, yes, they're pretty fly. For more info, go to www.coloradoflyball.com.

Colorado Disc Dogs Frisbee Competitions. These two events are part of an annual series of canine Frisbee contests put on by the Colorado Disc Dogs. The first is held in Thornton during the third weekend of May at the Thornton Rec Center (108th St. and Colorado Blvd.). Dogs compete in two categories: the minidistance, in which they receive points for catching distance and style in 60-second rounds (with bonus points for midair catches); and the freestyle, in which they demonstrate their best tricks. A two-day event, the Colorado

Canine Challenge, takes place the second weekend of August at Cornerstone Park in Littleton (Windermere and Belleview). In addition to the minidistance and freestyle, dogs can compete in the Quadruped, in which the winner is the owner who can throw the Frisbee the farthest and the dog who can then catch it. Bring your dog to participate or just to watch; no previous competitive experience is necessary. For more information, go to www.coloradodiscdogs.com.

Red Rocks Park and Amphitheatre. Red Rocks is a spectacular outdoor concert venue nestled among a natural amphitheater of—as the name implies—striking red sandstone. Though your dog is unable to come howl and cheer with the crowd during the annual summer concert series, he can pay a visit with you during nonevent times. You can even bring him onstage to play air guitar and imagine an appreciative audience of thousands before him—as long as he stays on a leash. Some hiking trails run through the park, including a 1.4-mile loop trail that starts at the Trading Post gift shop and goes by several of the park's unusual rock formations. To reach Red Rocks, take I-70 west from Denver to the Morrison exit (259); head south on Hwy. 93 for about 1.5 miles to the park entrance on the right. For more information, go to www.redrocksonline.com.

Buffalo Bill's Grave. Okay, so it's not quite Graceland, but your dog may be interested in sniffing out a bit of the Wild West with a visit to the final resting place of William F. Cody, a.k.a. Buffalo Bill. Rover won't be able to enter the Memorial Museum or gift shop, but he can walk with you (on leash) to the gravesite as well as enjoy the view from Lookout Mountain. From Hwy. 6, coming from Golden or Lakewood, turn west on 19th St. and follow the switchbacks up to the signed turnoff for the grave. From I-70 west coming from Denver, take Exit 256, make a right at the stop sign, and follow along Paradise and Charros Rds. to Lookout Mountain Rd. Go right at the T-intersection and follow Lookout Mountain Rd. to the signed turnoff for the grave. The museum is open 9 AM– 5 PM, every day, from May 1–October 31; 9 AM–4 PM, Tuesday through Sunday, from November 1 to April 30. Call 303- 526-0744 for additional information, or go to www.buffalobill.org.

The Museum of Outdoor Arts. Does your dog complain that he never gets to go to museums? Bring him to The Museum of Outdoor Arts, a "museum without walls," that showcases pieces by artists like Red Grooms, Guy Dill, and Harry Marinsky. The forty-plus pieces of artwork—90 percent of which is outdoor sculpture—are spread out among several locations. One grouping is at the sculpture garden outside the museum's indoor gallery and offices (1000 Englewood Pkwy., second floor of the Englewood Civic Center building), just east of Santa Fe Dr. and north of W. Hampden Ave. (Hwy. 285). Other sculptures are placed along Englewood Pkwy. Another significant grouping is at Samson Park in Englewood's Greenwood Plaza, just west of I-25 and north of E. Arapahoe Rd. (next to the Fiddler's Green Amphitheatre). Also check out the eight marble, stone, and bronze lion sculptures at the "Lion's Den," just north of E. Orchard Rd., off I-25. Call 303-806-0444 for more information or go to www.moaonline.org to download a map for a self-guided tour.

Bathing Beauty. Fido's been tromping through the mud all afternoon, and you don't want him to leave pawprints all over your hotel room. Lucky for you (he may have a different opinion), the Denver area has many self-service dog washes. In addition to the shops listed here, which focus on grooming and/or self-service washes, many pet-supply stores have do-it-yourself facilities, too (see Pet Provisions).

Heavenly Dog (2224 E. Tennessee St., Denver, 303-777-4665, heavenlydog .net) charges $15 for a basic bath, which includes shampoo and conditioner and use of brushes, chamois towels, dryers, and an apron. For $20, you can give your dog The Works Wash, which adds on ear, eye, tooth, and breath cleaner, and paw conditioner. And for $10 extra with any wash, you can use the store's Furminator and really get after your dog's undercoat. Closed Mondays.

Muddy Paws Bath House Self-Serve Dog Wash (4902 West 38th Ave., Denver,

A NOSE FOR WINE

The owners of Denver-based Cru Vin Dogs have a thing for canines. They donate 10 percent of profits from their wine sales to Canine Companions for Independence and the Morris Animal Foundation Canine Cancer Campaign, and they also contribute to other dog-related charities. Almost all of the wine is made by Cru Vin's own winemaker in Sonoma, with grapes sourced from various vineyards. Each release then sports breed-specific labels, such as greyhound sauvignon blanc and golden retriever chardonnay, and some are named for heroic dogs, like the Yogi cabernet-syrah, in honor of a bloodhound with the Aurora Police Department who worked on 476 cases. Stop by the winery's gallery at 1500 S. Pearl St. in Denver to view artwork by Cru Vin partner Jay P. Snellgrove, who also creates the limited-edition illustrations on some of the labels. The wine is available at some restaurants and retailers in Colorado and California, as well as online. 303-722-7363, 866-278-8461, www.cruvindogs.com.

303-433-4642, www.muddypawsbath house.com) provides circular tubs for easier washing (as well as a low walk-in tub for very large or older dogs), with sprayers that dispense both water and shampoo. The $15 wash ($10 for very small dogs) includes towels, brushes, and a dryer. If your dog is really brave (or maybe just incredibly dirty) try sticking him in the automatic pet spa ($18), which is like a walk-in washing machine—during the 30-minute cycle, 36 jets soap and wash your dog, then dry him. All you need do is watch through the window.

Puppy Love Suds and Snacks (3480 S. Galena, Denver, 303-755-0099, www .puppylovesudsandsnacks.com) has easy-access tubs and an array of natural deodorizing, brightening, and moisturizing shampoos and conditioners. Washes range $10–$25, depending on the size of dog, and include shampoo and conditioner, towels, brushes and combs, dryers, and nail clippers. Closed Mondays.

At **U-Shampooch** (7474 E. 29th Ave., Ste. 800, Denver, 303-321-5353; 10325 S. Progress Wy., Parker, 303-841-2880) a wash with everything included (all-natural shampoo and conditioner, towels, brushes, dryer) costs $16.

The Wag Shop (1222 E. 6th Ave. Denver, 303-282-1894, www.thewag shop.com) provides washing bays, basic shampoo and conditioner, and pet colognes, plus use of two towels, dryers, and grooming tools for $10–$16 per dog, depending on size. There's also the Big Tub, available on a limited basis for dogs over 100 pounds.

Mutt Puddles (8700 Wadsworth Blvd., Arvada, 303-403-9901; 3740 E. 120th St., Thornton, 303-255-7611; www.muttpuddles.net) offers rental of a small washing bay (for dogs under 20 pounds) for $10, a large one for $14. Prices include shampoo and cream rinse as well as use of a towel, blow-dryer, and grooming tools.

Spawlash (10351 Grant St., Unit 3, Thornton, 303-255-2205, www.spawlash .com) has custom tubs with nonslip rubber mats and a special insert to make it easier to wash small dogs; the $15 wash ($10 for dogs 10 pounds and under) includes shampoo and conditioner, a chamois drying cloth, brushes, and blow-dryer.

The Dirty Dog (1100 Hwy. 287, Unit 1100, Broomfield, 303-469-9490, www .dirtydoggrooming.com) offers a tub for small dogs and an elevated platform on the floor where you can wash your large dog for $12.50 ($10 for each additional dog). A wash includes shampoo and conditioner, towels, dryer, and grooming tools.

Shampooch Dog Wash (7250 W. 38th Ave., Wheat Ridge, 303-420-9220). A wash is $8–$18 depending on the size of dog, and includes everything you'll need to get your dog clean and dry, as well as the use of nail clippers, ear cleaner, and fragrances.

Laund-Ur-Mutt (12512-B Ken Caryl Ave., Littleton, 720-981-7387, www .muttspa.com) provides washing-bay rental and use of a dryer, towels, and brushes for $13.50 for the first half hour, $6 per additional half hour, and $5 per additional dog. You can buy shampoo, including one-wash-size bottles, at the store, or bring your own.

A Paw Spa (5950 S. Platte Canyon Blvd., Littleton, 303-798-7297, www.apawspalittleton.com) has a self-service wash in addition to its full grooming services; $15 (and $5 per additional dog) will let you get Rover clean, including shampoo and conditioner, towels, grooming tools, and a heatless dryer that won't burn your dog.

Sud Z Pup (139 W. County Line Rd., Littleton, 303-798-6099, www.pupnsuds .biz) charges $16 for a self-service wash, which includes shampoo, towels, grooming tools, and dryer. Closed Wednesdays.

Purr Y Paws (10417 S. Parker Rd., Parker, 720-851-0312, www.1wp.com/

go/purrypaws) offers washes for $10 ($15 if you have an exceptionally large dog), which covers everything, including natural shampoo and conditioner.

Pup N Suds (16522 Keystone Blvd., Parker, 303-841-5008, www.pupnsuds. biz) charges $16 for a wash, with shampoo, towels, grooming tools, and a dryer included. Closed Mondays.

A Barker's Dozen. Sometimes your dog deserves more than the standard Milk-bone. If your dog(s) aren't lucky enough to have a grandmother who bakes them homemade biscuits (like mine do!), bring them to one of the following stores with in-house bakeries or custom treats.

Cosmo's Retail Store and Bakery (10210 W. 26th Ave, Lakewood, 303-232-1477, 888-882-6766, www.cosmos retailstore.com) is one of Denver's longest-running pet bakeries. Though Cosmo himself was a cat, the bakery is known for its nutritious, natural dog treats, including grain-free and wheatless varieties. Perennial favorites include Barbecued Mail Carriers, honey-and-molasses-flavored Good Dog Stars, and Fresh Breath Frizbees, with mint and parsley. If Fido is allergic to wheat, try Broxie's Blueberry Scones, made with oatmeal, blueberry, and apple, or Rosie's Pumpkin Delights, which include oat flour and pure pumpkin. And if your dog's birthday is coming up, surprise him with one of Cosmo's personalized mutt cakes, a whole-wheat, oatmeal, and carrot cake with cream cheese and carob frosting.

At **For Paws Bakery** (19565 E. Main St., Parker, 303-840-5999, www.four paws.t83.net), dogs have close to twenty varieties of treats to sniff among, many named for the dogs who inspired them, such as Roxy's Kisses (filled cookie cups in carob or peanut butter flavors), Mia's Munchies (chicken-flavored crackers), and Georgie and Daisy's Breath Bombs, made with organic peppermint oil. Also popular are Pup Cakes, which include sunflower seeds and carrots, with peanut butter or white frosting. In addition to individual sizes, they're available as larger round or bone-shaped cakes.

Originally founded on the concept of Doggone Fresh Breath Mints, still the store's best seller, **Mouthfuls** (4224 Tennyson St., Denver, 720-855-7505, www.mouthfuls .net) also offers a tempting array of treats at its Bone Bar, where your dog can buy his favorites in bulk. Choose from biscuits like Lickable Livers (with flaxseed and kelp) and wheat-free veggie minis, which include cabbage, potatoes, peppers, and carrots, as well as blueberries. Though treats aren't made on-site, they are custom baked for the store. Other droolworthy items include Just Chicken! (freeze-dried chicken bites), Lickin' Logs (jerky sticks), and Savory Turkey and Potato Bites, which even include cranberry and sage.

The healthy canine will want to make **Remington and Friends Neighborhood Bakery** (278 S. Downing, Denver, 303-282-8188, www.remingtonandfriends.com) a must-sniff. Biscuits such as Doggone Danish (apple and honey), Tail-Wagging Veggie, and F. Liver Paté (named after Frank, the golden retriever customer who deemed it his favorite) are baked daily on the premises. And for that special day, bone-shaped, chicken-flavored birthday cakes can be made to order. Canon, Ranger, and Remington —all sons of the original Remington, the Irish setter who was the bakery's namesake—are usually present to help dogs whose taste buds are overwhelmed with their selection. Closed Sundays and Mondays.

The two Denver branches of the Kansas City–based **Three Dog Bakery** (231 Clayton Ln., Denver, 303-350-4499; 8000 E. Belleview Ave., Greenwood Village, 303-773-3647; www.threedog colorado.com) turn out all-natural doggie delectables like carrot cake (frosted, of course!), Beggin' for S'mores, made with rice flour and carob, and the Big Scary Kitty, a six-inch peanut-butter biscuit dipped in carob. Or treat Fido to a cup of Lickety Split doggie ice cream, available in peanut butter and mint-carob chip. The bakery caters to canine special occasions with four flavors of bone-shaped or round cakes. The stores also carry oven-baked dog food.

Wag N' Wash Healthy Pet Center bakes all-natural dog biscuits at each of its locations (323 Metzler Dr., Castle Rock, 303-814-9274; 2229 W. Wildcat Reserve, Highlands Ranch, 720-344-9274; 5066 S. Wadsworth Blvd., Littleton, 303-973-9274; www.wagnwash .com). Remo's Wag N' Treats, named for the black Lab who belonged to the chain's founders, include bark bars (made with rolled oats and molasses), multigrain ducks, puppy love biscuits (which include applesauce and carrots), and cheesie delights (with cheddar cheese). The stores also sell made-in-house deli items like liver brownies (a quick sell-out), peanut-butter pie, and beef loaf with corn and tomato sauce. Plus, you can order bone-shaped canine birthday cakes.

Doggie Paddling. Lakes, rivers, and even mud puddles are time-honored favorites for water-loving dogs. But urban dogs (or visitors) can also opt for the more civilized approach—an actual pool for swimming laps, playing canine water polo, or channeling their inner Michael Phelps. These four daycare and boarding facilities open their pools to the public at regular times each day.

For a great workout, bring Rover to the **Canine Fitness and Fun Center** (6336 Leetsdale Dr., Denver, 303-394-3647, www.caninefitnessandfuncenter.com), which has two indoor pools, one large one that's four feet deep for avid swimmers, one smaller, two-foot-deep pool for waders or small dogs. Both pools have safety

decks and ramps for easy entry. Half-hour group swims ($8.50 per dog), where your dog can join the daycare guests if space is available, run 9 AM–noon and 2:30–7 PM, Monday to Friday, and at 10 AM and 1 PM Saturday. You can also book a 20-minute private swim ($18) or a half-hour semiprivate group swim (two to four dogs, $14 per dog) noon–2 PM or 7–8 PM, Monday to Friday, or Saturday at various times between 9 AM and 4 PM. If your dog is swimming privately, you can be by the pool with him; otherwise, for safety reasons, you'll need to watch from the lobby.

City Bark LoDo (3150 Brighton Blvd., Denver, 303-296-3722, www.citybark .com) opens its chlorinated outdoor pool and "mountain area"—which has some manufactured hills and tunnels for dogs to play in—to all dogs Monday to Friday, 4–7 PM, and Saturday, noon–7 PM. Admission is $5 per dog.

Earth Dog Denver (370 Kalamath, Denver, 303-534-8700, www.earthdog denver.com), which took over the original City Bark location, makes its pool available for open swims Monday to Friday, 4–7 PM, and Saturday and Sunday, 2–6 PM, for $5 per dog. The pool ranges from one to four feet deep, with stairs leading in, and includes a waterfall. Poolside, there are rocks to climb on, a tunnel, and a railed platform known as the tree house that dogs can play on. You can rinse the chlorine off Rover afterward in the self-service dog wash ($10–$12).

Hobnob (8990 W. Colfax Ave., Lakewood, 303-233-8990, www.hobnobpet .com) has a four-feet-deep indoor saline pool (which means less skin-drying chlorine), with a ramp so older dogs can get in and out. Half-hour group swim sessions are offered Monday to Friday, 4–6:30 PM, and Saturday and Sunday, 11 AM–2 PM and 4–6:30 PM, for $8 per half hour, per dog. You can also reserve the pool for private swim sessions—for two or more dogs, the fee is $13 per half hour, per dog; for one dog, it's $17 per half hour. Towels are provided. Swimmers older than six months should be spayed or neutered, and you'll need to provide proof of vaccinations.

Colorado Petfitters, 2075 S. University, Denver, 303-282-0020, and 1590 Little Raven St., Denver, 303-825-2713, www.coloradopetfitters.com. The Denver area has long had a multitude of mountaineering stores to supply the gear needs of outdoor recreationists. Now dogs have a specialty gear store (with two locations) to call their own. Colorado Petfitters carries everything for the outdoor dog. Before heading to the mountains, bring Fido here to choose from a fine assortment of packs, booties, bowls, leashes, and treats. The store also sells pet-related books, premium dog food, doggie health foods, and maps. Your dog is welcome to accompany you inside; store policy is "if he pees on it, he buys it." The University Blvd. location also has a self-service dog wash; $10 covers washing-bay rental, shampoo, and use of towels, dryers, and grooming tools.

(Re)Tail Therapy. Denver has lots of great pet-supply stores, where you can find the right accessories for your dog, from outdoorsy to super stylish to conscience-soothing organic. A couple of boutiques, however, stand out for their unusual selections. **Zen Dog** (2401 15th St., Ste. 180, Denver, 303-744-7067, www.zendogonline.com) gives a literal meaning to downward dog—toys, for example, are placed low so that the intended audience can choose what he likes. Owner Alex E'Aton emphasizes healthy and earth-friendly pet items, like all-natural shampoos, essential oils, bamboo collars and leashes, and locally baked organic treats. You'll also find mod beds from Otis and Claude, stylish pet carriers from Pet Flys

and Sleepy Pod, and hip accessories from the Italian line Pet Ego, as well as a full line of dry and raw food. The store hosts weekly events, such as dog art shows, canine massage demos, animal communicator sessions, and holiday parties. Alex's three dogs—Bob, a Chihuahua, Otis, a mixed breed, and Rudy, a shepherd mix—are often in the store.

Dog Savvy (1402 Larimer St., Denver, 303-623-5200, www.dogsavvy.com), in bustling Larimer Square, gets lots of wags from local dogs—and kudos from local media—for its comprehensive collection of all things canine, as well as its dog "spa," where in addition to grooming, dogs can indulge in a blueberry facial. A self-service wash is also available, if you prefer to do the pampering. The store was a hot spot during the 2008 Democratic National Convention, with its "Bark for Barack" and "Bark Obama" T-shirts and bandannas. Of particular note are the large selection of collars and leashes (including vibrant ones from local company Walk-e-Woo); canine jerseys, leashes, and collars from all the Denver pro sports teams; colorful breed-specific magnets; and a gallery of dog art from local artists like pet portrait painter Shawndell Oliver. There's a small patio out front, with tables and chairs, where you can people-watch while your dog munches on an organic peanut-butter oatmeal cookie from the store's bakery case.

Shopping at Aspen Grove. Dogs can do more than just window-shop at many of the stores in this outdoor mall in Littleton (7301 S. Santa Fe Dr.). Look for the dog-friendly decals in the window, and you and your dog can while away an afternoon browsing through merchandise at Banana Republic, J. Jill, and Pottery Barn. For general information, go to www.shopaspengrove.com.

DOGGIE DAYCARE

Because there are so many boarding kennels in the Denver area, veterinarians that also offer boarding haven't been listed here (unless an animal hospital has a large daycare facility). But if you're having difficulty finding a place for your loyal companion to spend the day, you might try the vet option. And keep in mind that many of these places also offer grooming, training, self-service dog washes, and pet supplies and food.

Arvada

Action Kennel, 12975 W. 80th Ave., 303-423-2243, www.actionkennel.com. $10/day. Exercise time in the grassy play yards is $5/half-hour extra. Open 8 AM–5 PM, Monday to Thursday and Saturday; 8 AM–6 PM, Friday; 9–9:30 AM and 7–7:30 PM, Sunday.

The Barking Lot, 5890 Lamar St., 303-420-5388, www.the-barkinglot.com. $20/day; $12/half-day. The "lot" includes an outside play yard with pond. Open 7 AM–7 PM daily.

Indian Tree Pet Lodge, 9530 W. 80th Ave., 303-421-3758, www.indiantreepetlodge .com. $25/day; $18/half-day. Potential daycare dogs must go through a free half-day assessment first. Once they get the nod, they can enjoy playing in groups in the artificial turf play yards and wading in doggie pools in the summer, and you can watch the fun via Web cam. Open 7 AM–7 PM, Monday to Friday; 8 AM–5 PM, Saturday; noon–4 PM, Sunday.

Aurora

B&B for D.O.G., 10 S. Potomac, 303-361-0061, www.bbfordog.com. $17–$20/day, depending on size of dog. The facility includes a 10,000-square-foot play area with artificial turf and wading pools. Open 6:30 AM–9 PM, Monday to Friday; 7 AM–9 PM, Saturday and Sunday.

Broadview Kennels, 2155 S. Havana, 303-755-0471, www.americandogtrain .com. $9–$11/day, depending on the size of dog. Open 7 AM–5:30 PM, Monday to Friday; 7–11:30 AM, Saturday.

Camp Bow Wow DIA, Call for address, 303-340-4861, www.campbowwow.com/ us/co/aurora. $25/day; $12/half-day. Canine campers must go through a free interview day before being accepted. The Camp Bow Wow experience includes separate playgroups into which dogs are placed based on size and temperament; they have all-day access to indoor and outdoor play areas with dog-specific play equipment and, in warmer weather, wading pools. You can keep tabs on the great time your pooch is having via the online Camper Cam. Open 6:30 AM–7 PM, Monday to Friday; 7 AM–7 PM, Saturday; 7–11 AM and 3–7 PM, Sunday.

DIA Dog Club, 22351 E. Bayaud Ave., 303-344-3647, www.diadogclub.com. $20/day; $13/half-day. Dogs have an indoor playroom, plus four outdoor play areas on 6 acres, with play structures and agility obstacles, as well as wading pools in summer. They rest in their own indoor/outdoor kennels. The Dog Club also offers parking and shuttle service to and from Denver International Airport for an extra fee. Open 7 AM–6:30 PM, Monday to Friday; 7 AM–4:30 PM, Saturday and Sunday.

The Pup Stop, 2250 Chambers Rd., 303-343-7878, www.pupstop.com. $20/day. There's a large outdoor yard for avid runners, a smaller outdoor play yard with agility equipment, a generously sized concrete wading pool, and an indoor playroom. Open 7 AM–6 PM, Monday to Friday.

Rocwind Canine Center, 876 Ventura St., 303-364-8586, www.rocwindcanine center.com. $16/day. The large play area at this all-indoor facility, run by a long-time dog trainer, is climate controlled. Open 6:30 AM–7:30 PM, Monday to Friday; 7 AM–6 PM, Saturday and Sunday.

Tenaker Pet Care Center, 895 Laredo St., 303-366-2376, www.tenakerpetcare.com. $22/day. The facility includes a comprehensive agility course (training sessions on the course are among the center's other offerings) and an outdoor swimming pool that's open year-round. You can keep tabs on Fido via Web cams. A full-service veterinary hospital is also on the premises. Open 7 AM–7 PM, Monday to Friday.

Broomfield

Camp Bow Wow, 1705 W. 10th Ave., 303-469-9972, www.campbowwow.com/us/co/broomfield. $23/day. Canine campers must go through a free interview day before being accepted. The Camp Bow Wow experience includes separate playgroups into which dogs are placed based on size and temperament; they have all-day access to indoor and outdoor play areas with dog-specific play equipment and, in warmer weather, wading pools. You can keep tabs on the great time your pooch is having via the online Camper Cam. Open 6:30 AM–7:30 PM, Monday to Friday; 8–11 AM and 5–8 PM, Saturday and Sunday.

Colorado Dog Academy, 12180 N. Sheridan Blvd., 303-465-1703, www.codogacademy.com. $12/day. If your dog's not up for playing in groups with others (formed according to size, age, and temperament), he'll go on walks to ensure he gets outside exercise. Open 8 AM–5:30 PM, Monday to Friday.

Castle Rock

Beau Monde Kennels, 660 E. Happy Canyon Rd., 303-688-9578. $25/day. The kennel features a 1-acre fenced-in exercise and

play area for its guests, as well as heated indoor/outdoor runs. Open 7:30 AM–6 PM, Monday, Tuesday, Thursday, Friday; 7:30 AM–noon, Wednesday and Saturday.

Camp Bow Wow, 500 1st St., 303-814-8108, www.campbowwow.com/us/co/castlerock. $22/day; $15/half-day (after 12 PM). Canine campers must go through a free interview day before being accepted. The Camp Bow Wow experience includes separate playgroups into which dogs are placed based on size and temperament; they have all-day access to indoor and outdoor play areas with dog-specific play equipment and, in warmer weather, wading pools. You can keep tabs on the great time your pooch is having via the online Camper Cam. Open 7 AM–7 PM, Monday to Friday; 9–11 AM and 6–8 PM, Saturday and Sunday.

Paws Field, 780 Kinner St., 720-259-2515, www.pawsfield.com. $23/day; $12/half-day. This daycare takes its cues from baseball. As with any team, a tryout is required, which consists of a temperament test and a half-day trial visit ($12). Dogs play indoors and out, with separate areas for large and small dogs, play equipment, and wading pools in summer. Web cams let you watch the game on TV. If your dog is a standout, he may earn MVP or Rookie of the Month honors. Open 6 AM–6 PM, Monday to Friday; 8 AM–6 PM, Saturday; 7–9 AM and 4–6 PM, Sunday (for drop-off and pick-up only).

Tails Up, 401 S. Gilbert St., 303-660-9934, www.tailsup.com. $25/day. Dogs play together for an hour or so in the morning and again in the afternoon, in small groups based on size, age, and activity level. In between, they relax or nap in private rooms, which have full walls and glass windows. The 7,000-square-foot outdoor yard has small- and big-dog sections, synthetic turf, and climbing structures. You can add on extra play-time, a massage, training, or cuddle time ($10–$15). And there are Web cams. Open 7 AM–7 PM daily.

Denver

Allbrick Boarding Kennels, 8700 Zuni, 303-429-2433, www.allbrickkennels .com. $15/day. Affiliated with the Allbrick Veterinary Clinic, the parklike daycare area includes a 9,000-square-foot yard for outdoor play, divided in half for small and large dogs, with agility courses and shaded wading pools. Open 6:30 AM–6:30 PM, Monday to Friday; 7 AM–5 PM, Saturday.

Animal Lodge (at VCA Alameda East Veterinary Hospital), 9870 E. Alameda, 720-975-2800, www.aevh.com. $25/day; $16/half-day. In addition to a huge indoor playroom with agility equipment and toys and an outdoor yard with playground equipment, this 10,000-square-foot facility houses Alameda East's sports medicine center, including two indoor pools where your dog can work on the underwater treadmill or just go for a swim ($10–$40 extra). Log on to the lodge's Web cam to view all the fun from afar. Open 6 AM–8 PM daily.

Bark! Doggie Daycare + Hotel + Spa, 1277 Santa Fe Dr., 303-892-5556, www.bark denver.com. $24/day; $14/half-day. Your dog will have 3,000 square feet of indoor play space, including a separate room for smaller dogs, as well as 1,500 square feet to play outdoors, with playground equipment and wading pools. Open 6:30 AM–7 PM, Monday to Friday; 7 AM–6 PM, Saturday.

Barkly Manor, 5010 E. Colfax Ave., 303-997-6498, www.barklymanor.com. $24/day. While at the manor, dogs have 6,000 square feet of play space. Indoors, the play area has custom rubber floors,

and there's even a senior lounge, with a couch, for older guests. The outside yard has play equipment and wading pools in summer. Open 7 AM–7 PM, Monday to Friday; 9 AM–3 PM, Saturday.

Best Friends Forever Pet Care, 4613 E. 23rd Ave., 303-321-8900, www.bffpet care.com. $22/day. This small facility, staffed by the owner and his wife, accommodates only up to 18 dogs at a time. In addition to playtime, they go on two walks each day. Open 7 AM–7 PM, Monday to Friday.

The Big Backyard, 5310 E. Pacific Pl., 303-757-7905, www.the-big-backyard .com. $22/day; $15/half-day. In addition to the big backyard, which comprises three fenced areas with play equipment and wading pools in summer, the 8,000-square-foot facility has three indoor playrooms, with doggie doors to the outside yards. Naps at lunchtime include gentle music. Open 7 AM–6:30 PM, Monday to Friday; 8 AM–6 PM, Saturday.

Camp Bow Wow Denver Central, 1221 S. Cherokee St., 303-282-5484, www.camp bowwow.com/us/co/denver. $22/day; $12/half-day. This is the original Camp Bow Wow location, before the daycare chain took off nationwide. Canine campers must go through a free interview day before being accepted. The Camp Bow Wow experience includes separate playgroups into which dogs are placed based on size and temperament; they have all-day access to indoor and outdoor play areas with dog-specific play equipment and, in warmer weather, wading pools. You can keep tabs on the great time your pooch is having via the online Camper Cam. Open 6:30 AM–7 PM, Monday to Friday; 8–11 AM and 4–7 PM, Saturday and Sunday.

Camp Bow Wow LoDo, 3645 Brighton Blvd., 303-577-0232, www.camp

bowwow.com/us/co/denver3. $25/day; $14/half-day. Canine campers must go through a free interview day before being accepted. The Camp Bow Wow experience includes separate playgroups into which dogs are placed based on size and temperament; they have all-day access to indoor and outdoor play areas with dog-specific play equipment and, in warmer weather, wading pools. You can keep tabs on the great time your pooch is having via the online Camper Cam. Open 6:30 AM–7 PM, Monday to Friday; 7 AM–7 PM, Saturday; 7–11 AM and 3–7 PM, Sunday.

Camp Bow Wow Denver Southeast, 2125 S. Jasmine, 303-300-8284, www.camp bowwow.com/us/co/denver2. $21/day. Canine campers must go through a free interview day before being accepted. The Camp Bow Wow experience includes separate playgroups into which dogs are placed based on size and temperament; they have all-day access to indoor and outdoor play areas with dog-specific play equipment and, in warmer weather, wading pools. You can keep tabs on the great time your pooch is having via the online Camper Cam. Open 6:30 AM–6:30 PM, Monday to Friday; 7–10 AM and 4–7 PM, Saturday and Sunday.

Canine Fitness and Fun Center, 6336 Leetsdale Dr., 303-394-3647, www .caninefitnessandfuncenter.com. $25/day; $19/half-day. Your dog can't help but get in shape if he comes here. The facility includes two indoor swimming pools—one four feet deep, the other two feet—and indoor and outdoor play areas, including an activity room with tunnels, ramps, and mazes. Add on a swim session to your dog's day for $5–$10 extra, depending on the length. You can also drop off your dog for two hours of play or swim and play ($10–$15), as well as swim-only sessions (see Worth a Paws). Web cams let you view all the splashing

and playing. Open 7 AM–8 PM, Monday to Friday; 9 AM–4 PM, Saturday.

City Bark Denver, 2000 W. 8th Ave., 303-573-9400, www.citybark.com. $27/day; $16.50/half-day. A pre-daycare interview is required. Dogs get to play in five indoor, climate-controlled playrooms or in the outdoor dog park, which includes a swimming pool and hill and tunnel structures to climb over and through. And they get a well-deserved snack and nap midday. Web cams capture the goings-on. City Bark occasionally hosts Friday "yappy hours" in the dog park, with hot dogs and beer and suggested donations to benefit an animal-related nonprofit. Open 6:30 AM–7 PM, Monday to Saturday; 5–7 PM, Sunday.

City Bark LoDo, 3150 Brighton Blvd., 303-296-3722, www.citybark.com. $27/day; $16.50/half-day. A pre-daycare interview is required. Dogs get to play in four indoor, climate-controlled playrooms or in the outdoor dog park, which includes a swimming pool and hill and tunnel structures to climb over and through. And they get a well-deserved snack and nap midday. Web cams capture the goings-on. The dog park is also open to the public at certain times (see Worth a Paws). City Bark Lodo hosts an annual Halloween "yappy hour" in the dog park. Open 6:30 AM–7 PM, Monday to Saturday; 5–7 PM, Sunday.

Daily Wag, 1190 Yuma St. (off I-25 and 8th Ave.), 303-307-1638. www.dailywag .com. $24.50/day; $16/half-day. The facility has large play areas, indoors and out, with slides and other play equipment, and wading pools in summer. Check up on Fido via Web cam. Open 6:30 AM–7 PM daily.

Digstown, 2005 Willow St. (Stapleton area), 303-399-5500, www.digstown.us.

$26/day. At this purpose-built facility, dogs play in groups according to age, size, and temperament, in three indoor rooms and on close to an acre of land with obstacle courses, two wading pools (one with fountains), and shade. Open 6:30 AM–7:30 PM, Monday to Friday; 8 AM–7:30 PM, Saturday; 8–9:30 AM and 5–7:30 PM, Sunday.

Dog-Topia, 341 S. Lincoln, 303-722-2620, www.dog-topia.com. $22/day; $15/half-day. Dogs have unlimited access to the 3,000-square-foot outdoor play yard, which has jungle gyms and wading pools in summer. There are also separate large- and small-dog play areas. Open 6:30 AM–7 PM, Monday to Friday; 7 AM–7 PM, Saturday and Sunday.

The Downtown Dog, 3325 Brighton Blvd., 303-295-1421, www.thedowntowndog.com. $22/day; $12/half-day. Dogs must go through a free two-hour evaluation first. There's 5,000 square feet of inside and outside play space, with fun play structures. Dogs are never kenneled, and naptime is accommodated but not enforced. Open 6:30 AM–7 PM, Monday to Friday; 9–11 AM and 4–6 PM, Saturday and Sunday.

Earth Dog Denver, 370 Kalamath, 303-534-8700, www.earthdogdenver.com. $25/day; $15 half-day. In addition to indoor play areas, dogs get to enjoy a large outdoor swimming pool, with a waterfall, tunnels, rock hills, and agility equipment. The pool is also open to the public at certain times (see Worth a Paws). Open 6:30 AM–7 PM, Monday to Friday; 8 AM–6 PM, Saturday; 2–6 PM, Sunday.

Fetchers Dog Care, 2555 S. Santa Fe, 303-733-3313, www.fetchersdogcare.com. $25/day; $12/half-day. A pre-daycare interview is required. Dogs are never kenneled; they socialize in climate-controlled indoor play areas and in the large outside yard, where they can wade in the pools (in summer), play on the equipment, and, of course, fetch balls. Open 6 AM–9:30 PM daily.

Happy Dog Daycare, 3939 Newport St., 303-331-1364, www.happydogdenver.com. $25/day; $15/half-day. Once dogs have gone through the required meet-and-greet session, they can happily play indoors and out, as well as paddle in the 10-by-20-foot indoor swimming pool ($6 extra for a 15–20 minute session). Open 7 AM–8 PM, Monday to Friday; 8 AM–6 PM, Saturday.

Hounds on the Hill, 960 Lincoln, 303-830-1226, www.houndsonthehillLLC.com. $22/day; $17/half-day. The prescreening interview fee is $10 and it's refundable at the first daycare session. Dogs play in groups indoors and out, with play equipment and wading pools in summer. Open 7 AM–7 PM, Monday to Friday.

Little Doggie Daycare and Boarding, 1842 S. Parker Rd., 303-745-8538. $20/day; $25/day for puppies. The daycare specializes in small- to medium-sized dogs. Open 6:30 AM–6 PM, Monday to Friday; 7 AM–5 PM, Saturday and Sunday.

Mile High Mutts, 3500 Chestnut Pl., 303-296-3998, www.milehighmutts.com. $22/day. A free full-day evaluation is required before dogs can come to daycare regularly. This huge facility has 8,000 square feet for indoor play and a 12,000-square-foot outdoor yard, with summer wading pools, jungle gyms, and even a bubble machine. Small dogs need not feel overwhelmed; they have their own play areas, inside and out. Web cams let you keep tabs on your dog. Open 6:15 AM–7 PM, Monday to Friday; 6:30 AM–7 PM, Saturday and Sunday.

Mutt-Mutt Palace, 2347 Curtis St., 303-296-6888, www.mutt-muttpalace.com. $21/day; $11/half-day. A generous 4,000 square feet of indoor space includes two play areas, and there's a 2,000-square-foot yard outdoors. All play areas have plenty of equipment to climb on and play in, and wading pools are set up outside in summer. Open 7 AM–7 PM, Monday to Friday; 9 AM–5 PM, Saturday and Sunday.

Playful Pooch, 4000 Holly St., 720-941-7529, www.playfulpoochusa.com. $25/day. The facility has six different indoor and outdoor play areas, with equipment that includes an energy-dissipating game called Pitball, in which a dog bats a ball around inside a high-sided ring—watch your dog on the Web cam. Open 7–11 AM and 1:30–6 PM, Monday to Friday; 8–10 AM and 3–5 PM, Saturday and Sunday.

Englewood

City Bark Too–Englewood, 3320 S. Knox Ct., 303-783-9401, www.citybark.com. $20.75/day; $13/half-day. A pre-daycare interview is required. Dogs get to play in two indoor, climate-controlled playrooms. For $8 more, they also have the option of playing at City Bark Denver's outdoor pool and park, with transportation provided. All dogs get a well-deserved snack and nap midday. Web cams capture the goings-on. Open 6:30 AM–7 PM, Monday to Saturday; 5–7 PM, Sunday.

The Dog House, 1101 W. Quincy Ave., 303-781-4577, www.thedoghouserules .com. $18/day; $12/half-day. In addition to a large indoor play area, there's a 5,000-square-foot outdoor space, divided into two yards, with tunnels, play equipment, a large wading pool, and shaded areas. A doggie Web cam captures the action. Open 7 AM–7 PM, Monday to Friday; 8 AM–5 PM, Saturday; 9 AM–noon and 4–6 PM, Sunday.

Doggie Pause, 3220 S. Acoma St., 303-761-8743, www.doggiepause.com. $27/day. Dogs play together indoors and out, with play equipment and wading pools in summer. There's also a special playroom for small dogs. Puppies younger than five months can enroll in doggie day school, which combines training with daycare. Open 6:30 AM–7 PM, Monday to Friday; 6:30 AM–7 PM, Saturday and Sunday during the summer.

Evergreen

Bergen Bark Inn, 2989 Bergen Peak Dr., 303-679-0202, www.berganbarkinn .com. $25–$35/day. Open 8 AM–6 PM, Monday to Friday; 8 AM–5 PM, Saturday; 10 AM–5 PM, Sunday. Run by a licensed veterinarian and his wife, the "inn" facilities include a "serenity room" for dogs who prefer quiet and separate accommodations for older or special-needs dogs, as well as a large fenced yard for supervised play.

Evergreen Kennel and Grooming, 30596 Bryant Dr., 303-670-9792. $22/day; $11/half-day. New dog guests are required to come for a four-hour trial-run stay before they can be dropped off for a full day. There's lots of playground equipment in the outdoor area to keep dogs active. In summer, they can splash in the wading pool. Open 7 AM–6 PM, Monday to Saturday; 3–5 PM, Sunday.

Glendale

For the Love of Dog, 4751 E. Virginia Ave., 303-355-6700, www.fortheloveofdog .com. $29/day; $18/half-day. Inside, rubber-floored playrooms cater separately to large and small dogs. The 3,500-square-foot outdoor yard, where the bigger dogs spend most of their time, includes wading pools, play equipment, and, in summer, shade tarps that release a cooling mist on your dog. Water for the pools and for drinking is filtered. You can even book a personal training session for Fido on the canine treadmill ($5 for 10 minutes). Open 7 AM–6:30 PM, Monday to Friday; 10 AM–5 PM, Saturday.

PetsHotel at PetSmart, 4300 E. Alameda Ave., 303-399-0880, www.petsmart .com. $16–$20/day. The store differentiates between day camp and daycare. In the former, dogs get to play with each other from 9 to 5 in one of four indoor playrooms, which have toys and play equipment, with an hour off at noon to nap in private rooms. The cost is $20 a dog, and they're divided into playgroups by size and temperament. If your dog prefers not to socialize as much, you can put him in day care ($16); he'll get his own room to snooze in, with two 15-minute play breaks. Open 7 AM–9 PM daily.

Golden

The Alpine Dog House, 29600 Hwy. 40 (at Evergreen Pkwy.), 303-526-0664, www .alpinedoghouse.net. $15/day. Dogs can feel right at home at this daycare in an Evergreen residence. They can romp on 1.5 wooded acres, snooze on the furniture, or stay in their own room if they just want their privacy. Open 7 AM–7 PM, Monday to Saturday; 7 AM–4 PM, Sunday.

Camp Bow Wow, 13101 W. 43rd Dr., Unit 102, 303-271-9663, campbowwow .com/us/co/golden. $22/day; $12/half-day. Canine campers must go through a free interview day before being accepted. The Camp Bow Wow experience includes separate playgroups into which dogs are placed based on size and temperament; they have all-day access to indoor and outdoor play areas with dog-specific play equipment and, in warmer weather, wading pools. You can keep tabs on the great time your pooch is having via the online Camper Cam. Open 6:30 AM–7:30 PM, Monday to Friday; 8–11 AM and 4–8 PM, Saturday and Sunday.

Canines' Canyon, 24060 Hwy. 40, 303-526-9212, www.caninescanyon.com. $20/day; $10/half-day. Dogs must go through a half-day socialization evaluation before they can come for daycare. If they pass muster, they'll enjoy a huge indoor play area, with in-floor radiant heat, and a 7,500-square-foot fenced outdoor play yard, divided into three areas, with playground equipment and a true agility course. Plus they're promised ample hugs and belly rubs. Open 6:45 AM–7 PM, Monday to Friday; 7 AM–5 PM, Saturday; 3–5 PM, Sunday.

Rover Retreat, 17731 W. Colfax, 303-215-0413, www.roverretreat.com/golden. $24/day; $12/half-day. A trial day is required before dogs can come to daycare full time. Dogs play in groups based on temperament. Open 7 AM–7 PM, Monday to Friday; 7–10 AM and 4–7 PM, Saturday and Sunday.

Sage Valley Pet Center, 16400 W. 54th Ave., 303-279-6969, www.sagevalley .com. $20/day. All dogs get their own indoor/outdoor, climate-controlled runs, plus one-on-one playtime in one of the five play yards on the property and plenty of treats. Open 8 AM–6 PM, Monday to Saturday; noon–6 PM, Sunday.

Highlands Ranch

Dogtopia of Highlands Ranch, 6448 E. County Line Rd., 303-770-0776, www .dogdaycare.com/highlandsranch. $30/day. Dogs socialize in groups based on size and temperament, in indoor and outdoor playrooms, with play equipment and wading pools in warm weather. You can check in via Web cam. Open 7 AM–7 PM, Monday to Friday; 10 AM–5 PM, Saturday; 11 AM–2 PM, Sunday (drop-off and pick-up only).

VCA Tenaker Animal Hospital, 5790 E. County Line, 303-694-5738, www.vca

tenaker.com. $26/day. Dogs play outside most of the day, other than a one-hour nap in their own kennels. The play yard includes a heated swimming pool and wading pools for smaller dogs in summer, and shaded areas. Open 7 AM–7 PM, Monday to Friday.

Lakewood

The Den Doggie Daycare, 8700 W. 14th Ave., 303-237-4979, www.thedendog giedaycare.com. $23/day; $15/half-day. At this daycare-only facility, there are four separate play areas for dogs of different sizes and temperaments, as well as a large, shaded outdoor play yard, where dogs also socialize in smaller groups. Open 6:30 AM–6 PM, Monday to Friday.

Hobnob, 8990 W. Colfax, 303-233-8990, www.hobnobpet.com. $23/day; $17/half-day. In addition to two outdoor and two indoor play areas (with cushions and couches for taking a break), there's an indoor swimming pool, which your dog can take a half-hour dip in for $5 extra. The pool is also open to the public at certain times (see Worth a Paws). You can order treats for your dog to receive during the day, like ice cream or a meat-filled hoof chew, through the "minibar." Web cams let you check in. Open 7 AM–7 PM daily.

K-9 Castle, 5603 W. 6th Ave., 303-237-4901, www.k9castledoggydaycare.com. $22/day; $16/half-day. Dogs are free to play indoors and out, with play structures in the outside yard and Web cams for you to check in on the fun. Open 7 AM–7 PM, Monday to Friday; 8–10 AM and 6–7 PM, Saturday and Sunday.

Littleton

Camp Bow Wow, 8121 S. Grant Wy., 303-797-2267, www.campbowwow.com/us/co/littleton. $22/day. Canine campers must go through a free interview day before being accepted. The Camp Bow

Wow experience includes separate play-groups into which dogs are placed based on size and temperament; they have all-day access to indoor and outdoor play areas with dog-specific play equipment and, in warmer weather, wading pools. You can keep tabs on the great time your pooch is having via the online Camper Cam. Open 7 AM–7 PM, Monday to Friday; 9–11 AM and 6–8 PM, Saturday and Sunday.

Doggie Dude Ranch, 13906 Kuehster, 303-697-6824, www.littletondoggiedude ranchkennellessdogboarding.com. $22/day. This is a home-based boarding service run by a certified vet technician. Dogs have 3 fenced-in acres on which to romp and no cages or kennels. Arrangements made by appointment only. Note that though the address is officially Littleton, the house is located in the mountains, close to Conifer.

High Country Kennels, 8290 W. Coal Mine Ave., 303-979-3353. $10/day. Dogs stay in indoor/outdoor runs. Open 7:30 AM–5:30 PM, Monday to Friday.

PetsHotel at PetSmart, 8500 W. Crestline Ave. 303-948-6372, www.petsmart .com. $16–$20/day. The store differentiates between day camp and daycare. In the former, dogs get to play with each other from 9 to 5 in one of four indoor playrooms, which have toys and play equipment, with an hour off at noon to nap in private rooms. The cost is $20 a dog, and they're divided into playgroups by size and temperament. If your dog prefers not to socialize as much, you can put him in day care ($16); he'll get his own room to snooze in, with two 15-minute play breaks. Open 7 AM–9 PM, Monday to Saturday; 8 AM–7 PM, Sunday.

PetsHotel at PetSmart, 8695 S. Park Meadows Center, 303-799-1624, www .petsmart.com. $16–$20/day. The store differentiates between day camp and daycare. In the former, dogs get to play with each other from 9 to 5 in one of four indoor playrooms, which have toys and play equipment, with an hour off at noon to nap in private rooms. The cost is $20 a dog, and they're divided into playgroups by size and temperament. If your dog prefers not to socialize as much, you can put him in day care ($16); he'll get his own room to snooze in, with two 15-minute play breaks. Open 7 AM–9 PM, Monday to Saturday; 7 AM–7 PM, Sunday.

Northglenn

Camp Bow Wow, 11480 N. Cherokee St., Unit P, 303-254-9247, www.campbow wow.com/us/co/northglenn. $23/day. Canine campers must go through a free interview day before being accepted. The Camp Bow Wow experience includes separate playgroups into which dogs are placed based on size and temperament; they have all-day access to indoor and outdoor play areas with dog-specific play equipment and, in warmer weather, wading pools. You can keep tabs on the great time your pooch is having via the online Camper Cam. Open 6:30 AM–7:30 PM, Monday to Friday; 8–11 AM and 5–8 PM, Saturday and Sunday.

Parker

Camp Bow Wow, 10325 S. Progress Wy., 303-805-9739, www.campbowwow.com/us/co/parker. $25/day. Canine campers must go through a free interview day before being accepted. The Camp Bow Wow experience includes separate playgroups into which dogs are placed based on size and temperament; they have all-day access to indoor and outdoor play areas with dog-specific play equipment and, in warmer weather, wading pools. You can keep tabs on the great time your pooch is having via the online Camper Cam. Open 6:30 AM–7 PM, Monday to Friday; 7–10 AM and 4–7 PM, Saturday and Sunday.

City Bark Parker, 9835 Mangano Ln., 720-221-3267, www.citybark.com. $27/day. A pre-daycare interview is required. Dogs get to play in five indoor, climate-controlled playrooms or in the outdoor dog park, which includes a swimming pool, hill and tunnel structures, and an Astroturf surface. And they get a well-deserved snack and nap midday. Web cams capture the goings-on. City Bark occasionally hosts Friday "yappy hours" in the dog park, with hot dogs and beer and suggested donations to benefit an animal-related nonprofit. Open 6:30 AM–7 PM, Monday to Saturday; 5–7 PM, Sunday.

Club Pet, 10719 E. Parker Rd., 303-841-3227, www.clubpetkennel.com. $20/day; $12/half-day. At this large "pet resort," daycare guests go out twice a day in groups, based on size and disposition, to one of the fourteen outdoor play yards, with shade and wading pools. Plus they get a "country field walk" on the property's 25 acres and a stuffed Kong treat. You can check in via Web cam. Open 6:30 AM–7 PM, Monday to Friday; 8 AM–6 PM, Saturday; 3–5 PM, Sunday.

Smooch the Pooch, 10445 S. Parker Rd., 303-841-5155, www.smooch-thepooch.com. $20/day; $14/day. Three indoor playrooms, with equipment and toys, accommodate groups of dogs divided by size; outdoor play yards will eventually be available, too. Open 6:30 AM–6:30 PM, Monday to Friday; open on weekends for drop-off and pick-up only (no daycare).

Winston's Doggy Playhouse, 10530 S. Progress Wy., 303-805-9640, www.win stonsdoggyplayhouse.com. $23/day. A pre-daycare social evaluation is required. The playhouse provides cageless daycare, with fenced play areas indoors and out that have play equipment, toys, and a bubble machine. A separate "couch potato" area accommodates dogs who just want to chill. Open 6:30 AM–7 PM, Monday to Friday; 9 AM–2 PM, Saturday; 3–6 PM, Sunday (no daycare on weekends).

Westminster

Canine Campus, 8971 Harlan St., 303-650-3005, www.caninecampus.us. $22/day; $12/half-day. Dogs must pass an admissions test to be accepted. Canine students can play with others, indoors and out, or just nap as much as they want. A school lunch is also available for $2. Open 6:30 AM–6:30 PM, Monday to Saturday; overnight boarding only on Sunday.

The Dog and I, 8971 Harlan St., 303-426-5910, www.thedogandi.com. $22/day. Dogs are grouped by size and temperament and play in three indoor and outdoor areas. Open 7 AM–6:30 PM, Monday to Friday; 8–10 AM and 4–6 PM, Saturday and Sunday.

PetsHotel at PetSmart, 10460 Town Center Dr., 303-466-8409, www.petsmart.com. $16–$20/day. The store differentiates between day camp and daycare. In the former, dogs get to play with each other from 9 to 5 in one of four indoor playrooms, which have toys and play equipment, with an hour off at noon to nap in private rooms. The cost is $20 a dog, and they're divided into playgroups by size and temperament. If your dog prefers not to socialize as much, you can put him in daycare ($16); he'll get his own room to snooze in, with two 15-minute play breaks. Open 7 AM–9 PM, Monday to Saturday; 8 AM–6 PM, Sunday.

Watkins

Doggie Dude Ranch, 1600 S. Quail Run Rd., 303-366-2498, www.dogcatranch.com. $22/day. Located on a 20-acre ranch east of Denver, the facility includes a 1,500-square-foot indoor playroom and outdoor play areas, including a heated swimming pool. Dogs also get plenty of

rest, with three hours of nap or quiet time in the afternoon in individual rooms, plus home-baked biscuits and peanut-butter-stuffed Kongs. If Fido is really stressed, sign him up for a canine massage. Pick-up and delivery within the Denver metro area is available. Open 8 AM–6 PM daily.

Wheat Ridge

All About Paws, 4322 Xenon St., 303-420-0307, www.allaboutpaws.org. $18/day; $13/half-day. A pre-daycare interview is required. Dogs play together indoors and out, with playground equipment and wading pools in summer. Naptime is not enforced; dogs make their own schedules. Open 7 AM–7 PM, Monday to Friday.

Beds n Biscuits, 4219 Xenon St., 303-940-9188, www.bedsnbiscuits.com. $20/day. The focus here is mainly on overnight guests, but a small number of dogs come for daycare. Indoor kennels are climate controlled, and the outdoor play areas have wading pools in summer. Open 8 AM–6 PM, Monday to Friday; 8 AM–4 PM, Saturday; 2–5 PM, Sunday.

Best Friends Pet Care, 11440 W. 44th Ave., 303-422-2055, www.bestfriendspetcare.com. $18/day. Currently, dogs stay in indoor/outdoor kennels, with a one-on-one outdoor playtime session, and a walk to nearby Prospect Park ($8 extra). Plans call for a more social doggy day camp. Open 8 AM–6 PM, Monday to Friday; 8 AM–5 PM, Saturday; 3–6 PM for pick-ups only, Sunday.

Rover Retreat, 8175 W. 48th Ave., 303-432-8860, www.roverretreat.com/wheatridge. $24/day; $12/half-day. Dogs have unrestricted access to indoor and outdoor play areas. The 9,000-square-foot outside yard has lots of play equipment and toys, wading pools in summer, and shade canopies with misters in hot weather. Open

7 AM–7 PM, Monday to Friday; 7–10 AM and 4–7 PM, Saturday and Sunday.

PET PROVISIONS
Arvada
Paws 'n' Play, 7403 Grandview Ave., 303-420-2525, www.pawsnplay.com

Pet Empawrium and Spaw, 12393 W. 64th, 303-467-7777, www.petempawrium.com

PetSmart, 5285 Wadsworth Bypass, 303-456-1114, www.petsmart.com

Aurora
Pet Palace, 4082 S. Parker Rd., 303-699-4554, www.petpalaceusa.net. The store also has a self-service dog wash.

PETCO, 16960 E. Quincy Ave., 303-699-5061; 13750 E. Mississippi, 303-695-1223; 3511 N. Salida Ct., 303-371-2941; 24101 E. Orchard Rd., 303-627-5710; www.petco.com. All of these locations except the one at Salida Ct. also have self-service dog washes.

PetSmart, 40 S. Abilene St., 720-859-8122; 5520 S. Parker Rd., 303-690-4697; 7350 S. Gartrell Rd., 303-400-4778; www.petsmart.com

Brighton
PetSmart, 2435 Prairie Center Pkwy., 303-637-9232, www.petsmart.com

Broomfield
Paw-Wares, 1000 Depot Hill Rd., 303-469-1540, www.paw-wares.com

PETCO, 12163 N. Sheridan Blvd., 303-635-1540, www.petco.com. The store also has a self-service dog wash.

PetSmart, 16575 Washington St., 303-255-0644, www.petsmart.com

Willow Run Feed and Supply, 5700 W. 120th Ave., 303-466-5971, www.willowrunfeed.com

Castle Rock
Castle Rock Feed and Western Wear, 200 Perry, 303-688-3016

The Pet Stuff Place, Castle Pines Marketplace (I-25 and Castle Pines Pkwy.), 303-814-6060, www.thepetstuffplace.com

PetSmart, 4654 Milestone Ln., 720-733-6282, www.petsmart.com

Rampart Feed and Pet, Inc., 1233 N. Park, 303-688-7360

Wag N' Wash Healthy Pet Center, 323 Metzler Dr., 303-814-9274, www.wagnwash.com. The store also has a self-service dog wash, with three grades of washes.

Centennial
Paw Prints, 6842 S. Yosemite St. (Southgate Shopping Center, corner of Arapahoe and Yosemite), 720-482-6806, www.pawprints.biz

Samantha's Katz n' Dogz, 22978 Smoky Hill Rd., 303-627-7387, www.katzndogz.net

Conifer
Buster's Natural Pet Supply, 27122 Main St., 303-816-1848, www.bustersnaturalpetsupply.com

Healthy Pet Supply, 25797 Conifer Rd., 303-816-7003, www.healthypetsupplyonline.com

Denver
6th Ave. Pet Source, 810 E. 6th Ave., 303-733-6410, www.sixthavepetsource.com

A Pets Paradise, 913 Corona, 303-863-8151, www.apetsupplyparadise.com. A pet psychic comes to the store the second Saturday of every month.

C.B. Paws Denver, 278 Fillmore St., 303-322-7297, www.cbpaws.com

Chewy's Bonetique, 200 Quebec St., 303-344-2663, www.chewysbonetique.com. The store also has a self-service dog wash.

Ciji's Natural Pet Supplies, 2260 Kearney, 303-322-8000, www.cijisnaturalpet supplies.lbu.com

Colorado Petfitters, 2075 S. University, 303-282-0020; 1590 Little Raven, 303-825-2713, www.coloradopetfitters.com (see Worth a Paws)

Cosmo's Retail Store and Bakery, 10210 W. 26th Ave, Lakewood, 303-232-1477, 888-882-6766, www.cosmosretailstore .com (see Worth a Paws)

Dog Savvy, 1404 Larimer, 303-623-5200, www.dogsavvy.com (see Worth a Paws)

Doggie Delights on Broadway, 1432 S. Broadway, 303-777-5076

Lil Angel Pet Boutique and Gallery, 1014 S. Gaylord St., 303-777-0224, www.lil angelboutique.com

Mouthfuls, 4224 Tennyson St., 720-855-7505, www.mouthfuls.net (see Worth a Paws)

PETCO, 4100 E. Mexico Ave., 303-756-0892, www.petco.com

PetSmart, 2780 S. Colorado Blvd., 303-756-4199; 7505 E. 35th Ave., 303-393-9156, www.petsmart.com

Pet Station, 2300 S. Colorado Blvd., 303-757-6800, www.mypetstation.net. The store also has a self-service dog wash.

Quality Paws Natural Pet, 46 N. Broadway, 303-778-7297, www.qualitypaws.com

Remington and Friends Neighborhood Bakery, 278 S. Downing, Denver, 303-282-8188, www.remingtonandfriends .com (see Worth a Paws)

Sherlock Hound's Pet Deli, 4369 Stuart St., 303-433-3234, www.sherlockhound petdeli.com

Three Dog Bakery, 231 Clayton Ln., 303-350-4499, www.threedogcolorado.com (see Worth a Paws)

Whole Cat and Dog Too, 1540 S. Pearl, 303-871-0443

Zen Dog Pet Boutique, 2401 15th St., 303-744-7067, www.zendogonline.com (see Worth a Paws)

Englewood
PETCO, 9425 E. County Line Rd., 303-708-0616; 551 W. Hampden Ave., 303-761-0363, www.petco.com. The County Line Rd. location also has a self-service dog wash.

Evergreen
Chow Down, 3719 Evergreen Pkwy. (in the Evergreen North shopping center), 303-674-8711. The store also has a self-service dog wash.

Dogma Pet Supplies & Dog Wash, 29017 Hotel Wy., 303-526-7297, www.dogma colorado.com. The store also has a self-service dog wash with custom-designed tubs that don't require entry ramps and provide access from three sides.

Healthy Pet Supply, 1254 Bergen Pkwy., 303-679-1028, www.healthypetsupply online.com

Glendale

PetSmart, 4300 E. Alameda Ave., 303-399-0880, www.petsmart.com

Golden

Gold'n Paws, 710 Golden Ridge Rd., 303-278-8566, www.goldnpaws.com. The store also has a self-service dog wash.

PETCO, 17132 W. Colfax Ave., 303-384-0013, www.petco.com

Greenwood Village

Pet Outfitters, 5942 S. Holly, 303-290-0430, www.petoutfitters.com

Three Dog Bakery, 8000 E. Belleview Ave., 303-773-3647, www.threedog colorado.com (see Worth a Paws)

Highlands Ranch

Paw Prints, 6654 Timberline Rd., Unit C, 303-471-4230, www.pawprints.biz

Smooch the Pooch, 3624 E. Highlands Ranch Pkwy., 303-346-8009, www .smooch-thepooch.com

Wag N' Wash Healthy Pet Center, 2229 W. Wildcat Reserve, 720-344-9274, www.wagnwash.com. The store also has a self-service dog wash, with three grades of washes.

Lakewood

Curve Feed and Supply, 6750 W. Mississippi Ave., 303-934-1249

PETCO, 475 S. Wadsworth, 303-985-0050, www.petco.com

PetSmart, 160 Wadsworth Blvd., 303-232-0858, www.petsmart.com

Pets N' Stuff, 7777 W. Jewell, 303-989-5380, www.petsnstuffcolorado.com. The store also has a self-service dog wash.

Littleton

Lewis and Bark, 5623 S. Prince St., 303-347-6370

Laund-Ur-Mutt, 12512-B Ken Caryl Ave., Littleton, 720-981-7387, www.muttspa .com (see Worth a Paws)

Murdoch's Ranch and Home Supply, 12154 N. Dumont Wy., 303-791-7800, www.murdochs.com

PETCO, 8100 W. Crestline, 303-973-7057; 7460 S. University Blvd., 720-488-5222; www.petco.com. The S. University Blvd. location also has a self-service dog wash.

PetSmart, 8695 Park Meadows Dr., 303-799-3575; 8222 S. University Blvd., 303-220-0215; 7900 W. Quincy Ave., 303-971-0016; 8500 W. Crestline Ave., 303-948-6372; 8440 S. Kipling Pkwy., 720-922-8335; www.petsmart.com

Takoda's Pet Depot, 7735 W. Long Dr., 303-932-7387, www.petdepot.net/tako das.html

Wag N' Wash Healthy Pet Center, 5066 S. Wadsworth Blvd., 303-973-9274, www .wagnwash.com. The store also has a self-service dog wash, with three grades of washes.

Northglenn

PETCO, 450 E. 120th Ave., 303-255-4528, www.petco.com. The store also has a self-service dog wash.

PetSmart, 10600 Melody Dr., 720-929-9459, www.petsmart.com

Parker

Essential Pet, 17930 Cottonwood Dr., 303-805-5451, www.essential-pet.com

For Paws Bakery, 19565 E. Main St., 303-840-5999, www.fourpaws.t83.net (see Worth a Paws)

Muttz N' Stuff, 12620 Washington Ln., #303 (Meridian Business Center), 303-790-9490, www.muttznstuff.com. The store also has a self-service dog wash.

PetSmart, 11183A S. Parker Rd., 720-851-7790, www.petsmart.com

Westminster
Muttz Pet Goods and Gifts, 11225 Decatur St., 303-460-0117, www.muttzpet goods.com

PETCO, 6735 W. 88th Ave., 303-432-9230, www.petco.com. The store also has a self-service dog wash.

PetSmart, 10460 Town Center Dr., 303-466-2834, www.petsmart.com

Wheat Ridge
PetSmart, 3540 Youngfield St., 303-424-0123, www.petsmart.com

Walkers Quality Cage and Feed Supply, 4298 Kipling, 303-424-0305

Wardle Feed and Pet Supply, 7610 42nd Ave., 303-424-6455

CANINE ER
Arvada
Animal Urgent Care of Arvada, 7851 Indiana St., 303-420-7387, www.animal urgentcareofarvada.com. Open 5 PM–8 AM, Monday to Friday; 24 hours weekends and holidays.

Castle Rock
VCA Douglas County Animal Hospital (AAHA certified), 531 Jerry St. (off Hwy. 86), 303-688-2480, www.vcadouglas county.com. Open 24 hours.

Denver
VCA Alameda East Veterinary Hospital (AAHA certified), 9770 E. Alameda Ave. (2 blocks west of Havana), 303-366-2639, www.aevh.com. Open 24 hours.

Evergreen
Evergreen Animal Hospital, 32175 Castle Ct. (corner of Bergen Pkwy. and Hwy. 74), 303-674-4331, www.evergreenvet .com. A certified vet technician is at the clinic nights, weekends, and holidays.

Englewood
Central Veterinary Emergency Services (AAHA certified), 3550 S. Jason (inside Veterinary Referral Center of Colorado), 303-874-7387, www.vrcc.com. Open 4 PM–8 AM Monday to Friday; 24 hours weekends and holidays.

Highlands Ranch
Animal Hospital Specialty Center (AAHA certified), 5640 County Line Pl., 303-740-9595, www.ahscvets.com. Open 24 hours.

Lakewood
Animal Critical Care and Emergency Services, 1597 Wadsworth Blvd., 303-239-1200. Open 24 hours.

Littleton
Columbine Animal Hospital, 5546 W. Canyon Trail, 303-979-4040, www.col umbineanimal.com. A doctor is at the clinic nights, weekends, and holidays.

Animal ER, 221 W. County Line Rd., 720-283-9348. Open 6 PM–8 AM, Monday to Friday; 24 hours weekends and holidays.

Parker
Animal Emergency and Specialty Center, 17701 Cottonwood Dr., 720-842-5050, www.aescparker.com. Open 24 hours.

Westminster

Banfield 24-Hour Emergency Hospital, 7243 N. Federal Blvd, Ste. 15, 303-428-4368, www.banfield.net. Open 24 hours.

Northside Emergency Pet Clinic, 945 W. 124th Ave., 303-252-7722, www.emergencypetclinics.com. Open 5:30 PM–8 AM, Monday to Friday; 24 hours weekends and holidays.

Wheat Ridge

Wheat Ridge Animal Hospital (AAHA certified), 3695 Kipling, 303-424-3325, www.wheatridgeanimal.com. Open 24 hours.

RESOURCES

Denver Metro Convention and Visitors Bureau, 1555 California, Denver, 303-892-1112, 800-645-3446; www.denver.org

Denver Mountain Parks, 303-697-4545, www.denvergov.org/Mountain_Parks

Jefferson County Parks and Open Space, 303-271-5925, www.co.jefferson.co.us

South Platte Ranger District, Pike National Forest, 19316 Goddard Ranch Ct. (past the N. Turkey Creek Rd. turnoff from Hwy. 285 South), Morrison, 303-275-5610

Two
Boulder and Vicinity

THE BIG SCOOP

The communities in Boulder County, including Boulder, Louisville, Lafayette, Longmont, Lyons, and the mountain town of Nederland, provide lots of great outdoor opportunities for dogs, even though development in the area increases at a rate faster than a wagging tail.

Boulder is in general a dog-friendly town, though environmental and shared-use concerns have made dogs on trails the subject of occasionally heated debate. A local group known as FIDOS (Friends Interested in Dogs and Open Space) has become an advocate of canine rights, working to keep the majority of trails accessible to dogs. Given the occasionally lukewarm reception that some Boulder residents may give you and your dog, therefore, be sure to help your own Fido brush up on etiquette before hitting the trails.

Dogs are not allowed on Boulder's downtown, pedestrian-only Pearl Street Mall, which limits their sightseeing and shopping options somewhat. A leash law is enforced within the city limits of all towns in Boulder County, though not in unincorporated Boulder County. And though there's no direct ordinance against public tethering, the City of Boulder leash law can be interpreted as prohibiting it, so you're better off not tying up your dog outside a store.

TAIL-RATED TRAILS

Boulder dogs are lucky in that there are many trails in or near the city on which they can be off leash, though a stricter management plan introduced in 2006, known as the **Voice and Sight Dog Tag Program**, has curtailed their options somewhat (and if you're just visiting Boulder for a day or two, you may well want to pass up the process and just keep Fido leashed).

As a dog owner (or guardian, in Boulder parlance), you must first watch a short video on voice and sight control produced by the City of Boulder Open Space and Mountain Parks Department (voice/sight control means a dog must stay within your range of view and come immediately when called, no matter what distractions of other dogs, wildlife, or people may tempt him to do otherwise). Then you must purchase a special tag through the department ($15 for Boulder residents; $18.75 for nonresidents; $5 per additional tag) and make sure your dog(s) wear it when hiking off leash. You should also have a leash per dog handy at all times, and no more than two dogs per person can be off leash. Rangers will test your dog's obedience level on occasion (a pocketful of treats can be helpful in such situations—for your dog, not the ranger!). Anyone in your household who walks the dog must watch the video and register in the program, though one registration fee covers everyone. Note that the tag program applies only to City of Boulder trails, not Boulder *County* Open Space, where dogs generally have to be leashed.

The **Trailhead Leash Program** is one more component of Boulder's dog-management plan on trails and open space. You must keep your dog leashed at all trailheads (including the parking lot) and as you begin and finish your hike; look for the trail markers that indicate when your dog can be under voice and sight control on the trails that allow it. For more information, call 303-441-3440 or go to www.osmp.org.

No matter where you are, plastic pick-up baggies are considerately provided at many trailheads to encourage you to clean up after your dog's pit stops—use them!

The trail map put out by the Colorado Mountain Club (Boulder Group) includes many hiking options in addition to the ones suggested here. Look for it at the Chatauqua Park ranger's cottage as well as at local mountaineering stores. *Boulder Hiking Trails*, by Ruth and Glenn Cushman, is another good resource.

Boulder

Boulder Dog Parks

Regulations: Dogs must be vaccinated and have a current license; a guardian (owner) must be present at all times; clean up after your dog (poop bags and trash cans are on hand) and have a leash at the ready for each dog, if needed; leave female dogs in heat at home, as well as puppies younger than four months; no more than four dogs per guardian are allowed at one time. *Dogs can be off leash.*

Thanks to a cooperative effort between dog owners and the Parks and Recreation Department, Boulder is home to four off-leash dog parks, all of which have proven to be immensely popular. The parks are usually busiest after work and on weekends, and they're great places for owners to socialize, too.

The **Valmont Dog Park**, on the north side of Valmont Rd. between Foothills Pkwy. and 55th St., is on about 3 acres adjacent to a former chicken farm. Parking is available directly off Valmont (look for a green, aluminum-sided building on the street's north side). Though dogs may rue the fact that the farm no longer generates a pungent odor that used to permeate the neighborhood on warm summer days, their humans will appreciate its absence. The park is fenced on three sides, with one of the old farm buildings forming part of the fourth barrier. There's also a .25-acre fenced area for smaller dogs. A large shady tree at the park's entrance with a picnic table and chairs, and some other picnic tables and benches along the side of the park, give you a place to hang out while your dog romps. Water is available at the park in the summer.

The 2.25-acre **East Boulder Dog Park** is located on the west side of the East Boulder Community Center (north on 55th St. off S. Boulder Rd.), between the lake and the playing fields. It's the most popular of the dog parks; on a sunny Sunday afternoon, Clover and I watched 20 dogs frolic together, with the action temporarily broken up by two fights: one dog-on-dog, and one owner-on-owner (verbally). A small-dog park adjacent to the main dog park keeps the Chihuahuas separate from the Great Danes, if desired. Two picnic tables provide a place for owners to gather, and the nearby playground lets you drop off your two-legged kids to play while you take the four-legged ones to the park. Best of all, part of the lake and a small swimming beach are within the park, allowing your dog to try out a new stroke or play water polo with the other canines.

The **Howard Heuston Dog Park**, the first off-leash dog area to be established, consists of 1.25 acres within the larger community park (take 34th St. south from the Diagonal Hwy. for several blocks to its end). The dog park is outlined with markers rather than a fence, so you'll want to make sure that Fido's up for responding to voice commands before bringing him here; in fact, you must be registered through the Voice and Sight Dog Tag Program (see Tail-Rated Trails intro) to have your dog off leash here. No water is available.

Foothills Community Dog Park is the newest of Boulder's canine-friendly facilities. The community park is in north Boulder, between Locust Ave. and Lee Hill Rd., and west of Broadway; to reach the dog park, drive west on Violet from Broadway, go right on 10th St., and left on Cherry. Dogs have 2 fenced acres to play in, with separate small- and large-dog areas.

Marshall Mesa

Distance: 3.7 miles round-trip
Elevation gain: Approximately 200 feet
Trailhead: Take Hwy. 93 (S. Broadway) south out of Boulder to the intersection with Hwy. 170 (Eldorado Springs Dr.) and the turnoff for Eldorado Springs. Turn left; the trailhead is immediately on the right, up a short hill.

Dogs can be off leash, except in the vicinity of the trailhead, as part of the Trailhead Leash Program; signs along the trail indicate where you can switch from leash to voice control, and vice versa.

Though close to a major thoroughfare, the trails on Marshall Mesa convey the flavor of Boulder County's less-developed past, allowing you and your dog to experience some vestiges of a rural landscape among the ponderosa pines. In fact, cows sometimes roam on the mesa; if your pooch is prone to chase them, it's wise to keep him leashed. This was Clover's favorite evening hike when we lived in Boulder, as the views west to the foothills (and Longs Peak) provide good sunset watching.

Begin on the **Marshall Valley Trail**, which traverses left from the trailhead for .8 mile (if you look down the hill toward Marshall Dr., you'll see the original trailhead for Marshall Mesa, before it was rerouted in 2007. After a short climb you'll join up with the **Community Ditch Trail** (stay right at the T-intersection); this wide gravel service road parallels an irrigation ditch, usually filled during the spring and summer, where your dog can

Kip leashes up before a hike in Boulder.

have lots of fun frolicking in the water. After about 1.3 miles the trail meets up with the **Marshall Mesa Trail** to the right, which loops back to the Marshall Valley Trail in .9 mile, giving wet dogs a little under 2 miles to dry off before arriving back at the trailhead. (If you want a shorter hike, stay on the Community Ditch Trail past the intersection with Marshall Mesa; at the next trail intersection, keep right, then turn right onto the Coal Seam Trail to reach the trailhead.) As an added bonus for the literate canine, signs along the loop describe the history and geology of the mesa.

Mount Sanitas

Distance: Either 3.1 or 2.2 miles round-trip
Elevation gain: Up to 1,280 feet
Trailhead: Drive on Mapleton Ave. west from Broadway in downtown Boulder; after the Mapleton Center for Rehabilitation on the corner of 4th St., you'll see several parking turnouts on the right that

provide access to the trailhead. The recommended starting point is the picnic shelter right before the small bridge.

Dogs can be off leash, except in the vicinity of the trailhead, as part of the Trailhead Leash Program; signs along the trail indicate where you can switch from leash to voice control, and vice versa.

The Sanitas trails are doggie central in Boulder (some would say too much so—one overzealous dog hater spent hours mapping poop piles on his GPS to make a case for banning dogs from the trail). Your dog will love you for bringing him here if he's the social type, as there are always plenty of opportunities to do the doggie handshake (i.e., butt sniffing). And you'll enjoy the panoramic vistas of Boulder and the eastern plains offered at a couple of vantage points as well as the sense of being miles away from population density when you're really just a few minutes from downtown.

Clover's favorite route—best for the aerobically fit dog and owner—involves climbing the **Mount Sanitas Trail**, which branches off to the left after the bridge. You'll reach the summit after 1.2 miles of steady climbing. Descend .8 mile by the steep **East Ridge Trail** (shoes with good tread or hiking boots come in handy) and walk along the ridge past the trophy

Thanks to her voice-and-sight dog tag, Chica can hike off leash on many City of Boulder open space trails.

homes until you reach the top of the **Sanitas Valley Trail**. This wide gravel path descends gradually for 1.1 miles back to your launching point. (If you're into practicing your rock-climbing moves, there are some good bouldering sites along the hike up Sanitas—just look for the signs and chalk marks.)

A less strenuous alternative would be to forgo the vertical and hike along the **Valley Trail**, which affords views of rolling green hills capped by the famous Flatirons. Or your dog may prefer to hike up the Valley Trail and return on the 1-mile **Dakota Ridge Trail**, which begins to the right of the Valley Trail's "summit" and eventually rejoins this trail about three-quarters of the way down.

A small brook by the picnic shelter provides a cooling rest for your dog after hiking and socializing. A "swimming hole" about halfway up the Sanitas Valley Trail on the left is usually full of water in the summer, and a trickling rivulet on the trail's right provides the opportunity for some slurps. As there are no water sources on the Mount Sanitas Trail, you may want to bring extra water to share with your dog.

Twin Lakes Open Space

Access: From Boulder, take the Diagonal Hwy. (119) northeast to Jay Rd. and turn right. From Jay Rd., turn left (north) on 63rd St., then make a right on Nautilus Dr. (the entrance into an office park). Turn left at the next intersection and follow the road to its end, where there's a parking area. A wide gravel path to the southeast leads to the lakes.

Dogs can be off leash at West Lake; they must be leashed elsewhere.

This Boulder County Open Space parcel in the Gunbarrel neighborhood gives Boulder dogs a place to run off some steam off leash without having to go through the process of obtaining a voice-and-sight tag from the city (because it's a county, not a city, property). A little more than 3 miles of gravel trails encircle both lakes, which are reservoirs operated by the Boulder and Left Hand Irrigation Company since 1910. Visit West Lake with your dog and he can chase sticks or toys in the water, take a jog with you around the lake, and, perhaps, spot a great blue heron alighting. If you venture over to the slightly larger East Lake, Rover will have to be on leash. An irrigation ditch spanned by a small bridge separates the two lakes.

Chautauqua Park

Access: Drive west on Baseline Rd.; the park entrance is on the left after 9th St.

Dogs can be off leash, except in the vicinity of the trailhead, as part of the Trailhead Leash Program; signs along the trail indicate where you can switch from leash to voice control, and vice versa. Dogs must also be leashed on the lower McClintock Trail and on the large lawn area that fronts the Chautauqua Auditorium and restaurant.

This is perhaps Boulder's best-known spot for hiking and playing, with a stunning location at the base of the town's signature Flatirons. It's wise to avoid this area midday on warm, sunny weekends (summer or winter), when everyone and their dog seem to come here (pardon the play on words). Several trails originate from here, including the popular **Mesa Trail**, which runs almost 7 miles south to Eldorado Springs. For great views of Boulder, hike to **Saddle Rock** or **Royal Arch** (both are slightly more than 2 miles round-trip and involve some climbing). If you go to Saddle Rock and want to continue hiking up Green Mountain, your only option is to go right on the **Ranger Trail** and gain the summit this way; dogs are not permitted on the E.M. Greenman Trail. And note that the Ranger Trail is designated

on-corridor voice-and-sight control, so dogs shouldn't venture off the actual trail.

Flatirons Vista/ Doudy Draw

Distance: 5.6 miles round-trip
Elevation gain: 450 feet

Trailhead: Take Hwy. 93 (S. Broadway) south from Boulder. About 2 miles south of the stoplight at the Eldorado Springs turnoff, you'll see a fenced-in parking area on the right. The trailhead is here.

Dogs can be off leash, except in the vicinity of the trailhead, as part of the Trailhead Leash Program; signs along the trail indicate where you can switch from leash to voice control, and vice versa.

This is a popular trail with horseback riders as well as hikers and mountain bikers. If your dog has an aversion to equine creatures, note the number of horse trailers in the parking lot before setting out. Begin by hiking west on a service road, taking in, as the trailhead name implies, a beautiful vista of the Flatirons, the vertical rock slabs that front the foothills. After the third livestock gate, the trail narrows, winding along a ridge through fragrant ponderosa pine. It then follows a switchback down to a small gully, where you'll come to a dog rest stop (i.e., stream). After crossing, follow the trail sign to the right. A good turnaround point for your hike is a bridge you'll come to just before the **Community Ditch Trail**, which allows your dog another respite near water. Hiking farther would bring you to a final paved portion of the trail that ends at a trailhead on Eldorado Springs Dr. (Hwy. 170), a total of 3.3 miles from the Flatirons Vista trailhead.

Boulder Creek Path

Access: Runs 5.5 miles from the mouth of Boulder Canyon to east of 55th St.
Dogs must be leashed.

If possible, avoid bringing your dog on the downtown section of this often crowded paved path—in the wink of an eye he could easily become tangled up with the multitude of bicyclists, in-line skaters, runners, and amblers who use this popular route. The stretch of path that runs east of Foothills Hwy. and initially parallels Pearl St., however, offers more breathing space, especially on weekdays. See if your clever canine spots the pawprints embedded in the concrete just east of the office park on Pearl—they lead to a small, refreshing pool where dogs can partake of the waters while you relax on a nearby bench.

 Despite the many places in and around Boulder where you can hike with your dog, certain areas lie at the other end of the spectrum—that is, dogs are banned. Fido is not welcome on the following trails on City of Boulder and Boulder County Open Space as well as on Mountain Parks land:

- The **Goshawk Ridge Trail** and **Spring Brook Loop South Trail**, which branch off the Fowler Trail and the Spring Brook Loop North Trail south of Eldorado Springs Dr.
- The **Tall Grass Prairie Natural Area**, on either side of the lower Big Bluestem Trail (part of the Shanahan Ridge trail network)
- The 1.5-mile section of the **South Boulder Creek Trail** that runs south of South Boulder Rd.
- The **White Rocks section** of the **East Boulder Trail**, bounded to the south by Valmont Rd. and to the north by a trail through the **Gunbarrel Farm** open space area, which dogs are not allowed on either
- The **Prairie Dog Habitat Conservation Area** east of the Greenbelt Plateau Trail
- The **upper McClintock Trail**, a self-

guided nature walk between the Enchanted Mesa and Mesa Trails in Chautauqua Park

- The **E.M. Greenman** and **Long Canyon Trails**, accessed from the Realization Point Trailhead atop Flagstaff Mountain or via trails from the Gregory Canyon Trailhead
- The **Hogback Trail**, which branches off the Foothills Trail north of Wonderland Lake; all the land north and west of the Foothills Trail on the west side of Hwy. 36 (several "social trails" crisscross this area); and the land east of Hwy. 36 in this same area, bounded on the east by the Left Hand Trail and the south by Longhorn Rd.
- The **Sombrero Marsh Trail**, north of Baseline Reservoir
- The **Prairie Dog Habitat Conservation Area** east of the Cottonwood Trail
- Various city open space properties that have no established trails—check fence lines for No Dogs postings
- The **Hall Ranch** area north of Boulder, off Hwy. 36
- The **Heil Ranch** area, near the mouth of Lefthand Canyon
- The **Caribou Ranch** open space, northwest of Nederland

 South shore of Boulder Reservoir. During the summer, dogs are prohibited from this area.

Eldorado Springs

 Eldorado Canyon State Park
Access: From Hwy. 93 just south of Boulder, turn right on Hwy. 170 at the Eldorado Springs turnoff. The park is about 3 miles ahead.
Dogs must be leashed.
When your dog has had his fill of watching climbers attempt the numerous

technical routes for which "Eldo" is renowned, he'll probably be interested in doing a bit of hiking. At 2.8 miles round-trip, the **Rattlesnake Gulch Trail** begins off the one road through the park. It climbs gradually but steadily to a flat overlook, former site of the Crags Hotel, which burned in 1913. The only remains of this once-luxurious retreat are a couple of fireplaces, sections of the foundation, and scattered pieces of charred dinnerware—as well as a spectacular view of the canyon and the plains beyond on one side and the rugged Indian Peaks on the other. Though the trail continues to an upper loop near the railroad tracks (you might spot an Amtrak train traveling high above during your hike), the overlook makes a good turnaround point. The **Eldorado Canyon Trail** takes off from the end of the park road, climbing, at times steeply, through ponderosa pine and intersecting after 3.5 miles with the **Walker Ranch Loop Trail**, a popular mountain-biking area on Boulder County Open Space. Taking a left at the intersection puts you on the **Crescent Meadows Trail**, which leads to another parcel of state park land (known as Crescent Meadows). The trail eventually ends at the Gross Dam Rd.; the round-trip distance from the trailhead is 11 miles.

Lafayette

Great Bark Dog Park

Access: From the intersection of Baseline and 119th St., turn north onto 119th and drive for .2 mile to the large parking lot on the left.
Regulations: Dogs must be spayed or neutered, vaccinated, and have a current license; puppies must be four months or older; owners must be 18 or older, be present at all times, and have a leash on hand for each dog; clean up after your dog; no more than three dogs per owner are allowed at one time.

Dogs can be off leash.

The aptly named park is sure to elicit great big barks of joy from your dog, with a generous 6 acres for leash-free playing. A fenced inner circle area is set aside for small or timid dogs, with a canopied bench for owners. The larger area that rings it, also fenced, has a natural-surface path around the perimeter for leash-free strolls, with five canopied benches along it for resting and taking in the grand views of the snow-capped Indian Peaks to the west (as well as of the surrounding farmland that's sure to be a housing development one day). The park's only downside is that there's no shade or water for dogs.

Waneka Lake Park

Access: From South Boulder Rd. in Lafayette, head west and turn right (north) onto Centaur Village Rd. Turn left onto Caria at the stop sign, then drive up the hill and turn right into Waneka Park; park in the lot. Alternatively, you can access a second parking lot on the east side of the lake: turn right on Caria at the stop sign, then left at the intersection with Emma St.

Dogs must be leashed.

A 1.3-mile gravel foot and bike path runs along the periphery of the small reservoir that is the focal point of this 147-acre community park. The reservoir was dug out by the pioneering Waneka family on the site of a spring more than 100 years ago. The trail that encircles it is best for sociable dogs and people who won't mind sharing the path with bicycles and families. About half is shaded by trees and brush; the rest is open to sunshine, occasionally blustery winds, and a knockout view of the Front Range. The surrounding park has a playground and picnic gazebos, in addition to a small boathouse and pier with bathrooms and rowboat, canoe, and paddleboat rentals (the boathouse is open from Memorial Day through Labor Day).

Longmont

Longmont Dog Parks

Regulations: Dogs must be licensed and vaccinated; puppies younger than four months, dogs in heat, and aggressive dogs are not permitted; there's a limit of three dogs per person; owners must stay at the park and have a leash on hand for each dog; young children must be supervised by an adult; pick up after Fido. *Dogs can be off leash.*

Canine-friendly Longmont has an impressive six dog parks, which likely sets the record for dog parks per capita in Colorado. The first dog park, simply known as **Park #1**, is the 2.5-acre fenced park at 21st St. and Francis, which opened in the summer of 2000. A small covered shelter and several picnic tables around the park allow owners to take a breather while their dogs run themselves silly. Bring water, as there's no source handy. The one caveat is parking: You'll have to leave your car at either Garden Acres Park or Carr Park, both about a block and a half away on 21st St. (the neighbors will raise a howl if you park on the residential streets near the dog run). And do keep your dog on leash while walking to and from the off-leash venue.

Another dog park, **Park #2**, is at the intersection of Airport and St. Vrain Rds. Parking is available behind the Public Works building on Airport Rd. This 2.8-acre fenced park is adjacent to Longmont's small airport, so aviation-minded dogs may particularly enjoy a visit here. They'll also find some agility equipment to try their paw at and a water spigot.

The unfenced **Dog Training Area at Union Reservoir**, on the lake's south side, is paradise for water-loving hounds (and it's the rare dog that wouldn't put himself into this category). To reach the reservoir, east of Longmont, take Ken Pratt Blvd./Hwy. 119 (or, alternatively, 9th Ave. east from town) to E. County Line Rd (a.k.a. CR 1). Turn left (right if you're on 9th Ave.), then take a right (or left if you came from 9th) on CR 26, which leads into the park. The reservoir was actually a natural lake before it was tapped for water supply. The only downside is the $8 per vehicle admission fee (though you can get a season pass—$55 for Longmont residents, $65 for nonresidents). Dogs must be leashed elsewhere in the park.

Several community parks in Longmont offer .3-acre fenced **off-leash areas**. One is at **Stephen Day Park**, at the corner of E. Mountain View Dr. and Deerwood Dr. in east Longmont. Another is at **Rough and Ready Park** (or Ruff and Ready, in dog lingo), at 301 E. 21st Ave. in north-central Longmont. There's also a labyrinth in the park that your dog can accompany you in on leash. And a third area is at **Blue Skies Park**, at 1520 Mountain Dr. in west Longmont. The overall park has a flight theme, so there's a time line of flight development, with images from a pterodactyl to the Wright Brothers' plane to a rocket ship and others sandblasted into stone pavers. Bring water to all of these parks, as none is available on-site.

Golden Ponds Park and Nature Area

Access: Take 3rd Ave. west until it ends at the parking area for the park. *Dogs must be leashed.*

This pleasant oasis within Longmont provides a gentle stroll for you and Fido. Interconnected gravel paths encircle each of the four "golden" ponds (actually reclaimed gravel pits donated by Vernon Golden), with distances ranging from .55 mile to .8 mile. The ponds are popular for catch-and-release fishing, and ducks and cormorants share the waters with the fish. Dogs are understandably not allowed in the water (it is a nature area, after all), so water dogs may be a bit disappointed. Perhaps the stellar view of 14,259-foot Longs Peak and the mountains known as the Twin Sisters to the west will suffice as distraction. From the park you can also hook up with the paved St. Vrain Greenway, which runs 7.3 miles along the river that it's named after.

Louisville

Louisville Dog Parks

Regulations: Dogs must have current vaccinations; no puppies younger than four months, female dogs in heat, or aggressive dogs are allowed; there's a limit of three dogs per owner; owners must remain present and have a leash for each dog on hand; children must be under adult supervision; no food is allowed; clean up after your dog.
Dogs can be off leash.

The **Davidson Mesa Dog Run Area** is part of the Davidson Mesa Open Space, located on the west side of McCaslin Blvd., .5 mile south of South Boulder Rd. (parking is available). There's a fenced-in park of about 4 acres where dogs can play off leash, in addition to about 4 miles of surrounding trails that you and your leashed dog can enjoy. You may want to bring water for your dog, since none is on-site; try to avoid the heat of day in summer, as the yucca-filled terrain lacks shade. It can also be notoriously windy, but the sunset views are spectacular.

To reach the **dog park at the Louisville Community Park** (955 Bella Vista Dr.), drive south on Main St. from downtown Louisville until it ends in Rex St. Turn left and drive two blocks to County Rd. Turn right and drive the length of the park to Bella Vista Dr. Make a right here, and then another right to enter the park. The dog park is adjacent to the parking lot. This extremely social dog park consists of one fenced area of close to an acre, with a small pavilion for you to seek shade in while your dog plays. A small adjacent pond with beach area is also accessible, but it's separately fenced, and you'll have to decide whether or not you want your dog to swim in it, since it contains treated reclaimed domestic wastewater. The water is said to be safe for dogs to play in, as it's filtered and disinfected, but it's not considered potable for humans. Then again, if you think about the mud holes your dog probably likes to lie in and drink from, it's certainly no worse (and likely better).

Coal Creek Trail

Distance: 8 miles one way
Access: There are numerous access points for this trail. The western terminus is at McCaslin Blvd., just west of Hwy. 36 in Superior; the eastern end is at 120th St., a few blocks south of South Boulder Rd., in Lafayette. One easily accessible place to reach the trail is just east of 96th St., off the north side of Hwy. 42, where there is a trailhead and parking at the Aquarius Open Space parcel.
Dogs must be leashed.

This primarily flat pedestrian and bike trail follows Coal Creek for most of its length, winding through neighborhoods in Louisville and Lafayette. With its semirural character in parts, you and your dog may even forget you are still in town. There's water galore if Rover wants to splash in the creek. Parts of the trail have been paved for bicycles, though a dirt trail leading to the river often parallels the paved one.

Carolyn Holmberg Preserve at Rock Creek Farm

Distance: 2.8 miles of trails
Access: Take Dillon Rd. east from McCaslin Blvd. to 104th St. Go

south on 104th St. The trailhead is .7 mile ahead on the left.

Dogs must be leashed.

Don't confuse this Boulder County Open Space area with the monolithic Rock Creek subdivision visible from Hwy. 36. In fact, with the wide openness of this area, you and your dog might think you're in Nebraska, except for the stunning view of Longs Peak to the west. This would be a great place for a sunset walk. The most scenic hiking section, on the 1.5-mile **Mary Miller Trail**, goes around Stearns Lake (keep an eye out for the wildlife area closure signs) and travels on a wide, flat path through fields. From Stearns Lake, you can also hike south from the dam on the 1.3-mile **Cradleboard Trail**; after going through a horse pasture, stay to the right, where a dirt service road will eventually bring you out on 104th St. Cross the road and continue hiking along a stream known as Buffalo Gulch. The final section of trail borders a wetlands preserve, with a small pond, before ending at Brainard Dr.

 Harper Lake. Because the lake, off McCaslin Blvd. across from the Davidson Mesa Open Space, is home to a wildlife sanctuary and is part of the city's water supply, canines are verboten.

Lyons

 Bohn Park Off-Leash Dog Areas
Access: From Hwy. 36 (off the stretch of road between the turnoff to Boulder and downtown Lyons), turn south onto 2nd Ave. Drive a block and a half to the entrance to Bohn Park on the right.
Regulations: Dogs must have current vaccinations and a license; no aggressive dogs or females in heat; you must have a leash for each dog with you; no more than three dogs at a time per owner; your dog must always be supervised; children must be accompanied by an adult; clean up after your dog; no human food is allowed; don't leave behind toys, chairs, or water dishes.

Dogs can be off leash.

Part of the larger Bohn Park (and yes, it's pronounced "bone"), the main off-leash area consists of a generous 10 acres of fenced meadow where even the biggest dogs should be able to tire themselves out. This area is in the park's southernmost section, and a path from the main parking lot leads the way to it, past the playing fields and a couple of picnic areas. South of the dog park is another 10-acre parcel that's managed by Boulder County Open Space, so if you happen to venture that way, make sure your dog is leashed up.

Once your dog has played to his heart's content in the field, he'll want to check out the separate off-leash area along the St. Vrain River. From the parking lot, walk up 2nd Ave. and take the pedestrian underpass beneath the 2nd Ave. bridge. The dog beach area is right there and signs mark the boundaries.

Nederland

 Lost Lake
Distance: 3.2 miles round-trip
Elevation gain: 800 feet
Trailhead: From Nederland, take Hwy. 72 east. Make a right on CR 130 (toward Eldora Mountain Ski Resort). Stay on this road, going past the ski area turnoff and through the small hamlet of Eldora, after which the road turns to dirt. At the signed fork, stay left, to Hessie. In the spring, when the road past this point becomes streamlike, you may want to park near the fork. But if your vehicle has good clearance, the most available parking is at Hessie townsite, less than .25 mile farther along. The

trailhead is just up the road from here, at the North Fork of Boulder Creek. *Dogs can be off leash.*

On this particular trail, dogs can hike with their owners under voice control because the trail doesn't enter the Indian Peaks Wilderness. If you continue hiking on one of the other trails accessed from here, however, be ready to leash your dog as soon as you cross the wilderness boundary.

This area is extremely popular on weekends year-round; midweek would be the best time to explore it. The first part of this trail follows an old mining road up a gradual ascent. Midsummer, you'll be greeted by a colorful profusion of wildflowers on the slopes alongside the trail. After about .5 mile, cross a bridge over the South Fork of Boulder Creek and hike up parallel to it. A sign for Lost Lake soon indicates a turnoff to the left. From there, it's a short way to the lake itself, where your dog can frolic in the water while you pick out the mining ruins on the hillside across the lake.

CYCLING FOR CANINES

Of the handful of trails near Boulder where you can bike, only a few allow free-running dogs (and keep in mind that you'll have to comply with the Voice and Sight Dog Tag Program and keep Fido leashed in the vicinity of the trailhead): the **Community Ditch** and **Greenbelt Plateau Trails** on Marshall Mesa (see Tail-Rated Trails); the part of the **Community Ditch Trail** that also runs for 1.7 miles on the west side of Hwy. 93 (access this portion either by parking alongside Hwy. 93 or from the Doudy Draw trailhead off Eldorado Springs Dr. in order to avoid a dangerous crossing of the road with bike and dog in tow); the **Boulder Valley Ranch** and **Foothills Trails** off Hwy. 36, just north of Boulder (dogs are required to be leashed on the section of the Foothills Trail south of Lee Hill Rd., however);

and the **Teller Farm section of the East Boulder Trail**, which runs by two lakes between Valmont Dr. and Arapahoe Ave. east of Boulder. Note that the popular Walker Ranch and Betasso Preserve loop trails both have a leash law.

You'll have more biking options outside of Nederland. The "Mountain Bike Map of Boulder County," published by Latitude 40° and available at area bike and mountaineering shops, is a good resource. Try a section of the **Sourdough Trail**, a great moderate ride that runs 14.7 miles (one way) from Rainbow Lakes Rd. to Brainard Lake Rd.; access it by driving 7 miles north of Nederland on Hwy. 72 and turning left at the University of Colorado Mountain Research sign. (Other access points are from the Red Rock Trailhead, 14 miles north of Nederland on Hwy. 72 and left on Brainard Lake Rd.; the Beaver Creek Trailhead, 15 miles north of Nederland on Hwy. 72 and left on CR 96; and the Buchanan Pass Trailhead, 18 miles north of Nederland on Hwy. 72 and left on FR 114.) The **Switzerland Trail** follows a former narrow-gauge railroad track and has great views. There are several access points; one is reached via Sugarloaf Mountain Rd. out of Boulder Canyon, and another is about 3.5 miles past the town of Gold Hill, via Mapleton Ave./Sunshine Canyon Rd. out of Boulder. The trail runs about 4 miles down to Fourmile Creek from both of these starts. The **Bunce School Rd.** (now a jeep road) goes for about 6 miles from just past Peaceful Valley Campground, off Hwy. 72 north from Nederland, to Hwy. 7; you'll have to do an out-and-back to avoid riding on the highway. Water is available near or along all of these trails.

POWDERHOUNDS

You and your dog will need to venture into the mountains around Nederland to find reliable snow for skiing or snowshoeing. Note, however, that certain trails are completely closed to dogs from November 15 through April 30: the Brainard Lake snowshoe, Brainard Lake Cutoff, Beaver Creek, Mitchell Lake, Little Raven, Waldrop, CMC, CMC Cabin Cutoff, Pawnee Pass, Jean Lunning, Niwot Cutoff, and South St. Vrain Trails at the popular Brainard Lake area; the Jenny Creek and Guinn Mountain Trails by the Eldora Nordic Center; and the Buchanan Pass Trail in the northern Indian Peaks Wilderness.

Some good routes to consider include the **Sourdough Trail** (see Cycling for Canines); the unplowed road that leads to **Lefthand Park Reservoir**, which branches off the Brainard Lake Rd. before the winter closure gate (but note that dogs aren't permitted on the ski trails, listed above, that go off the road); the **Coney Flats Trail**, a jeep road that begins at Beaver Reservoir, off Hwy. 72 north of Ward; and the **Mammoth Gulch Road**, just past Tolland on the Rollins Pass Rd. outside Rollinsville. For more detailed descriptions of these routes as well as other options, refer to *Snowshoeing Colorado*, by Claire Walter.

CREATURE COMFORTS

Unless otherwise stated, dogs should not be left unattended in the room or cabin.

Boulder

$$ Foot of the Mountain Motel, 200 Arapahoe Ave., 303-442-5688, www.footofthemountainmotel.com. The small, simply furnished, wood-paneled rooms are contained in rustic-looking cabins built in the 1930s (the motel's two suites aren't pet friendly, though). There's a $5 fee per night, per pet, plus a $50 deposit. A big plus is the motel's location across the street from Boulder Creek and Eben G. Fine Park; though dogs must be leashed, the park and adjacent Creek Path provide great sniffing opportunities. You may leave your dog unattended in the room as long as you notify the front office and leave a cell-phone number.

$$–$$$ Best Western Boulder Inn, 770 28th St., 303-449-3800, 800-233-8469, www.boulderinn.com. Dogs are allowed in first-floor smoking rooms only, and a $100 deposit is required. Don't confuse this motel with the other Best Western in Boulder, the Golden Buff, which doesn't allow pets.

$$–$$$ Boulder Mountain Lodge, 91 Four Mile Canyon Rd., 303-444-0882, 800-458-0882, www.bouldermountainlodge.com. This motel complex, located streamside several miles from town, has a casual, summer-camp feel. In fact, campsites are available in addition to rooms, in summer. Dogs can be left in rooms, if necessary, with approval of the front office, but housekeeping will not come in. Keep your dog leashed when outside.

$$–$$$ Boulder Outlook Hotel, 800 28th St., 303-443-3322, 800-542-0304, http://boulderoutlook.com. This former Ramada Inn has been colorfully renovated and now bills itself as a zero-waste hotel. Dogs are allowed in outside-facing rooms only, for $10 extra per night, per dog, with a maximum fee of $30 per visit. They can be left unattended if housekeeping is notified; you can borrow a travel crate from the hotel if you want to keep Fido contained. Outside is a fenced dog run for pups to do their business, with poop bags. The Outlook also has a bar and grill, a regular slate of live music during the week, and an indoor courtyard recreation area with a chlorine-free heated pool and a pair of rocks for bouldering (in keeping with the active Boulder spirit).

 $$–$$$ Boulder University Inn, 1632 Broadway, 303-417-1700, www.boulderuniversityinn.com. Under the same ownership as the Quality Inn and Suites Boulder Creek, the motel also has the same pet policy: canine guests up to 75 pounds each (with a limit of two per room) pay an extra charge of $15 per night, per dog, to stay in designated rooms and must put down a deposit of $100. They get treats and a bandanna at check-in and you can request bowls to use during their stay. You can leave your dog unattended inside the room for a couple of hours as long as you give a cell-phone number. And the hotel has info on nearby hiking trails and dog parks, as well as veterinarians, groomers, and dogsitters.

$$–$$$ New West Inns, 970 28th St., 303-443-7800, 800-525-2149, www .newwestinnsboulder.com. Dogs are allowed in designated pet rooms for $10 extra per dog, per night.

$$$ Colorado Chautauqua Association, 900 Baseline Rd., 303-952-1611, www .chautauqua.com. Let your dog experience a bit of Boulder's intellectual past with a stay in one of these character-filled cottages in a stunning location at the base of the Flatirons. The adajcent Chautauqua Auditorium was built in 1898 and was for many years the hub of summer retreats for associates of the University of Texas, who came to attend lectures and concerts. Most of the cottages were constructed in the early 1900s, and today some are privately owned, while the others are rented out both nightly and long-term by the Chautauqua Association. The cottages were originally built as summer homes, and though most have been winterized, they definitely retain that "summer cabin at the lake" feel. Rentals range from studio/efficiencies to three bedrooms, and all have kitchens and necessary supplies. Pets are permitted in most of them for a fee of $10 per night, per pet, which is capped at $100 per visit if you're staying for multiple nights. You can leave your dog unattended for a short time as long as he remains relatively quiet, per-

haps while you enjoy a meal at the nearby dining hall. Among other events, the auditorium hosts concerts by local and national acts during the summer, and you can picnic on the lawn outside for free with your dog and still catch the music. And miles of trails start right outside the door in Chautauqua Park.

$$$ Quality Inn and Suites Boulder Creek, 2020 Arapahoe, 303-449-7550, 888-449-7550, www.qualityinn boulder.com. The same dog-loving owners run this more upscale Quality Inn and the value-priced Boulder University Inn. Canine guests up to 75 pounds each (with a limit of two per room) pay an extra charge of $15 per night, per dog, to stay in designated rooms and must put down a deposit of $100. They get treats and a bandanna at check-in, and you can request bowls to use during their stay. The hotel has info on nearby hiking trails and dog

Cisco, a former Boulder resident, loves playing and hates thunderstorms.

parks, as well as veterinarians, groomers, and dogsitters. The rooms are more nicely appointed than the typical Quality Inn; they even feature a framed picture of Samantha, the owners' dog. You can leave Rover inside for a couple of hours as long as you leave a cell-phone number. Hotel amenities include a pool, fitness center, and complimentary breakfast buffet, and out back is a small, fenced dog walk area with poop bags.

$$$–$$$$ Boulder Residence Inn, 3030 Center Green Dr., 303-449-5545, 800-331-3131 (national number), www.marriott.com. There's a $75 one-time fee for dogs at this all-suite hotel. You can leave your dog unattended in the room.

$$$–$$$$ Holiday Inn Express, 4777 N. Broadway, 303-442-6600, www.hiexpress.com. There's a nightly fee of $25, with a maximum of $50 per stay. If you leave your dog unattended in the room, he must be in a travel kennel.

$$$–$$$$ Homewood Suites, 4950 Baseline Rd. (behind the Meadows Shopping Center), 303-499-9922, 800-225-5466 (national number), www.boulder.homewoodsuites.com. There's a $50 one-time fee for dogs to stay in the apartment-style suites. You can leave your dog unattended as long as housekeeping is notified.

Longmont

$–$$ America's Best Value Inn, 3815 Hwy. 119, 303-776-8700, 888-315-2378 (national number). The motel has designated pet rooms on the ground floor (both smoking and nonsmoking available) and charges $10.29 extra per night, per dog. You can leave your dog unattended in the room as long as you let the front desk know; housekeepers won't come in during that time.

$–$$ Super 8 Del Camino, 10805 Turner Ave. (intersection of Hwys. 25 and 119), 303-772-0888, 800-800-8000 (national number), www.super8.com. There's a $10 fee per pet, per night.

$$ Countrywood Inn and RV Park, 1550 N. Main St., 303-776-2185, 877-776-2185, www.countrywoodinn.com. To stay in one of the motel rooms here, you must pay $7 extra per night, per dog, or a $50 one-time fee per dog for the week. Make sure your dog stays leashed outside, is cleaned up after, and is quiet.

$$ Days Inn Longmont, 3820 Hwy. 119, 303-651-6999, www.daysinn.com. Dogs can stay in first-floor rooms for a $20 one-time fee. If they're in a travel crate, they can stay unattended in the room.

$$ Ellen's Bed and Breakfast, 700 Kimbark St., 303-776-1676, www.ellensbandb.com. Your dog may well appreciate this alternative to Longmont's chain motels. Set in a 1910 Victorian house, Ellen's offers two rooms, one with a queen-size bed and private bath, the other with bunk beds and a shared bath. There's a $5 nightly pet fee. An outdoor hot tub is available. You are able to leave your dog unattended inside the room, at the discretion of the owners, though Fido may prefer to stay in the B&B's fenced yard. Two schnauzers serve as host dogs.

$$–$$$ Hawthorn Suites, 2000 Sunset Wy., 303-774-7100, www.hawthorn.com. Aside from a few standard rooms, all of the units are one-bedroom suites with kitchens and gas fireplaces. There's no charge for dogs who stay fewer than seven days; if they stay longer, there's a $100 one-time fee. They can be left unattended only if in a travel kennel. Rates include a breakfast buffet and an evening reception Monday to Thursday with drinks and appetizers.

$$-$$$ Longmont Residence Inn, 1450 Dry Creek Dr., 303-702-9933, www .marriott.com. Dogs must pay a $100 one-time fee to stay in the studio to two-bedroom suites, so it only makes sense to bring Fido here for an extended stay. You can leave your dog unattended inside as long as he doesn't make any excessive noise. All suites have kitchens, and the two-bedroom suites have fireplaces, too.

$$-$$$ Radisson Hotel, 1900 Ken Pratt Blvd., 303-776-2000, 888-333-3333 (national number), www.radisson.com. The hotel has both standard rooms and suites, with living room, kitchenette, and separate bedroom. Dogs are permitted with a $50 deposit (or credit-card imprint) and your signature on the pet release form. You can leave your dog unattended in the room if he's in a travel kennel.

$$-$$$ Super 8 Twin Peaks, 2446 N. Main, 303-772-8106, 800-800-8000 (national number), www.super8.com. Dogs can stay in smoking rooms only, for $10 per pet, per night.

$$$ Holiday Inn Express Hotel and Suites, 1355 Dry Creek Dr., 303-684-0404, 877-863-4780 (national number), www .hiexpress.com. There's a $30 one-time pet fee, and your dog can stay unattended in the room.

Louisville

$$-$$$ Comfort Inn, 1196 Dillon Rd., 303-604-0181, 800-228-5150 (national number), www.comfortinn.com. There's a $15 nightly charge, per dog, and a limit of two dogs per room. Dog guests must also be less than 100 pounds each.

$$-$$$ La Quinta Inn and Suites Boulder-Louisville, 902 Dillon Rd., 303-664-0100, 800-753-3757 (national number), www.lq.com. All you need do to stay here with your dog is sign the hotel's

pet waiver; among other things, it states that if you leave Fido unattended in the room and he becomes a nuisance, he'll be removed. So quiet, well-mannered dogs needn't worry.

$$-$$$ Quality Inn and Suites, 960 W. Dillon Rd., 303-327-1215, www.quality inn.com. There's a $15 nightly fee per dog. It's okay to have your dog unattended in the room.

$$-$$$$ Louisville Residence Inn, 845 Coal Creek Cir., 303-665-2661, www .marriott.com. There's a $100 one-time fee and a limit of three dogs per unit at this extended-stay hotel. Rooms range from studios to two-bedroom suites. Your dog can be unattended in your room, but unless he's in a travel kennel, housekeeping won't come in while he's alone.

Lyons

$$-$$$$ Stone Mountain Lodge and Cabins, 18055 North St. Vrain Dr. (Hwy. 36, 2 miles west of Lyons), 303-823-6091, 800-282-5612, www.stonemountainlodge .com. This complex on 45 acres includes motel rooms, updated cabins that date to the 1950s, an outdoor pool, and duck pond. Dogs are allowed in all of the motel rooms and three of the six cabins for $15 per pet, per night (or $45 for the week). You'll be asked to sign a pet agreement at check-in that spells out the rules; make sure you and your dog follow them, or you could face a $100 fine. Each motel room has a refrigerator, microwave, and coffeemaker, and a few have kitchenettes. Of the pet-friendly cabins, one is a studio with a kitchenette; the other two have one bedroom and a full kitchen, and one even has a private yard. It's okay to leave your dog unattended inside. There's also a fenced kennel where he can spend some time outside on his own while you're in your cabin (if you leave the property, he can't stay outside unattended). The two of you may want to explore the hiking trail up Stone Mountain, which begins behind the lodge; your dog can hike it under voice control, but he must be on leash elsewhere on the property. Note that various minimum-stay requirements apply during the year.

Nederland

$$$ Arapaho Ranch, 1250 Eldora Rd., 303-258-3405, www.coloradodirectory .com/arapahoranch. This 680-acre guest ranch near the Indian Peaks Wilderness offers 10 rustic cabins, all fully equipped, that range in size from two to four bedrooms. Before the first of June and after Labor Day, the cabins are available for nightly rentals, with a $5 fee per night, per dog. Otherwise, stays at the ranch are on a weekly basis, with a $50 one-time fee per dog. Families will find a variety of recreational opportunities close at hand (though horseback riding is no longer offered), and dogs will appreciate Middle Boulder Creek, which runs through the property. Open mid-May to October 1.

$$$ Best Western Lodge at Nederland, 55 Lakeview Dr., 303-258-9463, 800-273-5463, www.bestwesterncolorado.com. This is a particularly nice Best Western, built in log-cabin style with Southwest-accented decor in the rooms. Your dog can join you for $10 extra per night, per pet.

$$$ Sundance Lodge, 23942 Hwy. 119, 303-258-3797, 800-817-3797, www.sun dance-lodge.com. Dogs can enjoy a stay in one of the 12 cozy rooms, individually decorated with a mountain-themed decor, for $50 extra per visit. You can leave your dog unattended inside the room, perhaps while you go for a meal at the adjacent Sundance Café, a popular breakfast spot that also serves lunch and dinner. From mid-May to October, the lodge also offers horseback riding.

Chloe gets big air in Boulder.

CAMPGROUNDS

National forest campgrounds: **Kelly-Dahl Campground**, 3 miles south of Nederland off Hwy. 119 (46 sites); **Rainbow Lakes Campground**, off Hwy. 72, 7 miles north of Nederland (16 sites); **Pawnee Campground**, at Brainard Lake Recreation Area, 14 miles north of Nederland off Hwy. 72 (55 sites).

Union Reservoir, Longmont (see Tail-Rated Trails) (42 sites).

Meadow Park, Hwy. 7 and Railroad Ave., Lyons (10 sites).

Private campgrounds: **Boulder Mountain Lodge** (see Creature Comforts).

WORTH A PAWS

Only Natural Pet Store, 2100 28th St., #1C, Boulder, 303-449-5069, www .onlynaturalpet.com. Originally known as

Colorado Canines, the store merged with a Boulder-based natural pet products company and expanded in 2008. Think of it as a Whole Foods Market for dogs (and, in fact, it's practically next to the real Whole Foods). Your dog can sniff out his favorites from among an extensive selection of all-natural treats and dog food, as well as vitamins, shampoos and other pet-care items, and holistic remedies. You and he will also find gear for the active outdoor dog and environmentally friendly products, like cushy dog beds made in part from recycled plastic bottles, food bowls made of recycled glass, and hemp chew toys and leashes (if you don't think your dog's earthy enough, don't worry—there's lots of fun stuff here). The store hosts several events each month, ranging from info sessions with local vets to anesthesia-free teeth cleaning and canine massage demonstrations.

P.C.'s Pantry for Dogs and Cats, 2600 30th St., Boulder, 303-245-9909, www.pcspantry.com. Your dog's nose will start to quiver as soon as he enters this canine (and feline) bakery and smells some of the treats that are baking. And then he'll salivate in front of the display case as he tries to decide among the various-shaped biscuits flavored with ingredients such as yam, pumpkin, cheese, carob, peanut butter, and liver. Take-out deli items include five kinds of loaves (liver, turkey, chicken, salmon, and meat) and pierogies stuffed with hamburger, rice, and sun-dried tomatoes (and, yes, those are for dogs, not people). A selection of bowls, beds, leashes, toys, and gift items is also on hand. And P.C., in case you're wondering, is the CEO (cat executive officer).

Farfel's Farm, 906 Pearl St., 303-443-800-806-6994, www.farfelsfarm.com. This cozy emporium just off the west end of the Pearl St. Mall in downtown Boulder has an array of dog (and cat) treats and food, toys, and gear, as well as gifts for the people who love them. With more than 200 dog breeds represented (including "mutt"), chances are you can find something appropriate for your dog. Or you might just want to stop by and say hi to Farfel, a bearded collie. The store frequently hosts animal-related benefits, too. And you can arrange for a photography session for you and Fido, or any other pet; the store's owners are also professional photographers.

Blue Hills Dog and Cat Shoppe, 2255 Main St. (in the Horizon Park Shopping Center), Longmont, 303-651-2955, www.bluehillsdogandcat.com. In addition to a wide selection of natural foods and health-care items, Blue Hills has an on-site bakery, where dogs can choose from an array of organic treats, such as liver brownies, biscuits made from peanut butter and applesauce, or ones made of rice spelt and amaranth, flavored with mint or ginger, for canines who may be allergic to wheat.

Shop for the Dogs (and more). The Humane Society of Boulder Valley and the Longmont Humane Society both operate secondhand stores where you can purchase gently used clothing, furniture, and household items while steering needed money toward the shelters. Check out Boulder's Thrift and Gift Shop (5320 Arapahoe Ave., 303-415-0685) and Longmont's two Second Chance Thrift Stores (2351 N. Main St., 303-774-6517, and 1265 Bramwood Pl., 720-494-8348). All are open seven days a week.

A Cause for Paws. Your dog (and his leash) can accompany you in this long-time fundraiser for the Humane Society of Boulder Valley, which includes the 5K Doggie Dash and the 3K walkathon along the Boulder Creek Path. Both start at the Humane Society at 2323 55th St.

in Boulder. Ideally you would register in advance and collect pledges from fellow dog lovers. However, if you're just in town for the weekend (the walk takes place mid-September), you can register on the morning of the event. A pancake breakfast and pet expo, with various exhibitors, takes place after the race/walk. Call the Humane Society at 303-442-4030 or go to www.boulderhumane.org for more details.

Ella's Walk in memory of Meredith Hope Emerson. This 3-mile pledge walk in Longmont is held on the second weekend of May, to coincide with Be Kind to Animals Week. Originally known as Walk for Animals, the event was renamed in honor of a Longmont resident who died in 2008 (Ella is her black Lab). The course follows the St. Vrain Greenway from the Boulder County Fairgrounds through Rogers Grove to Golden Ponds and back, and proceeds benefit the Longmont Humane Society. You're encouraged to sign up in advance and collect a minimum of $100 in pledges (though you can also register the morning of the event), and you'll receive a T-shirt. The coinciding **Furry Friends Festival** includes agility dog demos, canine massage, pet-friendly booths and exhibits, and live music. Call the Humane Society at 303-772-1232 or go to www.longmonthumane.org for more info.

Canine Classic. The annual mid-April event at the Boulder Reservoir includes a 10K and 5K race for people and their leashed dogs. (Leashes can't be longer than six feet, each person can't have more than two dogs, and dogs must be at least six months old.) Less fit canines may choose to walk the course. And runners don't have to have a dog to participate. Prizes are awarded to the top adult and youth finishers in each race. If you register in advance, you'll receive a race T-shirt and goody bag. All of the money

raised through entry fees and pledges goes to local nonprofit MESA (Moving to End Sexual Assault). Stick around after the race for the Canine Expo, where you and your dog can check out pet-product exhibits, watch dog demos, and chow down on human and dog treats. For more information, call 303-443-0400 or go to www.movingtoendsexualassault.org.

Harvest Challenge 5K Run/Walk. The Institute of Taoist Education and Acupuncture (ITEA) in Louisville puts on this annual mid-September event as a fundraiser for its low-cost and free acupuncture clinics. Leashed dogs are encouraged to accompany their owners on the course, which goes along a section of the adjacent Coal Creek Trail. The event begins at the Caranci Pavilion in Louisville Community Park, 955 Bella Vista, and money is raised through entry fees and pledges. For more information, call 720-890-8922 or go to www.itea.edu. You can also register at www.active.com.

Dog Dayz at Scott Carpenter Pool, 1505 30th St. (at Arapahoe), Boulder. Before this City of Boulder pool shuts down for annual maintenance and winterization at the end of August/beginning of September, it opens up to the real doggie paddlers for several days of wet and wild fun. Dogs of all sizes and types swim, splash, chase tennis balls and Frisbees, and even practice belly flops off the diving board. Usually two sessions are held each day, for $5 per dog (or buy a punch pass for $45). And on a couple of weekend days, there's also a dog expo with exhibitors and services that cater to the furry, four-legged set. For more information, call 303-441-3427 or go to www.cityofboulder.gov.

Is your dog starting to smell like a Deadhead-type who's been on the road too long? A visit to a self-service dog wash may be just the ticket. At **Laund-Ur-Mutt,**

(Table Mesa Shopping Center [near King Soopers], Boulder, 303-543-9592, www.laundurmutt.com) washing bays rent for $12 for a half hour, which includes dog-friendly hoses, a scrubbing tool, and use of a dryer. Towels, at $1.25, and shampoo are extra. Or you can bring your own. Open Wednesday through Sunday.

PETCO (2480 Arapahoe, Boulder, 303-544-1888, and 205 Ken Pratt Blvd., #280, Longmont, 720-652-4642, www.petco.com) provides shampoo, towels, grooming tools, and a dryer at its self-service dog wash for $12 a wash at the Boulder location, $10 in Longmont.

Whole Pets (2835 Pearl St., Ste. B, Boulder, 303-444-4733, www.wholepets.com) also charges $12 a wash, which includes everything from shampoo to a dryer.

At **The Healthy Bone** (3140 Vista Village Dr., Erie, 303-828-2663, www.thehealthybone.com), a wash is $10–$15, depending on the size of dog, and includes shampoo, towels, grooming tools, and dryer. Closed Mondays.

Struttin Pup (2850 Arapahoe, Ste. 110, Lafayette, 303-665-3038, www.struttinpup.com) charges $12 for a wash, which includes a choice of natural shampoo, an apron for you, and use of towels, brushes, nail clippers, and a dryer.

At **Unleashed Ultimate Dog Center** (1617 Coalton Rd. [Safeway Plaza], Superior, 303-554-9343, www.unleashyourdog.com), you'll find custom non-slip tubs, with easy access for dogs to get into and for you to wash them from both sides; the $15 wash includes an apron, grooming tools, shampoo, and dryer.

Four Paws & Co. (1225 Ken Pratt Blvd., Longmont, 303-485-1565, www.fourpawsandco.com) charges $10 a wash, including shampoo, towels, grooming tools, and drying.

And **Happy Hounds** (1822 Sunset Pl., #2, Longmont, 303-774-8158, www.happyhoundscolorado.com) provides shampoo and conditioner, towels, dryers, grooming tools, and an apron for $10 a wash.

Dog Wash. Consider this a spa day for your dog. The washes are held monthly during the summer at the Lefthand Brewery, 1265 Boston Ave., Longmont. In addition to washers, groomers are on hand to coif drying fur and clip too-long nails, as well as massage therapists to give therapeutic treatments. You can even get your dog microchipped. Proceeds benefit the Longmont Humane Society (303-772-1232, www.longmonthumane.org).

DOGGIE DAYCARE
Boulder
Arapahoe Animal Hospital, 5585 Arapahoe Ave. (behind the Boulder Dinner Theatre), 303-442-7033, www.arapahoeanimalhospital.com. $24/day; $14/half-day. Dogs play in small groups together in the shaded play yard, with wading pools in summer. Open 7 AM–8 PM, Monday, Tuesday, Friday; 7 AM–6:30 PM, Wednesday and Thursday, 8 AM–6 PM, Saturday.

Broadway Animal Hospital and Pet Center, 1405 S. Broadway (1 mile south of Table Mesa Dr.), 303-499-5505, www.broadwayanimal.com. $20/day. Your dog will get to go out and play with the other dogs half a dozen times each day. Open 7 AM–7 PM, Monday to Friday. 8 AM–noon, Saturday.

Camp Bow Wow, 3631 Pearl St., 303-442-2261, www.campbowwow.com/us/co/boulder. $27/day; $18/half-day. Canine campers must go through a free interview day before being accepted. The Camp Bow Wow experience includes separate playgroups into which dogs are placed based on size and temperament; they have all-day access to indoor and outdoor play areas with dog-specific play equipment and, in warmer weather, wading pools.

You can keep tabs on the great time your pooch is having via the online Camper Cam. Open 6:30 AM–7 PM, Monday to Friday; 7 AM–10 AM and 4 PM–7 PM, Saturday and Sunday.

Cottonwood Kennels, 7275 Valmont Rd., 303-442-2602, 800-866-1406, www .cottonwoodkennels.com. $17-25/day, depending on size of dog. At this perennially popular farm-based daycare (and boarding facility), dogs are divided into small-dog and medium- to large-dog playgroups. Outdoor yards include agility equipment and swimming pools. Grooming is also available. Open 7:30 AM–6 PM daily.

Dog City, 2907 55th St., 303-473-9963, www.dogcityboulder.com. $27/day; $15/half-day; $6/hour. At this "interactive" daycare and boarding facility, dogs hang out and play with each other all day, both indoors and out; they also have places to rest if they get tuckered out. To top it off, there's a dog Web cam so you can check up on your pampered pooch over the Internet. Open 7 AM–7 PM, daily.

The Dog Spot, 5155 Arapahoe Ave., 720-565-3647, www.thedogspot.moonfruit .com. $28/day. The spot includes an outdoor play yard, with wading pools and sun shades, and indoor play areas with flooring made of recycled tires. A "lunch special" (a Kong stuffed with treats like jerky or kibble) and spa packages that include a bath, brushing, and nail trim are also available. Open 6:30 AM–6:30 PM, Monday to Saturday.

Doggie Depot, 4525 N. Broadway, 303-443-7297, www.doggiedepot.org. $24/day; $13/half-day. At this smaller daycare facility, dogs play outdoors and indoors in supervised groups according to temperament. Open 7 AM–6:30 PM, Monday to Friday.

Gunbarrel Veterinary Clinic, 55th St. and Diagonal Hwy., 303-530-2500, www .gunbarrelvet.com. $14/day. Open 7:45 AM–5:30 PM, Monday, Wednesday, Friday; 7:45 AM–7 PM, Tuesday and Thursday.

VCA All Pets Animal Hospital Boulder, 5290 Manhattan Cir. (at Hwy. 36 and S. Boulder Rd.), 303-499-5335, www .vcahospitals.com/all-pets-boulder. $32/day. Open 24 hours. (Note that the Allpets Clinic in Lafayette doesn't offer day boarding.)

Erie

A Lov-in Touch Pet Chalet and Spaw, 7019 Weld CR 5, 303-651-3999, www.alovin touch.com. $20/day; $22/day during holiday periods. The facility is located on 2 acres, where dogs can wear themselves out playing with each other and on pint-sized playground equipment. Especially deserving pets can also get a "spaw" service: massage, bath and brush, or nail trimming. Drop-offs are from 7:30–9:30 AM, and pick-ups are from 4:30–6:30 PM, Monday to Friday.

Bowhaus, 415 Jones Ct., 303-828-4989, www.bowhaus.biz. $22/day. Dogs all play together in the 13,000-square-foot outdoor fenced play yard and the 4,000-square-foot indoor play area. The kennel area has air-conditioning and radiant-heat floors. Drop-offs are from 7–9:30 AM, and pick-ups are from 4–6:30 PM, Monday to Friday.

Lafayette

Rover Retreat, 287 Hwy. 287, Ste. D, 303-604-6264, www.roverretreat.com/lafayette. $24/day; $12/half-day and weekends. Dogs play together at this indoor daycare, with naptime from noon to 2 PM. Open 7 AM–noon and 2–7 PM, Monday to Friday; 7–10 AM and 4–7 PM, Saturday and Sunday.

Longmont

Happy Hounds, 1822 Sunset Pl., #2, 303-774-8158, www.happyhoundscolorado.com. $25/day or $5/hour. Dogs are put in playgroups based on temperament and energy, with access to indoor and outdoor spaces. Open 7 AM–6 PM, Monday to Friday.

Pansy's K/9 Corral, 9232 CR 1, 303-682-2922, www.pansysk9corral.intuitweb sites.com. $15/day. At this kennel-free facility on a farm, dogs have lots of room to play together; there's also a pond for swimming. Daycare is available only on Tuesday, Wednesday, and Thursday. Open by appointment.

Timberline Dog Boarding Company, 6368 Ephesus Rd., 303-774-2052. $20/day. At this small home-based daycare (there's a maximum of 10 dogs at a time), all dogs play together under supervision in the .75-acre yard. When inside, they can relax in separate areas and watch the Animal Planet channel on TV. Open by appointment.

Whispering Pines Pet Resort, 14360 N. 83rd St., 303-776-3907. $18/day. The resort has indoor/outdoor runs and play yards on its 12 acres. Options like playgroups and walks are an additional $4/day. Open 7:30 AM–6 PM, Monday to Friday.

Louisville

The Divine Canine, 1141 South St., 303-464-1380, www.divinecanine.net. $19/day; $12/half-day. After playing in the outdoor play yard (with wading pools) and indoor fun room, dogs nap in individual crates between noon and 2 PM so they're rested to play again in the afternoon. Grooming services are also available. Open 7 AM–noon and 2–6:30 PM, Monday to Saturday.

Nederland

Peak to Peak Animal Hospital, 75 E. 2nd St., 303-258-7004. $20/day. Open 8 AM–6 PM, Monday to Friday; 8 AM–noon, Saturday.

Niwot

Dapper Dog Day Spa, 7960 Niwot Rd., 303-652-9191, www.dapperdogdayspa.com. $24/day; $18/half-day; $5/hour. There's a 2,400-square-foot indoor, climate-controlled area with play equipment, and dogs also go on walks to the park. Open 7 AM–6 PM, Monday to Friday.

Rollinsville

Simba Ranch, 700 Lump Gulch Rd., 303-258-3023, www.simbaranch.com. $20/day. Dogs must go through an initial meeting and short visit before being accepted for a full day of care. If everything goes well, they get to hang out at the 2.7-acre ranch, as well as go on walks in the area. Open 8 AM–6 PM, Monday to Saturday.

PET PROVISIONS

Boulder

Aqua Imports, 2690 28th St., 303-444-6971

Farfel's Farm, 906 Pearl St., 303-443-7711, 800-806-6994, www.farfelsfarm.com (see Worth a Paws)

Humane Society of Boulder Valley Sonnyside Retail Store, 2323 55th St., 303-442-4030, ext. 620, www.boulderhumane.org

Liberty Hardware, 691 S. Broadway (Table Mesa Shopping Center), 303-499-7211

McGuckin Hardware, 2525 Arapahoe Ave. (in the Village Shopping Center), 303-443-1822, www.mcguckin.com. You and your leashed dog are welcome to browse among the cornucopia of pet items and just about anything else you can think of.

WHAT'S IN A NAME?

So you consider yourself your dog's owner? Not anymore in Boulder, where, in the summer of 2000, a proposal was approved to change the designation "owner" to "guardian" in animal ordinances. The change was made in the hopes of enlightening people that dogs are not things that can be owned and then, perhaps, neglected or abused. To err on the safe side in typically forward-thinking Boulder, you could always just refer to yourself as Fido's "mom" or "dad."

Only Natural Pet Store, 2100 28th St., #1C, Boulder, 303-449-5069, www.onlynaturalpet.com (see Worth a Paws)

P.C.'s Pantry for Dogs and Cats, 2600 30th St., Boulder, 303-245-9909, www.pcspantry.com (see Worth a Paws)

PETCO, 2480 Arapahoe, 303-544-1888, www.petco.com

PetSmart, 2982 Iris (in the Albertson's shopping center), 303-939-9033; Walnut and 30th Sts., 303-449-0201, www.petsmart.com

Whole Pets, 2835 Pearl St., Ste. B, Boulder, 303-444-4733, www.wholepets.com

Erie
The Healthy Bone, 3140 Vista Village Dr., 303-828-2663, www.thehealthybone.com

Lafayette
Bark Avenue, 101 E. Chester St., 303-664-9663, www.barkavenue.com. The shop bills itself as a "pet department store."

Lafayette Feed and Grain, 816 E. Baseline Rd., 303-665-5055

Struttin' Pup, 2850 Arapahoe, Ste. 110, 303-665-3038, www.struttinpup.com

Longmont
Blue Hills Dog and Cat Shoppe, 2255 Main St. (in the Horizon Park Shopping Center), 303-651-2955 (see Worth a Paws)

Four Paws & Co., 1225 Ken Pratt Blvd., 303-485-1565, www.fourpawsandco.com

Murdoch's Ranch and Home Supply, 2255 Main St., 303-682-5111

PETCO, 205 Ken Pratt Blvd., #280, 720-652-4642, www.petco.com

PetSmart, 1125 S. Hover Rd., 303-702-9526, www.petsmart.com

Louisville
Front Range Pet and Supply, 1140 E. South Boulder Rd., 303-464-0956

Nederland
Nederland Feed and Supply, 45 E. 2nd St., 303-258-7729

Niwot
Niwot Rental and Feed, 291 2nd Ave., 303-652-2900

Superior
PetSmart, 402 Center Dr., Superior, 303-543-6060, www.petsmart.com

Unleashed Ultimate Dog Center, 1617 Coalton Rd. (Safeway Plaza), 303-554-9343, www.unleashyourdog.com

CANINE ER
Boulder
Arapahoe Animal Hospital (AAHA certified), 5585 Arapahoe Ave. (behind the Boulder Dinner Theatre), 303-442-7033, www.arapahoeanimalhospital.com. Open 7 AM–8 PM, Monday, Tuesday, Friday; 7 AM–6:30 PM, Wednesday and Thursday; 8 AM–6 PM, Saturday and Sunday.

Boulder Emergency Pet Clinic, 1658 30th St. (in the Sunrise Shopping Center), 303-440-7722, www.emergencypetclinics .com. Open 5:30 PM–8 AM, Monday through Friday; 24 hours weekends and holidays.

VCA Allpets Animal Hospital Boulder (AAHA certified), 5290 Manhattan Cir. (at Hwy. 36 and S. Boulder Rd.), 303-499-5335, www.vcahospitals.com/all-pets-boulder. Open 24 hours.

Longmont
Animal Emergency and Critical Care at Aspen Meadow Veterinary Specialists, 230 S. Main, 303-678-8844, www.aspen meadowvet.com. Open 6 PM–8 AM, Monday through Friday; 24 hours weekends and holidays.

RESOURCES
Boulder Convention and Visitors Bureau, 2440 Pearl St., Boulder, 303-442-2911, 800-444-0447, www.bouldercoloradousa .com

Boulder County Parks and Open Space, 303-678-6200, www.co.boulder.co.us/ openspace

Boulder Ranger District, Arapaho and Roosevelt National Forests, 2140 Yarmouth Ave. (off Hwy. 36 on the north end of town), Boulder, 303-444-6600

City of Boulder Open Space and Mountain Parks Department, 303-441-3440, www.osmp.org

FIDOS (Friends Interested in Dogs and Open Space), www.fidos.org

Nederland Visitor Center, 1st and Bridge St., Nederland, 303-258-3936, www .nederlandchamber.org

Three

Central City, Clear Creek County, and Vicinity

THE BIG SCOOP

Traveling dogs will find it all here: scenic trails, 14,000-foot mountains, welcoming lodging, and mountain air—everything within a short drive of Denver. One thing your dog won't be able to do, however, is frequent the casinos in Black Hawk and Central City; to the best of our knowledge, paw-friendly slot machines have yet to be invented.

All the towns in this area have leash laws, as do Clear Creek and Gilpin Counties, though the county leash ordinance is not enforced on forest service trails that allow dogs under voice control.

TAIL-RATED TRAILS

The area surrounding Mount Evans, south of Idaho Springs, has the most concentrated selection of trails in the vicinity. Because of their proximity to Denver, many of these trails receive heavy use, especially on summer weekends, something to keep in mind if you're into more solitary hiking with your dog. And most of the trails are in the Mount Evans Wilderness Area or the Mount Evans Elk Management Area—where dogs must be kept leashed, for all or part of their length. A great resource for the Mount Evans trails is *Foothills to Mount Evans: West-of-Denver Trail Guide*, by Linda McComb Rathbun and Linda Wells Ringrose.

If you and your dog are staying near Idaho Springs, refer to the "West of Denver" section in Chapter 1, Tail-Rated Trails, for more nearby options. And it's only a short drive to trails near Nederland (see Chapter 2) from the Central City area.

Herman Gulch
Distance: 5 miles round-trip
Elevation gain: 1,800 feet
Access: Take Exit 218 off I-70 (past Silver Plume). If you're coming from the east, turn right at the stop sign at the end of the exit ramp and double back on the dirt road that leads to the trailhead parking area; from the west, cross over the highway and turn right on the dirt road to the parking area.

Dogs can be off leash. Signage at the trailhead suggests that you leash your dog because of wildlife concerns, but as of this writing, there's no leash requirement.

This hike has become increasingly popular, especially with dogs and their owners, as the secret's out that a beautiful route hides behind the unmarked highway exit. The well-maintained trail first leads through a section of forest before popping out into a series of meadows, studded with colorful wildflowers in July and August. You'll then reenter the woods as you ascend the gulch, following closely along a stream. There are several nice areas along this stretch where you can sit on a downed log and enjoy a snack while Rover tests out the water. In the final .5 mile or so of trail, you'll hike above timberline, following a few steep switchbacks before reaching

Herman Lake, nestled right at the base of the Continental Divide, below the rocky slopes of 13,553-foot Pettingell Peak. Before heading back downvalley, take a breather on one of the boulders along the shoreline and soak in the rugged surroundings; your dog will probably want to brave the frigid water for a quick dip. If he's lucky, he may even find a snowfield or two in which to play.

Silver Dollar Lake
Distance: 3 miles round-trip
Elevation gain: 1,000 feet
Access: From the Georgetown exit (228) off I-70, follow the signs to Guanella Pass at the western end of town. From the beginning of Guanella Pass Rd. (at the mileage signs), drive 8.6 miles, past the Guanella Pass Campground, to a T in the road and a sign for the Silver Dollar Lake Trail. Turn right and drive 1 mile to the parking area at the side of the road and the trailhead.
Dogs can be off leash.

This short, scenic hike brings you and your dog to a lake, popular for fishing, near the base of the Continental Divide. The trail heads southwest from the parking area, winding through a stately forest of Douglas fir on a moderate ascent. Shortly after passing timberline, you'll reach the lake. To the southwest lies Square Top Mountain. After your dog enjoys splashing in the lake, you and he may want to do some exploring to the

Clover and Tansy show teamwork on the trail.

northwest to visit nearby Murray Lake, which is also above timberline, before hiking the return route.

Golden Gate Canyon State Park
Access: The park has several access points, a couple of which are near Central City and Black Hawk. From Black Hawk, take Hwy. 119 north for about 8 miles to Hwy. 46; the park visitor center is 4 miles east on Hwy. 46. Or continue on Hwy. 119 about 3 miles past the Hwy. 46 turnoff, then turn right on Gap Rd., which leads into the park. For more details, see Tail-Rated Trails in Chapter 1. 303-582-3707, www.parks.state .co.us/parks/goldengatecanyon.
Dogs must leashed.

Hells Hole
Distance: 7 miles round-trip
Elevation gain: 1,700 feet
Access: From Idaho Springs, drive southwest on Hwy. 103 for 6 miles. Make a right onto West Chicago Creek Rd. (FR 188) and drive for 3 miles. The trailhead is past the West Chicago Creek Campground at the end of the road.
Dogs can be off leash until the wilderness boundary, about 1 mile in.

Despite the ominous name, this is a beautiful hike, especially during the autumn when the aspen change color. It is also one of the less-crowded hikes in the Mount Evans area. Because the very first part of the trail passes by some quasi-picnic areas popular with families, you might have to keep a close eye on Fido or leash him up so he doesn't make a nuisance of himself. The trail begins in forested terrain and follows West Chicago Creek, crossing various tributaries as well. After about 1 mile, you'll start to climb away from the creek, gradually at first, then more steeply as the trail switchbacks up amid a high wooded canopy of pine, fir, and aspen. Gray Wolf Mountain and Sugarloaf Peak come into view to the south and east, respectively. Eventually you'll break out of the trees into a spectacular high-alpine, marshy meadow bounded by a rocky cirque that includes the 13,602-foot Gray Wolf. The trail ends among the scree in a basin at the bottom of the cirque—the Hells Hole.

CYCLING FOR CANINES

Most of the biking routes in this area follow four-wheel-drive roads rather than singletrack trails. One recommended option is the **Old Squaw Pass Rd.**, which parallels Hwy. 103 east of Mount Evans for 3.25 miles. The trail has four access points from the south side of Hwy. 103: 4.5 miles east of Echo Lake, 5.8 miles east, 7.4 miles east, and 8.4 miles east.

The **Devil's Canyon jeep road** runs for 2.5 miles one way, ending on a ridge with views of the Mount Evans area. There are also some loop options in this area, on the small network of jeep roads. Drive on Hwy. 103 from Idaho Springs for 10 miles, then make a left just after the big curve beyond the Ponder Point Picnic Area onto FR 246. The ride begins here. Bring extra water for Rover on Old Squaw Pass Rd. and Devil's Canyon.

The road up **Bard Creek** provides several miles of riding on an old mining roadbed that follows the path of the creek; access it via Bard Creek Dr. off US Hwy. 40 through Empire.

For more specifics on rides, pick up the "Four-Wheel Driving" information sheet from the Clear Creek Ranger District (see Resources) and the Trails Illustrated biking map for Idaho Springs/ Clear Creek County.

POWDERHOUNDS

The Clear Creek County area has several fine trails for ski touring or snowshoeing with your dog.

The 4-mile round-trip **Butler Gulch Trail** is a personal favorite because it holds snow well and has fun telemarking terrain in the bowls at trail's end (rife with avalanche danger, however). It can get quite busy on weekends, so a midweek tour, if possible, would be your dog's best bet. To reach the trailhead, take the Empire exit off I-70 and follow US Hwy. 40 west to the sharp switchback at Henderson Mine (about 8 miles past Empire). The ski begins across from a small parking area, on a road. Watch out for snowmobilers on this first part; soon the Butler Gulch Trail splits off to the left and you'll leave motorized traffic behind.

The **Old Fall River Rd.** to Fall River Reservoir is a 6-mile round-trip easy ski on gentle terrain. From Exit 238 off I-70, turn north on Fall River Rd. Drive 6.5 miles to a right-hand switchback. The trail, which follows a jeep road, travels west-northwest from here.

The **Waldorf Rd.**, which follows a very gradual, wide ascent off the Guanella Pass Rd. outside of Georgetown, also makes a good dog ski. With Sidney Mine as the turnaround point, it's a 7-mile round-trip. To access the trail, head up the Guanella Pass Rd. for 2.5 miles to a pair of switchbacks; at the second switchback, you'll see a small parking area on the right. The Waldorf Rd. begins near the parking area.

For more information on some of these and other routes, refer to *Snowshoeing Colorado*, by Claire Walter.

CREATURE COMFORTS

Unless otherwise stated, dogs should not be left unattended in the room or cabin.

Georgetown

$$ Georgetown Mountain Inn, 1100 Rose, 303-569-3201, 800-884-3201, www .georgetownmountaininn.com. The motel allows dogs in 10 rooms, a few of which have mountain-style handcrafted log furniture, for a $10 one-time fee. You can leave your dog unattended inside as long as he's in a travel crate.

$$ Georgetown Super 8, 1600 Argentine St., 303-569-3211, 800-884-3201, www .super8.com. The motel now accepts pets for $15 extra per night.

$$$$ All Aboard Inn, 605 Brownell St., 303-569-2525, www.allaboardinn.com. This bed-and-breakfast gives you and your dog the opportunity to stay in one of Georgetown's historic residences, a 130-year-old Victorian. The upper-floor suite, which has two bedrooms and a living area, as well as private bath and separate outside entrance, is dog friendly. If you leave Fido behind in the room, he'll need to be in a travel crate. And your dog is bound to meet Maynard, the B&B's host dog, an English mastiff who, at 160 pounds, may well outweigh you.

Idaho Springs

$$ 6 & 40 Motel, 2920 Colorado Blvd., 303-567-2691. Dogs are allowed only in smoking rooms, for a $10 nightly fee. The motel is situated along Clear Creek, where you can walk your dog on leash along the banks.

$$ H & H Motor Lodge, 2445 Colorado Blvd., 303-567-2838, 800-445-2893. Dogs are allowed in designated rooms at the motel for $5 extra per night, per pet.

$$–$$$ Columbine Inn, 2501 Colorado Blvd., 303-567-0948, www.columbine inncolorado.com. Dogs 35 pounds and under are allowed in several of the motel rooms, as well as a light, bright two-bedroom cottage with kitchen that's also on the property. The rooms, recently remodeled, are a notch above the typical motel room, with in-floor radiant heating and homey quilts. There's a $15 one-time fee for dogs.

CAMPGROUNDS

Golden Gate State Park. The easiest way to access the campgrounds is via Gap Rd., a right turn off Hwy. 119, about 11 miles north of Black Hawk. The Reverend's Ridge Campground (97 sites) and Aspen Meadow Campground (35 sites) are both in the northwest part of the park. In addition, Reverend's Ridge Campground has five camper cabins and two yurts available for nightly rentals ($60/night; each sleeps up to 6). Four of the cabins and one of the yurts are pet friendly, for $10 extra per night. There are also four backcountry shelters and twenty backcountry tent sites throughout the park.

National forest campgrounds: **Cold Springs Campground,** 4 miles north of Black Hawk on Hwy. 119 (38 sites); **Columbine Campground,** 2.1 miles northwest of Central City on CR 279 (47 sites); **West Chicago Creek Campground,** FR 188, off Hwy. 103, south of Idaho Springs (16 sites); **Guanella Pass Campground,** about 8 miles out of Georgetown on Guanella Pass Rd. (18 sites).

WORTH A PAWS

Mount Evans Rd. For the quickest way to take your dog to the top of a fourteener (that's a 14,000-foot mountain, or, in this case, 14,264 feet), drive him up the paved road to the top of Mount Evans. Take Hwy. 103 south of Idaho Springs to Echo Lake; the road to the summit begins here. Fourteen miles later, your dog will feel like he's standing on top of the world. And he'll probably get excited at seeing the mountain goats that usually hang around roadside—viewing them from behind a car window, of course. The road is open to the summit from Memorial Day to the day after Labor Day; $10 per car is collected just beyond Echo Lake.

Argo Gold Mill. Does your dog harbor a secret desire to don a helmet, grab a pickax, and burrow into a hillside? If so, he might be interested in accompanying you on a 45-minute tour of this former gold mill, which dates from 1913 and once supplied much of the gold for the Denver Mint. The mill is now on the National Register of Historic Places. The tour includes a van ride up to the Double Eagle Gold Mine, which you'll be able to walk 300 feet into. Look for the big red building on the hillside in Idaho Springs—it's hard to miss. Call 303-567-2421 (or look at www.historicargotours.com) for more information. Open May 1 to September 30.

Georgetown Loop Railroad. Unfortunately, dogs are no longer allowed on this scenic narrow-gauge train trip between Georgetown and neighboring Silver Plume. The railroad operates daily from Memorial Day through the first weekend of October.

DOGGIE DAYCARE
Idaho Springs
Happy Tails Dog Wash and Pet Supply, 1640 Miner St., 303-567-1102, www.happytailscolorado.com. $18/day; $9/half-day. Dogs can go outside in their runs at their leisure, and there's an indoor play area for cold winter days. Open 8 AM–6:30 PM, Monday to Friday; 9 AM–5 PM, Saturday; 11 AM–4 PM, Sunday. Earlier drop-offs can be arranged.

PET PROVISIONS
Idaho Springs
Happy Tails Dog Wash and Pet Supply, 1640 Miner St., 303-567-1102, www.happytailscolorado.com. In addition to grooming, the store has a self-service dog wash; the $18.95 price includes whatever you need to get your dog clean.

CANINE ER
Evergreen
Evergreen Animal Hospital, 32175 Castle Ct. (corner of Bergen Parkway and Hwy. 74), 303-674-4331, www.evergreenvet.com. Open 24 hours. Though the hospital is not in Clear Creek County, it's close enough to warrant the short drive.

RESOURCES
Clear Creek County Tourism Board, 303-567-4660, 866-674-9237, www.clearcreekcounty.org

Clear Creek Ranger District, Arapaho and Roosevelt National Forests, 101 Chicago Creek Rd., Idaho Springs, 303-567-3000

Georgetown Information Center, 1491 Argentine, 303-569-2405

Idaho Springs Visitor Information Center, 2060 Miner St., Idaho Springs, 303-567-4382, 800-882-5278

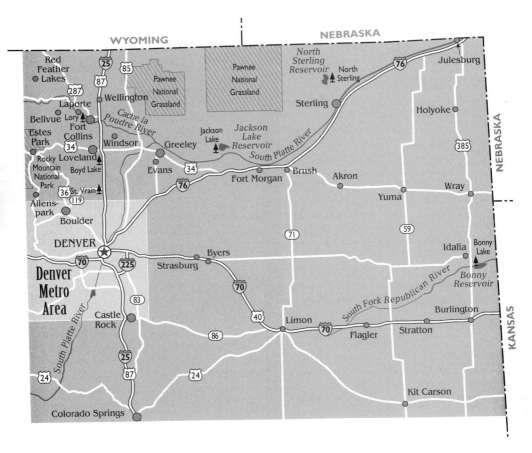

NORTHEAST COLORADO

Interstate Highways 25
State Highways 87
State Parks

0 10 20 30 40
Miles

N

Four
Fort Collins and Vicinity

THE BIG SCOOP

Close to the foothills of the northern Front Range, Fort Collins and neighboring Loveland offer a variety of opportunities for canine recreation. If you're looking for a more rustic getaway, the Poudre River Canyon (which begins about 10 miles northwest of Fort Collins) and the village of Red Feather Lakes (about 50 miles northwest of Fort Collins) have cabin resorts, many of which allow canine guests. And your dog can rest easy about his health during a visit to Fort Collins: Colorado State University is home to one of the best veterinary schools in the country, and the Veterinary Teaching Hospital operates a 24-hour critical care clinic.

You'll have to keep your dog leashed within Fort Collins and Loveland city limits; in unincorporated Larimer County areas, dogs may be under voice command.

Fort Collins opened one of the first dog parks on the Front Range in September 1998, and it's since been joined by two others. Loveland opened its own dog park in 2008 (see Tail-Rated Trails for all).

TAIL-RATED TRAILS

Dogs in Fort Collins can enjoy several open space areas, three major recreational trails within or close to town, and two parks with hiking trails just west of Horsetooth Reservoir. Except for the three dog parks, however, none include any off-leash dog areas. To find trails where Fido can hike leash free, head up scenic Poudre Canyon (though note that the popular Greyrock National Recreation Trail has a leash policy) or to the Red Feather Lakes area. One close-by option in the canyon—Young Gulch—is described here. The forest service office in Fort Collins (see Resources) has a good range of maps and trail descriptions for other hikes. *The Field and Trail Guide to Roosevelt National Forest*, published by the Poudre Landmarks Foundation, contains detailed hiking descriptions, too.

The City of Fort Collins Natural Areas Program occasionally offers trail-savvy-dog classes (970-416-2815 to register) for pooches who need to perfect their trail manners.

Young Gulch
Distance: Up to 10 miles round-trip
Elevation gain: 1,170 feet
Trailhead: Head north from Fort Collins on US Hwy. 287 to the turnoff for Hwy. 14 and Poudre Canyon (about 9 miles). Turn left onto a dirt road 12.8 miles up the canyon, just past the Ansel Watrous Campground on the right. Follow the dirt road to the parking area and trailhead.
Dogs can be off leash.

This is a perfect trail for the dog who likes to get his paws muddy. Water-loving hounds will appreciate the numerous creek crossings (none on bridges), which apparently run into the 40s (we lost count after about 20). There's really no set destination for this hike, and the scenic factor remains about the same throughout, so don't feel that you must cover all 5 miles (one way). You and your dog will have an enjoyable trip no matter how far you decide to go.

The easy-to-follow trail makes a very gradual ascent up a forested gulch, winding through sweet-smelling ponderosa and lodgepole pine, Rocky Mountain juniper, Douglas fir, and aspen. The last mile or so travels across an open meadow, where the trail narrows to a small footpath. A final climb up an old road brings you to a cattle fence signed for private property, and to the end of the trail; just beyond, you'll see Stove Prairie Rd.

Fort Collins Dog Parks

Regulations: Dogs must be licensed and vaccinated, and puppies under four months old are not allowed. You must have a leash on hand in case your pup gets unruly, and no more than three dogs per owner are allowed at one time. Dogs cannot be left unattended, and if your pooch is in heat, leave her at home. *Dogs can be off leash.*

At the **Spring Canyon Dog Park** (take Horsetooth Rd. west until just before it ends; a dirt parking area is on the right), a 3-acre fenced area provides plenty of room, as well as a pond, for dogs to romp, chase a ball, and socialize. There's also a separate area for small and shy dogs. The pond, usually water filled from late April through September, is fenced separately, with a gated entrance, so if you don't want to drive home with the aroma of wet dog in the car, you can keep Fido from going in the water. A seasonal water fountain is available (generally May to October) near the main park entrance. Poop-bag dispensers and trash cans are thoughtfully staggered around the park's perimeter. The dog park, which is part of the large Spring Canyon Community Park, is adjacent to the Pineridge Natural Area, 619 acres of short-grass prairie crossed by approximately 7 miles of wide dirt trails that are perfect for a pre- or postpark walk. You'll have to keep your dog on a leash in the natural area and pick up after him. The area abuts 40-acre Dixon Reservoir, where the Foothills Trail (see later description) begins.

The **Soft Gold Dog Park** (Hickory St. between N. College Ave. and Conifer St.) provides a 1-acre fenced area for pups to play; a water fountain and small pavilion are slated to be installed.

The **Fossil Creek Dog Park** (from E. Harmony, turn south on S. Lemay Ave.; the park entrance is about 1 mile farther on the right), part of the larger Fossil Creek Community Park, is about 1 fenced acre, including a separate area for small or shy dogs. The park has a gravel surface at its center, with a grassy perimeter that includes poop-bag dispensers and trash cans. While their dogs frolic—this is a popular park so there's bound to be company—owners can sit at several picnic tables or under a small pavilion. The seasonal water fountain (May–October) at the park's entrance includes a dog-level spout—a nice touch.

Loveland Dog Park

Access: From N. Lincoln Ave. (Hwy. 287) if you're heading north, or N. Cleveland Ave. if you're heading south (both streets are one way), turn west on 1st St. Take the next left onto S. Railroad Ave. and follow it to Fairground Park's south end; make a left onto Fire Engine Red Rd., then a left into the parking area for the dog park. Regulations: Dogs must be vaccinated, licensed, and older than four months. Make sure you clean up after your dog, don't bring food or drinks into the park, and don't let your dog jump on other people. If your dog is sick or in heat, leave her at home. *Dogs can be off leash.*

Part of the extensive Fairgrounds Park complex, which opened on the former site of the Larimer County Fairgrounds in 2008, the 1.5-acre fenced park provides a grassy play area, with a sectioned-off area for small dogs, as well as a few large rocks for dogs to practice their bouldering skills on. A small shelter at the center serves as a gathering spot for owners to socialize. Water is available from a drinking fountain for humans and dogs (though not in winter). The Big Thompson River runs tantalizingly close to the park but is just outside the fenced boundary; to access it, you'll have to walk from the parking area toward the playground; en route, you'll see a footbridge that crosses the river and leads into a paved riverside recreation path.

Foothills Trail

Distance: Runs 6.4 miles from Dixon Reservoir, near the south end of Horsetooth Reservoir, to Michaud Ln., near the north end of the reservoir.

Trailhead: To access the trail at Dixon Reservoir, head west from downtown Fort Collins on one of the major cross streets (e.g., Prospect) to Overland Trail (a road). Go south on Overland Trail to CR 42C and turn right. Just after the hairpin

Leo experiences his first river swim.

turn, look for the signed parking area for Dixon Reservoir and the Pineridge Natural Area.

Dogs must be leashed.

This is a great trail for water-loving dogs, as you start out near a small reservoir and eventually gain access to large, scenic Horsetooth Reservoir. The trail begins from the parking area and skirts a short portion of Dixon Reservoir's west side before descending a short hill and crossing CR 42C. The trail parallels a service road through the Maxwell Natural Area west of Colorado State University's Hughes Stadium, then switchbacks up a dry hillside of grassland, yucca plants, and sagebrush. Shortly after reaching the hilltop, cross Centennial Rd., the north–south artery for Horsetooth Reservoir, and look for the continuation of the trail at the northeast corner of the paved parking area. Stay left at the first fork. The trail goes along the bluffs above the reservoir before descending toward shoreline. Several spur trails lead down to the water, so your dog can take a dip, well deserved on a hot day. If you continue hiking, follow the trail along the shore; it eventually ascends and crosses Centennial Rd. again to the Reservoir Ridge Natural Area, ending at the parking area at Michaud Ln., adjacent to Claymore Lake.

If you want a shorter hike, or if your dog wants quicker access to water, you can access portions of the Foothills Trail from several parking areas off Centennial Rd. between Dixon Dam and Soldier Canyon Dam. You can also hike the trail around Dixon Reservoir, which is approximately 2 miles.

Horsetooth Mountain Open Space

Access: From College Ave. in Fort Collins, head west on Horsetooth Rd. (south of downtown). Drive 2 miles to Taft Hill Rd.; turn left, then take a right at the next traffic light (CR 38E). Follow the road around the southern end of Horsetooth Reservoir (you'll see signs for the park). The parking area will be on the right. There's a $6 entry fee.

Dogs must be leashed.

Formerly known as Horsetooth Mountain Park, the area offers 29 miles of trails, including an ascent to the distinctive Horsetooth Rock, from which you get an encompassing view of the peaks on the eastern side of Rocky Mountain National Park. (Note that with the exception of **Horsetooth Rock Trail** and **Horsetooth Falls Trail**, the trails are multiuse, so you'll be sharing them with bikes and horses.) Most people stick to the first couple miles of trails, hiking to Horsetooth and Culver Falls, and to Horsetooth Rock. So if you're looking for more solitude with your pooch, venture a little farther. You'll find water along the 2-mile-long **Spring Creek Trail** (which requires about 1.5 miles of hiking to reach) and the nearly 3-mile **Mill Creek Trail** (which begins at the end of the Spring Creek Trail). If you're really ambitious, you can even hike into neighboring Lory State Park via two of the trails. Backcountry camping is allowed in Horsetooth Mountain Open Space, so you can do longer hikes broken up by an overnight stay. Remember to keep your dog leashed at all times; rangers do patrol, and they have a no-tolerance policy, which means you're pretty much guaranteed a fine if Fido's romping freely.

Lory State Park

Access: From Fort Collins, take Hwy. 287 north. After passing through Laporte, go left on CR 52E to Bellvue. Drive about 1 mile to CR 23N; head south for about 1.5 miles to CR 25G, on the right, and the park entrance. Entry fee is $6 per vehicle.

Dogs must be leashed.

The park offers 20 miles of well-marked trails for you and your dog to enjoy together. A few options that your dog may prefer: the 1.2-mile **Well Gulch Nature Trail,** for hikers only, heads west from the park road, up a drainage with a stream at the bottom, then loops back down to the Homestead picnic area. The trail up to **Arthur's Rock,** which provides a panoramic view of Horsetooth Reservoir and Fort Collins, is also for hikers only; the route is 3.4 miles round-trip, and an intermittent stream alongside is a potential water source. If your dog wants to visit the water's edge, bring him on the **Shoreline Trail,** a 2-mile round-trip to the reservoir and back from the park road. There are also six backcountry campsites within the park, all of them along the 3.5-mile **Timber Trail,** where you can overnight with your dog. 970-493-1623, parks.state.co.us/parks/lory.

Poudre River Trail

Access: Runs 10.6 miles from Lions Park in Laporte, northwest of Fort Collins, to the CSU Environmental Learning Center, near the Prospect Ponds Natural Area. Some good places to access the trail, with parking available, are, from west to east, at the Taft Hill Rd. trailhead (north of W. Vine Dr.), Lee Martinez Park, and the Environmental Learning Center, off Ziegler Rd. (but note that dogs are not permitted in the Running Deer Natural Area adjacent to the Learning Center or the nearby Cottonwood Hollow Natural Area).

Dogs must be leashed.

This paved bike and hike path parallels the Cache La Poudre River, passing several open space areas and city parks along its route (Lee Martinez Park is especially popular with dogs and their owners). It's a great place to take your dog for a stroll that's close to town, and it's usually less traveled than the Spring Creek

Trail. As you head east from downtown, the trail passes through less-developed surroundings.

Spring Creek Trail
Access: Runs 6.9 miles from Spring Canyon Park to East Prospect Rd., where it ends in the Poudre River Trail. Park at Spring Canyon Park, at the southern end of Overland Trail (a road), or Edora Park (south of Prospect St.), near the trail's east end, for easy access with available parking.
Dogs must be leashed.

This paved trail follows Spring Creek and passes through several parks and open space areas. As it runs close to the Colorado State University campus, it's more of a transportation corridor than a hiking trail, but it nonetheless provides your dog with some off-street walking space.

Jackie takes a short rest while hiking.

Dogs are not allowed in two of Larimer County's open space areas: **Fossil Creek Reservoir Open Space** (off CR 32/Carpenter Rd., between Fort Collins and Loveland) and **Rimrock Open Space**, which borders the Devil's Backbone Open Space, west of Taft Hill Rd. between Fort Collins and Loveland. (Dogs are allowed on Devil's Backbone, which includes part of the 15-mile regional Blue Sky Trail, open to hikers, mountain bikers, and horseback riders).

Dogs are not allowed in the following natural areas managed by the City of Fort Collins: **Bobcat Ridge** (west of Masonville), **Cottonwood Hollow** (near the CSU Environmental Learning Center and Prospect Ponds), **Coyote Ridge** (off CR 19, midway between Fort Collins ands Loveland), **Running Deer** (adjacent to the CSU Environmental Learning Center), and **Soapstone Prairie** (25 miles north of Fort Collins).

CYCLING FOR CANINES

You'll have to head up Poudre Canyon to find the closest areas to town where you can ride with a dog. The 10-mile round-trip **Young Gulch Trail** (see Tail-Rated Trails) has the advantage of lots of water for dogs to run through; the first mile or so will have you walking up some rocky sections, but if you stick with it you'll reach some nice rolling singletrack. The 7-mile **Lower Dadd Gulch Trail**, 29 miles up Poudre Canyon off Hwy. 14, makes a moderate ascent up the gulch, with more than a dozen easily navigable stream crossings, before breaking out into meadows a couple miles in; the trail ends at Salt Cabin Rd. The **Mt. Margaret Trail**, just outside Red Feather Lakes, is a scenic, rolling 7-mile round-trip to the base of Mt. Margaret and back.

POWDERHOUNDS

To find consistent snow for skiing or snowshoeing, you and your dog will need to drive to Cameron Pass at the top of Poudre Canyon, about 65 miles west of Fort Collins on Hwy. 14. A great short tour follows an old jeep road to **Zimmerman Lake**, a 2.2-mile round-trip from the Zimmerman Lake parking area off Hwy. 14, past Joe Wright Reservoir and about 2 miles below the pass. Another tour begins at the pass summit and follows the **Michigan Ditch Rd.** south into the upper part of the Michigan River drainage; a 2.6-mile round-trip brings you to some old cabins and back, though you can easily ski farther along the ditch. See *Snowshoeing Colorado*, by Claire Walter, for more details on these and other routes.

CREATURE COMFORTS

Unless otherwise stated, dogs should not be left unattended in the room or cabin.

Bellvue

$$ Tip Top Guest Ranch, 1300 CR 41 (about 30 miles from Fort Collins, in Rist Canyon), 970-484-1215, www.tiptop ranch.com. This 6,400-acre ranch, with views of Rocky Mountain National Park, has three cabins where you and your dog can overnight. There's a $5 nightly fee for pets and a limit of two dogs per cabin. The cabins have separate living and bedroom areas, kitchenettes, electricity, and wood-burning stoves for heat, though no indoor plumbing (there's a central bathhouse). You can leave your dog unattended inside for short periods of time. Although you'll need to supply your own food for the most part, the ranch offers dinner rides on horseback. Campsites are also available at the ranch.

Fort Collins

$-$$ Motel 6 Fort Collins, 3900 E. Mulberry, 970-482-6466, 800-466-8356 (national number). Dogs less than 30 pounds are permitted, with a limit of one pet per room.

$-$$$ Fort Collins Lakeside KOA, 1910 N. Taft Hill Rd., 970-484-9880, 800-562-9168, www.fclakesidecg.com. Dogs (other than Rottweilers, Dobermans, and pit bulls) are allowed in the camping cabins for a $5 one-time fee per pet. You'll have to supply your own bedding and cooking gear; some of the cabins have electricity

but no running water, and the camping cottages and lodges have kitchenettes, private baths, and even air-conditioning. Be sure to keep your dog leashed when outside. You'll also have to break the news to Fido that he's not allowed to swim in the 9-acre lake on the property (then again, people aren't allowed to swim in it, either). The KOA also has an 18-hole minigolf course and paddleboats for use on the lake. Open year-round.

$$ Comfort Suites, 1415 Oakridge, 970-206-4597, 800-228-5150 (national number), www.comfortsuites.com. There's a $15 nightly fee and a 50-pound maximum weight limit for canine guests, and you can leave yours unattended in the room for a short time.

$$ Days Inn, 3625 E. Mulberry, 970-221-5490, 800-DAYS-INN (national number). The motel has some designated pet rooms, where dogs can stay for a $5 fee per night, per pet. You can leave your dog unattended in the room.

$$ La Quinta Inn Fort Collins, 3709 E. Mulberry, 970-493-7800, 800-735-3757 (national number), www.lq.com. Midsize and smaller dog guests, with a maximum of two, are usually placed in first- and second-floor rooms, with a $5 fee per night. If you're paying with cash, a $50 deposit is required.

$$ Lamplighter Motel, 1809 N. College, 970-484-2764. Dogs are $5 per pet, per night, and the motel doesn't accept pit bulls or Rottweilers.

$$ Ramada Inn, 3836 E. Mulberry, 970-484-4660, 800-2-RAMADA (national number). Dogs are usually put in outside-facing rooms. There's a one-time fee of $30.

$$ Super 8 Motel, 409 Centro Wy., 970-493-7701, 800-800-8000 (national number), www.super8.com. The motel requires a deposit of $10 for the first pet and $5 per additional pet (up to three dogs, total) if you're paying with cash. You can leave your dog unattended in the room if you sign a damage waiver first.

$$–$$$ The Armstrong Hotel, 259 S. College, 970-484-3883, 866-384-3883, www.thearmstronghotel.com. Dogs can get a sense of Fort Collins's architectural past with a stay at this historic Old Town boutique hotel, which first opened in 1923. There's a $15 per night, per pet fee, and a limit of two dogs per room. After deteriorating into a low-rent boarding house, the hotel shut its doors in 2000. It reopened in 2004 in its current state, after a thorough and historically accurate renovation. Pets are welcome in four of the rooms and suites (out of 41), which are individually furnished with either vintage-style pieces or sleek contemporary decor.

$$–$$$ Best Western Kiva Inn, 1638 E. Mulberry, 970-484-2444, 888-299-5482, www.bestwesternkivainn.com. The hotel has designated pet rooms for $10 extra per night, per pet.

$$–$$$ Hampton Inn, 1620 Oakridge, 970-229-5927, 800-426-7866 (national number), www.ftcollins.hamptoninn.com. Dogs are allowed with a $25 one-time fee. Quiet dogs can be left unattended in the room, but housekeeping won't come in during that time.

$$–$$$ Holiday Inn Express, 1426 Oakridge, 970-225-2200, 800-HOLIDAY (national number), www.holidayinn.com. Pets are allowed for a $30 one-time fee.

$$–$$$ Horsetooth Hideaway Bed and Breakfast, 4699 W. CR 38E, 970-222-2242, www.horsetoothhideaway.com. With Horsetooth Reservoir and a park right across the street, and a recently completed section of a hiking/biking trail nearby that runs all the way up to Greeley, the Hideaway is "dog heaven," says owner Alan Evans. And Horsetooth Mountain Open Space is just up the road. Dogs are accepted at the B&B on a case-by-case basis, with a $50 deposit, so hopefully yours will pass muster. The six suites all have full baths, fireplaces, kitchenettes, and private decks or patios, so staying here is more like being at a hotel than at your average B&B. There's also a small workout facility on-site.

$$–$$$ Mulberry Inn, 4333 E. Mulberry, 970-493-9000, 800-234-5548, www.mulberryinn.com. Some of this motel's rooms have hot tubs in them (for humans only, of course). There's a $5 fee per night, per dog.

$$–$$$ Quality Inn and Suites, 4001 S. Mason, 970-282-9047, 800-228-5151 (national number), www.qualityinn.com. Dogs under 90 pounds are allowed in designated rooms, with a $25 one-time fee per pet.

$$–$$$ Residence Inn by Marriott, 1127 Oakridge, 970-223-5700, 800-331-3131 (national number). For a $75 one-time fee, dogs are allowed on two of the three floors of this all-suite hotel, with a limit of two dogs per unit and a preference for those under 80 pounds. You can leave your dog unattended in your unit, and the hotel provides poop bags for your walks.

$$–$$$ Sleep Inn, 3808 E. Mulberry, 970-484-5515, 800-627-5337 (national number), www.sleepinn.com. There's a $10 one-time fee per dog to stay in one of the motel's designated pet rooms. You can leave your dog unattended in the room only if he's secure in a travel cage.

$$–$$$$ Best Western University Inn, 914 S. College, 970-484-1984, 800-528-1234 (national number), www.bwui.com. The motel has pet-specific rooms for $15 per night, per dog. No more than three dogs are allowed in one room.

$$$ Homewood Suites, 1521 Oakridge, 970-225-2400, www.homewoodsuites hilton.com. Your dog can join you at this all-suite hotel, where suites range from studios to two bedrooms, for a $75 one-time fee. He can be left unattended in the room as long as you notify the front desk, though housekeeping won't come in unless Fido is in a travel kennel. The rates not only include breakfast, but also a light dinner from Monday to Thursday (and each suite has cooking facilities, too).

$$$–$$$$ Hilton Fort Collins, 425 W. Prospect, 970-482-2626, 800-HILTON (national number), www.hilton.com. Dogs can stay in second- or third-floor rooms for a $50 one-time fee. If you leave your dog unattended inside the room, he must be in a travel kennel. Note that the other Fort Collins Hilton, the Hilton Garden, does not accept pets.

Laporte
$$ Fort Collins/Poudre Canyon KOA, Hwy. 287 at the entrance to Poudre Canyon, 970-493-9758, 800-562-2648, www.koa .com. Dogs are allowed in the camping cabins; you'll have to supply your own bedding and cooking gear. Open May 1 to September 30.

Loveland
$–$$ Kings Court Motel, 928 N. Lincoln Ave., 970-667-4035. Dogs can stay in smoking rooms only for $10 per night, per pet.

$$ Hiway Motel, 1027 E. Eisenhower Blvd., 970-667-5224. Dogs are allowed for $10 extra per night.

$$–$$$ Best Western Crossroads Inn, 5542 Hwy. 34, 970-667-7810, 888-818-6223, www.bwloveland.com. Dogs are permitted for $15 per night, per pet. You can leave your dog unattended in the room, but the housekeepers won't come in to clean during that time.

$$–$$$ La Quinta Inn & Suites Loveland, 1450 Cascade Ave., 970-622-8600, 800-753-3757 (national number), www .lq.com. The hotel has a limit of two dogs per room, with a maximum of 50 pounds of dog per room (so, for example, you could stay with your 50-pound Aussie shepherd or your two 25-pound beagles).

$$$–$$$$ Residence Inn Loveland, 5450 McWhinney Blvd., 970-622-7000, 800-MARRIOT (national number), marriot .com. Dogs up to 50 pounds are permitted, with a $75 one-time fee and a limit of two dogs per room. All rooms are suites with full kitchens and living areas. You can leave your dog unattended inside as long as he's in a travel crate. The Loveland outlet stores are next door, if you're dog is interested in sniffing out bargains.

$$$–$$$$ Embassy Suites, 4705 Clydesdale Pkwy., 970-593-6200, 800-EMBASSY (national number), www .embassysuites.hilton.com. The hotel prefers that dog guests be 50 pounds or under. There's a $50 one-time fee and a limit of one dog per room. All units are two-room suites with kitchenettes.

Poudre Canyon
$–$$ Trading Post, 44414 Poudre Canyon Rd. (55 miles from Fort Collins), 970-881-2215, www.tradingpostresort .com. This small complex across the road from the river has a general store and 12 cabins. Dogs are $2.50 per night, per pet, with a two-dog limit. The rustic cabins come with cold running water and, except

for one, wood-burning cookstoves; modern ones have kitchens and private baths. Keep your dog leashed on the property.

$$ Glen Echo Resort, 31503 Poudre Canyon Rd. (41 miles from Fort Collins), 970-881-2208, 800-348-2208, www.coloradodirectory.com/glenechoresort. At this riverside family resort, up to two dogs at a time are allowed only in the rustic cabins, which have no running water but do have shared baths and cooking facilities. There's a $10 fee per night, per dog. A restaurant and general store are on the premises. You can leave your dog unattended inside the cabin for a short time, and you're required to keep him leashed on the property. Open May 1 to October 1 and Thursday to Sunday outside of those dates.

$$ Sportsman's Lodge, 44174 Poudre Canyon Rd. (54 miles from Fort Collins), 970-881-2272, 800-270-2272, www.coloradodirectory.com/sportsmanslodge. "Sportdogs" are permitted in the 11 rustic one-room cabins (with shared baths and wood-burning cookstoves) or the one "modern" cabin, with kitchenette and private bath, for $5 extra per pet, per night.

$$–$$$ Archer's Poudre River Resort, 33021 Poudre Canyon Rd. (45 miles from Fort Collins), 970-881-2139, 888-822-0588, www.poudreriverresort.com. Dogs are allowed in 11 of the 15 cabins at this complex, which spans the Poudre River, for $10 per night, per dog. The fully equipped cabins range from studios to two bedrooms, and all are individually decorated. The owners ask that you keep your dog leashed on the 7.5-acre riverside property. A general store is on-site, as well as tent and RV sites.

Red Feather Lakes

$$ Alpine Lodge, 157 Prairie Divide Rd., 970-881-2933. Located about .5 mile from the village of Red Feather Lakes, the lodge has three fully furnished cabins and two mobile homes that you and one small dog at a time can stay in.

$$–$$$ Red Feather Ranch Bed and Breakfast and Horse Hotel, 3613 CR 68C, 970-881-3715, 877-881-5215, www.redfeatherranch.com. This bed-and-breakfast is set on 40 acres adjacent to the Roosevelt National Forest, and if your dog enjoys playing with others (there are a few resident dogs) and romping outdoors, he'll have a great time here. For a one-time fee of $15 each, dogs are allowed in any of the main lodge's five guest rooms, done up in casual mountain-style decor. Your dog can stay unattended for a short time as long as he promises to stay off the furniture. Facilities are also available for visiting horses. Nearby hiking, mountain-biking, skiing, and snowshoeing trails all start from the ranch.

$$–$$$ Trout Lodge, 1078 Ramona Dr., 970-881-2964, www.troutlodgerfl.com. You and your dog have your choice of six fully equipped cabins, ranging from studios to two bedrooms, in the village of Red Feather Lakes. Unless the dogs are small, there's a one-dog limit. You'll need to keep your dog leashed when outside. Open mid-April to October 31.

$$–$$$$ Beaver Meadows Resort, 100 Marmot Dr., 970-881-2450, 800-462-5870, www.beavermeadows.com. This 840-acre ranch, with its own trail network and frontage on the North Fork of the Poudre River, is dog heaven. For accommodations, dogs have their pick of condos, homey log cottages, or a cabin for a $20 one-time fee per dog (they're not allowed in the lodge rooms). All are equipped with kitchens, and some have wood-burning stoves or fireplaces and decks. Campsites and a camping cabin are also available. You can leave your well-behaved dog unattended inside. The resort maintains 25 miles of hiking/ mountain-biking/horseback-riding trails that spill over into the adjacent Roosevelt National Forest and you can bring your dog on them, leashed or under voice control. During the winter, about 4 miles of trails are designated for snowshoers and their dogs, while other trails are groomed for skiing (unless Fido knows how to cross-country ski in a track, he'll need to stay off them). Stables at the resort operate year-round. Summer activities also include fishing (on the river and in ponds), disc golf, and paddleboating. In winter, the resort also offers a tubing hill (with a rope tow that operates on weekends), two outdoor skating ponds, and horse-drawn sleigh rides. All of those activities are likely to build up your appetite; luckily, there's also a restaurant on the premises.

$$$–$$$$ Sundance Trail Guest Ranch, 17931 Red Feather Lakes Rd., 970-224-1222, 800-357-4930, www.sundance trail.com. This 140-acre dude ranch offers horseback riding, fishing, jeep rides, and easy access to trails in the adjacent Roosevelt National Forest. If your dog is one of the lucky ones (usually only one set of guests at a time can bring pets, unless each can vouch that their dog plays well with others), he can stay with you in one of the seven cabins or lodge suites, nicely done up in a mountain/western decor. And he can stay inside even when you're not there. Meals are served family-style in the lodge's dining room. From mid-May to the beginning of October, the ranch accepts guests on a weekly basis only, for an all-inclusive price from Sunday to Saturday. The rest of the year it operates as a bed-and-breakfast, with rates including dinner on the night of arrival and a horseback ride the next day.

$$$$ Mountain Rose, 160 Comanche Cir., 970-881-2503, 800-477-7673, www.the mountainrose.com. This upscale, amenity-filled cabin in Crystal Lake, about 4 miles from the town of Red Feather Lakes, offers you and your dog a stellar weekend getaway. There's a $50 one-time fee per pet and a limit of two dogs. The three-bedroom, two-bath cabin, on 5 wooded acres, can sleep up to eight. You can leave your dog unattended inside so long as you're sure he won't jump on the furniture or chew any of the decor. And you'll need to clean up after him outdoors. A hot tub is available for guests, too. Owners Maggie Mora and Marge Wolf emphasize that you and your dog should book early, as the cabin has become popular with guests. The website has an availability calendar.

Wellington

$ KOA Fort Collins North, Exit 281 off I-25, 970-568-7486, 800-KOA-8142, www.koa.com. Dogs are allowed in the camping cabins for a $5 one-time fee; you'll have to supply your own bedding and cooking gear.

CAMPGROUNDS

Boyd Lake State Park. East of Loveland off US Hwy. 34 (148 sites).

Larimer County Parks: **Carter Lake,** on CR 31, about 5 miles west of Loveland (5 campgrounds); **Horsetooth Reservoir,** east of Fort Collins via CR 38E (2 campgrounds); **Flatiron Reservoir,** off CR 18E, about 7 miles west of Loveland (1 campground); **Pinewood Reservoir,** at the end of CR 18E, about 10 miles from Loveland (1 campground).

National forest campgrounds: Several campsites are right off Hwy. 14 in Poudre Canyon, including **Ansel Watrous Campground** (19 sites); **Stove Prairie Campground** (9 sites); **Narrows Campground**

(15 sites); **Mountain Park Campground** (55 sites); and **Kelly Flats Campground** (29 sites). Campgrounds near Red Feather Lakes include the **Bellaire Campground**, Red Feather Lakes Rd. to FR 162 (26 sites); **Dowdy Lake Campground**, 1.5 miles from the village on FR 218 (62 sites); and **West Lake Campground**, 1 mile from the village on FR 200 (35 sites).

Private campgrounds: **Tip Top Guest Ranch** in Bellvue; **Fort Collins Lakeside KOA** in Fort Collins; **Fort Collins/Poudre Canyon KOA** in La Porte; **Archer's Poudre River Resort** and **Glen Echo Resort** in Poudre Canyon; **Beaver Meadows** near Red Feather Lakes; **KOA Fort Collins North** in Wellington.

RAILS AND TAILS

Fort Collins's most prominent canine was Annie, a shepherd/collie mix who was adopted by workers for the Colorado and Southern Railroad and became the station mascot.

Annie lived at the railroad depot until her death in 1948. The workers buried her outside the station, and though the depot no longer exists, you can still visit the grave, surrounded by an iron fence, on Mason St. just north of LaPorte Ave.

Annie is also commemorated by a life-size bronze sculpture, by local artist Dawn Weimmer, in front of the Fort Collins Library at 201 Peterson St. The annual Annie Walk (see Worth a Paws) is held in her honor.

WORTH A PAWS

Doggie Olympics. Do you think you have a potential gold medalist in the Hot Dog Retrieve, just waiting for an opportunity to demonstrate his skills? Or maybe your dog would prefer to strut his stuff in the 25-Yard Dash or the Obstacle Course. Bring him down to Fort Collins's City Park in September for the Doggie Olympics, where he can compete in these and other events, such as Best Tidbit Catcher and the Pentathlon. There are four levels of competition for each event, so the serious canine athlete as well as the habitual couch potato can participate. Proceeds benefit the Larimer Animal–People Partnership (LAPP). You can register in advance or on the day of the competition. For more information, call 970-226-4146 or go to www.colapp.org.

Fire Hydrant Five. Held in early May in Edora Park in Fort Collins, the Fire Hydrant Five consists of a 5K run for humans and a 3K fun run and 5K walk for leashed dogs and their owners. In addition to your registration fee, you and your dog can collect donations, all of which will benefit the Humane Society for Larimer County. Call the Humane Society at 970-226-3647 for more information or go to www.larimerhumane.org.

Flame Out Five. Dalmatian or no, your dog can join you for this 5K run/3K walk that raises money for the smoke-detector distribution program of the Poudre Fire Authority. It takes place on either the first or second Saturday in October, in conjunction with Fire Prevention Week. The course begins at Fire Station 3, at 2000 Matthews St., and goes through the surrounding residential district. Prizes are given to the top male and female runners with dogs, and there are treats for everybody. Call 970-221-6570 or go to www.poudre-fire.org for details.

The Fast and the Furriest. Rounding out Fort Collins's trio of owner/pet running events, this annual 5K run/1K walk takes place the third Saturday of April and benefits the Companion Care Fund of Colorado State University's veterinary program, which assists pet owners in paying for necessary animal care. Let your dog know he may face some unusual competition, as the run is open to all sorts of pets, as long as they're leashed or contained; one year a pet rat, a goat, and a snake were among the participants. The race, which is organized by vet students, begins behind the James L. Voss Veterinary Medical Center, at 300 W. Drake St.; afterward everyone gathers for food, fun, activities, and prizes for humans and pets. For more information, go to www.cvmbs.colo state.edu (click on Development, then Current Events).

Annie Walk. This family-friendly canine walk, held the fourth Saturday in August, honors Annie the railroad dog (see sidebar). The 1.5-mile course runs from the Fort Collins library's main branch (201 Peterson St.) through downtown to Annie's grave on Mason St. and back. Fuel up before the walk at the pancake breakfast put on by the Lions Club, and afterward stick around for the Annie lookalike, pet/owner lookalike, and tail-wagging contests, and games like doggie musical chairs. If your dog is still raring to go, let him try the agility and rally courses (in the latter, dogs perform tasks like sitting and staying or retrieving biscuits along the way to the finish line). The registration fees bring in funds for children's books and materials in the Fort Collins library system. Participants also get an Annie T-shirt. Contact the library at 970-221-6526 for more information or go to www.fcgov.com/library.

Payton Classic. Named after Colorado's first state champion Frisbee dog, this annual athletic event is held the third or fourth weekend in June at City Park in Fort Collins (1500 W. Mulberry St.). The competition has two components: the minidistance, in which dogs compete in 60-second rounds, earning points for catching distance and a bonus for mid-air catches; and the freestyle, in which they're judged on difficulty, execution, leaping agility, and showmanship while performing tricks. For more information, visit www.coloradodiscdogs.com.

Wagz Colorado, 132 N. College, Fort Collins, 970-482-9249, www.wagzcolorado .com. In addition to wagging his tail for the six flavors of biscuits, like bacon and cheese and peamutt butter, made at the in-store bakery (with all-natural ingredients from the local food co-op), your dog can browse the cornucopia of leashes and collars, toys, feeders, and outdoor gear from Ruffwear. Some of the store's more out-of-the-ordinary merchandise includes doggie bike trailers, William Wegman for Crypton dog beds and tote bags, and artisan jewelry. Exhibits of work from local artists who do dog and cat portraits rotate regularly. And in October, be sure to check out the Wagz Halloween costume parade down College Ave. through Old Town Fort Collins.

Arfy's Mercantile for Dogs & Cats, 2601 S. Lemay Ave., #4, Fort Collins, 970-493-1747, www.arfys.com. "The word *spoiled* isn't in our vocabulary. Dogs here are just overly loved," says owner Robin Loeb. Part of that love involves the on-site bakery, which turns out treats in seven flavors like peanut butter, carob, BBQ, and chicken, as well as canine birthday cakes. And all four-legged shoppers get one of Arfy's signature frozen liver treats ("They don't even have to do a trick," says Loeb). The store also carries a variety of learning-oriented toys, beds, feeders, chews (including hard-to-find buffalo bones), leashes, and collars, and human items like humorous signs for pet lovers and Life Is Good T-shirts. And, of course, there are things for cats, too, which we won't waste time on here! The first Saturday in October, bring your dog to the annual Arfypallooza, a day of fun activities and food for dogs, held in the store's parking lot.

Doggie Dips and Chips, 265C E. 29th St. (Orchard Center shopping plaza), Loveland, 970-461-1109, www.doggiedips andchips.com. The "dip" in the name of this canine emporium refers to the self-service dog wash, which has four tubs with spalike redwood surrounds. A wash is $14 for one dog, $25 for two, and includes shampoo, towels, an apron for you, and use of a professional dryer and grooming tools. The "chips" relates to the in-house biscuit bakery; once he's clean, your dog can sniff out six flavors of all-natural treats, including peanut-butter puppers and vegetabones, for dogs sensitive to corn and wheat. There's also a comprehensive selection of rawhides, toys, beds, and doggie-oriented craft items. Plus, Steve Fifer (who owns the store with his wife, Sandy) is a leathersmith who crafts custom collars and leashes.

Dirty dogs should try one of these do-it-yourself dog washes: in Fort Collins, **Laund-Ur-Mutt** (1721 W. Harmony, Unit 105, 970-223-8225) rents washing bays for $12 for the first half hour and $6 for each additional half hour. You'll have use of an apron, a scrub mitt, one towel per dog, combs and brushes, and the fur dryer. You'll need to supply your own shampoo or buy it from Laund-Ur-Mutt's stock. Closed Wednesdays.

    Biscuit's Dog Pawlour (2005 S. College, 970-484-3644, www.dogpawlour .com) offers a private wash room for $16 ($10 for small dogs) for the first dog, and $10 per additional dog. That includes shampoo, towels, and a dryer. Closed Mondays.

DOGGIE DAYCARE
Berthoud
Destiny's Kennel, 2683 CR 42, 970-532-1232, www.destinyskennel.com. $15/day. Dogs can enjoy playing in the fenced outdoor enclosure, splashing in kiddie pools, and getting treats during "cookie hour." Open 8 AM–6 PM, Monday to Friday; 9 AM–3 PM, Saturday; 9–10 AM and 5–6 PM, Sunday.

Happy Tails Dog Ranch, 18490 CR 1, 970-532-4040,www.happytailsdogranch.com. $17/day. There are 1.5 acres of fenced play yards in a country setting, with several wading pools, as well as an indoor play area with playground equipment for dogs. Open 7–9 AM and 4:30–6:30 PM, Monday to Friday.

Fort Collins
Andelt's Pet Motel, 3200 E. Mulberry, 970-484-5776. $15/day. Open 7:30 AM–12:30 PM and 1:30–5:30 PM, Monday to Friday; 7:30 AM–noon and 3:30–5:30 PM, Saturday; 8–9 AM and 3:30–4:30 PM, Sunday (for pick-up only).

Ashcroft Boarding Kennels, 5020 S. CR 3, 970-221-5689, www.ashcroftkennels .com. $15/day; $10 each additional dog. Open 7:30–9:30 AM and 4–6 PM, Monday to Friday; 7:30–10 AM, Saturday; 4–6 PM, Sunday.

Biscuit's Dog Pawlour, 2005 S. College, 970-484-3644, www.dogpawlour.com. $24/day; $15/half-day. A prescreening appointment is required for newcomers. Open 9 AM–7 PM, Tuesday to Saturday.

Camp Bow Wow, 4103 S. Mason St., 970-266-9247, www.campbowwowusa.com/colorado/fort-collins/. $22/day, $15 per additional dog. Canine Campers must go through a free interview day before being accepted. The Camp Bow Wow experience includes separate playgroups into which dogs are placed based on size and temperament; they have all-day access to indoor and outdoor play areas with dog-specific play equipment and, in warmer weather, wading pools. You can keep tabs on the great time your pooch is having via the online Camper Cam. Open 7 AM–7 PM, Monday to Saturday.

Country Squire Pet Resort, 3320 N. Shields, 970-484-3082, www.country squirepetresort.com. $22–$24/day, depending on the size of dog. Open 8 AM–5:30 PM, Monday to Friday; 8:30 AM–noon, Saturday.

Crystal Glen Kennel, 720 W. Willox Ln., 970-224-3118, www.crystalglen.net. $17–$19/day. The kennel, on 12 acres, also breeds golden retrievers. Daycare dogs play together in small groups and have access to a 4-acre fenced yard with agility equipment, as well as a stream and two pools to swim or wade in. Open 8 AM–1 PM and 3:30–6 PM, Monday to Saturday; 4–6 PM, Sunday (pick-up only).

Lazy Dog Ranch, 4417 E. Prospect Rd., 970-482-1103. $14/day. Dogs have 2.5 fenced acres to romp on. Open by appointment.

Moore Animal Hospital Pet Camp, 2550 Stover, 970-416-9101, www.mooreanimal hospital.com. $16/day. Dogs get three walks daily and time in the indoor play area. Open 7 AM–6 PM, Monday to Friday; 7 AM–noon, Saturday.

PetsHotel at PetSmart, 4432 S. College, 970-223-9020, www.petsmart.com. $16–$20/day. The store differentiates between day camp and daycare. In the former, dogs get to play with each other from 9 to 5 in one of four indoor playrooms, which have toys and play equipment, with an hour off at noon to nap in private rooms. The cost is $20 a dog, and they're divided into play-groups by size and temperament. If your dog prefers not to socialize as much, you can put him in daycare ($16); he'll get his own room to snooze in, with two 15-minute play breaks. Open 7 AM–9 PM, Monday to Saturday; 8 AM–6 PM, Sunday.

Peticular Care, 6108 S. College, Unit B, 970-223-1814, www.peticularcare.com. $18/day; $13/half-day. Dogs can play in the 4,440-square-foot indoor play area (covered with AKC–approved nonslip flooring) or a 2,000-square-foot outdoor yard with water features. Open 6:30 AM–6 PM, Monday to Friday; 8 AM–noon and 4–6 PM, Saturday.

Rover's Ranch, 4837 Terry Lake Rd., 970-493-5970. $13/day. Open 7 AM–6 PM, Monday, Thursday, Friday; 7–10 AM and 4–6 PM, Tuesday and Wednesday; 8 AM–noon, Saturday; 8–9 AM and 5–6 PM, Sunday (pick-up and drop-off only).

Loveland

Boyd Lake Veterinary Center, 3850 E. 15th St., 970-593-1717, www.boydlakevet.com. $19/day. The daycare facility includes a large, fenced outdoor play area carpeted with artifical turf and a full-size swimming pool. Open 6:30 AM–6 PM, Monday to Friday; 8 AM–noon and 3–6 PM, Saturday.

Creature Comforts Pet Retreat, 808 S. CR 23E, 970-669-2084, www.creaturecom fortspet.com. $18.50–$19.50/day. Optional exercise sessions include a 1-mile nature hike, for $3.50 extra, or a supervised play session, for $2.50 extra. Open 8 AM–5 PM, Monday to Friday; 8 AM–noon, Saturday; 9–10 AM and 4–5 PM, Sunday.

The Dog Club, 224 E. 29th St., 970-669-4245, www.lovelanddogclub.com. $21/day. Dogs play together in small groups, and a visit may include a bath, nail trim, and/or training. Open 6:30 AM–6:30 PM, Monday to Friday; 10 AM–5 PM, Saturday.

PET PROVISIONS
Fort Collins
Arfy's Mercantile For Dogs & Cats, 2601 S. Lemay Ave., #4, 970-493-1747, www .arfys.com (see Worth a Paws)

Biscuit's Dog Pawlour, 2005 S. College, 970-484-3644, www.dogpawlour.com

Cache La Poudre Feeds, 1724 N. Overland Trail, 970-482-5092

Jax Farm & Ranch, 1000 N. Hwy. 28, 970-484-2221, www.jaxmercantile.com

Northern Colorado Feeder's Supply, 359 Linden St., 970-482-7303

PETCO, 2211 S. College, 970-484-4477, www.petco.com

PetSmart, 4432 S. College, 970-223-9020, www.petsmart.com

Poudre Feed Supply, 622 N. College, 970-482-2741; 6204 S. College, 970-225-1255, wwwpoudrefeed.com

Vetline, 425 John Deere Rd. (behind the Ramada Inn), 970-484-1900, 800-962-4554. The store carries a complete line of animal vaccines, medications, and other medical supplies.

Wagz Colorado, 132 N. College, 970-482-9249, www.wagzcolorado.com (see Worth a Paws)

Laporte
The Old Feed Store, 3612 W. CR 54G, 970-493-0320

Loveland
Doggie Dips and Chips, 265C E. 29th St. (Orchard Center shopping plaza), 970-461-1109, www.doggiedipsandchips.com (see Worth a Paws)

PetSmart, 1715 Rocky Mountain Ave. 970-278-9178, www.petsmart.com

West Side Feed, 5623 W. Hwy. 34, 970-622-8658, www.westsidefeed.com

CANINE ER
Fort Collins
Fort Collins Veterinary Emergency Hospital, 816 S. Lemay, 970-484-8080, www.veterinaryemergencyhospital.net. Open 24 hours.

James L. Voss Veterinary Teaching Hospital (AAHA certified), 300 W. Drake Rd., 970-221-4535, www.cvmbs.colostate.edu/vth. Part of Colorado State University, the clinic is staffed 24 hours a day for emergency patients.

Loveland
VCA Veterinary Specialists of Northern Colorado, 201 W. 67th Ct. (off Hwy. 287 between Loveland and Fort Collins), 970-663-5760, www.vcavsnc.com. The clinic is staffed 24 hours a day for emergency patients.

RESOURCES
Canyon Lakes Ranger District, Arapaho and Roosevelt National Forests and Pawnee National Grassland, 2150 Centre Ave. Bldg. E, Fort Collins, 970-295-6700

Colorado Welcome Center/Fort Collins Visitor Information Center, Interstate 25 and Prospect Rd. (Exit 268), Fort Collins, 970-482-5821, 800-274-3678, www.ftcollins.com

Five

Greeley and Northeastern Plains

THE BIG SCOOP

For the most part, the plains of eastern Colorado are travel-through country (although the tourism organizations, which market part of the area as "Colorado's Outback," don't want you to think this). But frankly, unless your dog is fascinated by pioneer history or into long car rides, he'll want to keep heading toward the mountains. You will, however, find plenty of dog-friendly lodgings, most of them lower-priced motels.

Greeley, somewhat of a gateway to the plains and home to the University of Northern Colorado, is a town of great smells—for dogs. When the wind's blowing just right, evidence of the area's agriculture industry permeates the airwaves, so to speak. That's one of the few things dogs will find to enjoy, however, as all parks except two in Greeley are closed to canines. Luckily, one of them is an off-leash dog park. For a more scenic walk than the average curbside stroll, walk your dog along a portion of the Poudre River Trail.

TAIL-RATED TRAILS

The observant dog will note that there are three state parks in the region—Bonny Lake, North Sterling Reservoir, and Jackson Lake—but he might be disappointed to hear that only one (North Sterling) currently has hiking trails of note. They all make great destinations, however, to camp with your dog and hang out by the water on a hot day. Dogs are not allowed on any of the swim beaches, but there are other areas in each park with water access where Fido (on leash) can dip a paw. (For park locations, see the campgrounds section in Creature Comforts.)

Rover Run Park

Access: Follow W. 10th St. (Hwy. 34 business route) west from downtown Greeley to N. 59th Ave. Turn right on 59th and drive 1.1 miles to F St. Make a right on F. The dog park is .5 mile down on the left.

Regulations: Dogs must have current vaccinations and licenses; owners must clean up after their pooches and have a leash on hand; aggressive dogs, puppies younger than four months, or dogs in heat are not allowed; no glass containers can be brought into the park.

Dogs can be off leash.

Greeley's first (and only, so far) official dog park keeps things simple, with a little more than 3 fenced acres for pups to run and roam on, and a few picnic tables for owners to congregate at. There's no water source, so bring your own if your dog plans on playing hard. If you want to take Fido for a longer walk, the Poudre River Trail runs by the park (dogs must be leashed on the trail). The park is open during daylight hours only.

North Sterling Reservoir State Park

Access: From the Sterling exit off I-76, head west on

Max practices for a visit to the dentist.

Hwy. 14 (3rd Ave.) to 7th Ave. Turn right on 7th, then left at the T-intersection with CR 46. Go right at the next T onto CR 33, which will bring you to the park entrance. Entry fee is $6.

Dogs must be leashed.

The **South Shoreline Trail** runs for 5.5 miles along the 3,000-acre reservoir's south side. You can pick up the crushed-surface trail at the southernmost boat ramp on the east side of the lake; from there it runs down to the Inlet Grove Campground and then crosses a bridge before following the shore in an otherwise undeveloped section of the park. You'll be able to go as far as CR 29 before the trail ends at private property. 970-522-3657, www.parks.state.co.us/parks/northsterling

Pawnee Buttes

Distance: 4 miles round-trip
Elevation gain: 240 feet
Access: Depending on your starting-out point, head either east or west on Hwy. 14 to CR 390 (about 13 miles east of Briggsdale or 10 miles west of Raymer). At Keota, head north on CR 105 for 3 miles, then turn right on CR 104 and go another 3 miles to CR 111. Go left for 4.5 miles, then follow the signed road to the trailhead parking area, next to a windmill.

Dogs can be off leash.

The buttes are two dramatic, 300-foot-tall blocks of eroded sandstone within the Pawnee National Grassland, a short-grass prairie preserve. They top out at 5,500 feet elevation. Your dog will enjoy this hike most during the spring or fall, when intense daytime temperatures subside a bit. And you might enjoy it most in the spring, when the abundant wildflowers bloom. Regardless of when you choose to hike, bring plenty of water along. Because the area is home to several species of birds of prey that nest here in the spring, you might want to keep your dog on a leash if he's a wanderer. The easy-to-follow, primarily flat trail goes through a couple of drainages before ending at a fence line near the buttes. En route, your dog might sniff out yucca, prickly pear cactus, and rabbitbrush, as well as some juniper. If you decide to explore more of the grasslands, be aware that dogs are not allowed on the nature walk at the Crow Valley Recreation Area (in the southwest corner of the campground).

Poudre River Trail

Access: The trail has numerous access points. One place to pick it up from downtown Greeley is at Island Grove Regional Park, the trail's eastern terminus. Drive north on 14th Ave. until it dead-ends at the park.

Dogs must be leashed.

This recently completed paved trail runs for 20 miles between Island Grove Regional Park and the neighboring town of Windsor, tracing the contours of the Cache La Poudre River and crossing it at several points. Along the way it passes parks, wildlife areas, and historic sites.

One of the more scenic spots to explore with Fido is the 4-mile section of trail that runs from 95th Ave. to Hwy. 257 in Windsor, crossing the Kodak property en route and traveling through a riparian corridor that draws lots of wildlife. The portion of trail that runs by the Rover Run dog park is also a great place to wander. Head west from the park to eventually reach shady cottonwood groves; head east for more open land and great vistas of the river. For more trail specifics, go to www.poudretrail.org.

CREATURE COMFORTS

Unless otherwise stated, dogs should not be left unattended in the room or cabin.

Evans

$$ America's Best Value Inn, 800 31st St., 970-339-2492, 800-777-5088, www .americasbestvalueinn.com. Dogs are allowed for a $10 nightly fee per pet, with a maximum of $20 per pet. You can leave your dog unattended only if he's in a travel kennel.

$$ Motel 6, 3015 8th Ave., 970-351-6481, 800-4-MOTEL6 (national number), www.motel6.com. The Motel 6 policy is one small pet per room (although if your medium- to large-sized dog is well behaved, chances are the motel can accommodate him). There's a $5 one-time fee for one dog, $7.50 for two dogs. They can be left unattended if in a travel kennel.

$$ Select Stay Hotel, 3025 8th Ave., 970-356-2180, 800-753-3746 (national number), www.selectstay.com. There's a $15 one-time pet fee for one or two dogs, $25 for more than two. They can be left unattended only if in a travel kennel.

Greeley

$–$$ Greeley Inn, 721 13th St., 970-353-3216. There's a $10 fee per night, per pet, with a limit of two dogs per room. Dogs are relegated to the smoking rooms for the most part, and they can be left unattended, but housekeeping won't enter to clean the room during that time.

$$ Clarion Hotel, 701 8th St., 970-353-8444, www.clariongreeley.com. Formerly the Regency, the hotel still allows pets, with a $25 one-time fee and a maximum of two dogs per room. You can leave your dog unattended only if he's in a travel kennel.

$$ Days Inn, 5630 W. 10th St., 970-392-1530, 800-DAYS-INN (national number), www.daysinn.com. There's a $15 nightly fee per pet and a limit of two dogs per room. If you give your cell-phone number to the front desk staff, you can leave your dog unattended in the room.

$$ Super 8 Greeley, 2423 W. 29th St., 970-330-8880, 800-800-8000 (national number), www.super8.com. Dogs are welcome in any of the rooms for $15 per night, per pet.

$$–$$$ Country Inn and Suites, 2501 W. 29th St., 970-330-3404, 800-456-4000 (national number), www.countryinns .com. Dogs 25 pounds and under (a limit that's open to some interpretation) can stay in the motel's designated pet rooms for $20 nightly per pet. There's also a limit of three dogs per room.

$$–$$$$ Comfort Inn and Suites, 2467 W. 29th St., 970-330-6380, www.com fortinn.com. Dogs are charged $15 extra per night, per pet, with a limit of two dogs per room.

Windsor

$$ AmericInn Lodge & Suites, 7645 Westgate Dr., 970-226-1232, 800-634-3444 (national number), www.coloradolodges .com. Dogs under 25 pounds (which is sometimes loosely interpreted) can stay in designated pet-friendly first-floor rooms for $10 extra per night. The hotel is just off I-25.

$$–$$$ Super 8 Windsor, 1265 Main St., 970-686-5996, 800-800-8000 (national number), www.super8.com. There's a fee of $15 per pet, per night, but if you're staying for several nights, the fee is often negotiable.

NORTHEASTERN PLAINS
Akron

$$ Akron Motel, 60 Hickory Ave., 970-345-2028. This motel, which used to be a railroad lodge, allows dogs in some of its rooms for $10 per pet, per night. There's a nearby field where you can exercise Fido on leash.

$$ Lighthouse Inn, 625 E. 1st St. (Hwy. 34), 970-345-2231. There's a $5 one-time fee, per dog, at this 11-room motel.

Brush

$–$$ Budget Host Empire Motel, 1408 Edison, 970-842-2876, www.budgethost.com. There's a $5 one-time dog fee.

$$ Econo Lodge, 1208 N. Colorado Ave., 970-842-5146, 800-424-6423 (national number), www.econolodge.com. It's $10 per night, per pet, with a limit of two dogs per room. You can leave your dog unattended if he's in a travel kennel.

$$ Microtel Inn, 975 N. Colorado Ave., 970-842-4241, 800-771-7171 (national number), www.microtelinn.com. Dogs are allowed only in smoking rooms for $15 extra per night, per dog, with a maximum of two dogs per room.

Fort Lupton

$ Motel 6, 65 S. Grand Ave., 303-857-1800, 800-4MOTEL6 (national number), www.motel6.com. Dogs of any size, shape, or form who "won't terrorize the motel" are welcome.

Fort Morgan

$–$$ Central Motel, 201 W. Platte, 970-867-2401, www.centralmotel.biz. Dogs are allowed in most of the motel's rooms for a $10 one-time fee.

$–$$ Country Comfort Motel and RV Park, 16466 W. Hwy. 34, 970-867-0260, www.countrymotel.net. There's a $5 per night fee per dog. The motel is on 2.5 acres, so your pooch will have a chance to stretch his legs. And you can leave him unattended in the room if he's in a travel kennel.

$–$$ Sand's Motel, 933 W. Platte Ave., 970-867-2453, www.sandsmotelfm.com.

$$ Best Western Park Terrace, 725 Main St., 970-867-8256, 800-528-1234 (national number), www.bestwesterncolorado.com. With a $10–$15 one-time fee, depending on their size, dogs can stay in eight of the rooms.

$$ Rodeway Inn, 1409 Barlow Rd. (Exit 82 off I-76), 970-867-9481, 877-424-6423 (national number), www.rodewayinn.com. Dogs are allowed for $10 extra per night, with a limit of one dog per room.

Holyoke

$ Burge Hotel, 230 N. Interocean Ave., 970-854-2261. Dogs looking for a bit of history out on the plains may enjoy a stay at this quaint, 10-room hotel that was built in the late 1880s to house railroad employees. If you leave your dog unattended inside the room, he must be in a travel kennel.

$ Cedar Inn, 525 E. Denver, 970-854-2525. Dogs are allowed for $10 per dog, per visit. You can leave yours unattended in the room as long as you notify the front desk.

$$ Golden Plains Motel, 1250 S. Interocean Ave., 970-854-3000, 800-643-0451, www.goldenplainsmotel.com. Dogs are allowed in the motel's older rooms, for an $8–$10 one-time fee, depending on the number of dogs. If you leave your dog unattended in the room, he should be in a travel kennel.

Julesburg

$ Grand Motel, 220 Pine, 970-474-3302. One dog per room stays for free; after that, it's $5 for each additional dog.

$–$$ Holiday Motel, Hwy. 138, 970-474-3371. The motel charges $5 per dog, per night.

$$ Platte Valley Inn, I-76 and Hwy. 385, 970-474-3336, www.budgethost.com. It's smoking rooms only for dogs here, and $7 per dog, per night. There is a gravel and grass pet area where they can be walked on leash.

Sterling

$ Crest Motel, 516 S. Division Ave., 970-522-3753, www.thecrestmotel.com. The motel allows dogs in some of its rooms, but you must pay with a credit card.

$–$$ Colonial Motel, 915 S. Division, 970-522-3383. Dogs are permitted in any of the rooms for $5 per night, per pet.

$$ Ramada Inn, I-76 and E. Hwy. 6, 970-522-2625, 800-835-7275, www.ramada.com. Dogs are welcome in outside rooms with a $25 deposit.

$$ Super 8, 12883 Hwy. 61 (Exit 125 off I-76), 970-522-0300, 800-800-8000 (national number), www.super8.com. Dogs can stay for $10 extra per night, per pet.

$$ Travelodge, 12881 Hwy. 61 (Exit 125 off I-76), 970-522-2300, 800-578-7878 (national number), www.travelodge.com. Dogs can stay for $10 extra per night, per pet.

$$–$$$ Best Western Sundowner, Overland Trail St., 970-522-6265, 800-528-1234 (national number), www.bestwesterncolorado.com. Dogs are allowed in smoking rooms only for $10 per night extra. They can be left unattended inside in a travel kennel. There's a large yard outside the motel where dogs can exercise off leash.

Wray

$ Butte Motel, 330 E. 3rd, 970-332-4828. There's a $15 one-time pet fee. Dogs must be in a travel kennel at all times when in the room.

$$ Sandhiller Motel, 411 NW Railway, 970-332-4134, 800-554-7482. Dogs are accepted in smoking rooms only for $5 per dog, per night.

Yuma

$$ Harvest Motel, 421 W. 8th Ave., 970-848-5853, 800-273-5853, www.harvestmotel.com. Quiet dogs are welcome for $7 per night, per dog.

$$ Nelson Inn, 815 E. 8th Ave., 970-848-2774, 866-329-7695, www.nelsoninn.com. The motel has three dog-friendly rooms, for $10 per night, per pet.

$$ Sunrise Inn, 420 E. 8th Ave., 970-848-5465, 800-378-9166, www.sunriseinnyuma.com. There's a $10 per dog nightly fee, with a maximum of two dogs per room.

CENTRAL EASTERN PLAINS
Burlington

$ Hi-Lo Motel, 870 Rose Ave., 719-346-5280. Smaller dogs are allowed in certain rooms for a $10 fee per dog, per night.

$ Western Motor Inn, 2222 Rose Ave., 719-346-5371, 800-346-5330. Dogs are permitted in some rooms for $7 per night, per dog.

$–$$ Burlington Inn, 450 S. Lincoln St., 719-346-5555, www.burlingtoninn colorado.com. Pets are permitted in certain rooms, with a limit of one dog per room. There's a $7 fee per night, and a dog can be left unattended in the room.

$$ Chaparral Motor Inn, 405 S. Lincoln St. (Exit 437 off I-70), 719-346-5361. The motel allows dogs in designated rooms for $7 per night, per dog. A field where they can stretch their legs is beside the motel.

$$–$$$ Comfort Inn, 282 S. Lincoln St., 719-346-7676, 888-388-7676, www .comfortinn.com. The motel has designated pet rooms for a $50 deposit and a $15 nightly fee. Up to two dogs, each less than 50 pounds, are allowed per room.

Byers
$$ Budget Host Longhorn Motel, 457 N. Main, 303-822-5205. One dog per room is allowed, for $5 extra per night.

Flagler
$–$$ Little England Motel, 244 High St., 719-765-4812. This small motel allows dogs that are "housebroken and won't jump up on the bed," says the owner, who also expresses a preference for non-shedding dogs. Two dogs per room are allowed in some units, and you may be asked to put down a $10 deposit.

Idalia
$ Prairie Vista Motel, 26995 Hwy. 36, 970-354-7237. Two dogs maximum are allowed in a few of the motel's rooms.

Limon
$ First Inn Gold, 158 E. Main, 719-775-2385. Dogs less than 50 pounds are preferred, with a limit of two dogs per room. There's a $5 fee per dog, per night.

$ Limon KOA, 575 Colorado Ave., 719-775-2151, 800-562-2129, www.koa colorado.com. Dogs are allowed in the cabins (you'll need to bring your own bedding and cooking supplies).

$$ Econo Lodge of Limon, 985 Hwy. 24, 719-775-2867, www.econolodge .com. There's a $25 deposit and a $12.50 nightly fee per dog for the motel's designated pet rooms.

$$ Safari Motel, 637 Main, 719-775-2363. For $5 extra per night, per pet, dogs can stay in several of the motel's rooms.

$$ Super 8 Motel, 937 Hwy. 24, 719-775-2889, 800-800-8000 (national number), www.super8.com. Dog guests are welcome for a $10 one-time fee ($20 for two or more dogs) in five ground-floor rooms. You can leave your dog unattended inside.

$$ Tyme Square Inn, 2505 6th St., 719-775-0700. The motel offers four pet-friendly rooms. There's a $15–$50 one-time fee, depending on the size of the dog, and a two-dog limit per room.

$$–$$$ Best Western Limon Inn, 925 T Ave., 719-775-0277, 800-528-1234 (national number), www.bestwestern colorado.com. There are seven designated pet rooms; the fee for dogs is $20 per night, per pet.

Strasburg
$–$$ Denver East/Strasburg KOA and Kamping Kabins, 1312 Monroe St., 303-622-9274, 800-562-6538, www.koa.com. There's a $5 fee per night, per dog for dogs to stay in the camper cabins (bring your own bedding and cooking supplies).

Stratton
$$–$$$ Best Western Golden Prairie Inn, 700 Colorado Ave., 719-348-5311, 800-626-0043, www.bestwesterncolorado

.com. The motel has several rooms that dogs can stay in, with a $50 deposit and a $10 per dog nightly fee.

CAMPGROUNDS

Pawnee National Grassland. The campground is at the Crow Valley Recreation Area, about 25 miles east of Greeley near the intersection of Hwy. 14 and CR 77. There are 10 individual sites (seven single and three double), plus some group sites that must be reserved in advance.

State park campgrounds: **Bonny Lake State Park**, near Idalia, off Hwy. 385 (190 sites among four campgrounds); **Jackson Lake State Park**, northwest of Fort Morgan, off Hwy. 144 (260 sites among seven campgrounds); **North Sterling Reservoir State Park**, northwest of Sterling off CR 33 (141 sites among three campgrounds).

WORTH A PAWS

Paws and Sneakers. This annual 5K run/walk for dogs and their owners is held the first Saturday of April. The course winds through Riverside Park in Evans. The event's proceeds, raised through registration fees, pledges, and community sponsors, benefit the Humane Society of Weld County. Participation gets you a T-shirt, your pooch some goodies, and the both of you a great time.

After the run, stick around for the Canine Carnival, in which your dog can compete for honors such as best trick or best kiss. For more information, call the Humane Society at 970-506-9550 or go to www.weldcountyhumane.org.

DOGGIE DAYCARE

Evans

The Dog House, 1009 31st St., 970-353-9301, www.evansdoghouse.com. $12/day. This is a small, home-based daycare. Open by appointment only.

Greeley

Serious Fun at West Ridge, 6525 W. 28th St., 970-330-5150, www.seriousfun .wrah.net. $20/day. The facility is affiliated with the West Ridge Animal Hospital; dogs have indoor/outdoor areas to play in, and you can track Fido's day via the on-site Web cam. Open 7 AM–7 PM, Monday to Friday.

Camp Bow Wow, 3005 W. 29th St., 970-346-2275, www.campbowwow.com/us/co/greeley. $20/day, $15 per additional dog; $13/half-day. Campers must go through a free interview day before being accepted. The Camp Bow Wow experience includes separate playgroups into which dogs are placed based on size and temperament; they have all-day access to indoor and outdoor play areas with dog-specific play equipment and, in warmer weather, wading pools. You can keep tabs on the great time your pooch is having via the online Camper Cam. Open 7 AM–7 PM, Monday to Friday; 7 AM–10 AM and 4 PM–7PM, Saturday and Sunday.

RUFhouse Doggy Daycare, 2680 1st Ave., 970-395-9808. $2/hour. Dogs must pay a two-hour visit before coming to full-time daycare. A climate-controlled indoor space has futons and cushions for dogs to lounge on. Outside are 2 acres of play yards, with wading pools in summer, where dogs of all sizes play together. Open 7:30 AM–5:30 PM, Monday to Friday.

Tail Waggers, 3616 W. 10th St., 970-353-3736. $18/day. Dogs have access to indoor/outdoor runs. Open 6:30 AM–7 PM, Monday to Friday; 9 AM–5 PM, Saturday.

Windsor

K-9 Bed and Biscuit, 14253 Hwy. 392, 970-352-5330. $8/day. Dogs stay in indoor/outdoor runs and enjoy an outside play area several times a day. Open 8:30 AM–5:30 PM, Monday to Friday; 8:30 AM–4 PM, Saturday.

PET PROVISIONS

Fort Morgan
Murdoch's Home and Ranch Supply, 1207 W. Platte Ave., 970-542-1515

Greeley
PETCO, 4751 W. 29th St., 970-330-5941, www.petco.com. The store also has a self-service dog wash; a wash is $12 and includes shampoo, towels, and grooming utensils.

PetSmart, 2833 35th Ave., 970-330-3790, www.petsmart.com

Tail Waggers, 3616 W. 10th St., 970-353-3736

Windsor
Happy Paws, 510 Main St., 970-686-5547

CANINE ER

Burlington
Vondy and Powell Veterinarians, 11675 Hwy. 385, 719-346-7341. Open 7 AM–5 PM, Monday to Friday; by appointment on Saturday.

Evans
Pet Emergency Treatment Services, 3629 23rd Ave., 970-339-8700, www.pet emergency.net. Open 6 PM–8 AM, Monday to Thursday; 6 PM Friday–8 AM Monday, 24 hours on holidays.

Fort Morgan
Fort Morgan Veterinary Clinic, 1215 E. Burlington, 970-867-9477. Open 8 AM–5 PM, Monday to Friday; 9 AM–noon, Saturday.

Greeley
West Ridge Animal Hospital (AAHA certified), 8235 20th St., 970-330-7283, www.wrah.net. Open 8 AM–9 PM, Monday to Friday; 8 AM–5 PM, Saturday; 9 AM–1 PM, Sunday.

Limon
Limon Veterinary Clinic, 1005 Immel, 719-775-9773. Open 8 AM–5 PM, Monday to Friday; 8 AM–noon, Saturday.

Sterling
Veterinary Medical Clinic (AAHA certified), 211 El Camino St., 970-522-3321. Open 8 AM–5 PM, Monday, Tuesday, Thursday, Friday; 8 AM–noon, Wednesday and Saturday.

RESOURCES

Colorado Welcome Center, I-70 near Colorado/Kansas border, Burlington, 719-346-5554

Greeley Convention and Visitors Bureau, 902 7th Ave., Greeley, 970-352-3566, 800-449-3866, www.greeleycvb.com

Northeast Colorado Travel Region, 451 14th St., Burlington, 719-346-7019, 800-777-9075, www.northeastcolorado tourism.com

Pawnee National Grassland Ranger District, 660 O St., Greeley, 970-353-5000

Six
Estes Park

THE BIG SCOOP

This area's primary tourist draw—Rocky Mountain National Park—becomes a lot less attractive if you're visiting with your dog: you can't bring him on any hikes within the park. To the north, east, and south of Estes Park, however, is a range of national forest trails that you and your furry cohiker can enjoy together.

Dog guidelines to live by when in Estes: (1) remind your owner to keep you leashed within the city limits and not to leave you unattended in front of a store or restaurant; (2) leave the elk alone—they don't want to play with you; and (3) keep your paws off the park trails—otherwise your owner will have to pay a fine, which just might come out of your dog-treat allowance.

TAIL-RATED TRAILS

At one time, the forest service proposed a management plan that would have banned dogs completely from the eastern half of the Indian Peaks Wilderness Area, south of Rocky Mountain National Park, if compliance with the mandatory leash law was less than 90 percent five years after the plan's enactment. Although the plan was not approved, be extra diligent about keeping your dog leashed when in this area so that the ban idea is not resurrected (none of the trails described here are in the wilderness area). Note that if you decide to hike **St. Vrain Mountain** outside of Allenspark, you're supposed to turn around before reaching trail's end: part of the trail goes through a short section of Rocky Mountain National Park, and dogs are not allowed on this part. (You could also skirt this section alto-

gether by heading off trail, but you didn't hear it from me.) And though the **Twin Sisters Trail** is in a separate location, it's on national park property and is therefore off-limits to dogs. In addition to the trails listed below, you could hike with your dog in the **Pierson Park** and **Johnny Park** areas (see Cycling for Canines).

Crosier Mountain
Distance: 8 miles round-trip
Elevation gain: 2,010 feet
Trailhead: From the intersection of Hwys. 34 and 36 in Estes Park, take Hwy. 34 west, past the Stanley Hotel. Make a right onto Devil's Gulch Rd. After about 7 miles, you'll reach the hamlet of Glen Haven. Look for the Crosier Mountain Trail sign on the right, just before a horse-rental operation. You'll need to park across the street, however, as the road leading to the trailhead is a private drive.
Dogs can be off leash.

This is a marvelous hike that will capture both your and your dog's interest with a variety of terrain and landscape. Walk up the private road (you'll probably want to keep your dog on a leash during this part) and hook up with the actual trail on the right. Be aware that the trail gets high horse use in the summer, which means that if your dog is like most, he'll try to help himself to "snacks" along the way. The trail begins by switchbacking up, though not too steeply, through stands of ponderosa pine. At .5 mile, you'll pass a signed turnoff to the H-G Ranch, the first of a couple you'll come to. Shortly after, your dog can pause for refreshment at a small stream. The trail

On top of the world at Estes Valley Dog Park.

Regulations: Dogs must have collars and tags and be at least three months old; clean up after your dog and have a leash on hand for each dog; there's a maximum of three dogs per owner.

Dogs can be off leash.

The Estes dog park has it all: ample room to play, a swim area, an agility course, and awesome views. There are also buckets of water, poop bags, and trash cans. The park is divided into two sections, each ringed with a chain-link fence. In one, there's a large sandy expanse for dogs to run themselves silly—all that's needed is the scent of coconut oil, and you could swear you're at the beach. Dogs, in fact, do have the chance to swim in part of Lake Estes; a gate leads to the water from the park and, when it's warm, there's often a hoard of splashing pups. Dogs who enjoy a bit of a challenge head to the park's other section, where a two-way ramp, a tunnel, and a large frame that can be jumped through make up a short obstacle course. If you tire of watching your dog have fun, look up and take in the background of peaks in Rocky Mountain National Park, including the distinctive Twin Owls within rocky Lumpy Ridge.

then narrows and leads you to perhaps the most beautiful part of the hike, Piper Meadow, a vast expanse studded with wildflowers in the summer. The Mummy Range and other mountains in the park stretch out to the west. Stay left at the fork, and follow the trail as it crosses above the meadow. After passing another trail junction, you'll climb a series of switchbacks leading up the hillside above the meadow. Hike past another junction atop a small saddle. The next stretch goes through thick stands of lodgepole pine, passing yet another trail junction. The final .5-mile ascent to the summit gets rocky and quite steep. The trail ends at a spectacular vista atop the 9,250-foot peak, with views to Longs Peak.

Coulson Gulch

Distance: 5.6 miles round-trip

Elevation gain: 900 feet (which comes on the way out)

Trailhead: From the point where Hwy. 7 intersects it at Lake Estes, drive south on Hwy. 36 for just under 10 miles and take the turnoff for Big Elk Meadows (CR 47) on the right. Drive for 3.1 miles and veer left at the fork; after .5 miles on the dirt road, turn sharply left into a large parking area along a fence (the road continues on as the Johnny Park four-wheel-drive route). The last .1 mile is a little rough, so you may want to park at the side of the road if you have a low-clearance vehicle.

Estes Valley Dog Park

Access: The park is located at the corner of Community Dr. and North St. Vrain Ave. (Hwy. 36).

The trail begins next to three tall log posts (a four-wheel-drive road also goes out of the parking area—this is not the trail). *Dogs can be off leash.*

We met a couple of mountain bikers on this quiet, scenic trail who had just discovered it the weekend before and referred to it as the "ssshh" trail. After some debate over whether to publicize it, my friend Sean and I were outnumbered by our three dogs, who made a case for sharing it with their canine brethren as another alternative to the forbidden trails of the national park.

One of the features in the canine obstacle course at Estes Valley Dog Park.

The trail heads downhill through a meadow before entering an area of widely spaced ponderosa pine. A small stream runs alongside the trail through the gulch, providing refreshment for thirsty canines. Eventually, a short, steep climb leads you out of the gulch onto a side hill, from which you'll gain a nice view of the surrounding foothills. After switchbacking down again through the pines, you'll come to a small clearing with the remains of a cabin. Next up is a huge expanse of meadow known as Higgins Park (bring a tennis ball if Fido really wants to romp). At the meadow's south end, take a right on the dirt track and continue for about 25 minutes or so to the bridge over rushing North St. Vrain Creek. This makes a good spot for a well-earned doggie

paddle and is the turnaround point for this hike. If you're up for a longer excursion, however, you can continue across the bridge, following the **Button Rock Trail** west for about 1.5 miles, then heading north (right) on the little-used North **Sheep Mountain Trail**, which runs along a side creek. It's then possible to loop back to the Coulson Gulch trailhead via the Johnny Park four-wheel-drive road, for a total distance of about 8 miles.

Lily Mountain

Distance: 4 miles round-trip
Elevation gain: 1,006 feet
Trailhead: Take Hwy. 7 south from Estes Park. At 5.7 miles, look for a small parking pullout on the right as well as a small brown Lily Mountain sign and blue call-box sign. *Dogs can be off leash.*

A popular hike close to Estes Park, 9,786-foot Lily Mountain lies just outside the park boundary; therefore, dogs are allowed, and because it's on national forest land, they can even explore leash free. You'll need to bring water for the both of you, as there's none along the trail. Clover likes this hike because it remains primarily in ponderosa and lodgepole pine, which means she finds an ample supply of sticks to carry around. The first half of the trail parallels Hwy. 7, though as you make the moderate climb, the noise from the busy highway begins to fade. And during the ascent, you'll pass lots of vista points that look down into the Estes valley. The peaks of Twin Sisters rise directly to the east. Stay left at an unmarked fork; from this point, the trail switchbacks up the mountain. As you approach the top, the trail becomes harder to follow; look for the rock cairns. The final ascent involves a bit of rock scrambling, but nothing that the agile dog won't be able to handle. The reward is a panoramic view of the park's lofty peaks.

Lion Gulch

Distance: 5.6 miles roundtrip to Homestead Meadows

Elevation gain: 1,300 feet

Trailhead: From Estes Park, head south on Hwy. 36 for 8 miles. Then look for the parking area and trailhead on the right.

Dogs can be off leash.

The hike begins with a short descent down to the Little Thompson River. After crossing this, the trail follows a smaller stream on the ascent up the gulch, criss-crossing it several times via bridges and logs laid across. You'll enjoy the sweet smell of pine as you travel. Shortly before reaching the first meadow, a great spot for summer wildflowers, the trail turns into an old dirt road. Pause to read the trailside sign that will educate you and your dog about the Homestead Act of 1862, in case you've forgotten that part of your high-school history class. Once at the meadows, you can hike to as many as eight homesteads or a sawmill (distances range from .25 mile to 2 miles one way). The homesteads, which date from 1889 to 1923, are in various states of degeneration, but you'll still be able to appreciate their scenic settings. Fido, in the meantime, can enjoy the open terrain and, if thirsty, refresh himself at the horse trough in the first meadow.

Lake Estes Trail

Distance: 3.8-mile loop

Elevation gain: 120 feet

Access: The easiest place to pick up the trail is behind the chamber of commerce building, just east of the intersection of Hwys. 34 and 36.

Dogs must be leashed.

Great for a scenic stroll close to town, this paved path encircles Lake Estes, where your dog can do a bit of on-leash splashing in the water and, perhaps, gaze longingly at the ducks. And you'll get a nice view of the park's eastern peaks. A spur of the trail runs along the Big Thompson River from the lake to Riverside Plaza downtown.

Rocky Mountain National Park. In case your dog missed the explanation at the beginning of the chapter, here's a recap: the park is just not a dog-friendly place. Dogs can come along to campgrounds and picnic areas in the park as long as they're on a leash six feet long or less. And they can venture up to 100 feet from roadways or parking areas. That's it—all trails have been designated canine free. And in case you're thinking of leaving Fido in the car or tied up at a trailhead or campsite, that's a no-no, too. Your best bet is to stay at a place where you can leave your dog unattended in the room or to board him during the time you plan to be in the park.

CANINE COOL-OFF

Is Fido craving a cool drink in downtown Estes Park? Bring him to Riverside Plaza, where a fountain and surrounding pool (as well as the nearby Big Thompson River) can provide some relief.

CYCLING FOR CANINES

Several four-wheel-drive roads on national forest land provide good spots for taking the pooch for a pedal. The **Pierson Park** area is accessible from Fish Creek Rd., near the east end of Lake Estes. The **Johnny Park** area can be reached from either Hwy. 36 south (at the forest service access sign for Big Elk Meadows; see Coulson Gulch in Tail-Rated Trails) or from Big Owl or Cabin Creek Rds. off Hwy. 7 south. To reach **Pole Hill**, follow the Forest Access sign off Hwy. 36 north, just before the final descent into the Estes valley. The forest service office (see Resources) has maps of all these areas.

POWDERHOUNDS

Finding places to ski and snowshoe with your dog in the Estes Park area generally means having to venture southwest toward Nederland (see Chapter 2). The Estes valley does not hold snow for very long, making national forest trails iffy for skiing. Rocky Mountain National Park, of course, is off-limits, and trails just south of Estes are in the Indian Peaks Wilderness, where leashes are required.

CREATURE COMFORTS

Unless otherwise stated, dogs should not be left unattended in the room or cabin.

Allenspark

$$–$$$ Sunshine Mountain Lodge, 18078 Hwy. 7 (2 miles south of Allenspark), 303-747-2840, 888-747-2843, www.sunshinemtnlodge.com. Billed as a bed-and-breakfast and wellness retreat, the lodge allows you and your dog to enjoy some quiet time together in six simple but cozy mountain cabins on 5 forested acres. The pet fee is $10 per visit. (The main lodge is available only to groups and does not allow dogs). The cabins range from one to two bedrooms, and all but one have full kitchens. Two also have wood-burning stoves. Breakfast is included in the summer and on winter weekends.

$$$$ Lane Guest Ranch, 12 miles south of Estes Park off Hwy. 7, 303-747-2493, www.laneguestranch.com. A vacation at this family-oriented guest ranch is a treat for everyone, including the dog. In operation since 1953, the ranch accommodates up to 70 guests and has a staff of about 55. There are 25 cozy one- and two-bedroom cabin and A-frame units, most with private patios or decks, and more than half with private hot tubs. You can leave your dog unattended inside or on the deck while you go horseback riding or whitewater rafting. Other ranch offerings include guided hikes and fishing trips, evening entertainment, and a whole slate of children's activities. And of course there's plenty of hiking and biking nearby that you can do on your own with your dog (you'll need to keep your dog leashed on the 25-acre ranch property). The best deals are the weeklong package plans, which include three meals a day and all activities. And your pooch is sure to salivate when you tell him that free dog meals—steak, prime rib, or chicken breast—are available! Open beginning of June to beginning of September.

Drake

$$$$ Dripping Springs Inn and Cabins, 37 Dripping Springs Ln., 970-586-3406, 866-459-7687, www.drippingsprings.com. Dogs can have a restful stay at the inn's seven cabins overlooking the Big Thompson River (though not in the B&B rooms) for $15 extra per night, per dog. Though the guideline is dogs under 25 pounds, the owners do make exceptions, so if you have a well-behaved larger dog, just ask. There's a limit of two dogs per cabin, and you can leave your dog unattended inside as long as he's in a travel kennel and promises to stay quiet. The cabins, which sleep from two to six, vary in feel and decor, from rustic to southwestern to more contemporary. All have kitchens and large outdoor decks with private hot tubs; most have fireplaces. Be sure to keep your dog leashed outside. Open mid-May to mid-October.

Estes Park

$$–$$$ Colorado Cottages, 1241 High Dr., 907-586-4637, 800-468-1236, www

.colocottages.com. For an additional $15 per night, per pet, dogs are welcome in seven of the eleven cottages at this small resort, one of Estes Park's better values. Built in the early 1900s, the cottages have been hosting visitors to Estes ever since. Six of the canine-friendly units are studios; the other has one separate bedroom. All have fully equipped kitchenettes and wood-burning fireplaces. Outside, a hot tub, grills, and picnic tables are available for guests. Be sure to keep your dog leashed and picked up after. In summer, weather permitting, owners Carolyn and John Edrington host nightly campfires. Perhaps your dog can roast s'mores and sing songs with Dharma, the resident golden retriever. Closed in January.

$$–$$$ Columbine Inn, 1540 Big Thompson Ave., 970-586-4533, 800-726-9049, www.estescolumbineinn.com. This family-run motel allows dogs for $10 extra per night, per pet. In addition to standard rooms, three larger suites are available. All units are ground level, which makes taking out the pooch a bit easier. Open mid-May to early October.

$$–$$$ Elkhorn Lodge and Guest Ranch, 600 W. Elkhorn Ave., 970-586-4416, www.elkhornlodge.org. Does your dog like to sniff out historic sites? If so, he might like a stay at the Elkhorn, which is on the National Register of Historic Places and claims to be the oldest continuously operating guest ranch in the Rocky Mountains (since 1874). The accommodations, in varying degrees of aging rusticity, are spread among numerous buildings, all constructed more than a century ago: the 30-room main lodge; the nine-bedroom Coach House (Estes Park's original stagecoach stop), which is suitable for large groups; 10 one- to three-bedroom cottages (one was the first schoolhouse in Estes), two of which have cooking facilities; 13 studio cabins that sleep two each; five two- to four-bedroom "alpine houses," some with kitchens; and the Woodshed (originally an ice house), which has five small, basic motel rooms. Group camping facilities are also available, though they require a short hike to access. Dogs are $10 extra per visit (incidentally, if you're traveling with your parrot, you can bring him, too—at no extra charge). Activities at the ranch include horseback riding, fishing in a stocked trout pond (for the kiddies) or on the .25 mile of the Fall River that runs through the property, and hiking. Cruiser bike rentals are also available. One trail that starts from the ranch leads up 8,310-foot Man Mountain, known as a vision-quest site for early Native Americans. And, unlike hikes in the national park, your dog can join you on this one (as long as he's comfortable scrambling up rocks). Open from June through Thanksgiving.

$$–$$$ Estes Park KOA, 2051 Big Thompson Ave. (Hwy. 34), 970-586-2888, www.estesparkkoa.com. The campground, located across Hwy. 34 from Lake Estes, has both one- and two-room camping cabins (bring your own bedding and cooking supplies) and deluxe cottages, which include kitchens and bathrooms, gas fireplaces, and even TVs. Most dogs are allowed in both, with a maximum of three dogs and/or 100 pounds total per cabin or cottage. There's a $5 one-time fee per dog for the cabins; $10 per dog in the cottages. Dogs that are not permitted include Dobermans, Rottweilers, Fila Brasileiros, Japanese Tosas, Dogo Argentinos, and pit bulls. Keep your dog leashed at all times outside and take him to the designated pet walk area for his bathroom needs. Open May 1 to October 15.

$$–$$$ Machin's Cottages in the Pines, 2450 Eagle Cliff Rd., 970-586-4276, www.estes-park.com/machins. Dogs less than 25 pounds may stay in any of the

17 fully equipped, quaintly furnished cabins, which have from one to three bedrooms and fireplaces. There's a maximum of two dogs per cabin, and you can leave your dog unattended inside. Because the cottages are surrounded by national park, you won't be able to walk Fido very far from them. There's a three-night minimum stay. Open from late May through the end of September.

$$–$$$ National Park Retreats, 3501 Fall River Rd., 970-586-4563, www .nationalparkretreats.com. The 13-acre resort is located just outside the Fall River entrance to the park. Your dog is welcome to join you in the various lodging options: two motel-style rooms that sleep two; a pair of three-bedroom suites with full kitchens; and five fully outfitted cabins that sleep from four to ten. There's a $15 nightly fee per dog and a limit of two pets in a unit. Be sure to keep your dog leashed on the property. A two-night minimum stay is required from May 1 through October 31.

$$–$$$ Olympus Lodge, 2365 Big Thompson Ave., 970-586-8141, 800-248-8141, www.olympuslodge.com. About a quarter of the motel's rooms are pet friendly, with a nightly charge of $10 per dog (and a maximum of three dogs). All rooms have microwaves and refrigerators.

$$–$$$ Paradise on the River, 1836 Hwy. 66, 970-586-5513, 866-566-3422, www .paradiservcolorado.com. The location of paradise in this instance is along the Big Thompson River, about 1 mile from the national park. For $10 per pet, per night, up to two dogs each can stay in the one-bedroom, riverside Creek View cabin, as well as the 27-foot Moose Meadow RV permanently parked on-site. Both have full kitchens. (The other five cabins are off limits to dogs.) The canine welcome mat, however, is permanently rolled up

for Dobermans, Akitas, and pit bulls. Regular RV parking sites are also available. Open May 1 to mid-October.

$$–$$$$ 2 Eagles Resort, 1372 Big Thompson Canyon (about halfway between Estes Park and Loveland), 970-663-5532, 866-834-4724, www.2eaglesresort.com. The resort's 11 individually decorated units are like cabins, though only a few are actually freestanding. All but one have fully equipped kitchens, and some have fireplaces. One "cabin" is actually a mobile home that looks like a caboose from the outside. Dogs are permitted in nine of the units, with a $10 nightly fee per pet and a $250 credit card deposit. You must keep your dog leashed at all times when outside on the 5-acre property (you'll be able to take him to explore the Big Thompson River at property's edge). Open Memorial Day to November 1.

$$–$$$$ Discovery Lodge, 800 Big Thompson Ave. (Hwy. 34), 970-586-3336, 800-354-8253, www.estesdiscovery lodge.com. Dogs are allowed for $15 per night, per dog, with a maximum of three dogs per room. Most rooms have balconies, and the more upscale balcony suite rooms have fireplaces, too. The motel is on 5 wooded acres with a small catch-and-release fishing pond. The lodge also rents out a well-appointed two-bedroom log cabin with kitchen on 1.5 acres and the three-bedroom Heritage House, an older home; dogs are permitted at both, too.

$$–$$$$ Four Winds Budget Host, 1120 Big Thompson Ave. (Hwy. 34), 970-586-3313, 800-527-7509, www.fourwinds budgethost.com. The motel accepts dogs in designated rooms for $15 per dog, per night. In addition to standard rooms, two- and three-room suites and units with kitchens are available. A three-bedroom log house can also be rented (with a three-night minimum in summer).

$$–$$$$ Lazy R Cottages, 891 Moraine Ave. (Hwy. 66), 970-586-3708, 800-726-3728, www.lazyrcottages.com. These cottages situated 1 mile from the national park range from one to three bedrooms, with some that can sleep up to 14 people. Up to two dogs each are welcome in 10 of them for $15 per pet, per night. The cottages vary quite a bit in terms of decor, with some having more of a vintage mountain style and others more updated. All have fully equipped kitchens, and most of the dog-friendly ones have fireplaces, too. You can leave your dog unattended inside if he's in a travel kennel.

$$–$$$$ Rocky Mountain Park Inn, 101 S. St. Vrain Ave., 970-586-2332, 800-803-7837, www.rockymountainparkinn.com. At this full-service Holiday Inn hotel, dogs are permitted in first-floor rooms only, with a $30 one-time fee for up to three dogs per room. Facilities at the hotel include an indoor pool, restaurant, fitness center, and game room.

$$–$$$$ Rodeway Inn, 1701 N. Lake Ave., 970-586-5363, 800-458-1182, www.estesrodewayinn.com. Up to two dogs per room are allowed in certain ground-floor units at the motel (which doesn't include any of the suites). There's a $10 nightly fee per dog.

$$–$$$$ Rustic River Cabins, 2550 Big Thompson Ave., 970-586-8493, 800-530-3942, www.rusticrivercabins.com. For $15 a night extra, your dog can have his pick of eight fully equipped cabins (most are one bedroom), all with fireplaces and some with their own hot tubs. "I've had responsible pet owners, and they're better than some people with children," notes owner Tony Williamson. If you leave your dog alone in the cabin at all,

he should be in a travel kennel. And you can take Fido to explore the surrounding 15 acres along the Big Thompson River. Open March to end of December.

$$–$$$$ Silver Moon Inn, 175 Spruce Dr., 970-586-6006, 800-818-6006, www.silvermooninn.com. This nicely appointed motel allows one dog per room in eight of its standard rooms (unfortunately, none are the riverside units). You can leave your dog unattended inside if he's in a travel kennel. The complex is located right on the Fall River, about a block from downtown.

$$$ Braeside Cabin, 2179 Hwy. 66, 970-586-6845, www. braesidecabin.com. Formerly a sister property to the now-closed Braeside Bed and Breakfast, this renovated studio cabin sleeps two. Done up in a mountain cabin decor, with knotty-pine interior, cathedral ceiling, full kitchen, and wood-burning fireplace, it allows you and your dog to enjoy a great vista of the adjacent national park, and specifically Longs Peak, in comfort. Well-behaved dogs can be left unattended inside. Since there's no extra canine fee or deposit, "if the dog redecorates, we'd settle up at checkout," says the friendly owner. "But I've never had that happen," she adds. Make sure you keep it that way!

$$$–$$$$ Black Dog Inn, 650 S. St. Vrain Ave., 970-586-0374, 866-786-0374, www.blackdoginn.com. Up to two dogs at a time (no matter what their color) can stay with their owners in the inn's Mt. Olympus cottage for $12 per night, per pet. The updated, two-room cottage has Victorian-style furnishings, a large Jacuzzi in the bedroom, and a cozy sitting area. A fenced dog run is right outside the cottage. Though you can't leave Fido inside the run if you leave the property, he can hang out there while you get breakfast in the main lodge (where dogs aren't allowed), which was one of Estes Park's early houses, built in 1910. Note that the inn doesn't accept kids, even in the cottage.

$$$-$$$$ Bristlecone Inn, 215 Virginia Dr., 970-586-4370, www.bristleconeinn .com. Dogs are welcome in the inn's Deer Ridge log cabin, one of the more interesting structures they can stay in around Estes Park. Originally a forest service cabin that was built in 1909 in what is now the national park, it was moved to its present location near downtown in the 1960s. The one-bedroom cabin sleeps up to four and has a fully outfitted kitchen. With its abundance of interior wood and traditional mountain style, the cabin is a cozy refuge. There's a $200 pet deposit, and you can leave your dog unattended inside only if he's in a travel kennel.

$$$-$$$$ Castle Mountain Lodge, 1520 Fall River Rd., 970-586-3664, 800-852-7463,www.castlemountainlodge.com.Up to two "mature, well-mannered" dogs are allowed in each of about 10 of the cottages here, which range from one to three bedrooms, for a $15 fee per night, per dog. The knotty-pine-paneled cottages are fully equipped, and many have fireplaces. The pet policy clearly spells out the house rules, which include the admonition that "dogs who like to lie on the furniture must bring their own." Your dog will enjoy the scenic location on 35 acres along the Fall River, close to the national park; just make sure you keep him on his leash.

$$$-$$$$ Cliffside Cottages, 2445 Hwy. 66, 970-586-4839, www.cliffsidecottages .com. The three cute, homey cabins vary in size, sleeping from two to six, and all have fireplaces and full kitchens. In addition, owners Craig and Deanna Bigler have put in a fenced-in, grassy dog exercise area, where Fido can do his business and where you can also throw tennis balls for him. In fact, once they added a few lawn chairs to the enclosure, they've found it's a popular spot for guests to hang out with their dogs. You can leave your dog unattended inside the cabins, though if your pooch is friendly, the Biglers may also keep an eye on him for a few hours and bring him to the exercise area. Cliffside is on the western side of Estes Park, about 2 miles from the entrance to Rocky Mountain National Park. Open Memorial Day through mid-October.

$$$-$$$$ Estes Park Center YMCA, 2515 Tunnel Rd. (Hwy. 66), 970-586-3341, www.ymcarockies.org. The YMCA complex is scenically situated on 860 acres right next to the national park. Though dogs are not permitted in the lodge rooms or the "reunion cabins," you'll be able to choose from more than 200 fully equipped family cabins and vacation homes, ranging in size from two to four bedrooms and the majority with fireplaces, that can accommodate Fido for $10 per night, per dog, with a maximum of two dogs per unit. You can leave your dog unattended in the cabin; keep him leashed when outside it. The center offers an extensive slate of activities and recreation, including a fishing lake, indoor swimming pool, craft and design center, roller rink, minigolf course, volleyball and basketball courts, tennis, climbing wall, library, and museum.

$$$-$$$$ McGregor Mountain Lodge, 2815 Fall River Rd., 970-586-3457, 800-835-8439, www.mcgregormountain lodge.com. The lodge, near the national park's Fall River entrance, permits dogs in five of its cabins for $25 per night, per pet. The dog-friendly cabins range from one to two bedrooms and have full kitchens, fireplaces, and jetted bathtubs.

They're nicely appointed and more contemporary inside than many of the cabins in Estes. Make sure your dog is on his best behavior during your stay, which includes not jumping on the furniture, keeping out of the national park, which borders the property, and staying on his leash at all times when outside. If he's unsure about something, he can always check in with the lodge's two host dogs, Daisy, a Chesapeake retriever, and Tanner, a Bernese mountain dog. The lodge can provide a list of suggested doggie hikes as alternatives to hikes in the park, where dogs can't be on the trails.

$$$–$$$$ Shadow Pines Condos, 731 S. St. Vrain Ave., 970-667-1452, 877-333-6898, www.estesparkvacationcondos.com. This pair of two-bedroom, suburban-style rental condos that make up the Shadow Pines complex not only allows dogs but each one also has a private fenced yard for them. "We've had dogs from Chihuahuas to Great Danes," says the manager. The condos also have their own decks with hot tub and attached garages, as well as wood-burning stoves. You can leave your dog unattended inside. Once you tell Fido that the Estes dog park is within walking distance, however, he'll insist you take him there.

$$$–$$$$ Skyline Cottages, 1752 Hwy. 66, 970-586-2886, 602-274-6407 (in winter), www.skylinecottages.com. Your dog will join a long line of canine visitors with a stay at Skyline, as the owner has welcomed pets for more than three decades. The eight fully equipped cottages range in size from one-room units to two bedrooms. Most have fireplaces, and a couple have decks overlooking the Big Thompson River; three have separate spa rooms with jetted tubs. Skyline also rents two other small, one-bedroom cottages about .25 mile away; one has its own fenced pet yard where your dog can

relax on his own (as long as he's not a fence jumper) if you, say, go into Rocky Mountain National Park, which is just steps away. For all the cottages, there's a $12 fee per night, per pet, and you are able to leave your dog inside unattended. The property also features a large standalone riverside deck with picnic tables and other seating. Be sure to bring Fido by the office for a treat from the basket of dog biscuits; poop bags and plastic gloves are also dispensed. Open from the end of May through mid-October.

$$$–$$$$ The Stanley Hotel, 333 Wonderview Ave., 970-577-4000, 800-976-1377, www.stanleyhotel.com. Stephen King–loving dogs will appreciate a visit to the venerable Stanley, which served as the inspiration for King's book *The Shining* and, more recently, was the site of filming for a TV miniseries of the novel. If you train your dog to bark just right, he may even be able to freak out fellow guests with a passable imitation of the famous "red rum" line from the movie version of *The Shining.* In real life, the century-old Stanley, listed on the National Register of Historic Places, offers a range of rooms, suites, and villas, many furnished with antiques, though dogs are permitted only in the Manor House, adjacent to the main hotel, with a $50 one-time fee. You can leave Johnny, er, Rover unattended inside, but housekeeping won't come in while he's there. The hotel includes two restaurants and a small spa and also offers on-site ghost tours.

$$$–$$$$ Timber Creek Chalets, 2115 Fall River Rd., 970-586-8803, 800-764-4308, www.timbercreekchalets.com. These updated cabins on 11 acres at the foot of Castle Mountain, 2 miles from the Fall River entrance to the national park, allow up to two dogs in five units for a $15 nightly fee per pet. All have kitchens, and all but one have fireplaces. You can leave your dog unattended inside if he's in a travel kennel. The complex has an outdoor pool and hot tub.

$$$–$$$$ Triple R Cottages, 1000 Riverside Dr., 970-586-3708, 800-726-3728, www.rockymtnresorts.com. Dogs are welcome in all of these eight historic cottages near the national park for $15 per night, per pet. The two cabins that sleep up to eight have been remodeled and have fireplaces; the other, smaller cabins are more vintage in style (they date to the early 1930s, though they've been updated since). All have kitchens or kitchenettes. You can leave your dog unattended inside if he's in a travel kennel.

CAMPGROUNDS
Rocky Mountain National Park. The park has four campgrounds on the eastern side, and dogs are permitted at all of them.

National forest campgrounds: **Camp Dick** (41 sites) and **Peaceful Valley Campgrounds** (17 sites) are off Hwy. 72 (via Hwy. 7 south past Allenspark) at Peaceful Valley; **Olive Ridge Campground** (56 sites), off Hwy. 7, is near the Wild Basin area of the national park.

Private campgrounds: **Estes Park KOA** (see Creature Comforts).

WORTH A PAWS
International Dog Weight Pull Competition. Bring your dog to drool over the Arnold Schwarzeneggers of the canine world. Sanctioned by the International Weight Pulling Association, this two-day competition, held mid-February in the south parking lot of the Estes Park Convention and Visitors Bureau, allows about 50 dogs to show off their pulling prowess. Each dog is put into a competitive class based on his own weight. The competitors then vie to see who can pull the most weight on a sled on snow one day, the most wheeled weights the next. For more information, contact the visitors bureau at 800-44-ESTES or 970-577-9900 or go to www.estesparkcvb.com.

DOGGIE DAYCARE
Estes Park
The Animal House, 453 Pine River Ln., 970-586-4703, www.estesparkpetvet.com. $3/hour, with a minimum of $6. Affiliated with the Animal Hospital of the Rockies, the facility has indoor runs and a large outdoor play area. Open 8 AM–5 PM, Monday to Friday; 10 AM–11 AM and 4 PM–5 PM, Saturday, Sunday, and holidays.

Estes Park Pet Lodge, 1260 Manford Ave., 970-586-6898, www.estesparkpetlodge.com. $15/day. Part of the Animal Medical Center of Estes Park. Dogs stay in indoor/outdoor runs and also play in small groups in an outside yard. Drop-offs are 8–8:30 AM Monday to Friday, and 8–9:30 AM, Saturday and Sunday. Pick-ups are 4–4:30 PM daily.

Linda's Pet Care Services, 841 Dunraven St., 970-586-0340, www.lindaspetcareservices.com. $10/day; $18/day on Saturdays. Linda's bills itself as a home away from home for dogs and includes two indoor playrooms and an outdoor yard. Dogs are not confined to kennels and have ample opportunity to play together. Open 7:30 AM–5:30 PM, Monday to Friday; 10 AM–5 PM, Saturday; closed 11 AM–2 PM daily for naptime.

PET PROVISIONS
Estes Park
Estes Park Pet Supply, Upper Stanley Village, 970-586-8442, www.estesparkpetsupply.com. There's a self-service dog wash here, too; a wash is $16 and includes everything you need to get Rover clean and dry.

CANINE ER
Estes Park

Animal Hospital of the Rockies, 453 Pine River Ln., 970-586-4703. Open 8 AM–5 PM, Monday to Friday.

Animal Medical Center of Estes Park (AAHA certified), 1260 Manford Ave., 970-586-6898. Open 8 AM–5:30 PM, Monday to Friday; 8:30 AM–12:30 PM, Saturday.

RESOURCES

Estes Park Convention and Visitors Bureau, 500 Big Thompson Ave., Estes Park, 970-577-9900, 800-44-ESTES, www.estesparkcvb.com

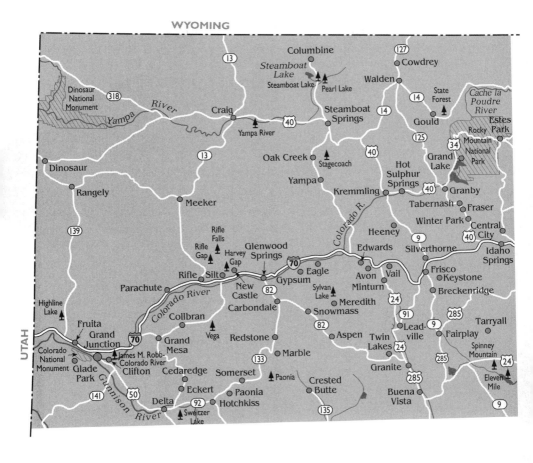

Dinosaur National Monument

318

Yampa River

Craig

Columbine

13

Steamboat Lake
Steamboat Lake ▲ ▲ Pearl Lake

127

Cowdrey

Walden

14

State Forest

Cache la Poudre River

Steamboat Springs

14

Gould

125

Rocky Mountain National Park

Estes Park

34

▲ Yampa River

13

Dinosaur

Rangely

139

Meeker

Oak Creek ▲ Stagecoach

Yampa

40

40

Hot Sulphur Springs

Kremmling

Tabernash ● Fraser

Grand Lake ●

Granby

40

Colorado R.

Heeney

9

Winter Park ●

Central City

Rifle Falls
Rifle Gap ▲ Harvey Gap ▲

Glenwood Springs

70

Edwards

Silverthorne

40

Idaho Springs

Rifle ● Silt ●

Gypsum

Eagle

Avon ● Vail

Frisco ●
Keystone

Parachute

Colorado River

New Castle

82

Sylvan Lake ▲

Minturn

24

Breckenridge

Highline Lake ▲

Fruita

Grand Junction

70

Collbran

Carbondale

Meredith

91

285

Tarryall

Snowmass

Lead-
ville

9

Fairplay

Colorado National Monument

Glade Park

141

Grand Mesa

Vega

Redstone

82

Aspen

Twin Lakes

24

Spinney Mountain

James M. Robb-
Colorado River

50

Clifton ● Cedaredge

133

Marble

285

Granite

Eleven Mile ▲

24

Somerset

▲ Paonia

Crested Butte

Buena Vista

285

9

Eckert

92

Paonia

Hotchkiss

135

Delta

▲ Sweitzer Lake

NORTHWEST COLORADO

●DENVER

🐾 Interstate Highways

🛡 State Highways

▲ State Parks

N

25 Interstate Highways

87 State Highways

0   10   20   30   40
Miles

Seven

Winter Park, Grand Lake, and Granby

THE BIG SCOOP

The area from Winter Park to the town of Grand Lake, which runs along the western side of the Continental Divide, has fantastic views of the rugged peaks along the Divide, several lakes nestled at the base of the mountains, and abundant recreational opportunities. And Grand Lake itself is Colorado's largest natural lake. So what's in it for Rover? Not quite as much as for you, unfortunately, primarily because dogs are not allowed on any of the trails in Rocky Mountain National Park, which lies adjacent to Grand Lake. And many of the other trails enter the Indian Peaks Wilderness area, where dogs must be leashed. But there are some great trails where your dog can hike off leash with you (including the Never Summer, Byers Peak, and Vasquez Wilderness Areas, where dogs can be under voice command) as well as suitable mountain-biking terrain for the both of you. And there's even a backcountry hut you can ski to with your dog!

Within the town limits of Winter Park, Fraser, Tabernash, Granby, Grand Lake, and Hot Sulphur Springs, you'll need to keep your dog leashed. In unincorporated parts of Grand County, you can walk your dog under voice command.

TAIL-RATED TRAILS

For additional trail information, stop by the Sulphur Ranger District office in Granby (see Resources), which puts out a few pamphlets with short hike descriptions, or look for an informative booklet, "The Official Hiking Guide to Grand County," by Susie Masterson, at local visitor centers. If you're starting a hike at the **Monarch Lake Trailhead**, note that dogs are required to be on leash on trails by the lake, even though it's not within the wilderness boundary. And you can hike with your dog at the **Winter Park Ski Area** as long as he stays on leash. Unfortunately, the **Baker Gulch Trail**, a four-tail-wag hike in previous editions of this book, is no longer accessible to canines; Rocky Mountain National Park used to waive its dog ban for the initial .5 mile of trail that goes through park land, but that policy has changed.

Devil's Thumb Pass
Distance: About 7 miles round-trip
Elevation gain: 2,155 feet
Trailhead: From Fraser take CR 8 off Hwy. 40 and drive for 4.6 miles to FR 128 (CR 8 takes several twists and turns along the way, so follow the signage). Turn left on FR 128 and drive just under 2 miles to a sign for Devil's Thumb Trail. Make a right and drive to the end of the road and the trailhead.
Dogs can be off leash until the wilderness boundary, about 3 miles in.

The trail, which is also designated as part of the 3,100-mile-long Continental Divide National Scenic Trail (CDT), brings hikers to Devil's Thumb, a prominent rock feature on the Continental Divide; from

Skijoring with your dog makes going uphill a cinch.

here you'll be treated to expansive views of the Fraser River valley, the Indian Peaks Wilderness area to the east, Winter Park Ski Area and surrounding peaks to the west and south, and the Never Summer Range to the north. From the trailhead, you'll hike along fairly level terrain. After a little more than .5 mile, the trail intersects the High Lonesome Trail coming in from the left. Stay right and cross Cabin Creek. The beautiful meadows you'll hike through are part of Devil's Thumb Park, a high-alpine plateau.

These meadows also allow you to glean a better understanding of forest succession. They started as beaver ponds (if you look closely you can still see where the waterline was). As the streams feeding the ponds continued to transport waterborne silt and sediment, the ponds gradually filled in, becoming the lush meadows surrounding you. In time, these meadows, too, will change: the rich soil will nourish lodgepole pine and spruce. And, in the far-off future, some enterprising beavers might take a liking to the landscape and use the trees to dam the stream, creating suitable habitat—and beaver ponds. And so it goes.

The trail now starts to climb abruptly toward the peaks to the east. Soon you'll be able to spot the Devil's Thumb, a lone spire rising from the ridgeline. The trail ultimately passes just south of the thumb

(it makes a good landmark, as the trail becomes faint near the ridgeline) into the Indian Peaks Wilderness area, where you'll need to leash Fido, and Devil's Thumb Pass, which straddles the Divide. Stop at the pass and savor the outstanding views in all directions before returning the way you came.

Columbine Lake

Distance: 5.6 miles round-trip

Elevation gain: 1,000 feet

Trailhead: Take CR 83 off Hwy. 40 at the south end of Tabernash (you'll see a sign for Devil's Thumb Ski Area and a forest access/Meadow Creek Reservoir sign). Stay left at the next two forks—the first left will put you on CR 84—following the signs to the reservoir, which is about 9 miles away. About .7 mile after FR 128 comes in from the right, you'll come to an unmarked fork; stay right. Once you reach Meadow Creek Reservoir, follow the sign to Junco Lake. The parking area and trailhead are by a small forest service cabin. Note that you'll have to pay a day-use fee of $5 per vehicle, as the trail is in the Arapaho National Recreation Area. Note that you'll have to pay a day-use fee of $5 per vehicle, as the trail is in the Arapaho National Recreation Area.

Dogs can be off leash until the wilderness boundary, about 1.75 miles in.

Begin hiking up an old road, which crosses a couple of streams and then ascends gradually through subalpine fir. At the entrance to a large meadow, you'll cross the wilderness boundary, which means it's time to leash up. Ahead on the right, Mount Neva comes prominently into view. The road skirts the meadow on the left, eventually becoming a narrower trail. Shortly after passing the turnoff for the Caribou Trail, you'll ascend away from the meadow into the woods; you should be on the left side of a creek. The trail then skirts a couple of other meadows before the final ascent to the lake. The last part of the trail is a bit trickier to follow, so you may want to let Rover sniff out the way. You'll ascend the left side of a scree-filled drainage, hiking next to a melodic stream. The trail then crosses a plateau, which includes some marshy areas, as it angles southeast toward the lake. The lake itself is at the base of a cirque and makes for a scenic lunch spot before the return hike.

Jim Creek Trail

Distance: About 3 miles round-trip

Elevation gain: About 820 feet

Trailhead: From Hwy. 40 west, .6 mile past the turnoff for Mary Jane Ski Area, make a right on an unmarked dirt road (it's actually FR 128). Drive 1.6 miles, staying left at the fork, to a small parking area by a water diversion dam. The trail begins on the right side of the parking lot, through the bushes. *Dogs can be off leash.*

This hike, which stays below tree line, doesn't include any spectacular vistas of the peaks on the Continental Divide or a specific destination. But your dog will be more interested in the fresh aroma of pine and spruce and the cooling waters of Jim Creek—as well as the fact that he can enjoy them leash free. During the summer, wildflowers dot sections adjoining the trail; this is also a nice fall hike, as a hillside of aspen rises above the trail. About the first .5 mile follows an old roadbed, gradually descending to creek level. The trail then winds uphill of the creek, alternately passing through stands of fir and alpine meadows. Eventually you'll cross a series of small streams coming down the hillside and come creekside again. A small open area makes a good turnaround point; the trail continues but gets increasingly sketchy from here onward.

A NATIVE CONNECTION

The Dog Trail, so called because the Native Americans who traveled it used dogs to carry their possessions, went through an area between Estes Park and Grand Lake.

ALL ACCESS

A barrier-free nature trail constructed by the Bonfils-Stanton Foundation and the Winter Park Outdoor Center allows a guide dog and his owner to enjoy a wilderness experience. The trail is located off Hwy. 40, across from the entrance to the Winter Park Ski Resort.

Rocky Mountain National Park. To reiterate (see Chapter 6), the park is just not a dog-friendly place. Dogs can come along to campgrounds and picnic areas in the park as long as they're on a leash six feet long or less. And they can venture up to 100 feet from roadways or parking areas. That's it—all trails have been designated canine free. And in case you're thinking of leaving Fido in the car or tied up at a trailhead or campsite, that's a no-no, too. Your best bet is to stay at a place where you can leave your dog unattended in the room or to board him during the time you plan to be in the park.

Shadow Mountain and East Shore Trails and part of the Knight Ridge Trail. Dogs are not allowed on the East Shore Trail, which runs along the east shore of Shadow Mountain Lake, or the Shadow Mountain Trail, which branches off it, because both are within Rocky Mountain National Park. Half of the 7-mile-long Knight Ridge Trail, starting at the Green Ridge Recreation Complex, also runs across park land, making it inaccessible to dogs. However, if you begin at the Roaring Fork trailhead at the end of CR 6, your dog can join you on the southern half of the trail, which goes through a portion of the Arapaho National Recreation Area and the Indian Peaks Wilderness area. Though dogs do not have to be leashed on the sections of trail in the recreation complex, keep a leash handy and a sharp eye out for wilderness boundary signs, as you will need to leash your dog on the sections of trail in the Indian Peaks Wilderness.

CYCLING FOR CANINES

Winter Park has developed a reputation for the quality and variety of its mountain-biking trails. But you won't be easily able to bike with Rover on the ski resort's network of trails, as dogs are required to be leashed on them. The **Creekside** and **Flume Trails** make an approximately 4-mile loop that begins and ends at the St. Louis Campground off CR 73, outside of Fraser. In the same vicinity, you can access the **Chainsaw Trail** (about 2 miles one way) and **Zoom Trail** (about 1.5 miles); the Chainsaw Trail goes out of CR 72 and intersects the Zoom Trail, which can also be accessed from CR 159. Water is available at places along all of these trails. For a different type of cycling adventure, bike 2.5 miles in to the **High Lonesome Hut**, outside of Tabernash. See Powderhounds for more details.

POWDERHOUNDS

Devil's Thumb Cross-Country Center, 3530 CR 83, 970-726-8231, www.devils thumbranch.com. This popular Nordic ski area, at the end of CR 83 out of Taber-nash, allows dogs on eight of its groomed ski trails: the 3.5-kilometer **Foxtrot,** the 3.5-kilometer **Left Field,** the 2-kilometer **Creekside,** the 1-kilometer **Elk Walk,** the 1-kilometer **Larkspur,** the 1.5-kilometer **Coyote,** the .5-kilometer **Horizon,** and the 2.5-kilometer **Ram's Curl.** Note that dogs

are not permitted on the snowshoe trails. A leash regulation is in effect, but there's no restriction on length, so you can outfit Rover with an extra-long leash to make skiing or snowshoeing with him in tow a bit more manageable. The center also rents skijoring equipment and offers clinics (see Worth a Paws). You'll have to pay a trail fee ($18) to access the dog-friendly routes; Fido is free.

Grand Lake Touring Center, 1415 CR 48, 970-627-8008, www.grandlakeski.com. The center, located about 2 miles west of Grand Lake, features two groomed dog loops for skiers and snowshoers as well as their canine companions. Both begin and end near the center's main building; the outer loop goes for about .75 mile, and the inner loop is approximately .3 mile. Dogs can be off leash as long as they don't run over to any of the neighboring Nordic trails. A few laps should tucker out Rover enough that you can check out the rest of the terrain while he snoozes in the car. Dogs are also permitted on the center's 1.5-mile snowshoe trail, though they must be kept leashed on it. You'll need to buy a $12 day pass; there's no extra charge for your dog.

High Lonesome Hut, 970-726-4099, www .lonesome-hut.com. A backcountry hut that your dog can come along to—wonders never cease! Actually, there are some good reasons why dogs aren't allowed at most huts, water supply being one of them (you don't want to be melting yellow snow!). But the High Lonesome has a well—and indoor plumbing—making the water source a moot point. The hut, which sleeps up to eight people, is a gentle 2.5-mile ski or snowshoe in from CR 84 out of Tabernash, in the Strawberry Creek region. You can either go the traditional route, humping your own pack with food and drink, or pay extra for the "hut master service," which includes gear transport and three meals a day. Either way, your dog will love being able to accompany you on a ski tour and telemark adventure. The hut is also available during the summer to hikers and mountain bikers.

Snow Mountain Ranch, Hwy. 40 north of Fraser, 970-887-2152, ext. 4173, www .ymcarockies.org. The Nordic ski area at this YMCA center has one dog-friendly groomed ski trail, the 1.6-kilometer **Travis' Trail,** on which your leashed dog can accompany you; it's also a popular route for skijoring and dogsled training runs. Dogs can also go on the ungroomed snowshoe trails and can generally be off leash; just make sure to keep Fido under control when you cross one of the ski trails. You'll need to pay a fee ($15, or $10 if you're a YMCA member) to use the ski and snowshoe trails; dogs are free.

CREATURE COMFORTS

Unless otherwise stated, dogs should not be left unattended in the room or cabin.

Fraser

$$–$$$ Pinnacle Lodge, 108 Zerex St., 970-722-7631, 800-834-9638, www.silver leafresorts.com/resorts/the-pinnacle-lodge. This newer hotel allows dogs in designated rooms for a $25 one-time fee. You may leave your dog unattended in the room.

$$–$$$ Rocky Mountain Inn and Hostel, 15 CR 72, 970-726-8256, 888-467-8351, www.therockymountaininn.com. A former bed-and-breakfast, the inn has five rooms, all with private bath, that are individually furnished in a comfortable B&B style, as well as dorm rooms. Dogs are welcome in two of the private rooms for $25 per night, per dog (they're not allowed to bunk up with others in the hostel rooms). All inn guests have access to a full kitchen, as well as laundry, common areas, and ski and bike storage.

$$$ Snow Mountain Ranch YMCA, Hwy. 40 north of Fraser, 970-726-4628 or 303-443-4743, www.ymcarockies.org. Located on almost 5,000 acres, the ranch has 45 fully furnished cabins, ranging from two to five bedrooms, in which you and your dog can stay (dogs are not permitted in the lodge rooms). All the cabins have fireplaces, and you can leave your dog unattended inside. When exploring the ranch property, you'll need to keep Rover on his leash. The complex also offers a restaurant, indoor pool, indoor climbing wall, tennis courts, miniature golf, and a Nordic trail system (see Powderhounds). Camping and RV sites are also available.

Granby

$$ Blue Spruce Motel, 170 E. Agate (Hwy. 40), 970-887-3300, 800-765-0001. Dogs are allowed in any room.

$$ Frontier Motel, 232 W. Agate (Hwy. 40), 970-887-2544, 800-367-3002, www .frontiermotelgranby.com. Under the same ownership as the Blue Spruce, the motel also allows dogs in any room.

$$ Homestead Motel, 851 W. Agate (Hwy. 40), 970-887-3665, 800-669-3605. Dogs pay a $10 one-time fee to stay here. Three units with kitchenettes are available.

$$$–$$$$ The Inn at Silver Creek, 62927 Hwy. 40, 970-887-4080, 888-878-3077, www.silvercreekgranby.com. This condo hotel, located near the family-oriented SolVista ski area at Granby Ranch, offers a range of rooms, from standards to studios, lofts, and suites with kitchenettes and fireplaces. Certain units within each type are pet friendly. There's a $25 one-time fee per dog. If you leave your dog unattended inside the room, housekeeping will not come in. The hotel complex includes an outdoor pool, hot tubs, bar and restaurant, tennis and racquetball courts, a fitness room, and a liquor store and hair salon.

$$$–$$$$ Shadow Mountain Guest Ranch, 5043 Hwy. 125 (8 miles from Granby), 970-887-9524, 800-64-SHADOW, www.coloradodirectory.com/shadowmtnranch. The seven fully outfitted log cabins at the ranch, which was first opened to guests in 1936, range from studios to three bedrooms, and some have fireplaces or woodstoves. The cabins date back to the 1920s and '30s, but have been updated. Rates include a full breakfast in the central lodge (except Monday and Thursday). You'll pay a $20 fee per night, per dog, to bring four-legged guests, and Fido can stay inside unattended, preferably in a travel kennel. But he'd probably rather be out with you, exploring the ranch's 80 acres leash free (though you'll want to keep him on leash around the cabins). Horseback rides are offered during the summer.

Grand Lake

$$ Bluebird Motel, 30 River Dr., 970-627-9314. There's a $15 one-time fee for one dog, an additional $10 if you have a second dog, and they're permitted in smoking rooms only. Note that the Peaks Point Cottages, which are affiliated with the motel, do not allow dogs.

$$ Elk Creek Camper Cabins and Campground, 143 CR 48 (near the park entrance), 970-627-8502, 800-ELK-CREEK, www.elkcreekcamp.com. Dogs are allowed in the 14 camper cabins for a $7 one-time fee per dog. "We're doggie people," says the owner, "but we don't want things getting torn up." You'll need to supply your own bedding. Four of the cabins are heated and are available for rental through approximately the end of March; the rest of the campground is open May 1 to September 30.

$$ Sunset Motel, 505 Grand Ave., 970-627-3318. The motel is under the same ownership as the Bluebird (see earlier entry) and shares the same pet policy.

$$–$$$ A Gathering Place, 207 Garfield, 941-623-3720, www.vrbo.com/86011. These six one- and two-bedroom cabins in town can be rented individually as well as together, for a large group. Dogs are allowed for $10 per night, per pet. Four have been remodeled with pine interior finishings and new kitchens and bathrooms; the other two are more rustic, but do have updated kitchens and baths. If you leave your dog unattended inside, he must be in a travel kennel. A fire pit and barbecue deck are on the property. And Fido might do a double take when he encounters the large bear outside the cabins; tell him to relax—it's made of recycled beverage cans, melted down and remolded. Open May 15 to October 1.

$$–$$$$ Columbine Cabins, 416 Grand Ave., 970-627-0800, www.columbinecabins.com. There's a $20 nightly fee to stay with your dog at these cabins in downtown Grand Lake. The complex consists of seven one-bedroom cabins, with knotty-pine walls, that sleep up to six; one two-bedroom cabin that sleeps up to eight; and two large "suites" that sleep up to 10 and 12. All have full kitchens. You can leave your dog unattended inside as long as you let the front desk know. Triangle Park, for quick walks, is across the street.

$$–$$$$ Spirit Lake Lodge, 829 Grand Ave., 970-627-3344, 800-544-6593, www.spiritlakelodge.com. Dogs are allowed in three of the rooms at this downtown Grand Lake motel for $10 extra per night, per dog, with a maximum of two dogs per room. Some rooms have fireplaces, and some have kitchenettes.

$$$ Daven Haven Lodge, 604 Marina Dr., 970-627-8144, www.davenhavenlodge.com. The lodge, a Grand Lake fixture since the 1930s, allows most dogs in one of its 12 cabins, No. 38, for an extra fee of $15 per night, per pet; the one exception may be black Labs, as the housekeepers have found their fur particularly difficult to get rid of. This one-bedroom cabin sleeps up to four and has a full kitchen. Particularly well-behaved dogs may be left unattended inside. You and your dog can also enjoy dinner together on the outdoor patio at the lodge's Backstreet Steakhouse (there is usually a limit of three dogs at a time, so keep that in mind if you see a pack of canines clamoring for steak). Make sure to greet Buddy, the resident border collie/Australian shepherd mix, who can often be found lying in front of the fireplace or on the floor of the lobby.

$$$ Mountain Lakes Lodge, 10480 Hwy. 34 (4 miles south of Grand Lake), 970-627-8448, www.mountainlakeslodge.com. "Dogs are always welcome," says Paul Parker, one of the owners of this folksy resort situated in a wooded area on a canal that connects Lake Granby and Shadow Mountain Lake. Ten connected, fully equipped log cabin units (some with gas fireplaces) are available, as well as one three-bedroom log house with a fenced yard (for a higher rate). The charmingly rustic cabins are individually furnished with handmade log furniture and quilts and have vaulted ceilings. There's a $25 nightly dog fee, and four-legged guests are greeted with blankets and food and water bowls to use during their stay, as well as, eventually, dog beds. If your dog is a nonchewer and nonbarker, you can leave him unattended inside. Each cabin also has a small, individually fenced yard behind it. You can walk Fido on the surrounding 2.5 acres of property, which has great views of the Indian Peaks, and on the pathway that runs along the canal for several miles in each direction. A two-night minimum stay on weekends applies.

$$$–$$$$ The Historic Rapids Lodge, 209 Rapids Ln., 970-627-3707, www.rapidslodge.com. Located on the eastern end of town, this unique lodgepole-pine lodge opened in 1915 and its name refers to its scenic site along the rushing Tonahutu River, which flows out of Rocky Mountain National Park. Dogs are welcome in the two one-bedroom cottages, located .5 mile from the main lodge, and in the three historic one-bedroom cabins adjacent to the lodge. (The original lodge rooms, condos, and suites are not pet friendly.) The cottages have full kitchens, while the cabins have kitchenettes. There's a $10 nightly fee per pet, and Rover should refrain from jumping onto the furniture. The restaurant is considered one of Grand Lake's best. The riverfront area behind the restaurant is off-limits to canines, so just be sure to walk your dog elsewhere. Note that minimum-stay requirements apply on summer weekends.

$$$–$$$$ North Shore Resort, 928 CR 64, 970-627-3220, 877-627-3220, www.northshore-resort.com. Under the same ownership as Mountain Lakes Lodge, the resort has the same friendly dog policies (see earlier entry). The 10 attached, cabinlike units have full kitchens and knotty-pine interiors. Most are one and two bedrooms, but there is one 1,200-square-foot, three-bedroom suite. Best of all for your dog is that Lake Granby is about 100 yards behind the hotel, and he can engage in romping and swimming to his heart's content. A nearby marina also rents boats. There's a two-night minimum stay on weekends.

$$$$ Moose Lake Lodge, 303-740-7441, www.mooselake-lodge.com. The lodge is actually neither a lodge nor located on Moose Lake. Rather, four houses are available for rent, all of them right on

Sun Valley Lake, a private body of water about 3.5 miles northwest of Grand Lake. The moose reference isn't for naught; you may well spot a moose or two wandering around the lakeshore. Three of the houses—Elk, Woolly, and Log—are pet friendly. Two have four bedrooms, the other has two bedrooms. In summer, the owners charge $15 per dog, per night, if you'll have a house full of people; if your group is small or you're visiting during quieter times of the year, there's usually no extra dog charge. Fido can be left unattended inside only if he's in a travel kennel; don't tie him up outside, since his barking may easily carry across, and around, the lake.

Hot Sulphur Springs

$$ Canyon Motel, 221 Byers Ave., 970-725-3395, 888-489-3719, www.canyonmotelcolorado.com. Up to two dogs per room are allowed for $10 extra per night. You'll also be asked for a credit-card number as a deposit. Some rooms have kitchenettes. The front desk staff can direct you and Rover to nearby walking and hiking venues.

$$ The Riverside Hotel, 509 Grand Ave., 970-725-3589, www.riverside-hotel.com. Built in 1903 and open as a hotel ever since, the Riverside provides a comfortable, historic experience. You and your dog can stay in one of several pet-friendly rooms, named for past female residents of the hotel (which was reputedly a brothel at one point long ago). Rover can hang out unattended in the room, perhaps while you enjoy a meal in the hotel's restaurant or a drink at the elaborately carved bar.

$$ Ute Trail Motel, 120 E. Hwy. 40, 970-725-0123, 800-506-0099, www.coloradodirectory.com/utetrailmotel. There's a $10 fee per night for dogs. Some units have kitchenettes.

Parshall

$$$–$$$$ Williams Fork Lodging, 1160 CR 373 (about 10 miles from Parshall), 970-725-3336, www.williamsforkvacationrentals.com. If you and your dog are looking for a fairly remote place where you can spend uninterrupted time together in nature, this may be your place. The lodging consists of the Stone Guest House on 40 acres. The house has two suites that sleep up to four, and each suite has a full kitchen, deck with BBQ grill, and private entrance. An outdoor hot tub is available to all guests. Rent the whole house or rent just the ground-floor Williams Peak Suite (the upper-level suite is off-limits to dogs unless you reserve the entire house). There's a $50 one-time fee per dog, and the Williams Peak Suite includes a dog bed, toys, dishes, and a dog door into a fenced kennel. If you need to leave your dog behind in the house, you can do so at your discretion. The owners, who live nearby, can also lend you an indoor kennel. Horses are welcome, too, and a corral is available. The property has 5 miles of trails that your dog can hike under voice command, and Williams Fork Reservoir is 3 miles away.

Tabernash

$$$$ Devil's Thumb Ranch, 3530 CR 83, 970-726-5632, 800-933-4339, www.devilsthumbranch.com. After varying its pet policy in recent years, the ranch has settled on allowing dogs in two of its cabins, Wrangler and Ranch Creek, for $50 extra a night for one dog and $25 extra for an additional dog, with a limit of two dogs per cabin (dogs aren't permitted in the lodge rooms). The lucky dog who stays here can relax in comfort in the luxe rustic furnishings of these new log cabins with wood-burning fireplaces. The Wrangler sleeps two in its loft bedroom and has a microwave and mini-fridge; the two-bedroom Ranch Creek sleeps four and has a kitchenette. You

Tansy and a little cowpoke in a dog-friendly cabin at Devil's Thumb Ranch.

can leave your dog unattended inside, but housekeeping may not come in during that time. There's plenty to do and see on the 5,000-acre ranch: hiking, mountain biking, fly-fishing, horseback riding, swimming, ice skating, a luxurious spa, and two eateries, including the much-lauded Ranch House restaurant. Devil's Thumb Cross-Country Center is also on the property, and you can take your dog on several trails (see Powderhounds for more details). During your stay, be sure to keep your dog leashed and pick up after him.

 $$$$ Wild Horse Inn, 1536 CR 83, 970-726-0456, www.wildhorseinncolorado.com. Though dogs can't stay in the B&B rooms at the inn, they are welcome in two of the on-site cabins, for $35 extra per night for one dog, or $50 for two dogs. Each cabin has a king-sized bed, fireplace, and kitchenette, and you can either walk over to the inn for breakfast or have it delivered to your door. One of the dog-friendly cabins is furnished in a chic western style; the other takes its cues from the Southwest, with Spanish tiles, brightly patterned stained-glass windows, and a kiva-style fireplace. Well-behaved

pets can be unattended inside, preferably in a travel kennel. The inn pampers its four-legged guests with a welcome basket that includes treats, a sleeping blanket to use during the stay, poop bags, and a towel for paw wiping.

Winter Park

$–$$$ Viking Lodge, 78966 Hwy. 40, 970-726-8885, 800-421-4013, www.skiwp.com. The Viking, around since 1953, bills itself as a traditional European ski lodge. Room sizes and amenities vary, ranging from the very small "Nordic" rooms to larger "Alpine" rooms, some with lofts and kitchens. There's also a suite with full kitchen and fireplace. Note that during ski season and on summer weekends, there are minimum-stay requirements of two or more nights.

$$–$$$ Beaver Village Resort, 79303 Hwy. 40, 970-726-5741, 800-525-3561, www.beavervillage.com. This old-time ski lodge, with its distinctive A-frame architecture, opened in 1939. For a $20 one-time fee, dogs are allowed in any of the lodge's hotel rooms, but not in the condos. Rates from mid-December to April include buffet breakfast and dinner (not gourmet-style but hearty). You can leave your dog unattended in the room, though housekeeping won't enter during that time.

$$–$$$ Sitzmark Lodge, Chalets and Cabins, 78253 Hwy. 40, 970-726-5453, www.coloradodirectory.com/sitzmark lodgechalets. This small, older complex offers six units: four are basically motel rooms, though the owner refers to them as "cabin rooms," since they're all housed in one quadplex building. The other two are cabins that sleep up to six and have full kitchens. The nightly dog fee ranges from $5 to $15, depending on the size and number of dogs. An RV park and campground are also on-site.

$$–$$$ Valley Hi Motel, 79025 Hwy. 40, 970-726-4171,888-706-4173,www.valley-hi-motel.com. Dogs are permitted in several rooms for $10 extra per night, per pet, usually with a limit of two dogs per room. If your dog is in a travel kennel, he can stay unattended in the room.

$$–$$$$ Best Western Alpenglo Lodge, 78665 Hwy. 40, 970-726-8088, 888-726-8088, www.wplodging.com. The motel has three pet-friendly rooms, with a $10 nightly charge per dog and a limit of two dogs per room. A hot breakfast buffet is included in the room rate.

 $$–$$$$ The Vintage Hotel, 100 Winter Park Dr., 970-726-8801, 800-472-7017, www.vintagehotel.com. One of Winter Park's more upscale hotels, the Vintage offers a variety of lodging options, ranging from regular rooms to studios with kitchenettes and fireplaces, as well as one- and two-bedroom suites, that you can share with your dog. There's a $25 one-time fee for one dog, plus $10 for each additional dog. You can leave Fido unattended inside your room, but housekeeping won't service the room during that time. The hotel hands out blankets and treats to canine guests. Your dog will also want to get his mug on the picture board of four-legged visitors that's in the lobby; a staffer will take his photo. The hotel restaurant is the Five Mountain Tavern.

 $$–$$$$ Winter Park Mountain Lodge, 81699 Hwy. 40, 970-726-4211, 866-726-5151, www.winterparkhotel.com. The dog-friendly units at this large lodge across the street from the ski area are the forest-view rooms, at the back of the hotel. There's a $25 one-time pet fee for one dog, plus $10 per pet for any additional dogs. When checking in, your dog

will receive treats and a paw-printed blanket to use during his stay. He can be unattended in your room; the hotel prefers that you leave a contact cell-phone number at the front desk. Lodge amenities include the Moffat Station Restaurant and Brew Pub, indoor swimming pool and hot tubs, and a ski shop.

CAMPGROUNDS
Rocky Mountain National Park. The park has one campground, Timber Creek (98 sites), on its western side.

National forest campgrounds: **Arapaho National Recreation Area**, which includes Lake Granby, Shadow Mountain Lake, Monarch Lake, Willow Creek Reservoir, and Meadow Creek Reservoir, has several campgrounds, among them **Stillwater Campground**, off Hwy. 34 (129 sites); **Green Ridge Campground**, off CR 66 (78 sites); **Sunset Point**, 1.5 miles east of Hwy. 34 on CR 6 (25 sites); **Arapaho Bay Campground**, at the end of CR 6 (84 sites); and **Willow Creek Campground**, off CR 40 at Willow Creek Reservoir (35 sites). Also available are **St. Louis Creek Campground**, 4 miles from Fraser off CR 73 (16 sites); **Byers Creek Campground**, 7 miles from Fraser off CR 73 (6 sites); **Idlewild Campground**, 1 mile south of Winter Park off Hwy. 40 (24 sites); and **Robbers Roost Campground**, 5 miles south of Winter Park on Hwy. 40 (11 sites).

Private campgrounds: **Elk Creek Camper Cabins and Campground** in Grand Lake; **Snow Mountain Ranch YMCA** outside of Winter Park; **Sitzmark Lodge, Chalets and Cabins** in Winter Park (see Creature Comforts for details on all).

WORTH A PAWS
Skijoring Clinics. Ever wish you could harness some of the energy your dog has when hiking or tugging at her leash? With skijoring you can, and the Nordic center

at Devil's Thumb Ranch, which offers clinics at least monthly in winter, is a great place to learn. The sport involves a harness for your dog, a waist belt for you, and a leash with a bungee-cord attachment that connects the two of you. You stand on your cross-country skis, your dog pulls, and off you go. When Clover and I took a skijoring lesson at Devil's Thumb, our instructor pronounced her a natural, and, like many dogs, she seemed to love having a job to do. Skijoring is also a great way to take your dog Nordic skiing while complying with the leash law required at some ski centers. For more information on Devil's Thumb, see Powderhounds.

DOGGIE DAYCARE
Fraser
Byers Peak Veterinary Clinic, 360 Railroad Ave., 970-726-8384. $20/day. Open 9 AM–12:30 PM and 2–5 PM, Monday to Friday; 10–10:15 AM for drop-offs and 6–6:15 PM for pick-ups, Saturday and Sunday.

Mountain Dawg Outfitters, 505 1/2 Zerex (Hwy. 40), 970-726-8451, www.mountain-dawg.com. $5/hour, with a maximum charge of $25/day. Up to four dogs at a time can be in daycare. Mountain Dawg is also a pet supply store, and daycare dogs can either stay in crates or hang out in the store, depending on temperament. A dog door leads to a yard for supervised play sessions, and dogs also get walks in summer (or whenever the snow has melted). Open 10 AM–6 PM, Tuesday to Saturday (hours may vary in the off-season).

Tabernash
Rocky Mountain Dog Ranch, 970-531-8776, www.rockymountaindogranch.com. $30/day. This home-based daycare (and overnight boarding facility) is on 50 acres, where dogs can hike and refresh themselves in the pond and creek. There's also a 5,000-square-foot fenced area and the doggie lounge, a sunroom where dogs can nab a well-earned snooze. Call for an appointment.

PET PROVISIONS
Fraser
Mountain Dawg Outfitters, 505 1/2 Zerex (Hwy. 40), 970-726-8451, www.mountain-dawg.com

Granby
Paw Paw Patch, 62543 Hwy. 40, # J, 970-887-3211

Grand Lake
Grand Lake Sports, 900 Grand Ave., 970-627-8124

CANINE ER
Fraser
Byers Peak Veterinary Clinic, 360 Railroad Ave., 970-726-8384. Open 9 AM–12:30 PM and 2–5 PM, Monday to Friday.

Granby
Brooks Veterinary Service, 12 E. Agate (Hwy. 40), 970-887-2417. Open 8 AM–5 PM, Monday to Friday; 8–11 AM, Saturday.

Granby Veterinary Clinic, 458 E. Agate (Hwy. 40), 970-887-3848. Open 9 AM–5 PM, Monday to Friday; 9 AM–noon, Saturday.

RESOURCES

Fraser Visitor Center, 120 Zerex St. (Hwy. 40), Fraser, 970-726-8312, www.frasercolorado.com

Grand Lake Chamber of Commerce Visitor Center, intersection of Hwy. 34 and W. Portal Rd., Grand Lake, 970-627-3402, 800-531-1019, www.grandlakechamber.com

Greater Granby Area Chamber of Commerce, 81 W. Jasper, Granby, 970-887-2311, 800-325-1661, www.granbychamber.com

Sulphur Ranger District, Arapaho and Roosevelt National Forests, 9 Ten Mile Dr., Granby, 970-887-4100

Winter Park/Fraser Valley Chamber of Commerce, 78841 Hwy. 40, Winter Park, 970-726-4118, 800-903-7275; www.winterpark-info.com

Eight

Steamboat Springs and North Park

THE BIG SCOOP

Steamboat Springs, with its ski-town sensibility (which means lots of dogs) and miles of trails in Routt National Forest close at hand, is a dandy place to take a dog. If you're looking for a truly get-away-from-it-all trip, head to the North Park area northeast of Steamboat. The region combines ample BLM and national forest land with a location remote enough that your dog can explore leash free to his heart's content without disturbing other hikers (keep an eye out for wildlife, though).

Leash laws are enforced within the city limits of Steamboat Springs. In Routt County, you can have your dog under voice command. In Jackson County (North Park), dogs can be under voice command on county land; individual towns have their own leash laws.

TAIL-RATED TRAILS

For more hiking ideas, pick up a "Trails Map" brochure at the Steamboat Springs Chamber Resort Association (see Resources) or a copy of *Hiking the 'Boat*, by Diane White-Crane (the author's dog accompanied her on all of the hikes). The three state parks in the Steamboat area—Stagecoach, Pearl Lake, and Steamboat Lake—primarily focus on water recreation, though all offer some lakeside hiking opportunities, with the longest trail following the southern shoreline of Stagecoach Reservoir. State Forest State Park, outside Walden, is described in more detail later in this section.

Steamboat Springs

Mad Creek/Swamp Park
Distance: 7.8 miles round-trip to the Mount Zirkel Wilderness Area boundary and back

Elevation gain: 637 feet

Trailhead: Head west from Steamboat Springs on US Hwy. 40 to CR 129 (you'll see a sign for Steamboat Lake). Turn right and drive 5.5 miles to the parking area and trailhead on the right.

Dogs can be off leash up until the wilderness boundary.

Be aware that this trail can get heavy horse use on summer weekends. You'll start out climbing up a rocky hill for the first few tenths of a mile. The trail then meanders along a shelf high above Mad Creek before dropping closer to creek level. After going through a livestock fence, you'll spot a footpath leading down to the creek, a side trip your dog will no doubt want to take. Shortly after, you'll reach a junction; stay right on Trail 1100 (the sign says Swamp Park). A forest service building known as the Mad House sits to the south. The trail becomes a narrow singletrack rolling through a pasture. When you come to a fork where a split-rail fence curves to the right, stay to the left. You'll hike through a beautiful stretch of open meadow on an old wagon road. The next section of trail meanders through stands of aspen and again parallels the creek, this time at dog's-eye level. At about 4 miles, you'll reach the clearly marked wilderness boundary, the turn-around point for this hike. Remember that if you decide to venture farther, Fido will need to leash up.

Steamboat Springs Off-Leash Dog Areas

Regulations: Owners must have completed the city's off-leash training program and carry proof of it with them; dogs must be vaccinated and licensed; there's a maximum of two dogs per owner; owners must have a leash on hand; clean up after your dog; dogs in heat, aggressive dogs, and puppies younger than four months are not permitted.

Dogs can be off leash.

In a program created through the cooperation of the Steamboat parks department and an advocacy organization known as the Responsible Dog Ownership Group of Steamboat, two parks in town allow dogs to romp off leash: **Rita Valentine Park**, between Hilltop Pkwy. and Anglers Dr., and **Spring Creek Park**, .5 mile in on the Spring Creek Trail (see below for directions). Dogs also have access to the lower Spring Creek Reservoir as part of the off-leash area. At each park, the off-leash areas aren't fenced but are delineated by bamboo poles around the perimeter.

In order for your pooch to enjoy these off-leash privileges, however, you must first watch a short video on owner responsibility, available at the parks department (245 Howelsen Pkwy.) for viewing there or to take home. After watching the video, you'll be asked to sign a "Manners in Off-Leash Areas" document, and you'll receive a tag that you—not your dog—will need to have on hand when you're at the off-leash areas. The "certification" is open to both Steamboat residents and visitors.

For more information, contact the parks department at 970-879-4300 or go to www.steamboatsprings.net.

Soda Creek

Distance: About 3.5 miles round-trip

Elevation gain: About 200 feet

Trailhead: From downtown Steamboat, take 3rd St. northwest from Lincoln Ave., then make a right at the next block onto Fish Creek Falls Rd. Shortly after, look for a sign for Buffalo Pass and make a left onto Amethyst. Follow Amethyst until it ends in a fork at Strawberry Park Rd.; bear right. You'll see a sign on the right that points toward Buffalo Pass. Drive up Buffalo Pass Rd. to Dry Lake Campground on the left. Park in the large lot across the road.

Dogs can be off leash.

This is considered an unofficial trail and is not maintained by the forest service, even though it's on forest service land, so you won't find any information on it at the local ranger district office.

Kylie samples some of Steamboat's famed champagne powder.

Begin by walking on a service road just past the campground sign. When the road forks, stay right; you'll come to a gate barring vehicle traffic as well as a small wooden Soda Creek sign. After this point, the road turns into a smooth, gentle trail, descending gradually through aspen and ferns toward Soda Creek. When you reach a three-way junction, stay right to follow the trail (though you should consider detouring down the middle path to allow your dog a dip in the creek). You'll eventually reach a large meadow, prime dog-frolicking ground and, during the summer, a first-rate place to view wildflowers. The trail, which begins to become less distinct, goes along the meadow's edge. The end of the meadow, where the trail pretty much peters out, makes a good turnaround point.

Steamboat Ski Area/ Mount Werner

Access: You and your dog can speed on up the Silver Bullet Gondola, which goes about halfway up the mountain, and hike back down. The gondola operates daily from 10 AM to 4 PM from mid-June through mid-August. From the last weekend of August to mid-September, it runs on weekends only. Tickets are $10–$20. Though dogs ride for free, you can buy a souvenir Critter Card for your dog, a Steamboat pass with his picture on it, for $10 ($5 gets donated to the Routt County Humane Society).

The resort requests that you keep your dog leashed.

Most of the summer trail network is open to mountain bikers, so if you're out on foot, your best options are the hikers-only **Vista Nature Trail**, which makes a 1.25-mile loop near the gondola, and the **Thunderhead Hiking Trail**, a 3.8-mile trip down to the gondola base area. 970-879-6111, www.steamboat.com.

Howelsen Hill Trail System

Access: From Lincoln Ave., head southwest on 5th St. for two blocks to Howelsen Pkwy. (cross the Yampa River along the way). Turn right on Howelsen and follow it as it turns left into the parking area. *Dogs must be leashed.*

Outside of ski season, this popular, close-to-town network offers 10 miles of hiking, mountain-biking, and horseback-riding trails on city-owned Emerald Mountain, on the southwest side of Steamboat Springs. (In the winter, the area is home to the Howelsen Hill Ski Area, and the terrain morphs into downhill ski trails.) Since you and your dog will likely share the trail with lots of other users, make sure your four-legged companion interacts well with bikers and horses before setting out for a hike. Other than Blackmere Dr., a dirt road that heads up to a hilltop quarry, the trails are primarily singletrack and afford outstanding views of town and Mount Werner, the site of Steamboat's other ski area. Your dog might be interested in sniffing out the sulphur cave near the beginning of the Mile Run Trail (it's roped off, so you can only peer into it). During the winter, Blackmere Dr. remains open to hikers (or snowshoers) and their dogs.

Spring Creek

Distance: 10.4 miles round-trip

Elevation gain: 1,200 feet

Trailhead: From downtown Steamboat Springs, drive northwest on 3rd St. for one block to Fish Creek Falls Rd. on the right. Turn left onto Amethyst shortly after, then right onto E. Spring St. (which is E. Maple on the left). Park along the road. From November 15 to April 15, the trail is closed after the first 1.5 miles for winter elk migration. *Dogs must be leashed.*

"All the dogs come here," says one local dog owner about Spring Creek. Unfortunately, this has also resulted in a bit of controversy over leash laws—there are a lot of noncomplying dogs, and property owners near the trail have been getting upset. So make sure you do your bit not to make things worse. The trail is also a popular mountain-biking route, so ask Rover to keep a nose out for riders flying downhill. The first part of the hike follows a single-lane dirt road for about .5 mile to the Spring Creek Reservoirs. The reservoirs make a pleasant destination in themselves, and a separate footpath encircles them. After passing the reservoirs, the road narrows and bends to the left; follow the signs to the right to access a newer, rerouted section of the trail. As you ascend the Spring Creek drainage via a consistent, but moderate, climb, you'll crisscross the creek several times over a series of bridges, giving your dog ample opportunity to hydrate. The Steamboat Ski Area becomes visible to the right as you gain elevation. The trail ends partway up Buffalo Pass, in a parking area across from the Dry Lake Campground.

Yampa Core Trail
Distance: Runs for 6.29 miles along the Yampa River, from the James Brown Bridge on Shield Dr. to Walton Creek Rd., east of town
Dogs must be leashed.

This paved recreation path runs along the river, passing by the southeastern edge of downtown Steamboat Springs, the Howelsen Hill Ski Area, and the rodeo grounds before reaching a more undeveloped area in riparian habitat. It's a great spot for a close-to-town stroll with your dog—just keep an eye out for bicyclists and in-line skaters.

The only time CharlieDog sits still long enough for photos is during water breaks.

Fish Creek Falls
Distance: A little under 1 mile round-trip to view the falls
Elevation gain: 100 feet
Trailhead: From Lincoln Ave. in downtown Steamboat Springs, head northwest on 3rd St. (you'll see a sign for Fish Creek Falls). Take a right at the next block, which is Fish Creek Falls Rd. The falls are 4 miles ahead (there's a $5 fee for parking). *Dogs must be leashed.*

From the main parking lot, take the gravel-surface Fish Creek Falls National Recreation Trail (the other two trails are paved) to the Historic Fish Creek Bridge, where your dog can salivate at the 283-foot-high waterfall. Reward him with a dip in the creek. If you're feeling ambitious (and are suitably prepared), follow the trail 2 miles farther to the Upper Falls or 5 miles total from the trailhead to Long Lake, at 9,850 feet. As dogs are allowed off leash on this national forest trail, this could turn your outing into a three- or four-wag hike.

North Park

State Forest State Park
Look for a park entrance off Hwy. 14 west, about 20 miles from Walden and just before Gould. Hwy. 14 also runs through the park before reaching Cameron Pass. There's a $6 entrance fee.
Dogs must be leashed.

With 70,000 mostly undeveloped acres along 28 miles from north to south, this is by far the biggest of Colorado's state parks. There are 14 established hiking trails throughout the park. The 1.6-mile round-trip **Lake Agnes Trail** is the most heavily used, as it's short and incredibly scenic, nestled near the 12,400-foot Nokhu Crags and 12,940-foot Mt. Richthoven, the highest peak in the Never Summer Range in nearby Rocky Mountain National Park. The 11-mile round-trip **American Lakes Trail** is nearby. The trailheads for these hikes are off Hwy. 14 toward Cameron Pass. The least-used trails are those to **Clear Lake** (14 miles round-trip) and **Kelly Lake** (13 miles round-trip). Both lakes are at timberline, and you'll hike through pine and spruce forest to reach them. The trailhead is accessed via a road heading north shortly past the park headquarters. The **Ruby Jewel Lake Trail** is a relatively short 3 miles round-trip if you're able to get all the way up the four-wheel-drive access road to the trailhead. As this road is often not passable to the end, you'll likely end up parking somewhere along it and extending the hike's mileage. During any of these hikes, but especially the less-traveled ones, keep an eye out for moose, the park's "specialty." 970-723-8366, www.parks.state.co.us/Parks/StateForest.

CYCLING FOR CANINES

The **Mad Creek Trail** (see Tail-Rated Trails) is a scenic ride you can take Fido on. So is the **Coulton Creek Trail**, off Seedhouse Rd. (CR 64) north of Steamboat, though you'll want to ride it as an out-and-back rather than as a loop to avoid 1.5 miles of road riding. A network of jeep roads just west of **Steamboat Lake State Park** and north of **Sand Mountain** is a less-frequented cycling area: begin on FR 42, which runs west out of CR 62, and follow FR 480 to the left and around to make a loop. The top of **Rabbit Ears Pass**

offers a couple of biking options: you and your dog can take an approximately 6-mile round-trip ride to the distinctive Rabbit Ears Peak by following FR 291, which branches out of FR 311 past the Dumont Lake Campground (park at the beginning of FR 291). Or drive farther on FR 311 to the Base Camp trailhead (Trail 1102). From here you can ride to **Fishhook Lake**, **Lost Lake**, and **Lake Elmo**, up to a 6-mile round-trip.

POWDERHOUNDS

Dogs aren't permitted at any of the Nordic touring centers in and around Steamboat, but **Rabbit Ears Pass** is one of the most popular backcountry ski and snowshoe areas. Several trails start here, including the **West Summit Loop**, a 3.5-mile tour that doesn't cross any avalanche terrain. Note that dogs aren't permitted on the groomed Bruce's Trail on the pass. There are also trails off **Seedhouse Rd.** (CR 64) north of Steamboat, out of the Hinman Park and Seedhouse Campgrounds—watch out for snowmobilers in this area. And the road itself is unplowed after a certain point, providing a wide, gentle grade for skiing or snowshoeing. Refer to *Snowshoeing Colorado*, by Claire Walter, for details on these and other routes.

CREATURE COMFORTS

Unless otherwise stated, dogs should not be left unattended in the room or cabin.

Columbine

$$–$$$ Columbine Cabins, 64505 CR 129, 970-879-5522, www.cabinsatcolumbine .com. Columbine, located about 30 miles north of Steamboat, was once an active gold-mining town. The only buildings that remain are these historic cabins (the oldest is from about 1890), which have been renovated to accommodate guests, and a general store. The 14 rustic cabins are furnished and vary in their amenities: most have wood-burning stoves to cook on as well as hot plates, though a few have more modern kitchen facilities; most rely on the central shower house for bathing and toilet facilities; and one lacks running water. There's a $10 fee per night, per dog, for the first three nights (no charge after that) and a maximum of three dogs per cabin. It'll be a step back in time for you, and your dog is sure to enjoy the surrounding Routt National Forest and miles of trails nearby. Bring your skis or snowshoes to explore in the winter, as there's a 1-mile maintained loop trail on the property, and your dog can accompany you on it under voice control. Open May 15 to March 31.

Gould

$$ Never Summer Nordic Yurts, 970-723-4070, www.neversummernordic.com. Despite the name of this backcountry yurt and cabin system in State Forest State Park, dogs are allowed in summer (and most of the fall) only, usually from June to sometime in November. The eight yurts—round, tentlike structures built on wood platforms—and two cabins sleep from five to nine, depending on which one you book. You can drive up to all of them except for the Grass Creek yurt, which requires a .3-mile hike in, and the North Fork yurt, 1.1 miles in by trail. There's a two-dog limit per yurt, and be sure to pick up after your four-legged family members. Since you'll be in the state park, your dog must be leashed when he's outside.

$$ North Park KOA, 53337 Hwy. 14, 970-723-4310, 800-KOA-3596, www.koa.com. Dogs other than Dobermans, Chows, pit bulls, Rottweilers, and wolf hybrids are allowed in the camper cabins (you'll need to supply your own bedding and cooking gear), and they must be kept leashed when outside. Open end of May through mid-November.

$$ Powderhorn Cabins, 35336 CR 21, 970-723-4359, www.gouldcolorado.com. There are 15 cabins, all fully furnished and with kitchens. Dogs are permitted only in the 12 rustic ones, which have use of a central bathhouse, with a $20 one-time fee. You'll need to keep your dog leashed on the property. State Forest State Park is just a couple hundred yards away. Open Memorial Day to November 15.

$$ State Forest State Park Cabins, 56750 Hwy. 14, 303-470-1144 (in Denver only), 800-678-2267, www.parks.state.co.us/Parks/StateForest. Dogs are allowed in the six rustic cabins alongside North Michigan Reservoir in the state park for $10 extra per night. Four of the cabins sleep up to six; the other two sleep up to 15 and 21 people. All have wood-burning or propane stoves and bunks with mattresses. Bring your own bedding and cooking supplies.

$$$ North Park Yurts, 970-723-4070, www.neversummernordic.com. Affiliated with the Never Summer Nordic Yurts, these three new yurts clustered on 30 acres bordering State Forest State Park allow dogs year-round. The 24-foot-diameter structures sleep up to seven on a mix of beds and futons, and each has a wood-burning stove, kitchen area with cooking supplies, and solar lighting. If you're visiting with your dog in winter, take care to keep the snow around the yurt pristine for those who may choose to melt snow for water rather than bring in their supply.

Kremmling

$$ Allington Inn and Suites, 215 W. Central Ave., 970-724-9800, www.allingtoninn.com. The motel, opened in 2009, permits dogs in designated rooms for $10 extra per night. Your dog can be unattended inside the room.

$$ Bob's Western Motel, 110 W. Park Ave. (Hwy. 40), 970-724-3266, www .bobswesternmotel.com. Luckily, Bob likes dogs, though only enough to let them stay in smoking rooms.

$$ Cliffside Inn, 113 N. 6th St., 970-724-8949, 877-254-3374, cliffsideinnkrem mling.net. Dogs are allowed in all rooms and can be left unattended as long as they don't disturb others by barking. Each room has a refrigerator.

Oak Creek

$$ Oak Creek Motel, 408 Willow Bend, 970-736-2343, www.oakcreekmotel.com. One dog per room is preferred at this 10-room motel, with a nightly fee of $10. You can walk your dog off leash on the 1.5-acre property.

Phippsburg

$$–$$$ Black Dog Inn, 21601 Hwy. 131, 970-736-2430, 888-250-2430 www.black doginn.net. This small, recently renovated hotel 30 miles from Steamboat welcomes dogs in any of its 11 rooms (one is a suite with separate bedroom, sitting area, and kitchen, and several others have kitchenettes), with a two-dog limit per unit. The inn is named for Bubba, the owners' black Lab.

Steamboat Lake

$ Steamboat Lake Camper Cabins, Steamboat Lake Marina, 970-879-7019, www .steamboatlakemarina.com. These 10 cabins allow dogs for $10 per pet, per night, with a limit of two dogs per cabin. Each one has electric heat, a small refrigerator, and a coffeemaker, but you'll have to bring your own bedding and do any cooking on an outdoor grill. Two bathhouses have showers and toilets.

$$–$$$ Dutch Creek Guest Ranch, 61565 RCR 62, 970-879-8519, 800-778-8519, www.dutchcreek.net. The ranch, on 100

acres across from Steamboat Lake and bordered by Routt National Forest, offers a total of nine modern, fully outfitted log cabins and A-frames. Dogs are allowed for a $10 fee per dog, per night, with a limit of two dogs per unit. The owners ask that you keep your dog leashed when around the main lodge and cabins and the horse area. The ranch offers horseback rides in the summer and sleigh rides in the winter. Breakfast is included, and dinner is available by reservation.

$$–$$$$ Steamboat Lake Outfitters, 60880 CR 129 (7 miles north of Clark), 970-879-4404, 800-342-1889, www .steamboatoutfitters.com. This guest ranch is just across the road from Steamboat Lake State Park. You and your dog have a choice of lodging options, with a $40 one-time pet fee and a two-dog limit per unit: four rustic cabins, all fully equipped, that sleep from two to eight guests; four new fully equipped cabins, with two bedrooms and two baths; or 12 bunkhouse rooms, each with two queen beds and private bath. You can leave your dog unattended inside if he's in a travel kennel. There isn't a strict leash law, though if a lot of other dogs are around, you might be asked to restrain yours. The ranch offers guided horseback rides and ATV tours in summer. A general store is on the premises as well as a restaurant that serves breakfast, lunch, and dinner.

Steamboat Springs

$$–$$$ Alpiner Lodge, 424 Lincoln Ave., 970-879-1430, 800-340-9169, www .alpinerlodge.info. Dogs are permitted at the motel with a $15 one-time fee.

$$–$$$ Rabbit Ears Motel, 201 Lincoln Ave., 970-879-1150, 800-828-7702, www .rabbitearsmotel.com. Your dog may not know what to make of the neon pink bunny head on this family-run motel's sign, but for a $15 one-time fee, he can stay at the motel and gaze at it all night, if he wants.

$$–$$$ Super 8, 3195 S. Lincoln Ave., 970-879-5230, 800-800-8000 (national number), www.super8.com. Third-floor rooms are pet friendly, with a limit of one dog per room and an additional fee of $15 per night.

$$–$$$$ Comfort Inn, 1055 Walton Creek Rd., 970-879-6669, www.comfortinn .com. Dogs are allowed in certain first-floor rooms for $20 per night, per dog.

$$–$$$$ Fairfield Inn and Suites, 3200 S. Lincoln Ave, 970-870-9000, www.mar riott.com/sbsfi. Dogs are permitted in standard rooms with two queen beds on the first floor. There's a $25 one-time fee, and a maximum of two dogs per room.

$$–$$$$ La Quinta Inn Steamboat Springs, 3155 Ingles Ln., 970-871-1219, 800-753-3757 (national number), www .lq.com. There's a $10 nightly, per pet fee, and dogs are put in designated rooms. You can leave Fido unattended if you can absolutely vouch that he won't bark; you'll need to hang out the Do Not Disturb sign, too.

$$–$$$$ Nordic Lodge Motel, 1036 Lincoln Ave., 970-879-0531, 800-364-0331, www.nordiclodgeofsteamboat.com. Most of the rooms and suites at this nicely kept up motel are pet friendly; there's a $10 nightly fee for dogs. You can leave yours unattended in the room if you leave a cell-phone number with the front-desk staff.

$$$–$$$$ Holiday Inn, 3190 S. Lincoln Ave., 970-879-2250, 800-654-3944, www.steamboathi.com. Dogs are welcome in first-floor rooms for $10 per night, per dog. You'll be asked to fill out a pet form at check-in and leave a cell-phone number

so if you leave your dog unattended in the room, the hotel can track you down if he makes a fuss.

$$$–$$$$ Perry-Mansfield Log Cabins, 40755 CR 36, 970-879-1060, 888-672-6938, www.steamboat-springs.com. These seven charming rustic cabins 1.5 miles from Steamboat are located on the expansive grounds of the Perry-Mansfield Performing Arts Camp, which has been in operation since 1913. If your dog is a budding thespian, he'll enjoy coming here, as well as exploring the surrounding 76 acres (on leash). Dogs are permitted for a $35 one-time fee, per pet. The fully equipped cabins have from one to five bedrooms and wood-burning fireplaces and are available to rent from early September through mid-May. You can leave your dog unattended inside if he guarantees he won't practice singing or barking. Note that there are two- to five-night minimum stay requirements, depending on time of year. Reservations are taken through Pioneer Ridge property management.

$$$–$$$$ Ptarmigan Inn, 2304 Apres Ski Wy., 970-879-1730, 800-538-7519, www.steamboat-lodging.com. You can stay at this slopeside hotel with your dog for a one-time fee of $25 during the summer only (which is basically defined as when the mountain is not open to skiing—mid-April to Thanksgiving). Because the gondola is open for summer hiking, there is still some advantage to being mountainside.

$$$–$$$$ Scandinavian Lodge, 2883 Burgess Creek Rd., 970-879-0517, 888-672-6938, www.steamboat-springs.com. The lodge consists of condos, from studios to three bedrooms. Dogs are allowed in four of the units, which range from studios to two bedrooms, for a $35 one-time fee per pet. You can leave your pooch unattended inside as long as you leave a cell-phone number with the property management company. Note that there are two- to five-night minimum stay requirements, depending on time of year. Reservations are taken through Pioneer Ridge property management (which also has several pet-friendly homes for rent).

$$$–$$$$ Sheraton Steamboat Resort, 2200 Village Inn Ct., 970-879-2220, www.starwood.com. The huge, slopeside Sheraton permits dogs in third-floor hotel rooms (not in any of the resort's condos) with a $35 one-time fee. There's a maximum weight total of 80 pounds per room, so you could stay, for example, with one large golden retriever or two medium-sized dogs. The hotel used to close seasonally but went to a year-round schedule in 2009.

Walden

$$ Lake John Resort, 2521 Jackson CR 7A (17 miles northwest of Walden), 970-723-3226, www.lakejohnresort.com. The resort, located alongside Lake John, has four cabins with kitchenettes and private baths for rent. There's a two-dog limit per cabin, with a $10 nightly fee per dog. The cabins are heated, though the water is shut off in the winter, so you'll have to use the bathrooms in the main building. You'll need to keep your dog leashed on the resort's 14 acres, but dogs do have swimming privileges in the lake. There's a general store on-site as well as a restaurant (open from the beginning of May to the end of September) and an RV park.

$$ North Park Inn and Suites, 625 Main St., 970-723-4271, www.northparkinn andsuites.com. The motel has six pet rooms, all with kitchen facilities, and charges $10 extra per pet, per night.

$$ Roundup Motel, 365 Main St., 970-723-4680, 866-689-2866. Dogs are welcome in any of the rooms for a $10 one-time fee. Rooms with kitchenettes are available.

$$ Westside Motel, 441 LaFever, 970-723-8589, www.geocities.com/westside_motel/. Five rooms at this simple, friendly motel are designated for pets. You can leave your dog unattended in the room for an hour or two, and the owner may even take him on a quick bathroom break.

Yampa

$–$$ Royal Motel, 201 Moffatt, 970-638-4538. The owner emphasizes that dogs should be well behaved and well trained to stay at this small motel, housed in a building from 1906 that has undergone some recent renovation. You'll be asked for just a $10 deposit. Two of the seven rooms have private baths.

$$ Oak Tree Inn, 98 Moffatt, 970-638-1000, www.oaktreeinn.net. This newer chain motel accepts dogs for $10 extra per night. You can leave Fido unattended in the room as long as he doesn't whine, bark, or cry, according to the printed pet policy.

$$–$$$ Van Camp Cabins, 303 Rich Ave., 970-638-4254, www.coloradovacation.com/cabins/vancamp. There's an $8 one-time fee per dog to stay in one of these seven one-room cabins (note that they don't have kitchen facilities or running water—a central bathhouse serves all guests). The cozily rustic decor includes custom log furniture and handmade quilts. Behind the cabins is a stream and a campfire area. You can also bring your horse. Open May 1 to December 1.

CAMPGROUNDS

State park campgrounds: **State Forest,** off Hwy. 14 near Gould (219 sites); **Stagecoach State Park,** 16 miles southeast of Steamboat Springs on CR 14 off Hwy. 131 (92 sites); **Pearl Lake State Park,** 26 miles north of Steamboat Springs, via CR 129 to CR 209 (36 sites; these campsites are closed through at least spring 2010 because of potential danger from falling trees killed by mountain pine beetles; dogs are not allowed in the park's two yurts); **Steamboat Lake State Park**, 27 miles north of Steamboat Springs, via CR 129 to CR 62 (188 sites; these campsites are closed through at least spring 2010 because of potential danger from falling trees killed by mountain pine beetles).

National forest campgrounds: **Hinman Park Campground**, 20 miles north of Steamboat Springs (13 sites), and **Seedhouse Campground**, 22 miles north of Steamboat (24 sites), are off Seedhouse Rd., via CR 129 north; **Dry Lake Campground**, 6 miles east of Steamboat Springs (8 sites), and **Summit Lake Campground**, 15 miles east of town (15 sites), are both on Buffalo Pass Rd.; **Meadows Campground**, 15 miles southeast of Steamboat Springs (30 sites), and **Dumont Lake Campground**, 22 miles (22 sites), are off Hwy. 40, on Rabbit Ears Pass; **Big Creek Lakes Campground**, west of Cowdrey via CR 6 and FR 600 (54 sites); **Aspen Campground** (7 sites) and **Pines Campground** (11 sites) are both on FR 740, just outside of Gould.

Private campgrounds: **North Park KOA** (see Creature Comforts).

WORTH A PAWS

Silver Bullet Gondola. Bring your dog aboard Steamboat Ski Area's gondola for a bird's-eye view of the surrounding valley. You can either hike down or make a return trip on the gondola. See Tail-Rated Trails for more details.

Felix and Fido, 601 Lincoln, Steamboat Springs, 970-870-6400, www.felixand fido.com. Felix and Fido bills itself as a dog and cat boutique store. Your dog may just turn up his nose at the abundance of cat-related paraphernalia, but he'll love sniffing out the selection of unique collars and leashes, bowls, dog packs, dog booties, treats, and squeaky toys. You'll enjoy browsing among the dog-themed items, including clothing, jewelry, accessories, and knickknacks—more than 125 different breeds of dogs are represented.

Crazy River Dog Contest. Local crazy canines and other river-savvy dogs turn out for this unique twist on stick retrieval, part of Steamboat's annual Yampa River Festival, held in late May. A stick is thrown into the Yampa; once it passes a certain point, a doggie contestant swims out and is timed on how long it takes him to get the stick and get out of the water. Once the field has been narrowed down to the top four dogs, there's a "stick-off": all four dogs go at once, and the winner is the one who comes up with the stick.

There's a $5 entry fee for the contest, which takes place at Yampa River Park on the Saturday of the festival. Any dog is welcome to participate, though "we'd hate for your dog to drown if you show up with a little city dog," quips one of the organizers. Call Back Door Sports at 970-879-6249 or go to www.backdoor sports.com for more information.

DOGGIE DAYCARE
Steamboat Springs
Mt. Werner Veterinary Hospital, 35825 E. Hwy. 40, 970-879-3486, www.mtwerner vet.com. $25/day. Open 9 AM–5:30 PM, Monday to Friday; 9 AM–noon, Saturday. Weekend day boarding available by appointment.

Red Rover Resort, 10 miles west of Steamboat Springs, 970-879-3647. $25/ day. The resort has a huge outdoor play yard. When you book an appointment, you'll receive the physical address. Open 8 AM–noon and 4 PM–8 PM daily.

RK Pet Ranch, 30265 Hwy. 131 (8 miles south of Steamboat Springs), 970-879-5639, www.rkpetranch.com. $20/day. Dogs have indoor and outdoor spaces for playing and also receive two long walks daily. Open 8 AM–10 AM and 4 PM–6 PM daily.

Yampa

Rocky Mountain Pet Resort, 27150 Watson Creek Tr., 970-638-0242. $20–$24/day depending on size of kennel. Dogs have access to the outdoor play yard three times a day. Open 7:30 AM–6:30 PM daily.

PET PROVISIONS
Steamboat Springs
Elk River Farm and Feed, 2680 Copper Ridge Cir., 970-879-5383, www.elkriverfarmandfeed.com

Paws 'n Claws 'n Things, 345 Anglers Dr., 970-879-6092

CANINE ER
Steamboat Springs
Mt. Werner Veterinary Hospital, 35825 E. Hwy. 40, 970-879-3486, www.mtwernervet.com. Open 9 AM–5:30 PM, Monday to Friday; 9 AM–noon, Saturday.

Pet Kare Clinic, 102 Anglers Dr., 970-879-5273, www.petkareclinic.com. Open 8 AM–8 PM, Monday to Thursday; 8 AM–5 PM, Friday; 9 AM–noon, Saturday.

Steamboat Veterinary Hospital, 1878 Lincoln Ave., 970-879-1041. Open 7:30 AM–6 PM, Monday to Friday; 8 AM–noon, Saturday.

RESOURCES
Bureau of Land Management/Parks Ranger District, Routt National Forest, 2103 Park Ave., Kremmling, 970-724-3000

Hahn's Peak/Bears Ears Ranger District, Routt National Forest, 925 Weiss Dr., Steamboat Springs, 970-870-2299

North Park Chamber of Commerce, 416 4th St., Walden, 970-723-4600, www.northparkvisitorsbureau.com

Parks Ranger District, Routt National Forest, 100 Main St., Walden, 970-723-2700

The Ski Haus, 1457 Pine Grove Rd., Steamboat Springs, 970-879-0385, 800-932-3019, www.skihaussteamboat.com, has a good selection of trail guides and maps to the area.

Steamboat Springs Chamber Resort Association, 125 Anglers Dr., Steamboat Springs, 970-879-0880, www.steamboat-chamber.com

Yampa Ranger District, Routt National Forest, 300 Roselawn Ave., Yampa, 970-638-4516

Nine
Summit County

THE BIG SCOOP

Summit County is a dog paradise, with plenty of great hiking, mountain-biking, and skiing opportunities as well as a variety of accommodations that actively welcome four-legged guests. When Denver or other areas along the Front Range become a bit too warm midsummer for those stuck with a permanent fur coat, mountain relief is but an hour's drive away among the towns of Silverthorne, Dillon, Frisco, and Breckenridge. And about 20 miles north of Silverthorne is Green Mountain Reservoir and the hamlet of Heeney (though your dog probably won't want to visit during Heeney's annual Tick Festival in mid-June!).

All of the principal Summit County towns have leash laws within their city limits. On county land, your dog can be off leash if he stays within 10 feet of you and is under voice control.

A canine fund-raising and advocacy group, LAPS (League for Animals and People of the Summit) meets monthly in Frisco and holds several events annually to benefit spay/neuter programs and assist the pets of local low-income families. Members are also working to establish another dog park in Summit County (currently there's only one, at Breckenridge's Carter Park).

TAIL-RATED TRAILS

What follows are but a few recommendations out of the many hiking options in the region. For more ideas, consult *The New Summit Hiker and Ski Touring Guide*, by Mary Ellen Gilliland.

Chihuahua Gulch
Distance: 6.2 miles round-trip
Elevation gain: 1,423 feet
Trailhead: From Dillon, head east on Hwy. 6, past Keystone Resort. Exit onto Montezuma Rd. About 4.5 miles from the exit, turn into a parking area on the left (across from the Western Skies bed-and-breakfast). Peru Creek Rd. begins just beyond the parking area. Drive 2.1 miles to a parking pullout on the right; the trailhead is on the left. *Dogs can be off leash.*

With a name like Chihuahua, this hike begs exploration by dogs. When I brought Clover and her hiking companion Tundra here, they had a great time on this spectacularly beautiful trail that ascends between the backside of Arapahoe Basin Ski Area and Grays and Torreys Peaks, a pair of 14,000-foot mountains, to Chihuahua Lake. Because the hike involves several stream crossings, it's best to wait until the spring runoff has subsided before tackling it. Begin by climbing steadily up a four-wheel-drive road. Stay left at a fork, which will bring you to the first stream to ford. The ascent levels off as you enter a vast meadow, with two more stream crossings. After the beaver ponds, take the left trail fork and stay left again after another stream crossing. At the end of the meadow, the trail resumes its climb. The final approach to the lake involves scrambling up a steep, but short, talus slope to the left. You'll first reach a small pond; continue downslope to reach the emerald green lake, which shimmers at the base of a cirque of rocky peaks.

Waiting to hit the Rainbow Lake Trail. From left: Spencer, Copper, Whistler, Dulce, Sally, Ryder, and Charlie.

Wilder Gulch

Distance: 6 miles round-trip
Elevation gain: 1,000 feet
Trailhead: Turn off I-70 at the Vail Pass rest area and park in the main lot (by the restrooms). Look for a footpath through the grass, designated by a small sign that says No Vehicles Off Roads. Follow this path for about .5 mile as it goes down a hill, crosses a small stream, and climbs a gentle hill on the other side; it will bring you to Wilder Gulch. (Though you can also access the trail from the bikeway, you'd spend the first .5 mile of your hike uncomfortably close to the interstate.)

Dogs can be off leash.

Turn right at the junction with the Wilder Gulch Trail, which climbs gradually along Wilder Creek. You'll ascend through wildflower-studded meadows surrounded by lodgepole pine. Stop occasionally to enjoy the views of Ptarmigan Hill at the head of the gulch ("hill" is definitely a misnomer), and Jacque Peak, Copper Mountain, and the Tenmile Range to the east. Eventually you'll come to an expansive meadow. Here the slope intensifies somewhat as it climbs through cool and fragrant stands of spruce. If your dog's a mycophile, let him know to keep an eye out for the big brown caps of boletus mushrooms, which grow in profusion in August and September. In about

another mile you'll come to a junction with four-wheel-drive Wearyman Road, our turnaround point; if you're game to keep going, turn left and climb for an additional 2 miles to Ptarmigan Pass, which offers great views of the Gore and Tenmile Ranges.

French Gulch

Distance: About 6 miles round-trip
Elevation gain: Approximately 1,200 feet
Trailhead: From Frisco, head south on Hwy. 9 to CR 450 just before Breckenridge (there's a 7-Eleven store on the corner). Turn left (east) and follow the road as it curves right under a railroad trestle structure marking the French Creek subdivision. Make a left at the stop sign. Then drive past numerous mine tailings and structural remains for about 3.5 miles until you came to a gate across the road. Park on the side of the road.

Dogs can be off leash.

French Gulch is a favorite among locals but is less crowded than many of the other Summit County trails, meaning that, especially on a weekday afternoon, you and your dog may be able to hike in relative solitude. The trail is actually an old mining road, a remnant of the area's past excavation industry. Past the gate, you'll start out walking up the road, which goes gradually uphill. About 1.5 miles into your hike, you'll pass some beaver ponds on the right, a good place for your dog to take a stick-retrieving break. After crossing a meadow a little farther along, the trail climbs more steeply. Go either way at the fork; the trails rejoin shortly after. Pass an orange metal gate marked Road Closed on the right. You'll cross a small stream twice within a short distance and then emerge into a beautiful wildflower-studded meadow. The trail continues up the meadow's right side and eventually crosses another small stream. After passing through a stand of timber, you'll come out into yet another glorious meadow, framed by the barren, red-hued slopes of Mount Guyot on the left and Bald Mountain on the right, both 13,000-plus-foot peaks. This was our turnaround point, though you could continue hiking for about .75 mile more up the ridge at the head of the meadow to French Pass, just above 12,000 feet, for a vista of both Breckenridge and the peaks to the east.

Crystal Lake

Distance: 4 miles round-trip
Elevation gain: 2,124 feet
Trailhead: Drive south from Breckenridge on Hwy. 9 for 2.5 miles to Spruce Creek Rd. (you'll see a sign for the Crown subdivision). Turn right and continue on Spruce Creek Rd. for 1.2 miles to the trailhead parking area.

Dogs can be off leash.

This popular hike follows a jeep track up to Lower Crystal Lake, nestled at the base of a cirque. Begin by walking along Spruce Creek Rd. for about .25 mile, to where Crystal Rd. takes off to the right. The wide, rocky trail ascends somewhat steeply for about the first .5 mile through stands of lodgepole pine, Douglas fir, blue spruce, and aspen; it then levels out to a more gradual ascent. As you hike, you'll become aware of Crystal Creek in the gully to the left, though it remains out of paw-dipping range. Not too far from the trailhead, you'll pass the Burro Trail coming in from the north. About 1 mile later, the Wheeler National Recreation Trail crosses your route. At this point, the trail breaks out above treeline and follows a short, steep ascent onto a shelf. You may glimpse lovely Francie's Cabin off to the right, part of the Summit Huts Association and available for winter use by reservation only (but dogs are not allowed). It's then a steady uphill to the lake, through wildflower-filled meadows

bordered by craggy Mount Helen to the south. At the lake, your dog can play in the water and sniff out the remains of an old cabin while you savor the scenery. If you're inspired to make the hike longer, it's possible to climb up on a trail that winds north and then southwest to Upper Crystal Lake, hidden from sight at the base of Crystal Peak, which rises to the west from Lower Crystal Lake.

Dog Park at Carter Park

Access: From Main St. in downtown Breckenridge, head east (away from the ski area) on Adams Ave. for four blocks to High St. Turn right on High and park at the end of the street.
Regulations: Dogs must have current rabies and ID tags; female dogs in heat are not allowed; dogs must be under voice and visual control at all times; pick up after your dog; children must be under adult supervision.

Dogs can be off leash.

Nikko is suited up for a spring hike in the high country.

The 1-acre park, a popular social spot for Summit County pooches and their people, is the happy result of dogged citizen involvement in determining an appropriate area where dogs can run while other park users can still go about their business. After a period of trial and error, the final location is now right at the High St. entrance to the larger Carter Park. A split-rail fence with wire-mesh inserts defines the grassy dog-specific area. Some benches and a permanent summer water source are planned; in the meantime, park users have been keeping bowls of water filled. If your dog wants to get the inside sniff on Breckenridge and the area, this is the place to come.

North Tenmile Trail

Distance: 4 miles round-trip to the Eagles Nest Wilderness boundary

Elevation gain: approximately 1,000 feet

Trailhead: Head west on I-70 past Silverthorne to Exit 201. Stay right at the end of the exit ramp and park in the gravel lot by the trailhead. If coming from Frisco, drive west on Main St. and cross under I-70 to reach the parking area.

Dogs can be off leash up until the wilderness boundary.

This pleasant hike follows an old mining road, alternating between stands of pine and spruce and grassy clearings. Follow the dirt road from the parking area. Right before a large green water tank on the left, take the road that branches off to the right. At the next junction, either option works; they rejoin shortly after. Then stay right at a fork shortly afterward, as the road takes a short climb. From here on, it's easy going. The trail parallels North Tenmile Creek, with many good access points for dogs, including a crystal-clear beaver pond. The wilderness boundary was our turnaround point, though you could continue

for another 1.5 miles to an intersection with the Gore Range Trail. If you do keep hiking, remember to leash up Fido once you cross that wilderness area line.

Boulder Lake

Distance: 5.46 miles round-trip

Elevation gain: 828 feet

Trailhead: From the intersection of Hwy. 9 and Rainbow Dr. in Silverthorne, head north on the highway for 7.9 miles to FR 1350. Make a left. After 1.4 miles, you'll turn left at a fork (a sign indicates the Rock Creek trailhead, from which this hike begins). From there, it's another 1.6 miles to the end of the road and the trailhead parking area.

Dogs must be leashed.

This hike doesn't have any outstanding views until the lake, but it covers forested terrain in the Eagles Nest Wilderness that's interesting while not involving any challenging climbs. From the trailhead, head southwest on the Rock Creek Trail, a wide, smooth path that's sort of like a wilderness highway. Don't worry—you won't be on it for long. After .3 mile, the Gore Range Trail, a 50-mile long route that traverses the eastern slopes of the mountains it's named after, intersects. Go right on this trail, which heads slightly uphill into a glade of lodgepole pine, with a small group of ponds and wetlands off to the right. You and your dog will gain a small ridge while hiking through a stand of aspen. The trail then arcs west before traveling north again, through a blissfully shady (in summer) stand of mixed conifers. Traverse up and down another low ridge before descending via a series of intermittent switchbacks to Boulder Creek, where your dog will likely want a quick drink. Cross the creek on rocks and logs and turn left onto the Boulder Creek Trail, which comes in from the northeast. After about .25 mile of gentle to moderate climbing, you'll arrive at your destination, Boulder Lake, a serene pool encircled by dense evergreens, with a classic Rocky Mountain backdrop: peaks in the Gore Range, standing like sentinels as they soar toward 13,000 feet.

Rainbow Lake

Distance: Approximately 2 miles round-trip

Elevation gain: 150 feet

Trailhead: From Main St. in Frisco, go south on 2nd St. until its end; cross the bike path and, if you're driving, park in the dirt lot.

Dogs can be off leash.

This short hike is great for a close-to-town canine workout. It's also a good place to spot columbine in July and August. From the parking lot, take a right on the paved bike path, toward Breckenridge and Keystone (keep your dog leashed on the path). Walk about an eighth of a mile to an opening in the trees on the right. Then go straight across a clearing and pick up the wide path that leads to a boardwalk across fragile wetlands. After crossing a stream, the trail ascends gradually through lodgepole pine, aspen, and blue spruce. You'll cross an old road and another trail before reaching the lake. For a loop option, look for the blue diamond marker at the right of the lakeside clearing. Almost immediately, you'll come to another dirt road; take a right. Stay to the right when the trail converges with another road, right at the fork shortly after, and right at the junction that follows. When you pass a small wooden post on the right, marked with arrows, turn left, and you'll be back at the original trail on which you came up.

Tenderfoot Trail

Distance: 2.5 miles round-trip

Elevation gain: 621 feet

Trailhead: Head east on Hwy. 6 from Silverthorne. At the stoplight turnoff toward Dillon, make a left, then an immediate sharp right. Signed parking for the trail is .6 mile ahead on the right.

Dogs can be off leash.

In this trail's favor are its accessibility and views. However, the constant drone of traffic from I-70 reminds you that you haven't escaped civilization. This is a dry area, so bring water. Walk up the hairpin curve in the road and past the water treatment plant to access the trail. Follow a dirt road for .25 mile to a trail sign pointing left and uphill. Wend your way through an odd gate contraption and you'll be on the trail. As you hike, you'll enjoy wonderful views of Buffalo Mountain and the Gore Range to the north, as well as Dillon Reservoir and Peaks 1 through 10 beyond. The trail switchbacks gently up Tenderfoot Mountain, first through sagebrush, then aspen, and, finally, lodgepole pine. The second bench along the trail, from which you can see Breckenridge and Keystone Resorts, is a good turnaround point. After this, the trail gets considerably steeper and less maintained as it heads to the summit of Tenderfoot.

Keystone Mountain

Access: The eight-person River Run Gondola takes you and your dog from the middle of River Run Village, on Keystone's east side, to the top of Dercum Mountain in less than 12 minutes. Each car's floor-to-ceiling windows mean everyone can enjoy the views, whether you're at human eye level or dog eye level. The gondola runs from 9 AM to 4 PM from late June through the beginning of September. Tickets are $8–$12. Call the Keystone Activities Desk, 970-496-4386, for more information or go to www.keystoneresort.com.

Dogs must be leashed.

Because the mountain receives quite a lot of fast, downhill mountain-bike traffic, one recommended hike where you and your dog are less apt to get tangled up in someone's spokes is the **11-7 Trail**, a 1.75-mile loop atop Dercum Mountain that gets little use by mountain bikers. If you and Fido want to hike back down the mountain rather than take the gondola, use the hiker-only **Jackstraw Rd.**

 Cucumber Gulch Preserve. Dogs are not permitted on any of the trails at this wildlife preserve and open space property between downtown Breckenridge and Peak 8 of the ski area.

CYCLING FOR CANINES

Summit County is filled with great riding spots, and because many routes follow trails or old mining roads on national forest property, they're also dog friendly, as long as you keep an eye on distance. **Wilder Gulch, Crystal Lake, Rainbow Lake**, and **North Tenmile Trail** up to the wilderness area boundary (see Tail-Rated Trails for more info) all make suitable dog rides. Or try an out-and-back on the jeep road along **Tenderfoot Mountain** (see Tenderfoot Trail in Tail-Rated Trails; keep following the dirt road you start out on instead of taking the trail uphill). For more ideas, check out *The Mountain Bike Guide to Summit County*, by Laura Rossetter.

POWDERHOUNDS

There are many excellent backcountry ski and snowshoe trails throughout Summit County. Some routes that follow roads, which means more room for both skiers/snowshoers and dogs to maneuver, include **Peru Creek, Webster Pass**, and **Deer Creek**, off Montezuma Rd.; **Keystone Gulch; French Gulch** and **Sally Barber Mine**, outside of Breckenridge; **North Tenmile Trail** near Frisco; and **Mayflower Gulch**, south of Copper Mountain via Hwy. 91. Refer to *Snowshoeing Colorado,* by Claire Walter for other options.

Breckenridge Nordic Center, 1200 Ski Hill Rd., Breckenridge, 970-453-6855, www.breckenridgenordic.com; **Frisco Nordic Center**, 18454 Hwy. 9 (on Dillon Reservoir), 970-668-0866, www.frisco nordic.com. These two Nordic centers, under the same ownership, offer a few dog-friendly options. At Breckenridge, leashed dogs are permitted in the Peak 7 area (known as **New Nordic World**), which includes the 11-kilometer groomed **Siberian Loop** and a snowshoe trail that's about 6 kilometers out and back; at Frisco, though dogs are not permitted on the ski trails, they can run alongside their owners, on leash, on all 20 kilometers of snowshoeing trails. You'll need to buy a $15 trail pass (Fido is free), which is good within the same day at either center, as well as at the Gold Run Nordic Center in Breckenridge (see below). Open mid-November to mid-April.

Gold Run Nordic Center, 200 Clubhouse Dr., Breckenridge, 970-547-7889, www .goldrunnordic.com. The ski and snow-shoe trails at Gold Run, operated by the town of Breckenridge, occupy what in summer is the municipal golf course, about 3 miles north of town, as well as some forest service land. Dogs and their owners can explore 12.2 kilometers of groomed trails together in the Nordic center's **Peabody Placer area**, and dogs can be under voice control. You'll need to purchase your $15 daily trail pass (dogs are free) at the day lodge; then drive about 1.5 miles to the Peabody trailhead. From there, you and Fido can ski the 2.2-kilometer **Peabody Trail**, the 5-kilometer **Hoodoo Voodoo Trail**, and the 5-kilometer **Preston Loop Trail**, which leads to a historic townsite. The Nordic center also rents and sells skijoring equipment. Open mid-November to early April.

CREATURE COMFORTS

Unless otherwise stated, dogs should not be left unattended in the room or cabin.

Breckenridge

$$–$$$$ Breckenridge Mountain Lodge, 600 S. Ridge St., 970-453-2333, 888-400-9590, www.breckresorts.com. Dogs are permitted in most of the rooms at this ski-area-owned property in Breckenridge's historic downtown. There's a $20 nightly fee per dog. Rooms are comfortably furnished in rustic mountain style, with peeled-log furniture. You can leave your dog unattended inside the room, but housekeeping won't come in during that time.

$$–$$$$ Great Divide Lodge, 550 Village Rd., 970-547-5550, 888-400-9590, www.breckresorts.com. This 208-room, full-service hotel owned by the resort is just 50 yards from the ski area's Peak 9. Dogs can stay in designated rooms for a $30 nightly fee per dog, with a $150 deposit. Rooms are large, with upscale furnishings, and hotel amenities include an indoor pool, hot tubs, a fitness room, business center, and bar and restaurant.

$$–$$$$ Lodge at Breckenridge, 112 Overlook Dr., 970-453-9300, 800-736-1607, www.thelodgeatbreck.com. This luxury lodge, located off the road to Boreas Pass, accepts dogs for a $20 nightly fee for up to two dogs (additional dogs are another $10 per night). Rooms are furnished in an upscale rustic style, with peeled-log furniture and beams. Mountain-view rooms, with hand-painted armoires, nicely appointed kitchenettes, and gas fireplaces, are definitely the nicest of the bunch. The one-notch-down standard rooms are on the small side. All upper-level rooms have balconies; if you appreciate views, ask for a room with a dramatic vista of the Tenmile Range. You can leave your dog unattended inside if he's well behaved and quiet, as long as

you provide a cell-phone number to the front desk. The lodge also rents out two three-bedroom homes that are adjacent, and dogs are permitted in one of them.

$$–$$$$ The Village at Breckenridge, 535 S. Park Ave., 970-453-5192, 888-400-9590, www.breckresorts.com. This ski-area-owned, ski-in/ski-out hotel at the Peak 9 base area allows dogs in four of its 60 recently renovated hotel rooms (note that dogs aren't allowed in the individually owned condo suites that are also part of the Village complex). There's a $30 nightly fee per dog, with a limit of two dogs per room. Your dog can be unattended inside, but housekeeping won't come in to clean unless he's in a travel kennel. The Village includes a fitness center, indoor/outdoor pool, nine hot tubs, ski shop, pub, and, in winter, a childcare center.

$$$–$$$$ Tannhauser Lodging, 420 S. Main St., 970-453-2136, 800-433-9217, www.tannhauserlodging.com. Comfortable but not luxurious, these condos are conveniently located in downtown Breckenridge and, most important, your dog can stay, too. "Most of our dog guests are better behaved than the human ones," notes Rick, the manager. Almost half of the one- and two-bedroom units in the complex allow pets with a $40 one-time fee. You can leave your dog unattended inside.

Copper Mountain

$$$–$$$ Copper Mountain Lodging, 888-219-2441, www.coppercolorado.com. All of the lodging at the base of the Copper Mountain ski area is made up of condos and townhouses located in various neighborhoods along the length of the base village. The ski resort handles rentals of these properties, which range from hotel-style rooms to five-bedroom units, and some are dog friendly. Since each one is individually owned, the welcome mat for dogs varies among units, not overall buildings; call for specifics. There's a $15 nightly fee per dog, and you can leave Rover unattended in the room as long as he has a travel kennel to stay in.

Dillon

$$–$$$ Best Western Ptarmigan Lodge, 652 Lake Dillon Dr., 970-468-2341, 800-842-5939, www.ptarmiganlodge.com. The motel, located across from the Dillon Marina and a lakeshore path, accepts dogs in two of its buildings for a $15 one-time fee per pet. You can leave Fido unattended in your room, perhaps while you grab a bite at the adjacent Arapahoe Café, but housekeeping won't enter during that time.

$$–$$$ Dillon Super 8, 808 Little Beaver Tr., 970-468-8888, 800-800-8000 (national number), www.super8.com. The motel accepts dogs from April 1 to December 15, for a $15 one-time fee per dog.

Fairplay

$$ Hand Hotel Bed and Breakfast, 531 Front, 719-836-3595, www.handhotel .com. Built as a hotel in the 1930s, the Hand has since been converted to a B&B. The 11 rooms, all with private bath, are individually decorated with a western theme that commemorates Fairplay's history. Canine guests are welcome in all but one of the rooms, for $5 extra per night, per dog, and particularly quiet, well-mannered dogs may be left unattended inside if they're in a travel kennel.

$$ Western Inn Motel & RV Park, 490 W. Hwy. 285, 719-836-2026, 877-306-3037, www.thewesterninn.com. Dogs are welcome at this family-run motel for a $10 one-time fee per dog. They can be unattended inside the room as long as they don't disrupt other guests. There's a designated walking area behind the motel where your dog can do his business.

Frisco

$$–$$$ Snowshoe Motel, 521 Main St., 970-668-3444, 800-445-8658, www .snowshoemotel.com. This older motel in the heart of downtown Frisco has some designated pet rooms, where up to two dogs can stay for a $10 one-time fee. You can leave your dog unattended in the room if he's in a travel kennel and promises not to bark.

$$–$$$ Summit Inn, 1205 N. Summit Blvd., 970-668-3220, 800-745-1211, www.newsummitinn.com. At this pet-friendly, chain-style motel, dogs are invited to stay for $10 per night each. Your four-legged traveler can stay unattended in the room if he's in a travel kennel, and a sheet of pet rules spells out other important stuff for him to know.

$$–$$$ The Woods Inn, 205 S. 2nd Ave., 970-668-2255, 877-664-3777, www .woodsinn.biz. You and your adult dog (no puppies, please) can stay in any of the 12 eclectically furnished units at this bed-and-breakfast just off Frisco's Main St. Accommodations range from comfortable bedrooms to multiroom suites with kitchens. There's a $25 pet charge per visit, and the pet policy states that your dog be well behaved and chaperoned. "The only thing that bothers me is barking pets," says owner Les Kennedy. Of special interest is the building that houses the breakfast area and fireplace lounge—this structure was originally a hunting lodge, built in the early 1930s, and was then moved from the old town of Dillon (now flooded by the Lake Dillon reservoir) to Frisco in the late 1940s.

$$–$$$$ Best Western Lake Dillon Lodge, 1202 N. Summit Blvd., 970-668-5094, 800-727-0607, www.lakedillonlodge.com. Dogs are allowed in designated rooms only, with a $20 one-time fee.

$$–$$$$ Hotel Frisco, 308 Main St., 970-668-5009, 800-262-1002, www.hotel frisco.com. Most of this well-appointed small hotel's rooms are dog friendly, including a two-bedroom suite and a one-bedroom apartment with kitchen, for an extra $10 per night, per pet. Hannah, the resident yellow Lab, will make sure your dog receives a friendly greeting ("She's almost the owner," says one of the managers), and Buddha, a Chihuahua, may be on hand, too. There's a stash of dog treats at the front desk, and your dog can request a bed and feeding bowls to use during his visit. He may be able to lounge unattended in your room if you leave a cell-phone number with the staff. If you check out the Pets Welcome section on the hotel's website, you'll see an assortment of happy canine visitors that have stayed here.

$$–$$$$ Ramada Ltd., 990 Lake Point Dr., 970-668-8783, 800-272-6232 (national number), www.ramadafrisco.com. Located within walking distance of Lake Dillon, the motel allows dogs for $10 per night in its first-floor rooms.

$$$–$$$$ Holiday Inn Frisco, 1129 N. Summit Blvd., 970-668-5000, 800-782-7669 (national number), www.holiday inn.com. Dogs are allowed in designated pet rooms for a $25 one-time fee.

Heeney (Green Mountain Reservoir)
$$–$$$ Melody Lodge, 1534 CR 30, 970-468-8497, 800-468-8495, www.melody lodgecabins.com. The lodge accepts mature dogs (i.e., those older than one year) for $10 per night, per pet. There are five studio to two-bedroom, fully equipped cabins, which vary in age and decor. It's about a three-minute walk to the reservoir. You must keep your dog on a leash on the lodge's 5.5 acres. Open mid-May to mid-November.

$$$–$$$$ Heeney Hideaway Cabins, 158 Green Mountain Ave., 970-724-0775, www.heeneyhideaway.com. Of these three cabins, "mature, quiet" dogs who are at least 12 months old are allowed in the comfortably rustic, two-bedroom Green Mountain Getaway, which sleeps up to eight and has a kitchen, wood-burning stove, washer/dryer, and out-door gas grill. The pet charge is $10 per night, per dog, with a limit of two. Your dog must be in a travel kennel if you leave him unattended inside the cabin.

Keystone
$$–$$$$ Arapahoe Inn, 22859 Hwy. 6, 970-513-9009, 888-513-9009, www .arapahoeinn.com. For $20 extra per night you can stay with your dog at this basic motel next to the Keystone base village. There are, however, only two pet-friendly rooms (out of 60), so you'll want to reserve well in advance.

$$–$$$$ Inn at Keystone, 970-496-3658, 877-753-9786, www.keystoneresort .com. Your dog can join you in any of the second-floor rooms at this hotel in the middle of Keystone's mountain base village, from which you can easily hook into one of the many walking/biking paths that run through the area. There's a $25 nightly pet fee, and your pooch will be greeted with treats at check-in. You'll receive poop bags for cleaning up after Rover and a special Do Not Disturb sign to hang outside the room if you leave your dog unattended inside. The front desk also has a list of local pet resources.

Silverthorne
$$ First Interstate Inn, 357 Blue River Pkwy., 970-468-5170, 800-462-4667 (national number), www.1stinns.com. Dogs are permitted in all rooms.

$$–$$$ **Quality Inn and Suites,** 530 Silverthorne Ln., 970-513-1222, 800-422-6423 (national number), www.quality inn.com. The hotel allows dogs in standard rooms, for $10 per night, per dog, with a $50 deposit.

$$–$$$$ **Days Inn,** 580 Silverthorne Ln., 970-468-8661, 800-329-7466 (national number), www.daysinn.com. Dogs are permitted in any of the rooms, with a $5 charge per dog, per night. You can leave your dog unattended in the room only if he's in a travel kennel.

$$–$$$$ **La Quinta Inn and Suites Dillon Silverthorne,** 560 Silverthorne Ln., 970-468-6200, 800-753-3757, www.lq.com. Dogs 50 pounds and under are permitted in designated rooms.

CAMPGROUNDS

National forest campgrounds: **Blue River Campground**, 9 miles north of Silverthorne off Hwy. 9 (24 sites); **Dillon Reservoir** has five campgrounds, for a total of 323 sites, plus one group campground; **Cataract Creek Campground** (5 sites), **Elliot Creek Campground** (24 sites), **McDonald Flats Campground** (12 sites), **Prairie Point Campground** (22 sites), and **Willows** (25 sites) are all at Green Mountain Reservoir in Heeney.

WORTH A PAWS

Keystone River Run Gondola. Enjoy a scenic summertime trip on the Keystone gondola with your dog. You can either hike back down or take the gondola. See details in Tail-Rated Trails.

Canine 4K Feline No-Way Walk/Run. This annual race, held the first Saturday of August, is a fundraiser for LAPS, the League for Animals and People of the Summit. You and your leashed dog follow a course that begins and ends at the Frisco gazebo, in the Historic Park on Main St. Registration fee (around $22, slightly more on race day) includes a T-shirt for you and a goody bag for your canine companion. And if you'd like to run or walk in honor of your cat—dog or no dog—you're welcome to participate in the event, too. Following the race, stick around for the Mountain Mutt contest, in which your dog can vie for prizes in categories such as best singing dog and closest pet-owner lookalike, as well as a silent auction. You can register in advance of the race at the Summit County Animal Shelter, 970-668-3230; race-day registration is also available. Your dog must show proof of current rabies vaccination to participate, and there's a maximum of two dogs per person. For more information, go to www.summitlaps.com.

DogTerra. Held the first Saturday of March, this annual winter fund-raiser for the League for Animals and People of the Summit (LAPS) takes place at the Gold Run Nordic Center in Breckenridge. Your dog and you can participate in several activities: snowshoeing, skijoring on the Nordic trails, the "dogstacle" (a dog/owner obstacle course), or the Frisbee/Chuckit! catch. Prize drawings are held during the morning, and all canine participants get dog treats and water, while their humans can wake up with coffee and donuts. Entrance fees are about $20 per dog ($5 per additional dog with the same owner), and registration takes place the morning of the event. Your dog must have a current rabies tag, and human participants can't have more than two dogs each. For more information, go to www .summitlaps.com or call the Nordic center at 970-547-7889.

Animal Rescue of the Rockies' 5K Run and Fun Walk. Held annually in mid- to late August at Breckenridge's Carter Park, this event raises money for a local rescue group that places homeless pets in foster homes and, eventually, permanent homes. The 5K race, which starts at the park and follows some singletrack mountain trails, is for humans only, but dogs and their people can both enjoy the 3K Fun Walk, which follows a trail through the park and then picks up another trail behind the ice rink before looping back. Afterward, everyone gathers in the park for snacks and socializing. For more information, call 970-389-8324 or go to www.animalrescueoftherockies.org.

For Pets' Sake Thrift Shop, 203 N. Main St., Breckenridge, 970-453-4339. This cleverly named store sells a variety of secondhand items, including clothing and housewares. It's completely volunteer staffed, and all of the proceeds go to the Animal Rescue of the Rockies, which fosters pets and finds homes for them. Open Tuesday through Saturday. For more information, go to www.animalrescueof therockies.org.

Marina Mutt Contest. Started in 1997, this fun, land-based social event is put on for dogs and their owners by the Lake Dillon Marina on Labor Day. There are three categories of canine competition: best trick, best pet/owner lookalike, and best howl. No entrance fee is required, but your dog can win cool prizes from local businesses. Even if your dog is the noncompetitive type, bring him down just to socialize. The marina is located at 150 Marina Dr. (take a right on Lake Dillon Dr. when heading east on Hwy. 6, then a left on Lodgepole, which will bring you near the marina). Call 970-468-5100 or go to www.dillonmarina .com for specifics.

Colorado Disc Dog Frisbee Competition. One of a series of canine Frisbee events in the state, this annual competition takes place in Silverthorne's Rainbow Park in July. Dogs participate in the minidistance,

earning points for catching distance and a bonus for midair catches, and the freestyle, in which they're judged on difficulty, execution, leaping agility, and showmanship while performing tricks. Colorado Disc Dogs puts on the events. For more information, go to www.coloradodisc dogs.com.

The Breckenridge Barkery, 100 N. Main St., Breckenridge, 970-547-1986, www .thebreckenridgebarkery.com. This dog emporium stocks lots of breed-specific items, like ornaments and pictures, as well as cute retro-style advertising prints of various types of hounds. Your dog will find lots of toys, leashes, and treats to sniff out, as well as gear (e.g., backpacks, booties to protect paws) that he might want for hiking the nearby peaks.

DOGGIE DAYCARE
Breckenridge
DnR Kennels, 0115 Gateway Dr. (CR 950), 970-453-6708, www.dnrkennels .com. $25/day. Dogs go out to the 1-acre fenced play yard at least twice a day. Open 8 AM–6 PM, daily.

The Dog House, 229 Continental Ct., 970-453-5301, www.breckenridgedoghouse .com. $30/day; $23/half-day (five hours or less). Dogs can play in groups and/or relax in a climate-controlled kennel. They'll also get walks every two hours. Open 7:30 AM–6 PM, Monday to Friday; 8:30 AM–5 PM, Saturday. Sunday daycare and pick-up and drop-off can be arranged.

Dillon
The Dog Den, 850 Little Beaver Tr., 970-262-9076, www.dillondogden.com. $30/day; $23/half-day (five hours or less). Dogs have two indoor play areas and a large outdoor yard to choose from. Open 7 AM–6:30 PM, Monday to Friday; 8 AM–5:30 PM, Saturday.

PET PROVISIONS
Breckenridge
Paws & Claws Pet Supply, 1705 Airport Rd., 970-547-9633. In addition to food and other supplies, there's a self-service dog wash. The $18 fee includes everything you'll need to get Fido sweet smelling again.

Frisco
The Barnyard, 104 Main, 970-668-0238

Elk Mountain Trading Company, 121 Summit Blvd., 970-668-0495

CANINE ER
Frisco
Frisco Animal Hospital (AAHA certified), 700 N. Summit Blvd., 970-668-5544. Open 8 AM–5:30 PM, Monday to Friday; 8 AM–noon, Saturday.

RESOURCES
Breckenridge Welcome Center, 203 S. Main St., Breckenridge, 970-453-2913, 877-864-0868, www.gobreck.com

Dillon Ranger District, White River National Forest, 680 Blue River Pkwy., Silverthorne, 970-468-5400

South Park Ranger District, Pike National Forest, 320 Hwy. 285, Fairplay, 719-836-2031

Summit County Chamber of Commerce Visitor Center, 246 Rainbow Dr., Silverthorne (in the Green Village section of the Outlets at Silverthorne), 970-468-5780, 800-530-3099, www.summitchamber.org

Ten
Vail, Leadville, and Vicinity

THE BIG SCOOP

Situated smack-dab in the middle of the mountains, Vail and Leadville offer the avid outdoor canine lots of trail mileage to sniff out. The more refined dog might prefer Vail, with its faux-Tyrolean decor and upscale boutiques—and where the arm that reaches out to pet him is likely to be sporting a Rolex. The dog with an interest in Colorado's past will relish a visit to Leadville, whose ties to its mining roots are still strong. About the only place your dog won't enjoy is Beaver Creek Resort—because he can't. Dogs are not allowed anywhere in Beaver Creek unless they belong to property owners at the resort. Rumor has it that even Olympic gold medalist Picabo Street was deterred when she tried to bring her pooch along.

In Vail, dogs must be on a leash in Vail Village and Lionshead, on any bike path, and in all public parks (except the designated off-leash dog areas—see Tail-Rated Trails). Anywhere else in the city limits, as well as in unincorporated areas of Eagle County, dogs can be under voice control as long as they're within 10 feet of their owners.

In Leadville, a leash law is in effect within the town and in Lake County. Though in general it's not actively enforced on national forest trails, be aware that you could receive a warning or a ticket if the sheriff's office receives a complaint about an off-leash dog on forest service land. There's also a law against public tethering in Leadville, meaning you can't tie up your dog in front of a store or restaurant, for example, and leave him unattended, even for a few moments.

TAIL-RATED TRAILS

If you're looking for a place to wander in Vail that's close at hand, bring your dog to the **paved walkway/bike path** that follows **Gore Creek** (from Vail Village to Lionshead, the route parallels W. Meadow Dr. instead of the creek). Or check out the **Vail Nature Center**, next to Ford Park, where a network of four short interpretive trails goes through a meadow and riparian habitat (your dog can be under voice command here). For more hiking options in the beautiful mountains surrounding Vail, refer to *The Vail Hiker and Ski Touring Guide,* by Mary Ellen Gilliland. In Leadville, stop by the chamber of commerce (see Resources) and pick up a copy of the chamber-issued hiking and mountain-biking guides.

Leadville

Midland Trail
Distance: 5.5 miles round-trip
Elevation gain: 600 feet
Trailhead: From Hwy. 24 in Leadville, take 6th St. west. In approximately 2 miles, you'll come to a T-intersection (Leadville's recreation center will be on your right). Turn right and continue straight on the paved road to Turquoise Lake. As you reach the lake,

continue past the dam. You'll climb two separate hills that afford wonderful overlooks of the lake before coming to FR 105, a dirt road bearing to the left. Turn here. The trailhead is 3.75 miles ahead (you'll pass the Native Lake trailhead en route). The last .25 mile to the parking area is rough; if you have a low-clearance car, you'll probably need to park alongside the road and walk that last part. Across the road from the parking area is the trailhead and a sign describing the Colorado Midland Railroad.

Dogs can be off leash, except for the .5 mile of trail that goes in and out of the Mount Massive Wilderness midhike.

This high-altitude hike will let your dog sniff around one of the ghost towns for which Colorado is renowned. Many of these former towns have some connection to the state's fabled mining past. This one does, too, but in a roundabout way.

Douglass City was a wild and woolly construction camp built high above Turquoise Lake and Leadville to house workers building the Hagerman Tunnel. The tunnel was built in 1888 and used until 1897 as a route for the Colorado Midland Railroad between the silver mines of Aspen and the smelters of Leadville. At 11,528 feet, the tunnel was the highest ever built, featuring a 1,100-foot-long curved trestle (both the trestle and the tunnel were engineering marvels at the time). The path to Douglass City and the Hagerman Tunnel follows the former railroad grade.

The trail starts out over rough cobble and rocks, but it soon smooths out to a gradual doubletrack. Throughout the ascent, you'll enjoy spectacular views of the valley you just traveled through, as well as the northern flank of Mount Massive. After about 1.5 miles, the grade comes to an abrupt end; this is where the long trestle once stood. If you look hard, you can see where the railroad grade resumes, 1,100 feet across the valley.

Don't hike to it! Instead, turn around to see a small trail climbing the hill to the left 50 feet behind you. Continue up this trail, which is a bit steeper and more rocky. At the four-way intersection in the trail shortly after, turn left to take a shortcut to the site of Douglass City. No standing structures remain; in fact, many of the "buildings" of Douglass City were tents. Eight saloons and one dance hall were among the first buildings up and among the busiest, as long as the work lasted. You'll see a few of their remains among the rocks and wildflowers.

Continue climbing past the town, toward a steep rock wall. Soon you'll come to remnants of the tunnel-making operation; high above and to the right is the old railroad grade leading to the tunnel. Follow the trail up the hill to the railroad grade and turn left. In less than 100 yards you'll see the entrance to the tunnel and, just inside, ice. The tunnel was used only briefly by the Colorado Midland. It cost James J. Hagerman, the tycoon who owned the rail line, millions to construct and almost as much to keep open. The high elevation and fierce winter conditions caused so many problems that the Midland was soon routed through another tunnel, the Busk-Ivanhoe (now called the Carlton), which allowed the trains easier passage. Enjoy the coolness of the tunnel's mouth and the quiet dripping sounds from deep within. Your pooch may be tempted at the sight of emerald green Opal Lake below, which can provide a welcome splash on the hike down.

Big Willis Gulch
Distance: 11 miles round-trip
Elevation gain: 2,400 feet
Trailhead: From the town of Twin Lakes, drive west on Hwy. 82 for 2 miles. Turn left and follow the dirt road down to the parking area.
Dogs can be off leash.

This gorgeous hike has a great mix of varied terrain: aspen groves, evergreen forest, expansive meadows, ample water for dogs, and an above-treeline lake nestled between high peaks as the ultimate destination. From the parking area, cross Lake Creek on a wooden bridge into a grove of shady cottonwood. Stay left at the fork shortly after. A series of beaver ponds ahead on the left gives your dog the chance to take a quick swim before the trail suddenly takes a turn for the steeper, with an efficient elevation gain. Bear right at the next fork (the left branch goes to Upper Twin Lake). The trail's grade mellows but will still keep you breathing a bit harder as it ascends through a large stand of aspen; in the fall, you'll get a wonderful color show at this point.

The trail eventually tops out beside an old aqueduct. As you follow it, you'll soon hear the rushing waters of Willis Creek. Stay right after crossing the creek on a wooden bridge (going left would take you back down to the Upper Twin Lake trail). After a steady but moderate ascent that parallels the creek at first, then gradually veers away, bear right at yet another fork. Cross Little Willis Creek on a few logs. The trail turns into an old doubletrack path. Cross Willis Creek via logs, then enjoy the next section of the hike, as it's relatively flat. If you're backpacking, there are several nice spots to camp along this stretch.

Before long you'll pop out into a splendid meadow, with the flanks of 13,933-foot Mount Hope as the backdrop. Next, cross a large scree slope and then begin a long but easy hike up the narrow, long valley of upper Big Willis Gulch. You'll have to do a bit of whacking through willow brush, but the trail is not difficult to follow. Pass a shallow tarn off to the left—this is not Willis Lake—and keep going until you reach the lake, cradled between the lowest flank of Mount Hope and a ridge to the west at about 11,800 feet in elevation. To access the water, cross the talus slope that descends to the lake and pick your way down the first grassy gully. While your dog dips his paw or perhaps paddles through the chilly water, find a rock to lean against, listen to the gentle lapping of waves, and gaze up at the pair of 13,000-plus-foot peaks that reign over the end of this classically U-shaped glacial valley.

Turquoise Lake Trail

Distance: 6.4 miles along the lakeshore

Elevation gain: 55 feet

Trailhead: From Hwy. 24 in Leadville, take 6th St. west. In approximately 2 miles, you'll come to a T-intersection (Leadville's recreation center will be on your right). Turn right and continue straight on the paved road to Turquoise Lake. As you reach the lake, continue straight toward the dam, but don't drive onto it. Park at the pullout on the left immediately before it. Cross the road and start down the singletrack that contours along the shoreline. The other main access point for the trail is at the May Queen Campground, though you can also pick up the trail at various points along it.

Dogs can be off leash (though you may want to leash your dog in the vicinity of the campgrounds the trail skirts).

This beautiful trail is a great hike. It never strays farther than 25 yards from the water—most times it's a lot closer than that—and winds around several secluded coves with sparkling water and sandy beaches. During the summer, the trail is fairly popular, especially close to the dam. Expect to see plenty of other hikers and cyclists if you go on a holiday weekend. (Hint: Go off-season if you can. On a beautiful autumn day, we had the trail completely to ourselves.) You'll savor spectacular views of the two highest peaks in the Rocky Mountains, Mount Elbert (14,433 feet) and Mount

Massive (14,421 feet), which dominate the skyline across the water. After approximately 4 miles, you'll encounter the remains of abandoned mines—remnants of Leadville's rip-roaring mining heyday. A sign alongside the trail enumerates many of the dangers posed by the abandoned mine shafts and suggests you turn around here. Don't, but take the warnings to heart, and make sure your dog (and you) stay on the trail, which passes safely through the dilapidated remains. (While you're in Leadville, you may want to stop by the National Mining Hall of Fame and Museum, 120 W. 9th St., which offers fascinating displays and artifacts on mines and mining. Your dog won't be able to accompany you inside, however.) After 6.4 miles, the trail reaches the May Queen Campground at the northern terminus of the lake.

Vail

Meadow Mountain

Distance: 9 miles round-trip
Elevation gain: 2,006 feet
Trailhead: From the Minturn exit off I-70, drive .5 mile to the Holy Cross Ranger District Forest Service office on the right. There's ample parking in the large lot. You'll find the trailhead at the parking lot's southwest corner.

Dogs can be off leash.

This area used to be the location of the short-lived Meadow Mountain ski area, which operated only from 1966 to 1969, when it was purchased by Vail and the lifts were sold to A-Basin. From late spring (after the mud dries up) through early autumn, the trail, actually an old road, is a great venue for hiking and mountain biking. In the winter months, it's shared by snowshoers, cross-country skiers, and snowmobilers. And the mountain lives up to its name, providing plenty of meadows for Rover to romp in and chase down a few sticks.

Clover and the author during a high-summer backpacking trip.

Begin by walking through a gate and heading south on the trail/road. The trail starts to switchback soon after, although the climb is continuously gradual as you ascend through sagebrush and stands of aspen. Inside 30 minutes, you'll find yourself among sloping ranchlands, where some old cabins still stand. (Apparently, lettuce was grown here in the 1920s.) Beyond these ranchlands, the grand vistas are endless, as you catch sight of the rugged Gore Range to the northeast and the Tennessee Pass area to the southeast. Locals who hike this trail claim that the reflected light of sunsets are one of a kind here. Eventually, you'll climb high enough to glimpse both Vail and Beaver Creek ski runs. At about 2 miles the trail makes several switchbacks in a row, and the tree scenery changes to spruce and fir. At 2.7 miles, you'll reach a fork. Stay to the right for a final switchback or two. The last 100 yards are noticeably steeper. You'll be rewarded by more gorgeous meadows, which host an incredible variety of wildflowers during July and August. At mountaintop you'll come to a small cabin, complete with a table and chairs, known as the line shack. It's a perfect rest stop before you head back down the trail.

Vail Off-Leash Dog Areas

Regulations: Dogs must be supervised at all times; owners must have a leash in hand for each dog; pick up after your dog; no aggressive dogs.

Dogs can be off leash.

Tucked away on Vail's east end, the 7.3-acre **Bighorn Park** (on Meadow Dr., east of the Vail Racquet Club) allows dogs to be off leash throughout the park, except for the playground (which, in a twist on the usual dog park setup, is the only part of the park that's fenced in). Dogs will find plenty of places to play here, whether it's chasing Frisbees on the grassy lawn, swimming circles in Bighorn Pond, or trotting down to dip a paw in Gore Creek, just north of the pond. Owners, meanwhile, can hang out at the picnic tables, stroll the gravel path around the pond, or just enjoy the visual backdrop of the East Vail Chutes, a favorite, though avalanche prone, venue for backcountry skiers.

At **Stephens Park** in West Vail (off S. Frontage Rd. just west of Exit 173 on I-70), the unfenced off-leash area consists of the park's northern portion, bounded on one side by the parking area and on the other by Gore Creek, which bisects the park. It includes a large field for dogs to romp in and an easily accessible "beach" area on Gore Creek. Once he crosses the bridge to the south side of Gore Creek, Fido will have to be leashed up.

West Grouse Creek

Distance: 9 miles round-trip
Elevation gain: 2,965 feet
Trailhead: Take the Minturn exit off I-70 and drive south on Route 24 toward Minturn and Leadville. After approximately 1 mile, immediately across from the Meadow Mountain Business Park, you'll see the parking area and trailhead for the Grouse Lake and West Grouse Creek trails.

Dogs can be off leash until the wilderness boundary, 4.6 miles in.

This is not a destination hike per se; it offers no holy grail, no pot o' gold, no ultimate goal. It is, however, a great trail on which to completely enjoy the process of hiking with your dog. It's also a trail that sees little traffic, so you and your dog can exult in sharing the many sensations that accompany a hike with little chance of interruption.

The first thing to do when you get on the trail is stop, close your eyes, and inhale; you'll pick up the unmistakable savory smell of sagebrush. Don't get used to this smell on your hike, however; you'll soon ascend out of the semiarid basin and pass through several distinct vegetative zones as you hike. The sagebrush quickly gives way to towering lodgepole pine—each one straining to get at the light high above.

After .25 mile, bear right at the fork, continuing on the West Grouse Trail (the trail to the left will lead you to Grouse Lake). Climb a gentle grade that parallels the creek. In a little under 1 mile, you'll come to an old road; continue straight across it, staying on the hiking trail. Eventually you'll come to another fork; bear right, descending to a small log bridge spanning the creek. Cross the bridge and climb into a beautiful high meadow. In late summer, you may be lucky enough to spot some ripe wild raspberries along the trail. Behind you, to the east, are fabulous views of the Holy Cross Wilderness Area. The trail meanders alternately through wet spots close to the creek and talus, continuing to gradually climb. At about 4 miles the trail will diverge from the creek, and at 4.5 miles you'll pass the first of two Waterdog Lakes along this trail, a small, remote pool in the trees. You'll find it—hopefully—by bushwacking off to the right of the trail as you ascend. As you bushwack, remember which way you came because you'll need to retrace your steps. This is the turnaround point for our trail description; if you choose to keep hiking, you'll need to leash up your dog as you cross the signed wilderness boundary.

Lost Lake

Distance: 6.8 miles round-trip

Elevation gain: About 800 feet

Trailhead: Take the Vail exit (176) off I-70 and head west on N. Frontage Rd. for approximately 1 mile to Red Sandstone Rd. Turn right and drive up a few switchbacks until you come to a dirt road bearing left (FR 700). Turn here and drive for 6 miles to the trailhead on the right.

Dogs can be off leash.

Unlike the other destination hikes just north of Vail, Lost Lake sits just outside the border of the Eagles Nest Wilderness, so your dog can hike with you under voice command. The trail traverses a ridge that separates the Piney River and Red Sandstone Creek and maintains an easy grade for much of the way (which also makes it popular with hikers, as well as mountain bikers who are riding the trail as part of a longer loop).

Start out hiking through a wonderfully shady forest of soaring lodgepole pine, spruce, and subalpine fir interspersed with groves of aspen. After 2 miles, you'll come to a junction; the left fork heads to Piney Lake. Stay straight. Shortly after, you'll top out on the trail's high point. Begin the slight descent to the lake, passing FR 720, which comes in on the right. Hike through several clear-cut areas, which were logged by the forest service in the 1980s.

The trail forks just before the lake; bear right to reach the water, where Rover will likely want to take a well-deserved dip. While he cools his paws, take in the vista of the rocky, imposing peaks of the Gore Range in the background. The trail continues past the lake and ends about .75 mile later at the eastern Lost Lake trailhead, reached via a rough four-wheel-drive road, but our hike stopped at the lake.

North Trail

Distance: 11.6 miles end to end

Elevation gain: Varies

Trailhead: There are several places to access the trail system, all on the north side of I-70. One such point is from Buffehr Creek Rd. From the West Vail exit (173), drive east on N. Frontage Rd. for .5 mile. Turn left on Buffehr Creek Rd. and drive .5 mile to the bridge; there's a parking pull-off just beyond it.

Dogs must be leashed (this is nonwilderness, but there's a special leash order on the trail).

The North Trail, which was constructed in the late 1990s, etches the hillsides on the north side of I-70, across from the Vail ski area. Though you never entirely escape hearing the underlying rush of highway traffic while on it, the trail system provides ample hiking close to town and stellar views of the Holy Cross Wilderness and, from some places, the Gore Range behind it.

For a short stroll with your dog that includes views and water, begin from the Buffehr Creek access point described above. Cross Buffehr Creek on the bridge. You'll traverse an aspen-groved hillside on a well-maintained trail before arriving at a signed fork for the North Trail system; stay right. A series of moderate switchbacks leads upward. At the plateau, you'll come to another signed fork for the North Trail. Stay right again. The trail descends back down to the level of Buffehr Creek. En route, you'll pass a beaver pond, giving your dog a chance to cool his paws and belly. This makes a good turnaround point. If you're up for a longer hike (3.2 miles total, one way), cross the creek on some large stones and climb up the opposite hill out of the drainage. Go right at the fork all the way at the top to stay on the North Trail. The trail meanders through an aspen grove before switchbacking down to Red Sandstone Rd. and another trailhead access point.

Upper Piney River Trail

Distance: 5 miles round-trip to Piney River Falls
Elevation gain: 600 feet
Trailhead: From the Vail exit (176) off I-70, take N. Frontage Rd. west. After approximately 1 mile, turn right onto Red Sandstone Rd. You'll climb through a few switchbacks and come to a dirt road bearing left (FR 700). Turn here and follow the signs to Piney River Ranch (9 miles). Park in the public parking lot outside of the fence. Note that in the past, owners of the ranch were blocking access to dogs on the short stretch of trail that crosses their property (too many unleashed dogs were chasing the horses). The forest service hammered out a compromise and rerouted the first part of the trail. You will still be crossing ranch property, however, so please be extravigilant about keeping your dog on his leash so that the ranch owners won't be inclined to re-restrict access. *Dogs must be leashed (this is wilderness area).*

This is a hike with a view: you'll be entering a broad valley flanked by cliffs of red sandstone. As the trail contours along Piney Lake's left shore, you may marvel at the sheer rock walls of the Gore Range reflected in the water. You'll most likely see waterfowl and maybe spot the beaver that live in the lodge at the east end of the lake. As you near the east shore, where the creek enters the lake, you'll see a sign and trail register indicating you are about to enter the Eagles Nest Wilderness Area. After approximately .25 mile,

bear right at the fork (the left one goes to Soda Lakes). Enjoy the vistas of rock walls ahead of you; aspen on the slopes to your left (incandescent in autumn!); and spruce, fir, and pine across the valley. The rock has weathered into rugged spires, sharp horns, knife-edge ridges, and jagged arêtes, offering a striking and photogenic backdrop.

After about 2 miles you'll come to another fork in the trail. Bear left, which will start to bring you up and around the cirque you've been admiring throughout your journey. You'll enter a forest of aspen and pine, which should send your dog's nose into overdrive; the trail will become a bit more rugged as it climbs through the rocks and trees. As you climb you'll encounter several forks along the trail; stay right on the main-travel route. It will soon bring you along a ridge, crossing several small streams, and, ultimately, to a wonderfully scenic overlook of the valley and Piney Lake beyond. You may be tempted to stop here, but less than .25 mile away is Piney River Falls. It's a bit of a scramble to the falls, but their ambience and the always spectacular vistas make it well worth your collective efforts. If you've been hiking during midafternoon, turn around periodically on the way back, as the steep rock walls turn lustrous hues of apricot and orange as the afternoon light slowly fades.

Booth Creek Falls Trail

Distance: 4 miles round-trip to the falls; 8.2 miles round-trip to Booth Lake
Elevation gain: 1,400 feet to the falls; 3,080 feet to Booth Lake
Trailhead: Take the East Vail exit (180) off I-70 and head west along Frontage Rd. In less than 1 mile you'll see Booth Falls Rd. on your right. Drive to the trailhead at the end of the road (.25 mile) and park. Please be careful not to block or park in the nearby driveways.

Dogs must be leashed (this is wilderness area).

Climb about .25 mile through open, wildflower-studded meadows to exit the noise and bustle of Vail Valley, and you'll soon travel through cool stands of aspen, white fir, and blue spruce (Colorado's state tree). Keep an eye out for hummingbirds, which are plentiful in the lower areas during summer. You'll hear the rush of Booth Creek to your left as you climb high above it. After 2 miles, the trail opens up to reveal vistas of the classic U shape of this glacially sculpted valley, with the creek bed etching a deep notch at its base. You'll also see evidence of recent avalanches all around.

Before reaching the falls you'll cross two smaller creeks, providing your dog with the opportunity to cool off. After approximately 2 miles you'll reach Booth Falls, which are quite impressive as they cascade 80 feet through a sheer notch in the schist. You'll definitely want to linger here on one of the many perches that loom directly over the plunge.

You might be tempted to turn around at the falls—don't. The falls are a portal to the incredibly beautiful high-alpine environment beyond. Immediately after the falls, the trail winds directly alongside the brook through cool and fragrant spruce groves, then climbs somewhat more steeply for a short stretch. Soon it brings you through the grass and wildflowers of a high mountain meadow, which is surrounded by the steep-sided mountains that make up the Gore Range.

Ultimately you'll come to Booth Lake, which sits at the base of a high cirque, surrounded by towering walls of schist—the predominant rock in the Gore Range. In addition to being breathtakingly beautiful and a great place to kick back, it also offers good fishing (and swimming for those with a fur suit).

 Vail Mountain. Though dogs are not allowed to ride *up* the gondola, you can take Rover hiking on the mountain's summertime trail network. And if he's tuckered out afterward, he is allowed to join you on a gondola ride *down*. A summer trail map lays out the options, and the hiking trails are separate from the biking trails so that pedestrians and downhill cyclists don't suffer any overly close encounters (a few trails, designated multiuse, are open to both, but you can easiliy avoid these). Pick up the **Berrypicker Trail** behind the gondola loading station in Lionshead. The trail climbs for 5.5 miles to Eagles Nest, where you can grab a cold libation and enjoy live music on the deck throughout the summer. You can also find water for your dog here (the hike itself is dry). You'll be treated to spectacular views of Mount of the Holy Cross and the surrounding peaks in the wilderness area. *Dogs must be leashed.*

CYCLING FOR CANINES

The **Turquoise Lake Trail** outside of Leadville is a mellow bike ride that dogs also will enjoy, while the **Meadow Mountain Trail** near Minturn includes a gradual climb (see Tail-Rated Trails). The **Lost Lake Trail**, ridden from the east side, combines forest service roads and a bit of singletrack. It's about a 10-mile round-trip if you ride an out-and-back to the lake starting from Lost Lake Rd. (FR 786), a little more than .7 miles up Red Sandstone Rd. from Vail's N. Frontage Rd.; you can shorten the distance by driving part of the way up FR 786 if you have a high-clearance vehicle. Near Leadville, the 6-mile round-trip ride on the **Interlaken Trail** leads along rolling singletrack to an abandoned resort from the late 1800s that's undergoing some restoration; your dog will also have access to the Twin Lakes at various points along the trail.

POWDERHOUNDS

Tennessee Pass Nordic Center. Located at the base of Ski Cooper, northwest of Leadville, the Nordic center (formerly known as Piney Creek) has 25 kilometers of trails for skiing and snowshoeing. And your dog is welcome to accompany you on all of them! You'll have to purchase a trail pass; Fido is free. 719-486-1750, www.tennesseepass.com

At the **Vail Nordic Center**, on the Vail Golf Course, dogs are allowed on the 15 kilometers of snowshoe trails (not any of the ski trails) and must be leashed. 970-476-8366, www.vailnordiccenter.com

As for backcountry trails, there's national forest land aplenty where you can ski or snowshoe with a canine companion. A trail system begins on the south side of Tennessee Pass; the **Powder Hound Loop** would be especially appropriate. Pick up a Lake County ski map at the Leadville Ranger District (see Resources). Note that the trails beginning at the Leadville Fish Hatchery are not really appropriate for skiing with dogs, unless you're skijoring, as they enter a designated wilderness area, where leash rules apply.

The Vail Pass area keeps getting busier and busier, with skiers and snowmobilers alike. Instead, bring your dog to one of the unplowed forest service roads off Hwy. 24 south of Minturn, such as the **Tigiwon Road** (FR 707) or **No Name Road** (FR 705), or skin or shoe up the gentle grade of the **Meadow Mountain** road (see Tail-Rated Trails).

CREATURE COMFORTS

Unless otherwise stated, dogs should not be left unattended in the room or cabin.

LEGAL BEAGLES

If your dog stays in Vail for more than two weeks, you'll have to get him a local license. Call the animal shelter in Eagle at 970-328-DOGS for details.

Avon

$$$–$$$$ Comfort Inn Beaver Creek, 161 W. Beaver Creek Blvd., 970-949-5511, 800-423-4374, www.comfortinn.com. Dogs under 50 pounds each are allowed in first-floor rooms for a $50 one-time fee. Note that dogs are not allowed in the lobby.

 $$$$ Ritz-Carlton Bachelor Gulch, 0130 Daybreak Ridge, 970-748-6200, 800-241-3333, www.ritzcarlton .com. Located in Bachelor Gulch amid the Beaver Creek ski area (though accessible by road) the Ritz puts on a four-star experience for its canine clientele for a $125 one-time fee. The large rooms start at 450 square feet and are impeccably furnished in a luxe mountain style. Dog amenities include biscuits from the hotel's pastry kitchen, a Ritz-logoed bed, and food and water bowls in the room. And if Fido is feeling a bit overworked after hiking or snowshoeing on nearby trails, book him an in-room dog massage, available through the spa. If you happen to be staying at the Ritz without your pooch and are feeling a bit lonely, you can take Bachelor, the resort's resident yellow Lab, on a hike or snowshoe; through its Loan-a-Lab program, the Ritz will supply you with a trail map, a fanny pack with a water bottle, dog biscuits, a leash, and the opportunity to donate to the Eagle River Humane Society—and Bachelor, of course. Reservations are recommended, as Bachelor is a pretty popular pup.

$$$$ Westin Riverfront Resort and Spa, 126 Riverfront Ln., 970-790-6000, 866-949-1616, www.westin.com/river frontavon. Among the newest of the Vail area's luxury hotels, the Westin doesn't overlook the comfort of its four-legged guests, providing dogs with a canine version of Westin's signature Heavenly Bed. Visiting canines will also find food and water bowls awaiting them in the room and a welcome package with biscuits and clean-up bags. The one restriction is a limit of 80 pounds of dog per room; you could stay with one large dog, for example, or two 40-pound dogs. The rooms, appointed with warm, contemporary furnishings, range from studios to three bedrooms. Studio units include kitchenettes, and the larger units include full kitchens; all have gas fireplaces. You can leave your dog unattended inside, but housekeeping won't enter during that time. The resort also has a large spa, restaurant and wine bar, and a gondola right outside the door whisks you (but not your pooch, since dogs aren't allowed in Beaver Creek) up to the Beaver Creek ski area.

Eagle

$$ Sylvan Lake State Park Cabins and Yurts, 10200 Brush Creek Rd., 970-328-2021, www.parks.state.co.us/parks/sylvanlake. Dogs are permitted in two of the park's eight camper cabins near the lake for $10 extra per night, as well as in one of the three yurts up East Brush Creek (9.5 miles from the lake). The cabins and yurt sleep up to six people each; bring bedding and cooking supplies for both.

$$$ Holiday Inn Express, 0075 Pond Rd., 970-328-8088, 800-HOLIDAY (national number), www.hiexpress.com/eagleco. Certain rooms are pet-friendly, with a $40 one-time fee for dogs, and a limit of two dogs (or perhaps three particularly small ones).

$$$–$$$$ Best Western Eagle Lodge, 200 Loren Lane, 970-328-6316, 800-780-7234 (national number), www.bestwestern.com. The motel charges a $10 nightly fee, per pet, and requires a $150 deposit if you're paying in cash. There's a limit of two dogs per room, and pit bulls are not permitted at the motel. You'll be asked to sign a pet release form at check-in saying

that if you leave your dog unattended in the room, you'll take responsibility for the consequences of any destructive behavior or excessive barking.

Edwards

$$$–$$$$ Inn and Suites at Riverwalk, 27 Main St., 970-926-0606, 888-926-0606, www.innandsuitesatriverwalk.com. Though not nearly as beautiful as the striking lobby, the rooms in this hotel are spacious and comfortable. Dogs are also allowed in some of the one- to three-bedroom condos adjacent to the hotel, which have gas fireplaces and jetted tubs. There's a $25 fee per dog for the first night of your visit, with a $5 charge for each additional night, as well as a limit of two dogs per room (or condo). If you need to leave Fido unattended inside your room, the front desk staff asks that you leave a cell-phone number with them.

Granite

$$ Win-Mar Cabins, intersection of Hwys. 24 and 82, 719-486-0785, 800-694-6627, www.winmarcabins.com. These ten fully equipped cabins, situated at the turnoff for Independence Pass, aren't in the most scenic setting, but the location—about halfway between Leadville and Buena Vista—is convenient. Dogs under 10 pounds are permitted with a $50 deposit. From May to mid-November, all cabins are available; during the winter only a couple are kept open.

Leadville

$ Leadville Hostel, 500 E. 7th St., 719-486-9334, www.leadvillehostel.com. This small, friendly hostel in a converted ranch house several blocks off the main street is actually one of the nicer places to stay in Leadville. It welcomes dogs for a $5 one-time fee "provided that the owners are nice, they have the dog under control, and the dog gets along with other people," says owner "Wild" Bill Clower. Of the 11 rooms, some are private, with their own bathroom, and others are dormitory-style, with several beds and shared bath. All have homey touches like quilts, which make it feel more like a bed-and-breakfast than a hostel. Dogs generally aren't placed in the dorm rooms, unless everybody there agrees to it. Guests have use of the kitchen and the large common areas. If you need to leave your dog unattended for a short time, you can leash him up outside, where there's plenty of space to do so. This is a popular place for runners to stay while they engage in high-altitude training, and some bring their dogs. Perhaps yours will be inspired to shed that puppy fat in the company of such athletic canines.

$$ Alps Motel, 207 Elm St., 719-486-1223, 800-818-ALPS, www.alpsmotel.com. Dogs are allowed in some of the rooms at this homey, eight-unit motel for $18 a night for one dog, plus an additional $12 for a second dog. There's a limit of two dogs per room.

$$ Hitchin' Post Motel, 3164 Hwy. 91 (3 miles north of Leadville), 719-486-2783, 888-824-0422, www.hitchinpostmotel.org. Your dog is welcome to hang his hat in any of the rooms here. The motel is on 7.5 acres, with some frontage on the East Fork of the Arkansas River, and you can exercise your dog off leash on the property, away from the main area.

$$ Mountain Peaks Motel, 1 Harrison Ave., 719-486-3178, 877-487-3178, www.mountainpeaksmotel.com. There's a $5 fee per night, per dog, at this small, vintage motel. The motel also offers a large hostel room with 19 beds; dogs, understandably, are not permitted here.

$$–$$$ Silver King Motor Inn, 2020 N. Poplar, 719-486-2610, 800-871-2610, www.silverkinginn.com. The Silver King underwent an extensive renovation to turn it into one of Leadville's fancier motels. For an additional $10 per night, per pet, dogs can stay in one of the eight designated pet rooms (none of the suites, which have full kitchens, are pet friendly).

$$–$$$ Timberline Motel, 216 Harrison Ave., 719-486-1876, 800-352-1876, www.timberlinemotel.net. Located in the heart of downtown, the Timberline has basic rooms but is definitely more tourist-oriented than some of the other nearby motels. Three of the 15 rooms are family-style, which means they have two queen beds. There's a $7 fee per night, per dog, and a pet rules page clearly spells out the dos and don'ts for Fido.

$$$–$$$$ Leadville Inn, 127 E. 8th St., 719-966-4770, www.leadvilleinn.com. You have to like a B&B that touts being dog friendly at the top of its list of amenities. The homey, but not stuffy, inn welcomes canine guests in any of its nine rooms for a $10 one-time fee. Five rooms are in the main house, a Victorian built in 1895, and four are in the adjacent carriage house; all have private baths. You can leave your dog unattended inside, preferably in a travel crate, for a short time. Three host dogs live here, so your dog will have lots of company to sniff out. When not exploring the trails around Leadville, you and your dog can relax in the garden, which has a small gazebo and hot tub.

Minturn

$$$$ Pando Cabins, Hwy. 24 at Camp Hale, 719-486-2656, 888-949-6682, www.novaguides.com. For a $20 one-time fee, your dog can step back in history during a stay at these cabins located near Camp Hale, the one-time ski-training ground for the Tenth Mountain Division troops, who courageously fought in the Alps during World War II. The three two-bedroom modern log cabins come fully equipped with kitchens, gas fire-places, decks overlooking Camp Hale, and southwestern decor. You can leave your dog unattended inside if he has a travel kennel to stay in. And if he's not into the historical aspect, he'll certainly enjoy romping leash free on the surrounding 80 acres. The cabins are operated by Nova Guides, which runs rafting, fishing, jeeping, ATV, and mountain-bike trips in the summer and rents snowmobile and has dogsled tours in the winter.

Redcliff

$$$ Redcliff Ski Lodge, 206 Eagle St., 866-563-1222, www.redcliffskilodge.com. The town of Redcliff is a small hamlet tucked in the upper Eagle River Valley, right off Hwy. 24 and at the southern end of the dirt Shrine Pass Rd. (the latter is closed in winter). The lodge consists of two buildings that house seven large, recently remodeled condos, ranging in size from one to three bedrooms. Your well-behaved dog can be left unattended inside at your discretion. There's a three-night minimum stay.

Twin Lakes

$$ Twin Peaks Cabins, 6889 Hwy. 82 (.5 mile west of Twin Lakes Village), 719-486-2667. Located on the road to Independence Pass, Twin Peaks offers two fully equipped cabins as well as a four-bedroom mobile home for rent. Well-mannered dogs are allowed, with a $10 charge per night. The owner, who loves dogs but not necessarily the messes they make, emphasizes that they should be kept on a leash at all times outside and that you should walk Fido away from the property to do his business. Open mid-May to mid-October.

$$-$$$ Mount Elbert Lodge, Hwy. 82 (4 miles west of Twin Lakes Village), 719-486-0594, 800-381-4433, www.mount-elbert.com. The lodge, a former stagecoach stop with an idyllic setting on the banks of Lake Creek, makes a great dog destination. Though dogs are not allowed in the B&B rooms of the main lodge, they are welcome in any of the eight cozily decorated, fully furnished cabins for $15 per night, per pet. Cabins range from one to four bedrooms, and in winter, six of them are available to stay in. If your dog would like to explore Mount Elbert itself—Colorado's highest peak—the Black Cloud trail to the summit starts right outside the door.

Vail

$$$-$$$$ Antlers at Vail, 680 W. Lionshead Pl., 970-476-2471, 800-843-8245, www.antlersvail.com. About a quarter of the 90-some individually owned condos in this very-near-to-slopeside, recently refurbished complex allow dogs. For $15 per night, per pet, you and your dog can stay in comfort in units that range from studios to three bedrooms, all with full kitchens and gas fireplaces (none of the four-bedroom condos are pet friendly). Dogs can be left unattended in the condos as long as you leave a cell-phone number at the front desk. The Antlers is located alongside Gore Creek; a creekside trail runs right behind the building. And the staff is more than willing to dispense free dog biscuits at the front desk.

$$$-$$$$ Holiday Inn Apex Vail, 2211 N. Frontage Rd. West, 970-476-3890, 866-317-2739, www.apexvail.com. The hotel has been extensively renovated and updated from its former incarnation as the West Vail Lodge, and with amenities like granite/marble baths and high-thread-count bed linens, it's now one of the nicest Holiday Inns you can stay in. Only three rooms are dog friendly, however; one smoking and two nonsmoking. There's a $25 fee per night, per pet, and dog guests must weigh less than 50 pounds.

$$$–$$$$ Lift House Condominiums, 555 E. Lionshead Circle, 970-476-2340, 800-654-0635, www.lifthousevail.com. Most of these individually owned studio condos just steps from the gondola allow dogs for $25 per night, per pet. There's a maximum of two dogs per unit. Each condo is equipped with a gas fireplace and kitchenette. If you leave your dog unattended in the room, he must be contained in a travel kennel. Bart & Yeti's restaurant (see sidebar) is just downstairs.

$$$$ Lodge at Vail, 174 E. Gore Creek Dr., 970-476-5011, 877-528-7625, www .lodgeatvail.rockresorts.com. The lodge's extremely plush rooms and suites (which are really one- to three-bedroom condos) are furnished in a style that evokes a very high-end ski chalet, so if your pooch answers to the name of Heidi and yodels instead of barks, she'll be right at home here. The hotel has designated pet rooms for an additional fee of $50 per night and with a limit of one dog per room. You can leave your dog lounging unattended in the room if you need to, perhaps while you get a papaya-pineapple wrap at the new spa or partake of the amazing lunch buffet at the in-house Cucina Rustica restaurant.

$$$$ Sonnenalp, 20 Vail Rd., 970-476-5656, 800-654-8312, www.sonnenalp .com. At this beautiful, Bavarian-inspired hotel (there is, in fact, a sister property in Germany), dogs are permitted in certain rooms for a $100 one-time fee per pet. Most of the rooms are suites, ranging from 490 to 1,600 square feet and are luxuriously appointed with custom wood furniture, gas fireplaces, and bathrooms with radiant-heated floors. You can leave your dog unattended inside or arrange for dogsitting through the concierge, at $15 an hour. If your dog is alone and creates a nuisance, however, the hotel will likely send up someone to petsit, at a rate of $20 an hour. There's a full spa on-site, as well as four restaurants and an indoor-outdoor pool. Note that dogs are not permitted at One Willow Bridge, a condo complex that the Sonnenalp also oversees.

CAMPGROUNDS

State park campgrounds: **Sylvan Lake State Park,** 16 miles south of Eagle on W. Brush Creek Rd., has two campgrounds (44 sites).

National forest campgrounds: **Gore Creek Campground,** Hwy. 6, 2 miles from the East Vail exit off I-70 (25 sites); **Camp Hale Memorial Campground,** Hwy. 24, south of Minturn at Camp Hale (21 sites); **Turquoise Lake,** outside of Leadville (see Tail-Rated Trails for directions), with 8 campgrounds, for a total of 261 sites; **Lakeview Campground,** FR 125, off Hwy. 82 near Twin Lakes (59 sites).

SNIFF AND BE SNIFFED

When in Vail, bring your dog to Bart & Yeti's restaurant, named after Bart, a golden retriever, and Yeti, a spaniel mix, who used to frequent the place. Woodrow, a cocker spaniel, carries on their legacy. Bart mixed with the movers and shakers, siring dogs belonging to Henry Kissinger, Nelson Rockefeller, and Clint Eastwood (Liberty, former president Ford's dog, was the lucky gal). Enjoy a meal with your dog on the outside patio (though a local dog or two has also been known to sneak into the bar area).

WORTH A PAWS

Leadville, Colorado & Southern Railroad Company. Bring Fido on a scenic, open-passenger-car train ride along the old Colorado & Southern high line. Though it's ultimately up to each day's conductor to give the final say on whether a leashed dog is allowed, chances are good yours will make the grade. The two-and-a-half-hour round-trip brings you north of Leadville toward Fremont Pass, up to the Climax molybdenum mine and back again, with a short stop at the French Gulch water tower. The train runs daily from the end of May to the beginning of October, with two runs a day between mid-June and mid-August. Catch it at the historic depot, 326 E. 7th St. in Leadville. For price information, call 866-386-3936 or go to www.leadville-train.com.

Mountain Dog Biscuit and Gifts, 100 E. Meadow Dr., #33, 970-479-8488, www .mountaindogvail.com. This dog (and, despite the name, cat) emporium caters to active pups who want to be stylish, too. Your dog can sniff out things like Ruff-wear dog packs so he can keep his things handy on the trail and Swiss-made Alpen Schatz leather collars so he can look suitably Alpine while in Vail. There's also a selection of leashes, dog bowls, beds, and elevated feeders, and breed-specific papier-mâché clocks and charms for dog-devoted owners.

Teva Mountain Games Dog Competitions. This annual early June outdoor-adventure sports extravaganza draws pro and amateur mountain bikers, kayakers, climbers, trail runners, paragliders—and extreme canines. What started as one distance dock-jumping event for dogs in 2007 has

Dogs let fly at the dock-jumping competition during the annual Teva Mountain Games in Vail.

morphed into a trifecta of events: the big air, where dogs are judged on the distance they jump from dock to water; extreme vertical, in which dogs compete to see who can jump the highest off a dock; and speed retrieve, where dogs are timed on how quickly they can jump off the dock and nab a rubber toy suspended above the water. Dogs of all experience levels, from newbies to veterans, can register to compete. We entered Tansy in the inaugural dock-jumping competition; she was in third place—until the fourth dog went. Despite the fact that her seven-plus-foot jump paled in comparison to the winning jumps of 20-something feet, we told her that it's about having fun, not winning. And she definitely had fun. For more information, go to www.tevamountain games.com.

DOGGIE DAYCARE
Avon
Eagle-Vail Animal Hospital, 40843 Hwy. 6, 970-949-4044, www.eaglevailvet .com. $26/day. Open 8 AM–5 PM, Monday to Friday.

Vail Doggie Day Spa and Lodging, 41199 Hwy. 6, 970-949-0922, www.vaildoggie .com. $31/day; $20/under six hours, $12/ two hours. Dogs are divided into groups of similar temperament and have three indoor play areas. They're also walked every three hours. Open 7:30 AM–7 PM, Monday, Wednesday, Thursday, Friday; 8 AM–6 PM, Saturday and Sunday; no daycare on Tuesday.

Walkin' the Dog, 281 Metcalf Rd., #201, 970-476-8197. $40/day. Dogs have access to an indoor play area and a 1.5-acre fenced outside yard. Pick-up and drop-off can be arranged, and the daycare also offers hour-long group dog hikes ($30), which includes pick-up and drop-off. Open 7:30 AM–6:30 PM, Monday to Friday.

Leadville

Cold Nose Warm Heart Pet Care, 329 Hwy. 24, 719-486-2014. $15/day. Dogs play together indoors and outdoors at this home-based daycare. Open daily by appointment.

PET PROVISIONS

Avon

Avon Pet Centre, 730 Nottingham Rd., 970-949-6467, www.avon-pet-centre.com

Eagle-Vail Animal Hospital, 40843 Hwy. 6, 970-949-4044, www.eaglevailvet.com

Edwards

The Pet Spot, 0429 Edwards Access Rd., Ste. 204, 970-926-5786

Wags & Whiskers, 34520 Hwy. 6, Unit C10, 970-926-8768

Leadville

Cold Nose Warm Heart Pet Care, 329 Hwy. 24, 719-486-2014

CANINE ER

Avon

Avon Pet Centre (AAHA certified), 730 Nottingham Rd., 970-949-6467, www.avon-pet-centre.com. Open 8 AM–5:30 PM, Monday to Friday; 9 AM–4 PM, Saturday.

Eagle-Vail Animal Hospital/Vail Animal ER, 40843 Hwy. 6, 970-949-4044/970-845-2286, www.eaglevailvet.com. Open 8 AM–5 PM, Monday to Friday. The ER part of the hospital is open from 6 PM Friday–8 AM Monday.

Leadville

Leadville Veterinary Clinic, 728 Front St., 719-486-1487. Open 9 AM–5 PM, Monday to Friday (closed Thursday).

RESOURCES

Leadville/Lake County Chamber of Commerce, 809 Harrison Ave., Leadville, 719-486-3900, 888-532-3845, www.visit leadvilleco.com

Holy Cross Ranger District, White River National Forest, 24747 Hwy. 24, Minturn, 970-827-5715

Leadville Ranger District, San Isabel National Forest, 810 Front St., Leadville, 719-486-0749

Vail Valley Partnership (Chamber and Tourism Bureau), 970-476-1000, 800-525-3875, www.visitvailvalley.com

Eleven

Aspen

THE BIG SCOOP

Aspen is one of the dog-friendliest towns we've visited. So friendly, in fact, that Clover and I moved here shortly after the first edition of *Canine Colorado* came out. A comment I overheard one day while strolling downtown sums it up: "All the dogs here seem so happy," said a woman to her companion, glancing at Clover.

Dogs are welcome on the downtown pedestrian mall, which includes several fountains. The one at the corner of Hyman and Mill—columns of water of varying heights that spurt unpredictably through a grate—is especially appealing to dogs. We've rated several hotels "exceptionally dog friendly." Dogs are permitted on local buses in Snowmass Village (though not on the Roaring Fork Transportation Authority ones that go in and out of Aspen). And your dog need not worry about missing out on any of the chichi shopping opportunities for which Aspen is renowned; almost every store allows Clover and Tansy as customers (and they knows exactly where some of them keep a stash of dog biscuits).

The leash situation in Aspen and environs merits some explanation. Technically, a leash law is in effect in Aspen and Snowmass as well as throughout Pitkin County. Historically, it hasn't been rigorously enforced on a consistent basis. But as more people (and dogs) move into Aspen, and trail use increases, conflicts have been on the rise. The trail descriptions here reflect the leash laws as they're written, but as you and your dog are out and about, you'll certainly notice a large contingent of off-leash dogs. So with this information in mind, use your common sense and discretion as to how you control your dog.

TAIL-RATED TRAILS

This is only a small sampling of the many gorgeous trails in the Aspen area. For more ideas, consult *Aspen Snowmass Trails*, by Warren Ohlrich, or the "Aspen/ Crested Butte/Gunnison Recreation Topo Map," put out by Latitude 40°. The Aspen Ranger District of the White River National Forest Service also has a sheet of off-leash hikes (see Resources). And if your dog wants an instant "in" with Aspen's canine social scene, take him up **Smuggler Mountain Rd.**, on the east side of town near the Centennial condo complex. Especially after work, there's a steady parade of hikers, mountain bikers, and dogs heading up and down this dirt road. And dogs can be off leash. The most popular destination is a viewing platform about 1.5 miles up, from which you can catch your breath and enjoy a vista of Aspen and, beyond, Mount Sopris.

Hunter Creek/ Hunter Valley Trail
Distance: About 4 miles round-trip
Elevation gain: 1,500 feet
Trailhead: Take Main St. to Mill St. north, bear left onto Red Mountain Rd. after the bridge, then take an immediate right onto Lone Pine Rd. Trail access is via the first left, into the Hunter Creek condos parking lot (you'll need to park on the street, however). The trailhead is close enough to town that you can walk to it. There is an upper access point farther up Red Mountain Rd. via a right turn onto

Chica and Kim Raupp on a spring ski outing on Mount Hayden.

Hunter Creek Rd.; however, the lower access offers proximity to the creek.
Dogs must be leashed up until the forest service boundary.

This trail has it all for dogs: water, trees, and a meadow to frolic in. Begin by following Hunter Creek, crossing it via bridges several times. As you ascend, you'll get increasingly better views of Aspen Mountain. The trail becomes steeper and more rocky before reaching the Benedict Bridge, where it merges with the trail from the upper access. Shortly after the bridge, consider a short detour up the hillside to Verena Mallory Park (look for the spur trail to the right and the park sign), where you'll find an overlook, with bench, that provides great views of Aspen and the Elk Mountains. Then continue on the now-wide main trail as it climbs steeply, crossing a private drive along the way. At the national forest boundary sign (where you can unleash as long as your dog stays under voice control), the trail opens up into the spacious meadows of Hunter Valley. Follow the wide trail through and to the left, where you'll come to the Tenth Mountain Bridge, 1.5 miles from the trailhead. The meadow beyond is home to several old cabins. To make a short loop, follow the trail east through this meadow. When you come to another smaller bridge, cross over and come back down the path along the south side of the creek. Rejoin the main Hunter Valley Trail near the Tenth Mountain Bridge. Head back to the trailhead the way you came up.

Aspen Mountain

Access: During June, July, and August, and on September weekends after Labor Day, the Silver Queen Gondola whisks hikers to the top of 11,212-foot Aspen Mountain. Not only can your dog accompany you (at no charge) but you can purchase a souvenir dog gondola pass with your loved one's picture on it for $10 at the gondola ticket office. The gondola operates 10 AM to 4 PM, and tickets are $23–$26. 970-925-1220, www.aspen snowmass.com
Dogs should be leashed near the restaurant and gondola unloading station; once you begin hiking on the ridge or down the mountain, you'll be primarily on national forest land and leashing your dog is at your discretion.

Once at the top, you can choose to stroll out along Richmond Ridge (there's a short nature walk loop, but you can also hike for miles on a four-wheel-drive road), hike 4.5 miles to the bottom of the gondola via Summer Rd., or take the shorter (2.5 miles) but more precipitous Ute Trail down. A popular locals' routine is to hike up Aspen Mountain, then ride the gondola down. You can also dine alfresco with your dog at the Sundeck Restaurant; on Saturdays at 1 PM during the Aspen Music Festival, students give free concerts mountaintop, and on Sundays from mid-June through the end of August, there are free bluegrass concerts outside the Sundeck, from noon to 3 PM.

Sunnyside Trail

Distance: About 4 miles round-trip

Elevation gain: About 1,300 feet

Trailhead: Take Hwy. 82 west out of Aspen. Just after the road jogs right, then left, you'll cross Castle Creek; turn right at the traffic light onto Cemetery Ln. After 1.5 miles you'll see a small parking area on the left; the trail begins on the right. You can also access the trail via a new extension that begins off the Rio Grande Trail. Doing so will add about 1 mile round-trip to your hike, but parking is more prevalent. After turning onto Cemetery Ln., drive for about 1 mile and look for the large parking area on the left, just after you cross the Roaring Fork River. Hike west on the Rio Grande Trail for a few minutes and look for the signed Sunnyside Trail heading up on the right.

Dogs can be off leash.

This trail features easy access from town as well as scenic views. Because it climbs up a dry, south-facing slope, dogs will enjoy it most in the early morning or evening on warm days (or anytime on cooler days). However, the trail's middle section, which passes a couple of irrigation ditches, does bring four-leggeds closer to water for at least part of the way. The narrow trail contours steeply up the hillside. As you hike, you'll gain great views of Aspen Mountain, Aspen Highlands, and Buttermilk; the Maroon Bells will soon reveal themselves behind Buttermilk. After a level section where the trail follows a ditch for a stretch, giving your dog a perfect wading opportunity, it crosses another ditch and resumes climbing, traversing a series of long switchbacks up the side of Red Mountain.

A good turnaround spot is the radio tower, which you'll come to shortly after entering a large aspen grove, where the trail temporarily levels out again. If you're up for a longer hike, continue uphill until you reach a signed intersection with the **Shadyside Trail**, which peels off to the left. The trail, which lives up to its name, follows a not-quite-2-mile loop through the forest; stay right at the first two trail intersections to rejoin the Sunnyside Trail, from which you can retrace your route back down the mountain. The Shadyside extension is particularly appealing because, though it's relatively close to town, you and your dog's chances of encountering other hikers are about as good as finding a hotel room for under $100 in Aspen.

Crown Mountain Dog Park

Access: From the intersection of Hwy. 82 and Valley Rd. in Basalt/El Jebel (just past City Market if you're coming from downtown Basalt), turn south onto Valley Rd., then stay right at the fork immediately after. The entrance to Crown Mountain Park is just ahead on the left. Once you enter the roundabout at the park entrance, take the first right. Then bear right just before the park's playground. A left turn shortly after will bring you to a parking lot.

Regulations: Dogs must be licensed and current on vaccinations; no puppies younger than four months or dogs in heat; no aggressive dogs or excessive barking; clean up after your dog; dogs can't wear

Tansy rarely stops long enough to sniff the wildflowers.

spiked or choke collars; children 16 and under must be with an adult; there's a limit of three dogs per person; no smoking or food, except for dog treats, is allowed inside the fence.

Dogs can be off leash.

If you're in the Basalt area, this generously sized dog park—part of a larger complex that includes playing fields, tennis courts, and an extremely creative children's playground—is a great place to let Fido run. The dog park contains two grassy side-by-side enclosures, each individually fenced. There's a bench in each side for owners to hang out on and, because the tennis courts are next door, your dog may well discover a stray ball or two lying around. A water fountain for both people and pups is just outside the entrance gate, along with a poop-bag dispenser; there's also a water pump and dog bowl inside one half of the park.

Difficult Creek

Distance: 4.8 miles round-trip

Elevation gain: 1,340 feet

Trailhead: Head east on Hwy. 82 from downtown; from the spot where you must turn left to follow the highway (at Original St.), it's 3.5 miles to the Difficult Campground parking area on the right. When the campground is open (generally from the end of May to the end of September), drive down to the picnic area day-parking lot on the right; the trailhead is at the southeast corner of the lot. When the campground is closed, you'll have to walk .6 mile down a paved road to the trailhead.

Dogs must be leashed (this is wilderness area).

Don't let the name of this trail mislead you—it's actually a moderate hike. And because the route is mostly in pine and fir forest, this is a good hike for dogs on a hot day. After leaving the parking lot, stay left at the first fork, then follow the brown-and-white designated-route markers to a wooden bridge that spans the Roaring Fork River. The trail leads to Difficult Creek, then climbs away from the creek for a while before rejoining it (you'll cross another small stream en route). You'll eventually pass through a clearing, where your dog may be able to spot the remains of some log cabins, and arrive at a sign indicating that the trail is not maintained beyond this point. This is the "official" turnaround spot.

Rio Grande Trail

Distance: 44 miles from Herron Park in downtown Aspen to 23rd St. in Glenwood Springs.

Access: The trail has multiple access points throughout the Roaring Fork Valley. One that's just a short walk from downtown Aspen is to take Main St. to Mill St. north (away from Aspen Mountain), then left on Puppy Smith St. Catch the trail across the street from the post office.

To reach an unpaved portion of the trail, drive Main St. (Hwy. 82) west out of Aspen. Just after the road jogs right, then left, you'll cross Castle Creek; turn right at the traffic light onto Cemetery Ln. After crossing the Roaring Fork River at about 1 mile, look for the parking area on the left.

Dogs must be leashed. Also, dogs are not permitted on about 5.5 miles of the trail farther downvalley—the stretch that begins in Emma, outside Basalt, and runs to the Catherine Bridge on CR 100 in Carbondale.

This popular trail along the Roaring Fork River follows the old Denver & Rio Grande railroad bed, so it remains fairly level throughout, with a slightly perceptible 2 percent grade along its length. If your dog is into jogging, this trail is a perfect venue. If you head downvalley (left) on the trail, the first 2 miles are paved. At Cemetery Ln., the trail surface switches to gravel for the next 6 miles. (About 1 mile from this juncture, look for the small, tropical-style waterfalls cascading down a rock face next to the trail. Your dog will probably want to take a dip or sip from the crystal-clear pool at the bottom.) As you travel farther west, the Roaring Fork drops away into a canyon while the trail comes out onto a plateau behind the Aspen Airport Business Center (a hot, dry stretch on a summer afternoon). After traversing the sagebrush-filled expanse on the wide trail for another mile or so, you'll cross McLain Flats Rd. and pick up the trail on the other side. If you and your dog are industrious hikers, continue until the trail dips down near the funky Woody Creek Tavern across the road, 8 miles from Aspen. Enjoy lunch on the patio, then call a taxi to shuttle you back to town.

If you head upvalley (right) on the trail (from the Aspen post office), you'll travel under Mill St. and then past the Aspen Art Museum before reaching the John Denver Sanctuary after about .25 mile (look for the song lyrics inscribed on huge, granite boulders). The shallow pools formed by the Roaring Fork River at this point are a popular spot for local dogs to splash and swim.

Hogan and Marley in the Maroon Bells–Smowmass wilderness area.

Ute Trail

Distance: About 2 miles round-trip

Elevation gain: 1,700 feet

Trailhead: This trail is also within walking distance of downtown. Head east on Ute Ave. for about .4 mile. Shortly after you come to a house with a multitude of windows, look for the small wooden trail sign on the right (across from a parking pullout for Ute Park). *Dogs must be leashed.*

Because of its proximity to town and its low mileage, the Ute Trail is an efficient way to exercise your dog (as well as yourself). This short trail switchbacks steeply up the lower third of Aspen Mountain. The reward is a bird's-eye view of town from the rock outcroppings at the end. Don't forget water for your dog, as there's no source on the trail—actually, you'll both need it after tackling the lung-busting climb. You can also hike all the way to the top of Aspen Mountain from the Ute, if your dog is up for an even more intense workout; follow the trail to the left just before the rock outcroppings and stay left at the fork shortly after. Farther up the mountain you'll join up with some of the ski area service roads. And if you're tuckered out after topping out, two-leggeds and four-leggeds alike can ride the gondola down.

Maroon Bells

Access: Take your dog to view two of Colorado's best-known peaks, the 14,000-plus-foot Maroon Bells. From mid-June to Labor Day and on weekends in September, cars are not permitted to drive up to the Bells between 8:30 AM and 5 PM, unless you're camping, backpacking, or have an infant in a car seat. (A $10 pass per car is required for cars entering before and after these hours.) The best way to get there is to board a Maroon Bells–bound Roaring Fork Transit Authority bus at the base of the Aspen Highlands ski area on Maroon Creek Rd. Though dogs aren't permitted on any other Aspen buses, they are allowed on this one route, and for free (people pay $6). Call 970-925-8484 for more information. *Dogs must be leashed due to the heavy use of the area.*

The 1.5-mile **Maroon Lake Scenic Trail** lives up to its name, providing stunning views of the nearby Bells. (Note that dogs are not allowed within 100 feet of Crater Lake, which is 1.75 miles up the Maroon-Snowmass Trail.) To give your dog a chance to enjoy the beauty of this area while encountering relatively few people, hike the beautiful **Maroon Creek Trail**, which runs 4.5 miles from the upper Maroon Lake parking lot down the valley to the East Maroon Portal. The bus can then pick you up along Maroon Creek Rd. for the trip back to town.

Conundrum Creek Trail
Distance: 17 miles round-trip
Elevation gain: 2,500 feet
Dogs must be leashed.

The only reason this extremely popular backpack route is included here is so you'll be aware of its restrictions. The trail leads up a scenic valley to a pair of wonderfully situated hot springs pools (and eventually to Gothic, near Crested Butte), but the trip is not a lot of fun for dogs. For starters, neither Clover nor I (with both of us wearing packs) enjoyed being linked to each other for 8.5 miles. Because the hot springs see heavy use, camping is limited to designated sites, which become even more limited if you're with a dog. And dogs cannot be brought over to the east side of Conundrum Creek, where the hot springs are. In fact, as of summer 2009, the forest service was even considering an outright ban on dogs here. So if the thought of tying your dog to a tree, out of sight, while you luxuri-

ate in the springs evokes a pang of guilt, leave Fido at home for this one.

Ashcroft Ghost Town. The town of Ashcroft, 10 miles up Castle Creek Rd., was established by silver prospectors in 1880, and today some remaining structures, including a couple that have been rehabilitated enough for you to walk into, provide a glimpse into the past (there's a $3 entrance fee). Your dog, unfortunately, will have to stay behind. But you can make a quick tour of Ashcroft in about 15 minutes, so leaving him in the car, with windows open, of course, wouldn't be problematic. And then you can take him for a hike on one of the nearby trails in the Castle Creek valley.

Hallam Lake Nature Preserve. As might be expected, dogs are not allowed at this 25-acre oasis that is home to the Aspen Center for Environmental Studies.

Lake Christine and Toner Creek State Wildlife Areas. These two areas near Basalt—the first a 4,000-acre preserve on Basalt Mountain, the second up the Fryingpan Valley—are managed by the Colorado Department of Wildlife. Lake Christine was a popular dog-walking spot in the past; however, the DOW banned dogs in May 2000 from both areas because too many dog owners were ignoring the leash requirement.

North Star Nature Preserve. Dogs are prohibited from this 175-acre open-space-area-cum-nature-preserve on the east side of Aspen (though somehow cross-country ski trail grooming machines and para-gliders alighting from the sky are not considered disruptive to the nature idyll). Ironically, the private development of 15,000-square-foot houses that abuts the preserve also bans dogs from entering. You can walk with your leashed dog on the **East Aspen Trail**, which runs adjacent to the preserve's north boundary; just keep Fido from crossing the fence.

CYCLING FOR CANINES

The **Government Trail** is an area classic that runs 9.8 miles between Snowmass Village and Aspen. The best way to bike it is to start from Snowmass, and you'll want to set up a car shuttle if you ride the whole trail. The **Hunter Valley Trail** (begin from the upper access—Red Mountain Rd. to Hunter Creek Rd.) is Aspen's bike central, and it leads to several great rides in the Four Corners area (see Tail-Rated Trails). But to comply with the leash regu-lation, you'll need to walk your bike and dog the first .5 mile or so of the trail.

Other options are the 10-mile round-trip ride on the four-wheel-drive **Lincoln Creek Rd**. from Grizzly Reservoir to the ghost town of Ruby (before the reservoir the road, though verging on four-wheel-drive, is heavily trafficked), and the unpaved continuation of **Castle Creek Rd**. (a couple of miles past Ashcroft) toward Pearl Pass, for as long as you want to ride. The dirt roads and trails on the flanks of **Basalt Mountain**, past Missouri Heights and Spring Park Reservoir from El Jebel, also provide some nice, not-too-technical riding. And the 8-mile out-and-back to **Hay Park**, a beautiful, wildflower-studded meadow reached from the Thomas Lakes trailhead for Mount Sopris, is a great midsummer ride. For more detailed information about these routes, look at the single-sheet ride descriptions issued at the Aspen Ranger District office (see Resources) or check with one of the bike shops in town.

POWDERHOUNDS

In addition to the suggestions below, the **Hunter Creek/Hunter Valley Trail** (see Tail-Rated Trails) makes a great ski or snowshoe outing.

Dogs are allowed on several of the trails groomed by the Aspen Nordic Council: **Bernese Boulevard** at the **Aspen Cross-Country Center**, which traces the perimeter of the Aspen Golf Course for 2 miles; the 1.5-mile **Marolt Trail**, on the Marolt Open Space on the west end of Aspen; and the **Rio Grande Trail**, which has a groomed track for 20 miles between Aspen and Basalt. Dogs can be under voice control on the first two of these trails; they must be leashed on the Rio Grande Trail. For more information, go to www.aspennordic.com.

At the **Snowmass Club Cross-Country Ski Center**, the 5-kilometer Anderson Ranch Loop is dog friendly, and access is free. Dogs can be under voice control. Call the center at 970-923-5700 for details.

Though dogs are not allowed on the trails at the Ashcroft Ski Touring Center, they can accompany their skiing or snow-shoeing owners on the unplowed section of **Castle Creek Rd.**, which begins at the Nordic center and eventually passes a couple of the Alfred E. Braun system backcountry huts (some avalanche-slide paths do cross the route) and heads up to Montezuma Basin. Dogs can be off leash provided they refrain from trotting over to any of the nearby Nordic trails. And you can lunch at the Pine Creek Cookhouse as long as you access it via the road (as opposed to the trails) and tie up your dog at least 100 yards from the restaurant.

From the beginning of November through Memorial Day, **Independence Pass Rd.** is closed to vehicles just past the Difficult Creek Campground, 3.5 miles east of Aspen. One of the better doggie social scenes occurs here. There is some potential for avalanches the farther up the pass you venture, but for the first couple of miles the danger is minimal. **Maroon Creek Rd**. is closed to cars past the T Lazy 7 Ranch during the winter. You can hike, snowshoe, or ski (there's a maintained track on the side of the road) with your pooch. On both of these roads, you'll occasionally have to dodge some snowmobile traffic.

For those into uphill snowshoeing, you can bring your leashed dog with you to the Snowmass ski area to ascend the trails.

CREATURE COMFORTS

Unless otherwise stated, dogs should not be left unattended in the room or cabin.

Aspen

$$$–$$$$ Aspen Meadows, 845 Meadows Rd., 970-925-4240, 800-452-4240, www.aspenmeadows.com. Design-minded dogs may enjoy a stay at the Meadows, a Bauhaus-inspired complex on the campus of the Aspen Institute. There's a $100 one-time pet fee. The clean-lined rooms, which start at 500 square feet, are furnished with classic midcentury-modern furniture and include microwaves and refrigerators. Most of the dog-friendly ones are on the first floor. You can leave your dog unattended inside as long as you alert the front desk, so that housekeeping won't go in during that time. Make sure to pick up a copy of the walking tour pamphlet so that you and your dog can visit the artwork on the grounds, which includes murals by Bauhaus architect and artist Herbert Bayer (who also designed many of the Aspen Institute's buildings), a Buckminster Fuller geodesic dome, and the Andy Goldsworthy indoor/outdoor sculpture Stone River.

$$$–$$$$ Hotel Aspen, 110 W. Main St., 970-925-3441, 800-527-7369, www .hotelaspen.com. All of the hotel's rooms are dog friendly, with a $20 nightly fee per dog for the first three nights of your stay. Rooms are large, and each

has a small, semienclosed patio area or, for second-level rooms, a balcony. All rooms have microwaves; some have gas fireplaces. Jacuzzi rooms come with a private hot tub on the balcony. Paepcke Park, across the street, offers your dog a chance to stretch his legs.

 $$$–$$$$ Limelight Lodge, 355 S. Monarch St., 970-925-3025, 800-433-0832, www.limelightlodge.com. The Limelight recently underwent a complete rebuild; rooms are spacious and much more luxe than during the hotel's former incarnation. Suites come with full kitchens, and most other rooms have refrigerators and microwaves. Luckily, what hasn't changed is the hotel's dog-friendly policy. Pets are allowed in first-, second-, and fourth-floor rooms for $25 per night, per dog. A place mat and food and water bowls are available for canine guests, and dogs can be left unattended inside the room if in a travel kennel. The motel's location across from Wagner Park, where many local dogs frolic during the day, is a plus.

$$$–$$$$ Molly Gibson, 101 W. Main St., 970-925-3434, 800-356-6559, www.molly gibson.com. Under the same ownership as the Hotel Aspen, across the street, the Molly Gibson is also pet friendly, with a $20 nightly fee per dog for the first three nights of your stay. The courtyard rooms are a tight squeeze, but the hotel has a variety of room types and sizes, up to two-bedroom apartments with full kitchens.

 $$$$ Hotel Jerome, 330 E. Main St., 970-920-1000, 877-412-7625, www.hotel jerome.com. This Aspen landmark dates to 1889, when Jerome B. Wheeler, one of the town's founding fathers, created a hotel to rival the Ritz in Paris. It has since been restored to its former opulence, and canine guests are welcome, for a $75 one-time fee. They're given a dog bed and water and food dishes to use during their stay, as well as welcome treats on arrival—there's also a ready stash of biscuits at the outside bellhop's stand, which all the local dogs know about. You can leave your dog unattended in your large Victorian-style room so long as you hang the Pet in Room sign to alert housekeeping.

 $$$$ The Little Nell, 675 E. Durant, 970-920-4600, 888-843-6355, www.thelittlenell .com. If you have the money, there are few better places than The Little Nell to take a dog. The pet fee is $100 per stay, and the pampering begins at check-in, where dogs are presented with a customized treat and brass ID tag with The Nell's phone number on it, while owners get a "petiquette" booklet. Dog beds and food and water dishes are supplied during the stay, and The Nell offers a room service pet menu, with options like beef tenderloin and grilled chicken with carrots and brown rice. All of the spacious rooms, which start at 600 square feet, have gas fireplaces, and some have balconies. Dogs can be left unattended in the rooms; put up the Privacy sign to let the housekeepers know. The staff is also willing to watch your dog down in the lobby, if things aren't too hectic, or periodically take him for a short walk. And Glory Hole Park, a pleasant oasis with two small ponds, is down the street, at the corner of Original St. and Ute Ave.

$$$$ The Residence, 305 S. Galena, 970-920-6532, www.aspenresidence.com. Your pampered pooch can luxuriate in one of this small, centrally located boutique hotel's seven apartment-style suites. Each one is lavishly furnished with antiques, museum-quality artwork, Ralph Lauren linens, and upholstered walls and ceilings.

Five have full kitchens; the others have kitchenettes. Max, a Chinese crested (a small, white, fluffy-type dog) is the resident canine.

 $$$$ The Sky Hotel, 709 E. Durant Ave., 970-925-6760, 800-882-2582, www.thesky hotel.com. The Sky (part of the dog-friendly Kimpton Hotel Group) is one of Aspen's hippest gathering spots, thanks to the 39 Degrees bar/lounge and the adjacent year-round outdoor pool and hot tub. Though dogs aren't allowed in the pool or bar area, they are permitted in half of the hotel's rooms. Your dog can request food and water bowls, as well as a dog bed (with a leopard-print cover that matches the in-room robes). The staff also doles out treats, and dogs are welcomed by name via the dog-shaped chalkboard on the front desk. When booking, look into the hotel's Howlin' at the Sky pet package, which includes a discounted room rate and a day of doggie daycare or a dog walk.

 $$$$ The St. Regis Aspen, 315 E. Dean St., 970-920-3300, 800-454-9005, www .stregisaspen.com. First-class Fidos are welcome in any of the rooms, which are furnished in a luxe mountain style, for a $100 one-time fee. They'll have an extra-thick dog bed, ceramic food and water bowls, and a place mat at their disposal during the stay, as well as a supply of biscuits that gets replenished daily. The St. Regis also has a canine room service menu with dishes such as braised beef stew, salmon and scrambled eggs, and chicken with root vegetables. Dogs cannot be left unattended in the rooms, but you can arrange for dog walking or pet-sitting through the concierge, which works with a local pet-care service.

Meredith (Ruedi Reservoir)

$$–$$$$ Double Diamond Ranch Bed & Breakfast, 23000 Frying Pan Rd., 970-927-3404. If your dog can play well with others, he can stay with you at this 85-acre ranch surrounded by the White River National Forest and about five minutes from Ruedi Reservoir. He'll have his pick of two rooms in the main ranch house, each with private bath, or a cabin with full kitchen (as well as a Jacuzzi). And he can even run leash free on the ranch as long as he doesn't bother the resident horses or mules.

Snowmass

$$$–$$$$ Silvertree Hotel, 100 Elbert Ln., 970-923-3520, 800-837-4255, www.silvertreehotel.com. There's a $25 per night fee for dogs at the Silvertree, a full-service slopeside hotel with a three-story atrium lobby and lots of steel-and-glass accents. The rooms are of average size and are comfortable, though not ultra-luxe. You must sign a pet waiver when you check in, assuming liability for any damage your dog may inflict during your stay.

$$$–$$$$ Snowmass Mountain Chalet, 115 Daly Ln., 970-923-3900, 800-843-1579, www.mountainchalet.com. This slopeside hotel accepts dogs in two of its rooms for $10 per night, per pet, in the summer and $20 in the winter, with a limit of two dogs per room. You and your dog will usually be booked in a ground-floor room for easy walking access. The recently remodeled rooms are comfortably furnished with log furniture. Rates include a hot breakfast year-round and in winter a light soup lunch. You can leave your dog unattended in the room as long as you're sure he won't bark so much as to disturb other guests.

$$$–$$$$ Wildwood Lodge, 40 Elbert Ln., 970-923-3550, 800-837-4255, www.wildwood-lodge.com. The Wildwood is affiliated with the Silvertree and has the same pet regulations (see above). And you can enjoy many of the Silvertree's amenities, such as access to the health club. The rooms are fairly standard motel style; there are also six suites, four of which have fireplaces.

CAMPGROUNDS

Forest service campgrounds: **Difficult Campground,** 3.5 miles east of Aspen on Hwy. 82 (47 sites). **Weller** (11 sites), **Lincoln Gulch** (7 sites), and **Lost Man** (10 sites) campgrounds are farther east on Hwy. 82, as the road ascends Independence Pass. Campgrounds off the road to the Maroon Bells are **Silver Bar** (4 sites), **Silver Bell** (5 sites), and **Silver Queen** (6 sites).

TWICE THE FUN

Visit the canine-themed Double Dog Pub (303 E. Hopkins Ave.), where pictures of local pups line the entry stairwell and the chalkboard signs above the bar have dog-inspired quips and quotes. The pub is affiliated with the Steak Pit restaurant next door and serves great burgers and prime-rib sandwiches, so even though you can't bring Fido inside with you, you can bring him an excellent doggie bag.

WORTH A PAWS

Borrow-a-Dog. If your dog wants a friend to play with, or even if you're in Aspen without your dog and could use some surrogate canine companionship, check out this popular year-round program at the Aspen/Pitkin County Animal Shelter (101 Animal Shelter Rd.). For nothing more than your signature on a release form, you can borrow a shelter dog, for a few hours or a whole day. Seth Sachson, shelter director, will match you with an appropriate dog. Call 970-544-0206.

Happy dogs, and their people, during the annual K-9 Uphill at Buttermilk Mountain, outside Aspen.

Silver Queen Gondola. Take your dog on the ski gondola up Aspen Mountain and buy him a souvenir pass. See details in the Tail-Rated Trails section.

Canine Fashion Show. If your dog has a penchant for dressing up, and you're in town during mid-January Wintersköl festivities, enter him in the annual fashion show at Aspen's Paepcke Park. Judges award prizes for categories such as most adorable, funniest, and, because this is Aspen, best celebrity look-alike. There's no fee; just show up with your decked-out pooch. www.aspenchamber.com

K-9 Uphill. Aspen local Erik Skarvan organizes this annual snowshoe climb for dogs (on leash) and people up Buttermilk Mountain. It usually takes place the second Saturday of April, after Buttermilk Ski Area has closed for the season. Your dog can choose between the competitive and the recreational divisions and look forward to treats at the top of the 2,000-vertical-foot course. This is the one time you *want* your dog to be a puller! After the uphill (you'll also need to walk downhill), there's a barbecue and a huge raffle with both dog and human prizes. Registration fees benefit the

Aspen Animal Shelter and the Valley Dog Rescue in Basalt. 970-925-1069, www.sundogathletics.com

Aspen Music Festival Concerts. Is your dog a closet Chopin fan? Does he like to snooze to Brahms? Give him a little cultural exposure by bringing him to the David Karetsky Music Lawn, the grassy area outside Aspen's Benedict Music Tent, to hear any of the world-class concerts that take place almost daily from mid-June to mid-August. Dogs are welcome provided they are on leash and cleaned up after (and preferably don't howl during the performance). The best part for humans is that it doesn't cost anything to bring a blanket and listen to the concert—the tent's louvered sides let the music emanate clearly. www.aspenmusicfestival.com

Independence Ghost Town. Your dog can envision what life might have been like for a miner's dog in the late 1800s at this former gold-mining community, which dates from 1879 and is believed to be Aspen's first mining camp. Several tumbledown cabins dot the site, scenically situated beneath the Continental Divide. You can find the ghost town by driving 13.5 miles up Hwy. 82 from Aspen on Independence Pass. There are no official interpreters on-site, but a brochure available in a dispenser at the parking pullout details the town's history.

DOGGIE DAYCARE
Aspen
The Aspen Boarding Kennel, 101 Animal Shelter Rd., 970-544-0206, www.dogsaspen.com. $40/day. You can watch your dog play via the kennel's Web cam. A half-hour river walk for your pooch is $30 extra. Open 7 AM–6 PM daily.

Basalt
Alpine Meadows Ranch and Kennel, 0329 Holland Hills Rd., 970-927-2688. $15/ day for a stay in the heated kennels, with feeding and ball-playing sessions or a short hike as well. Open 9 AM–noon and 3–5 PM daily.

PET PROVISIONS
Aspen
Aspen Wags to Riches, 101 Animal Shelter Rd. (in the Aspen/Pitkin County Animal Shelter), 544-9247, www.aspenwags toriches.com

C. B. Paws, 420 E. Hyman Ave., 970-925-5848, www.cbpaws.com

Rocky Mountain Pet Shop, 107 S. Monarch, 970-925-2010, www.rockymountain petshop.com. The store also has a self-service dog wash. For $15, you get use of shampoo and conditioner, towels, a dryer, and brushes.

El Jebel
RJ Paddywacks, 19400 Hwy. 82 (next to City Market), 970-963-1700. The store also has a self-service dog wash. It's $15 a wash, which includes shampoo and conditioner, towels, grooming tools, and use of a dryer.

CANINE ER
Basalt
Valley Emergency Pet Care, 180 Fiou Ln. (one block off Hwy. 82 from Basalt Ave. intersection), 970-927-5066. The clinic is about 15 minutes from Carbondale and 25 to 30 minutes from Glenwood Springs. Open 5 PM–8 AM, Monday to Friday; 24 hours on Saturday, Sunday, and holidays.

RESOURCES
Aspen Chamber Resort Association, 425 Rio Grande Pl., 970-925-1940, 800-670-0792, www.aspenchamber.org

Aspen Ranger District, White River National Forest, 806 W. Hallam, 970-925-3445

Snowmass Village, 866-352-1763, www .snowmassvillage.com

The Ute Mountaineer, at 308 S. Mill St., 970-925-2849, www.utemountaineer.com, is a good resource for trail maps and hiking/ biking guides.

Twelve
Glenwood Springs and Vicinity

THE BIG SCOOP

Three hours west of Denver, and just about an hour down the road from Aspen, Glenwood Springs makes a pleasant destination in and of itself or a more affordable base camp for exploring the mountains around its tonier sister city. (Your dog, however, will have to sit out the natural hot springs for which Glenwood is famed.) About 40 minutes south of Glenwood Springs, the one-street town of Redstone—lined with galleries and antiques stores—and the funky hamlet of Marble also invite a visit. While in Glenwood, be sure to stop by the canine-loving Chamber Resort Association, where Clover scored lots of complimentary dog biscuits.

Leashes are the law within Glenwood and Carbondale city limits, but they are optional in unincorporated Garfield County. Be sure to note that the leash law includes an ordinance against public tethering (i.e., you can't leave your dog tied up and unattended outside a store or other business), which can make getting food when it's too warm to leave Fido in the car—on most summer days—problematic.

TAIL-RATED TRAILS

Because Glenwood Springs is in a canyon, most of the nearby trails offer vertical climbs. For strolling on the flats, try the paved Glenwood Canyon Recreation Path (see specifics below). A helpful resource is the "Trail and City Map," which you can pick up at the Glenwood Springs Chamber Resort Association (see Resources).

Carbondale

Red Hill
Distance: Varies
Elevation gain: Approximately 1,000 feet from trailhead to Mushroom Rock

Trailhead: At the intersection of Hwys. 82 and 133 in Carbondale, turn into the gravel parking lot just north of the intersection, off CR 107.

Dogs can be off leash.

This trail network on BLM land is a popular spot for local hikers and mountain bikers. The vegetation—piñon pine and juniper—set against a contrasting background of red rock and red dirt (hence the name) is reminiscent of Colorado's Front Range, compared to the more alpine setting of much of the Roaring Fork Valley. There's no parking directly at the trailhead, so you'll need to walk along CR 107 for about .25 mile from where you left your car—you'll likely want to leash up Fido on this section. Once at the trailhead, on the left of the road, peruse the map there to scout out your options among the 14-plus miles of trails. No matter which route you decide on, you'll begin with a healthy climb, either up the **Mushroom Rock Trail** or the **Three Gulch Trail**. Once you top out, the trails meander through meadows full of fragrant sage and pine forest. Bring water for both you and your dog, especially on a warm summer day, as none is available along the trails.

Carbondale
Dog-Friendly Areas

Regulations: Dogs must be licensed; no aggressive dogs; owners must have a leash on hand and pick up after their dogs; no female dogs in heat are permitted; children 12 and under must be under adult supervision.

Dogs can be off leash.

With the dramatic massif of Mount Sopris as a backdrop, the **Doggie Park** has one of the best pooch-park views in Colorado. To reach it, head south on Hwy. 133, from the intersection with Main St., for about .3 mile to Hendrick Rd. Turn right, then take the first left onto Holland Dr. and park along the street; the dog park is on the west side (note that Hendrick Park, on the east side of Holland Dr., does not allow dogs). The 2.9-acre fenced area provides ample room for pups to socialize, and a fire hydrant in the middle is a winsome prop. Only some small trees dot the park, so shade is limited. A couple of picnic tables and a water fountain with dog bowls round out the features.

Glassier Park, 3 blocks south of Main St. on Weandt Blvd., across from Glassier Dr., provides .5 acre for well-controlled dogs to shake their legs out. The park, adjacent to Carbondale's former middle school, is unfenced and sits right along the road, so if your dog tends to ignore you when he's playing, this wouldn't be the best venue for him. It is a picturesque little spot, with a grassy cover, a few large trees, and a small ditch along one edge that is water filled in summer.

Glenwood Springs

Jesse Weaver

Distance: About 6.25 miles round-trip

Elevation gain: About 1,600 feet

Trahilhead: From Glenwood Springs, head east on I-70 to Exit 119 (No Name).

Make a left at the top of the exit ramp, then follow the paved road to the signed trailhead parking area.

Dogs can be off leash.

This trail is usually less crowded than the neighboring one up Grizzly Creek, and since it parallels No Name Creek, which descends in a series of incredibly picturesque rapids, it's a good pick for a hot day. Begin by walking uphill on a narrow dirt road, past a couple of houses. A short trail diversion to the right bypasses a green gate (if the gate is open, you can stay on the road). No Name Creek rushes by on the left—as it constitutes part of the Glenwood water supply, make sure Fido doesn't relieve himself near the water. If you look above the creek, you'll see some mining remains and, perhaps, some rock climbers, as the first part of the trail has some popular climbing routes. Cross the creek on a concrete bridge, then continue following the dirt road to the right (the left track ends at a boarded-up tunnel). The trail narrows immediately after and runs close to the creek. A little more than 1 mile in, it switchbacks up and away from the creek at a fork; to the right is a scenic, but precipitous, overlook above the water, which would make a good turnaround point for a shorter hike. The trail then continues as a steady, though not strenuous, uphill, with the rush of rapids in the creek below a constant companion. Although you can hike for several more miles, our goal was the bridge over the cascading falls, a little more than 3 miles from the trailhead. When it's time to head back, return the way you came.

River Run Dog Park

Access: From the intersection of Grand Ave. and 20th St., drive into the Safeway parking lot and park behind the US Bank building, adjacent to the supermarket. From the northwest corner of the lot, locate and take a small path that crosses the old railroad tracks. You'll come out on the paved Glenwood recreation path. Walk right. The dog park is a couple hundred yards away on the left, just past a group of picnic tables.

Regulations: None posted

Dogs can be off leash.

The 2-acre park, on a bluff above the Roaring Fork River, is sectioned into two fenced areas. With a mostly gravel surface, it's like a big playground for dogs, with several large boulders to hop around and over, fire hydrants, tunnels, a doghouse, and some balancing structures divided between the two sections. There's a bench and picnic table but no permanent water source, though a large portable water dispenser was by the front gate when we visited. Despite the name, the park doesn't actually have access to the river, which runs below it. And it has a somewhat hardscrabble vibe—there's not much green in or around the park. But your dog is unlikely to mind.

Jeanne Golay Trail

Distance: 4 miles round-trip
Elevation gain: 1,600 feet
Trailhead: Take 7th St. west from Grand Ave. to the T-stop at Midland. Make a right and then take the next left on Red Mountain Dr. and follow it to its end. There's a parking area just before the closure gate, adjacent to the trailhead.

Dogs can be off leash.

Named after two-time Olympic cyclist and US Bicycling Hall of Famer Jeanne Golay, a Glenwood Springs resident, this hike follows a dirt road up Red Mountain, through what was once the Glenwood Springs ski area. The area closed in the early 1950s, but some of the lift structures remain. Begin by following the road; then cut through an open area to the left of the first water tank you'll come to. (This shortcut allows you to avoid walking through the city's

Mush, Tansy! Griffin gets a sled ride.

water treatment plant.) Hike up the narrow footpath at the far end—a real lung buster. You'll soon meet up again with the road. The road keeps to a gradual grade; as you ascend, Glenwood Springs unfolds below. About two-thirds of the way up, a bench provides a rest spot with a panoramic view of almost-13,000-foot Mount Sopris and the Elk Mountains. The road ends at the summit, where the old ski lift used to unload. You'll encounter some shady areas along the way, but this hike is primarily hot and dry (a stream does flow by the trailhead). Your dog might enjoy it most in the early morning or evening.

Boy Scout Trail

Distance: About 6 miles round-trip
Elevation gain: About 2,000 feet

Access: From Grand Ave., take 8th St. 4 blocks east to the end. There's no trailhead parking lot—just a couple of spaces on the street—so if you're staying downtown, consider walking to the trail.

Dogs can be off leash, keeping in mind the following: although the first .5 mile is within city limits, the trail is not regularly patrolled by animal control. If your dog harasses or injures another hiker or biker, however, you may be cited, among other things, for having a dog off leash. If you're sharing the trail with a lot of other users, it's probably best to keep your dog leashed.

Because this hike is dry and largely unshaded, it's best for dogs as an evening outing during the summer. Begin by walking down the driveway on the left of 8th St. to the actual trail. You'll face a short, steep climb before the trail levels off to a more gradual ascent as it snakes around the hillside. Enjoy the bird's-eye view into Glenwood Canyon below. After about .5 mile, your dog will find brief respite in the shade of piñon pines. The trail continues to ascend steadily through sage and oak brush. At the T-intersection, go left, then take the next right, about 200 feet ahead (if you stayed straight, you'd be on the Forest Hollow Trail). The final section of trail is less traveled and becomes narrower and rockier as it climbs steadily for another .5 mile before topping out at an old campground on Lookout Mountain. The only remaining signs of the campground are some picnic tables and a fire grate. Up to the left, you'll see the end of Lookout Mountain Rd. Savor the views of Mount Sopris and other high peaks of the Elk Range to the south before returning the way you came.

Instead of doing an out-and-back hike, you can take an alternate route that adds several miles but allows you to loop back into Glenwood Springs. At the T-intersection mentioned above, go right instead. You'll then follow a dirt track that wraps around a ridge on the west side of Lookout Mountain. Once you contour around the ridge and begin heading downhill, you'll reach a four-way intersection of dirt roads. Turn right and follow a somewhat overgrown dirt track northwest along wide switchbacks down a hillside of sagebrush, juniper, and gambel oak. You'll have a vista of Glenwood Springs below and Red Mountain across the valley. At the distinct intersection with the wide dirt Cemetery Rd., almost at the bottom of your descent, head

downhill (left). You'll shortly intersect with the end of Palmer Ave. and 12th St., just a few blocks east of Glenwood's main street, Grand Ave.

Glenwood Canyon Recreation Path

Distance: Runs 16 miles from the Vapor Caves, at the east end of 6th St., to about 2 miles west of the Dotsero exit off I-70. *It's suggested, but not required, that dogs be leashed.*

This paved multiuse trail runs the length of spectacular Glenwood Canyon, bordering the Colorado River. Although your dog probably won't appreciate the much-touted engineering marvels of the highway above, he may well enjoy a walk by the water. The best place to access the path near Glenwood is at the No Name exit (119) just east of Glenwood Springs, as the first mile or so of trail from Glenwood runs directly adjacent to the highway. There are some great doggie play spots in the river accessible from here.

Rifle

Rifle Falls State Park

Access: From the Rifle exit off I-70, west of Glenwood Springs, travel north on Hwy. 13. After about 5 miles, take a right on Hwy. 325; the park is 9.8 miles ahead on the right. There's a $6 entrance fee. *Dogs must be leashed.*

Since you can't take your dog to Hanging Lake (see below), bring him here to see a triple waterfall. Once inside the park, go left to access the falls; there is a day-use parking area where the road ends. From there, it's a short walk to the falls. Your dog will appreciate their spray on a hot day. After viewing the plunging water, hike on the **Coyote Trail**, a short 20- to 30-minute walk that meanders past limestone grottos and caves, and a small

Daly contemplates life lakeside.

Hanging Lake. This great hike up to a gorgeous tropical-style waterfall with—well, never mind, because your dog can't see it anyway. Because of the immense popularity of this trail, dogs are not allowed, period.

Harvey Gap State Park. With the exception of hunting dogs during hunting season, dogs are not allowed in this park, which contains Harvey Gap Reservoir. There are no hiking trails here anyway, so your dog probably won't regret the lack of access.

CYCLING FOR CANINES

The **Red Mountain Trail** is easy to bike, though it involves a healthy climb, as it follows a dirt road in fairly good shape. Just remember to allow your dog time to catch up with you on the ride down. **Red Hill**, outside Carbondale, is a popular biking area; the initial climb to access the rest of the trail system is fairly technical, so depending on your biking skills, your dog may outpace you on the way up. You can conceivably bike with your dog on the **Glenwood Canyon Recreation Path**, since leashes are not a requirement, but keep in mind that weekends, especially, are busy with other cyclists and your dog will be running on pavement. (See Tail-Rated Trails for all of the above.) Another option is the 7-mile round-trip **Burnt Tree Ridge Trail** (#18 on the Glenwood "Trail and City Map"), which follows an old four-wheel-drive road about 15 miles east of Glenwood Springs. Or investigate the **Roan Cliffs** area outside of Rifle. A biking map is available at the Bureau of Land Management office in Glenwood Springs (see Resources); the northwest section, accessible from Piceance Creek Rd. outside of Rio Blanco, is generally less used by motorized vehicles than the eastern section.

stream before taking you to the top of the falls (you'll be glad to have your dog on a leash here!). Descend via the trail marked Difficult (it's not, really), and you'll come out by the drive-in campsites. If your dog is into botany, he'll appreciate the trailside markers that identify native plants and trees. The 1.5-mile one-way **Squirrel Trail** (did Rover's ears just prick up?), which follows an irrigation ditch for most of its length, is another option for a short walk; it's part dirt road, part path. If you decide to overnight in the park, stay at one of the walk-in campsites, which you'll pass along the Squirrel Trail. Note that if you hike the **Bobcat Trail**, which connects the park to the nearby Rifle Falls State Fish Hatchery, you and your dog will have to turn around before you reach the hatchery, as pets are not allowed on the property. 970-625-1607, www.parks .state.co.us/parks/riflefalls.

POWDERHOUNDS

It's primarily backcountry as far as finding a good location near Glenwood Springs to ski with your dog. The Sunlight Mountain Nordic Center discourages dogs on its trails, and the Four Mile Park area, which is on national forest land, is popular for snowmobiling, making it less than ideal for the four-legged set. The Spring Gulch Nordic trail system, outside of Carbondale, does not permit dogs. See *Snowshoeing Colorado*, by Claire Walter, for a couple of ideas.

CREATURE COMFORTS

Unless otherwise stated, dogs should not be left unattended in the room or cabin.

Carbondale

$$–$$$ BRB Crystal River Resort, 7202 Hwy. 133, 970-963-2341, 800-963-2341, www.cabinscolorado.com. Located about 7 miles south of Carbondale, with .5 mile of private frontage on the Crystal River, the resort is a great play spot for a dog, especially if you book one of the cabins right on the river. There are 13 studio to two-bedroom rustic log cabins (as well as tent and RV sites), and dogs are allowed for $10 per night, per pet, with a limit of two dogs per cabin. All cabins have kitchens, and some have fireplaces. You must keep your pet leashed outside. Note that there's usually a two-night minimum stay on weekends. Open mid-April to mid-November.

$$$–$$$$ Comfort Inn and Suites, 920 Cowen Dr. (near the intersection of Hwys. 82 and 133), 970-963-8880, 800-473-5980, www.comfortinnaspen-carbondale.com. Dogs are allowed in the rooms here (not the suites) for $25 per night, per pet, with a limit of two per room. There's a jar of treats at the front desk for canine guests and a place for them to walk down to the Roaring Fork River behind the hotel. You can leave

your dog unattended inside the room for a couple of hours if he's in a travel crate and you leave a cell-phone number with the front desk staff.

$$$–$$$$ Days Inn, 950 Cowen Dr. (near the intersection of Hwys. 82 and 133), 970-963-9111, 800-944-3297, www.carbondaledaysinn.com. This very pet-friendly Days Inn permits dogs for $10 per night, per dog. You and your dog can access the Roaring Fork River from behind the hotel for a quick walk/swim.

$$$$ The Lodge on the Roaring Fork, 0635 CR 106, 970-963-5806, www.thelodgeontheroaringfork.com. This newer B&B, which is, indeed, within easy access of the Roaring Fork River, welcomes dogs in one of its five rooms for $25 extra per night. You can leave your dog unattended inside; the room's bathroom is so big that some guests have even put their dogs there to hang out for a short time. With .25 mile of river frontage, some informal trails on the property, and the paved Rio Grande Trail running directly behind the lodge, your dog will have plenty of places to sniff and swim. Shadow, the host golden retriever, may be able to show him around ("Water dogs are in heaven here," says owner Jason Siegal). In addition to a full breakfast, the lodge hosts a daily happy hour, with Fat Tire on tap, wine, sodas, and cheese and crackers.

Debeque

$$$$ Kessler Canyon, 0655 CR 209, 970-283-1145, 866-548-3267, www.kesslercanyon.com. This 23,000-acre luxury sporting retreat about 45 minutes west of Glenwood Springs accepts dogs on a case-by-case basis (the resort also has its own kennel of 50 dogs on-site that accompany guests on the guided game and bird hunts offered). Only 30 guests at a time can stay here, either in the guestrooms in one of two small lodges or in four upscale cabins. Dogs can be left unattended inside if they're kenneled. Rates include three meals daily, as well as wine with dinner and an open bar (and airport transport to and from Grand Junction, if needed). The resort often hosts groups (it has meeting and conference facilities), but also accommodates individual guests.

Dotsero

$$–$$$ A. J. Brink Outfitters at Sweetwater Lake, 3406 Sweetwater Rd. (25 miles west of Gypsum), 970-524-7344, www.brinkoutfitters.com. This well-established rustic resort and stables are on 400 acres adjoining the Flattops Wilderness above Glenwood Springs. Four motel rooms as well as six one- to three-bedroom cabins, all with kitchen facilities, are available to you and your dog (as well as campsites). They're outfitted in a style that the woman I spoke with laughingly referred to as "early American garage sale." Dogs must be kept leashed on the property, though they're certainly welcome to dip a paw in the lake. In addition to horseback riding, the resort rents out rowboats and canoes to use on Sweetwater Lake, and there's a restaurant, too. Open Memorial Day to mid-November (a few cabins remain open in the winter).

Glenwood Springs

$$ Red Mountain Inn, 51637 Hwy. 6 & 24, 970-945-6353, 800-748-2565, www.redmountaininn.com. The inn, near the West Glenwood exit off I-70, offers cabins or motel rooms, and dogs are allowed in both, for $10 per pet, per night. The rooms are modern, clean, and comfortable. All cabins have full kitchens, and some have fireplaces. There's a small pet-walking area on the premises where well-behaved dogs can be unleashed. You may be able to leave your dog unattended in your room for a short time, but only if he's in a travel kennel.

$$–$$$ Ramada Inn and Suites, 124 W. 6th St., 970-945-2500, 800-332-1472, www.ramadaglenwood.com. Dogs are allowed in all rooms except those on the third floor for a $15 nightly fee. Dogs who promise not to raise a ruckus may be left unattended in the room for short periods of time.

$$–$$$ Quality Inn and Suites on the River, 2650 Gilstrap Ct., 970-945-5995, 800-228-5151 (national number), www.qualityinn.com. The hotel has designated pet rooms for $10 extra per night.

$$–$$$ Starlight Lodge, 121 W. 6th St., 970-945-8591. The motel, 1 block from the hot springs, allows dogs in designated rooms.

$$$–$$$$ Glenwood Canyon Resort, 1308 CR 129, 970-945-6737, 800-958-6737, www.glenwoodcanyonresort.com. With easy access to the Colorado River, the Glenwood Canyon bike path (which runs alongside the resort), the Jess Weaver Trail (see Tail-Rated Trails), and airy and bright recently built log cabins with decks, the resort, by the No Name exit off I-70, is an idyllic place for a vacationing dog. Just make sure you've trained yours to be well-behaved (whenever problems arise, "it's never the dog, it's always the owners," quips Ken, one of the managers). And book early, as just three of the eight fully equipped, one-bedroom cabins are dog friendly, for an additional fee of $25 per pet, per night. There's a limit of one large dog or two small- to medium-sized dogs per cabin. The cabins also have sleeping lofts, so they can accommodate up to six, as well as vaulted ceilings, gas fireplaces, and air-conditioning. Note that there's a two-night minimum stay on summer weekends. The resort has RV and tent sites, too, as well as camper cabins, though the latter aren't open to dogs. Keep your pet leashed outside, though he can go down to the small swim beach and take a dip in the Colorado. In summer, Rock Gardens Rafting at the resort offers raft, kayak, jeep, and bike tours.

$$$–$$$$ Hotel Colorado, 526 Pine St., 970-945-6511, 800-544-3998, www .hotelcolorado.com. Let your dog be part of history with a stay at this elegant hotel, listed on the National Register of Historic Places, which boasts many past luminaries among its guests, including President Theodore Roosevelt. There's a $25 fee per pet, per night. Legend has it that the teddy bear originated at the hotel, a fact your dog may appreciate if he's a fluffy-toy aficionado. Rooms and suites are individually decorated with Victorian-style furniture, and the suites are definitely a notch up from the standard rooms (called "classic doubles"). Guest dogs receive biscuits on check-in.

$$$–$$$$ Hotel Denver, 402 7th St., 970-945-6565, 800-826-8820, www.the hoteldenver.com. The rooms and suites here are modern and comfortably furnished, though the building dates from the early 1900s. All are individually decorated with antiques or antique-style pieces, and some have hardwood floors and exposed brick walls. Many are pet friendly (though not the recently refurbished Denver rooms or the Cupola suite), and you can leave your dog unattended in them as long as you leave a cell-phone number with the front desk staff. If you and your dog want more privacy, opt for the St. James Room, which is actually a small one-bedroom house across the street, with a fenced yard and private hot tub. The Glenwood Canyon Brewing Company, which serves its own microbrews and a full menu, is conveniently located off the lobby. You may well smell the aroma of hops.

Marble

$$ Beaver Lake Retreat, 105 E. Marble, 970-963-3608, 866-963-3608, www .beaverlakeretreat.com. This small, eclectic lodge, with seven units that range from standard rooms to a small apartment to a bunk room, often hosts groups but also does individual nightly rentals when a yoga group, say, hasn't taken over the premises. Dogs are considered on a case-by-case basis; one room in particular is dog friendly, with its own entrance for easy outside access. There's a $10 nightly pet fee. Guests also have use of the lodge kitchen. The complex is located on the edge of town, with a view over Beaver Lake and of the surrounding Elk Mountains and a network of hiking trails close at hand. Your dog can be on the property with you under voice control, and, if your dog likes to boat, he can join you in one of the canoes the lodge lends out to use on the lake.

$$–$$$ Beaver Lake Lodge, 201 E. Silver St., 970-963-2504, www.beaverlake lodge.com. Located in the town of Marble (such that it is, with a population of 85), the main lodge building was a schoolhouse in the late 1800s. Though dogs are usually not permitted in the lodge guest rooms, they're welcome in the five cabins for a $15 one-time fee per pet. Built more than a century ago as homes for some of the men who worked in the town's marble quarry, the cabins have been recently updated; each has a kitchen and porch, and a "new" rustic but cozy feel, with hardwood floors, log furniture, and handmade quilts. A great hike, the Carbonate Creek Trail, starts just up the road. Open mid-May through the end of October.

$$$ Chair Mountain Ranch, 0178 CR 3, 970-963-9522, www.chairmountainranch .com. The ranch is situated on 8 acres by the Crystal River, between Redstone and Marble, and dogs are allowed in any of the five two-bedroom cabins for a $5 fee per night, per pet. The cabins have full kitchens and overlook a small pond. You can leave your dog unattended for a few hours inside as long as he's not a barker or a chewer. The owners do ask that you keep your dog leashed on the ranch property because of the abundance of chickens and ducks. Open Memorial Day through mid-November.

New Castle

$$ Elk Creek Campground, 581 CR 241, 970-984-2240, www.elkcreekcamping .com. Dogs are allowed in three of the cabins at this former KOA, as well as at the campground as long as they're leashed (you'll need to provide your own sleeping and cooking gear). An enclosed dog area is available, and your dog can run off leash here, but you must supervise him.

$$–$$$ Rodeway Inn, 781 Burning Mountain Ave., 970-984-2363, www.rodeway inn.com. Dogs can stay for $10 extra per stay, per dog, with a $25 deposit.

Parachute

$$$–$$$$ Holiday Inn Express Hotel and Suites, 221 Grand Valley Wy., 970-285-2330, www.hiexpress.com. There's a $25 pet fee per visit.

Redstone

$$–$$$ Redstone Cliffs Lodge, 433 Redstone Blvd., 970-963-2691, 888-652-8005, www.redstonecliffs.com. Located in the heart of Redstone, an almost impossibly charming little place, the lodge offers standard rooms with kitchenettes and one- and two-bedroom suites with full kitchens in a low-slung log building. For $15 a night per pet your dog(s) can join you, with a limit of two dogs per unit. All are furnished in a casual western style, with log furniture and classic quilts. The Crystal River flows right behind the lodge, and you and your dog

can enjoy the view from the large grassy back lawn.

$$$ Redstone Inn, 82 Redstone Blvd., 970-963-2526, 800-748-2524, www.redstone inn.com. Dogs are permitted in four of the terrace rooms at this turn-of-the-century hotel, a member of the Historic Hotels of America, for $15 per pet, per night. You can leave your dog unattended in the room, but housekeeping won't come in to clean during that time. The terrace rooms are in a 1950s-era addition to the hotel, and they're large and comfortable but don't feature the Arts and Crafts decor (with original Stickley furniture) of the rooms in the hotel's main section. They do open on to a parking lot for easy dog-walking access. And dogs can romp, leashed, on the inn's 22 acres, which include a pool and tennis courts. The inn usually offers specials during the annual Sled Dog weekend, held in January or February, when races take place near Redstone.

 $$$–$$$$ Avalanche Ranch, 12863 Hwy. 133, 970-963-2846, 877-963-9339, www .avalancheranch.com. The ranch has long been a beloved spot for vacationing canines in Colorado. Thirteen rustic-style cabins are situated on 36 acres where dogs can romp unleashed; there's also .5 mile of private frontage on the Crystal River, a stocked pond for fishing or canoeing, and a slew of family-friendly games and activities. The dog fee is $12 per pet, per night, with a maximum of two dogs per cabin. The decor is mountain themed, and while the cabins are not upscale, they're cozy, cute, and spotless. Along with full kitchens for human convenience, doggie towels are provided in each cabin, and dogs receive biscuits upon check-in. A more modern loft apartment and a three-bedroom, two-bath house are also available for nightly rentals; your dog may enjoy playing "pioneer pooch"

in the restored shepherd's wagon, which is now a cozy bedroom heated by a woodstove that can be rented along with the house. The ranch's annual Apple Festival the first Saturday of October, with a pig roast and band, is a great time for both dogs and people.

Rifle

$$ Buckskin Inn, 101 Ray Ave., 970-625-1741, 877-282-5754, www.buckskininn .com. Almost all of the motel's rooms are pet friendly. It's possible to leave your dog unattended in the room for under an hour (say, to grab a bite to eat) if you check first with management. There's a nice grassy area outside the motel to walk your dog; just make sure you keep him on a leash and clean up after him.

$$ Red River Inn, 718 Taughenbaugh Blvd., 970-625-3050, 800-733-3152, www .redriverinn.com. Dogs are allowed in four of the rooms for $10 per pet, per night.

$$ Rusty Cannon Motel, 701 Taughenbaugh Blvd., 970-625-4004, 866-625-4004, www.rustycannonmotel.com. Four smoking rooms are set aside for guests with pets. There's a $50 deposit, and $25 of that will be refunded at the end of your stay if your dog has left his room in good shape.

$$$ La Quinta Inn and Suites Rifle, 600 Wapiti Ct., 970-625-2676, 800-753-3757 (national number), www.lq.com. Dogs are allowed in designated rooms for $10 per night, per pet, with a limit of two per room. They can be left unattended if kenneled in a travel crate.

CAMPGROUNDS

State park campgrounds: **Rifle Falls State Park**—see Tail-Rated Trails for directions (20 sites); **Rifle Gap State Park,** on Hwy. 325 outside of Rifle, just a few miles before Rifle Falls State Park (89 sites).

National forest campgrounds: There are a number of campgrounds along Coffee Pot Rd. (FR 600), 2 miles north of Dotsero off I-70, including **Coffee Pot Spring Campground** (15 sites) and **Deep Lake Campground** (45 sites); **Bogan Flats Campground,** on the Marble road off Hwy. 133 (37 sites); and **Redstone Campground,** about 1 mile north of Redstone (37 sites).

Private campgrounds: **A.J. Brink Outfitters** at Sweetwater Lake outside Dotsero; **Glenwood Canyon Resort** just east of Glenwood Springs; **Elk Creek Campground** in New Castle (see Creature Comforts).

WORTH A PAWS

Did Fido get too muddy from hiking through the forest or rolling around in dirt at the dog park? Freshen him up with a visit to the self-service dog wash at **High Tails Dog and Cat Outfitters** (50633 Hwy. 6 and 24, Glenwood Springs, 970-947-0014, 888-448-2457, www.hightailsdog andcat.com). A wash ranges $12–$23, depending on the size of dog, and includes shampoo (which is premixed with warm water in a spray faucet) and use of brushes and grooming tools, towels, and dryers. Afterward you can give him some free biscuits as a reward for enduring the indignity of a bath while you enjoy a cup of free coffee. Closed Sundays.

DOGGIE DAYCARE
Carbondale

Aspen Valley Pet Care, 16480 Hwy. 82, 970-963-2744. $20/day; $15/half-day. A stay here includes the use of indoor and outdoor runs, as well as exercise and playtime, with wading pools in summer. Open 8 AM–noon and 2–6 PM, Monday to Saturday; 2–6 PM, Sunday.

The Little Tail, 955 Cowen Dr., 970-704-0403, www.redhillvet.com. $20/day. Affiliated with the Red Hill Animal

Health Center, this boarding facility bills itself as the "five-paw pet resort of the Rockies." A stay includes time in the indoor play yard. Open 7 AM–7 PM, Monday, Tuesday, Thursday; 7 AM–5:30 PM, Wednesday and Friday; 8 AM–4 PM, Saturday; 3–4 PM, Sunday.

Skyline Ranch and Kennels, 0356 CR 101, 970-963-2915. $8/day. Open 7:30 AM–5 PM, Monday to Saturday; 8 AM–4 PM, Sunday.

Glenwood Springs
High Tails Dog and Cat Outfitters, 50633 Hwy. 6 and 24, 970-947-0014, 888-448-2457, www.hightailsdogandcat.com. $25/day; $15/half-day. The indoor play space has a rubber floor, splash pools, and equipment for dogs to climb and play on. Open 7 AM–7 PM, Monday to Thursday (the store is open but there's no daycare on Friday and Saturday).

Rifle
Cedar Hill Kennel, 2094 CR 326, 970-876-2451. $14/day; $10/half-day. Dogs get to play much of the day in this ranchlike setting with a pond. Open 8 AM–6 PM, Monday to Saturday; 2–6 PM, Sunday.

PICNIC IN THE PARK
A nice place to eat in the company of your dog is Veltus Park, in Glenwood Springs, off of Midland Ave. between 8th and 10th Sts., on the banks of the Roaring Fork River.

PET PROVISIONS
Glenwood
High Tails Dog and Cat Outfitters, 50633 Hwy. 6 and 24, 970-947-0014, www .hightailsdogandcat.com

PETCO, 105 E. Meadows Rd. (Glenwood Meadows shopping center), 970-945-1527, www.petco.com

Rifle
Jak Raimi's Exotic Pets, 120 E. 3rd, 970-625-3868

CANINE ER
Basalt
Valley Emergency Pet Care, 180 Fiou Ln. (1 block off Hwy. 82 at Basalt Ave. intersection), 970-927-5066. The clinic is about 15 minutes from Carbondale and 25 to 30 minutes from Glenwood Springs. Open 5 PM–8 AM, Monday to Friday; 24 hours on Saturday, Sunday, and holidays.

Parachute
Parachute Veterinary Clinic, 120 W. 1st St., 970-285-0356. Open 9 AM–4 PM, Monday, Wednesday, Friday; 9 AM–5 PM, Tuesday and Thursday.

Rifle
Town and Country Veterinary Hospital, 1595 Railroad Ave., 970-625-2971. Open 9 AM–5 PM, Monday to Friday; 9 AM–12 PM, Saturday.

RESOURCES

Bureau of Land Management, 2300 River Frontage Rd., Silt, 970-947-2800

Eagle Ranger District, White River National Forest, 125 W. 5th St., Eagle, 970-328-6388

Forest Supervisor's Office, White River National Forest, 900 Grand Ave., Glenwood Springs, 970-945-2521

Glenwood Springs Chamber Resort Association, 1102 Grand Ave., Glenwood Springs, 970-945-6589, www.glenwood chamber.com

Rifle Ranger District, White River National Forest, 0094 CR 244, Rifle, 970-625-2371

Sopris Ranger District, White River National Forest, 620 Main St., Carbondale, 970-963-2266

Summit Canyon Mountaineering, 8th and Grand Ave., Glenwood Springs, 970-945-6994, 800-360-6994, www.summit canyon.com, has an extensive collection of guidebooks and maps.

Thirteen

Northwestern Colorado

THE BIG SCOOP

The area of Colorado that's west of Craig and north of I-70 embodies the wide open spaces of the West. This is desert and canyon country, though even in the summer temperatures are cooler than in the Grand Junction area, for example, usually topping out in the 80s. But the very characteristic that can make it an appealing place for you and your dog to visit can also be its downfall—there's not a lot here. The principal towns are Craig, Meeker, and Rangely, all small, with just a few even smaller ones dotting the landscape. There's lots of BLM land where you can hike with your dog off leash, but the developed trails are few (and you can't bring your dog on the trails in Dinosaur National Monument). For forested, mountainous terrain, head east of Meeker into the White River National Forest and the Flat Tops Wilderness Area—one of the few wilderness areas in the state where dogs can hike off leash as long as they're under voice control. Several guest ranches in this region welcome canine visitors, and one even offers a dog-friendly backcountry yurt.

TAIL-RATED TRAILS

BLM Land

Almost all BLM land in this part of the state is undeveloped, meaning there aren't established trailheads or regularly maintained trails. *But you can bring your dog anywhere, and he can be off leash.* Just be sure to bring a topo map along, as well as lots of water.

The land on either side of Harpers Corner Rd., which leads from the Dino-saur National Monument visitor center outside of Dinosaur to the park itself, is BLM managed. On the west side of the road is the **Bull Canyon Wilderness Study Area**, and on the east side is the **Willow Creek Wilderness Study Area**. From the Plug Hat Butte picnic area, 3.5 miles up Harpers Corner Rd. from the visitor center, you can take a 4- or 5-mile round-trip hike into **Lower Buckwater Draw**; you'll find a waterfall in the draw during spring. For more hiking suggestions, stop by the BLM office in Meeker (see Resources), which has some printed route descriptions. *Exploring Colorado's Wild Areas*, by Scott S. Warren, also has information about hiking routes on BLM land in northwestern Colorado, as well as for other areas throughout the state.

Dinosaur National Monument. The monument straddles Utah and Colorado and includes Echo Park, at the confluence of the Green and Yampa Rivers, the site of a proposed dam that was scuttled in a celebrated showdown between the federal government and the Sierra Club in the 1960s. Although the monument's name comes from dinosaur bones discovered in the area, you can only actually see the fossils at the Dinosaur Quarry, 7 miles north of Jensen, Utah. The park's Canyon Area Visitor Center is 2 miles east of Dinosaur, Colorado. A $10 entrance fee is charged only on the Utah side of the monument.

Dogs are not allowed on trails, anywhere else in the backcountry, or on river trips through the park. You can bring your dog to the campgrounds and picnic areas as long as he's always on a leash. A .25-mile paved trail forms a short loop by the Plug Hat Butte picnic area, 3.5 miles from the Canyon Area Visitor Center on Harpers Corner Rd.; your dog can accompany you on this short stroll, which provides a spectacular panorama of the surrounding country. 970-374-3000, www.nps.gov/dino

CYCLING FOR CANINES

The BLM office in Craig (see Resources) has a handy pamphlet called "Mountain Bike Routes of Moffat County." Note that there's a leash law throughout Moffat County, so unless a bike route is actually on BLM or national forest land (and not all of the ones listed in the pamphlet are), it won't be practical for Fido to come along. **The Yampa Valley Trail** runs for 100 miles from the town of Maybell to within Dinosaur National Monument. You can access a singletrack section of it from Deerlodge Rd., about 20 miles west of Maybell, near the Cross Mountain turnout.

POWDERHOUNDS

Ute Lodge, 30 miles east of Meeker in the White River National Forest, has its own yurt that you can ski or snowshoe to and overnight at in the company of your dog. See Creature Comforts for details.

CREATURE COMFORTS

Unless otherwise stated, dogs should not be left unattended in the room or cabin.

Craig

$$ Elk Run Inn, 627 W. Victory Wy., 970-826-4444, 888-696-9720, www.elkrun inn.com. Dogs are permitted in all of the rooms at this recently remodeled motel. All units have kitchenettes.

$$ Traveler Inn, 2690 W. Hwy. 40, 970-824-7066, 800-458-7228. Dogs are welcome for a $10 one-time fee, though they're not allowed in the front desk area.

$$–$$$ Bear Valley Inn, 755 E. Victory Wy., 970-824-8101, www.bearvalley-inn.com. The motel accepts pets in designated rooms for $10 per night, per pet. They can be left unattended in the room for short periods of time.

$$–$$$ Super 8, 200 S. Hwy. 13, 970-824-3471, www.super8.com. Dogs are allowed in all of the rooms.

$$–$$$$ Best Western Deer Park Inn and Suites, 262 Commerce St., 970-824-9282, 888-328-1155 (national number), www.bestwesterncolorado.com. The motel charges a $10 one-time pet fee.

$$$–$$$$ Holiday Inn, 300 S. Hwy. 13, 970-824-4000, 800-HOLIDAY (national number), www.holidayinn.com. There's a $50 pet deposit if you're paying with cash.

$$$–$$$$ Candlewood Suites, 92 Commerce St., 970-824-8400, www.candle woodsuites.com/craignorthwest. This recently built extended-stay hotel has two pet rooms, available to dogs under 80 pounds. There's a $75 one-time fee for a stay of six days or less, and a $150 one-time fee for stays of seven days or longer. The rooms range from studios to one bedrooms, all with kitchenettes, and your dog can be unattended inside if he has a travel kennel to hang out in.

Hamilton

$$ Williams Fork Lodge, 17559 S. Hwy. 13, 970-826-0399. This five-room bed-and-breakfast allows dogs on a case-by-case basis, generally for $15 extra per night. The rooms share two common bathrooms, and the breakfast is continental. "Nothing in this place is real frilly," says Deb, the owner. One room, which has three lodgepole-pine bunk beds, can sleep six or seven. The log house sits on 4 acres along the Williams Fork River, and hiking trails in the White River National

Forest are nearby. The B&B's host dog is a blue heeler/Australian cattle dog mix named Shea.

$$$$ Creekside Guest Cabin, 18291 S. Highway 13, 970-756-5001, www.creek sideguestcabin.com. With a credit card as a deposit, your dog is welcome to join you at this modern, two-bedroom log cabin right on the Williams Fork River. The 1,400-square-foot house can sleep up to eight and includes a kitchen, washer/dryer, and gas fireplace. You'll have 80 acres of property, with .75 mile of river frontage, virtually to yourself (the owners live next door in a large log house). If you leave your dog unattended, he should be in a travel kennel if inside the cabin or secured outside on the wraparound covered porch.

Dinosaur

$$ Hi-Vu Motel, 122 E. Brontosaurus Blvd., 970-374-2267. This is the only place in Colorado where your dog can stay at an address that sounds like it's out of *The Flintstones*. This very basic motel allows dogs in two of its six rooms. A designated pet walking area is adjacent. Open mid-May to mid-November.

Meeker

$–$$ Ducey's White River Resort, 12830 CR 8 (14 miles east of Meeker), 970-878-4378. This small resort has four one-bedroom cabins, equipped with kitchenettes but not bathrooms (those are in separate buildings). You must keep your dog leashed at all times on the property and be sure to clean up after him. The White River runs through a part of the property. Of late, the cabins have been rented out seasonally to workers in the area, but check with the owners about nightly rentals. Open April 1 to November 15.

$–$$$ Ute Lodge, 393 CR 75 (30 miles east of Meeker), 970-878-4669, www .utelodge.com. Eight cabins, from one to three bedrooms, are at the lodge, which is on 310 acres near the Flat Tops Wilderness Area. Six of the rustic yet cozy log cabins are fully outfitted; two are without kitchen facilities and share a bathhouse. Dogs are $5 extra per night, per dog. Or you and your dog may prefer a very civilized camping experience in the Ute Lodge tent, which has cots, electric lights, and a woodstove; each night is $25 a person. Your dog can explore the lodge's property, which includes a private fishing lake and a creek, preferably on a leash. Horseback riding is also available from the lodge, and during the winter you can ski or snowshoe with your dog to the lodge's own yurt, about 2 miles from the main complex (in summer, you can reach it with a four-wheel-drive vehicle). The yurt sleeps up to five or six people, for $20 per person, and has coal and propane stoves, cooking supplies, propane lamps, and an outhouse. Tent and RV sites are also on the property. Open May 1 to mid-November (with the exception of the yurt, which is available year-round).

$$ Mesa House Bed and Breakfast, 100 Mesa Dr., 970-878-5319, www.mesa housebb.com. Up to two dogs, preferably under 40 pounds each, are allowed in one of the B&B's three rooms, the Cabin Room, for $10 extra per night, per dog. The room has a private bath, a queen bed, and a futon that can also sleep two. At night, the owners request that you keep your dog in a travel crate in the room; you can rent one from them if your dog doesn't have his own.

$$ Rustic Lodge, 173 1st St., 970-878-3136. Though they're not permitted in the motel rooms, dogs are allowed in the lodge's seven cabins (with kitchenettes), which are actually not quite as rustic inside as they look on the outside. There's a $7 nightly pet fee. The cabins vary in size and sleep from four to eight people. If you need to leave your dog unattended inside, he should preferably be in a travel kennel.

$$ Trappers Lake Lodge, 7700 Trappers Lake Rd. (50 miles east of Meeker), 970-878-3336, www.trapperslake.com. Located waaayy out there, the lodge is surrounded by the Flat Tops Wilderness. For $10 extra per night, per pet, you and your dog(s) can stay in one of 15 primitive cabins; some have propane heat, some wood-burning stoves, and all share a central bathhouse. You can leave your dog unattended inside the cabin. Dogs are not allowed in the lodge, however, and they need to be kept leashed on the lodge's 11 acres so as not to interfere with the resident working dogs. And make sure your dog stays off the bed! Activities at the lodge include horseback riding, fishing, and boating. There's a restaurant, too. Open Memorial Day to October 31.

$$ Valley Motel, 723 Market St., 970-878-3656. There's a $20 nightly pet fee at this motel right in town.

$$ Valley View Lodge, 981 8th St., 970-878-9808, www.valleyvulodge.com. This friendly bed-and-breakfast on a scenic hillside overlooking Meeker accepts dogs on a case-by-case basis in its three rooms, one of which has its own bath. Canine guests pay $10 extra per night and should have a travel kennel to stay in if they're left unattended in the room. There's a hot tub and outside grill you can use. The premiere attraction for dogs is the close-by 57-acre Dorcas Jensen Memorial Park, an open space area that backs up to BLM land and offers plenty of hiking, running, and stick-or tennis-ball-chasing opportunities.

$$–$$$ The Brick House Bed and Breakfast, 687 Garfield St., 970-878-5055, www.meekercolorado.com/brickhouse. Good dogs—ones "who don't sleep in the beds or beg breakfast from other guests," says owner Evie Chambers—can stay with you at this historic B&B on a case-by-case basis. Built as a boarding house in 1904 (by the same builders who constructed Denver's Brown Palace hotel and the Redstone Castle, in Redstone), the house has three guest rooms, furnished in antiques. Meeker's downtown business district is a couple of blocks away.

$$–$$$ Buford Lodge, 20474 CR 8 (22 miles east of Meeker), 970-878-4745, www.bufordstoreandlodge.com. This historic lodge is located on 235 acres along the North Fork of the White River, bordering the national forest. Ten rustic log cabins are fully furnished but have no bathrooms or running water; there's a central bathhouse for guests. And you'll prepare your meals on a wood-burning cookstove. The oldest of the cabins is more than 100 years old; the "youngest" is about 75 years old. You can also rent two modern cabins, which do have full baths. In addition to the cabins, the lodge has a grocery store, gas station, and a small museum on the premises, as well as tent and RV sites. And with hiking trails nearby, as well as off-leash privileges on the lodge's property, you won't have any reason to leave Rover behind. Open May 1 to November 15.

$$–$$$$ Meeker Hotel and Cafe, 560 Main St., 970-878-5255, www.the meekerhotel.com. No doubt your dog will be intrigued by the numerous elk and deer heads that adorn the lobby walls. The hotel, built in 1896, is on the National Register of Historic Places, and the rooms, though not incredibly luxurious, are cozy and furnished with antiques; many have hardwood floors. Several of the 24 rooms are dog friendly, with a $10 nightly fee. Generally, canine guests should be 50 pounds or under, but larger dogs may be considered. The range of accommodations includes two apartments, with kitchens and exterior entrances, and five two-bedroom suites.

$$$–$$$$ Bufordview Lodge, 40905 CR 17 (22 miles east of Meeker), 970-878-5590, www.bufordviewlodge.com. Accommodations at the lodge include a two-room suite with private outside deck that can sleep up to four and a three-bedroom guest cabin, also with its own deck, that sleeps six. Smaller dogs are welcome in either one for $25 per pet, per visit, and they can be left unattended inside as long as they're in a travel crate. The 3-acre property sits about 300 feet above the White River and has a stellar view of Lake Avery. Nearby trails lead into the national forest, and in winter, you can cross-country ski along the plowed county road. Note that there's a two-night minimum stay on weekends. The resident Lab and border collie can show your dog around.

$$$$ Thunderbird Lodge, 40434 CR 17 (20 miles east of Meeker), 970-878-4806, 877-808-3845 (this reservations number goes to family members living in Germany, who are eight hours ahead of Colorado time), www.thunderbird lodgellc.com. This cozy three-bedroom, two-bath log house on 40 acres bordering the White River National Forest sleeps up to 10. Your dog can join you with a $50 deposit. You can leave Fido unattended inside, though with the Flat Tops Wilderness and numerous trails and lakes nearby, he'll likely want to spend all of his time out exploring with you. A two-night minimum stay is required, and during the Meeker Sheepdog Trials and hunting season, longer stays are required.

Rangely

$$ Budget Host Rangely Inn, 117 S. Grand, 970-675-8461. Dogs can stay for $10 extra per night, per pet.

$$$ Adora Inn, 206 E. Main St., 970-675-5036. Dogs can stay for $10 extra per night, per pet.

CAMPGROUNDS

Dinosaur National Monument. The park has six established camping areas, three in Colorado: **Gates of Lodore**, **Deerlodge Park**, and **Echo Park** (46 sites total).

Bureau of Land Management campgrounds: Camping is allowed anywhere on BLM land.

Private campgrounds: **Buford Lodge** and **Ute Lodge** outside of Meeker (see Creature Comforts).

FEELING SHEEPISH

Canine spectators are discouraged from attending one of Meeker's most famous events—the Meeker Classic Sheepdog Championship Trials, in early September. Leave Fido at home and promise him you'll share some good tips.

DOGGIE DAYCARE
Craig

Canines Unlimited, 1592 W. Victory Wy., 970-824-6364, www.caninesunlimited training.com. $15/day; $10/half-day. There's also a self-service dog wash here; $20 per wash includes shampoo, grooming tools, towels, and the use of a dryer.

Honey Rock Dogs Boarding Kennel, 1202 Rose St., 970-824-9518. $10/day. The kennel can accommodate up to two dogs at a time for daycare. Each dog gets a climate-controlled indoor run, and all dogs at the kennel get to visit the 1,600-square-foot outdoor exercise yard during the day. Open 7:30 AM–noon and 4–5 PM, Monday to Saturday.

PET PROVISIONS
Craig
MJK Sales & Feed, 290 Ranney, 970-824-6583

Murdoch's Ranch and Home Supply, 2355 W. Victory Wy., 970-824-4100

CANINE ER
Craig
Bear Creek Animal Hospital, 2430 E. Victory, 970-824-5964. Open 8 AM–5:30 PM, Monday to Thursday; 9 AM–5:30 PM, Friday; 8 AM–noon, Saturday.

Meeker
W R Veterinary Clinic, 338 E. Market, 970-878-5647. Open 8 AM–noon and 1:30–5 PM, Monday to Friday.

RESOURCES
Blanco Ranger District, White River National Forest, 220 E. Market St., Meeker, 970-878-4039

Bureau of Land Management, 455 Emerson St., Craig, 970-826-5000

Bureau of Land Management, White River Field Office, 220 E. Market St., Meeker, 970-878-3800

Colorado Welcome Center, 101 Stegosaurus Freeway (Hwy. 64), Dinosaur, 970-374-2205

Meeker Chamber of Commerce, 710 Market St., 970-878-5510, www.meeker chamber.com

Moffat County Visitor Center, 360 E. Victory Wy., Craig, 970-824-5689, 800-864-4405, www.craig-chamber.com

Fourteen

Grand Junction and Vicinity

THE BIG SCOOP

The Grand Valley is dinosaur country. The legacy of these giant reptiles that roamed the area millions of years ago lives on in museums and fossil sites. But if your dog is already panting at the thought of humongous bones, you'll have to break the news to him that most of the dinosaur-related attractions don't allow dogs. Still, there's plenty to do. Spring and fall are the best times to visit Grand Junction and points west if you're a dog; the summer can be just too darn hot, and there aren't very many trees under which to seek respite or creeks to jump into in the desert. If you are in the area during the "nondog"-day months of June, July, or August, consider escaping to the forested lakes of Grand Mesa for the sake of your fur-coated companion.

In addition to the expected leash law throughout Grand Junction, there's an enforced pooper-scooper law in all city parks. (Of course, you should be cleaning up after your dog on the sidewalks as well.) Neighboring Fruita also requires that dogs be leashed. You don't have to go far, however, to find miles of unrestricted dog territory. Though surrounding Mesa County has a leash law, it is not actively enforced in national forest or Bureau of Land Management (BLM) areas. And since the BLM—one of the least regulatory land overseers—manages much of the area surrounding Grand Junction, those trails are a particularly good bet for leash-free dog hikes.

TAIL-RATED TRAILS

There are hundreds of miles of trails on Grand Mesa, which contains the Grand Mesa National Forest. Unfortunately, many of them are open to all-terrain vehicle (ATV) use as well as to hikers, bikers, and horseback riders. For good dog-hike options, consider the **Coal Creek Trail** (described here) or the **Kannah Creek Trail** (8.75 miles one way), neither of which permit motorized use. Both can be accessed from Carson Lake off of Lands End Rd. The **Lake of the Woods Trail** (about 11.5 miles round-trip to Cottonwood Lake #1) is another good possibility. Note that on the popular **Crag Crest Trail**, dogs must be leashed.

Coal Creek Trail
Distance: 9 miles one way
Elevation gain: 1,800 feet
Trailhead: The trail, which heads up (or down) Grand Mesa, can be accessed from a lower or an upper trailhead. Hiking from the upper access is not usually available until June, when the snow has melted enough to open the top section of Lands End Rd. To reach the lower trailhead, drive south on Hwy. 50 from Grand Junction for about 12 miles to the Lands End Rd. turnoff to the left. Go about 14 miles (the road turns to dirt after 9 miles) to the Wild Rose Picnic Area on the right. The trail begins at the far side of the parking lot. To reach the upper trailhead, head west on Lands End Rd. (sometimes referred to as Rim Dr.)

from Hwy. 65 for 3.1 miles; turn left on the Carson Lake Rd. Take the road until its end at Carson Lake. The trail begins just below the lower parking area.
Dogs can be off leash.

From the lower trailhead, the well-maintained trail climbs at a fairly gradual pace toward the rim of the mesa. You'll cross several streams in the first .5 mile or so. Get your dog to stop long enough so you can admire the wonderful vista of the Kannah Creek Basin below and the Uncompahgre Plateau to the southwest. As the trail ascends the mesa, it winds by large stands of aspen—making this a good candidate for a fall hike—as well as small, scrubby oakbrush. Unless you've arranged a car shuttle at Carson Lake, you'll probably want to turn around before reaching the mesa top.

Whitewater Creek Trail

Distance: 7.5 miles one way to rim of Grand Mesa; 3.5 miles farther to West Bench Trail
Elevation gain: About 1,900 feet to Grand Mesa rim
Trailhead: Take Hwy. 50 east from Grand Junction. When you reach the town of Whitewater (about 12 miles out of Grand Junction), turn left onto Reeder Mesa Rd. (just before mile marker 41). After 2.2 miles, make a left onto Whitewater Creek Rd. From there, it's 2.5 miles to the trailhead on the right side of the road (if you reach Lumbardy Ranch, you've gone a little too far). There's a small, informal parking pullout on the right. Look for the sign that says Grand Mesa Slopes, Mark's Trail.
Dogs can be off leash (but watch for cows in early spring and late fall).

This is an excellent fall hike. During the summer the lower reaches are hot, though the climate becomes pleasant when you reach the higher elevations. Remember to bring lots of water. If you

traveled the entire length of this trail, you'd hike from desert to subalpine zone, as it eventually climbs steeply up a basin to the top of Grand Mesa, connecting to the West Bench Trail. Chances are, however, that you and your dog will stick to the sand and sage of the first several miles. And you may well be able to enjoy some quality solitary hiking time together, as the trail is not heavily used. Moreover, it's free from the dirt-bike and ATV traffic of nearby areas, as it's designated for hiker use only. The trail is well marked at regular intervals with wooden stakes indicating WWC. Pay attention to your route, however, so you can return the same way—there's a network of cow trails that could get confusing. Whitewater Creek is, despite its name, slow moving and green. But Clover didn't seem to mind; it gave her a respite from the arid surroundings.

Scotland Trail

Distance: About 3 miles round-trip
Elevation gain: About 400 feet
Trailhead: From the visitor center atop Grand Mesa, drive 2.7 miles on Hwy. 65 (toward Cedaredge) to a pullout on the right where you can park (you'll see a small pond across the highway and a four-wheel-drive track). You may not realize this is a trailhead until you see a small trail marker that indicates you're at trail # 752, Scotland.
Dogs can be off leash.

The bonnie dog will enjoy this wee hike through meadow and trees to the lovely Scotland Park Reservoir. Clover also found the stick selection to be quite good. The one caveat is that this trail is open to ATVs, so you'll likely encounter some motorized traffic as you hike. From the parking pullout, a doubletrack winds up through a meadow into a stand of aspen, and then eventually fir. The trail continues this pattern, alternating between cool forest stands and open areas lush with wildflowers in July and August. After a traverse across a long meadow and a short climb, you'll reach the reservoir, tucked away in trees to the right. You'll have to pick your way down, as no maintained trail leads to the water. Though the main trail continues past the reservoir, we retraced our steps after stopping to gaze out at the lily pad–studded lake and retrieve a few sticks from its shallows.

Canyon View Dog Park

Access: The dog park is at the northwest end of Grand Junction's Canyon View Park. The park entrance is off 24 Rd., just before it crosses I-70. After driving into the park, turn left at the stop sign and drive to the farthest road; park along the fence line.

Regulations: Dogs must have current vaccinations, license, and ID tags; owners must clean up after their pets and carry a leash for each dog they're supervising; dogs must be at least four months old; no female dogs in heat; kids under 12 cannot enter the park, and kids between 12 and 16 must be accompanied by an adult; no food, human or dog, is allowed in the park.

Dogs can be off leash.

Grand Junction's first (and only, as of this writing) dog park opened in 2006 and was an immediate hit with local canines. The 3.2-acre rectangular fenced park isn't exactly a picture-perfect dog oasis—it's adjacent to the interstate and there's no shade—but there's plenty of room to play, as well as a few picnic tables where owners can hang out. During warm weather, there's also a pond for pooches to splash around in (it's drained during the winter). The park is divided into sections, each with its own entrance: one for small and/or senior dogs and one for larger, more active dogs.

Gunnison Bluffs Trail

Distance: Up to 6.7 miles one way, with some options for loops along the way

Elevation gain: About 100 feet

Trailhead: From Grand Junction, drive east on Hwy. 50. About 4.5 miles from the bridge over the Colorado River, turn right onto the Mesa County landfill access road. Just before the gated entrance to the landfill, turn left onto Coffman Rd. and go 1.5 miles to the trailhead, which has a large parking area on the right.

Dogs can be off leash.

The trail, a wide dirt track, is accessible to hikers, bikers, and horseback riders. Though just a few miles from Grand Junction, you may well feel like you're miles from anywhere, with only your dog(s) and some birds for company. Head out into a landscape—big sky, hills barren except for sagebrush—that dwarfs you and your dog. That's also your cue that this shadeless setting can be uncomfortably warm on a blazing hot day, so during the summer, save this hike for early mornings or early evenings. The track gradually heads toward the river but remains high, tracing the bluffs above it, as the trail name implies, so your dog won't be able to get within paw-dipping distance. In the distance ahead of you, the flat-topped monolith of Colorado National Monument rises up; when you retrace your steps, you'll be looking at the flat-topped monolith of Grand Mesa. At 3.5 miles from the trailhead, you'll meet up with a section of the **Old Spanish Trail** (see later description), which you can take back to the parking area to make a loop hike (several unmarked paths along the way also connect the two trails). Or continue north on the Gunnison Bluffs Trail. There's no set destination to this hike, so turn around whenever you or Fido feels like it.

McDonald Creek

Distance: About 4 miles round-trip
Elevation gain: 400 feet
Trailhead: From Grand Junction, head west on I-70 for 30 miles to the Rabbit Valley exit (Exit 2). Cross over the highway and pass a parking area for Rabbit Valley Recreation Area. Take the next right. The dirt road is narrow and bumpy, and you may well need a high-clearance vehicle to negotiate it. Follow the small Kokopelli's Trail decals on brown posts along the road for about 2.3 miles. Just after a small parking pullout on the right, watch for a sign to McDonald Creek and a road to the left. After taking this left, follow the road all the way to a small parking area at the trailhead.

Dogs can be off leash.

The McDonald Creek Cultural Resource Area is part of the BLM's Rabbit Valley Recreation Management Area. One of the beauties of this trail is that no motorized vehicles—or even bikes—are permitted. As you'll quickly surmise from driving to the trailhead, the rest of the Rabbit Valley area is a vast playground for ATVs, jeeps, and motorcycles.

First of all, don't be fooled by the name—there's no actual creek here, just a sandy wash, so bring along plenty of water on this desert hike. The trail allows for some exploring, as several paths wind through the wash, though you'll always be heading south. You'll soon be immersed in a landscape of sculpted sandstone, red sand, and pungent sage. Keep an eye out for rock art as you hike; four panels supposedly grace the canyon (we only spotted three). The trail ends at a set of railroad tracks (stay alert) along the Colorado River. Though it would be difficult to access the river from here, a small tributary comes in near the trail's end, and your dog can take a well-deserved dip.

For another hikers-only venue in the area, try the 5-mile round-trip **Rabbit's Ear Trail**, which leads to the Ruby Canyon overlook of the Colorado River. You can reach it by staying on the road from the I-70 overpass instead of turning right as for McDonald Creek. Drive 4.4 miles to the signed trailhead on the right, where there's also a small parking area.

Old Spanish Trail

Distance: About 4 miles one way
Elevation gain: About 100 feet
Trailhead: Head east on Hwy. 50 from downtown Grand Junction. About 2.5 miles from the bridge over the Colorado River (past the fairgrounds), make a right onto 28 1/2 Rd. Make an immediate left at the T-intersection (a brown-and-white Old Spanish Trail sign directs you to parking) and then an immediate right. A signed gravel parking area is on the right.

Dogs can be off leash.

Situated in the Orchard Mesa section of Grand Junction, this area has some historical significance: the North Branch of the Old Spanish Trail, which was used first by traders and trappers and then by wagon trains in the 1800s, passed through.

Don't pack up your dog's leash just yet; you'll have to walk through a few neighborhood streets to actually reach the trail. Once there, the route follows a wide dirt track that stretches off into the distance. This is not the most scenic hike—there are no trees, and you won't actually see much of the river—but it's a great place that's close to town for exercising your dog. And although there's no shade, your dog may enjoy a stiff breeze off the river rippling through his fur. Several small, unmarked paths from the Old Spanish Trail head toward the river and intersect with the **Gunnison Bluffs Trail** (see earlier description).

231

Colorado Riverfront Trails
Distance: Varying lengths
Access: An extensive trail system has been developed at various points along the Colorado River. The system is divided into several main portions, and more will eventually be established: the **Palisade Trail**; the **Corn Lake** section of James M. Robb-Colorado River State Park; **Las Colonias**; **Watson Island**; and the **Riverside Park**, **Audubon Trail**, **Blue Heron Trail**, and **Connected Lakes** sections of James M. Robb-Colorado River State Park, collectively known as the Redlands Loop. For more detailed information on specific trails, including access points and mileages, pick up the "Colorado Riverfront Trails" brochure, produced by the Colorado Riverfront Commission, at the Grand Junction Visitor Center (see Resources).
Dogs must be leashed.

One recommended hike begins at the Audubon trailhead and continues to Connected Lakes, a series of reclaimed gravel pits that have been turned into lakes. It's about 4 miles round-trip. To access the Audubon Trail, take Grand Ave. west from downtown (toward Colorado National Monument). Cross the Colorado River; at the intersection with Power Rd., turn right, then veer left to stay on Power Rd. (don't follow the sign for Connected Lakes that points right). Drive to the end of the paved road, where you'll reach a gravel parking area and see a trail sign.

Clover and I enjoyed a pleasant amble along this paved trail, which is partially shaded by cottonwoods and borders riparian habitat as it runs along the Redlands Canal. Once at Connected Lakes, your dog will have his choice of gravel trails that wind around and between the lakes. There's lots of water here, obviously, as well as cooling breezes off the river. Note that if you drive into the park rather than hike in via the Audubon Trail, you'll have to pay the standard entrance fee.

Highline State Park
Distance: 3.5-mile loop
Elevation gain: Minimal
Trailhead: To reach the park, which is northwest of Grand Junction in Loma, take I-70 west to the Loma exit (Exit 15). Head north on Route 139 for about 5 miles to Q Rd., then make a left and drive 1.2 miles to 11.8 Rd. Turn right; the park entrance is about 1 mile ahead. The entrance fee is $6.
Dogs must be leashed.

The park, with two lakes, is a welcome oasis of grass, trees, and water in the midst of arid surroundings, with 8 miles of trails. The **Highline Lake Trail** is an easy, mostly level stroll along a combination of dirt road and wide gravel path that circles the lake. While you gaze at the Book Cliffs to the northeast, your dog can amuse himself by splashing in the water and watching the water-skiers go by. Clover particularly enjoyed our evening walk here. There are several bird-watching blinds at the far side of the lake, so take care that your pooch doesn't disturb any birders who may be present (as well as the birds they're watching). Note that dogs are not allowed on the park's swim beach. 970-858-7208, www.parks .state.co.us/parks/highlinelake

Rabbit Valley Trail through Time
Distance: 1.5-mile loop
Elevation gain: 100 feet
Trailhead: From Grand Junction, head west on I-70 for 30 miles to the Rabbit Valley exit (Exit 2). Turn right and drive to the trailhead parking area straight ahead.
Dogs can be off leash.

This is the only dinosaur-related activity in the Grand Junction area in which your dog can participate. In addition to a working dinosaur quarry on the premises, an interpretive trail highlights dinosaur fossil imprints as well as the geology of the area. You may want to keep your dog on his leash so he's not tempted to start his own quarry excavation—and remind him that fossil collecting is prohibited by law on all BLM lands.

HOT DOGS

Heatstroke is a real risk to your dog when exercising in desert country. If you notice him having difficulty breathing, panting to excess, or refusing to go any farther, get him water immediately; even better, immerse him in water, if possible.

Colorado National Monument. Your dog can view the wondrous cliffs and canyons of the monument out the car window or from within the confines of the campground, but he's not allowed to set paw on any of the trails.

Riggs Hill and **Dinosaur Hill**. Dogs are not allowed at either of these outdoor fossil–viewing sites.

CYCLING FOR CANINES

The area around Grand Junction offers lots of riding opportunities, and nearby Fruita has become something of a mountain-biking mecca. The good news is that many of the rides are on BLM land, so your dog is free (literally) to accompany you. The bad news is that you'll definitely want to keep your rides on the shorter side so that your dog doesn't die of heatstroke in the desert. For descriptions and maps of some of the classic routes, pick up a copy of *Grand Junction Trails and Camping Guide,* by Nattana Johnson and Christopher Schnittker, at a local bike shop. Over the Edge Sports, 202 E. Aspen Ave. in downtown Fruita, is a helpful source of maps and information, as is Single Tracks, 150 S. Park Sq.

The **Gunnison Bluffs** and **Old Spanish Trails** (see Tail-Rated Trails) offer good riding opportunities on fairly level terrain. You and your dog may also want to check out part of the **Tabeguache Trail**; there's a trailhead off Hwy. 141, reached by driving Hwy. 50 east from Grand Junction toward the town of Whitewater. For more information on some other short rides (**Horsethief Bench**, a 3.4-mile loop, or **Rabbit Valley**), pick up the brochure "Biking Guide to the Grand Valley," put out by the Grand Valley Natural Resources and Tourism Council, at the Grand Junction visitor center.

Grand Mesa is another good biking choice, and it offers the advantage of fir, spruce, and aspen to make your ride (and your dog's run) a little cooler. Try the **West Bench Trail**, which runs about 5.5 miles from the Mesa Lakes Ranger Station to Powderhorn Ski Area, or the 11.5-mile (round-trip) **Lake of the Woods Trail**, which ends at Cottonwood Lake #1, allowing your dog to go for a welcome swim.

POWDERHOUNDS

The Grand Mesa is the place to head for wintertime recreation with your dog. The Grand Mesa Nordic Council maintains trails at three different sites on the mesa—Ward, County Line, and Skyway. You and Fido can explore the designated dog loop and dog trail at County Line, as well as the Ward Creek Trail. Otherwise, the groomed trails are off-limits to dogs. For more information, call 970-434-9753 or go to www.gmnc.org.

Some recommended backcountry trail areas on the mesa (none of which cross through avalanche terrain) include **Water Dog Reservoir, Griffith Lakes,** and **Deep Creek**. The 11-mile round-trip **West Bench Trail**, which starts from the Mesa Lakes Ranger Station, is also a popular winter ski or snowshoe tour. Stop in at the forest service office in Grand Junction (see Resources) for maps and more trail info.

CREATURE COMFORTS

If you can trust your dog on his own, it's a good idea to find lodging where you can leave him unattended while you go out to eat, for example. The high temperatures in the Grand Junction area make it especially inadvisable to leave your dog in the car.

Unless otherwise stated, dogs should not be left unattended in the room or cabin.

Cedaredge

$ Aspen Trails Campground, Store, and Cabins, 1997 Hwy. 65 (3 miles north of Cedaredge), 970-856-6321. Dogs can stay in either of the two camper cabins here with a $25 deposit. You'll have to bring your own sleeping bag; the cabins do have electricity. There's a soda fountain, gift shop, and deli on-site. Open April through the end of October.

$ Howard Johnson Inn, 530 S. Grand Mesa Dr., 970-856-7824, 888-855-2700 (national number), www.howardjohnson cedaredge.com. Several designated pet rooms are available, for a $10 fee per night, per dog.

$$ Lovett House Bed and Breakfast, 210 N. Grand Mesa Dr., 970-856-4375, www .logcabinbedandbreakfast.com. If your dog, like many, takes an intense interest in the mailperson, he'll be overjoyed to find out that he can stay in an actual former post office. The house, built in 1891, was Cedaredge's original post office as well as a longtime postmaster's residence. Now a Colorado State Historic Site, the bed-and-breakfast has three rooms (all with private baths and private entrances); one, Sam's Room, is canine friendly, with a king bed for humans, a dog bed for four-legged guests, and its own entrance into a fenced yard. You can stroll the surrounding 1.5 acres with your dog, then later relax in the B&B's living room, which has a large rock fireplace and an ultracozy vibe.

PARKS FOR PUPS

Looking for a shady respite in Grand Junction? Bring your dog to Hawthorne Park, just a few blocks north of downtown west of 5th St., or Whitman Park, a few blocks in the other direction of downtown, also west of 5th St. Sherwood Park, bounded by Orchard Ave., 5th St., North Ave., and 1st St., is a popular dog spot, with its grassy expanse and paved path on its perimeter.

$$ Tri-R Motel, 885 S. Grand Mesa Dr., 970-856-3222, 877-877-4732. Dogs can stay for $5 extra per night, per dog, at this small motel on the edge of Cedaredge. Three of the eleven units have kitchenettes.

Clifton

$$–$$$ Best Western Grande River Inn and Suites, 3228 I-70 Business Loop, 970-434-3400, 877-434-3404, www.bestwestern colorado.com. Dogs 25 pounds and under can stay, and management emphasizes that only adult dogs are welcome. There's a $20 fee per nights, per dog.

Collbran

$$ Alpine Motel, 102 Spring St., 970-487-3220, 877-557-7173, www.collbran alpinemotel.com. All the motel requires for dog guests is a credit-card imprint as a deposit and that they don't jump up on the beds.

$$ Vega State Park Camper Cabins, 800-678-2267, www.parks.state.co.us/Parks/Vega/Cabins. The park, 12 miles east of Collbran, has five simple cabins that sleep up to six people each, adjacent to one of the campgrounds. Dogs are allowed in three of them for $10 extra per night. Each cabin has electricity, a small refrigerator, a microwave, and a propane stove for heat. You bring your own bedding and cooking supplies.

Fruita

$-$$ Balanced Rock Motel, 126 S. Coulson, 970-858-7333. The motel allows dogs in smoking rooms only for a $5 nightly fee.

$$ H Motel, 333 Hwy. 6 & 50, 970-858-7198. There's a $5 fee per night, per dog, but dogs can stay in smoking rooms only.

$$ Super 8 Motel, 399 Jurassic, 970-858-0808, 800-800-8000, (national number), www.super8.com. Dogs can stay in pet-designated rooms, with a credit-card imprint as a deposit and a $5 fee per night, per pet.

$$-$$$ Comfort Inn, 400 Jurassic, 970-858-1333, 800-228-5150 (national number), www.comfortinn.com. Designated pet rooms are on the second and third floors of the motel. Your dog can be left unattended if he's in a travel crate.

$$-$$$ La Quinta Inn & Suites Fruita, 570 Raptor Rd., 970-858-8850, 800-753-3757 (national number), www.lq.com. Dogs are allowed in any of the rooms and suites, and can be left unattended as long as they're in a travel kennel.

Gateway

$$$-$$$$ Gateway Canyons, 43200 Hwy. 141, 970-931-2458, 866-671-4733, www.gatewaycanyons.com. This large adobe-style resort in canyon country 55 miles southwest of Grand Junction offers lodging in two varieties, and dogs are welcome in one of them: the 16-room Dolores River Inn (the more upscale Kiva Lodge is off-limits to canines). The pet fee is $30 per night, per dog, and four-legged guests receive a dog bowl with treats at check-in. The resort includes a restaurant, spa, retail outlets, an incredible auto museum, and an adventure center that offers mountain biking, climbing, fly-fishing, kayaking, rafting, horseback riding, and off-road driving tours. If you and your dog just want to soak in some of the gorgeous surrounding scenery, walk right from the resort to nearby Lumsden Canyon, where a new loop trail for hikers and mountain bikers was built by the BLM and volunteers.

Grand Junction

$ Grand Junction KOA, 2819 Hwy. 50, 970-242-2527, www.koa.com. In addition to the campground, dogs are permitted in the camper cabins, which are heated in winter and air-conditioned in summer (you'll have to bring your own bedding and cooking supplies). There's a $10 one-time fee per dog. The KOA also has an enclosed area—the "bark park"—where your dog can play leash free with other canine campers.

$-$$ Prospector Motel, 547 Hwy. 50 South, 970-242-4891, www.prospectormotelgrandjunction. Dogs are allowed in all rooms, with a $10 one-time fee. Some rooms have kitchenettes. You can leave your dog unattended in your room.

$$ Columbine Motel, 2824 North Ave., 970-241-2908. The motel charges $10 per night, per dog.

$$ El Rio Rancho Motel, 730 Hwy. 50 South, 970-242-0256. There's a $5 fee per night for small dogs and $10 per night for large dogs.

$$ Monument Inn, 1600 North Ave., 970-245-5770. Dogs are allowed in designated rooms for $10 extra per night, per pet.

$$ Motel 6, 776 Horizon Dr., 970-243-2628, 800-466-8356 (national number), www.motel6.com. The official policy is one small dog per room, though it's loosely interpreted as anything smaller than a Great Dane, say.

$$ Affordable Inns, 721 Horizon Dr., 970-243-6050, www.affordableinnsof colorado.com. Dogs can stay in designated pet rooms for $10 extra per night. You can leave your dog unattended in the room if you let the front desk know so that housekeeping doesn't enter during that time. A small dog-exercise area is behind the motel.

$$ America's Best Value Inn, 754 Horizon Dr., 970-245-1410, 800-544-3782 (national number), www.americasbest valueinn.com. The motel allows dogs in almost all of the rooms. If you stay more than two nights, a $10 per night, per dog fee kicks in.

$$ Country Inns of America, 718 Horizon Dr., 970-243-5080, 800-990-1143, www.countryinnsgj.com. The motel has several designated pet rooms, available for a $10 nightly fee per dog.

$$ Grand Vista Hotel, 2790 Crossroads Blvd., 970-241-8411, 800-800-7796, www.grandvistahotel.com. At this large, full-service hotel near the airport, dogs can stay in first-floor rooms for a $10 nightly fee. Your dog can stay unattended inside, as long as you provide the front desk with a cell-phone number.

$$ Holiday Inn Grand Junction, 755 Horizon Dr., 970-243-6790, 888-489-9796, www.holidayinn.com. With close to 300 rooms, there's bound to be room at the inn for your dog, or at least when the first-floor pet rooms are available. For human recreation, there's a pool, fitness center, and game rooms.

$$ Mesa Inn, 704 Horizon Dr., 970-245-3080, 888-955-3080. The motel has designated pet rooms, available for a $10 one-time fee per dog.

$$ Super 8 Motel, 728 Horizon Dr., 970-248-8080, 800-800-8000 (national number), www.super8.com. With a $5 nightly fee, up to two dogs per room are allowed in designated pet units.

$$ Two Rivers Inn, 141 N. 1st St., 970-245-8585, www.tworiversinns.com. This family-owned motel allows dogs for $15 extra per night.

$$ West Gate Inn, 2210 Hwy. 6 & 50, 970-241-3020, 800-453-9253, www .westgateinnco.com. This large, chain-style motel has several pet rooms, and you can leave your dog unattended unless he causes an audible problem.

$$–$$$ Best Western Sandman Motel, 708 Horizon Dr., 970-243-4150, 866-363-0915 (national number), www.best westerncolorado.com. The motel charges a $25 one-time fee for a dog to stay in one of the designated pet rooms.

$$–$$$ La Quinta Inn and Suites Grand Junction, 2761 Crossroads Blvd., 970-241-2929, 800-753-3757 (national number), www.lq.com. You can leave your dog unattended in the room (or suite) if you leave a cell-phone number with the front desk.

$$–$$$ Quality Inn of Grand Junction, 733 Horizon Dr., 970-245-7200, 800-790-2661, www.choicehotels.com. The motel has four pet rooms and charges $10 extra per night.

$$–$$$ Ramada Inn, 752 Horizon Dr., 970-243-5150, 800-2-RAMADA (national number), www.ramada.com. Dogs are allowed for a $10 fee per night, per pet.

$$–$$$$ Hawthorn Suites, 225 Main St., 970-242-2525, 800-527-1133 (national number), www.hawthorn.com. The hotel is located in downtown Grand Junction, away from motel row on Horizon Dr. and within walking distance of some parks. You can stay with your dog in any of the suites here, which range from studios to two bedrooms, some with full kitchen and others with kitchenette. There's a $25 per night pet fee that maxes out at $125 (so if your stay is longer than five nights, you won't be charged any more than that). You can leave your dog unattended in the room, but housekeeping will only come in to clean if he's in a travel kennel.

$$$–$$$$ Residence Inn by Marriott, 767 Horizon Dr., 970-263-4004, 800-936-1903 (national number), www.marriott .com. The hotel charges a rather steep $100 one-time fee for dogs, but if you're here for a longer stay, it might be worth it. The suites receive a thorough professional cleaning after canine guests check out. You can leave your dog unattended inside, and someone at the front desk might even be able to check on Rover or bring him down to the back office to hang out.

Grand Mesa

$$–$$$ Grand Mesa Lodge, Hwy. 65 (near milepost 28), 970-856-3250, 800-551-6372, www.coloradodirectory.com/ grandmesalodge. The lodge offers 14 one- and two-bedroom fully equipped and simply furnished but cozy log cabins in which dogs are allowed for $10 per dog, per night (dogs aren't permitted in the property's motel rooms). Your dog may want to explore Island Lake, the largest lake on the mesa, right behind the lodge buildings; you can rent a canoe or rowboat at the lodge. Fido can be left unattended in the cabin, and be sure to keep him leashed at all times around the property.

$$–$$$ Mesa Lakes Resort, Hwy. 65 (near milepost 36), 970-268-5467, www .coloradodirectory.com/mesalakesresort. Water dogs will love visiting Mesa Lakes, as it lives up to its name by being within walking distance of seven lakes. Established in 1920, the resort offers very basic motel rooms, small, summer camp–like rustic cabins (no running water, but there is electricity), and a handful of 1940s-era cabins; dogs can stay in all, with a two-dog max per unit. Your best bet is one of the two-bedroom cabins near Beaver Lake, with spacious living areas and an authentic vintage feel. The resort offers snowmobile tours in the winter, and miles of backcountry trails are readily accessible year-round. There's an on-site cafe with home-style meals that serves breakfast, lunch, and, occasionally, dinner.

$$$–$$$$ Spruce Lodge Cabins, 2120 AA50 Rd. (near milepost 22), 970-856-6240, 877-470-6548, www.sprucelodge colorado.com. The lodge offers 11 studio and one-bedroom cabins (that sleep up to six, thanks to extra futons), all recently remodeled, with kitchenettes and private baths. Unless your dog is a pit bull, Rottweiler, or Doberman, he can join you for $10 extra per night, per dog (two dogs max). There's also an on-site bar and restaurant, and you can leave your dog unattended in the cabin in a travel kennel while you check them out. Seven acres surround the cabins that your dog can sniff out on leash.

Mesa

$$$ The Wagon Wheel Motel, 10900 Hwy. 65, 970-268-5220. Located 7 miles from the Powderhorn ski area, this nine-room motel allows dogs basically in name only, as four-legged guests must be five pounds or less. If your dog does happen to be this small, he can stay with you for $10 extra per night (that would be $2 per pound).

Palisade

$$ The Orchard House Bed and Breakfast, 3573 E. 1/2 Rd., 970-464-0529, www .theorchardhouse.com. This B&B in the heart of Palisade's wine country accepts "well-behaved, well-socialized pets who stay off the furniture." The four rooms, in fact, are named after the owners' pets (three cats and, in the past, a dog). Three of the rooms have private baths, and all rooms are furnished in a streamlined country style. Though you can't leave your dog unattended inside the room, an outside kennel is available where he can hang out on his own.

$$$ Pearadice Farm Carriage House, 629 35 Rd., 970-464-5751, www.homeaway .com/search/colorado/palisade/region: 24283. This charming little guest house, 2 miles west of Palisade, provides the perfect escape for you and your dog (considered on a case-by-case basis) in Colorado's wine country. Built as a carriage house in the late 1890s and later used as a fruit pickers' bunkhouse, the completely renovated cottage has a full kitchen, bedroom with queen bed, another room with a single bed, and a cathedral-ceilinged living room. Owners Frank and Jackie Davidson live in the adjacent Victorian farmhouse on the 6-acre property, which includes a pear orchard and horse pastures (horse guests are welcome, too). Your dog should be well mannered and not prone to chew his surroundings (he will have to put down a $200 deposit as insurance).You can leave your dog unattended in the guest house for an hour or two at a time, but there's also a small fenced backyard where he may prefer to hang out. One special extra for humans is getting fresh organic eggs each day from the resident chickens.

CAMPGROUNDS
Colorado National Monument. Just west of Grand Junction, access off Hwy. 340, or off I-70 at the Fruita exit. The Saddlehorn Campground, near the visitor center, has 80 sites.

State park campgrounds: **Highline Lake State Park**—see Tail-Rated Trails for

directions (31 sites); **James M. Robb-Colorado River State Park/Island Acres**, Exit 47 off I-70, 5 miles east of Palisade (80 sites); **James M. Robb-Colorado River State Park/Fruita**, Exit 19 off I-70 (57 sites); **Vega State Park**, Hwy. 330, 12 miles past Collbran (109 sites).

Bureau of Land Management campgrounds: **Rabbit Valley**—see McDonald Creek in Tail-Rated Trails for directions.

National forest campgrounds: **Grand Mesa** has 10 campgrounds, with a range of 11 to 41 sites each.

DOGGIE DAYCARE
Clifton
Upper Valley Kennels, 3460 G Rd., 970-464-5713. $14/day ($22 for two dogs) lets your dog choose between 30 inside/outside temperature-controlled runs. "We can be accommodating and flexible, because we live here," says owner Donna Bondurant. Open 8 AM–6 PM, Monday to Saturday; 4 PM–6 PM, Sunday.

Fruita
Pet Particulars, 242 S. Mulberry, 970-858-0818. $11/day ($20 for two dogs). Dogs have individual kennels and an outdoor play area but generally don't play with other boarders. Open 8 AM–8:30 AM and 5 PM–5:30 PM, Saturday to Monday; 8 AM–5:30 PM, Tuesday to Friday.

Grand Junction
All Pets Center, 424 S. 5th, 970-241-1976, www.gjvet.com. $9/day. Open 7 AM–6 PM, Monday to Friday; 8 AM–5 PM, Saturday.

The Pet Spa, 2509 Industrial Ct., 970-241-8499. $7.50/day ($12.50 for two dogs). The "spa" differentiates between doggie daycare and day boarding. So if you ask about doggie daycare, you'll be told they don't offer it. If you simply ask about a place to board your dog during the day, they can do it. Open 8 AM–5:30 PM, Monday to Saturday; 9–9:30 AM (for drop-off) and 5–5:30 PM (for pick-up) Sunday.

Your Best Friends Boarding Kennel & Grooming House, 2708 Hwy. 50, 970-244-8865. $8/day ($14 for two dogs). Indoor kennels have in-floor radiant heat and piped-in music to soothe your pooch. Outdoors, there are four large play yards. Open 7 AM–5 PM, Monday to Friday; 8 AM–noon and 5 PM–6 PM, Saturday; 5 PM–6 PM, Sunday.

PET PROVISIONS
Fruita
Pet Particulars, 242 S. Mulberry, 970-858-0818

Grand Junction
Green Fields Seed and Feed, 520 S. 9th St., 970-241-0979

Mesa Feed Mart, 715 S. 7th St., 970-242-7762

Murdoch's Ranch and Home Supply, 3217 I-70 Business Loop, 970-523-7515

PETCO, 2464 Hwy. 6 & 50, 970-241-8340, www.petco.com. The store has a self-service dog wash. It's $12 a wash, which includes shampoo, towels, grooming tools, and a dryer. The one catch is that you'll need to show proof of your dog's rabies vaccination on paper, not just via his tag.

PetSmart, 2428 F Rd., 970-255-9305, www.petsmart.com

The Pet Spa, 2509 Industrial Ct., 970-241-8499

Your Best Friends Boarding Kennel & Grooming House, 2708 Hwy. 50, 970-244-8865. There's also a self-service dog wash here; $15 gets you everything you need to make Fido shine: shampoo, tools, towels, and dryers.

CANINE ER
Fruita
Kokopelli Animal Hospital (AAHA certified), 456 Kokopelli Blvd., Unit E, 970-858-4299, www.kokopellianimalhospital.com. Open 8 AM–5:30 PM, Monday and Friday; 7:30 AM–6 PM, Tuesday and Thursday; 8 AM–noon, Wednesday.

Grand Junction
All Pets Center (AAHA certified), 424 S. 5th, 970-241-1976, www.gjvet.com. Open 7 AM–6 PM, Monday to Friday; 8 AM–5 PM, Saturday.

Veterinary Emergency Center, 1660 North Ave., 970-255-1911. Open 6 PM–8 AM, weeknights; 24 hours weekends and holidays.

RESOURCES
Bureau of Land Management, 2815 H Rd., Grand Junction, 970-244-3000

Colorado Welcome Center, 340 Hwy. 340, Fruita, 970-858-9335

Fruita Chamber of Commerce, 432 E. Aspen, Fruita, 970-858-3894, www.fruitachamber.org

Grand Junction Visitor and Convention Bureau, 740 Horizon Dr. (at I-70), Grand Junction, 970-256-4060, 800-962-2547, www.visitgrandjunction.com

Grand Mesa Visitor Center, Grand Mesa, 970-856-4153. Open Memorial Day through end of October

Grand Valley Ranger District, Grand Mesa/Uncompaghre/Gunnison National Forests, 2777 Crossroads Blvd., Grand Junction, 970-242-8211

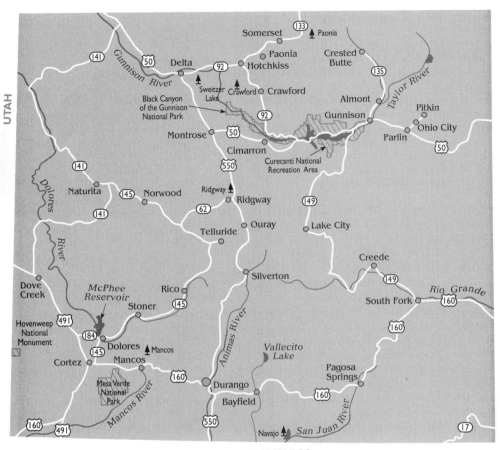

UTAH

Somerset
133 ♠ Paonia
Paonia
Crested
141
50
Delta
92
Hotchkiss
Butte
135
Gunnison River
Sweitzer
Lake
Crawford
Crawford
Almont
Taylor River
Black Canyon
of the Gunnison
National Park
92
Gunnison
Pitkin
Ohio City
Montrose
50
Parlin
50
Cimarron
550
Curecanti National
Recreation Area
141
Naturita
145
Norwood
Ridgway ♠
149
Dolores
62
Ridgway
141
Telluride
Ouray
Lake City
River
Creede
Dove
Creek
McPhee
Reservoir
Rico
Silverton
149
Rio Grande
South Fork
160
Stoner
145
Hovenweep
National
Monument
491
184
Animas River
160
Dolores
Mancos ♠
Vallecito
Lake
Pagosa
Springs
Cortez
145
Mancos
Mesa Verde
National
Park
Mancos River
160
Durango
Bayfield
160
160
491
550
San Juan River
17
Navajo ♠

NEW MEXICO

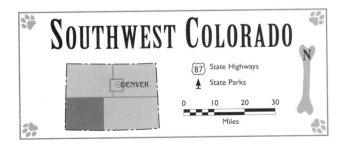

SOUTHWEST COLORADO

⊙ DENVER

87 State Highways
♠ State Parks

0   10   20   30
Miles

N

Black Canyon Area

THE BIG SCOOP

Not quite desert, not quite mountains, the area surrounding the Black Canyon of the Gunnison River will give your dog a taste of high plateau country. And the eponymous national park is one of the few where dogs can actually do something besides sit in the car.

The hub towns are Montrose and Delta, about half an hour's drive apart. Montrose has a leash law in both the city and county. Delta's leash law is imposed within city limits but not in surrounding Delta County.

TAIL-RATED TRAILS

FYI, the three state parks within this region—Paonia, Crawford, and Sweitzer Lake—focus on water recreation. Hiking opportunities are limited to a .5-mile nature trail and slightly longer shoreline trails at Crawford and a short canal road at Sweitzer. For some trail ideas in the West Elk Wilderness Area east of Crawford and the western part of the Curecanti National Recreation Area (dogs must be leashed in both locations), pick up the "North Fork Trails Network" brochure at the Delta Visitor Center or the Forest Supervisor's Office in Delta. Or ask for trail descriptions for the Uncompahgre Basin Resource Area at the BLM/forest service office in Montrose (see Resources).

Delta

Confluence Park

Access: Head south on Gunnison River Dr. from Main St. to reach the park entrance.

Dogs must be leashed.

There are about 5 miles of trails in this 265-acre park, formerly an abandoned industrial site, situated at the junction of the Gunnison and Uncompahgre rivers. If you're driving through Delta on a longer trip, a visit here is a great way for your dog to stretch his legs. It's also a good destination for a late afternoon or evening stroll. The nicest section of the wide gravel trails that loop around and through the park is by the waterfowl habitat area. For the most direct access, begin walking from the boat ramp on the Gunnison River (at the end of Gunnison River Dr., within the park, turn right and follow the road into a parking area). Another section of trail encircles Confluence Lake. Make sure to keep your dog on the trail with you throughout the park; he may encounter some hazards if he frolics in the water.

Montrose

Duncan Trail

Distance: 3 miles round-trip
Elevation gain: 840 feet
Trailhead: Drive north from Montrose for 9 miles on Hwy. 50 and turn right onto Falcon Rd., just before Olathe. Travel 3.6 miles to the end of the paved portion of the road, then follow it left as it turns into Peach Valley Rd. Staying left at the next fork you come to, drive 4.8 miles to the BLM sign for access to the Duncan Trail on the right. It's about 1.7 miles to the trailhead, where there's a parking area; stay left at the one fork you'll come to. It's inadvisable to drive on the dirt roads when they're muddy; apparently they turn into a sort of quicksand that will trap your car. And

though four-wheel drive is recommended for the access road off Peach Valley Rd., my low-clearance vehicle made it all the way to the trailhead. Note that because this trail is part of an area designated as the Gunnison Gorge Wilderness (under BLM oversight), there's a $3 day-use fee per person, payable via a self-service fee station at the trailhead.

Dogs can be off leash (even with the wilderness designation).

Less heavily used than the neighboring Chukar Trail, this is a rewarding hike for the intrepid dog. And it provides the access to the Gunnison River Gorge that your dog is unable to enjoy in the national park. The trail begins by traversing a hillside for .5 mile or so before beginning the descent to the river. At this point, it gets rather steep—a pair of hiking boots or good shoes is a must. Navigation also gets a little tricky before the final descent to the river. Look for the path of least resistance, as there seem to be several options. To avoid getting minicliffed-out right before the river, stay to the left and somewhat high in the last gully (you'll be able to see the river from here). Once at the river, your dog can cool off in the current while you relax to the water's soothing rush and muster the energy for the climb back up. Try the nearby **Ute Trail** if you want a more gradual, but longer (9 miles round-trip), hike; the access road is about 2.4 miles past the Duncan Trail turnoff.

 Black Canyon of the Gunnison National Park
Access: South Rim, 15 miles east of Montrose via Hwys. 50 and 347; North Rim, 11 miles south of Crawford, via Hwy. 92 and the North Rim Rd. The entrance fee is $15 per vehicle, which gives you a week's pass.

Dogs must be leashed.

The spectacular canyon for which the park is named reaches depths of close to 2,700 feet and is just 40 feet wide at its narrowest point. Unlike at many other sites managed by the National Park Service, dogs actually have a few—albeit short—hiking options at the monument. We'll start with the no-no's. Pets are not permitted on the North Vista and Deadhorse Trails (both on the canyon's north rim); on the Oak Flat and Uplands Trails (near the visitor center on the south rim); or on the Warner Point Nature Trail (at the end of South Rim Rd.). They are also not allowed in the inner canyon or designated wilderness areas.

You can bring your pooch along on the approximately 1-mile-long **Rim Rock Trail**, which leads from the South Rim Campground to the visitor center, and on two very short nature trails: **Chasm View**, by the North Rim Campground; and **Cedar Point**, off South Rim Rd. And your dog is welcome to gaze down to his heart's content from any of the overlooks—just be sure to keep a tight rein on him if he suffers from vertigo! Bring plenty of water to share for hiking.

You can also access the Gunnison River by driving down East Portal Rd. (the turnoff is before the South Rim Campground as you're entering the park). The paved road is steep (up to 16 percent in grade) and windy, but once at the bottom, which is actually part of the adjacent Curecanti National Recreation

Summit and Clover, best of buddies.

Area, your leashed dog can sniff along the riverbank to his heart's content. The road is generally open mid-April to mid-November.

In the winter, South Rim Rd. is unplowed past the visitor center and is open for cross-country skiing, but not to dogs. 970-641-2337, www.nps.gov/blca.

CYCLING FOR CANINES

The Uncompahgre Plateau west of Montrose offers lots of varied biking opportunities, including the originations of the **Tabeguache Trail**, which travels 142 miles to Grand Junction, and the **Paradox Trail**, which links up with Kokopelli's Trail 100 miles later in Utah. (Of course, just bike a few miles of these multiday trails if Fido is in tow.) Because the BLM and forest service oversee the land on which the trails pass, your dog will be able to run leash free beside your bike. For route descriptions, look for pamphlets on the Tabeguache and Paradox Trails at the BLM/forest service office in Montrose (see Resources) or check out *Bicycling the Uncompahgre Plateau*, by Bill Harris.

CREATURE COMFORTS

Unless otherwise stated, dogs should not be left unattended in the room or cabin.

Cimarron

$$ Cimarron Lodge, 84340 Hwy. 50 (look for the lodge sign in Cimarron), 970-249-8579. The lodge, on 85 acres, has four fairly new motel rooms with kitchenettes and welcomes dogs for $10 per dog, per visit. The resident border collie can show your dog the ropes. Open May 1 through mid-November.

$$ Pleasant Valley Cabins and Campground, 84100 E. Hwy. 50, 970-249-8330, www.pleasant-valley.biz. There's a $5 nightly fee per dog to stay in one of the seven one-room cabins on the Little Cimarron River, five with kitchenettes. A general store and small café are on-site. You can leave your dog unattended if he's in a travel crate. Open May 1 to November 15.

$$$–$$$$ The Inn at Arrowhead, 21401 Alpine Plateau Rd. (5.5 miles off Hwy. 50), 970-862-8206, www.arrowheadinn.net. The dog with a yen for British culture will particularly enjoy a sojourn here, where rates include a traditional English breakfast (for humans) and annual events such as Burns Night (in honor of the Scottish poet), a huge St. Patrick's Day party, and a Highlands festival. Dogs are allowed in any of the spacious rooms and suites, all with fireplaces, for $25 extra per night, per dog. The inn is within 1 mile or so of trails on BLM land, and, in winter, a groomed cross-country ski trail starts just off the property. Closed April 1 to mid-May and mid-Nov. to beginning of December.

Crawford

$$ Bid-U-Well Guest Ranch, 33732 B 25 Rd. (9 miles out of Crawford), 970-921-7070. The ranch has a building with two bedrooms that are rented out separately (both nonsmoking), a sitting room, and shared bath. You'll get a full homemade breakfast that can be served either near your room or in the main house (other meals are available on request). Dogs are each $4–$8 extra per night, depending on the size of dog, and you'll need to keep yours leashed outside, but there are 122 acres, with some hiking trails, to explore. A kennel space is also available if you need to leave your dog unattended. The ranch is home to an assorted populace of horses, cows, goats, chickens, cats, and dogs; you're welcome to bring your own horse, too. Owner Ann Critchley touts the ranch's panoramic views and relaxing atmosphere. "We treat everybody like family," she says.

$$ Crawford Country Store and Motel, 313 Hwy. 92, 970-921-5040, www.crawford countrystore.com. Dogs are welcome at this 10-room motel for a $30 one-time fee and can be left unattended in the room if they're in a travel kennel or are very well mannered. Two rooms have kitchenettes, and the attached general store has everything from food to fishing supplies to a tanning bed.

$$ Last Frontier Lodge, 40300 D Lane, 970-921-5150, www.coloradodirectory .com/lastfrontierlodge. This bed-and-breakfast on 10 acres near Crawford Reservoir offers eight rooms in a rustic-style log house. Two rooms have private baths; the others share a bath. Dogs are $10 extra per visit, per dog, and can be left unattended in the room for a short time, if necessary. You and your dog will have a stellar view of the lake from the lodge's long, covered porch, and some trails also lead down toward the water.

Delta

$–$$ El-D-Rado Motel, 702 Main, 970-874-4493. There's a $5 fee per dog, per night. You can leave your dog unattended in the room for a couple of hours.

$–$$ Westways Court Motel, 1030 Main, 970-874-4415, 877-874-4415, www.west wayscourt.com. The 10 log cabin units (two with kitchenettes) at this motel were built in the mid-1940s and are now classically vintage. If your dog is well behaved and clean, he can join you for a $10 nightly fee per pet.

$$ Four Seasons River Inn and RV Park, 676 Hwy. 50, 970-874-9659, 888-340-4689, www.fourseasonsriverinn.com. All of the units consist of two rooms with full kitchens. There's a $5 one-time fee per dog and a two-dog maximum per room. You can walk Fido on leash down to the Gunnison River, which runs along the property.

$$ Rodeway Inn, 2124 S. Main, 970-874-9726, 800-621-2271, www.rodewayinn .com. The motel offers designated pet rooms for $10 extra per night, per dog. There's a maximum of two dogs per room, and each dog must be 50 pounds or under.

$$–$$$ Best Western Sundance, 903 Main, 970-874-9781, 800-626-1994, www.bestwesternsundance.com. Dogs are $10 per night, per pet, and you can leave your dog unattended in the room for a short time; for example, to grab the full breakfast that's included in the room rate.

$$–$$$ Comfort Inn, 180 Gunnison River Dr., 970-874-1000, www.comfort inn.com. The motel accepts dogs in any rooms for $10 extra per night, per dog.

$$ La Casita Guest House, 21099 H Rd. (6 miles east of Delta, off Hwy. 92), 970-874-3244, www.lacasitaranch.com. The petite adobe guest house, shaded by cottonwood trees, is furnished in a traditional southwestern style, including a beehive fireplace and a kiva ladder leading to the sleeping loft. It shares 30 acres with a working cattle ranch, and "nice dogs," says the owner, are very welcome (as are horses). You can also leave Fido unattended in the casita if need be.

Hotchkiss

$$ North Fork Motel, 492 Hwy. 133, 970-872-2137, www.coloradodirectory .com/northforkmotel. This small motel in downtown Hotchkiss permits dogs in its six rooms (two have kitchens). You may leave your dog unattended in the room only if he's in a travel kennel.

$$$$ Casa Encantada Bed and Breakfast, 2690 O Rd. (11 miles from Hotchkiss), 970-399-7090, www.casaencantadabb.com. The accommodation here is actually a separate casita, enclosed in an adobe courtyard, that sleeps up to four. There are two bedrooms and baths, a full kitchen, and a living room with a beehive fireplace, furnished in southwestern decor. You can leave your dog unattended inside if necessary. The owners, Marilee and Charles Gilman, also raise organic produce and operate the Upland Game Club for bird hunters on their Four Directions Farm.

Montrose

$–$$ Blue Sky Inn and Extended Stay, 1150 N. Townsend, 970-249-4595, www.blueskyinn.com. This older motel has remodeled rooms with unexpected homey touches like quilts and cottage-style furniture. Dogs are permitted in all of the rooms, with a limit of two per room. They can be left unattended inside for up to an hour.

$$ Affordable Inns, 1480 Hwy. 550, 970-249-6644, 888-681-4159, www.affordable innsofcolorado.com. The motel allows dogs in certain rooms for a one-time $10 fee. There's a maximum of two or three dogs per room, depending on size, and certain breeds are not permitted.

$$ America's Best Value Inns, 1417 E. Main, 970-249-4507, www.usainnsof america.com. Dogs are permitted for $10 extra per night in smoking rooms only. They can be left unattended in the room.

$$ Black Canyon Motel, 1605 E. Main, 970-249-3495, 800-348-3495, www.toski .com/black-canyon. The motel has select pet rooms and allows small dogs only, with a limit of two per room, for $5 per night, per dog. The motel also has a grassy dog-walking area where four-legged guests can do their thing off leash.

$$ Canyon Trails Inn, 1225 E. Main, 970-249-3426, 800-858-5911, www.canyon trailsinn.com. Dogs can stay in designated rooms for $5–$10 extra per night.

$$ Country Lodge, 1624 E. Main, 970-249-4567, www.countrylodgecolorado.com. Dogs are permitted in all rooms, many of which are decorated in themes inspired by nature, fishing, and even John Wayne, with warm accents like knotty-pine-paneled walls and quilts. Some have kitchenettes, too. A three-bedroom cabin adjacent to the motel, with full kitchen, is also available.

$$ Rodeway Inn, 1705 E. Main, 970-249-9294, 877-424-6423 (national number), www.rodewayinn.com. Dogs can stay in four of the rooms for $10 per night, per dog.

$$ Western Motel, 1200 E. Main, 970-249-3481, 800-445-7301, www.western motel.com. The motel has four designated pet rooms. Dogs under 30 pounds are preferred, for $5 nightly per dog, plus a $25 deposit if you're paying with cash. Your dog can be left unattended in the room.

$$–$$$ Best Western Red Arrow Motel, 1702 E. Main, 970-249-9641, 800-468-9323, www.bestwesterncolorado.com. For $10 extra per dog, per night, you can stay in one of the motel's 12 designated pet rooms.

$$–$$$ Hampton Inn, 1980 N. Townsend, 970-252-3300, www.hamptoninn.com. Dogs can stay in designated pet rooms, and there's a maximum weight of 50 pounds total for all dogs in a room.

$$–$$$ Quality Inn and Suites, 2751 Commercial Wy., 970-249-1011, 800-424-6423 (national number), www .qualityinn.com. Dogs are welcome in all rooms for a $10 nightly fee per pet and can be left unattended inside.

$$$ Holiday Inn Express, 1391 S. Townsend, 970-240-1800, 800-550-9252, www.hiexpress.com. Dogs may stay in one of six pet-friendly rooms.

CAMPGROUNDS

Black Canyon of the Gunnison National Park, 15 miles east of Montrose via Hwys. 50 and 347. The monument has two campgrounds, one on the north rim (13 sites), one on the south rim (88 sites). There's also a small campground (15 sites) on East Portal Rd., in what is actually part of the Curecanti National Recreation Area.

State park campgrounds: **Crawford State Park**, 1 mile south of Crawford on Hwy. 92 (66 sites); **Paonia State Park**, 16 miles north of Paonia on Hwy. 133 (13 sites).

National forest campgrounds: **McClure Campground**, 12 miles north of Paonia Reservoir on Hwy. 133, at the top of McClure Pass (19 sites); **Erickson Springs Campground**, 6 miles down CR 12 (turn off Hwy. 133, right before Paonia Reservoir; 18 sites).

Private campgrounds: **Pleasant Valley Cabins and Campground** in Cimarron; **Four Seasons River Inn and RV Park** in Delta (see Creature Comforts).

DOGGIE DAYCARE
Crawford
Cottonwood Ranch and Kennel, 3994 G Dr., 970-921-7100, www.cottonwood ranchandkennel.com. $25/day ($20/day per dog for two or more dogs); includes food and multiple walks. Owner Ted Hoff is also well known as a dog trainer. Open 7:30 AM–6:30 PM, Monday to Saturday; by appointment on Sunday.

Delta
Canine Cottage, 1557 G96 Ln., 970-874-2547. $10/day. The owners live on-site, and the kennel area includes indoor/outdoor runs and a large play area. Day boarding is by appointment, with flexible pick-up and drop-off times offered daily.

Deleff Kennels, 1951 B 50 Rd., 970-874-4058. $10–$12/day, depending on the size of dog. Open 7 AM–6 PM, Monday to Saturday.

Montrose
Camp Bow Wow, 330 Denny Ct., 970-249-5999, www.campbowwow.com/montrose. $20/day; $12/half-day. A preboarding interview is required. The Camp Bow Wow experience includes separate playgroups into which dogs are placed based on size and temperament; they have all-day access to indoor and outdoor play areas with dog-specific play equipment and, in warmer weather, wading pools. You can keep tabs on the great time your pooch is having via the online Camper Cam. Open 7 AM–7 PM, Monday to Friday; 8–10 AM and 5–7 PM, Saturday and Sunday.

PET PROVISIONS
Delta
Sisson's Feed and Seed, 405 W. 5th St., 970-874-8376

Montrose
Camp Bow Wow, 330 Denny Ct., 970-249-5999, www.campbowwow.com/montrose

Alantis Aquatics and Pets, 16367 S. Townsend Ave., #1, 970-249-1797

Murdoch's Ranch & Home Supply, 2151 S. Townsend, 970-249-9991

CANINE ER
Delta
Delta Veterinary Clinic, 1520 Bluff St., 970-874-4486. Open 8 AM–5 PM, Monday to Friday; 8 AM–noon, Saturday.

Dorr Veterinary Hospital, 1070 Hwy. 92, 970-874-5785. Open 8 AM–5 PM, Monday to Friday; 8 AM–noon, Saturday.

Grand Mesa Veterinary Hospital, 1534 Hwy. 50, 970-874-8041. Open 8 AM–5:30 PM, Monday to Friday.

Two Rivers Veterinary Clinic, 443 Dodge St., 970-874-1441. Open 8 AM–5 PM, Monday to Friday.

Montrose

Alta Vista Animal Hospital, 1845 E. Main, 970-249-8185. Open 8 AM–5 PM, Monday to Friday.

Morningstar Veterinary Clinic, 717 N. Cascade Ave., 970-249-8022. Open 8 AM–5 PM, Monday to Friday (until 7 PM on Thursday); 8:30 AM–noon, two Saturdays per month.

Montrose Veterinary Clinic, 2260 S. Townsend Ave., 970-249-5469. Open 8 AM–5:30 PM, Monday to Friday, 8 AM–noon, Saturday.

San Juan Veterinary Clinic, 822 Spring Creek Rd., 970-249-4490. Open 8 AM–5:30 PM, Monday to Friday, 8 AM–noon, Saturday.

RESOURCES

Bureau of Land Management/Ouray Ranger District, Uncompahgre National Forest, 2505 S. Townsend, Montrose, 970-240-5300

Delta Area Chamber of Commerce and Visitor Center, 301 Main St., Delta, 970-874-8616, www.deltacolorado.org

Forest Supervisor's Office, Grand Mesa, Uncompahgre, and Gunnison National Forests, 2250 Hwy. 50, Delta, 970-874-6600

Montrose Visitors and Convention Bureau, 1519 E. Main, Montrose, 970-252-0505, 800-873-0244, www.visit montrose.net

Paonia Ranger District, Gunnison National Forest, North Rio Grande Ave., Paonia, 970-527-4131

Sixteen
Gunnison, Crested Butte, and Lake City

THE BIG SCOOP

Dogs on the go will find attractions aplenty in the Gunnison area: forested hikes, rugged mountains to climb, and lots of water. Just be sure to keep an eye on your dog when you're both out enjoying the natural environment—wildlife and livestock harassment by otherwise well-meaning dogs is a perennial problem in the region.

Gunnison has the expected leash law within city limits. In Gunnison County, dogs can legally be under voice control.

For a generally dog-friendly, laid-back mountain town, Crested Butte has fairly strict dog regulations: there's a leash law within city limits, public tethering (i.e., tying up your dog outside a shop while you run in) is verboten, and dogs are allowed in only one of the five town parks (Totem Pole, at Maroon Ave. and 3rd St.). Nevertheless, dogs here seem to enjoy themselves as much as in any of the ski towns, and your dog won't be at a loss for encountering other butts to sniff. There's also a leash law in the Crested Butte South neighborhood, even though it's technically in unincorporated Gunnison County. Mt. Crested Butte, which is the separate town at the ski area, allows dogs to be under voice control instead of on leash, and the no-public-tethering rule is confined to the ski resort's immediate base area.

Lake City (population 350), tucked in the mountains 55 miles south of Gunnison, requires dogs to be on leash; they can be under voice control in surrounding Hinsdale County. Unfortunately, dogs must refrain from setting paw in the town park.

TAIL-RATED TRAILS

There is limitless hiking in the Gunnison and Uncompahgre National Forests and BLM lands of which this region is largely composed. I've highlighted just a few of the most accessible trails. For more ideas, consult the "Aspen/Crested Butte/Gunnison Recreation Topo Map" put out by Latitude 40° and *Hiking in Heaven: A Crested Butte Trail Guide*, by Denis B. Hall. Keep in mind that many of the well-known hiking trails around Crested Butte are in wilderness areas, so your dog will have to stay on a leash. And because the town is a legendary mountain-biking hub, choose nonwilderness trails carefully if you want to avoid dodging avid cyclists. In addition, if you want to find some close-to-town places where your dog can romp off leash, check out the dog-friendly brochure compiled by the Paradise Animal Welfare Society (PAWS). The brochure not only has lodging suggestions and info on pet stores and vets, but it also maps out five parcels of land adjacent to downtown Crested Butte (including the Peanut Lake area detailed below) where dogs can be leash free. Look for the brochure at the visitor center in Crested Butte.

Crested Butte

Copley Lake

Distance: 4 miles round-trip
Elevation gain: 1,100 feet
Trailhead: From Crested Butte, head west on Whiterock Ave., which turns into Kebler Pass Rd. Take note of your mileage at the bridge that crosses Coal Creek on the edge of town. From there, drive 4.5 miles on the pass road to a parking pullout on the left (if you see mile marker 27, you've gone too far).

Dogs can be off leash.

This little known yet scenic trail should afford you and your dog a chance to take in some of the mountain splendor that surrounds the butte in relative solitude. From the parking pullout, cross the road and look for a path heading up the hillside, to the left of Elk Creek. You may not even think you're on a trail at first as you hike up this steep pitch of dirt and rock rubble. But the trail soon melds into a nice, distinct doubletrack (a former mining road) that goes up a classic mountain drainage—think rushing creek, the sweet smell of fir in the air, wildflowers poking up midsummer—and climbs at a steady pace. When the trail intersects with another old jeep track, which goes to the former Standard Mine, stay left. The lake is .2 mile ahead. Plan to spend some time here, as it will be hard to tear yourself away from this serene setting: Copley Lake nestled within an open meadow, with views of Mount Owen and Ruby and Purple Peaks to the northwest.

Green Lake

Distance: 9 miles round-trip
Elevation gain: 1,600 feet
Trailhead: This hike to a gorgeous mountain lake begins right in Crested Butte, at the Nordic Center at 2nd and Whiterock.

Dogs can be off leash (though you may want to leash up Fido on the short sections of dirt road that travel through private subdivisions).

Begin hiking up the dirt track that ascends from the left of the Nordic Center parking lot. At the top of the bench, go right on the dirt road (Journey's End Rd.). Look for the Green Lake trail sign on the left (it's by a small pullout, though no parking is available here). Cross a short meadow before entering a thick stand of aspen and conifer; there's not much water for your dog here, but it's nice and shady. The trail gradually switchbacks up the lower portion of Gibson Ridge for a little under 1 mile. When it levels out, make the short traverse to the next trail sign, where you'll stay left and join up with an old, rocky jeep road, known as Baby Head Hill, which climbs directly up for the next .3 mile. At a signed fork, the trail descends slightly and contours above a creek for about .4 mile before ending at a well-maintained dirt road (Wildcat Trail in the Trapper's Crossing subdivision). Go right. The actual Green Lake Trail is about .5 mile farther along the road; look for the trail sign. (Unfortunately, you can't just drive to this point from town because the road leading to it is private.) From here, the trail is distinct all the way to the lake, as it winds through wildflower meadows

Allie guards her camp in Crested Butte.

and forest. Just before reaching the lake, pass by a trail that climbs steeply up to the right. The lake itself lives up to its name and is picturesquely situated at the base of an alpine cirque below 12,055-foot Mount Axtell. Midsummer, the water temperature may even be warm enough for both you and your dog to enjoy a dip.

Woods Walk to Peanut Lake

Distance: About 3.6 miles round-trip

Elevation gain: Approximately 50 feet

Trailhead: From the intersection of Whiterock and 1st St. in Crested Butte, walk or drive west on Whiterock (which turns into Kebler Pass Rd.) for .3 mile to Treasury Hill Rd. on the right. The trailhead, which is marked by a brown carsonite post, is between Treasury Hill Rd. and the Trapper's Crossing housing development immediately west. If you've driven, look for a small parking pullout off the pass road, just west of the trailhead.

Dogs can be off leash.

Head into the woods from the trail marker. You'll first pass a trail branch coming in from the right. At the next fork, stay right. The trail goes through a thick stand of aspen, then opens into a wildflower-filled meadow. Continue hiking northwest until you draw near a distinctive house; turn left here. The trail then parallels Peanut Lake from above, with Crested Butte Mountain and Gothic Mountain dominating the view. Although your dog won't be within paw-dipping access of the lake, you will cross a stream he can get wet in. The trail eventually veers right at a fence line by the old Peanut Mine and descends about 50 feet to Peanut Lake Rd. If you want to make a loop, walk back on the road along the lake; just before you reach pavement, on the edge of downtown Crested Butte, take the small footpath up to the right.

Stay on the straight, narrow path past a branch-off to the left, until you meet up with your original route by the house.

Another alternative is to continue on the **Lower Loop Trail**, which would add approximately 4.6 miles round-trip. After descending to Peanut Lake Rd., head left and cross the cattle guard. The signed Lower Loop Trail starts in about .2 mile. Eventually the trail splits into an upper and a lower tier; both tiers end at the road that goes up to Gunsight Pass. Take one route out and return on the other.

You can also access Peanut Lake Rd. from town by walking to the end of Butte Ave., 4 blocks north of Elk Ave. This will make for a shorter hike, but you'll forsake the lovely woods part of the hike described above.

Crested Butte Mountain

The ski area is open for hiking (and mountain biking) in the summer, though you won't be able to ride up the Silver Queen chairlift with your dog. Instead, follow the **Silver Queen Trail** (the summer service road) from the base area to the top of the Silver Queen chair, a distance of 4.3 miles. Watch for bike traffic on the first half of the trail; the upper half, from the top of the Red Lady chairlift to the top of Silver Queen, is for hikers only. From there, trail signs will point you in the direction of the steep 1.8-mile round-trip hike to the peak, where you'll top out at 12,162 feet, rewarded by a stunning panoramic view of the Elk Mountains and the backside of the Maroon Bells.

Dogs can be off leash.

Gunnison

Curecanti National Recreation Area

Curecanti, administered by the National Park Service, encompasses an area from about 5 miles west of Gunnison to the border of the Black Canyon of the Gunnison National Park. Its centerpiece is 20-mile-long Blue Mesa Reservoir, created by three dams constructed along the Gunnison River. There are also seven established hiking trails in the recreation area. The Elk Creek Visitor Center, off Hwy. 50 west, has a brochure that describes them. The 1.5-mile round-trip **Neversink Trail**, which provides good bird-watching opportunities, is the closest one to Gunnison, just off Hwy. 50, 5 miles from town. For a less frequented hike that's also near water, try the 4-mile round-trip **Curecanti Creek Trail**, accessed from Hwy. 92 north, 5.7 miles from the junction with Hwy. 50. Your dog will have to pass on the guided boat tours of Morrow Point Lake.

Dogs must be leashed throughout the recreation area, including all trails.

Hartman Rocks

Access: From downtown Gunnison, head west on Hwy. 50 for approximately 1.5 miles to CR 38 (Gold Basin Rd.). Turn left and drive for 2.4 miles to the parking area on the right.

Dogs can be off leash.

This 160-acre recreation area, which abuts 8,000 acres of BLM land, has a network of trails looping over and around hilly terrain, with sage, piñon, and juniper as the primary vegetation. There's no set destination—let your dog lead the way to wherever his nose takes him. The trails are divided into "single track" trails, which permit nonmotorized and motorized use (except for ATVs and 4x4s), and nonmotorized-only trails, which are open to mountain bikers, horses, skiers, and hikers. You and your dog will likely want to avoid the former, but in order to connect various segments of the nonmotorized trail network, you will have to hike some short stints on the single track trails. Because the area is

dry and hot, you'll want to avoid bringing Fido here midday during the summer. Bring plenty of water for the both of you, though your dog might be lucky enough to come across one of the water-filled stock tanks on the backside of the hill.

Signal Peak

Distance: Up to approximately 8 miles round-trip
Elevation gain: 1,250 feet
Trailhead: From Main St. (Hwy. 135) in Gunnison, head east on Georgia Ave. Follow the road as it bends to the left, becoming Escalante Dr., and partially circumnavigate the Western State College campus. Turn into a parking lot on the right, just after the water storage tanks on the right and just before the athletic field. (Alternately, park in the lot on the left just before the water towers and look for a small brown Colorado Trail Spur sign and a locked gate on the right. Climb over a cow stile and follow the trail markers, which have white peaks on them.)

Dogs can be off leash.

The route up Signal Peak that this trail follows is actually a spur of the Colorado Trail. Although the hike is not necessarily rewarding enough to merit covering the entire 8 miles (unless you're on a bike), it's nice to have an option so close to town where your dog can hike with you leash free. Bring lots of water. The trail you want begins through the fence at the edge of the first parking area mentioned above. Either take the straight shot up to the first radio tower or, for a more gradual ascent, hike left along the dirt road and follow the marker for Parcours. Once on top of the hill, hike along the ridge toward the second radio tower. The trail follows a dirt road through the sagebrush and affords a nice panorama of the Gunnison Valley and the surrounding mountain ranges. Signal Peak is the cone-shaped feature to the northeast. Your dog might also just be interested in exploring the network of dirt roads and singletrack that winds around the radio tower hills. And if he's into disc golf, there's a course along here, too.

Lake City

Alpine Gulch

Distance: About 5 miles round-trip
Elevation gain: About 1,200 feet

Trailhead: From Hwy. 149 in Lake City, turn west onto 2nd St. and then make a left onto Bluff St., which will run into CR 20 (follow the signs for the Alpine Loop Scenic Byway). Drive for 2 miles to a parking pullout on the left.
Dogs can be off leash.

Tansy bags a peak in the San Juans near Lake City.

This hike doesn't have a set destination, but it leads to a beautiful, high valley, with lots of water for your dog to splash in along the way. Follow the series of steps that leads down from the parking pullout and cross Henson Creek on the bridge. At first, the trail parallels Alpine Creek as it slices through a tall, narrow canyon (the sharp-eyed dog might be able to spot a mine shaft in one of the canyon walls). After about .5 mile, the canyon begins to open up and the trail ascends away from the creek, settling onto a bench high above while the creek

disappears into a deep gulch. Water-loving pups needn't worry, though; the creek and the trail soon meet back up, and lots of little cascades translate into refreshing pools for hot-under-the-collar canines. Plus, you and your dog will need to cross the creek via logs half a dozen times. When you arrive at a signed fork, take the West Fork branch to the right (the left fork leads up toward Grassy Mountain and turns into the Williams Creek Trail—if you set up a car shuttle along the road past Lake San Cristobal, you could do a 13.5-mile point-to-point hike). Cross the creek one more time on logs, then tackle a steep but relatively short climb, which follows the West Fork of Alpine Creek below. Eventually, you'll cross a section of open terrain, then descend back to creek level and cross it. From here the trail climbs back up to the grassy slopes above, gradually growing less distinct. Hike upvalley as long as you want, enjoying the views of the unnamed, 13,000-plus-foot peaks that define the valley, before retracing your steps.

CYCLING FOR CANINES

Any mountain-biking dog worth his snuff will want to say he's been to the butte to bike, and several trails fit the bill for canine cycling companionship. The **Woods Walk** (see Tail-Rated Trails) is a nice, gentle ride, as is biking on **Peanut Lake Rd.** The **Lower Loop Trail** (described briefly in the Woods Walk entry) is a popular ride to do with dogs. For something more technical, try **Snodgrass Mountain** as an out-and-back ride of a few miles, driving to the trailhead past Mt. Crested Butte—the loop that bikers usually do involves riding on trafficked roads. Or drive up Brush Creek Rd. south of town and tackle the 5.5-mile **Farris Creek Loop**.

In Gunnison, **Signal Peak** and **Hartman Rocks** (see Tail-Rated Trails) are both suitable for taking your dog along on a ride.

POWDERHOUNDS

Two great places to ski or snowshoe with your dog in Crested Butte are **Slate River and Washington Gulch Rds**. Both are unplowed after a certain point and provide wide-open touring in breathtakingly scenic surroundings. See *Snowshoeing Colorado*, by Claire Walter, for details on these and other options. In the Lake City area, the **East Lakeshore** area, by Lake San Cristobal, includes an unplowed public road. The **Danny Carl** area, between Slumgullion and Spring Creek Passes on Hwy. 149 south, features a meadow as well as forested terrain. Note that dogs are not allowed at any of the yurts along the Hinsdale Haute Route system outside of Lake City.

DOGGIE PADDLING

Crested Butte dogs who are feeling a little hot under the collar like easily accessible Long Lake (a.k.a. Meridian Lake) to cool off—directly off Washington Gulch Rd.

Crested Butte Nordic Center, 620 2nd St., 970-349-1707, www.cbnordic.org. Of the 50 kilometers of trails that the Nordic Center maintains in and around Crested Butte, about 14.5 kilometers are dog friendly. These include the **Town Ranch Loops** (a.k.a. the Big Wag), by the high school, and the adjacent **Riverbend Loop**, which constitute 5.5 kilometers of trails groomed for classic and skate skiing. The 9-kilometer round-trip **Pooch's Paradise Trail**, which starts at the end of Butte Ave. and goes out past Peanut Lake, is the other groomed dog-friendly venue. Dogs can be under voice control on all of them. Pooch's Paradise requires a trail pass ($15), which includes a free dog pass. The Town Ranch and Riverbend trails are free for skiers and visiting dogs; locals who use these trails must purchase a $35 season pass for Fido (though a season pass from the Nordic Center comes with a dog pass at no extra charge).

CREATURE COMFORTS

Unless otherwise stated, dogs should not be left unattended in the room or cabin.

Almont

About 10 miles north of Gunnison on the way to Crested Butte, this small town is home to several cabin resorts. A few of the resorts listed here are closer to Taylor Reservoir, about a half-hour drive northeast of Almont.

$$–$$$ Almont Resort, 10209 Hwy. 135, 970-641-4009, www.almontresort.com. The 90-acre resort at the confluence of the Taylor and East Rivers has 20 units that range from small historic cabins (one was Almont's original post office) to modern houses that can be rented in whole or in sections. However, about half of the cabins don't have kitchen facilities, something to keep in mind if you're planning a cooking vacation. Depending on the size of dog, there's a $10–$15 nightly pet fee, per dog. Dogs can be left unattended inside or secured outside your lodging; the resort advises that you keep your dog leashed when outside because of the proximity to busy Hwy. 135. There's a restaurant on-site, as well as a stable that offers horseback rides and a fly shop that has guided fishing trips.

$$–$$$ Holt's Guest Ranch, 1711 CR 55 (2 miles from Taylor Reservoir), 970-641-2733 (summer only), 970-641-0700 (year-round). The ranch has 24 fully equipped cabins that sleep anywhere from two to ten people, and dogs may stay for a $5 fee per night. "We don't particularly like dogs," admits the owner, "but we've been accepting them for so long that we'll continue to do so." You must keep your dog leashed when he's outside. Open mid-May to mid-September.

$$–$$$ Taylor Park Trading Post, 23044 CR 742, 970-641-2555, www.taylor

parktradingpost.com. Thirty-three cabins, fully furnished, can be shared with your dog, for $5 extra per pet, per night. They range in size from studios to two bedrooms, and some have additional sleeping lofts. A general store, restaurant, and RV sites are also at the trading post, which is .5 mile from Taylor Reservoir. Closed beginning of November to December 24.

$$–$$$$ Three Rivers Resort and Outfitting, 130 CR 742, 970-641-1303, 888-761-3474, www.3riversresort.com. Situated where the Taylor and East Rivers flow into the Gunnison (hence the name), the resort has two vacation homes and 53 fully outfitted cabins, from studios to four bedrooms, some along the Taylor River. Dogs must pay $10 each, per night. (Dogs aren't permitted in the lodge rooms.) You can leave your dog unattended inside; he must be leashed when outside on the resort's property. The resort also offers guided rafting, kayaking, and fly-fishing trips (for humans only).

$$$–$$$$ Harmel's Guest Ranch, 6748 CR 742, 970-641-1740, 800-235-3402, www.harmels.com. This popular guest ranch offers a variety of accommodation options, from studios to three-bedroom cabins (some with kitchens) and lodge rooms, duplexes, and a fourplex. What's most important is that your dog can accompany you in any of them, for a $10 per night fee, per dog (unless he's a Doberman, pit bull, Chow, huskie, Akita, Rottweiler, Canary dog, Staffordshire terrier, or wolf hybrid—none of which are allowed on the ranch). Fido can be left unattended inside, as long as you let the front desk staffers know so they can alert the housekeepers. The ranch is on 150 acres surrounded by the Gunnison National Forest, and your dog can hike on the property with you (keep him leashed) and cool off in the Taylor River. Horseback riding, rafting, fishing, and children's

activities are also available. Three lodging plans are available: accommodations only; room and three meals a day; room, three meals a day, and most ranch activities. There's often a three-night minimum stay. Open mid-May to mid-September.

Crested Butte
$$ Crested Butte International Lodge and Hostel, 615 Teocali Ave., 970-349-0588, 888-389-0588, www.crestedbuttehostel.com. Dogs on a budget should check out this particularly nice hostel, where they can stay in the private rooms (with shared or private bath), the larger family rooms, or the two two-bedroom apartments with living room and kitchen. The downside is that the $30 per dog nightly fee can negate the savings, but the hostel can be flexible on the fee, depending on the length of your stay and the size of dogs. Your dog can stay unattended in the room, preferably in a travel kennel. Unfortunately, he won't be able to hang out with you in the hostel's common areas.

$$–$$$$ The Grand Lodge Crested Butte, 6 Emmons Loop, 970-349-8000, 888-823-4446, www.grandlodgecrestedbutte.com. This large hotel near the ski area base allows dogs in first-floor rooms only, for $30 extra per dog, per night. The suites include kitchenettes. Canine guests get a small package of treats and poop bags at check-in and can request dog beds during their stay. You'll receive a Dog in Room sign to hang on the door so the housekeepers will know of Rover's presence.

$$–$$$$ Purple Mountain Lodge, 714 Gothic Ave., 970-349-5888, 877-349-5888, www.purplemountainlodge.com. In a twist on many other place's policies, only dogs 30 pounds or more can stay at this B&B. "Bigger dogs tend to be quieter dogs," says owner Chris Haver. The pet fee is $10 per night, per dog, with a maximum of two dogs per room.

The house was built as a mining office in 1927 and moved to its current site in town in the 1970s. All five rooms have private baths, and guests have access to a communal refrigerator and microwave. You can leave your dog unattended in the room for a few hours (not for a ski day, say), as long as he's not a big barker and won't jump up on the bed. There's a day spa on-site where you (not your dog) can get a massage or herbal wrap, and a hot tub on the back deck.

$$$ Old Town Inn, 708 6th St., 970-349-6184, 888-349-6184, www.oldtowninn .net. Four dog-friendly rooms are available at this comfortable, well-priced motel on the edge of Crested Butte for $10 extra per night. Upon check-in, Fido will get a small bag of dog treats and a brochure of pet-friendly areas around town compiled by the Paradise Animal Welfare Society. The rates include an extensive continental breakfast set out each morning.

$$$–$$$$ Elizabeth Anne Bed and Breakfast, 703 Maroon Ave., 970-349-0147, www.crested-butte-inn.com. As long as your dog is not an annoying barker, he's very welcome here. The B&B has five rooms, all with private bath, appointed with Victorian-style furnishings. Your first dog stays for free; if you have additional dogs, there can be a charge of $10–$20 extra per night, depending on the size and type of dog. You can leave your dog unattended in the room at the B&B owners' discretion or, if you prefer, Rover could hang out on one of the dog leads in the yard for a couple of hours, perhaps with the company of Baxter, the host dog, who's a black Lab.

$$$–$$$$ Pioneer Guest Cabins, 2094 Cement Creek Rd. (CR 740), 970-349-5517, www.pioneerguestcabins.com. If your dog wants a more woodsy getaway

that's still close to Crested Butte (8 miles), book him a stay in one of these eight utterly charming log cabins, all with kitchens and fireplaces, that are actually within the national forest. Half of the cottages were built in 1939 to accommodate guests at a former nearby ski area that closed in the 1950s; the other half date to the 1960s. There's a $15 nightly dog charge for the first dog, $10 for the second, with a two-dog limit per cabin. In general, Rottweilers, Chows, pit bulls, and Dobermans are discouraged, but the owners admit they can be flexible on this policy. As long as your dog stays off the furniture and doesn't bark excessively, or if he has a travel kennel, you can leave him unattended inside the cabin. Outside, keep him leashed right around the cabins, but once you head away from them, he can be under voice control. Several trails begin nearby, and a forest service trail along Cement Creek borders the property. There's usually a two-night minimum stay, and from July to mid-August a seven-night minimum.

POOPER SCOOPERS

Crested Butte residents know that come spring, flowers aren't the only things that pop up; melting snow often unearths mounds of dog poop that have spent several months conveniently hidden. Local artist (and "Grand Poobah") Kate Seeley organizes the annual Poofest, a community event held in late April or early May, in which dog owners and good citizens pick up as much dog poop as they can find in a morning; the results are weighed and prizes given out for the biggest haul.

$$$–$$$$ San Moritz Condominiums, 18 Hunter Hill Rd., 970-349-5150, 800-443-7459, www.sanmoritz condos.com, www.petfriendlycrestedbutte .com. Dog-friendly condos are a rare find at a ski area. "We love pets," says the manager of these ski-in/ski-out condos, which range from two to four bedrooms. Not all are pet friendly, but for the ones that are, there's a $200 deposit and a $10 nightly fee for one dog, $15 per night for two dogs, with a maximum charge of $75 per stay. Dog sheets are provided to protect the furniture if your dog just can't keep his paws off the bed or couch. You can leave your dog unattended inside (preferably in a travel kennel) as long as he doesn't bark the day away (though the housekeepers will leave clean linens and towels outside your door when Fido guards the condo). There's usually a three-night minimum stay during the summer; three to five nights during the winter.

 $$$$ The Ruby Bed and Breakfast, 624 Gothic Ave., 970-349-1338, 800-390-1338, www.therubyofcrested butte.com. The B&B has six nicely appointed rooms, warmly furnished with a mix of antiques and all with private baths. But what your dog really wants to know is that he'll stay in comfort, supplied with his own bed, food and water dishes, and a bottomless plate of home-made dog treats in the room. But he does need to abide by the house rules, which include no more than two dogs per room, staying off all furniture, and not being unattended in the room (even for breakfast), unless he has a travel crate to stay in (and there's a two-hour limit in that case). Rover will also need to provide proof of current vaccinations before checking in. And if you do have to leave your dog behind, the Ruby's owners, Andrea and Chris, provide dogsitting ($10 an hour per dog), several walk and hike options (prices vary), and even doggie spa services through a local groomer. Two cozy sitting areas with fireplaces, an indoor hot tub, a grassy backyard with a small deck, and loaner cruiser bikes round out the amenities. And if Fido's gotten a bit dirty from

hiking or biking, dog towels and wipes are available, along with an outdoor washing station—and even shampoo—to rinse off if he likes. The host dog is River, a Catahoula mix who loves to play.

 $$$$ Elevation Hotel and Spa, 500 Gothic Rd., 970-251-3000, 800-810-7669, www.elevationhotelandspa .com. This trendy hotel that opened at the base of the ski area in 2008 greets its four-legged guests with a VIP (Very Important Pet) package. The pet fee is $30 per night, per dog, and includes treats, a dog bed, food and water bowls, ID tags with the hotel's address, and an info sheet with dog-friendly hiking (or in winter, snowshoeing) suggestions. Plus, a portion of each pet fee is donated to the local Paradise Animal Welfare Society. If your dog needs a short outing during your stay, the hotel staff is usually available to take him on a quick walk. And when the weather's nice, you and Fido can dine on the deck at 9380 Prime, the hotel restaurant. And, of course, you can indulge in a treatment at the on-site 11,000-square-foot spa. The hotel closes during off season, early April to late May and October to mid-November.

$$$$ The Inn at Crested Butte, 510 Whiterock Ave., 970-349-2111, 877-343-2111, www.theinnatcrestedbutte.net. Dogs are welcome in four rooms at this small, elegant boutique hotel for $15 extra per night, per dog, with a limit of two per room. A small spa is on-site.

Gunnison

$–$$ Alpine Inn and Suites, 1011 Rio Grande Rd., 970-641-2804, 866-299-6648, gunnisonalpineinn.com. This former Ramada Inn has several pet-friendly rooms near the exits, with a $10 one-time fee. You can leave your dog unattended in the room.

$–$$ Gunnison Inn, 412 E. Tomichi, 970-641-0700, 866-641-0700, www.gunnisoninn .com. The inn's motto is that it's "pet and planet friendly" (and note that "pet" comes first). Dogs can stay in one of the 16 first-floor rooms for $10 extra per night, per dog, and they receive welcome kits with treats, a water bowl and dog bed, and a Wipe Your Paws mat to go outside the room. As for the planet part, the motel uses compact fluorescent lights and organic products for cleaning and toiletries. Legion Park is across the street.

$–$$ Gunnison KOA Kampground, 105 CR 50, 970-641-1358, 800-562-1248, www .gunnisonkoa.com. Canines are allowed in the camping cabins and cottages for $5 per night, per dog (you'll have to bring your own bedding and cooking gear for the cabins; the cottages have kitchens, bathrooms, and even fireplaces). The campground has an off-leash dog park, as well as a pond that's divided for paddle boating on one side and trout fishing on the other. Open May 1 to October 15.

$–$$ Island Acres Motel, 38339 W. Hwy. 50, 970-641-1442, www.islandacres resort.com. This 1950s-era motel—renovated but still with a '50s flair, thanks to period pieces in the rooms—allows dogs in all rooms for $5 extra per night, and a dog contained in a travel kennel can be left unattended inside. Sixteen rooms have fully equipped kitchens. The motel is on 3.2 shady acres, so there's ample space to walk Fido. Open May 1 to mid-November.

$–$$ Swiss Inn Motel, 312 E. Tomichi, 970-641-9962, www.swissinn.com. Small dogs (poodle-sized) get the nod here. Light wood–paneled walls and individually decorated bedspreads give the motel a homier feel.

$$ ABC Motel, 212 E. Tomichi, 970-641-2400. The motel has some pet-designated rooms for $10 per night, per dog. Your dog can be unattended only if he's in a travel kennel.

$$ Ferro's Ranch Resort, 3200 Soap Creek Rd., 970-641-4671, www.ferrosbluemesa .com. The ranch is actually located 26 miles west of Gunnison, on the northwest side of Blue Mesa Lake and within spitting distance of the Curecanti National Recreation Area. You and your dog will have your choice of two fully outfitted quaint log cabins, two RVs, one mobile home, or one cabin with everything but running water. Dogs should be leashed on the post's 40 acres when horses are around; Ferro's offers guided fishing trips and horseback rides, and guests can also bring their own horse along. A general store is on-site. The friendly owner put in a plug for his cats, saying that they're entertained by visiting dogs and vice versa. Open May 1 to end of November.

$$ Lake Fork Resort, 940 Cove Rd. (25 miles west of Gunnison), 970-641-3564, 800-368-9421, www.bluemesaresort.com. Just a hop, skip, and a jump from Blue Mesa Lake, this resort has six fully equipped one-bedroom cabins. Dogs are permitted with a $15 one-time fee per dog. You must keep your dog leashed on the surrounding 36 acres. Open mid-April to early October.

$$ Long Holiday Motel, 1198 W. Hwy. 50, 970-641-0536. Dogs are assessed a $5 nightly fee, per dog, to stay in one of the motel's designated pet rooms.

$$ Rodeway Inn, 37760 W. Hwy. 50, 970-641-0500, 877-424-6423 (national number), www.rodewayinn.com. The motel charges $10 a night per dog for its designated pet rooms. Dogs should be 40 pounds or under, and there's a limit of two per room. If you call in advance to reserve a room, you'll be able to get a pet-accommodating nonsmoking room, but if you just show up with your dog, you'll likely get put in a smoking room.

$$ Super 8, 411 E. Tomichi, 970-641-3068, www.super8.com. Nonaggressive dogs (e.g., no pit bulls) can stay in designated rooms for $10 per night, per dog up to 20 pounds and $15 nightly for dogs that weigh more.

$$ Western Motel, 403 E. Tomichi Ave., 970-641-1722, www.westernmotel-co.com. There's a $10 fee per night, per dog. Your dog can be unattended in the room for reasonable periods of time. Legion Park, across the street, provides ample dog-walking opportunities.

$$–$$$ Affordable Inns at Tomichi Village, 41883 Hwy. 50 East, 970-641-1131, 800-641-1131, www.affordableinns.com. The motel has designated pet rooms for $10 extra per night, per dog.

$$–$$$ Days Inn, 701 W. Hwy. 50, 970-641-0608, 888-641-0608, www.daysinn gunnison.com. Dogs are allowed in designated rooms for a $10 one-time fee, per dog. There's a limit of two dogs per room, and you can leave your pooch unattended inside if you leave a cell-phone number at the front desk.

$$–$$$ Lost Canyon Resort, 8264 Hwy. 135 (8 miles north of Gunnison), 970-641-0181, www.coloradodirectory.com/lostcanyonresort. The resort's 17 studio to two-bedroom log cabins are scenically situated on 10 acres along the Gunnison River. About half of the fully equipped cabins also have fireplaces or wood-stoves. Your dog can explore the property off leash as long as you're there to supervise him.

$$–$$$ Quality Inn, 400 E. Tomichi, 970-641-1237, 800-424-6423, www.qualityinn.com. The motel has designated pet rooms, for an extra nightly cost of $15 per dog. Management would prefer that you not leave Fido unattended in the room, but if you have a particularly well-behaved dog and need to leave him behind for a quick dinner, say, you could do so as long as you leave a cell-phone number at the front desk.

$$–$$$ Water Wheel Inn, 37478 W. Hwy. 50, 970-641-1650, 800-642-1650, www.waterwheelinnatgunnison.com. Dogs can stay in five of the rooms at this large motel on the edge of Gunnison's golf course for $5 per night, per dog. You can leave your dog unattended inside at your discretion for short periods of time. Rooms have microwaves and refrigerators, and rates include a breakfast buffet with hot items.

$$–$$$$ Rockey River Resort, 4359 CR 10, 970-641-0174, www.colorado directory.com/rockeyriverresort. For $5 per night, per dog, your pooch(es)—up to two per unit—can join you in one of these 15 cabins, ranging from studios to three bedrooms, on 7 acres along the Gunnison River. The cabins have full kitchens, and all except two have bathrooms; there's a shower house for occupants of those two cabins. Dogs must be leashed when outside. One cabin is available during the winter. Open May 1 to October 31.

$$–$$$$ Wildwood Resort and Cabin Rentals, 1312 W. Tomichi Ave., 970-641-1663, 866-770-1663, www.wildwood motel.net. The dog with a penchant for gangster history might enjoy a stay at this in-town resort on 6 acres, built by the Chicago Mafia in 1929. The smaller cabinettes, recently remodeled, sleep two to four and have full kitchens. Larger cabins, which were built in 2004, are two stories, with two to three bedrooms, two bathrooms, and a kitchen. Dogs are welcome in certain ones for $7 extra per night, per dog, with a limit of two per unit.

$$$$ Rockin 3AR Cabin, 14255 CR 730, 970-641-2394, www.rockin3ar.com. This small, picturesque log cabin in the Ohio Creek Valley, about 17 miles northwest of Gunnison, sleeps four to six people, with one bedroom, a living room, and full kitchen. There's also a hot tub. Your dog can join you, as can your horse. The cabin is adjacent to proprietors Walter and Bunny Kelley's own house on 5 acres, and they can provide petsitting and meals (at additional cost) if you make advance arrangements.

Lake City

$$ Alpine Moose Lodge, 1221 Hwy. 149, 970-944-2415, 800-650-1221, www.alpinemooselodge.com. The motel has a few rooms that accommodate dogs, for $20 nightly per dog for the first one or two nights, and $15 nightly for stays longer than that. There's also a limit of two dogs per room. Two restaurants, one upscale, one more casual, are also at the lodge.

$$ Town Square Cabins, 231 Gunnison Ave., 970-944-2236, 800-787-3160, www.townsquarecabins.tripod.com. These eight fully equipped log cabins (studios and two bedrooms) are definitely on the funky side, with slanting floors and vintage furnishings. "They're old and rustic, but I keep them clean, and the beds are good," says the owner. And they are dog friendly, with a $10 one-time fee per dog. It's okay to leave your dog unattended inside if you're sure he won't chew up anything. When exercising your pooch, note that dogs are not allowed in the town park, across the street. A convenience store, gas station, and laundromat are located on-site.

$$–$$$ Alpine Village, 631 N. Silver, 970-944-2266, www.alpinevillagecolorado.com. These 11 one- and two-bedroom, fully equipped older log cabins are located in town. There's a $20 one-time fee. The owners are considering pulling up the welcome mat for dogs, however, as they've unfortunately experienced damage due to inconsiderate four-legged guests (or, more likely, their owners). Open June 1 to September 30.

$$–$$$ Castle Lakes Cabins and Campground Resort, CR 30 (Cinnamon Pass Rd.), 970-944-2622, www.castlelakes.com. Dogs are welcome in the resort's 13 furnished one- or two-bedroom cabins and authentically retro RV trailers, all with kitchens and baths, as well as at the tent and RV sites. The setting is gorgeous, on 41 acres 3.5 miles past Lake San Cristobal and near 14,000-plus-foot Redcloud and Sunshine Peaks. It's also along the Alpine Loop Scenic Byway, and jeep rentals are available on-site. The two Castle Lakes are on campground property and are popular for fishing. Open May 15 to October 1.

$$–$$$ Lake City Resort, 307 S. Gunnison Ave., 970-944-2866, www.coloradodirectory.com/lakecityresort. The eight cabins range from studios to two bedrooms and come with all the necessities. There's a $10 one-time fee. Although the cabins are in town, there's a grassy area around them where you can exercise your dog on leash. Open May 1 to October 15.

$$–$$$ Matterhorn Mountain Motel and Cabins, 409 N. Bluff, 970-944-2210, www.matterhornmotel.com. Two of the Matterhorn's 12 nicely appointed motel rooms as well as both of the fully outfitted cabins allow dogs under 25 pounds, with prior approval only. The pet fee is $10 extra per night, per dog. The cabins are available May 15 to October 1; the motel is open year-round.

$$–$$$ Wagon Wheel Resort, 249 Hwy. 149, 970-944-2264. The resort, on the south edge of town, has 13 cabins ranging from efficiencies to two bedrooms, all fully equipped. Up to two dogs per cabin are welcome for $8 per pet, per night, and can be left unattended inside for an hour or so tops "as long as they don't raise heck." Though the cabins look well worn on the outside, they're actually quite charming inside, decorated with touches like chenille bedspreads and painted lamps in the style of a country bed-and-breakfast. For dogs, there's ample grass outside for sniffing around; for kids, there's a play area with swings. Open mid-May through mid-November.

$$–$$$ Woodlake Park, 2690 Hwy. 149 (2.5 miles south of Lake City), 970-944-2283 (June-Sept.), 817-536-4079 (Oct.-May), 800-201-2694, www.woodlakeparkcolorado.com. The campground, on the Lake Fork of the Gunnison River, includes two camper cabins (bring your own bedding), three fully equipped cabins, an "apartment," which is part of a larger structure, and a fully equipped trailer. Tent and RV sites are also available. Open May 15 through September 30.

$$$ Lakeview Property Management, 970-944-2401, 800-456-0170, www.lakeview-inc.com. The management company rents three dog-friendly units. Two are cabins at the former Lakeview Resort on Lake San Cristobal, Colorado's second-largest natural lake, just outside Lake City. The third is an efficiency apartment in a duplex cabin along the Lake Fork of the Gunnison River, on the edge of town. For all, there's a $17 fee per night and a one-dog limit. If you leave your dog unattended inside, he must be in a travel kennel. Note that from mid-June to mid-August, there's a six-night minimum. Open Memorial Day to the end of September.

$$$–$$$$ Old Carson Inn Bed and Breakfast, 8401 CR 30 (Cinnamon Pass Rd.), 970-944-2511, 800-294-0608, www.oldcarsoninn.com. The well-behaved dog who wants more upscale accommodations in Lake City may be able to stay at this secluded, seven-room B&B, which on occasion actually allows dogs (though the official policy is no pets, since the owners have had some unfortunate experiences in the past). The inn is in a modern log and frame house, and the room where dogs are most likely to stay has a queen-size bed, antique furnishings, and a private entrance for discreet dog walking. Each of the spacious rooms has a private bath, and the house includes a lovely deck with a hot tub and hanging baskets with flowers spilling out of them. Kia the husky is the inn's four-legged greeter. Open Memorial Day to the end of September.

$$$–$$$$ The Texan, 860 CR 142, 970-944-2246, 877-220-1179, www.texanresort.com. The resort encompasses 38 rustic log cabins, many of them built in the 1940s, on the edge of Lake City. The pet policy is a bit tedious, so you'll probably want to have a really compelling reason to stay here yourself if you want to bring Fido along. Dogs are allowed with advance written notice only; you must send in a photo of your dog, along with proof of rabies vaccination and liability coverage (most likely, through your homeowners insurance). If your dog makes the cut, there's a fee of $10 extra per night, or $50 a week. The cabins range from one bedroom to a nine-bedroom lodge that sleeps up to 16, all with full kitchens and some with fireplaces. The Lake Fork of the Gunnison River runs through the property, and you can bring Fido down to the water on leash. In the middle of summer, there's usually a seven-night minimum stay.

$$$$ Cozy Corner, 9501 N. Hwy. 149 (8.5 miles north of Lake City), 970-944-

7008, www.cozycorner.info. The "corner" is actually a lovely four-bedroom log vacation house, on 17 wooded acres, that sleeps up to eight, as well as your dog(s). You can leave your dog unattended inside at your discretion. "We're dog people ourselves, and we trust that other dog owners won't cause any problems or damage," says the friendly owner. There's a three-night minimum stay.

$$$$ Vickers Ranch, Hwy. 149 (2 miles south of Lake City), 970-944-2249, www .vickersranch.net. Located on 1,800 acres just south of Lake City, the ranch, in operation since 1929, has 19 log cabins, ranging in size from two to four bedrooms, all with kitchens and fireplaces. There's a $15 per night, per pet fee, with a limit of one large or two small dogs per cabin. Your dog will want to do some sniffing around on this vast expanse of land—the Lake Fork of the Gunnison River runs on the property, and there are four ponds—but you'll have to keep him leashed because of the cattle and horses. The ranch has guided horseback trips and rents jeeps. Open May 1 to mid-November.

Ohio City
$$ Sportsmans Resort, 116 CR 771, 970-641-3720, www.pitkincolorado.com. The resort, in a town of about 50 people, has eight fully equipped older cabins that sleep from two to six. You can leave your dog unattended inside at your discretion. Open from Memorial Day to mid-November.

Parlin
$ 7 11 Ranch, 5291 CR 76 (5.3 miles north of Parlin), 970-641-0666. This working cattle ranch on 600 acres will let your dog be a guest as long as he doesn't chase the cattle. There are six fully equipped rustic cabins that share a central bathhouse. (There's also a bunkhouse with 10 beds available for rental, but dogs are allowed only on a case-by-case basis.)

You can leave your dog unattended inside the cabins or, if he prefers, in one of the ranch's outside kennels. When outside on the property, your dog doesn't have to be on a leash as long as you can keep him under your voice control. The ranch offers guided horseback rides, including multiday trips that your dog might be able to accompany you on (check with the ranch for details on the dog regulations for these). Open mid-March to Thanksgiving.

$$ Q T Corner, 1 Earl Ave., 970-641-0485. The Q and T in the name stands for Quartz Creek and Tomichi River, two excellent fishing venues that meet on the property of this small complex just off Hwy. 50. The five fully equipped riverside cabins include four studios with separate kitchen areas, as well as a larger family cabin with two bedrooms and two baths. There's a $10 one-time fee for dogs, and you can leave your dog unattended inside on a case-by-case basis. RV sites are also available. Open Memorial Day to mid-November.

Pitkin
$ Pitkin Hotel, 329 Main St., 970-641-2757, www.pitkincolorado.com. To get away from it all, your dog might enjoy a stay at this historic, funky hotel, which dates back to 1904. Downstairs is a large space that used to be full of used books and secondhand items but is being renovated; upstairs are seven private rooms, all with shared baths, as well as two bunkrooms, which sleep eighteen and six. The teeny town of Pitkin, about 30 miles northeast of Gunnison, has one restaurant that hasn't been in operation recently, so you'll have to fend for yourself, though you're welcome to bring your own food and use the hotel kitchen to whip up a meal. The hotel is "run like a youth hostel," says longtime innkeeper JoAnn Bannister. Rather than leave your

dog unattended in the room, the owner prefers that you leash him up outside the hotel (though there's really no place in Pitkin you'd be going without him). Open beginning of June to end of September.

$$ Quartz Creek Lodge, 100 2nd St., 970-641-6174,www.thequartzcreeklodge.com. Despite the name, the six attached, updated, country-style cabin units that make up the lodge are actually located on Armstrong Creek in Pitkin. They vary in size, from one room to a living area with separate bedrooms; four have full kitchens, and two have minifridges and microwaves. There's a $15 one-time fee per dog, and you can have your dog under voice control on the lodge's property.

$$–$$$ Silver Plume General Store, 204 9th St., 970-641-3866, pitkincolorado .com. The store has two dog-friendly apartments for overnight rentals on its second floor: a studio and a three bedroom, both with kitchens. The store itself is Pitkin's only source for basic groceries, deli sandwiches, ice cream, and gas. Open mid-May to end of November.

Sargents

$–$$$ Tomichi Creek Trading Post, 71420 Hwy. 50, 970-641-0674, www.tomichi creektradingpost.com. This roadside complex includes camper cabins, fully equipped cabins, a bunkhouse, tipis, and RV and tent sites, and dogs can stay in any of them. "As long as they're well behaved, we're dog friendly," notes the owner. The three camper cabins sleep up to four (bring your own bedding) and have microwaves and minifridges, but no running water; there's a central bathhouse. The two creekside larger cabins, with kitchens and baths, each have one bedroom plus a loft and can sleep up to 10. The bunkhouse above the garage is one open room, plus bathroom, that sleeps up to 12 and includes kitchen facilities. You can leave

your dog unattended inside your unit; keep him leashed outside. A general store and restaurant are also on-site.

CAMPGROUNDS

Curecanti National Recreation Area, west of Gunnison along Hwy. 50, has major developed campgrounds at Stevens Creek (53 sites), Elk Creek (160 sites), Lake Fork (90 sites), and Cimarron (21 sites); smaller campgrounds around Blue Mesa Reservoir are at Dry Gulch (9 sites), Red Creek (2 sites), Ponderosa (28 sites), and Gateview (6 sites).

National forest campgrounds: **Cement Creek Campground,** 4 miles up Cement Creek Rd. outside of Crested Butte (13 sites); **Lake Irwin Campground,** at Irwin Lake, west of Crested Butte on Kebler Pass Rd. (32 sites); **Cold Spring, Lodgepole, Lottis Creek, North Bank, One Mile,** and **Rosy Lane Campgrounds** are all along Taylor Canyon Rd. between Almont and Taylor Reservoir; **Lakeview Campground,** overlooking Taylor Reservoir (68 sites); **Williams Creek Campground,** on CR 30 past Lake San Cristobal, outside Lake City (23 sites); **Slumgullion Campground,** off Hwy. 149 south of Lake City (19 sites).

Private campgrounds: **Gunnison KOA; Castle Lakes Campground** and **Woodlake Park** near Lake City; **Tomichi Creek Trading Post** in Sargents (see Creature Comforts).

WORTH A PAWS

Blessing of the Animals. The second Sunday of each September, Crested Butte's historic Union Congregational Church, built in 1882, holds this special gathering for local (and visiting) four-legged parishioners. After a brief service, the animals go up to the altar, and each one gets an individual blessing. "We've had a couple of cats, a turtle, a bird, and a guinea pig, but mostly dogs," says Reverend Kelly Jo Clark. Not only will your dog get blessed, but he'll be visiting one of the oldest churches on Colorado's Western Slope. 403 Maroon Ave., 970-349-6405

Mountain Tails, 510 Elk Ave., Crested Butte, 970-349-5606, www.mountain petstore.com. This pet store deserves special mention. There's an enticing array of items for dogs (and cats, too), including specialty collars and leashes, backpacks, booties, toys galore, and gourmet treats. You'll also find pet-themed items such as picture frames, mugs, cards, and jewelry. It's hard to say who will have more fun shopping—you or Fido.

DOGGIE DAYCARE
Crested Butte
Oh-Be-Dogful Pet Ranch, 336 Buckley Dr., #B, 970-349-5047. $26/day; $17/half-day. Once your dog passes the on-site "interview" (a screening process to see if he plays well with others and is basically nonaggressive), he'll spend the day in both the indoor and outdoor play yards, with small kennel rooms available for feeding and naps. Open 7:30 AM–6 PM, Monday to Friday; 9 AM–5 PM, Saturday, Sunday, and holidays. Earlier drop-offs and later pick-ups can be arranged.

Gunnison
Critter Sitters and Outfitters (part of Gunnison Veterinary Clinic), 98 CR 17, 970-641-0460. $13/day. Open 8:30 AM–5:30 PM, Monday to Friday; 8:30 AM–noon and 5–6 PM, Saturday; 4–6 PM, Sunday.

Tomichi Pet Care Center, 106 S. 11th St., 970-641-2460. $14/day. Open 8 AM–5:30 PM, Monday to Friday; 9 AM–noon, Saturday.

PET PROVISIONS
Crested Butte
Mountain Tails, 510 Elk Ave., 970-349-5606, www.mountainpetstore.com

Gunnison
Critter Sitters and Outfitters, 98 CR 17, 970-641-0460

Mountain Mutts, 811 N. Main St., 970-641-2945

CANINE ER
Crested Butte
Animal Hospital of Crested Butte, 418 Belleview Ave., 970-349-1700, www.animalhospitalofcb.com. Open 8:30 AM–5 PM, Monday to Friday.

Gunnison
Town & Country Animal Hospital (AAHA certified), 1525 Hwy. 135, 970-641-2215. Open 8 AM–5:30 PM, Monday to Friday; 8 AM–noon, Saturday.

RESOURCES
The Alpineer, 419 6th St., in Crested Butte, 970-349-5210, www.alpineer.com, has maps, guidebooks, and friendly, knowledgeable advice about area trails.

Bureau of Land Management, Gunnison Resource Area, and **Gunnison Ranger District,** Gunnison National Forest, 216 N. Colorado, Gunnison, 970-641-0471

Crested Butte/Mt. Crested Butte Chamber of Commerce, 601 Elk Ave., Crested Butte, 970-349-6438, 800-545-4505, www.cbchamber.com

Gunnison Country Chamber of Commerce, 500 E. Tomichi Ave. (Hwy. 50), Gunnison, 970-641-1501, 800-323-2453, www.gunnison-co.com

Lake City Chamber of Commerce, 800 N. Gunnison Ave., Lake City, 970-944-2527, 800-569-1874, www.lakecity.com

Seventeen
Telluride, Ouray, and Silverton

THE BIG SCOOP

All three of these mountain towns are dog-friendly havens, with Telluride earning top honors. "Telluride has more dogs than people," claimed the guy behind the counter at the local pet supply store. While this may or may not be true, any town that sets aside designated Puppy Parking areas in its business district is definitely in step with the canine set. And poop bags are amply provided throughout town.

Telluride's leash laws match its laid-back atmosphere: dogs can be under voice control almost anywhere. The exceptions—where dogs must be leashed—are Colorado Ave. and anyplace within 1 block north and south of it, and Town Park. (Note that during Telluride's many weekend summer festivals, dogs are not allowed at all in the park.) In Mountain Village—the area halfway up the ski mountain that is a town in itself—dogs must be leashed in the village center, i.e., the commercial district and around the gondola; elsewhere they can be under voice control. Note that not only can you not tie up your dog to anything in the village center (while you go into a store or restaurant, say), but dogs cannot be left unattended in vehicles in Mountain Village parking lots. So if you bring your dog to Mountain Village, he's coming with you everywhere. The only place in Telluride that truly bans dogs is the Lawson Hill subdivision (by Society Turn). Leashed dogs can ride the gondola connecting downtown Telluride and Mountain

Village; about every fourth cabin is designated for pets.

Ouray, ringed by mountains on three sides, provides a spectacular setting. Your dog, however, will probably prefer to spend most of his time exploring the nearby trails rather than dodging kids and RVs on the town's busy main street. There is a leash law within city limits.

With only one paved road, Silverton would seem to be the kind of town where dogs roam the streets; in fact, we did see a couple of dogs on the loose during our visit. Nevertheless, there's a leash law within city limits (though not in surrounding San Juan County).

TAIL-RATED TRAILS

The area around Telluride, Ouray, and Silverton is filled with spectacular mountain hikes, many of them steeped in mining history. Some of the most accessible are described here. For more options, check out *Telluride Hiking Guide*, by Susan Kees; *Ouray Hiking Guide*, by Kelvin B. Kent; and, for Silverton, *Hiking Trails of Southwest Colorado*, by Paul Pixler. "Hiking Trails of Ouray County," a brochure and map put out by the nonprofit Ouray Trail Group, is another helpful resource.

Ouray

Gray Copper Gulch
Distance: 4.7 miles round-trip
Elevation gain: 1,140 feet
Trailhead: Head south out of

Ouray on Hwy. 550. From the sign for Box Canyon Falls on the edge of town, drive 7.6 miles to CR 20 on the left (the turnoff for the Ironton Nordic trail system). Turn onto the county road and bear left at the sign for Brown Mountain and Corkscrew Pass, at .2 mile in. Drive across the creek, stay right at the next fork shortly after, and park near the trailhead sign.

Dogs can be off leash.

If the prospect of hiking to a stunningly lovely high-alpine valley with several waterfalls appeals to your dog, then this is his trail. Begin by following a four-wheel-drive road steadily uphill (you'll pass a couple of side roads along the way). After a good snow year, parts of this road may be wet and muddy, which may well thrill Fido. At an intersection with another road at .7 mile in, heed the trail marker—a white diamond on a brown

Clover and Todd Hartley investigate mining ruins along the Gray Copper Gulch Trail south of Ouray.

background—and stay straight; a sign-in register will be just uphill. The road narrows to a singletrack trail and wends its way gradually uphill, then drops to Gray Copper Creek, where there's a makeshift log crossing. Now you'll start the climb into that aforementioned alpine valley. Can you or your dog spot the old mine opening in the cliff behind Gray Copper Falls? The trail ascends steeply through a stand of spruce, then traverses above the cliff with the mineshaft and follows the creek upstream. During the last stage of the hike, you'll notice a few buildings and some discarded mining equipment in the creek, which is now within paw-dipping range. These are the remains of the former Vernon Mine. The trail ends at a cairn with a stick in the middle, on the edge of a huge, remote basin flanked by the ridge of distinctive Red Mountain No. 1. Before retracing your steps back down, let your dog frolic here while you soak in the calming vibes of a serene and beautiful location that seems even more secluded than it already is.

Bear Creek National Recreation Trail

Distance: About 6 miles round-trip to the first creek crossing

Elevation gain: About 1,600 feet

Trailhead: Drive south out of Ouray on Hwy. 550. At about 2 miles from the signed turnoff for Box Canyon Falls, you'll pass through a tunnel; a parking area is immediately after it on the left. The trailhead is across the road, on the south side of the tunnel (which you'll actually hike on top of).

Dogs can be off leash.

The most taxing part of this trail is the beginning section, which switchbacks dramatically up the side of the canyon. You'll encounter loose slate and quartzite along the first half of the trail; Clover didn't have a problem with it, and neither did Bruno, a 10-year-old shepherd mix we met on the trail (who had a bandaged paw, no less). But if your dog's a tender-foot, keep an eye on him. At the top of the switchbacks, you'll be rewarded with a picture-perfect view of Red Mountain as well as a peek down the precipitous drop into Bear Creek Gorge. The narrow trail, built by miners in the late 1800s, has been carved out of the canyon's sides—if your dog has a fear of exposure you might want to keep him leashed. At 2.5 miles, pass the ramshackle remains of the Grizzly Bear Mine. About .5 mile beyond, the trail descends to the creek, traveling through grasses and fir, with some good resting spots for you and your dog. Eventually the trail crosses a side creek. This was our turnaround spot, but you can continue another mile or so farther to the ruins of the Yellow Jacket Mine, and even beyond.

Weehawken Trail

Distance: 6.2 miles round-trip
Elevation gain: 1,500 feet
Trailhead: Take Hwy. 550 south from Ouray. At the first switch-back, turn right at the national forest access sign for Camp Bird Mine and Box Canyon Falls, then stay left at the fork. Follow the Camp Bird road for 2.6 miles to a small parking area at the trailhead, on the right.

Dogs can be off leash.

This would be a particularly nice hike in the fall, when the aspens change. Begin by switchbacking up a wooded hillside on a narrow trail. Ascend first through an open meadow, then through aspens, all to the symphonic rumbling of Canyon Creek. Past the junction where a trail to the Alpine Mine heads off to the right (another good hike, which ends at a breathtaking over-look of Ouray), the trail snakes around a hillside, heading up the Weehawken Val-ley. Imposing volcanic cliffs rise across the

ravine. After crossing an avalanche basin, hike along a narrow shelf in the forest—with some breathtaking drop-offs, so take care to be sure-footed and sure-pawed—to the trail's eventual end at Weehawken Creek, where your dog can take a dip before the return hike out.

Ridgway

Blaine Basin

Distance: 6.4 miles round-trip
Elevation gain: 1,400 feet
Trailhead: From the intersec-tion of Hwy. 550 and Hwy. 62, head west on 62 for 4.8 miles. Then turn left onto East Dallas Creek Rd. (CR 7, which turns into FR 851). At .3 mile, stay left and at 2 miles from the start, stay right. Follow the right-hand branch at 8.2 miles, cross-ing East Dallas Creek. At 8.8 miles you'll come to a parking area and a locked gate. Don't worry if you see lots of cars—most of their occupants are going to Blue Lakes, a popular destination that starts from the same trailhead.

Dogs can be off leash.

Shade, water, and marvelous views are your frequent companions on this stellar hike. At the fork just after the trailhead, go left (the right leads to Blue Lakes) and cross East Dallas Creek on a bridge. Then hike up the doubletrack for about 1 mile. Just before the doubletrack hits Wilson Creek, the route you want to follow veers off to the right and uphill (look for a cairn and a white diamond on a tree). Cross the creek a little farther upstream via a series of logs and at the junction shortly after, take the right switchback, which should be marked, to stay on the Blaine Basin Trail. After running through a clearing, the trail again reaches the creek, and you'll see it continue on the other side; resist the temptation to try to cross here and instead follow a path through the trees for about 80 yards upstream to a better crossing, with lower-lying logs. On our visit, fluorescent pink tape marked some trees on the opposite side of the creek at this point. Once you cross the creek yet again not too much later, listen for the roar of a magnificent waterfall, which you'll soon be able to view through the trees. At a fork bear left, then stay right at the next fork (the left branch heads to Wilson Creek). Here's where the serious uphill begins. If you need motivation to keep going, stay focused on the glimpses you'll catch through openings in the forest of the north face of 14,150-foot Mount Sneffels and two subpeaks. Once the climb tops out, your reward will be Blaine Basin, an open, hanging valley of breathtaking beauty, bursting with wildflowers midsummer and fronting the toothy peaks of Cirque Mountain, Kismet, Sneffels, and Blaine Peak. Your dog's reward will be even more water to splash around in, as well as lots of meadowland to sniff out. From here, some hearty (and prepared) hikers who got an early start will continue on to a summit attempt of Sneffels, but this is the turnaround point for most.

Ridgway State Park

Access: The park is just off Hwy. 550 a couple miles north of Ridgway and is divided into three distinct sites: Pa-Co-Chu-Puk (try saying that one 10 times fast!), Dutch Charlie, and Dallas Creek.

Dogs must be leashed.

Fourteen miles of trail, both paved and gravel, meander through the park. For a complete listing, pick up the trails guide at the visitor center. A few your dog may particularly enjoy: **The Dallas Creek Trail**, a 1-mile loop, begins at the Confluence Nature Area in the Dallas Creek site, following the creek and then ascending a small hill to provide a nice vista of the nearby San Juan Mountains. The **Piñon Park Trail**, in the Dutch Charlie site, runs

a little more than .5 mile from the visitor center to the marina. And the 3.5-mile (one way) **Enchanted Mesa Trail** skirts the edge of the mesa from Dutch Charlie to Pa-Co-Chu-Puk, with views of both the reservoir and the mountains. Be sure to bring water on this hike, as the terrain is dry. And, as in all Colorado state parks, dogs are not allowed on the swim beach at Ridgway. 970-626-5822, www.parks .state.co.us/parks/ridgway

Telluride

Jud Wiebe Trail
Distance: 2.7-mile loop
Elevation gain: 1,200 feet
Trailhead: From Colorado Ave. in town, walk 3 blocks north on Aspen St. to where the road deadends. The trailhead is here. (You can also access the Sneffels Highline Trail from here, a 13-mile loop; because the trail enters a designated wilderness area, however, remind your dog to leash up.)
Dogs can be off leash.

Immediately past the trailhead, go left on the bridge over Cornet Creek. Then stay straight as the trail contours across a hillside. You'll ascend steadily, while gaining a bird's-eye view of Telluride along with a face-to-face view of the ski area. Your hiking companion in the fur coat will appreciate reaching the shady respite of aspens and, eventually, fir. The trail next opens up into a hillside meadow, from which you'll be looking directly at Bridal Veil and Ingram Falls. Descend through a lovely aspen stand before crossing another creek and hiking through more fir. When you reach an old road, go right. The trail descends back into town via a series of switchbacks; hiking boots with good tread will help you keep your footing on the loose rocks. The trail ends at a gate opening onto Tomboy Rd. Turn right to head back to town. After passing a couple of houses balanced on the hillside, you'll wind up at the top of Oak St.

Bear Creek Trail

Distance: About 5 miles round-trip

Elevation gain: About 1,000 feet

Trailhead: From Colorado Ave., head south on Pine St. for 3 blocks to the end of the road and the trailhead.

Dogs can be off leash.

This has to be the most popular trail in Telluride, judging from the many people we encountered, and it's no surprise why: it's a relatively short hike, starting from town, with a worthwhile payoff—the thundering Bear Creek Falls at trail's end. The trail follows an old mining road above Bear Creek up a fairly gradual ascent, passing in and out of forest and meadows. The road ends at a very large rock. From there, it's a short hike up one of the footpaths to the bottom of the falls, where your dog can enjoy the cool spray.

River Trail

Distance: Approximately 4 miles from Town Park to Hwy. 145

Access: You can access it from the southwest corner of the parking lot in the park or by heading south on any of the side streets in town.

Dogs can be off leash.

This extremely pleasant gravel trail runs along the banks of the San Miguel River, crisscrossing it several times. Your dog will be able to enjoy water-splashing as well as social sniffing opportunities. The trail remains pancake flat for its whole length. Maintenance ends past the Telluride town limits, so the condition of the trail slowly deteriorates as you head farther west.

CYCLING FOR CANINES

You can find several good biking options close to Telluride, including the **Bear Creek** and **River Trails** (see Tail-Rated Trails). Regarding Bear Creek, unless your dog enjoys dodging lots of unaware hikers, early morning or early evening would be the best times to ride. The popular **Mill Creek Trail**, a 7-mile loop that begins past the gas station west of town and winds up at the beginning of the Jud Wiebe Trail, is another recommended possibility; you can ride out of town on the paved bike path that begins near the high school so you and your dog won't have to bike on the road. The **Galloping Goose Trail** (part of it is known as the **Ilium Trail**) follows an old railroad bed for 18 miles, from Society Dr. in Telluride to Lizard Head Pass. Given the fairly gentle grade, riding a portion of the trail would make a good canine cycling outing. Because parking is limited at the Society Dr. trailhead, pick up the trail off of South Fork Rd. (also known as Ilium Valley Rd.). Head west from Telluride on Hwy. 145; after about 6 miles, look for a sign indicating National Forest Access/South Fork Rd. After you've turned left, it's about 3.5 miles to the trailhead, on the left; parking is across the street.

Ouray and Silverton are not as conducive to canine mountain biking, as most of the areas where you can reasonably ride are on county or four-wheel-drive roads that have their share of vehicle traffic.

POWDERHOUNDS

Telluride has several canine-friendly options for skiing and snowshoeing; be extra vigilant, however, in picking up after your canine friend, as poop on trails has been a bone of contention. Dogs are allowed off leash on the 4.9-kilometer groomed **Trout Lake Trail**, which descends an old railroad grade from the top of Lizard Head Pass, 18 miles south of town, to the lake. They are also permitted off leash on the 5 kilometers of groomed trails at **Priest Lakes**, 7.6 miles south of Telluride off Hwy. 145; on the .5-kilometer, packed-snow **Dog Run Loop** in Town Park (on leash); and on a couple of the trails adjacent to the groomed **Valley Floor** network west of Telluride—the 2.5-kilometer **River Trail**, which is on the other side of the river from the groomed trails, and the 3-kilometer **Boomerang Trail**, which leads up to Mountain Village. The Valley Floor system is relatively new, and the placement of trails and dog regulations are still evolving, so call the Telluride Nordic Center at 970-728-1144 or go to www.telluridenordic.com for the latest info. **Mountain Village** maintains 15.5 kilometers of groomed trails for skiing and snowshoeing that meander around the **Telluride Golf Course** and over to the Peaks Hotel, and dogs are welcome on all of them and can be under voice control. You can also ski or snowshoe with your dog along the **River Trail** in Telluride (see Tail-Rated Trails).

Dogs are not allowed on the groomed Nordic Center trails in Telluride's Town Park (other than the dog loop, which isn't actually part of the center) or on the TopAten Nordic trails at the Telluride ski area.

The Ouray Nordic Council oversees a trail system south of town; dogs are now permitted on all trails, both groomed and ungroomed, and they can accompany you off leash. Just make sure to pick up after your dog. Access the system from the **Ironton** trailhead, 8 miles south of Ouray on Hwy. 550 on the left side, or the **Silver Belle** trailhead, 10 miles south of town, also on the left. See *Snowshoeing Colorado*, by Claire Walter, for details on these and other options. Dogs aren't allowed on the groomed Nordic trails at Top of the Pines, a former Girl Scout camp near Ridgway that's now managed by Ouray County.

CREATURE COMFORTS

Unless otherwise stated, dogs should not be left unattended in the room or cabin.

Naturita

$–$$ Naturita Lodge, 431 Hwy. 97, 970-865-2700. Under the same ownership as the Ray Motel, the lodge has the same pet policy, too. Note that check-in is at the Ray.

$–$$ Ray Motel, 123 Main St., 970-865-2700. Designated pet rooms are available by advance reservation only.

Ouray

$$ Ouray KOA, 225 CR 23, 970-325-4736, www.koa.com. Dogs are allowed in the camper cabins (you'll have to supply your own bedding and cooking gear) for $5 extra per night, with a maximum of two dogs per cabin. This KOA does not allow pit bulls, Dobermans, or Rottweilers. Open May 1 through September 30.

$$ Timber Ridge Motel, 1550 N. Main St., 970-325-4856, 888-325-4856, www.timberridgelodgeouray.net. The motel, which bills itself as a "base camp for adventure," has designated about 10 rooms for four-legged guests, for an extra fee of $10 per night, per dog. Each room has a microwave and minifridge. Make sure you don't leave your dog unattended inside your room, as you'll be charged $125 if you violate that rule. The motel backs up to the Uncompahgre River Trail for easy dog-walk access.

$$–$$$ Ouray Victorian Inn, 50 3rd Ave., 970-325-7222, 800-846-8729, www.ouraylodging.com. This nicely appointed motel has eight pet rooms, with a $10 nightly fee for dogs. Your dog can be unattended inside the room only if he's in a travel kennel; the motel also offers dog-walking services for a small extra fee (around $5). Note that dogs are not allowed in the Victorian Inn Townhomes.

$$–$$$ River's Edge Motel, 110 7th Ave., 970-325-4621, 866-739-4917, www.rivers edgeouray.com. This simply furnished but homey motel is pleasantly situated on a side street and along the Uncompahgre River. There's a $10 fee per night to stay with your dog. Rooms with kitchens are available.

$$–$$$ Riverside Inn and Cabins, 1805 N. Main St., 970-325-4061, 800-432-4170, www.ourayriverside inn.com. This motel is located aside the Uncompahgre River, as the name implies, though it also fronts busy Hwy. 550. Dogs are welcome in ground-floor units, which include standard rooms as well as three suites with kitchenettes or kitchens, and 11 cabins alongside the river. Hand-carved log furniture throughout is a nice switch from standard motel furnishings. For the 10 camper cabins, you supply your own bedding and use a central bath-house; the cabins have heat and electricity. There's also the fully outfitted Imogene cabin, with kitchen and bath, which sleeps up to four. You and your dog can pick up the 2-mile, gravel Uncompahgre River Trail right behind the inn.

$$–$$$$ Best Western Twin Peaks Lodge and Hot Springs, 125 3rd Ave., 970-325-4427, 800-207-2700, www.bestwestern colorado.com. Dogs are permitted in smoking rooms only, for $10 extra per night. The hotel has its own mineral springs soaking and whirlpool tubs; as you can't leave your dog unattended in the room, you'll have to find somewhere else for him to hang out if you partake of these amenities.

$$–$$$$ Comfort Inn Ouray, 191 5th Ave., 970-325-7203, 800-438-5713, www.ouray comfortinn.com. The motel has designated pet-friendly rooms for $20 extra per night, usually per dog. There's a maximum of two dogs per room. Rover can be left unattended inside as long as you provide a contact number at the front desk.

Placerville

$$$–$$$$ Blue Jay Lodge, 22332 Hwy. 145, 970-728-0830, 888-605-2578, www .thebluejaylodge.com. Located 12 miles from Telluride, this small, elegant lodge welcomes dogs in four of its fourteen rooms for a $30 one-time fee for one dog and a $35 fee for two. Unless you have particularly small dogs, there's a limit of two dogs per room. The pet-friendly rooms are all on the first floor with access to private patios. The on-site café serves breakfast, lunch, and dinner.

Ridgway

$$ The Adobe Inn, 221 Liddell St., 970-626-5939. Salsa-loving dogs on a budget might want to check out this eclectic Mexican restaurant that rents out three simple but comfortable hostel-style rooms with shared bath (which you'll also share with the restaurant customers during dinner, FYI). Although in general dogs are not to be left unattended in the room, the owner may make an exception if you have a particularly well-mannered, quiet dog.

$$ Ridgway State Park Yurts, 28555 Hwy. 550, 303-470-1144 (in Denver only), 800-678-2267, www.parks.state.co.us/parks/ridgway. For $10 per night extra, dogs are allowed in one of the three yurts in the park's Dutch Charlie area. Each yurt sleeps up to six people and has electricity and a gas stove for heat. You'll need to supply your own bedding and cooking supplies (and maybe a camp stove; there's a grill outside the yurt and a microwave and small refrigerator inside).

$$–$$$ Ridgway Ouray Lodge and Suites, 373 Palomino Tr. (intersection of Hwys. 550 & 62), 970-626-5444, 800-368-5444, www.ridgewaylodgeandsuites.com. Formerly a Super 8, the hotel allows dogs in designated rooms for a $15 nightly fee per dog.

$$$–$$$$ Chipeta Sun Lodge and Spa, 304 S. Lena, 970-626-3737, 800-633-5868, www.chipeta.com. The dog looking for a holistic getaway might enjoy a stay at the adobe Sun Lodge, which offers a solar-heated pool and hot tub, herbal soaking tubs, yoga classes, spa treatments, and a southwestern-style restaurant. Dogs are allowed in some of the condos (thought not the lodge rooms or kiva suites) for a $35 one-time fee per pet. The studio to two-bedroom condos have full kitchens, gas fireplaces, and two-person jetted tubs in the bathroom. Dog beds are provided for canine visitors.

Silverton

$$ Canyon View Motel, 661 Greene St., 970-387-5400, www.canyonviewmotel.com. Biscuits in the room at this dog-loving motel await your dog when you check in. Though you can't leave your dog unattended in the room for a long period of time, you'll likely be able to leave him while you go out to dinner, say, with prior approval from the staff.

$$–$$$ Inn of the Rockies/Alma House Bed and Breakfast, 220 E. 10th St., 970-387-5336, 800-267-5336, www.innoftherockies.com. It's a lucky dog who gets to stay in the beautifully decorated rooms at this luxurious, but not stuffy, Victorian-themed B&B—not only because it's an exceedingly genteel place in which to stay, but also because dogs are accepted on a case-by-case basis. You'll be asked to sign a damage waiver for your dog and pay a $10 one-time fee. The house dates from 1898 and now has nine guest rooms, almost all with private bath, including three suites. Though you can't leave your dog unattended in the room for any length of time, he can stay in there while you eat the organic foods breakfast that's served or check out the inn's hot tub. The owner is a former guide at Silverton Mountain, so he can give you the inside scoop on this backcountry-style ski area.

$$–$$$ Red Mountain Motel and Campground, 664 Greene St., 970-387-5512, 888-970-5512, www.redmtmotelrvpk .com. In addition to motel rooms (which have kitchenettes), four two-room cabins are available, each with kitchen and bath. There's no standard pet fee, but you'll be charged $20 if your dog makes a mess of your room. He can be left inside unattended if he's in a travel kennel. Although the complex is open year-round (and includes Silverton/Molas Pass Snowmobile Tours), only the cabins are open in winter.

$$–$$$ Villa Dallavalle Inn, 1257 Blair St., 970-387-5555, 866-387-5965, www.villa dallavalle.com. This comfortable B&B allows dogs in all of its seven rooms, furnished with antiques and family memorabilia, for a $15 one-time fee. All have private baths. The inn's building, a one-time grocery store, was constructed in 1901.

$$$ Elevated Sleep and Supper, 1337 Blair St., 970-903-4132, www.sleepandsupper .com. This renovated 1903 Victorian cottage provides you and your dog with a civilized way in which to get a glimpse of Silverton's past. The house sleeps up to four and is colorfully decorated, with rotating art by various local artists. You can leave your dog unattended inside; there's also a yard (with grill and fire pit), though it's not fully fenced. Instead of breakfast, you can order a four-course dinner to be served at the house ($40–$80 per person), as the owner is also a caterer; if you prefer to do your own cooking, use the full kitchen, which can be prestocked with food if you want.

$$$ Smedley's Suites, 1314 Greene St., 970-387-5713, www.smedleysuites.com. This small guesthouse has three suites—all with private bath, kitchen, bedroom, and living room—and accepts dogs on a case-by-case basis. Two of the suites have sun porches, and each is furnished in a mix of antique and more contemporary furnishings. Smedley's is under the same ownership as the Pickle Barrel restaurant next door. Your dog might be interested to know it's also located above an ice-cream parlor and coffee shop.

$$$ St. Paul Ski Lodge and Backcountry Hut, 970-799-0785, www.skistpaul.com. Though dogs are not allowed during the winter, when backcountry skiers frequent this rustic lodge and adjacent hut, they can visit during the summer, when the hut is rented out by the week. The hut is 1 mile east of Red Mountain Pass and is reachable by four-wheel-drive vehicles or by foot (a .5-mile hike). It sleeps up to six and has a propane cookstove and oven, running water, and a woodstove for heat.

$$$–$$$$ Wyman Hotel and Inn, 1371 Greene St., 970-387-5372, 800-609-7845, www.thewymanhotelandinn.com. The Wyman building dates from 1902—it's now on the National Register of Historic Places—and has housed everything from offices to a dry goods store to a Studebaker dealer. Today it's a plush, antique-filled hotel that allows up to two 40-pound dogs in three second-story rooms for a $25 one-time fee per dog. High tea is served daily at 4 PM, and refined canines are not left out—biscuits are on hand "for our four-legged friends," says the manager. Closed April and November.

Telluride

$$–$$$$ Telluride Mountainside Inn, 333 S. Davis St., 970-728-1950, 888-728-1950, www.telluridemtnlodging.com. Located at the bottom of the ski area near Lift 7, the hotel has about 15 pet-friendly rooms, including two suites, for $30 extra per night. You can leave your dog unattended in the room, but the housekeepers won't enter during that time. Reservations for the hotel are handled by Telluride Alpine Lodging.

$$$–$$$$ Montana Placer Inn, 210 S. Oak St., 970-728-3388, 800-376-9769, www.telluridehotels.com. At this small inn housed in a historic Victorian, two of the four rooms are dog friendly, for $30 extra per night. All rooms, furnished in an updated Victorian style, have gas fireplaces, private balconies, and wet bars with a small refrigerator. Leaving Fido unattended inside is okay, but you won't receive housekeeping service while he's there. Reservations are handled by Telluride Alpine Lodging.

$$$–$$$$ Mountain Lodge at Telluride, 457 Mountain Village Blvd., Mountain Village, 970-369-5000, 866-595-8084, www.mountainlodgetelluride.com. Most of the accommodations at the lodge are dog friendly; these include standard rooms, studios, one- to two-bedroom condos, and seven large cabins with three to six bedrooms. There's a $50 nightly pet fee that maxes out at $150 per stay. The decor throughout is a comfortably clubby traditional mountain style, with lots of wood accents, leather chairs, and gas fireplaces.

$$$–$$$$ Wildwood Canyon Inn, 627 W. Colorado Ave., 970-369-1275, 877-332-1275, www.wildwoodcanyoninn.com. One room at this nicely appointed bed-and-breakfast is pet friendly, and it has a private entrance on the ground floor. But note that dogs can't set paw anywhere else in the inn. Either one large dog or two medium-sized pups can stay in the room, and they can be unattended if necessary, perhaps while you check out the third-floor outside hot tub.

$$$$ Camel's Garden, 250 W. San Juan Ave., 970-728-9300, 888-772-2635, www.camelsgarden.com. For a $40 one-time fee, up to two dogs can join you for a stay in one of 10 ground-floor rooms at this luxury ski-in/ski-out hotel (pets are not permitted in the resort's condos). Each of the generously sized rooms has a fireplace. The Atmosphere Spa and X Café, popular for après ski, are at the hotel.

$$$$ Fairmont Heritage Place, Franz Klammer Lodge, 567 Mountain Village Blvd., Mountain Village, 970-728-3318, 888-728-3318, www.fairmont.com/klammerlodge. Named after the Austrian skier who won the Olympic downhill in 1976, this ultra-high-end lodge allows dogs in certain units for $20 per night, with a maximum of two dogs each. The rooms are large two- and three-bedroom residences that are sold as fractional shares but also rented out individually. Each one includes a full kitchen with upscale appliances, gas fireplace, two master bedrooms, and balcony with a gas grill. You can leave your pooch behind to bask in luxury while you're out for a few hours.

 $$$$ Hotel Columbia, 300 W. San Juan Ave., 970-728-0660, 800-201-9505, www.columbiatelluride.com. Dogs love the Hotel Columbia, where they are truly welcomed. And you'll love the individually decorated, luxuriously appointed rooms and suites (if your dog really likes to stay in high style, book him in the penthouse suite). Rooms and suites on the second and fourth floors are dog friendly, and there's a $20 nightly fee. Upon check-in, your pooch will receive a small bag of biscuits, which he can replenish from the treat jar at the front desk, and you'll get poop bags as a gentle reminder to clean up

after him on your walks through town. Food and water bowls and dog beds are also available on request. You can leave your dog unattended in the room, but housekeeping won't come in during that time. The hotel staff can also recommend dog-walking and sitting services. The hotel's Cosmopolitan Restaurant is a long-time Telluride standout.

 $$$$ Hotel Telluride, 199 N. Cornet St., 970-369-1188, 866-468-3501, www.thehoteltelluride.com. This luxurious condo hotel, where rooms are furnished in an upscale mountain theme, welcomes dogs with a packet of treats and dog-pertinent info on Telluride. All rooms are pet friendly for a $100 one-time fee. There's a limit of two dogs per room, and together they can't weigh more than 140 pounds. Rover can stay unattended in the room as long as you leave a cell-phone number at the front desk. Rates include a full breakfast; the hotel includes a fitness center, small spa, and a bistro that serves light dinners.

$$$$ Lumiere, 118 Lost Creek Ln., Mountain Village, 970-369-0400, 866-530-9466, www.lumieretelluride.com. One of Telluride's newest, and chicest, hotels, the Lumiere allows dogs in all of its suites and residences, which range from studios to four bedrooms, for a $125 one-time fee. That includes the Tower, an over-the-top, 7,500-square-foot house adjacent to the hotel, with a home theater and private elevator. No matter what type of lodging you choose, a personal-stay attendant will be at your beck and call during your visit. And if you and your dog want a ride into Telluride from the hotel's Mountain Village location, just summon the Lumiere's hybrid SUV shuttle. If you leave your dog unattended in the room, he should preferably be in a travel crate, but if he's particularly well behaved, he can likely be free to roam—just let the front desk know your plans.

$$$$ The Peaks Resort and Golden Door Spa, 136 Country Club Dr., Mountain Village, 970-728-6800, 866-282-4557, www.thepeaksresort.com. For a $150 one-time fee (and an extra $100 for an additional dog), well-heeled canines can join their owners at this luxe hotel and spa, one of the original lodging properties in Mountain Village. Though you can't leave your dog unattended in the room, the concierge can book a local dogsitter, perhaps while you indulge in one of the Golden Door's signature spa treatments. Alas, the much-touted dog spa, which debuted in 2004, has closed—Clover very much enjoyed the massage she received there when it was open (and my husband was very jealous!).

POOCH PARKING

If you're running into a store (for 30 minutes or less) in downtown Telluride, put your pooch in designated Puppy Parking. The biggest spot is on the 100 block of S. Fir, conveniently across from Baked in Telluride, and there's another one on N. Pine. You're encouraged—not required—to tie up your dog here. Whatever you do, don't tie your dog to the bumper of your car—there's a town ordinance against doing so.

CAMPGROUNDS

Ridgway State Park, off Hwy. 550, just north of Ridgway. The park has 283 sites total among its three recreation sites.

Town Park, Telluride. Located at the east end of town (33 sites).

National forest campgrounds: **Matterhorn Campground,** off Hwy. 145, west of Telluride (28 sites); **Amphitheatre Campground,** 1 mile south of Ouray off Hwy. 550 (35 sites); **South Mineral Camp-**

Telluride thoughtfully provides parking spots for its four-legged residents and visitors.

ground, 5 miles west on FR 585 (turn off from Hwy. 550 about 2 miles north of Silverton; 26 sites).

Private campgrounds: **Ouray KOA** in Ouray and **Red Mountain Motel and Campground** in Silverton (see Creature Comforts).

WORTH A PAWS

Jeep touring. The San Juan Mountains are probably the most popular area in Colorado for four-wheeling, and several companies will allow your dog either in a rental jeep or on a guided tour. Ouray Mountain Adventures (125 3rd Ave., Ouray, 970-325-427), Ouray Riverside Inn Jeep Rentals (1804 N. Main St., Ouray, 970-325-4061), and Red Mountain Jeep Rentals (694 Greene St., Silverton, 970-387-5512) permit dogs in their rentals as long as you clean the interior of dog hair and muddy pawprints before returning the vehicle. Switzerland of America Jeep Tours (226 7th Ave., Ouray, 970-325-4484) will let your dog come along if you arrange for a private tour; you may be able to bring Fido on one of the group tours, depending on how big he is and how amenable your coriders are to sharing space with a dog. The tours are available from mid-May to mid-October.

Bridal Veil Falls, Telluride. Bring your dog (he can be off leash) to see Colorado's tallest free-falling waterfall (325 feet), at the east end of Telluride's box canyon. Drive east on Colorado Ave. past the Liberty Bell Mill to the beginning of a jeep road. Park either in the lot at the bottom or in one of the switchback turnouts off the jeep road. From here, it's about a 1-mile hike to the bottom of the falls and about another mile to the top, by the Bridal Veil Hydroelectric Plant (now restored as a private residence as well as a functional plant).

Box Canyon Falls and Park, Ouray. Your dog will have to forgo viewing this popular Ouray attraction. (But did you really want to pay to see a waterfall, anyway?) Instead, take him to see Lower Cascade Falls, a short walk (leash required) from the east end of 8th St.

Telluride Bluegrass Festival (the third weekend in June). Do yourself and your dog a favor and leave him behind. Dogs are not allowed in Town Park (where the performances take place) during the fest; in fact, dogs are not allowed in Town Park during Telluride's summer festivals, which take place almost every weekend. Most of the campgrounds erected for the long weekend don't allow dogs either. To top it off, the only way you can get into town by vehicle during the festival is via special shuttle buses, which—you guessed it—don't take dogs. Put a tape of Charles Sawtelle and the Whippets on the kennel sound system and let Fido do his paw-tapping at home.

DOGGIE DAYCARE

Norwood

San Miguel Veterinary Clinic, 40775 Hwy. 145, 970-327-4279. Starting at $15/day. A limited number of spaces are available. Open 8 AM–5:30 PM, Monday to Friday; 8 AM–noon, Saturday

Ridgway

Little Paws Dog Care, 133 CR 4 (10 minutes north of Ridgway), 970-626-5653, www.littlepawsdogcare.com. $15/day. This home-based, kennel-free facility accepts dogs 30 pounds and under, and only up to six dogs at a time. Dogs can play in a fenced yard and get daily walks. Pick-ups and drop-offs can be arranged for an extra fee. Open 7 AM–7 PM daily.

PET PROVISIONS

Telluride

Telluride Pet Supply, 138 E. Colorado Ave., 970-728-0484

CANINE ER

Norwood

San Miguel Veterinary Clinic, 40775 Hwy. 145, 970-327-4279. Open 8 AM–5:30 PM, Monday to Friday; 8–noon, Saturday.

Ridgway

Ridgway Animal Hospital, 635 N. Cora, 970-626-5001. Open 8 AM–4 PM, Monday, Tuesday, Thursday; 8 AM–noon, Wednesday; 8 AM–3 PM, Friday.

Telluride

Telluride Veterinary Clinic, 547 1/2 W. Pacific Ave., 970-728-4461. Open 8:30 AM–5:30 PM, Monday through Friday; until 7 PM on Thursday.

RESOURCES

Between the Cover Books, 224 W. Colorado Ave., Telluride, 970-369-0967, and **Ouray Mountain Sports,** 732 Main, Ouray, 970-325-4284, carry good selections of guidebooks and maps.

Norwood Ranger District, Uncompahgre National Forest, 1150 Forest, Norwood, 970-327-4261

Ouray Chamber Resort Association, 1230 Main (in front of the Hot Springs pool), 970-325-4746, 800-228-1876, www .ouraycolorado.com

Ouray Ranger District, Uncompahgre National Forest, 2505 S. Townsend, Montrose, 970-240-5300

Ridgway Area Chamber of Commerce, 150 Racecourse Rd., 970-626-5181, 800-220-4959, www.ridgwaycolorado.com

Silverton Visitor Center, 414 Greene St., 970-387-5654, 800-752-4494, www .silvertoncolorado.com

Telluride Visitor Services, 630 W. Colorado Ave., 970-728-6475, 888-605-2578, www.visittelluride.com

Eighteen
Mesa Verde and Vicinity

THE BIG SCOOP

Your four-legged companion won't be able to join you in viewing this area's main attraction—Mesa Verde National Park—but you'll still be able to explore much of the fascinating history and natural beauty of the area surrounding the "Green Table." And if your dog really wants to have something to tell his stay-at-home friends about, drive him 38 miles southwest from Cortez to the Four Corners National Monument (admission is $3), where he can put one paw in each state.

In 2000, 164,000 acres of Bureau of Land Management land was designated as the Canyons of the Ancients National Monument. The monument primarily encompasses the region west of Hwy. 491 and north of CR G, including Lowry Pueblo and Sand Canyon. Though there is a more obvious "official" presence on the lands in question, there aren't specific entrance gates or fees for the trails, and dogs are still permitted everywhere. The designation was made chiefly to protect the more than 6,000 archaeological sites in the area.

Activity in the area surrounding Mesa Verde is centered in the small towns of Cortez, Dolores, and Mancos, which form a triangle. All three towns have leash laws. Surrounding Montezuma County only requires that dogs be kept under voice control.

Cortez Centennial Park, located behind the Colorado Welcome Center in Cortez, provides a nice expanse of green for the dog who's feeling carbound, as well as 2.5 miles of paths. And in the Lizard Head Wilderness, about halfway between Cortez and Telluride off Hwy. 145, your dog can hike under voice command in the shadow of the reptilian-shaped monolith for which the area is named.

TAIL-RATED TRAILS

Trails in the region range from hot, sandy desert hikes to routes through the heart of the forest. The Visitor Information Bureau in Cortez puts out a great brochure with detailed descriptions, called "Guide to Scenic Hiking Trails in Mesa Verde Country." All the trails are on national forest (nonwilderness) or BLM land, and there are lots of leash-free jaunts on which to take your dog. A few other options are described here.

Mancos State Park/ Chicken Creek Trail

Distance: Up to 16 miles round-trip

Elevation gain: Up to 1,000 feet

Trailhead: From Mancos, head north on Hwy. 184 for .25 mile, then east (right) on CR 42. Go 4 miles to CR N, and turn left, which leads to the park entrance (there's a $6 entrance fee). To reach the trailhead, drive over the dam and around to the north side of Jackson Gulch Reservoir, where you'll see a parking area and trailhead sign on the left.

Alternate access: If you don't want to pay the

state park entrance fee, you can meet up with the upper portion of the Chicken Creek Trail by hiking west and downhill from the Transfer Campground. To reach the campground, continue past the turn-off for CR N (described previously) and take FR 561 for approximately 3.5 miles to the Transfer Recreation Area.

Dogs must be leashed on the portion of trail that begins in the state park; they can be off leash on national forest land.

This trail would be a good one for a dog during the day in summer—there's access to water as well as the pleasant shade of spruce and ponderosa pine once you reach the creek. Begin by hiking through a meadow. After about .25 mile, when the trail bends to the right, it forks in the grass; stay to the left. Continue walking through tall grasses and, in summer, colorful wildflowers. Hike across and down a small clearing, after which you'll pass through a fence; this is the park boundary. The trail heads down a wide, gradual pitch to Chicken Creek. From here, it runs alongside the creek, crisscrossing the water several times and allowing your dog to cool his paws. Because this is an out-and-back hike, follow the creek bed for as long as you like. One note of caution: because the trail receives a lot of horse use, the first mile may be heavily cratered when the dirt dries after a rainstorm.

Sand Canyon Trail

Distance: 12 miles round-trip

Elevation gain: Up to 1,000 feet (from south to north; the northern trailhead is the high point)

Trailhead: From Cortez, drive south on Hwy. 160/491. Make a right onto McElmo Rd. (also known as CR G). Go 12.5 miles to a trailhead parking area on the right. Alternate access is from the north, at Sand Canyon Pueblo: drive north from Cortez on Hwy. 491 for 5.3 miles; make a left on CR P. Go 4.5 miles, then left on CR 18,

at the T-intersection. After .5 mile, follow the road as it makes a sharp curve to the right, turning into CR T. Turn left on CR 17 (1.4 miles); drive for a little over 3 more miles (follow the road as it bears right, becoming CR N). Look for a small parking area and BLM signage for Sand Canyon Pueblo on the left.

Dogs can be off leash (though since this trail does get heavy use, especially on weekends, keep a leash at the ready).

This is true desert hiking, best to do in the spring or fall. Be sure to bring a lot of water. As the Sleeping Ute mountain formation snoozes to the south, head north from the parking area at the southern trailhead, traveling across slickrock before picking up the red dirt trail. Your dog will have the chance to sniff out piñon, juniper, yucca, and prickly pear cactus. The level trail, which is easy to follow, is also marked with the occasional rock cairn. Along the way, the dog with an archaeological bent will enjoy viewing several Ancestral Puebloan (also called Anasazi) cliff dwellings, the first of which is in a large dome about .5 mile from the trailhead. Other trail highlights include intriguing rock formations and sculpted canyons.

If you begin hiking from the north, the trail starts out somewhat rootier and rockier as it descends into the canyon. You may also want to walk the short interpretive trail around the Sand Canyon Pueblo, near the trailhead.

PAWS ON THE TRAIL

If your dog tends to wander off trails, it's a good idea to keep him leashed in the desert so he doesn't damage the fragile cryptogamic soil, which can take up to 100 years to form.

Dolores Walking Trail

Distance: About .5 mile

Access: At either the 4th St. Bridge (take 4th St. south

from Hwy. 145 through Dolores) or behind Joe Rowell Park, off Hwy. 145 north just before entering downtown Dolores. *Dogs must be leashed.*

This wide gravel trail that runs along the Dolores River is great for a short stop or, if you're staying in Dolores, a morning or evening walk with Fido. Hot and thirsty canine travelers will appreciate the easy river access.

Dominguez and Escalante Ruins Hike

Distance: 1 mile round-trip
Elevation gain: About 150 feet
Trailhead: The hike starts at the Anasazi Heritage Center, 27501 Hwy. 184, in Dolores.
Dogs must be leashed.

A paved trail winds up a gradual ascent to the Escalante Ruins, which were first documented by Spanish Franciscan friars in the eighteenth century and then excavated in 1976. Several shaded picnic tables are available along the trail for dining alfresco with your dog. At the top, take in the panoramic view of the surrounding area, including McPhee Reservoir and Mesa Verde. The Dominguez ruins are located right next to the museum building.

Mesa Verde National Park.

As with all national parks, dogs are not allowed on any of the trails here. Their presence in the park is limited to parking lots and campgrounds (always on leash) and the Far View Lodge.

Ute Mountain Tribal Park.

The park, which contains about 125,000 acres, is a primitive area near Towaoc containing hundreds of Ancestral Puebloan ruins, and admission is only with a Ute guide, by prior reservation. Dogs are discouraged as visitors,

mainly because of the archaeological work in progress. The staff member I spoke with relayed an incident in which a dog had run off, only to come back carrying a vertebra in its mouth. To prevent similar scenarios, consider day-boarding Fido in Cortez if you want to visit the park. The Cortez Animal Bed and Breakfast is the closest facility (see Doggie Daycare).

CYCLING FOR CANINES

Sand Canyon (see Tail-Rated Trails) is a scenic cycling option, best to do with your dog when temperatures are moderate and early or late in the day, when the trail is not as busy. Biking from south to north gives you better riding terrain, and turning around before the trail gets too rocky will keep the round-trip distance under 10 miles (check at the Anasazi Heritage Center in Dolores—see Worth a Paws—before you go to find out if the off-leash policy has changed, since Sand Canyon is now part of the Canyons of the Ancients National Monument). Or try the 10-mile round-trip **Cannonball Mesa** ride, which begins off McElmo Rd. about 8 miles past the Sand Canyon trailhead. For a detailed route description, pick up the brochure "Mountain and Road Bike Routes" that's put out by the Visitor Information Bureau in Cortez.

POWDERHOUNDS

Note that though the groomed trails in the Chicken Creek area near Mancos are on national forest land, the volunteers who maintain the ski trails ask that you leave Fido at home in winter. To access trails where you can ski or snowshoe with your dog, head northeast of Dolores up Hwy. 145 to the **Lizard Head Pass** area (see Chapter 17). Pick up maps at the Mancos-Dolores Ranger District (see Resources).

CREATURE COMFORTS

Unless otherwise stated, dogs should not be left unattended in the room or cabin.

Cortez

$–$$ America's Best Value Inn, 440 S. Broadway, 970-565-7778, 800-578-7878. The motel has several pet-friendly rooms, for a $5 one-time fee per dog. Dogs can be left unattended inside the room for a short time.

$–$$ Aneth Lodge, 645 E. Main, 970-565-3453, 877-515-8454. Up to three dogs each are allowed in all rooms.

$–$$ National 9 Sand Canyon Inn, 301 W. Main, 970-565-8562, 800-524-9999 (national number), www.sandcanyon.com. The motel has only two pet-friendly rooms, for $5 per dog, per night.

$–$$ Super 8, 505 E. Main, 970-565-8888, 800-800-8000 (national number), www.super8.com. The motel prefers small to medium-sized dogs, but if your larger dog appears well behaved, he'll likely make the cut. You can leave your dog unattended in the room as long as you let the front desk know so housekeeping won't enter during that time, and there's a small dog-walking area in back of the motel.

$$ Budget Host Inn, 2040 E. Main, 970-565-3738, 888-677-3738, www.budgethostmesaverde.com. The motel has a selection of pet-friendly rooms for $10 per dog, per night, and with a maximum of two dogs per room.

$$ Cortez/Mesa Verde Inn, 640 S. Broadway, 970-565-3773, www.cortezinn.com. Up to two dogs per room are permitted in designated rooms for $6 per dog, per night. There's a walking path behind the motel, with grass and trees, where you can exercise your leashed dog.

$$ Cortez/Mesa Verde KOA, 27432 East Hwy. 160, 970-565-9301, 800-KOA-3901, www.cortezkoa.com. Dogs other than Rottweilers, pit bulls, and Dobermans are allowed in the camper cabins (bring your own bedding and cooking supplies). There's also a 4-acre fenced pet area in which your dog can play with other campers. Open April 1 to October 15.

$$ Days Inn, 430 N. Dolores Rd. (Hwy. 145/160), 970-565-8577, 800-DAYS-INN (national number), www.daysinn.com. One dog per room is allowed in the motel's designated pet rooms for an extra fee of $10 per night.

$$ Jolly Rancher Bed and Breakfast, 12751 CR 25, 970-564-9101, 888-564-9101, www.thejollyrancher.com. The B&B, on 15 acres 3 miles from Cortez, will accept small dogs on a case-by-case basis, for a $12–$15 nightly fee per pet, depending on how small your dog is, and with a maximum of two dogs. An outside kennel is also available, where your dog may be able to stay if he's not jolly enough to go in one of the three guest rooms or the one-bedroom guesthouse. All units are large, with private baths, and the guesthouse also has a kitchen. There's a horse barn and corral, so if you have a traveling horse, bring him along, too.

$$ Tomahawk Lodge, 728 S. Broadway, 970-565-8521, 800-643-7705, www.angelfire.com/co2/tomahawk. Up to two dogs per room are allowed in designated pet rooms.

$$–$$$ Best Western Turquoise Inn & Suites, 535 E. Main, 970-565-3778, 800-547-3376, www.bestwesternmesaverdehotel.com. The motel has pet-designated rooms and charges a $15 one-time fee per stay for up to three dogs per room. You can leave your dog unattended inside if he's in a travel kennel.

$$–$$$ Comfort Inn, 2321 E. Main, 970-565-3400, 866-348-6112, www.comfortinn.com. "We're very pet friendly," said a front-desk staffer at the hotel. Indeed, dogs are allowed in any of the rooms for $10 per visit, with a limit of two dogs per room, and can be left unattended inside for a couple of hours at a time.

$$–$$$ Econo Lodge, 2020 E. Main, 970-565-3474, www.econolodge.com. The motel has seven designated pet rooms, as well as a designated pet relief area outside. Dogs are $10 extra per night, per pet and can be left unattended inside only if in a travel kennel.

$$–$$$ Rodeway Inn, 1120 E. Main, 970-565-3761, www.rodewayinn.com. Dogs are permitted in first-floor rooms for $10 per night, per pet, with a two-dog limit per room. You can leave Fido unattended inside if necessary.

$$$ Far View Lodge, Mesa Verde National Park, 970-529-4422, 800-449-2288, www.visitmesaverde.com. The lodge is one of the few places in the park where you can take your dog with you. Up to two dogs each are allowed in standard, or "comfort," rooms. A $50 deposit is required, as well as a $10 nightly fee per dog. Though your dog can't hike with you in the park, there are some pathways around the lodge where the two of you can stroll together. The lodge is open from mid-April to mid-October.

$$$ Holiday Inn Express, 2121 E. Main, 970-565-6000, 800-626-5652, www.coloradoholiday.com. The motel will try to place you and Fido in a first-floor room for your stay and requests a $50 deposit if you're paying in cash. There's a maximum of two dogs per room, and when Fido needs to stretch his legs, you can walk him on leash in a large area out back.

Dolores
$–$$ Dolores River Cabins and RV Park, 18680 Hwy. 145, 970-882-7761, 800-200-2399, www.doloresriverrv.com. This is a popular place for vacationing dogs, and yours is bound to make some new friends during a stay. The cabins include four full-service units and six camper ones (bring your own bedding to the latter). Dogs are allowed in all, with a $100 deposit, and they can be left unattended if they promise not to bark. You'll find a pet-walking area near the road as well as one by a pond; the owners ask that you keep your dog leashed. There's also a walk along the Dolores River behind the cabins. Open April 15 to mid-November.

$–$$$ Priest Gulch Lodge, Cabins, and Campground, 27646 Hwy. 145 (25 miles north of Dolores), 970-562-3810, www.priestgulch.com. Dogs may stay in three of the resort's full-service cabins, the one camper cabin (which comes with bedding), or the RV sites, but not the lodge rooms. There's a $5 nightly pet fee, per dog, and a limit of two dogs per unit. One of the dog-friendly cabins is actually a duplex, and each side sleeps up to six people. If your dog is a swimmer, he'll enjoy the riverside Toll House cabin. The complex is on 30 acres bordering the Dolores River, which your dog is welcome to explore on a leash. Open May 1 to October 31.

$$ Groundhog Lake RV Park and Campground, FR 533, 970-565-9093, 505-330-3658, www.groundhoglake.com. This isolated mountain setting (32 miles from Dolores) may be just what your dog is looking for. In addition to the campsites, two cabins are available: a three-bedroom house with full kitchen that sleeps up to 10 and a one-room bunkhouse with kitchenette. The latter does not have running water, so you'll have to use the campground bathhouse. There's a $25 one-time fee for dogs. Keep your dog leashed on the property. Open June 1 to November 15.

$$ The Rio Grande Southern Hotel, 101 S. 5th St., 970-882-2125, 866-882-3026, www.rgshotel.com. This former railroad hotel dates to 1893 and is on the National Register of Historic Places. Among the distinguished guests (along with your dog, of course, if you stay here) were Theodore Roosevelt and novelist Zane Grey. The seven cozy rooms (three with private bath) are furnished with turn-of-the-century antiques. Dogs could be left unattended inside on a case-by-case basis, but a more appealing option is the hotel's large fenced backyard, where your dog could keep company with the owners' dog. The hotel restaurant dishes up hearty, home-cooked food, and breakfast is included in the room price.

$$–$$$ Circle K Ranch, 27758 Hwy. 145 (26 miles northeast of Dolores), 970-562-3826, 800-477-6381, www.ckranch .com. Dogs are allowed in the ranch's eight motel units and three of its fully equipped cabins, for a $10 nightly fee per pet and a $50 deposit. (They're not permitted in the ranch's lodge rooms or the three dorm-style bunkhouses). The ranch is on 80 acres along the Dolores River, bordered on three sides by national forest land. You must keep your dog leashed and pick up after him outside. Horseback riding and guided fly-fishing outings are offered in summer, and hunting outfitting in the fall. You can also get meals, with advance reservations, at the main ranch house. Though the ranch stays open year-round, cabins are the only lodging option from November until mid-May, with a three-night minimum during that time.

$$–$$$ Dolores Mountain Inn, 701 Hwy. 145, 970-882-7203, 800-842-8113, www.dminn.com. For a $10 one-time fee, your dog can be a guest at this smoke-free motel in what passes for downtown Dolores. In addition to standard rooms, one- and two-bedroom suites with kitch-ens are available. You'll be asked to sign a pet agreement that requires, among a few other stipulations, that Fido go off motel property for his bathroom breaks.

$$–$$$ Outpost Cabins, Motel, and RV Park, 1800 Hwy. 145, 970-882-7271, 800-382-4892, www.doloreslodgings .com. For $8 per dog, per night, the Outpost allows most dogs (no Dobermans, Rottweilers, or pit bulls) in all of its lodging options: ten motel rooms (some with cooking facilities), five country-style furnished cabins (all with full kitchens), and, of course, the RV park. There's a maximum of two dogs per unit. A large deck overlooks the Dolores River, a great space for hanging out and watching the current go by. A path runs from the motel to one of the Dolores town parks nearby.

$$$ Green Snow Oasis, 28434 Highway 145, 970-562-7669. Located north of Dolores, near Rico, these five cute, rustic log cabins, all fully outfitted and with woodstoves, are along the Dolores River. Your dog can stay, too, at no extra charge. Each cabin has one main-level room and a second-story sleeping loft. You can leave Rover unattended in the cabin at your discretion; be sure to keep him leashed on the small property. Open May 15 to November 1.

$$$ Lebanon Schoolhouse Bed and Breakfast, 24925 Road T, 970-882-4461, 877-882-4461, www.lebanonschoolhouse .com. This is probably the only chance your dog could have to stay overnight in a schoolhouse, and, to be expected, he should be on his best behavior. Dating from 1907, the converted building features an intriguing mix of architecture, with two separate living room/kitchen areas, five antique-furnished bedrooms, including a master suite and the bell-tower room, and a separate small guesthouse that used to be the teacher's residence.

Dogs are permitted to stay overnight in two of the rooms, usually for a $20 nightly fee per dog. Though you won't be able to leave your dog unattended here, there's a nice fenced-in area outside where he can relax while you go out to dinner. And the "schoolyard" features colorful gardens and a picnic area. The two resident dogs may teach your dog some new-school tricks.

$$$ The Red Elk Lodge, 27060 Hwy. 145 (about 22 miles northeast of Dolores), 970-562-3849, 520-625-1000 (November to April), www.redelklodge.com. The lodge is actually a duplex log house; each side has one bedroom and a loft, in addition to a full kitchen. Dogs are $10 a night extra, per pet. If you need to leave Rover behind, there's an outside kennel he can stay in. The property, surrounded by national forest land, straddles both sides of the Dolores River. Open June through the end of November.

$$$$ Dunton Hot Springs, 52068 CR 38 (18 miles east of Dolores), 970-882-4800, www.duntonhotsprings.com. This secluded luxury resort surrounded by the San Juan National Forest is definitely one of the more unusual places in Colorado you and your dog can stay together. Dunton is actually a former gold miners' ghost town that was refurbished after it was privately purchased in 1994. The cabins, though unassuming from the outside, are the epitome of rustic luxe inside, with Western antiques, animal-hide rugs, and art from around the world. Dogs are welcome in two of the twelve: the Dunton Store (yes, originally the town's general mercantile) and the New House cabin for $50 extra per night, per dog. Both of these cabins sleep up to four, and the store has its own hot springs soaking pool in the back. You can leave your dog unattended inside the cabin while you soak in the resort's hot springs or eat a meal (all are included in your stay) in the main lodge, originally Dunton's saloon and dance hall. Your dog may want to take a dip in the West Fork of the Dolores River, which runs through the property. There's also a two-story library in a restored barn and a small gym on-site, and spa treatments can be arranged. Meanwhile, miles of trails nearby let you and Rover spend some quality time together.

$$$$ Fox Den River Cabin, 24516 Hwy. 145 (12.5 miles northeast of Dolores), 214-770-8805, www.foxdenrivercabins.com. This three-bedroom log house, outfitted in a rustic country style, has a prime location on the Dolores River, with a yard that slopes right down to the water for easy access. The house also has a huge moss rock fireplace, a nicely appointed kitchen, and an additional sleeping loft, so it can accommodate up to 14 people. Your dog can join you for a $100 one-time fee, and there's a two-night minimum for any stay. You can leave your dog unattended inside.

$$$$ Sophia Peace Center, 19581 CR 31 (12 miles north of Dolores), 970-882-4920, 877-246-0567, www.sophiaretreatcenter.org. The center, run by a Christian mystical group, accepts dogs on a case-by-case basis in its two cottages, about 1 mile from the main lodge, where retreats are often held by various groups. The pet fee is $20 per night for one dog and another $10 if you have a second dog. The cottages, built in 1982, are refurbished, and one sleeps up to six, while the other sleeps up to twelve; both have kitchens. If he's in a travel kennel, your dog can be unattended inside the cabin. In addition to enjoying the peaceful setting, on 30 acres surrounded by national forest, you and your dog can stroll the short walking paths on the grounds and even wander through the center's labyrinth.

Clover enjoys a visit to the exclusive Dunton Hot Springs resort, built on the site of a former gold-mining ghost town.

Dove Creek

$–$$ Country Inn Motel, 442 W. Hwy. 491, 970-677-2234. The motel charges $5 per dog, per night, and all rooms are nonsmoking.

Mancos

$ A&A Mesa Verde Camper Cabins and RV Park, 34979 Hwy. 160 (directly across from the entrance to Mesa Verde), 970-565-3517, 800-972-6620, www.mesaverde camping.com. In addition to tent and RV sites, the A&A has four camping cabins where you can stay with your small to medium-sized dog (roughly defined as "below knee level" when your dog is standing) for a $3 one-time fee, per dog. You'll have to bring your own bedding, and there are no cooking facilities, though the cabins do have heaters. Open April 1 to November 1.

$$–$$$ Enchanted Mesa Motel, 862 W. Grand Ave., 970-533-7729, 866-533-6372, www.enchantedmesamotel.com. At this small motel on the outskirts of Mancos, dogs 30 pounds and under pay $5 extra per night, while larger dogs pay $10 per night.

$$$–$$$$ Echo Basin Dude Ranch, 43747 CR M, 970-533-7000, 800-426-1890, www.echobasin.com. Dogs can stay in the twenty log A-frame cabins, three modern condolike cabins, or tent and RV sites on this 600-acre former working ranch turned rustic resort. A canine cabin stay is $10 per night, per dog, with a two-night minimum. You can leave your four-legged dude unattended in the cabin for a couple of hours only if he's in a travel kennel; be sure to keep him leashed when exploring the ranch's vast property. The ranch itself offers a generous helping of activities, including horseback riding (you can bring your own horse, too), an outdoor pool, volleyball and basketball courts, a nine-hole putting green, and a driving range. There's even an outdoor amphitheater on the grounds where acts such as .38 Special and Styx have played (can your dog hold up a cigarette lighter in his paw?). Open Memorial Day to mid-September.

$$$–$$$$ Sundance Bear Lodge, 38890 Hwy. 184 (4 miles north of Mancos), 970-533-1504, 866-529-2480, www .sundancebear.com. You and your dog will find a welcoming retreat at the lodge, tucked away on 80 acres close to national forest land. Accommodations consist of two rooms in the main house, a pond-side renovated log cabin, and a modern guest house that can be rented whole or partially. Canine visitors are permitted in the cabin and the guest house. The diminutive one-bedroom-plus-loft log cabin is the real thing and has a kitchenette and gas fireplace. You can rent it either with breakfast included or not; in the guest house, you're on your own for breakfast. A dog can be left unattended inside the cabin only, preferably inside a travel kennel, though owner Susan Scott notes that most dogs prefer to hang out outside in their kennels if they need to be left behind. And your dog can explore the lodge's property with you off leash as long as he gets along with everyone else around; perhaps Chester, an Australian shepherd/border collie mix, will show him the best places to sniff. Another dog, Oreo, two cats, and two horses round out the animal hospitality committee.

$$$$ River Bend Bed and Breakfast, 42505 Hwy. 160 (1 mile east of Mancos), 866-403-7063, www.riverbendbandb.com. Though dogs can't stay in the bed-and-breakfast rooms in the main house, they're very welcome in the adjacent two-bedroom cabin, dubbed La Casita. The cabin has a full kitchen (breakfast is not part of the stay when you're out here) and can sleep up to eight. It's also air-conditioned, and you can leave Fido unattended inside. With 6 acres to sniff out, there's lots of room for your dog to stretch his legs; just be sure to clean up after him and have a leash at the ready when other guests are around.

Rico

$$–$$$$ Rico Hotel, 124 S. Glasgow Ave. (Hwy. 145), 970-967-3000, 800-365-1971, www.ricohotel.com. Your dog will certainly soak up some atmosphere at the hotel, built in 1925 as a boarding house for the Argentine Mine Company. Dogs are welcome in the seven first-floor rooms (one has a shared bathroom, the rest have their own) for $10 per night, per pet. At the end of the day, when you and Fido are exhausted from exploring the stunning peaks that surround the town, the vaulted-ceiling lobby with large stone fireplace is an inviting place to recoup your energy. For humans, the

Argentine Grille serves innovative cuisine at very moderate prices, and breakfast is included in the room rate.

CAMPGROUNDS

Mesa Verde National Park. Off Hwy. 160, about 10 miles east of Cortez. The park's Morefield Campground has 435 sites.

Mancos State Park. See Tail-Rated Trails for directions (33 sites).

Forest service campgrounds: **McPhee Campground**, at McPhee Reservoir near Dolores (71 sites); **House Creek Campground**, also on the reservoir, reached via FRs 526 and 528 from Dolores (60 sites); **Transfer Campground**, north of Mancos on FR 561 (12 sites); **Mavreeso Campground** (19 sites), **West Dolores Campground** (18 sites), and **Burro Bridge Campground** (14 sites) are located on FR 535, 12.5 miles from Dolores on Hwy. 145 East.

Private campgrounds: **Cortez/Mesa Verde KOA** in Cortez; **Dolores River Cabins & RV Park, Groundhog Lake RV Park and Campground, Outpost Cabins, Motel, and RV Park,** and **Priest Gulch Lodge, Cabins, and Campground** in Dolores; **A&A Mesa Verde Camper Cabins & RV Resort** and **Echo Basin Dude Ranch** in Mancos (see Creature Comforts).

WORTH A PAWS

Anasazi Heritage Center, 27501 Hwy. 184, Dolores, 970-882-5600, www.co.blm .gov/co/st/en/fo/ahc.html. Though your dog can't accompany you inside the museum to view the exhibits on Ancestral Puebloan culture and artifacts on display, you're welcome to secure him to one of the benches outside while you wander through. The dog-friendly management can sometimes supply water dishes, and you can always fill up your dog's own dish from the "icy-cold water fountain," in the words of one museum staffer. Your dog can join you on the short hike up to the Dominguez and Escalante ruins; see Tail-Rated Trails for more information.

The Heritage Center is open year-round except on Thanksgiving, Christmas, and New Year's Day. Hours are 9 AM–5 PM from March to October; 9 AM–4 PM November to February. There's a $3 admission fee to the museum from March to October; it's free otherwise.

ANCIENT PUPS

Yes, there was a canine component to Ancestral Puebloan culture; the "ancient ones" kept dogs for work and companionship.

Lowry Pueblo. Excavated from 1930 to 1936, the pueblo dates from AD 1060. Its style reflects the cultural traditions of both early Chacoan architecture and also those styles found at Mesa Verde. You and your dog can take a self-guided tour of the pueblo and the adjoining Great Kiva, as long as your dog remains on his leash. To reach the ruins, head north from Cortez on Hwy. 481 to Pleasant View (about 18 miles). Turn left on CR CC and drive 9 miles to reach the pueblo. For more information, call 970-882-5600.

Hovenweep National Monument. The monument, established in 1923, lies about 43 miles west of Cortez, straddling the Colorado-Utah border. The Square Tower Ruins, in Utah, are accessible by car; the other five Ancestral Puebloan sites require short hikes. Your leashed dog is welcome to accompany you on this walk back through time (around AD 1200). Bring lots of water. The entrance fee is $6 per vehicle. For more information, call 970-562-4282 or to go www.nps.gov/hove.

DOGGIE DAYCARE
Cortez

Cortez Adobe Animal Hospital, 11314 Hwy. 145, 970-565-4458, www.cortez adobe.vetsuite.com. $10.50–$13.50/day, depending on the size of dog. Dogs get supervised outdoor playtime. Open 7:30 AM–5 PM, Monday to Friday; 9 AM–noon, Saturday.

Cortez Animal Bed and Breakfast, 6815 Hwy. 160, 970-564-1385. $12/day. Your dog will have plush accommodations in the indoor/outdoor heated kennels as well as four yards to play in with his fellow boarders. Open 8 AM–5 PM, Monday to Friday; 8–10 AM and 3–4 PM, Saturday; and 8–9 AM and 3–4 PM, Sunday. Other pick-up times can be arranged in advance for an additional fee.

PET PROVISIONS
Cortez
Bond's Gourmet Pet Foods, 121 N. Pinon Dr., 970-565-2762

Cortez Animal Bed and Breakfast, 6815 Hwy. 160, 970-564-1385

CANINE ER
Cortez
Cedarwood Animal Clinic, 1819 E. Main, 970-565-6531, www.cedarwoodanimal-clinic.com. Open 8 AM–5 PM, Monday to Friday.

Cortez Adobe Animal Hospital, 11314 Hwy. 145, 970-565-4458. Open 7:30 AM–5 PM, Monday to Friday; 9 AM–noon, Saturday.

Montezuma Veterinary Clinic, 10411 Hwy. 491, 970-565-7567. Open 8 AM–4 PM, Monday to Friday; 8 AM–noon, Saturday.

Vibrant Pet Animal Hospital, 25628 CR

L, 970-565-3196, www.vibrantpet.com. Open 7:30 AM–5 PM, Monday to Friday; 9 AM–noon, Saturday.

Mancos

Mancos Valley Veterinary Hospital, 299 W. Frontage, 970-533-1060. Open 8 AM–noon, and 2–5 PM, Monday to Friday.

RESOURCES

Colorado Welcome Center, 928 E. Main St., Cortez, 970-565-8227, 800-253-1616, www.mesaverdecountry.com

Dolores Visitor Center, 201 Railroad Ave., Dolores, 970-882-4018, www.doloreschamber.com

Mancos Visitor Center, 171 Railroad Ave., Mancos, 970-533-7434, www.mancosvalley.com

Dolores Ranger District, San Juan National Forest, 29211 Hwy. 184, Dolores, 970-882-7296

Nineteen
Durango and Vicinity

THE BIG SCOOP

Dogs will find plenty to do in Durango, from sniffing out good hikes near town to wagging their tails at the world-class mountain bikers who frequent many of the trails. In addition, the resort area of Vallecito Lake, some 20 miles northeast of Durango, contains numerous dog-friendly accommodations (most along the order of cabins and campgrounds) and is surrounded by national forest land and hiking trails. It's also permissible for dogs to be under voice control in the Weminuche and South San Juan Wildernesses, both within the San Juan National Forest. And Pagosa Springs, an hour east of Durango, boasts the "world's largest hot springs" (for people only) in addition to nearby national forest trails (for dogs and people).

Note that in addition to the expected leash and dog-waste cleanup laws, Durango City Code prohibits tied-up dogs being left unattended on public property (and animal control says they actively enforce this). In other words, if you want to leave your dog outside while you dash in for a bagel and coffee, don't. (For your dog's safety, find a friendly passerby who's willing to dogsit for a few minutes rather than leave your pet in the car on a warm day.) Within surrounding La Plata County, dogs can legally be off leash as long as they are under voice control and within your sight. In Pagosa Springs, dogs must be leashed; outside of city limits, in Archuleta County, they can be under voice control.

TAIL-RATED TRAILS

With the nearby San Juan National Forest as well as several trails in town, Durango is somewhat of a hiking mecca for dogs. The pamphlet "Hiking in and around Durango," available at the Durango Area Chamber Resort Association, describes other good options in addition to those given here.

Durango

Red Creek

Distance: 6.4 miles round-trip

Elevation gain: 1,800 feet

Trailhead: From Main Ave. in town, turn east on 32nd St. (by City Market). Make a right on CR 250 (toward Lemon Lake and Vallecito Lake), then go left at the next stop sign (CR 240). After a little over 7 miles, turn left on CR 246 (at the sign marked Colvig Silver). Stay on this road for 1.2 miles, where you'll come to a gate; you may have to open (and close) it. After driving another .3 mile, you'll see a small clearing on the right and another road leading up from it; you may want to park here, as the road gets a little rough after this point. If your car has four-wheel drive, continue straight through to the trailhead at road's end. *Dogs can be off leash.*

This is a good hike for the active dog; you and he can enjoy a peaceful route through aspen, pine, and spruce, accompanied by the symphony of the rushing creek. The trail follows Red Creek for most of the way, fording it several times, until about the last .5 mile, when it veers away to switchback steeply to the top of Missionary Ridge. If you're feeling more ambitious, it's possible to make a longer loop hike (around 13 miles): take a right on Missionary Ridge where the

Red Creek Trail intersects the Missionary Ridge Trail (it's not signed). Look for the next distinct trail to the right after a short, steep climb. Descend down the ridge between Red Creek and the north fork of Shearer Creek; you'll end up back at the road, about 3 miles from the Red Creek trailhead.

Durango Dog Park

Access: Recommended parking is at Schneider Park: from Hwy. 160 immediately west of where it crosses the Animas River, take Roosa St. north to the park, which is just ahead on the right. From there, backtrack on the paved Animas River Trail and take the short trail extension that goes under the highway. Cross the small bridge over Lightner Creek to enter the dog park.

Regulations: Dogs must have current vaccinations, license, and ID tags; owners must clean up after their pooches.

Dogs can be off leash.

More than six years in the planning (because of the various government agencies that had a say in the matter), this 5-acre playground for Durango dogs reflects persistence and dedication on the part of local dog advocates. So ask your dog to give a howl of thanks as he enjoys romping in this unfenced, grassy area bordered by Smelter Mountain, Lightner Creek, and the Animas River. An unmaintained

Treats always taste better at 14,000 feet.

dirt path parallels the river, and several other short paths meander through the park. Once your dog tires of playing, he can cool off at the side of the river (the park offers no shade) and watch the rafters and kayakers go by; during spring runoff, however, when the water flows deep and fast, make sure your dog stays away from all but the shallowest eddies.

Colorado Trail/ Junction Creek

Distance: 8 miles round-trip
Elevation gain: 1,000 feet
Trailhead: From Main Ave. in town, turn west on 25th St., which turns into Junction Creek Rd. After 3.4 miles, turn left into the gravel parking area, just after the cattle guard.

Dogs can be off leash.

This hike begins at the southwest terminus of the 468-mile Colorado Trail, completed in 1988. This portion of the trail offers excellent hiking, biking, and horseback riding, so be prepared to meet lots of other outdoor enthusiasts. In fact, you may want to leash your dog if trail use is particularly heavy during your hike to avoid conflict. Climb a fairly gentle grade for the first 2.5 miles. As it ascends, the trail clings to the side of a steep-walled ravine, providing breathtaking views. At 2.5 miles, cross a bridge and begin climbing a series of switchbacks for the next 1.5 miles to Gudy's Rest. The spectacular overlook is named for Gudy Gaskill, the driving force behind the construction of the Colorado Trail. Stay awhile and let your dog savor the view before heading back the way you came.

Falls Creek Meadow

Access: From Main Ave. in town, turn west on 25th St., which turns into Junction Creek Rd. Turn right at the sign for Falls Creek onto CR 205 and note your mileage. Pass by a small subdivision and Chapman Lake, then look for a national forest sign on the right; the road turns to dirt near this point. At 1.4 miles from your turn onto CR 205 is a pullout on the right, next to a couple of large boulders.

Dogs can be off leash.

This is an easily accessible, close-to-town spot for dogs who just want some more room to roam. From the parking pullout, an unmaintained track runs into the spacious meadow, with lots of room for Fido to run, catch a Frisbee, or just run circles around you. You may be tempted to start a hike from this area; don't, as doing so may well lead to inadvertently trespassing on unsigned private land.

Animas Mountain

Distance: 9.2-mile network of trails

Elevation gain: 1,500 feet

Trailhead: From Main Ave. in town, turn west on 32nd St. At the T-intersection with W. Fourth Ave., make a right. The road ends in a small parking lot at the trailhead. (There's also a trailhead on the west side of this park, on Birket Dr. off Junction Creek Rd., but parking is limited.)

Dogs must be leashed.

Check out the sign at the trailhead to see the various loops available on this hike. The trail is dry, so bring water for you and your pooch.

Begin by climbing a series of gradual switchbacks; as you climb, the scenic Animas River Valley unfolds below. And you may hear the distinctive whistle of the Durango-Silverton narrow-gauge train as it leaves town. Follow the route as it ascends through piñon, juniper, and stands of ponderosa pine. You'll eventually come to a series of vista points where you and your dog can enjoy views of the La Plata Mountains to the west and the Animas River as it snakes its way from the north through verdant flatlands. Either

turn around once you've had your fill of views or continue up the trail, which eventually loops back to the trailhead. When you come to an unmarked junction near the bottom of the mountain, stay left and head down the switchbacks to return to the parking area.

Animas River Trail

Distance: 5 miles one way

Access: An easy place to access the trail is behind the Durango visitor center in Santa Rita Park (formerly Gateway Park), where parking is available.

Dogs must be leashed.

Enjoy an easy stroll along this approximately 5-mile paved trail that follows the Animas River through Durango. The trail runs close enough to the river that your dog can dip his toes in. And several parks along the way offer opportunities for a "green break."

Durango Mountain Park

Access: From Main Ave. in town, turn west on 22nd St., which turns into Montview Pkwy. Drive until the road ends; several parking spots are available along the street. (There's also another trailhead 1 block south on Leyden St.)

Dogs must be leashed.

This 271-acre area, popular with mountain bikers (it's also known as the Test Tracks), has about 12 miles of crisscrossing trails. A map gives the lay of the land, but trails are not named. There are several other access points, in addition to the two described above, from any of the streets that back up to the park. You'll encounter two starting options from the Montview access: go left on the trail at the road's end. A couple of hundred feet later, another trail comes in from the north, which ascends up along a ridge. Or stay on the lower trail and hike in the shade. You may have to do some puddle jumping in the spring. During the summer, the area is quite dry. Let your dog decide the route since there's no particular destination for these hikes.

Pagosa Springs

In addition to the trail described below, **Town Park** and the adjoining short, paved **River Trail** along the San Juan are pleasant respites for a dog. During our visit to town, we enjoyed watching an agile black Lab jumping in and out of the river to retrieve a stick while kayakers played in the current nearby.

Reservoir Hill

Distance: 6 miles of trails on 137 acres

Trailhead: From Hot Springs Blvd. off Hwy. 160, make a left on San Juan St. (across from the visitor center). Take the first right, which leads directly to the parking area.

Dogs must be leashed.

There are an infinite number of short loop hikes within the network of trails here. All the routes are clearly marked with signs on the trees. You can ascend to various overlooks, including ones of the town, the hot springs, Wolf Creek Pass, and Pagosa Peak. A hike up to the San Juan overlook is a relatively quick way to view a nice panorama; your dog will discover lots of ponderosa pine and gambel oak to sniff through at the top as well as what could only be Paul Bunyan's picnic table.

There's no water along the trails, but you can fill up a water bottle at pumps at the main trailhead (in summer) and at the water tower overlook.

CYCLING FOR CANINES

Because Durango offers such a bonanza of biking opportunities, it's easy to pick up tips from locals on suggested rides. Some areas to consider for short rides with Rover include **Horse Gulch**, accessible from E. 8th Ave. and 3rd St. in

Golden retrievers Clover and Susie among the golden aspens.

Durango (your dog might enjoy the 4-mile Meadow Loop—go right at the first intersection you'll come to); **Lime Creek Rd.** (FR 591), off Hwy. 550, a couple miles north of Durango Mountain Resort (ride this old stagecoach route out and back for as long as you want); **Cascade Divide Rd.** (FR 579), an out and back on a lesser-traveled four-wheel-drive road, reached from Durango Mountain Resort via Hermosa Park Rd. (FR 578) to Relay Creek Rd. (FR 580); or the **Tuckerville Trail**, which starts at mile marker 11 off Middle Mountain Rd. near Vallecito Lake and follows an old jeep road to a former mining site. Stop by Hassle Free Sports, 2615 Main Ave., Durango, 970-259-3874, for maps and more specifics.

POWDERHOUNDS

Chimney Rock Archaeological Area. Though dogs are not allowed here during the summer, the forest service says that you're welcome to bring yours along as a ski or snowshoe partner in the winter. The 3.5-mile road up to the archaeological area is unplowed from about November to March, providing for an easy winter workout. To reach the area, drive 17 miles west from Pagosa Springs on Hwy. 160. At the Route 151 turnoff (by Lake Capote), turn south and continue for about 3 miles to the Chimney Rock entrance.

Vallecito Nordic Club Trail System. A local Nordic club maintains about 15 kilometers of groomed trails on the southeast side of Vallecito Lake that wind along an unplowed road as well as through campgrounds and surrounding area. The trailhead is at the Old Timers Forest Service Campground. Your dog can accompany you, and he can be off leash; the club suggests a $5 donation per dog, per season. www.pinevalleyski.com

NO TRAINING

One attraction that dogs will have to skip is the Durango & Silverton Narrow Gauge Railroad. If you opt to take the full-day trip on this historic coal-fired steam train, your dog can wait in comfort at one of several boarding kennels in Durango (see Doggie Daycare).

CREATURE COMFORTS

Unless otherwise stated, dogs should not be left unattended in the room or cabin.

Bayfield

$$ Horseman's Lodge, 7100 CR 501, 970-884-9733. Located halfway between Bayfield and Vallecito Lake, the motel allows dogs in any of its nine units, some with kitchenettes. The nod usually goes, however, to smaller, nonshedding dogs, as too many large, furry dogs have made their mark on bedspreads and furnishings; you'll be asked for a deposit if you're traveling with a big dog. It is okay to leave a dog unattended in the room.

Durango

$ Durango East KOA & Kamping Kabins, 30090 Hwy. 160, 970-247-0783, 800-

562-0793, www.durangoKOA.com. Dogs are allowed in the cabins (you'll need to supply your own sleeping and cooking gear), 7 miles east of town. There's a dog walk along a creek where you can bring your leashed companion. Open May 1 to October 15.

$ Lightner Creek Camper Cabins & Campground, 1567 CR 207 (Lightner Creek Rd.), 970-247-5406, www.camplightner creek.com. Dogs are allowed in the camper cabins as well as in the campground at this 27-acre site about 4 miles west of Durango; they're not allowed in the fully equipped cabins or lodge rooms. The camping cabins are bare bones—you must bring sleeping bags and cooking equipment, and they have 12-volt lighting but no electricity. Be sure to keep your dog leashed when outside. Open May 1 to September 1.

$-$$ Budget Inn, 3077 Main Ave., 970-247-5222, 800-257-5222, www.budget inndurango.com. The motel has designated pet-friendly rooms. Dogs pay $10 extra per night and, if paying with cash, a $20 deposit.

$-$$ Days End, 2202 Main Ave., 970-259-3311, 800-242-3297, www.days enddurango.com. You'll pay a $10 fee per night, per pet; however, dogs are not permitted in the motel's newest building. You can leave Fido unattended inside the room if you sign the pet release.

$-$$ Travelodge, 2970 Main Ave., 970-247-1741, 800-578-7878. Dogs 50 pounds and under can stay in one of the selected pet rooms for a nightly fee of $8 per pet.

$-$$$ Siesta Motel, 3475 Main Ave., 970-247-0741, 877-314-0741, www.durango siestamotel.com. The motel allows one dog per room in certain units for a $10 nightly fee.

$–$$$ Wapiti Lodge, 21625 Hwy. 160 West, 970-247-3961. The motel has some pet-friendly rooms for a $10 nightly fee.

$$ Adobe Inn, 2178 Main Ave., 970-247-2743, 877-247-9615, www.durango lodging.com. A $20 deposit and $10 nightly fee are required for canine guests, who can be left unattended in the room.

$$ Alpine Inn, 3515 N. Main Ave., 970-247-4042, 800-818-4042, www.alpine inn.info. The motel accepts dogs in some of its rooms for a $5 nightly fee.

$$ Caboose Motel, 3363 Main Ave., 970-247-1191, 877-527-1191, www.caboose moteldurango.com. Small- to medium-sized dogs, one per room, can stay in designated pet units for a $10 fee per night. Nine of them have full kitchens.

$$ Dollar Inn, 2391 Main Ave., 970-247-0593, 800-727-DRGO, www.dollarinn .com. Dogs are welcome to stay in the motel's rooms for a $5 fee per night, and you may be able to leave your dog unattended in the room for an hour or two.

$$–$$$ Best Western Durango Inn & Suites, 21382 Hwy. 160 West, 800-547-9090, 970-247-3251, www.durangoinn .com. The motel accepts dogs in the winter only (defined as approximately mid-October through mid-May) for a $15 nightly fee.

$$–$$$ Holiday Inn, 800 Camino del Rio, 970-247-5393, 800-HOLIDAY (national number), www.holiday-inn.com/durango co. Dogs are welcome for a $10 fee per night, per pet.

$$–$$$ Iron Horse Inn, 5800 N. Main Ave., 970-259-1010, 800-748-2990, www.ironhorseinndurango.com. All of the motel's rooms are bilevel, with a double bed, sitting area, and fireplace downstairs and a queen bed upstairs in a small loft area. You can leave your dog unattended inside. For safety, dogs are generally put in rooms away from the train tracks (the Durango-Silverton narrow-gauge train runs directly behind the motel several times a day, if your dog wants to come out and wag his tail at the waving passengers).

$$–$$$ Quality Inn, 2930 N. Main Ave., 970-259-5373, 877-424-6423. The motel has designated pet rooms and charges a $10 nightly fee per dog; there's a limit of two dogs per room.

$$–$$$ Super 8 Durango, 20 Stewart Dr., 970-259-0590, 800-800-8000 (national number), www.super8.com. About half of the rooms are pet friendly, with a $10 nightly charge per dog. Quiet dogs can be left unattended inside.

$$–$$$$ Doubletree Hotel, 501 Camino del Rio, 970-259-6580, 800-222-TREE (national number), www.doubletree .hilton.com. One of the more upscale accommodations in town that accepts pets, the hotel prefers to put dogs in the lower-level river-facing rooms. You'll pay a $15 fee per night. A nice bonus is that the dog park (see Tail-Rated Trails) is just a short walk away, via the paved Animas River Trail that runs behind the hotel.

$$$ Lou's Bed and Breakfast, 3115 E. 2nd Ave., 970-259-0505, www.lousbandb .com. Up to two large or three small dogs are allowed at this two-guestroom B&B along the Animas River. Each room has a private entrance, private bath, and kitchenette. An outside dog run is available for times when you may need to leave Fido behind.

$$$–$$$$ The Nugget Cabin, 48721 Hwy. 550 (.5 mile south of Durango Mountain Resort), 970-385-4742 or 970-749-4742, www.nuggetcabin.com. Owner Dale Butt, who rents out this two-bedroom, 900-square-foot log cabin with outdoor hot tub, says dogs are "always welcome, as they always should be." That's nice to hear, as the other lodging properties near the ski area have stopped permitting pets. There are no restrictions on four-legged occupants, so you can leave yours unattended in the cabin for a few hours (and go skiing, perhaps).

$$$–$$$$ Residence Inn by Marriott, 21691 Hwy. 160 West, 970-259-6200, 800-331-3131 (national number), www.marriott.com. Dogs up to 35 pounds are permitted with a $75 one-time fee. Rooms are configured as studios or one or two bedrooms, all with kitchens. You can leave your dog unattended inside, but housekeeping won't come in during that time, and the hotel will request a cell-phone number from you in case your dog becomes a loud barker. The Durango dog park (see Tail-Rated Trails) is a short stroll away.

$$$–$$$$ Rochester Hotel, 726 E. 2nd Ave., 970-385-1920, 800-664-1920, www.rochesterhotel.com. The most interesting place for dogs to stay in Durango is this tastefully updated historic hotel, especially if yours is a fan of Western movies. Two of the hotel's 15 Western flick–themed rooms are available for dog stays for $20 extra per night, per dog, and both open onto a lovely fenced-in courtyard garden (though the dog rooms may be relocated as the hotel undergoes some renovations). Guest dogs are greeted with their own bed in the room. Room rates include a full gourmet breakfast. Note that the affiliated Leland House Bed & Breakfast, across the street, does not accept dogs.

Pagosa Springs

In addition to the properties listed below, numerous individual cabins and houses for short-term rental are listed on the chamber of commerce website (see Resources), many of which will consider pets.

$ Pagosa Riverside Cabins & Campground, 2270 E. Hwy. 160, 970-264-5874, 888-785-3234, www.coloradodirectory.com/pagosariversidecamp. As the name implies, the campground has 1,100 feet of frontage on the San Juan River. Dogs are allowed in the two rustic cabins and the one slightly less rustic cabin, which has bathroom and kitchen facilities (bring your own bedding for all). Keep your dog on his leash when outside and be diligent about picking up after him. Open April 15 to November 15.

$–$$ Sportsman's Supply & Campground, 2095 Taylor Ln. (18 miles north of Pagosa Spgs.), 970-731-2300, www.sportsmanscampground.com. The campground has seven cabins, five fully equipped and two camper cabins, that dogs can stay in. Keep your dog leashed and clean up after him when exploring the campground's 10 acres. One cabin remains open year-round; the other cabins and the campground are open May 15 to November 15.

$$ Alpine Inn of Pagosa Springs, corner of Piedra Rd. and Hwy. 160, 970-731-4005, 866-628-9570, www.alpineinnofpagosasprings.com. Certain rooms are pet friendly for an additional fee of $10 per night, per dog, and with a limit of two dogs per room.

$$ Bruce Spruce Ranch, 231 West Fork Rd. (16 miles northeast of Pagosa Spgs.), 970-264-5374, www.brucespruceranch.com. Dogs are welcome in all of the ranch's 14 rustic log cabins, which have only cold running water but basic kitchen setups (a central bathhouse is available for showers). They're also permitted in the RV and tent sites, on 40 acres bordered by national forest land. The large group facility known as the Faris House Lodge, however, does not allow pets. There's a $4 fee per night, per pet, for the cabins. Dogs must be kept leashed when outside. The cabins are open from the end of May to the end of October (the group facility stays open year-round).

$$ Pagosa Springs Inn, 519 Village Dr., 970-731-3400, 888-221-8088, www .pagosaspringsinnsuites.com. The hotel has some designated pet rooms (none of the suites are included). Dogs must be approximately 50 pounds or under, and there's a $10 per pet, per night fee, with a maximum of two pets per room.

$$ Piedra River Resort, Hwy. 160 and Piedra River (20 miles west of Pagosa Spgs.), 970-731-4630, 800-898-2006, www .horsebackriding.com. Dogs are allowed to stay in any of six one- and two-bedroom, fully equipped cabins for $10 extra per visit, per dog. Keep your dog leashed (and picked up after) on the resort's 7 acres. As the website address implies, the resort also offers horseback riding. Open mid-April to mid-November.

$$ Pinewood Inn, 157 Pagosa St. (Hwy. 160), 970-264-5715, 888-655-7463, www.pinewoodinn.com. There's a $10 fee per night, per dog, to stay in one of the pet-designated rooms. One two-room cabin with kitchen is also available, and some of the motel rooms have kitchenettes.

$$ San Juan Motel, 191 E. Pagosa St., 970-264-2262, 800-765-0250, www .sanjuanmotel.net. Dogs are permitted in the motel's older rooms and in three of the on-site cabins (only one has a kitchen) for a $17.50 one-time fee. Campsites are available year-round, too, for dogs who may want to brave winter's chill.

$$ Skyview Motel, 1300 Hwy. 160 West, 970-264-5803. Dogs are welcome in designated rooms for a $7 fee per night, per dog, with a maximum of three dogs per room. They can be left unattended inside only if they're in a travel kennel.

$$–$$$ Econo Lodge, 315 Navajo Trail Dr., 970-731-2701, 800-553-2666 (national number), www.econolodge.com. Dogs 50 pounds and under are allowed in standard rooms, with a $10 fee per night, per pet, and a maximum of two dogs per room.

$$–$$$ Elk Meadows River Resort, 5360 E. Hwy. 160, 970-264-5482, 866-264-5482, www.elkmeadowsresort.com. Dogs are welcome in the five recently built or remodeled cabins and one apartment at this resort 5 miles east of Pagosa Springs, along the San Juan River. There's a $30 one-time fee for one dog, $50 for two dogs. The cabins range from studios to two bedrooms and have kitchen facilities. You may leave your pet unattended inside if you think he'll behave himself; keep him leashed when outside on the resort's 22 acres. In summer, campsites are also available.

$$–$$$ Indian Head Lodge, 631 Williams Creek Rd. (FR 640; 24 miles north of Pagosa Spgs.), 970-731-2282. For a one-time fee of $10 per pet, dogs are allowed in the four cabins here, two of which come with kitchen facilities. Well-behaved dogs may be left unattended inside. The property is on an acre surrounded by national forest land and is near Williams Creek Reservoir. Open end of May to mid-November.

$$–$$$ Mountain Landing Guest Quarters, 345 CR 600 (Piedra Rd.), 970-731-5345, 877-301-4129 x5345, www .mountainlanding.net. The guest quarters at this hotel are actually one- and two-bedroom condos. Dogs up to approximately 60 pounds can stay for an additional $10 per night, and there's usually a limit of one pet per condo. If your dog is an aspiring aviator, he might be into the decor touches that play off nearby Stevens Field airport, such as a driveway that resembles a runway and garages that look like airplane hangars.

$$–$$$ Oak Ridge Lodge, 158 Hot Springs Blvd., 970-264-4173, 866-472-4672, www. oakridgelodgepagosa.com. Dogs can stay for $15 extra per visit, per pet, in designated rooms. You can leave your dog unattended in the room.

$$$–$$$$ America's Best Value Inn High Country Lodge, 3821 Hwy. 160, 970-264-4181, 800-862-3707, www.highcountry lodge.com. You and your dog can enjoy one of the lodge's 10 cabins, which range in size from studios to two bedrooms and have fireplaces and kitchen facilities, or stay in one of the 22 guest rooms. There's a $25 pet fee the first night, $10 for each additional night. The lodge is on 15 acres, and national forest trails are nearby.

$$$–$$$$ Fireside Inn, 1600 E. Hwy. 160, 970-264-9204, 888-264-9204, www. firesidecabins.com. As far as dogs go, "just bring them and make sure they behave," say the operators of these studio, one-, and two-bedroom cabins, almost all of which are pet friendly. There's a $7.50 fee per night, per dog, with a limit of two dogs each. All of the units have kitchenettes or full kitchens. Just 1 mile from downtown Pagosa Springs, the cabins are on 10 acres bordering the San Juan River.

$$$–$$$$ The Springs Resort and Spa, 165 Hot Springs Blvd., 970-264-4168, 800-225-0934, www.pagosahotsprings .com. Ten of the standard rooms at the hotel, which is hot-springs central for Pagosa, are dog friendly, with a $20 nightly fee and a limit of three dogs per room. There are 17 natural hot springs around the property and a spa adjacent to the hotel.

Vallecito Lake

$$ Sawmill Point Lodge, 14737 CR 501, 970-884-2669, 800-884-2669. The lodge, across the road from the marina, has eight basic motel rooms with kitchenettes. Dogs are allowed in some of them for $20 per night, per dog, and can be left unattended inside if in a travel kennel.

$$–$$$ Bear Paw Lodge, 18011 CR 501, 970-884-2508, 877-884-2508, www .bearpawlodge.com. Dogs 30 pounds and under are permitted to stay in any of the lodge's seven one- to three-bedroom cabins, which have fireplaces or woodstoves. There's a $10 fee per night, per pet. Dogs have to stay off beds and furniture in the cabins, and they must be kept leashed when exploring the wooded property. The lodge is about 1 mile from the lake. Open May 1 to October 31.

$$–$$$ Blue Spruce RV Park and Cabins, 1875 CR 500, 970-884-2641, 888-884-2641, www.bluesprucervpark.com. The complex, about 1.5 miles from the lake's north end, allows up to two dogs each in eight of its country-style cabins (built in 2005) and apartments. The units range from studios to two bedrooms, and all have either kitchenettes or kitchens. The setting—14 acres bordering the national forest—is great for dogs, and Rover can explore off leash with you in the undeveloped portion of the property.

$$–$$$ Deer Willow, 18843 CR 501, 970-884-4193, www.deerwillow.com. These two fully equipped cabins, one a studio and one two bedroom, allow up to two dogs each for $10 nightly per pet. Built in the 1970s, they were remodeled in 2000. The north end of the lake is about 1.5 miles away. Open mid-May to mid-October.

$$–$$$ Durango Resort on Vallecito Lake, 14452 CR 501, 970-884-2517, 866-280-5253, www.durangoresortonlake.com. The resort allows dogs in about half of its 22 lakeside cabins. They range from studio size to one that can sleep up to 14 people, and all have full kitchens. There's a $15 fee per night, per pet, and a limit of two dogs per cabin. The lakefront location makes this an ideal base for water-loving hounds. Open beginning of May to mid-October.

$$–$$$ Lone Wolf Lodge, 18039 CR 501, 970-884-0414, www.lonewolflodge.com. For an extra $10 per night, per pet, up to two dogs per unit can stay in any of the six fully outfitted cabins here, which are a bit north of the lake. Keep your dog leashed when outside.

$$–$$$ Pine River Lodge, 14443 CR 501, 970-884-2563, www.pineriverlodge.com. You'll find a creative collection of 29 cabins, some lakeside, some across the road, all different from each other. Dogs are permitted in all but three of the cabins provided they're not larger than Lab size and pay a $10 fee per night, per pet.

$$$–$$$$ Croll Cabins, 4557 CR 501A, 970-884-2083, www.crollcabins.com. Five of these six lakeshore cabins allow pets for $10 per night, per dog. The cabins, all entirely different, range from two to four bedrooms and have full kitchens and wood-burning fireplaces. Two of them have outside fenced areas where your dog can hang out. Otherwise, if you need to leave your dog behind, you might be able to arrange for petsitting through the owner's granddaughter for a very reasonable hourly rate. Make sure Fido stays off the furniture in your cabin and keep him leashed everywhere on the property. Open mid-May to mid-October.

$$$–$$$$ Eagle's Nest, 18903 CR 501, 970-884-2866, www.eaglesnestcabins andhomes.com. The Eagle's Nest complex, 1 mile from the lake's north end, permits dogs in any of its three homey cabins (think lots of knotty pine), all of which have three bedrooms and a kitchen. There's a $10 fee per dog, per night. Open May 1 to October 31.

$$$$ High Tree Cabin, 970-884-7438, www.hightreecabins.com. "All sizes, shapes, and colors [of dogs] are welcome" at this cozy, knotty-pine-paneled A-frame a couple of miles away from the lake. The one-time fee ranges from $5 to $20, depending on the size and number of your dogs and the length of your stay. You can leave your dog unattended inside at your discretion. The cabin sleeps up to six, in two bedrooms and a loft, and includes a gas fireplace in the living room, a large back deck overlooking the wooded half acre of property, and an outside fire pit for toasting s'mores. Open May 1 November 1.

CAMPGROUNDS

National forest campgrounds: Three campgrounds (**Florida**, **Miller Creek**, and **Transfer Park**) are at Lemon Reservoir, 17 miles northeast of Durango, via CRs 240 and 243; Vallecito Lake has seven campgrounds, including the 80-site **Vallecito Campground**; **Junction Creek Campground** is just west of Durango on 25th St. (44 sites); **East Fork Campground** (26 sites), **Wolf Creek Campground** (26 sites), and **West Fork Campground** (28 sites) are all reached via Hwy. 160 east from Pagosa Springs, heading up Wolf Creek Pass.

Private campgrounds: **Durango East KOA** and **Lightner Creek Campground** in Durango; **Bruce Spruce Ranch**, **Pagosa Riverside Campground**, and **Sportman's Supply and Campground** in Pagosa Springs (see Creature Comforts for all).

OFF CAMPUS

In what may be a disappointment to the erudite canine, dogs are not allowed anywhere on the Fort Lewis College Campus, located on the eastern end of town.

WORTH A PAWS

Humane Society Thrift Stores

Both the La Plata County Humane Society and the Humane Society of Pagosa Springs operate secondhand stores. The La Plata store is at 1111 S. Camino del Rio (north of Walmart) in Durango (970-385-4322), and the other is at 269 Pagosa St. (Hwy. 160) in Pagosa Springs (970-264-6424). Both stores carry everything from clothing to home accessories and allow you to be a double do-gooder: not only will you be recycling whatever you buy, but proceeds go directly to the humane societies.

 Chimney Rock Archaeological Area. Guided tours only are available at the site of this one-time Ancestral Puebloan community, located between Durango and Pagosa Springs, but dogs are not allowed to participate. One kennel is available at the visitor center, where your dog can wait for you, and it's available on a first-come, first-serve basis. Dogs are welcome in wintertime (see Powderhounds). Call 970-883-5359 for more information.

DOGGIE DAYCARE

Durango

Akunow Kennel, 3705 CR 250, 970-259-8848, 800-516-0144, www.wonuka.com. $20/day. Located on 56-acre Wonuka Farm, the daycare facility has indoor kennels, and dogs get regular walks. Pickup and delivery can be arranged. Open 7 AM–9 PM every day.

Happy Paws Pet Spa, 1301 E. Florida Rd., 970-259-7917, www.happypawspetspa

.com. $2/hour. Dogs get to run free during the day, unless you request a kennel for yours. A water fountain made entirely of dog bowls is canine art, of a sort. Open 7:30 AM–5:30 PM, Monday to Friday.

Healthy Hounds & Fat Cats, 21738 Hwy. 160, Ste. B, 970-375-9700, www.healthy houndsandfatcats.com. $20/day; $14/half-day. Dogs can play in the large backyard (which has wading pools in summer) and in a 1,200-square-foot indoor playroom. Open 7 AM–6 PM, Monday to Friday; 5 AM–5 PM, Saturday. Earlier drop-offs and later pick-ups can be scheduled by appointment.

Puppy Love, 130 CR 234, 970-259-3043, 800-521-3843. $20–25/day, depending on size of dog. For an extra fee, the kennel will allow Durango & Silverton Narrow Gauge Railroad passengers to drop a dog off early or pick him up late. (The kennel is 10 minutes from the train station.) Regular hours are 7 AM–5:30 PM, Monday to Friday; 7 AM–noon and 2–5:30 PM, Saturday; 8–8:30 AM and 4–4:30 PM, Sunday.

Willow Tree Kennels, 6510 CR 203, 970-259-0018, www.willowtreedurango.com. $21–$25/day, depending on the size of dog (plus $5 if a dog isn't spayed or neutered). There's a $25 additional fee for dogs whose owners are taking the Durango & Silverton train and need an earlier drop-off or later pick-up. Regular hours are 8 AM–noon and 1–5 PM, Monday to Saturday; 8–10 AM and 3–4 PM, Sunday.

Ignacio

Pampered Pets, 2943 CR 321, 970-883-2220, www.frontier.net/~pwccinc. $15–$19/day, depending on the size of dog. In addition to playtime, dogs are walked twice a day, and, during warmer weather, they'll get to swim in a big pond on the property. Drop-off and pick-up are by appointment; pick-up and delivery to where you're staying can also be arranged, at an extra charge.

PET PROVISIONS
Bayfield
Village Feed & Supply, 39987 Hwy. 160, 970-884-4347

Durango
Creature Comforts, 305 S. Camino del Rio (in the Centennial Shopping Center), 970-247-2748

Healthy Hounds & Fat Cats, 21738 Hwy. 160, Ste. B, 970-375-9700, www.healthy houndsandfatcats.com

CANINE ER
Durango
Alpine Animal Hospital (AAHA certified), 2910 Main Ave., 970-247-5771, www.alpineanimaldurango.com. Open 7:45 AM–5:30 PM, Monday to Friday; 8 AM–noon, Saturday.

Durango Animal Hospital (AAHA certified), 2461 Main Ave., 970-247-3174. Open 8 AM–5:30 PM, Monday to Friday; 8 AM–3 PM, Saturday.

Riverview Animal Hospital (AAHA certified), 670 S. Camino del Rio, 970-247-8545, www.riverviewanimal.com. Open 7:30 AM–5:30 PM, Monday to Friday; 8–noon, Saturday.

Pagosa Springs
San Juan Veterinary Hospital (AAHA certified), 2197 E. Hwy. 160, 970-264-2629, www.sanjuanvethospital.com. Open 8 AM–5 PM, Monday to Friday; 8 AM–5 PM, Saturday (summer only).

RESOURCES
San Juan Public Lands Center (Bureau of Land Management/San Juan National Forest), 15 Burnett Ct., Durango, 970-247-4874

Columbine Ranger District East, San Juan National Forest, 367 Pearl St., Bayfield, 970-884-2512

Durango Area Tourism Office, 111 S. Camino del Rio, Durango, 970-247-0312, 800-525-8855, www.durango.org

Pagosa Ranger District, San Juan National Forest, 180 Pagosa St., Pagosa Springs, 970-264-2268

Pagosa Springs Area Chamber of Commerce, 402 San Juan St., Pagosa Springs, 970-264-2360, 800-252-2204, www.pagosa-springs.com

Vallecito Lake Chamber of Commerce, 970-247-1573, www.vallecitolakechamber.com

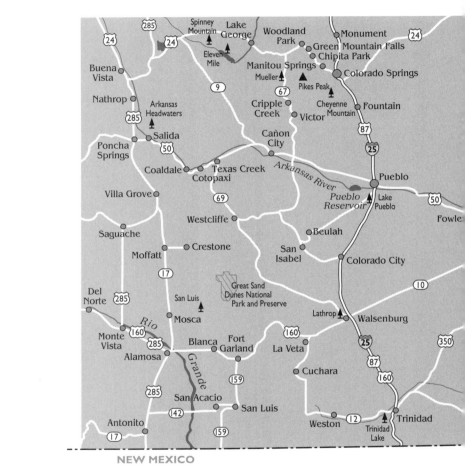

NEW MEXICO

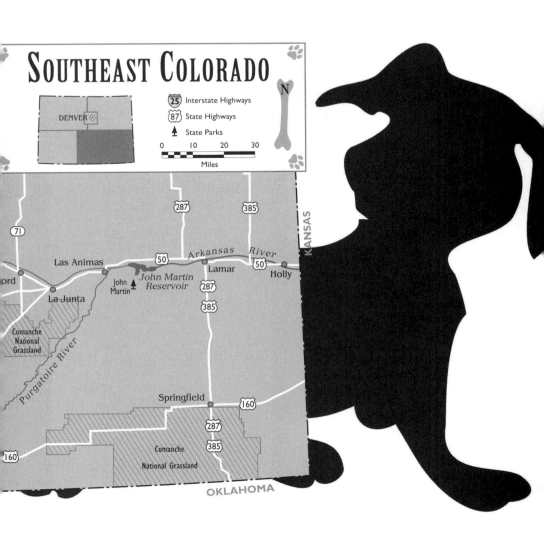

SOUTHEAST COLORADO

🐾

- 🛣 **25** Interstate Highways
- 🛡 **87** State Highways
- ▲ State Parks

N 🦴

DENVER ⊗

0 10 20 30
Miles

71

287

385

KANSAS

Las Animas 50 *Arkansas River* Lamar 50 Holly

ord

John Martin ▲ *John Martin Reservoir* 287

La Junta

385

Comanche
National
Grassland

Purgatoire River

Springfield 160

287

160

385

Comanche
National Grassland

OKLAHOMA

303

Twenty

San Luis Valley and Vicinity

THE BIG SCOOP

The San Luis Valley, 100 miles long and 50 miles wide, and bordered by the Sangre de Cristo Mountains to the east and the rugged San Juans to the west, encompasses a large portion of south-central Colorado. Though towns are few, small, and far between, your dog will exult in the thousands of acres of Rio Grande National Forest that stretch across the area. You'll be pleased that a wide variety of accommodations welcomes dogs, from remote cabin resorts to luxury inns. There's even a motel in Monte Vista from which you and your dog can watch movies at the drive-in theater next door. Note that dogs will have to pass up a ride on the Cumbres and Toltec Scenic Railroad, one of the area's few "organized" attractions, which runs between Antonito and Chama, New Mexico.

TAIL-RATED TRAILS

Great Sand Dunes National Park and Preserve
Access: Located 35 miles northeast of Alamosa via Hwy. 160 east and Hwy. 150 north. Entrance to the park is $3 per adult, and your pass is valid for a week. *Dogs must be leashed; they are primarily allowed only in the park and preserve's southeast corner.*

The sand dunes are the closest thing to the beach that your dog can experience in Colorado—minus all the water. At heights of up to 750 feet (higher than many midwestern ski areas), the dunes are the tallest in North America. Though your dog might not quite appreciate the stunning contrast between snowcapped peaks in the background and 30 square miles of sculpted sand, he'll certainly enjoy burrowing his nose in something new and different. You can bring him to the dunes play area, adjacent to the Dunes Parking Lot; the turnoff is just past the Visitor Center, on the left, and is the most popular part of the park to explore. There are no set trails across the dunes, so you're free to explore, as long as Fido stays leashed. In June, July, and August, the temperature of the sand can get as high as 140°—which will burn paw pads—so stick to hiking during the early morning or evening if you visit during those months. The only water you'll find is that of Medano Creek, which borders the dunes on the east and typically flows from late March to mid-July, so bring plenty along.

You can also take your dog on the short **Montville Nature Trail**, a .5-mile gravel-surface loop across the road from the Visitor Center; the **Wellington Ditch Trail**, which runs for about 1 mile between the Montville Trail and the Piñon Flats Campground; and the **Dunes Overlook Trail**, a .5-mile spur off the Sand Ramp Trail from the campground. The **Sand Ramp Trail** ultimately leads to the park's backcountry area and campsites; unfortunately, if you're planning a backpacking trip within the park, your dog won't be able to join you, as he's not allowed past the Point of No Return parking lot on this route. You and Fido, can however, hike the .5-mile **Sand Pit Trail** from that parking area to the Sand Pit picnic area alongside the dunes. And if you choose to take a four-wheel-drive trip (or even a hike) on the rugged **Medano Pass Primitive Road**, which starts at the Point of No Return, your dog can join you (and at the roadside car camping sites along it, too). For a change of pace from the sand, head east on the 7-mile round-trip **Mosca Pass Trail**, which borders Mosca Creek and climbs to 9,750-foot Mosca Pass. The trail is in the preserve up to Mosca Pass (after that point, it's national forest land), so your dog will have to hike on leash. 719-378-6399, www.nps.gov/grsa

San Luis State Park

Access: From Alamosa, head east on Hwy. 160 for 14.4 miles and turn north onto Hwy. 150. After 13.5 miles (a few miles before you reach the sand dunes), turn left onto Six Mile Ln.; the park entrance is 8 miles farther on the right. Entrance to the park is $6 per vehicle.

Dogs must be leashed.

Although the park does not contain the actual sand dunes of its well-known neighbor, the arid environment is desert-like, with only a few hardy plant species and a couple of shallow lakes. From the park, you and your dog are treated to a vista of extremes—the snowcapped four-teeners of the Sangre de Cristo Mountains fronted by the golden hues of the nearby Great Sand Dunes. (Stay until sunset and you and your four-legged friend may catch a stunner!)

There are two lakes at the park: the larger San Luis Lake, popular for water recreation, and the much smaller Head Lake, in the park's wildlife area. Four miles of connected wide gravel trails meander along the eastern half of San Luis Lake, past a wetlands area, and about three-quarters of the way around Head Lake. The northern part of the park—the wildlife area—is closed to visitors from February 15 to July 15. 719-738-2376, www.parks.state.co.us/parks/sanluis

Alamosa National Wildlife Refuge

Access: Located 3 miles east of Alamosa, off Hwy. 160. There's no entrance fee.

Dogs must be leashed.

The refuge is an 11,000-plus-acre preserve for thousands of migratory birds on the Rio Grande. Dogs are permitted on both of the trails: the 2-mile **Rio Grande Nature Trail** is a loop that begins and ends near the main parking area and traces the river for about a quarter of its length; the **Bluff Nature Trail** meanders for 1.5 miles (one way) in the park's southeast corner. 719-589-4021, www.fws.gov/alamosa

Clover on the trail to Mount Lindsay in the Sangre de Cristos.

CYCLING FOR CANINES

Four interconnected loop trails start just below the parking area for **Zapata Falls Recreation Area** (approximately 11 miles north of the Hwy. 160/150 intersection, or about 4 miles south of the entrance to the Great Sand Dunes, via a 3.5-mile gravel road that climbs east off Hwy. 150). Combine these loops of mellow, well-maintained singletrack, or various portions of them, for rides of anywhere from a couple of miles to 10. Afterward, you and your dog can cool off in the spray of nearby Zapata Falls, a .5-mile hike from the parking area (be sure your dog watches his footing around these powerful, 50-foot falls; reaching their base requires a bit of wading through South Zapata Creek and then venturing briefly up a narrow gorge).

CREATURE COMFORTS

Unless otherwise stated, dogs should not be left unattended in the room or cabin.

Alamosa

$–$$ Alamosa KOA and Kamping Kabins, 6900 Juniper Ln., 719-589-9757, 800-562-9157, www.alamosakoa.com. Dogs are allowed in the three camper cabins here (you'll need to provide your own sleeping and cooking gear), about 3.5 miles east of Alamosa. Open mid-March to December 31.

$–$$ Days Inn Alamosa, 224 O'Keefe Pkwy., 719-589-9037, www.daysinn .com. There's a $10 per visit charge to stay with your dog in one of the designated pet-friendly rooms.

$–$$ Valley Motel, 2051 Main, 719-589-9095, 800-726-0078. Dogs are charged a nightly fee based on their size, from $5 to $20. So if you're traveling with your Great Dane, say, you might want to have him crouch on the way in.

$$ Alamosa Lamplighter Motel, 425 Main, 719-589-6636, 800-359-2138, www .alamosalamplightermotel.com. Some rooms at this basic motel are pet friendly for an additional—and somewhat unusual—fee of $6.77 per night, per pet.

$$ Best Western Alamosa Inn, 2005 Main, 719-589-2567, 800-459-5123, www.best westerncolorado.com. Dogs under 20 pounds can stay in one of five pet-friendly rooms at the motel for $15 extra per dog, per night.

$$ Inn of the Rio Grande, 333 Santa Fe Ave., 719-589-5833, 800-669-1658, www .innoftherio.com. Dogs are permitted to stay in any of the rooms at this nicely appointed motel with a $25 deposit. You can leave your dog unattended inside the room if he's quiet—extra points if he's crated in a travel kennel. A restaurant and a water park (for human kids) are on-site.

$$ Super 8 Alamosa, 2505 W. Main, 719-589-6447, www.super8.com. The motel charges a $10 fee per visit, per dog.

$$–$$$ Holiday Inn Express Hotel and Suites, 3418 Mariposa, 719-589-4026, 888-465-4329 (national number), www .hiexpress.com. Dogs can stay for a $5 nightly fee.

Antonito

$–$$ Mogote Meadow Cabin and RV Park, 34127 Hwy. 17 (5 miles west of Antonito), 719-376-5774, 800-814-0129, www .mogotemeadow.com. Two two-bedroom cabins and one mobile home (as well as an RV park and camping sites) on 7 grassy acres are available to you and your dog, as long as he's 30 pounds or under. There's a $5 fee per night, per pet. Your dog can be left unattended in your cabin as long as he's in a travel kennel; keep him leashed when you're exploring together outside. Open May 1 to November 15.

$–$$ Ponderosa Campground and Cabins, 19234 Hwy. 17 (16 miles west of Antonito), 719-376-5857, www.colorado directory.com/ponderosacampcabins. The campground, along the Conejos River, also has six furnished cabins available, three equipped with a refrigerator and a hot plate for cooking and three with kitchenettes and private baths. Dogs are welcome with a $20 fee per visit and as long as they're kept leashed when outside. Open mid-May to September 30.

$$ Conejos River Anglers, 34591 Hwy. 17 (5 miles west of Antonito), 719-376-5660, www.conejosriveranglers.com. The specialty here is guided fly-fishing trips on the close-by Conejos River, which, unless you know how to transform fish into beefsteak, probably won't excite your dog very much. Nonetheless, he's welcome to join you in any of the four two-bedroom, fully equipped cabins for a $5 nightly fee. The owners also rent out a separate two-bedroom log cabin 15 miles west of Antonito on the Conejos River that's dog friendly. Open April 1 to November 10.

$$ Narrow Gauge Railroad Inn, 5200 Hwy. 285, 719-376-5441, 800-323-9469, www.narrowgaugerailroadinn.info. Dogs are accepted with a $10 one-time fee at this motel adjacent to the Cumbres and Toltec Railroad station. There's also an RV park here.

Former greyhound racers Crema and Spro enjoy a life of leisure.

$$ Platoro Valley Lodge and Cabins, FR 250 (about 45 miles west of Antonito), 719-376-2321, 325-223-1968 (Nov.– April), 877-752-8676, www.platorovalley cabins.com. Twelve rustic cabins, some multiroom and fully equipped, some single room with no cooking facilities, sit on this 2-acre site in "downtown" Platoro. Dogs (usually one per visit) are permitted in most of the cabins for $10 extra per night. A continental breakfast for all guests is served daily in the main lodge. Open Memorial Day to October 31.

$$ Twin Rivers Guest Ranch and RV Park, 34044 Hwy. 17 (5 miles west of Antonito), 719-376-5710, 800-873-6981, www.twnrvrs.com. For larger dogs (e.g., retriever size), there's a two-dog limit in these eight fully equipped cabins, which are on 13 acres by the Conejos River. For all dogs, there's a $10 one-time fee per pet. Keep your dog on a leash on the property. Open May 1 to October 31.

$$–$$$ Conejos Cabins, FR 250 (about 46 miles west of Antonito), 719-376-2547, 417-842-3279 or 877-376-2547 in winter, www.conejoscabins.com. Near Platoro Reservoir and well into the Rio Grande National Forest, west of Antonito, these rustic log cabins on the banks of the Conejos River afford you and your dog relative solitude. The 10 one- and two-bedroom cabins are fully equipped, and four have fireplaces. There's a limit of one dog per cabin, with a $10 fee per night. Make sure to keep your dog leashed when he's outside. Open Memorial Day to mid-October.

$$–$$$ Conejos Canyon River Ranch, 25390 Hwy. 17 (14 miles west of Antonito), 719-376-2464, www.conejos ranch.com. Choose from among the eight lodge rooms (breakfast included) or eleven fully equipped one- to three-bedroom cabins. Part of the ranch's main building is more than a hundred years old. There's a $10 one-time fee for dogs, who will probably be eager to explore the ranch's 15 acres within the Rio Grande National Forest—which they can do leash free—or play along the mile of Conejos River frontage. If you do need to leave Fido behind for any length of time (say, to ride the Cumbres and Toltec Scenic Railroad), there are four kennels at the ranch; the three resident dogs may keep your dog company, too. A restaurant is on the premises, and horseback rides are also available. Open May 1 through October 31.

$$–$$$ River's Inn and Swiss Cottage Bed and Breakfast, 317 River St., 719-376-6029, www.antonitobedandbreakfast .net. Dogs are considered on a case-by-case basis at this B&B in downtown Antonito. Those that pass muster can stay in one of the four guest rooms, each with hardwood floors and antique furnishings, for $10 extra per night. Two of the rooms have private baths; the other two share a bath. The house itself dates from 1907, and the rooms vary in size and decor, which accounts for the range of rates. You can leave your dog unattended inside only if he's in a travel crate; other options would be to contain him in the inn's fenced yard or see if owner Ursula Armijo Knobel might be able to keep an eye on him. The Swiss Cottage is a separate guesthouse behind the main house that is currently under renovation and will eventually be available for nightly rentals.

$$–$$$ Skyline Lodge, 23040 FR 250 (about 46 miles west of Antonito), 719-376-2226, 719-580-5386 in winter, www.skylineranchreserve.com. Operating since 1945, the lodge, in the former gold- and silver-mining town of Platoro, is among the more remote accommodations listed for Antonito. Luckily, a restaurant and a general store are on-site (as well as

stables and a guide service for hunting and fishing trips). You could have an idyllic stay here with your dog in either one of the six lodge rooms or one of thirteen fully outfitted cabins. There's a $20 one-time pet fee. Dogs can be left unattended inside; they must stay on leash with their owners on the property, which is next to the Conejos River. Open Memorial Day to October 30.

$$$ Gold Pan Acres, 120 Conejos Ave., Platoro (about 45 miles west of Antonito), 719-376-5543, 254-634-5722 (Nov.–April), www.goldpanrv.com. This complex, on 100 acres on the eastern edge of Platoro, includes an RV park, a general store, and a "family cabin," a three-bedroom-plus-loft, 2,500-square-foot house that can sleep up to 16. Up to two dogs are welcome, too, for $10 per night, per pet, and there's a seven-day minimum for renting the cabin. Four new cabins were slated to open in summer 2009, and at least some, if not all, will be pet friendly; inquire for details. Keep your dog leashed when outside. Open Memorial Day to October 31.

Creede

$–$$ Bruce's Snowshoe Lodge, 202 E. 8th St. (at Hwy. 149), 719-658-2315, 866-658-2315, www.snowshoelodge.net. The motel allows dogs in about half of its rooms for $10 extra per night, per dog.

$$–$$$ The Old Firehouse Bed and Breakfast, 123 N. Main St., 719-658-0212, 800-609-7369, ext. 705, www.theold firehouse.com. Now a restaurant in addition to a B&B, the building, which dates to 1893, was indeed Creede's firehouse for many years, as well as a general store in its earliest years. For a $20 one-time fee, dogs under 20 pounds (which, ironically, excludes dalmatians) are welcome to stay in one of the four rooms, all nicely appointed with antique furnishings and exposed brick walls. One of the four units is actually a two-room suite, and all have private bath. A restaurant downstairs serves Italian-style fare for dinner, as well as breakfast and lunch. Open May 1 to September 30.

$$–$$$ RC Guest Ranch, 37531 Hwy. 149 (17 miles southwest of Creede), 719-658-2253, www.rcguestranch.com. The ranch, which has operated for more than 100 years, accepts dogs in its nine authentic log cabins, which range from one to three bedrooms and have kitchens and baths. You'll need to keep your dog leashed on the surrounding 50 acres. The ranch also offers horseback trail rides and pack trips, as well as fishing and hunting trips into the nearby Weminuche Wilderness. You can bring your own horse here, too. Open May 15 to November 1.

$$$ The Club at the Cliffs, 719-873-5266, 361-749-6251 ext. 2206 (Nov.–April), www.clubatcliffs.com. This pair of quaintly furnished cabins on the banks of Willow Creek, on the outskirts of Creede, are dog friendly on a case-by-case basis. Each cabin sleeps up to four, and both have full kitchens. One is a century-old miner's cabin, and the other dates to the mid-20th century. There's a $20 one-time fee for dogs and a two-dog limit. You can keep your dog unattended inside if he's secured in a travel kennel. Open May 1 to October 31.

Crestone
$$ Casa Alegria Bed and Breakfast, 1986 Lost Cave Wy., 719-256-5116, www .casaalegria.crestonecolorado.com. Dogs who are into sustainable-building techniques may leap at the chance to stay at this strawbale house, which has adobe floors and walls, radiant heating, and Mexican tile accents. The B&B room has its own bath, private entrance, and an attached screened-in porch. There's

a two-dog limit, and a pet fee of $8 per night for up to two nights (if you stay longer, the fee won't exceed the $16). Owner JoAnn DeHavelin asks that you keep your dog on a leash when outside (the area her house is in, known as the Baca, has a strictly enforced leash law), and to let her know if your dog is an on-the-bed sleeper—she'll provide another blanket. The host dog is a Shih Tzu and loves to play with the four-legged guests.

$$ The Coll House Bed and Breakfast, 1019 Moonlight Wy., 719-256-4475, www .collhouse.com. This homey B&B about 3 miles from downtown Crestone has a variety of accommodations, and dogs are welcome in all for $10 per night, with a limit of two. Of the three standard rooms in the house, two have private baths. There's also a studio that sleeps up to four people with a full kitchen, woodstove, and separate entrance, and a one-bedroom apartment, with a private entrance and a kitchenette, that can sleep up to six. The trailhead to Willow Lake, a popular hike in the area, is within walking distance. And since B&B owner Marcia Heusted is also a certified bodyworker, you can arrange for in-room massage or a variety of other treatments, including intuitive readings for you and your dog.

$$ White Eagle Village, 67485 CR T (4 miles west of Crestone), 719-256-4865, 800-613-2270, www.whiteeaglevillage .com. This nonsmoking hotel and retreat center offers a few designated pet rooms for $10 extra per night. In keeping with Crestone's wellness vibe (both physical and spiritual), an acupuncture center is on-site and a fleet of massage therapists is on call.

Del Norte
$$ Country Family Inn, 1050 Grand Ave., 719-657-3581, 800-372-2331, www .countryfamilyinn.com. This basic motel

also has a café that comes in handy if you or your dog need a snack.

Fort Garland

$ The Lodge, 825 Hwy. 160, 719-379-2880, www.thelodgemotelcolorado.com. All 12 rooms are pet friendly, with a $5 one-time fee. You can leave your dog unattended inside as long as you let the front desk know. All rooms have microwaves and refrigerators. The Lodge can also accommodate your horse, with advance reservations.

Moffatt

$$ Willow Spring Bed and Breakfast, 223 Moffatt Wy., 719-256-4116, www.willow-spring.com. Dogs with responsible owners are welcome to stay at this nine-room B&B, housed in a hotel built in 1910. In keeping with the historic theme, the rooms, all of which share baths, are furnished with antiques, and Oriental rugs warm up the communal living room and parlor on the first floor.

Monte Vista

$–$$ Rio Grande Motel, 25 N. Broadway, 719-852-3516, 800-998-7129, www.rio grandemotel.net. There's a $5 fee per pet, per night. Your dog might prick up his ears at the wildlife-themed decor.

$$ Best Western Movie Manor, 2830 W. Hwy. 160, 719-852-5921, 800-771-9468, www.bestwesterncolorado.com. Unique in its own right, your stay here can be enhanced by the company of your dog. True to its name, the Movie Manor provides big-screen entertainment (from May to September) via the drive-in theater next door. Your room is equipped with speakers, so you can just lie on the bed and watch away. Dogs are restricted to smoking rooms only, however, and there's a $10 fee per night, per dog.

$$–$$$ Pecosa Inn, 1519 Grand Ave., 719-852-3584, 888-732-6724, www .pecosainn.com. The motel includes an indoor pool and hot tub.

Mosca

$ Great Sand Dunes Oasis and Camper Cabins, 5400 Hwy. 150 North (at the entrance to the national monument), 719-378-2222, www.greatdunes.com. Dogs are allowed in the four camping cabins (bring your own bedding) but not in the motel rooms. Make sure your dog is on leash when outside. Open April 1 to November 1.

$$–$$$ Great Sand Dunes Lodge, 7900 Hwy. 150 North (at the entrance to the national monument), 719-378-2900, www.gsdlodge.com. The motel allows dogs in some rooms with a $10 per-night fee and $15 per night for two dogs. Open mid-March to mid-October.

Saguache

$–$$ Saguache Campground and Lodge, 21495 Hwy. 285, 719-655-2264. This small motel also has a restaurant on-site, the Gunbarrel Steak House, which is open Thursday to Monday. Two of the motel rooms have kitchenettes.

South Fork

$–$$ The Inn Motel, 30362 Hwy. 160 West, 719-873-5514, 800-233-9723, www.innsouthfork.com. It's $5 per night, per dog, for canine guests, with a maximum fee of $25 per stay. Three two-bedroom cabins are also available for rent. You can leave your dog unattended inside for a short while if he's in a travel kennel.

$–$$$ Spruce Lodge, 29431 Hwy. 160 West, 719-873-5605, 800-228-5605, www .sprucelodges.com. The lodge, a log structure built in 1924 to house local sawmill workers, offers B&B rooms (not dog friendly) as well as three fully equipped cabins where your dog can stay with you.

A $20–$50 fee will be assessed at checkout if your dog has done any damage to your cabin.

$$ Allington Inn and Suites, 0182 E. Frontage Rd., 719-873-5600, 800-285-6590, www.allingtoninn.com. Dogs can stay in five of the rooms at this larger motel (it was formerly a Comfort Inn) for a $10 nightly fee per pet.

$$ America's Best Value Inn/Wolf Creek Lodge, 31042 Hwy. 160, 719-873-5547, 800-874-0416, www.wolfcreekskilodge.com. Eleven of the rooms are pet friendly, for $10 per pet, per night. Some motel rooms are also available with kitchenettes, and three of these are dog friendly. If you're not cooking for yourself, Nino's restaurant at the lodge serves American and Mexican food.

$$ Budget Host Ute Bluff Lodge, 27680 Hwy. 160 West, 719-873-5595, 800-473-0595, www.utebluﬄodge.com. The lodge offers seven cozy cabins (from studios to three bedrooms), with kitchens and gas fireplaces, and motel rooms, and dogs are welcome in select ones for $5 per pet, per night. Extra bedspreads are available for your dog's sleeping comfort. Keep your dog leashed around the lodge and cabins and while walking up to the bluff on the property; past the bluff, it's okay to let Fido off his leash so he can explore the rest of the surrounding 17 acres, adjacent to national forest land.

$$ Chinook Lodge and Smokehouse, 29666 Hwy. 160 West, 719-873-1707, 888-890-9110, www.chinooklodge.net. Your dog will probably start salivating as soon as you tell him that the lodge's 11 cabins, on 8.5 acres, are next to a smokehouse. All kinds of smoked meats are for sale, as well as smoked trout and salmon. As for the cabins, they were built in the late 1800s and have been used for guest lodging since 1908. They range in size from one to two bedrooms, and most have kitchens and rock fireplaces. Dogs pay a $5 nightly fee. Open mid-May to September 30.

$$ Goodnight's Lonesome Dove Cabins, 180065 Hwy. 160 West (6 miles west of South Fork), 719-873-1072, 800-551-3683, www.goodnightslonesomedove.com. Dogs are permitted in the 10 fully outfitted log cabins, ranging from one to three bedrooms, for a $15 one-time fee per pet. They must stay on leash when outside the cabins. Rocky, the resort's canine mascot, will be happy to show your dog around. In summer, RV and tent sites are available, too, as well as a minigolf course.

$$ Grandview Cabins and RV Park, 613 Hwy. 149 West, 719-873-5541, 800-713-3251, www.grandview.com. All of the 12 fully furnished cabins (some have fireplaces) are dog compatible. There's a $10 fee per night, per pet. Open April 15 to Thanksgiving.

$$ Lazy Bear Cabins, 29257 Hwy. 160 West, 719-873-1443, 877-873-1443, www.lazybearcabins.com. For $5 a night, per dog (with a maximum charge of $25 per stay), up to two dogs are welcome in any of the nine two-bedroom, fully out-fitted cabins. They can be left unattended inside as long as they're in a travel kennel but, more likely, your dog would enjoy sniffing around the surrounding 3 acres under voice control with you.

$$ Rainbow Lodge, 719-873-5571, 888-873-5174, www.rainbowsouthfork.biz. Dogs are welcome in the 16 one- and two-bedroom cabins, all with kitchens, at this complex right in the town of South Fork. You can leave your dog unattended inside for a short time, if necessary. Keep your dog leashed outside the cabins;

there's room to take him for a stroll. A small grocery and fly-fishing gear rental shop is at the lodge.

$$ South Fork Lodge and RV Park, 0364 Hwy. 149, 719-873-5303, 877-354-2345, www.coloradodirectory.com/southfork lodge. Dogs can stay the 12 fully furnished cabins for a $5 nightly fee, per dog, with a limit of two dogs per cabin. The owners ask that you be extradiligent about not letting Fido on the bed. You can leave your dog unattended in the cabin if he's in a travel crate, and you must keep him on a leash when outside.

$$–$$$ Wolf Creek Ranch Ski Lodge, 177022 W. Hwy. 160 (9 miles west of South Fork), 719-873-5371, 800-522-9653, www.wolfcreekco.com. The lodge complex is halfway between South Fork and the Wolf Creek ski area. For a $20 per pet one-time fee, your dog can join you in any of seven fully equipped cabins or eight basic motel rooms with kitchenettes. The cabins (two are really two-story houses) vary widely in size and style; some have fireplaces, woodstoves, or hot tubs, and three are right on the South Fork of the Rio Grande. The ranch offers summer horseback rides and winter horse-drawn sleigh rides.

$$–$$$$ Foothills Lodge and Cabins, 0035 Silverthread Ln., 719-873-5969, 800-510-3897, www.foothillslodgeandcabins .com. For a $7 per-night, per-pet fee (with a maximum charge of $50 per visit), the lodge happily accommodates dogs in four of its log cabins, all with full kitchens, three of its lodge cabins, which are attached dwellings, and its off-site cabin. Four units are always pet friendly, while the other four allow dog guests on a case-by-case basis, though it's clear where owner Karen Kovacik's sentiments lie. "We'd rather have the animals than the people," she admits. Two of the lodge

cabins are two-bedroom units with kitchens, and the third dog-friendly one is basically a motel room. The lodge also rents out the two-bedroom, two-bath alpine cabin, 3 miles away, which sleeps up to 10 and has a fenced enclosure for dogs. Exceptionally well-behaved, quiet dogs may be able to be left unattended inside their cabins or in an outside pet enclosure (the Elk cabin also has one); talk to the lodge staff. You must keep your dog leashed outside. Daisy, Bugsy, and Hailey are the lodge's official canine greeters.

$$–$$$$ Riverbend Resort, 33846 Hwy. 160 West, 719-873-5344, 800-621-6512, www.riverbend-resort.com. For a $10 one-time fee, per pet, Rover can stay with you in one of the 12 fully equipped studio to four-bedroom cabins with fireplace at this resort that once did double service as a movie set for National Lampoon's *Vacation.* Although you should keep your dog leashed when walking around the property, he can play along some of the resort's .75 mile of private frontage on the South Fork of the Rio Grande under voice control. RV and tent sites are available, too.

$$$–$$$$ Cottonwood Cove Lodge and Cabins, 13046 Hwy. 149 West (13 miles from South Fork), 719-658-2242, www .cottonwoodcove.com. Dogs are welcome in the resort's cabins, though not in the lodge, for a $20 one-time fee per pet. All of the 28 fully outfitted cabins are pet friendly. They range from studio size to three bedrooms, and some are on the river. There's a restaurant on the premises that specializes in homemade pie, among other things, and the lodge offers rafting trips, horseback rides, and jeep rentals. Open Memorial Day to mid-November.

Villa Grove

$$ Bonanza Inn Bed and Breakfast, 49130 CR LL 56, 719-655-2834 (712-683-5726,

Nov. 15–May 1), www.bonanzainnbbrv .com. Four of the six B&B rooms are dog friendly, with a limit of one dog per room. Each is simply furnished with log furniture and knotty-pine interiors and has a private bath. Outside the house is a deck with hot tub. Pets are also welcome in the on-site RV park, but not in the cabin. If you leave your dog unattended, he must be in a travel kennel. Open Memorial Day weekend to mid-October.

$$ Inn at Villa Grove, 34094 Hwy. 285, 719-655-2203. This small motel has three rooms and accepts dogs with a $10 one-time fee. You can leave your dog unattended in the room. Also on-site is the Villa Grove Trade, a convenience/general store with a deli.

$$–$$$ Joyful Journey Hot Springs Spa, 28640 CR 58 EE, 719-256-4328, 800-673-0656 (pin #4328), www.joyful journeyhotsprings.com. Is your pup stressed out from chasing too many sticks or tennis balls? Bring him to this mineral hot-springs resort for a nature-focused spa getaway. He can stay with you in two of the on-site yurts (furnished with beds) or any of the three tipis (available Memorial Day weekend to the end of October; bring a sleeping bag) for $20 extra per night. RV and tent sites are also pet friendly, though not the resort's lodge rooms. When you're ready for a soak in one of the three outdoor pools or a massage, facial, or body wrap, Fido can stay in the on-site kennel, which has two large spaces. Keep him on a leash when you're walking through the resort's outdoor common areas.

CAMPGROUNDS
Great Sand Dunes National Monument, 35 miles northeast of Alamosa via Hwys. 160 and 150. The Piñon Flats Campground (88 sites) is open year-round.

San Luis State Park. See Tail-Rated Trails for directions. The Mosca Campground has 51 sites.

National forest campgrounds: **Highway Springs Campground,** west of South Fork on Hwy. 160 (11 sites); **Big Meadows Campground,** at Big Meadows Reservoir, FR 410 off Hwy. 160, west of South Fork (60 sites); **River Hill Campground** (23 sites), **Thirty Mile Campground** (39 sites), and **Lost Trail Campground** (7 sites) are all on FR 520 by Rio Grande Reservoir, off Hwy. 149, 21 miles southwest of Creede; **Mogote Campground** (40 sites) and **Aspen Glade Campground** (32 sites) are both on Hwy. 17 west of Antonito; **Trujillo Meadows Campground,** by Trujillo Meadows Reservoir at Cumbres Pass, west of Antonito on Hwy. 17 (50 sites); **North Crestone Campground** (13 sites) on Alder St. in Crestone.

Private campgrounds: **Alamosa KOA** in Alamosa; **Mogote Meadow, Ponderosa Campground,** and **Twin Rivers Guest Ranch and RV Park** in Antonito; **Great Sand Dunes Oasis** at the entrance to Great Sand Dunes National Monument; **Goodnight's Lonesome Dove Cabins** and **Riverbend Resort** in South Fork; **Joyful Journey Hot Springs Spa** in Villa Grove (see Creature Comforts for all).

DOGGIE DAYCARE
Alamosa
Alamosa Valley Veterinary Clinic, 7038 Hwy. 160, 719-589-2615. $10–$14/day, depending on the size of dog. Open 8 AM–5:30 PM, Monday to Friday; 8 AM–noon, Saturday.

Dog Days Inn Pet Hotel, 603 Lava Ln., 719-589-3988, www.dogdaysco.com. $2/hour. There's a large outdoor dog run, as well as indoor kennels. Open 7:30 AM–1 PM and 3:30 PM–6 PM, Monday to Friday; 7:30 AM–noon and 3:30–6 PM,

Saturday; 7:30–10 AM and 4–6 PM, Sunday.

Monte Vista
Alpine Veterinary Hospital, 2835 Sherman, 719-852-2561. $17–$23/day, depending on dog size. Open 8 AM–5:30 PM, Monday to Friday; 9 AM–noon, Saturday.

PET PROVISIONS
Alamosa
Alamosa Valley Veterinary Clinic, 7038 Hwy. 160, 719-589-2615

Dog Days Inn Pet Hotel, 603 Lava Ln. 719-589-3988. There's also a self-service dog wash, for $8 per dog, which includes shampoo, towels, grooming tools, and drying.

Monte Vista
Alpine Veterinary Hospital, 2835 Sherman, 719-852-2561

Monte Vista Animal Clinic, 1851 Hwy. 160, 719-852-5504

CANINE ER
Alamosa
Alamosa Valley Veterinary Clinic, 7038 Hwy. 160, 719-589-2615. Open 8 AM–5:30 PM, Monday to Friday; 8 AM–noon, Saturday.

Creede
Creede Animal Clinic, 24251 W. Hwy. 149, 719-658-2614. Open 7 AM–noon, Monday to Friday.

Monte Vista
Alpine Veterinary Hospital, 2835 Sherman, 719-852-2561. Open 8 AM–5:30 PM, Monday to Friday; 9 AM–noon, Saturday.

Monte Vista Animal Clinic, 1851 Hwy. 160, 719-852-5504. Open 8 AM–noon and 1–5 PM, Monday to Friday; 8 AM–noon, Saturday.

RESOURCES
Colorado Welcome Center/Alamosa Convention and Visitors Bureau, 601 State Ave., Alamosa, 719-589-4840, 800-258-7597BLU-SKYS, www.alamosa.org

Conejos County Tourist Information, 719-376-2049, 800-835-1098, www.conejos vacation.com

Conejos Peak Ranger District, Rio Grande National Forest/Bureau of Land Management, 15571 CR T-5, La Jara, 719-274-8971

Creede/Mineral County Chamber of Commerce, 1207 N. Creede Ave., Creede, 719-658-2374, 800-327-2102, www.creede .com

Divide Ranger District/Creede Office, Rio Grande National Forest, 304 S. Main, Creede, 719-658-2556 (closed from mid-November to mid-April)

Divide Ranger District/Del Norte Office, 13308 W. Hwy. 160, Del Norte, 719-657-3321

Saguache Ranger District, Rio Grande National Forest/Bureau of Land Management, 46525 Hwy. 114, Saguache, 719-655-2547

San Luis Valley Visitor Center, 947 1st Ave., Monte Vista, 719-852-0660

South Fork Visitor Center, 28 Silver Thread Ln., South Fork, 719-873-5512, 800-571-0881, www.southfork.org

Supervisor's Office, Rio Grande National Forest, 1803 W. Hwy. 160, Monte Vista, 719-852-5941

Twenty-One
Arkansas River Valley and Vicinity

THE BIG SCOOP

The San Isabel National Forest figures prominently in the area described in this chapter, which includes the Arkansas River towns of Buena Vista, Salida, and Cañon City as well as Monarch Pass to the west and the Wet Mountains to the south. This translates into a wide range of dog-friendly hikes, many with no leash requirements. The buff dog might want to hike up one of the eleven 14,000-plus-foot peaks that dot the Sawatch Range in

Pam Seidler and Cisco pause near Ptarmigan Lake.

the area west of Hwy. 285. You can also bring Fido to several more traditional tourist attractions. However, he will have to sit out the raft trips that draw crowds to the area during the summer.

All the major towns in this vicinity have leash laws in effect. Chaffee County (which includes Buena Vista, Salida, and Poncha Springs) permits dogs to be under voice control. In Fremont County (home to Cañon City), dogs must be leashed everywhere (though the county does not patrol forest service trails). And, unfortunately, all town parks in Salida are closed to canines.

TAIL-RATED TRAILS

The forest service offices in Salida and Cañon City and the BLM office in Cañon City can provide details on the hundreds of trails in the area. In addition, the Cañon City visitor center (see Resources) has a brochure with local trail descriptions.

Buena Vista

Ptarmigan Lake
Distance: 6.6 miles round-trip
Elevation gain: 1,500 feet
Trailhead: From the intersection of Hwy. 285 and Cottonwood Pass Rd. in Buena Vista, drive 14.5 miles up the pass road to the trailhead parking on the left.
Dogs can be off leash.
The lake is a classically beautiful tarn tucked into the mountains just east of the

Continental Divide. And unlike the hikes on the north side of Cottonwood Pass Rd., this one is not in designated wilderness, so Rover can hike under voice control. You'll begin your hike by crossing Middle Cottonwood Creek immediately after the trailhead, then following a steady though gradual ascent through thick stands of spruce and subalpine fir, with an occasional view of high peaks to the south. After a little more than 1 mile, cross a forest service road and pick up the trail on the other side. When you eventually hit a few switchbacks and cross Ptarmigan Creek, you're almost at your destination. To reach Ptarmigan Lake, veer left off the trail at an obvious junction and go slightly downhill (the trail continues to a saddle). While your dog cools off in the water, enjoy the views of the 13,000-foot peaks that abut the lake on three sides. Look northeast, and in the distance you'll see the imposing flanks of 14,196-foot Mount Yale.

Chica on the trail to Mount Harvard, a fourteener near Buena Vista.

Barbara Whipple Trail

Distance: 1.4 miles round-trip (with shorter options available)

Elevation gain: About 375 feet

Trailhead: Head east on Buena Vista's Main St. until it ends at River Park. There's ample parking here.

Dogs must be leashed.

This short trail network that starts at the Arkansas River offers great views of town, the water, and the Collegiate Peaks to the west. And several kiosks along the trail give info about Buena Vista, past and present. From the parking area, cross the bridge and pick up the trail on the other side. You and your dog then have a few options: you can follow the main Whipple Trail as it traverses south on a bench above the river, then snakes its way up a piñon-sagebrush hillside where it ends at a junction with the Midland Trail (the old railroad grade). Or stay left shortly after the bridge and take the Whipple Trail's designated Steep Shortcut (if you're moderately fit it's not so bad—our 19-month-old hiked it, with hand-holding). Then go right at the next intersection to catch a hillside traverse. When you meet up again with the main Whipple Trail shortly after, go left to climb to the Midland Trail intersection; or, if you want an even shorter loop hike, stay right and follow the trail as it traverses above the river and back to the bridge.

Before or after your hike, take some time to explore the short gravel trails that run north and south along the Arkansas on the parking area side of the river. Your dog can cool off, and you and he can watch kayakers surf and spin on the waves in the kayak park play holes along this stretch of water.

Buena Vista Wildlife Trail.

This short trail along Cottonwood Creek, reached via CRs 306 and 361, accesses a popular fishing area and is on land owned by the Division of Wildlife; dogs are not permitted.

Monarch Pass

Waterdog Lakes

Distance: 4 miles round-trip

Elevation gain: 1,275 feet

Trailhead: From the intersection of Hwys. 50 and 285

at Poncha Springs, take 50 west (toward Monarch Pass) for 15 miles. Parking is at the side of the highway on the left. The trail begins on the opposite side of the road. *Dogs can be off leash.*

The name alone may cause your dog's ears to prick up with interest. The trail leads to a pair of lakes scenically situated right at the base of the Continental Divide near the top of Monarch Pass. From the trailhead, cross a small stream and follow the gradual ascent through cool, fragrant stands of ponderosa pine and Douglas fir. The trail steepens during the final approach to Lower Waterdog Lake until breaking out onto a grassy hillside—studded with wildflowers midsummer—just before the lake. An informal trail leads to the upper lake, about an eighth of a mile farther.

Florence

Newlin Creek Trail

Distance: 5.4 miles round-trip
Elevation gain: 1,360 feet
Trailhead: From its intersection with Hwy. 50 in Cañon City, head south on 9th St. (Colorado 115) to the town of Florence. From here, continue south on Hwy. 67 for 4.6 miles to CR 15. Turn right. From this point, it's 6.5 miles to the trailhead. Once you pass the Florence Mountain Park, the road becomes a little rougher and rutted, but a regular (i.e., lower profile) car should be able to handle it. At 2.8 miles from the start of CR 15, bear right. Bear right again at 4.4 miles. The road ends at a parking area. *Dogs can be off leash.*

The trail begins on an old logging road. It's not until about .5 mile in that you'll actually encounter Newlin Creek, a merry little meandering stream rife with cascades. After you cross over to the creek's south side, via a bridge, the narrow, rock-walled canyon opens up. Some interesting rock features still appear,

however, on the north side. The invigorating scent of ponderosa pine accompanies your hike along the Newlin drainage, a moderate uphill throughout. Fido is apt to enjoy the multiple creek crossings (on rocks and logs). There's no lake destination for this hike, but if your dog is goal oriented, go as far as the meadow, where you'll find a sign marking the remains of the Herrick Sawmill, from 1887. You'll be face to face with the remains of a steam boiler from the operation; a small map shows the sites of other mill ruins in the vicinity.

Cañon City

Arkansas Riverwalk

Distance: About 7 miles of trail along the Arkansas River (which includes the 1.2-mile loop in John Griffin Park)
Access: There are a few different access points, but this one is the most central: from Hwy. 50 in Cañon City, head south on Raynolds Ave. (the second traffic light in town if coming from the east). After crossing the Arkansas (in less than 1 mile), look for a trailhead sign and a large parking area on the left. *Dogs must be leashed.*

Although just a short distance from busy Hwy. 50, the wide gravel riverfront trail seems miles away. It's just you and your dog, the rushing of the water, and the rustle of cottonwood leaves in this verdant setting. Benches are strategically placed in shady spots along the route. If you're looking for a good jogging path for you and the pooch, this is the place. Head west (under the bridge) from the parking area, and you'll get a nice view of the jagged Sangre de Cristo Mountains rising to the west. This direction will bring you to the loop around John Griffin Park, a 75-acre nature area that also has some unmaintained paths leading through it.

Clover contemplates the view from atop Mount Columbia.

CYCLING FOR CANINES

Mountain-biking options abound in this area, but keep in mind that many of the ones you'll see mentioned in guides involve riding on dirt roads with vehicle traffic. When you want to take your dog along, try a section of the **Rainbow Trail**, which runs for 100 miles from southwest of Salida to Music Pass south of Westcliffe. One of the best parts to try is the one known as **Silver Creek**, which runs for 13 miles from the west end of the Rainbow Trail to Hwy. 285. Motorized vehicles (e.g., dirt bikes) are prohibited from a portion of the route. Reach the trail by driving 5 miles south of Poncha Springs on Hwy. 285. You can access a 5.2-mile section of the **Midland Bike Trail** by going almost 2 miles east of Johnson Village on Hwy. 285/24, then turning north on CR 304 to the trailhead; what's known as the Half Gentleman's Loop starts here. The **South Fooses Creek Trail**, which includes 3 miles of jeep road and 3 miles of singletrack, is another good ride. Take Hwy. 50 about 4 miles west of Maysville to CR 225 south.

POWDERHOUNDS

Dogs in search of snow have lots of great trails to sniff out in the area. One to try is the **South Fooses Creek Trail** (see Cycling for Canines).

The **Browns Creek Trail** is an 11-mile round-trip ski or snowshoe to picturesque Browns Lake. Take Hwy. 285 about 11 miles north of Salida to CR 270. Drive 1.5 miles to CR 272; drive on this for 2 miles to an intersection, where you'll turn left. The trailhead is 1.5 miles farther.

North Cottonwood Creek Rd. runs into the heart of the Collegiate Range, near the base of the Continental Divide. From the stoplight in Buena Vista, drive north to CR 350. Take a left, then a right at the intersection with CR 361. A sharp left will bring you onto CR 365 and to a plowed parking area, from where you'll commence skiing.

CREATURE COMFORTS

Unless otherwise stated, dogs should not be left unattended in the room or cabin.

Buena Vista
$–$$ Arrowhead Point Campground and Cabins, 33975 Hwy. 24 (5 miles north of Buena Vista), 719-395-2323, 800-888-7320, www.arrowheadpointresort.com. In addition to the tent and RV sites, dogs may stay in the deluxe cabins, yurts, or rustic cabins (for all, bring your own bedding or rent it). There's a $5 nightly charge per pet and a maximum of two dogs per unit. The rustic cabin is camper-style, while the deluxe cabins have a refrigerator, microwave, sink, and bath, and the yurts have fridges. All have fire-pit grills outside. Amenities at the campground include a minigolf course, playground, and volleyball courts, as well as a free shuttle service to go rafting. And if your dog has to stay behind, the campground has several on-site kennels where he can stay; inquire about fees.

$–$$ Great Western Sumac Lodge, 428 Hwy. 24, 719-395-8111, 888-786-2290, www.sumaclodge.com. Adult dogs are allowed in designated rooms with a $20 deposit and an $8 nightly fee per dog, with a maximum of two dogs per room.

$–$$ Topaz Lodge, 115 Hwy. 24 North, 719-395-2427, 800-731-5906, www .topazlodge.biz. The motel, part of which dates to the early 1900s, allows up to two dogs each in most rooms.

$–$$$ Alpine Lodge Motel, 12845 Hwys. 24 & 285 (Johnson Village), 719-395-2415, www.vtinet.com/alpine. The motel permits dogs in four rooms for $10 per dog, per night. You can leave your dog unattended in the room as long as he's in a travel kennel.

$$ Arkansas Valley Adventures (AVA) Rafting and Cabins, 40671 Hwy. 24 (13 miles north of Buena Vista), 800-370-0581, www.coloradorafting.net. Up to two dogs each are allowed in any of the five log cabins, attractively furnished with handmade log furniture. All cabins are one room, with two double beds; three have kitchenettes. Though you can't leave your dog unattended inside, you may be able to arrange for dogsitting with the office staff. Keep your dog leashed on the property, where there's plenty of room to run with him. Campsites are available here, too, and the cabin operators also offer raft trips. Open mid-May to the end of September.

$$ Buena Vista KOA, 27700 CR 203, 719-395-8318, 800-562-2672, www .buenavistakoa.com. One dog per cabin is permitted in the camper cabins for $7 extra per night—except for Rottweilers, pit bulls, and Dobermans. Bring your own bedding for the cabins (note that you can't cook inside them).

$$ Sagewood Cabins, 38951-B Hwy. 24 (11.5 miles north of Buena Vista), 719-395-2582, www.coloradodirectory.com/ sagewoodcabins. You and your dog (or two) can enjoy a quiet, relaxing stay in these fully furnished log cabins, decorated in a country style with some antiques. A few of the cabins have fireplaces. There's a $10 fee per dog, per night. You'll need to keep your dog leashed on the property, but the San Isabel National Forest is right next door.

$$ Vista Court Cabins and Lodge, 1004 W. Main, 719-395-6557, 800-241-0670, www.vistacourtcabins.com. Dogs are allowed in five of the seven lodge rooms and any of the eight quaint one- and two-bedroom log cabins, which have full kitchens, for $7 extra per night, per dog. A three-bedroom rental house here is also pet friendly. There's a limit of two dogs in each unit, and it's possible to leave Fido unattended inside if he's in a travel kennel. You'll need to keep your dog leashed on the surrounding 2 acres.

$$–$$$ A Riverhouse Inn, 12753 Hwys. 24 & 285 (Johnson Village), 719-395-6494, 800-497-7238, www.ariverhouse inn.com. This bed-and-breakfast on the Arkansas River has six rooms that sleep from two to four, all with private bath and each named for its view. All of them are potentially dog friendly—pets are accepted on a case-by-case basis—for a $40 one-time fee. You can leave your dog unattended in the room, perhaps while you go on one of the shorter rafting trips offered by the company that owns the B&B. Breakfast is continental, but you also have access to the kitchen (plus, rooms have coffeemakers and mini-fridges), as well as the living room, outdoor hot tub, and patio and yard. It's just a short hike down to water level if your pooch wants to dip his paws in the river. Rafting and adventure packages that include discounted lodging are available.

$$–$$$ Best Western Vista Inn, 733 Hwy. 24, 719-395-8009, 800-809-3495, www .bestwesterncolorado.com. The motel has just two pet-friendly rooms. There's a two-dog maximum per room and a $25 nightly fee per pet. There's a nice outdoor hot tub complex and ample open space behind the motel where you can walk your dog.

$$–$$$ Piñon Court Motel, 227 Hwy. 24 North, 719-395-2433, www.pinon courtcabins.com. The motel rents out studio and one-bedroom cabins with fully equipped kitchens. Eight are pet friendly, with a nightly fee per dog of $5–$15, depending on the type of dog, and a maximum of two dogs in a cabin. You can leave your dog unattended inside only if he's in a travel crate. There's a park across the street where your leashed dog can stretch his legs.

$$–$$$ Super 8 Buena Vista, 530 Hwy. 24, 719-395-4090, 866-944-0808, www .super8bv.com. Canine guests are usually put in end rooms, for easier outdoor access, with a $25 one-time fee.

$$–$$$ Thunder Lodge, 207 Brookdale Ave., 719-395-2245, 800-330-9194, www.thunderlodge.com. The lodge, on Cottonwood Creek in downtown Buena Vista, offers seven log cabins with full kitchens that sleep from two to six, plus dog. A maximum of two dogs per cabin is preferred.

$$$ Cottonwood Vista Bed and Breakfast, 20597 CR 306 (7 miles from Buena Vista), 719-395-2704, www.cotton woodvista.com. One well-behaved dog at a time, and one party of guests at a time, are welcome at this log-house B&B near the mountains. The two bedrooms share a bathroom, so "we like people to know each other," says Linda, the owner. The house is on 10 acres surrounded by national forest, and a main attraction midsummer is watching the scores of hummingbirds drawn to the feeders on the balcony. Open May 1 to October 31.

$$$ Woodland Brook Cabins, 226 S. San Juan, 719-395-2922, www.woodlandbrook cabins.com. Your dog will find a haven at Woodland Brook. Fifteen fully equipped log cabins, ranging from studios to two bedrooms, are situated on 5 acres within walking distance of town. Built in 1910, they're clean and comfortable while retaining a rustic mountain cabin charm. Most have fireplaces. Appealing touches include colorful quilts and curtains and dried flower arrangements. "We love animals," says owner Riaan van Niekerk, who has two of his own dogs as proof. Visiting dogs can explore the grounds off leash as long as they are under voice control, and they can perhaps pick up a few Frisbee-catching pointers from the resident dogs.

$$$$ Cottonwood Hot Springs, 18999 CR 306, 719-395-6434, www.cottonwood-hot-springs.com. Dogs are allowed in the four small, rustic log cabins at this hot springs resort (not in the lodge rooms) for $10 per pet, per night for small dogs, $15 for medium to large dogs. Each cabin has a full kitchen, but they're nothing fancy; the big appeal is that each has its own private soaking pool, so you can enjoy the springs without having to ditch your dog. There's a two-night minimum stay. Keep Fido leashed when he's outside.

Cañon City
$ Fort Gorge RV Park and Campground, 45044 Hwy. 50, 719-275-5111, 866-341-7875, www.fortgorge.com. One small dog (usually 10 pounds and under) is allowed in the three camper cabins (bring your own bedding or rent it here) at this complex located close to the Royal Gorge Bridge. You can only cook outside the cabin. Open May 1 to October 15.

$ Mountainview RV Park, 45606 Hwy. 50 (6 miles west of Cañon City), 719-275-

0900, 877-717-0900, www.mtviewcamp .com. In addition to the RV and tent sites, dogs are allowed in two of the camper cabins (bring your own bedding) with a credit-card imprint as a deposit. Be sure to keep your dog leashed everywhere on the property. "We're dog lovers," says the owner, "and, in fact, we often prefer pets to children!" If Fido likes pizza, he'll want to visit the pizza parlor at the park.

$ Travel Inn Motel, 2980 E. Main St., 719-275-9125, 800-310-0406, www .coloradovacation.com/inns/travel. Dogs 40 pounds and under can stay in certain rooms for a $20 deposit.

$–$$ Holiday Motel, Hwy. 50 and 15th St., 719-275-3317. With a $25 deposit (if you're paying with cash) and a $5 nightly fee per pet, dogs are allowed in some of the motel's rooms.

$–$$ Parkview Inn Motel, Hwy. 50 and 3rd St., 719-275-0624, www.parkview innmotel.com. Dogs are allowed in a few rooms for $5–$10 extra per night, with a maximum of two dogs per room.

$$ Budget Host Royal Gorge Inn, 217 N. Raynolds, 719-269-1100, 866-495-8403, www.royalgorgeinn.com. Small dogs get the nod for $10 per night.

$$ Royal Gorge/Cañon City KOA, 559 CR 3A, 719-275-6116, 800-562-5689, www .koa.com. Dogs are welcome in the camper cabins (bring your own bedding or rent it here). Be sure to keep your dog leashed around the campground. This activity-filled KOA includes a go-cart track, pool, minigolf course, and playground, as well as a restaurant. Open April 15 to October 1.

$$ Super 8 Cañon City, 209 N. 19th St. (at Hwy. 50), 719-275-8687, 800-800-8000 (national number), www.super8.com.

The motel has three rooms that a dog 30 pounds and under can stay in for a $30 nightly fee; the preference is for one dog per room, unless you have two dogs that are really small.

$$–$$$ Best Western Royal Gorge, 1925 Fremont Dr., 719-275-3377, 800-231-7317, www.bestwesterncolorado.com. Four dog-friendly rooms are available, with a one-time fee of $50 and up, depending on the size of dog. You can leave your dog unattended in the room, but management emphasizes that you must take complete responsibility if your pet damages anything.

$$–$$$ Holiday Inn Express, 110 Latigo Ln., 719-275-2400, 888-465-4329 (national number), www.hiexpress.com. Dogs can stay in designated pet rooms (all on the first floor) for $15 per night, per pet, with a limit of two dogs per room. Fido can be unattended inside only if he's in a travel kennel.

$$–$$$ Quality Inn & Suites, 3075 E. Hwy. 50, 719-275-8676, 800-525-7727, www.qualityinn.com. The motel has designated pet rooms.

$$$ Comfort Inn, 311 Royal Gorge Blvd., 719-276-6900, www.comfortinn.com. Dogs are welcome for a $10 one-time fee.

Coaldale

$–$$$ Big Horn Park Resort, 16373 Hwy. 50, 719-942-4266, www.bighornpark .com. The resort has a combination of motel rooms, camper cabins (a.k.a. mini bunkhouses), and fully equipped two-bedroom log cabins (as well as tent and RV sites). Dogs are allowed in some of each, for $12 per dog, per night, and a maximum of two per unit. The owner emphasizes that only nonaggressive breeds are allowed, so if you're traveling with your Rottie, say, you'll need to look elsewhere

Shanda, the former mayor of Guffey.

Perhaps the coolest town government in Colorado belongs to the unincorporated town of Guffey, northwest of Cañon City off Hwy. 9 (population: about 25). The mayor's post has traditionally been held by a local "Democat" or "Repuplican." Shanda, a golden retriever, took office in 1993, when her feline predecessor, Whiffy Legone, retired from politics. In 1998, Monster the cat assumed a co-mayorship with Shanda and now he is the sole mayor. You can visit him in his office at the Guffey Garage.

and your dog a slate of options for $5 extra per night: camping cabins (bring your own sleeping bag), furnished cabins without kitchens, motel rooms, and fully equipped cabins with kitchenettes. And there's access to the river for when your dog wants to cool off. Dogs must be kept on a six-foot leash when outside; there's to be "no barking, no biting, no fighting"; and all poop must be picked up. Open April 1 to October 31.

Florence

$$ Super 8 Florence, 4540 Hwy. 67, 719-784-4800, 800-800-8000 (national number), www.super8.com. There's a $20 one-time fee to stay with one dog, and $30 if you have the maximum of two dogs.

Guffey

$–$$ Rustic Cabins, 719-689-3291, www.guffeycolorado.com. "We encourage you to bring your dog," says Colleen Soux, who, with her husband, runs these six funky cabins located at various sites in Guffey (all within walking distance). Fitting for a town that elects dogs and cats as its mayor. Dating to the 1880s, the cabins are indeed rustic, with no running water and limited electricity. Each has an outhouse, and there's a central shower house. They range from a semi-underground cabin that used to be a general store and sleeps two to the honeymoon cabin, which sleeps up to five. Your dog can be unattended inside (perhaps if he's in the midst of a game of "pioneer dog"); keep him on leash outside so he doesn't chase the small local deer herd.

(no matter how sweet she is to you). Keep your dog leashed outside (where there's .5 mile of frontage on the Arkansas River). Open April 1 to January 1.

Cotopaxi

$–$$ Cotopaxi Arkansas River KOA and Loma Linda Motel, 21435 Hwy. 50, 719-275-9308, 800-562-2686, www.colorado campingkoa.com. This KOA offers you

Howard

$–$$$ Banderas Bunkhouse, 10281 Hwy. 50, 719-942-3811, www.banderasbunk house.com. This 3-acre property on the Arkansas River accommodates guests in three cabins (with kitchens), six basic motel rooms, and tent and RV sites. It accommodates dogs, too, for $5 per night, per dog, with a limit of two per cabin or room. You can't leave your dog unattended inside, but one of the neighbors runs a dog-boarding service, and you can arrange for petsitting through her. In addition to fishing, the Bunkhouse regularly offers wagon and buggy rides, which your dog is welcome to join in on, and, by advance reservation, a cowboy sing-along dinner show. A café is also on-site. Open beginning of April to end of December.

Monarch Pass Area

$$$ Monarch Mountain Lodge, 22720 Hwy. 50 (near the top of Monarch Pass), 719-539-2581, 800-332-3668, www.monarchmountainlodge.com. This 100-room lodge, across from the Monarch ski area, allows dogs in eight first-floor rooms only, for a $15 one-time fee per pet. You can leave Fido unattended in the room for a couple of hours.

$$ Wagon Wheel Guest Ranch, 16760 CR 220, 719-539-6063. This small, well-established guest ranch in Maysville, about halfway up Monarch Pass, has six cozy one-room cabins, all fully furnished and with extra touches such as handmade quilts and curtains. Dogs can recreate on leash with their owners on the surrounding 2.5 acres. Open Memorial Day to Labor Day.

$$$–$$$$ River Suites Luxury Cabins and Villas, 16724 W. Highway 50, 719-539-6953, www.riversuites.com. These nine cabins on the North Fork of the South Arkansas River (got that?) in Maysville are all dog friendly. The cabins sleep from four to twelve, and all have full kitchens, vaulted ceilings, and private hot tubs. Depending on your definition of luxury, these cabins may seem more middle of the road than luxe, but they are comfortably appointed with everything you need for a woodsy getaway.

Nathrop

$$–$$$ Hahns Haven Bed and Breakfast, 15656 CR 289A, 719-395-8432 www.hahnshaven.com. Dogs are welcome in all four rooms (one with private bath) at this idyllic little B&B, where your pooch can fall asleep to the restful music of Chalk Creek right out the door. In fact, pet-loving owner Melody Ann Hahn highlights "the ever-changing menagerie of animal visitors" on her website. You can leave your dog unattended in your room, though he'd probably rather hang out with you in the game room (with pool table), by the fireplace in the homey living room, or on the deck (with hot tub) overlooking the creek.

$$$ La Roca de Tiza Bed and Breakfast, 16420 CR 289A, 719-395-8034, www.larocabandb.com. With a paws-up from Stimpy, the resident cat (as well as a thumbs-up from owner Cheri Radway), dogs can stay in one of the three guest rooms (two share a bath) at this lovely post-and-beam house. There's a $10 nightly fee per dog, and you can leave Rover unattended in the room with advance approval. The B&B's name translates as "the rock of chalk," reflecting its location on 5 acres alongside Chalk Creek and near the distinctively white Chalk Cliffs. In addition to breakfast, your stay includes a cookie and chocolate basket in your room and an evening glass of wine. You and your dog can relax by the two large fireplaces or on the deck, which has a hot tub.

Poncha Springs

$$ Poncha Lodge, 10520 Hwys. 50 & 285, 719-539-6085, 800-315-3952, www.ponchalodge.com. Dogs get the okay in designated rooms, for $10 per night, per pet, with a limit of two dogs in a room. For doing his business and walking, Fido will need to stay on the large sandy area and not venture onto the property's grassy lawn. The rooms at this small motel have knotty-pine interiors.

$$–$$$ Rocky Mountain Lodge and Cabins, 446 E. Hwy. 50, 719-539-4143, www .coloradodirectory.com/rockymtnlodge. Up to two dogs per unit are permitted in five of the rooms at the motel and in both of the one-room cabins (with kitchens) with a $20 deposit.

Salida

$–$$ Aspen Leaf Lodge, 7350 W. Hwy. 50, 719-539-6733, 800-759-0338, www .aspenleaflodge.com. The motel has designated pet rooms, with a choice between smoking and nonsmoking. There's a $5 nightly fee per dog.

$–$$ Budget Lodge, 1146 Rainbow Blvd. (Hwy. 50), 719-539-6695, 877-909-6695, www.budgetlodgesalida.com. Homier than your average low-priced motel, with individually decorated rooms, some with full kitchens, the lodge allows up to two dogs per room for a $10 one-time fee.

$–$$ Mountain Motel, 1425 E. Hwy. 50, 719-539-4420, 866-542-3094, www .mountainmotel.net. The motel has six newer rooms and three cabins (two with kitchenettes); dogs are permitted in all, with a limit of two per unit.

$–$$ Travelodge, 7310 W. Hwy. 50, 719-539-2528, 800-234-1077, www.salida travellodge.com. Dogs are allowed for $5 per dog, per night, in designated rooms, as well as in the motel's four small cottages (which have microwaves and fridges).

$–$$ Woodland Motel, 903 W. 1st St., 719-539-4980, 800-488-0456, www.wood landmotel.com. You've got to love a place like the Woodland, which has its priorities straight: the motel's list of amenities is preceded by the word *pets*. Canine guests are greeted with their own quilted dog cushion (so he'll stay off the furniture), food and water bowls, and biscuits on check-in. Their owners will appreciate the motel's simple but well-kept standard rooms, efficiency units, and two-bedroom suites with full kitchens. There's a limit of two or three smaller dogs per room, or one very large dog. You can leave your dog unattended in the room for an hour or so as long as you let the front desk staff know, and there's an alley behind the motel for convenient dog walking.

$$ American Classic, 7545 Hwy. 50, 719-539-6655, 800-682-8513, www.american classicinn.com. Dogs are permitted in four rooms, for $5 extra per night, per pet. You'll also be asked to sign a release form, taking responsibility for any damage done and agreeing that you won't leave Fido unattended in the room.

$$ Circle R Motel, 304 E. Hwy. 50, 719-539-6296, 800-755-6296, www.the circlermotel.us. Dogs are welcome for $5 extra per night, per pet, and can be unattended in the room if in a travel kennel. One unit with a kitchenette is available, and there's a hot tub outside the motel.

$$ Great Western Colorado Lodge, 352 W. Rainbow Blvd. (Hwy. 50), 719-539-2514, 800-777-7947, www.gwsalida .com. It's $10 per dog, per night here.

$$ Simple Lodge, 719-650-7381, 224 E.

TREATS FOR EVERYONE

If your dog is hankering for some road snacks, stop by Bongo Billy's in Salida (300 W. Sackett) and pick up treats baked by the local Colorado Barkery. Flavors include Cheesy Bonz and Peanut Butter Delights. You'll find a yummy array of coffee drinks, baked goods, and sandwiches to choose from.

1st St., www.simplelodge.com. The lodge is actually a hostel situated in a completely refurbished (with many salvaged and recycled materials) two-story building from 1883 that originally housed railroad workers. One well-mannered dog is allowed in each of the two private rooms (not the communal bunk rooms) for a $5 one-time fee. Fido can go anywhere in the hostel, except the kitchen, as long as you accompany him.

$$–$$$ Days Inn, 402 E. Hwy. 50, 719-539-6651, www.daysinnsalida.com. The motel has only one pet room and charges a $10 one-time fee for up to two dogs to stay in it.

$$–$$$ Salida Gateway Inn and Suites, 1310 E. Hwy. 50, 719-539-2895, www.salidagatewayinnandsuites.com. Dogs up to 30 pounds can stay in one of the motel's designated standard pet rooms for $10 extra per dog, per night. Up to two dogs per room are allowed, and they can be left unattended. There's a gravel alley in back of the motel where you can walk your dog off leash if he's well behaved.

$$–$$$ San Isabel Bed and Breakfast, 15914 CR 260 (10 miles north of Salida), 719-539-5432, 866-361-1755, www.sanisabelbandb.com. This friendly B&B offers four rooms in a newer log house, and all can accommodate dogs. There's a $10 nightly charge per dog, $5 of which the B&B owners then donate to the Ark-Valley Humane Society. The two upper-level rooms share a bath, as do the two lower-level ones; the latter also have a common lounge area between them. Three host dogs live at the B&B (as well as a cat) and, more often than not, says the owner, they play with visiting canines on the 5.5-acre fenced grounds. If you need to leave Rover behind, he can stay in the outdoor kennel. Horses are also welcome; there's a barn and corral.

$$–$$$ Silver Ridge Lodge, 545 W. Hwy. 50, 719-539-2553, 877-268-3320, www.silverridgelodge.com. Small dogs are permitted in two rooms, with advance approval, for $10 per dog, per night.

$$–$$$ Super 8, 525 W. Rainbow Blvd., 719-539-6689, 800-800-8000 (national number), www.salidasuper8.com. Dogs are allowed in any room, and there's a dog-walking area behind one of the motel buildings.

$$$$ The Tudor Rose Bed & Breakfast & Chalets, 6720 CR 104 (1.5 miles from Salida), 719-539-2002, 800-379-0889, www.thetudorrose.com. Though dogs can't stay in the B&B rooms, they are allowed in two of the five nicely appointed chalets recently built on the 37-acre property. There's a $10 nightly fee per dog (with a maximum of two dogs), as well as a $25 deposit. Each chalet has one bedroom and a sleeping loft and accommodates up to six; amenities include a full kitchen, fireplace, vaulted ceilings, and log trim for a woodsy mountain touch. Fido can be unattended inside as long as he's in a travel kennel. You can bring your horse here, too; stables are on-site.

San Isabel

$$–$$$ The Lodge at San Isabel, Hwy. 165 (10 miles north of Rye), 719-489-2280, www.coloradodirectory.com/lodgesan isabel. This family-style resort in the Wet Mountains includes nine cabins situated on the shores of Lake Isabel (although some have kitchens, you'll have to bring your own cooking and serving dishes). There's a $15 one-time fee, per dog, and a limit of two dogs per cabin. Open mid-May through October.

$$–$$$ Pine Lodge, 18488 Hwy. 165, 719-489-2686, www.thepinelodge.net. Located within a couple hundred yards of Lake Isabel, these eight rustic cabins, which sleep from two to six, are dog friendly, for $5 per pet, per night, with a maximum of two dogs. Five have full-kitchen facilities; the other three have a microwave, refrigerator, and sink. You can let your dog sniff outside under voice control.

Westcliffe

$$ The Courtyard Country Inn Bed and Breakfast, 410 Main St., 719-783-9616, www.courtyardcountryinn.com. The B&B, which is centered around a charming, plant- and flower-filled courtyard, has two pet-friendly rooms, for $10 extra per dog, per night. If you leave Rover unattended inside, he must be in a travel kennel. The courtyard includes portable outdoor fireplaces, a small fish pond, and a pair of waterfalls and is a perfect place to relax on a summer evening and enjoy the complimentary evening cocktail (some nights, outdoor movies are shown). The B&B's canine greeters are Cody, a collie, and Lily, a golden retriever, and they share their home with two cats and a rooster, so if your dog is the sociable type, he can make some friends.

$$ Westcliffe Inn, 57975 Hwy. 69 (at Hermit Rd.), 719-783-9275, 800-284-0850, www.westcliffeinn.com. About half of the motel's 28 rooms are dog friendly (and all rooms are on the ground floor, for easy outdoor access). There's no charge for one dog; if you have two dogs, there's a $5 nightly charge that covers both. All rooms have refrigerators and microwaves.

CAMPGROUNDS

Arkansas Headwaters Recreation Area. Part of the state parks system, the recreation area consists of 150 miles of the Arkansas River and the area immediately surrounding it. Several campgrounds along the way are accessible by vehicle, including **Ruby Mountain** (22 sites) and **Hecla Junction** (22 sites), off Hwy. 285 south between Buena Vista and Salida;

and **Rincon** (8 sites) and **Five Points** (20 sites), off Hwy. 50 east of Salida.

National forest campgrounds: **Cottonwood Lake Campground,** south on CR 344 from Cottonwood Pass Rd. (28 sites); **Collegiate Peaks Campground,** west of Buena Vista on Cottonwood Pass Rd. (56 sites); **Cascade Campground,** 9 miles west from Nathrop on Chalk Creek Rd. (21 sites); **Monarch Park Campground,** Hwy. 50, near the top of Monarch Pass (36 sites); **Oak Creek Campground,** south of Cañon City on 4th St. to CR 143 (15 sites); and **Alvarado Campground,** southwest of Westcliffe—take Hwy. 69 south to Schoolfield Rd. west (47 sites).

Private campgrounds: **Arkansas Valley Adventures (AVA) Rafting and Cabins, Arrowhead Point Campground and Cabins,** and **Buena Vista KOA** in Buena Vista; **Cotopaxi Arkansas River KOA** in Cotopaxi; **Big Horn Park Resort** in Coaldale; **Mountainview RV Park, Fort Gorge Campground,** and **Royal Gorge/Cañon City KOA** in Cañon City; and **Banderas Bunkhouse** in Howard (see Creature Comforts for all).

WORTH A PAWS

Royal Gorge Bridge and Park. Your dog won't want to miss one of Colorado's most popular tourist attractions. The gorge boasts the world's highest suspension bridge, which spans the Arkansas River at 1,053 feet. Dogs are not allowed on the incline railway, aerial tram, or other rides, but you can take your leashed pooch on a walk across the bridge. And there are four dog kennels, available on a first-come, first-serve basis, which Rover can stay in while you go on one of the rides. The Royal Gorge Park encompasses 5,000 acres with lots of scenic overlooks that you and your dog can enjoy together. The park and bridge are located 8 miles west of Cañon City, via Hwy. 50, and are open year-round. The entrance fee ranges $18–$22, depending on time of year. For more information, call 719-275-7507 or 888-333-5597, or go to www.royalgorge bridge.com.

Buckskin Joe Frontier Town and Railway. Let your dog experience the Wild West during a visit to Buckskin Joe's (and he won't have to run behind a covered wagon to get there). A re-created western town, the park allows leashed dogs to join you in touring the "historic" buildings, watching staged gunfights, and, of course, stocking up on souvenirs. Or maybe your dog would like to try his paw at panning for gold. Buckskin Joe's also operates the Royal Gorge Scenic Railway, which will take you and Fido on a 30-minute round-trip ride to the rim of the gorge. The park is open mid-May to mid-September. From Memorial Day to Labor Day, hours are 9 AM–6 PM; hours are shorter during the rest of May and September. The railway stays open from March to October; hours are 9 AM–7 PM, Memorial Day to Labor Day, with shorter hours before and after those dates. Located 8 miles west of Cañon City, at Royal Gorge. For more information and ticket prices, call the park at 719-275-5149 or the railway at 719-275-5485, or go to www.buckskin joe.com.

Monarch Scenic Tram. The gondola whisks you and your leashed dog from the top of Monarch Pass to 12,000 feet in a matter of minutes, giving you a bird's-eye view of the neighboring peaks. There's a glass-enclosed observatory at the top for your viewing comfort, though you're free to wander around outside as well. This is a good option for the dog who doesn't want to work too hard for a panoramic vista. The gondola runs continuously throughout the day from May 15 through September 15. Call 719-539-4091 for current ticket prices or more information.

Bishop Castle. Your dog is welcome to tour this massive stone and iron work-in-progress with you as long as you keep him under control. Since 1969, Jim Bishop has worked on creating the castle-like structure, which is intended for public use, completely on his own. There's no admission charge, and the castle is open year-round. To reach it, drive 6 miles north from Lake San Isabel on Hwy. 165. You'll see a sign on the right side of the road; park alongside the road and cross it to get to the castle.

Arf Walk. Held annually in late September or early October, the walk benefits the Ark-Valley Humane Society. Leashed and fully vaccinated dogs and their owners meet at Riverside Park in Salida (the only time dogs can sniff out this usually off-limits site) and go on a 2.25-mile stroll through downtown. After the walk, participants can browse the dog-related exhibits or enter contests for closest dog/owner look-alike, waggiest tail, and biggest and smallest dogs. Funds are raised through the registration fees, and all humans get a T-shirt. Water stations are set up along the walk route; owners should bring plastic bags to pick up after their pets. For more information, contact the Ark-Valley Humane Society at 719-395-2737 or go to www.ark-valley.org.

Buena Vista Canine Classic. This annual half-day event for dogs of all athletic abilities takes place mid-August at the soccer fields at Buena Vista's River Park and, through registration fees, raises funds for the Ark-Valley Humane Society. Dogs who enjoy big air can strut their stuff in the Frisbee competition's two divisions: toss and catch, and freestyle. Those who like going under, over, or around things will want to try their paws at the agility course, while good listeners can test their skills on the rally course, a type of obstacle course where dogs must perform certain tasks, like walking around cones or sitting and staying, as they move through it. And sled-dog wannabes can check out dryland mushing; teams from Colorado Mountain Mushers give demonstrations and offer tips. For more information, go to www .bvk9classic.com.

Royal Gorge Route Railroad. Unfortunately, dogs are not able to accompany their owners on this two-hour train ride along the Arkansas River through Royal Gorge. However, the railroad operators will help you find petsitting options for your four-legged traveler. The train operates year-round. Call 719-276-4000 or 888-724-5748, or go to www.royalgorgeroute.com for more information.

DOGGIE DAYCARE
Cañon City
Country Kennels, 301 Fourmile Ln., 719-275-5681. $18/day. Dogs stay in indoor/outdoor runs. Open 8:30–10 AM and 4–5 PM, Monday to Saturday.

Fremont Veterinary Hospital, 2418 Florence St., 719-269-3349, www.fremont vethospital.com. $8–$11.75/day, depending on the size of dog. Open 8 AM–5 PM, Monday to Friday; 8 AM–noon, Saturday.

Kenline Veterinary Clinic, 1426 S. 9th St., 719-275-2081. $15–$19/day, depending on the size of dog. Open 8 AM–5 PM, Monday to Friday (closed Thursday); 9 AM–1 PM, Saturday.

Nathrop
Double J Cross Kennel, 17605 Hwy. 285, 719-539-4080. $15/day. Open 7 AM–6 PM, Monday to Friday; weekends by appointment.

Penrose
KLB Boarding Kennel, 1355 R St., 719-372-6831. $17–$24/day. Dogs stay in indoor/outdoor runs with piped-in music and go on daily walks on the 5-acre property. Open 7:30 AM–6 PM, Monday to Friday; 8 AM–5 PM, Saturday; 3–6 PM, Sunday.

Salida
Mountain Shadows Animal Hospital, 9171 W. Hwy. 50, 719-539-2533, www .salidavet.com. $5/day. Open 8 AM–noon and 1:30–5:30 PM, Monday to Friday; 8 AM–noon, Saturday; 6–7 PM, Sunday (for pick-ups).

Wag-N-Tails Pet Boarding and Grooming, 10525 CR 120, 719-539-9246, www.wag-n-tails.net. $12/day. The indoor/outdoor kennels have heated floors indoors. Open 8 AM–5:30 PM, Monday to Friday; 8–10 AM and 5–6 PM, Saturday and Sunday.

Silver Cliff
Dundee Memorial Animal Care Center, 1200 Broadway, 719-783-3770, www .dundeememorial.com. $10–$18/day. Open 8:30 AM–5 PM, Monday to Friday.

PET PROVISIONS
Buena Vista
Martin Feed, 15415 CR 306, 719-395-4044

Canon City
All Star Pets, 708 Main St., 719-275-7387

Salida
Murdoch's Ranch and Home Supply, 201 E. Rainbow Blvd. (Hwy. 50), 719-539-2767

Silver Cliff
Dundee Memorial Animal Care Center, 1200 Broadway, 719-783-3770

Feed Barn, 110 N. Mill St., 719-783-9398

CANINE ER

Buena Vista

Buena Vista Veterinary Clinic, 30400 Hwy. 24 North, 719-395-8239; after hours: 719-395-6408. Open 8:30 AM–noon and 1:30–5 PM, Monday to Friday; 9 AM–noon, Saturday.

Cottonwood Veterinary Service, 104 Isabel Ct., 719-395-8900, www.cotton wooddvm.com. Open 8 AM–5 PM, Monday to Friday.

Cañon City

Fourmile Veterinary Clinic, 151 Fourmile Ln., 719-275-6318. Open 8:30 AM–5 PM, Monday to Friday.

Fremont Veterinary Hospital, 2418 Florence St., 719-269-3349, www.fremont vethospital.com. Open 7:30 AM–6 PM, Monday to Thursday; 7:30 AM–5 PM, Friday; 8 AM–noon, Saturday.

Kenline Veterinary Clinic, 1426 S. 9th St., 719-275-2081. Open 8 AM–5 PM, Monday to Friday (closed Thursday); 9 AM–1 PM, Saturday.

Poncha Springs

Animal Care Center of Chaffee County PC (AAHA certified), 120 Pahlone Pkwy., 719-539-1086. Open 7 AM–5 PM, Monday to Friday

Salida

Mountain Shadows Animal Hospital, 9171 W. Hwy. 50, 719-539-2533, www .salidavet.com. Open 8 AM–noon and 1:30–5:30 PM, Monday to Friday; 8 AM–noon, Saturday.

Silver Cliff

Dundee Memorial Animal Care Center, 1200 Broadway, 719-783-3770, www .dundeememorial.com. Open 8:30 AM–5 PM, Monday to Friday.

RESOURCES

Cañon City Chamber of Commerce, 403 Royal Gorge Blvd., Cañon City, 719-275-2331, 800-876-7922, www.canoncity .com

Chaffee County Online Visitor's Guide, www.coloradoheadwaters.com

Custer County Chamber of Commerce, 2 Bassick Pl., Westcliffe, 719-783-9163, www.custercountyco.com

Buena Vista Area Chamber of Commerce, 343 Hwy. 24 South, Buena Vista, 719-395-6612, www.buenavistacolorado.org

Heart of the Rockies Chamber of Commerce, 406 W. Hwy. 50, Salida, 719-539-2068, 877-772-5432, www.salida chamber.org

Salida Ranger District, Pike/San Isabel National Forests, 325 W. Rainbow Blvd. (Hwy. 50), Salida, 719-539-3591

San Carlos Ranger District, Pike/San Isabel National Forests, and **Royal Gorge Field Office,** Bureau of Land Management, 3028 E. Main St., Cañon City, 719-269-8500

Twenty-Two
Pueblo and Points Southeast

THE BIG SCOOP

This chapter covers an area from the southeast plains of Colorado to Trinidad, about 20 miles north of the New Mexico border, up through the Cuchara Valley, and north to Pueblo, the metropolis of the region. It's a lot of territory for your dog to sniff, but the attractions he'll most want to explore tend to be spread out. Pueblo and the eastern plains, especially, can be ovenlike during the summer, so for your dog's sake, plan excursions to areas near water (see Tail-Rated Trails, below, for some ideas). The dry Comanche National Grasslands area is best suited for a spring or fall visit.

In Pueblo, dogs must be leashed within city limits; on county land, they can be under voice control. Because the extensive River Trail system is overseen by the city, dogs must be kept leashed on all of the trails.

TAIL-RATED TRAILS

**Bark Park
at Pueblo City Park**
Access: From Pueblo Blvd., turn east on Goodnight into City Park's west-side entrance. After entering the park, take the first right and follow the road past the pool and one softball field. The dog park is on the right (look for the bone-shaped sign). Parking is available along the street or in the lot past the next softball field.
Regulations: Dogs must have current vaccinations, license, and ID tags; females in heat and puppies younger than six months are not allowed; owners are legally responsible for their dogs and their dog's actions; dogs must be within owners' sight and under voice control; dogs showing aggression must leave the park immediately; no digging is allowed—and any holes dug must be filled; children under 12 must be under adult supervision; owners must clean up after their dogs.
Dogs can be off leash.

Pueblo City Park has it all: a zoo, disc golf course, skate park, pool, kiddie rides, tennis courts, ponds, playgrounds, and now a dog park. The fenced park is a converted athletic field, spread out between two softball fields. The 2.5 grassy acres provide ample room for dogs to stretch their legs; Tansy enjoyed a vigorous game of tennis-ball chasing when we visited. A small hill along one side lets dogs up their aerobic workout. There's little shade, other than a few trees in each corner, but picnic tables are strategically placed right under them. A bilevel water fountain just inside the entrance provides hydration, and poop bags and a trash can are also by the entrance.

Vogel Canyon (Comanche National Grasslands)
Distance: 2.25 miles round-trip
Elevation gain: Minimal
Trailhead: The route to Vogel Canyon feels something like driving down an airport runway, so flat and open is the landscape.

From La Junta, take Hwy. 109 south for 13 miles. Look for a sign to Vogel Canyon on the right and turn onto CR 802. After 1 mile, turn left (at another sign) onto FR 505A and proceed 2 miles to the parking lot.

Dogs are requested, but not required, to be on leash.

Hiking Vogel Canyon is a bit like a step back in time to the frontier days of the prairie. You and your dog will likely be the only ones there. Four trails begin at the trailhead; a pleasant loop combines portions of three of them. Start on the **Canyon Trail**, making your way through a cattle guard just past the parking area. The trail is marked by large stone cairns as it makes a gradual descent among large stands of juniper. It soon heads through the namesake grasslands, which also feature flowers and cacti. Eventually you'll reach some standing pools of water— actually a spring—where your dog may want to cool off, as the canyon is otherwise hot and dry. You'll see a three-way fork here, as well as a cairn; turn right to take the **Mesa Trail**. After crossing a dry streambed, go left, then through the fence opening, and follow the diagonal tracks in the grass. The trail is fairly clear, with some cairns along it.

Keep hiking below a series of rock outcroppings, ignoring any cairns you may spot above, until you come to a rectangular foundation. These are the remains of a stagecoach stop that operated in the 1870s. Just beyond them are three cairns in front of a rocky area. Scramble east up through the rocks, keeping to the left. At the top, look to the northeast for another cairn. Once you reach this cairn, you should be able to spot another to the east. The rest of the Mesa Trail follows a series of cairns. Shortly after climbing over a stile, your route intersects with the **Overlook Trail**, a wide gravel path. A left brings you back to the trailhead.

Lake Pueblo State Park

Access: From Pueblo, take Hwy. 50 west to Pueblo Boulevard. Turn left (south) and drive about 4 miles to Thatcher Ave.; turn left (west), and drive 6 miles to the park entrance. (You can also access the park from the north, farther west on Hwy. 50, via McCulloch Blvd.)

Dogs must be leashed.

The park boasts 34 miles of trails. The longest one, the paved 8.9-mile **Pueblo Reservoir Trail**, runs along the north and eastern sides of the lake, connecting the three campgrounds, two marinas, and the visitor center; it also ties into the **Pueblo River Trail** system (see later entry). The most scenic portion of the trail runs east from the Juniper Breaks Campground to the Rock Canyon area. The trail network on the park's south shore consists of technical singletrack that's extremely popular with mountain bikers; in other words, not the best dog-walking venue.

Note that dogs are not allowed at the Rock Canyon swim beach area. 719-561-9320, www.parks.state.co.us/parks/lakepueblo

Lathrop State Park

Access: From Walsenburg, head west on Hwy. 160 for a little more than 3 miles to the park entrance on the right. There's a $6 entrance fee.

Dogs must be leashed.

The hiker's-only **Hogback Trail**, an easy 2-mile loop, winds through large stands of piñon and juniper as it ascends, via a series of moderate switchbacks, the Hogback Ridge. From the top, you'll have a nice view of the twin Spanish Peaks to the south and the Wet Mountains to the north—and, on a clear day, Pikes Peak. Pamphlets for a self-guided nature tour are available at the trailhead, which is on the north side of Martin Lake. Bring enough water for you and your dog, as the trail is dry.

The paved **Cuerno Verde Trail** encircles Martin Lake, forming a 3-mile loop. Note that dogs are not allowed on Martin Beach.

For picnicking with your dog in a less-frequented area of the park, try the North Martin Inlet. 719-738-2376, www.parks.state.co.us/parks/lathrop

Pueblo River Trails

A paved trail system runs for about 35 miles through Pueblo, east–west along the Arkansas River and north–south along Fountain Creek. The Arkansas River Trail connects with the paved trails in Lake Pueblo State Park. *Dogs must be leashed.*

Although there are numerous trail access points in Pueblo, by far the nicest place to pick up the trail is at the Nature and Raptor Center of Pueblo, just west of downtown. The most straightforward way to get there is to take Hwy. 50 west from town to Pueblo Blvd. Turn left (south) and travel about 2.5 miles to Nature Center Rd. on the right (it's W. 11th St. on the other side of Pueblo Blvd.). Take the road to its end, where there's lots of parking at the Nature Center complex.

From here, either head east toward town (after about 2 miles, the trail is not

Emma and Lucy think about their next outdoor adventure.

as scenic, however) or head west, where 3.5 miles of trail brings you to the state park. Hiking near the Nature Center is especially serene. The mighty Arkansas just purrs along at this point, and abundant cottonwood drape over the river. A small network of gravel paths begins behind the Nature Center and goes by the river, allowing your dog to dip his paws in. The Nature Center includes a large picnic area as well as a coffee shop, the Coyote's Den, with outdoor seating—perfect for enjoying a latte by the river with your dog. If you're looking for a short walk closer to the center of town, the **Runyon Lake Trail** travels 1.2 miles around its namesake lake. Parking is available at the end of Juniper, by Runyon Field.

Trinidad Lake State Park

Access: From Exit 14A off I-25 at Trinidad, follow the signs for Route 12; the park is about 3 miles west on Route 12, on the left. There's a $6 entrance fee. *Dogs must be leashed.*

The park has several hiking trails, the busiest of which is the 1-mile **Levsa Canyon** self-guided nature trail. For more secluded hiking with your dog—though you'll need to keep an eye out for mountain bikers—try the 4-mile (one way) **Reilly Canyon Trail** starting from its west end. To reach the trailhead, drive about 3 miles past the main park entrance and take a left at the Cokedale turnoff to access the Reilly Canyon entrance. Cross over two cattle guards; the trailhead is about 200 yards past the second one, on the left. The trail is hot and dry, so early morning—as well as spring and fall—are the best times to hike here with your dog. Bring lots of water. The trail meanders, with moderate ups and downs, through piñon and juniper woodlands along a mesa above the lake. You and your dog can enjoy photo-worthy views of the lake as well as of square-topped Fisher's Peak, which looms above Trinidad.

You can also reach this trail from the east via the first .25 mile of the Levsa Canyon Trail, which begins at the Carpios Ridge Campground at the main park entrance. The Reilly Canyon Trail, clearly marked, branches off to the west. Hiking from east to west, you'll encounter a fairly steep descent into Levsa Canyon.

To allow your panting pooch access to the lake, continue on the road to Reilly Canyon (see above), past the trailhead. Once the road turns east, it dead-ends shortly afterward, close to the lake. Also at this junction, **Old Hwy. 12**, now unmaintained, heads west. Park your car along the shoulder and take your dog for a solitary walk near the Purgatoire River. The road ends about 1 mile later, at the park's western boundary.

The 2.5-mile **South Shore Trail**, while providing scenic views of the lake, follows a rather overgrown roadbed next to railroad tracks. Skip it. 719-846-6951, www.parks.state.co.us/parks/trinidadlake

CREATURE COMFORTS

Unless otherwise stated, dogs should not be left unattended in the room or cabin.

Colorado City

$$ Days Inn Colorado, 6670 W. Hwy. 165 (I-25 at Exit 74), 719-676-2340, 800-329-7466 (national number), www.daysinn.com. Dogs are permitted in designated rooms for $10 extra per night, per pet, with a maximum of two dogs per room.

Cuchara

$$–$$$ Dodgeton Creek Inn, 40 Cuchara Ave. East, 719-742-5169, www.sangres.com/riversedge. "We allow well-behaved dogs and extremely well-behaved children—and we prefer the dogs," quips owner Mike Moore. Formerly a sister property to the River's Edge B&B, which

DOGS ON THE DECK

The town of Cuchara is a popular dog spot. The Dog Bar & Grill, on the town's main street, originally got its name because so many dogs would hang out in front of the bar (and sometimes inside). Now that there's a restaurant, too, dogs need to stay outside, but Rover is welcome to join you for a meal on the deck.

is a now a private house, the inn, on Dodgeton Creek, has eight comfortable guest rooms, six with private baths and five with kitchenettes. You can leave your dog unattended in your room at your own discretion, but he'll probably be more eager to explore the adjacent national forest land, about 30 yards away. In addition to breakfast, human guests can enjoy complimentary wine in the evening.

$$–$$$ Yellow Pine Guest Ranch, 15880 Hwy. 12, 719-742-3528, www.yellowpine.us. Since 1927 this 400-some acre ranch has greeted guests at its location within walking distance of the town of Cuchara yet bordered by the San Isabel National Forest. It also welcomes dogs on a case-by-case basis (certain breeds, like Chows and Rottweilers, don't get the welcome mat) with a $25 one-time fee and a $25 deposit, which you'll get back if there's no damage or excessive fur left behind. The nine cabins sleep anywhere from two to eight and have kitchens and, in most cases, fireplaces. You can leave Fido unattended inside, preferably in a travel kennel. Ranch activities include horseback riding and fly-fishing (in addition to a stocked trout pond, 1 mile of the Cucharas River flows through the property) and Thursday night BBQs. Open May 1 through October 31.

Eads

$$ Econo Lodge, 609 E. 15th St., 719-438-5451, 877-424-6423 (national number), www.econolodge.com. Dogs are allowed in any of the rooms for $10 per night, per pet.

Fowler

$–$$ Bushy's Blue Sky Motel, 2nd and Hwy. 50, 719-263-4271. Dogs are permitted in four smoking rooms only. They can be left unattended inside if they're in a travel kennel.

La Junta

$ La Junta Travel Inn, 110 E. 1st St., 719-384-2504. Dogs pay a $10 one-time fee.

$–$$ America's Best Value Inn and Suites, 1325 E. 3rd St., 719-384-2571, 888-315-2378 (national number), www.americas bestvalueinn.com. Only the standard rooms, not the suites, are pet friendly. There's a limit of one dog per room, with a $10 nightly fee. All rooms have microwaves and refrigerators.

$–$$ La Junta KOA, 26680 Hwy. 50, 719-384-9580, 800-562-9501 (national number), www.koa.com. Dogs are allowed in two of the camper cabins for a $10 one-time fee (bring your own bedding and cooking supplies). Keep your dog leashed at the campground, which includes a playground and pool, unless Fido is taking a run around the fenced on-site dog park.

$$ Mid-Town Motel, 215 E. 3rd St., 719-384-7741, www.midtownlajunta.com. At this very clean, renovated motel, run by a friendly East Coast émigré named Nick, dogs are welcome for $10 per night, per pet, and a credit-card imprint as a deposit. You can leave your dog unattended inside the room.

$$ Stagecoach Motel, 905 W. 3rd St., 719-384-5476, www.stagecoachlj.com. The motel allows dogs in designated rooms, up to two per room, for a $10 nightly fee per pet.

$$$ Holiday Inn Express, 27994 Hwy. 50, 719-384-2900, 800-HOLIDAY (national number), www.hiexpress.com. Dogs can stay in ground-floor rooms for $20 per night, per pet. You can leave Fido unattended in the room as long as you put up the Do Not Disturb sign.

Lamar

$–$$ Holiday Motel, 404 N. Main St., 719-336-9754, www.holidayhotellamar .com. Dogs are permitted in certain rooms for $10 extra the first night, $5 extra each additional night.

$$ Best Western Cow Palace Inn, 1301 N. Main, 719-336-7753, 866-363-0915 (national number), www.bestwestern colorado.com. Canine guests are allowed in designated rooms, for $15 extra per dog, per night, as well as a $100 deposit. You can leave your dog unattended in the room as long as he's in a travel kennel; just make sure he doesn't plan on barking 'til the cows come home.

$$ Blue Spruce Motel, 1801 S. Main, 719-336-7454, www.bluesprucelamar.com. Certain rooms are pet friendly, with a $5–$10 fee per night, per dog, depending on the size of dog. You can leave yours unattended inside for a short time, but housekeeping won't come in while he's there.

$$ Chek-Inn, 1210 S. Main St., 719-336-4331, www.chek-inn.com. Designated dog-friendly rooms are $5 extra per night, per pet.

$$ Country Acres Motel and RV Park, 29151 Hwy. 287, 719-336-1031, 888-336-1031, www.lamarcountryacres.com. This small motel considers dogs on a case-by-case basis. If your dog makes the grade, you and he can stay together in one of eight rooms furnished according to theme, which range from planetarium to rodeo, for $10 extra per night, per dog.

$$ Days Inn, 1302 N. Main, 719-336-5340, 800-329-7466 (national number), www.daysinn.com. The motel has only one pet-friendly room, for small dogs only with a $10 nightly fee. And your small dog must be in a travel kennel at all times, even when you're in the room with him.

$$ Lamar Inn, 1201 N. Main, 719-336-7471. Up to two dogs each can stay in certain rooms for an $8 nightly fee per pet.

$$ Lamar Super 8, 1202 N. Main, 719-336-3427, 800-800-8000 (national number), www.super8.com. All of the rooms are dog friendly.

Las Animas

$$ Best Western Bent's Fort Inn, 10950 E. Hwy. 50, 719-456-0011, 866-363-0915 (national number), www.bestwestern colorado.com. There's a $10 nightly fee per dog, and certain rooms are pet friendly. You can leave your assuredly well-behaved dog unattended in the room.

La Veta

$$ Ranch House Inn, 1012 S. Cherry St., 719-742-5234, www.theranchhouseinn .com. This small, homelike inn permits up to two small dogs (the owner doesn't specify a weight limit but Fido should probably be under 20 pounds) in one of its five themed guest rooms for a $10 nightly fee. All rooms have microwaves and refrigerators. The inn is located south of downtown, across from the golf course.

$$–$$$ Deer Tracks by the River Cabins and RV Park, 404 Oak St., 719-742-6404. Dogs can add their pawprints to the deer tracks at this complex 2 blocks from La Veta's Main St. "We're a laid-back place," says owner Nancy Wooldridge. In addition to the RV and tent sites, dogs may stay in the seven cabins for a $10 one-time fee per pet for bigger dogs, $5 for smaller

ones. The updated cabins, built sometime in the 1920s or '30s, range from studios to one bedroom, and the larger ones sleep up to six. They're equipped with microwaves and refrigerators. Your dog can hang out inside unattended as long as he doesn't bark the whole time. The Cucharas River runs along the property, and your dog can explore his surroundings on leash. Open June 1 through November 30.

$$$ La Veta Inn, 103 W. Ryus, 719-742-3700, 888-806-4875, www.lavetainn .com. This historic inn in downtown La Veta allows dogs in its six Southwest Family Suites for $10 extra per night, per pet (the inn rooms and several other suites are not pet friendly). The suites, which sleep up to four, are in an addition to the original 1876 building and have Saltillo-tiled floors and kitchenettes. Your dog can be unattended inside if he's in a travel kennel. Francisco's restaurant at the inn serves southwestern dinners.

$$$ Sulphur Springs Guest Ranch, 5218 Indian Creek Rd. (CR 421), 719-742-5111, www.sulphurspringsranch.com. Located 5 miles west of La Veta, this 160-acre ranch is bordered by the San Isabel National Forest and affords you and your dog a peaceful retreat (despite the name, no hot springs are actually on the property). Lodging is in five updated cottages that date from the 1920s, all with wood-burning stoves and full kitchens. Though no pet fees are assessed up front, you'll be asked to pay a $25 cleaning fee if your dog leaves any unwanted deposits in the cabin. Hiking trails at the ranch, some of which extend into the national forest, include several that ascend the rock wall, a notable feature that's geologically related to the nearby Spanish Peaks. Open May 1 to October 31.

Pueblo

$ Motel 6 I-25, 4103 N. Elizabeth, 719-543-6221, 800-4-MOTEL6 (national number), www.motel6.com. You can leave your dog unattended in the room if you let the front desk staff know.

$ Valustay Inn and Suites, 2001 N. Hudson, 719-542-3750. Dogs are accepted in designated rooms with a $100 deposit and a $25 one-time fee. The motel prefers smaller dogs and has a limit of two dogs per room. You can leave yours unattended in the room.

$ Pueblo KOA & Kamping Kabins, 4131 I-25 North, 719-542-2273, 800-KOA-7453, www.koa.com. Dogs are allowed in the camping cabins (you'll need to bring your own bedding and cooking supplies) for a $5 one-time fee. In addition to a pool and hot tub, the campground has a playground, a nature trail, and a fenced-in dog run where your dog can socialize with other four-legged campers.

$–$$ Motel 6 West, 960 Hwy. 50 West, 719-543-8900, 800-4-MOTEL6 (national number), www.motel6.com. Dogs can stay in any of the rooms.

$–$$ USA Motel, 414 W. 29th St., 719-542-3268. There's a $10 nightly fee per dog.

$$ Econo Lodge, 4615 N. Elizabeth, 719-542-9933, 877-424-6423 (national number) www.econolodge.com. Dogs are permitted, but here's the catch: Rover must be in a travel kennel at all times, even when you're in the room (if you don't have a kennel, the motel can lend you one). There's a $10 nightly fee per dog and a $30 deposit.

$$ Microtel Inn, 3343 Gateway Dr., 719-242-2020, 888-771-7171 (national number), www.microtelinn.com. Dogs are welcome with a $50 deposit and a $10 one-time fee. Rover can be left unattended in the room if he's in a travel kennel.

$$ Piñon Inn, 4803 N. I-25, 719-545-3900 or 719-545-6560. There's a $10 fee per night, per pet for dogs to stay in designated rooms at this motel and truck stop.

$$ Super 8, 1100 Hwy. 50 West, 719-545-4104, 800-800-8000 (national number), www.super8.com. The motel has several rooms that dogs can stay in for $10 per pet, per night.

$$–$$$ Best Western Eagleridge Inn and Suites, 4727 N. Elizabeth St., 719-543-4644, 866-545-4818, www.bestwestern colorado.com. There's a $15 nightly fee per pet. You can leave your dog unattended inside the room.

$$–$$$ GuestHouse Inn and Suites, 730 N. Sante Fe, 719-543-6530, 800-21-GUEST (national number), www.guest houseintl.com. Dogs get the nod for one of the several pet rooms, with a $25 one-time fee per pet.

$$–$$$ Holiday Inn, 4530 Dillon Dr., 719-542-8888, 888-465-4329 (national number), www.holidayinn.com. Dogs are welcome in second-floor rooms for a $20 one-time fee. There's generally a limit of two dogs per room, and you can leave Rover unattended inside as long as you let the front desk know so they can alert the housekeepers.

$$–$$$ La Quinta Inn and Suites Pueblo, 4801 N. Elizabeth St., 719-542-3500, 800-753-3757 (national number), www .lq.com. The motel prefers dog guests who weigh 20 pounds or less. You can leave your dog unattended in the room, but you must leave a cell-phone number at the front desk.

$$–$$$ Ramada Inn, 4703 N. Freeway, 719-544-4700, 800-272-6232 (national number), www.ramada.com. With a $15 one-time fee, dogs may stay in certain rooms.

$$–$$$ Sleep Inn, 3626 N. Freeway, 719-583-4000, 877-424-6423 (national number), www.sleepinn.com. Up to two dogs per room can sleep in the motel's designated pet units, for $15 extra per night, per dog.

Rocky Ford

$$ Arkansas Valley Bed and Breakfast, 301 N. 12th, 719-254-7999, www.arkansasvalleybedandbreakfast.com. Well-behaved dogs can stay in any of the guest rooms in this 19th-century house. Rooms are furnished in a simple country style (not stifling, as in some B&Bs), and all share bathrooms. It's okay to leave your dog behind in your room, if necessary. Breakfast in summer features Rocky Ford melon, the town's farm-fresh specialty.

$$ High Chaparral Inn, 1319 Elm Ave., 719-254-4006, 888-254-9898. Dogs are welcome in designated rooms.

Springfield

$–$$ J's Motel, 265 Main St., 719-523-6257. Dogs can stay for $10 extra per night, per pet.

$$ Starlite Motel, 681 Main St., 719-523-6236. There's a $10 nightly fee per dog.

Trinidad

$–$$ Downtown Motel, 516 E. Main, 719-846-3341. Dogs are allowed with a $5 nightly fee each and a limit of two dogs per room. The motel is, indeed, in downtown Trinidad.

$–$$ Frontier Motel, 815 Goddard Ave., 719-846-2261. Up to two dogs each are permitted in designated rooms for $5 per night, per dog.

$$ Best Western Trinidad Inn, 900 W. Adams, 719-846-2215, 866-363-0915 (national number), www.bestwesterncolorado.com. Dogs 20 pounds and under get the okay to stay in the designated pet rooms. They can be left unattended if they're in a travel kennel.

$$ Budget Host Trinidad, 10301 Santa Fe Trail Dr., 719-846-3307, 800-BUD-HOST (national number), www.sangres.com/budgethost.htm. Dogs must be 25 pounds or less to stay in one of the motel's designated pet rooms. There's a $10 nightly fee per dog.

$$ Budget Summit Inn, 9800 Santa Fe Trail Dr., 719-846-2251. Dogs are welcome in outside-facing rooms for a $10 one-time fee.

$$ Quality Inn, 3125 Toupal Dr., 719-846-4491, www.qualityinn.com. Dogs pay $15 per night extra to stay in one of the designated pet rooms. There's a maximum of three dogs per room, and you can leave your dog unattended inside.

$$ Super 8 Motel, 1924 Freedom Rd. (Exit 15 off I-25), 719-846-8280, 800-800-8000 (national number), www.super8.com. Only one dog per room can stay in the designated pet-friendly units here, for a $15 one-time fee.

$$ Trail's End Motel, 616 E. Main, 719-846-4425. There's a $10 nightly fee per dog, and the motel has certain pet-friendly rooms.

$$ Trinidad Motor Inn, 702 W. Main, 719-846-2271, 877-846-2271, www.trinidadmotorinn.com. There's a $6 nightly pet fee.

$$–$$$ Holiday Inn, 3130 Santa Fe Trail, 719-845-8400, 800-HOLIDAY (national number). Dogs are allowed in first-floor rooms with a $20 one-time fee.

$$–$$$ La Quinta Inn & Suites, Trinidad, 2833 Toupal Dr., 719-845-0102, 800-753-3757 (national number), www .lq.com. There's a $10 one-time fee for minidogs (under 10 pounds) and a $20 fee for the rest. Two dogs per room are permitted, and it's okay to leave yours unattended for a short while.

Walsenburg

$–$$ Country Budget Host, 553 Hwy. 85/87, 719-738-3800, 800-BUD-HOST (national number). Dogs, preferably smaller ones, are allowed in smoking rooms only for $10 extra per night. There's a limit of two dogs per room.

$$ Knights Inn, 22808 Hwy. 160, 719-738-2167, www.knights.com. The motel charges $10 per night, per pet, for dogs to stay in designated rooms.

$$–$$$ Best Western Rambler Motel, Hwy. 85/87, Exit 52 (off I-25), 719-738-1121, 866-363-0915 (national number), www.bestwesterncolorado.com. The motel accepts dogs 50 pounds and under in designated rooms. There's a $10 nightly fee per dog.

$$$ Rio Cucharas Inn, 77 Taylor Rd., 719-738-1282. The motel seems to have been through its ups and downs regarding condition and ownership. Nonetheless, dog guests are allowed for $10 nightly per pet. In addition to motel-style rooms, the inn has three more expensive suites, each with fireplace.

CAMPGROUNDS

John Martin Reservoir State Park. About 16 miles east of Las Animas and 2 miles south of Hasty, off Hwy. 50 (213 sites).

It's full throttle ahead for Kip.

Lake Pueblo State Park. See Tail-Rated Trails for directions (401 sites).

Lathrop State Park. See Tail-Rated Trails for directions (103 sites).

Trinidad Lake State Park. See Tail-Rated Trails for directions (73 sites).

National forest campgrounds: Camping is allowed in the parking area at **Vogel Canyon** (see Tail-Rated Trails for directions).

Private campgrounds: **Deer Tracks by the River Cabins and RV Park** in La Veta, **Pueblo KOA,** and **La Junta KOA** (see Creature Comforts).

WORTH A PAWS

Bent's Old Fort National Historic Site. Eight miles east of La Junta and 15 miles west of Las Animas, on Hwy. 194. An influential frontier trading post on the Arkansas River, Bent's Fort was in operation from 1833 to 1849. Today, a reconstruction operated by the National Park Service allows visitors to experience the fort's heyday through tours and interpretive activities. Your dog is welcome to accompany you into the fort's plaza as long as you keep him on a leash. He won't be able to go with you inside the fort's rooms, however, so the best plan would be to go with a partner who can trade dog-watching duty with you in the plaza. Open 8 AM–5:30 PM daily, June 1 to August 31; 9 AM–4 PM the rest of the year. There is a $3 entrance fee. 719-383-5010, www.nps.gov/beol

Feet and Fur. If you and Fido are in the Pueblo area mid-June, sign yourselves up for this annual fund-raising 5K walk. The course begins and ends at Pueblo's City Park, off of Pueblo Blvd. and Goodnight Ave. The walk is followed by contests, including pet/owner look-alike, best trick, best kisser (dogs, that is!), and the "real dawg" dog show. You and your dog can also get pet care information and various freebies at booths set up in the park and view demonstrations by local 4-H groups and police K-9 units. Money raised through registration fees and pledges benefits Pueblo Animal Services, the 4-H Mighty Dogs Club, CSU Extension Office, Pet Project, and the Animal Welfare Society. For more information, contact Pueblo Animal Services at 719-544-3005 or go to www.puebloanimalservices.org.

Whisker Ball. Is the only kind of ball your dog knows the kind that bounces on a tennis court? Treat him to a Cinderella-like experience and bring him to a real ball. The Whisker Ball, held at the end of October or beginning of November, takes place at Pueblo's Sangre de Cristo Arts and Conference Center and benefits Pueblo Animal Services. In addition to a catered dinner (for people only), the evening includes live and silent auctions, a "runway show" of shelter dogs, and recognition of a local animal advocate. Black tie is optional, but leashes are required for four-legged ballgoers. For tickets and more information, contact Pueblo Animal Services at 719-544-3005 or go to www.puebloanimalservices.org.

Four Paw Spa, 3853 Goodnight Ave., Pueblo, 719-320-3074. Is your lovable pooch starting to smell up the backseat after rolling in that suspicious-looking stuff out at the reservoir? Bring him here for a quick spruce-up. For $12 you can clean your dog in one of the special wash bays—shampoo, towels, and blow dryer are provided. You'll need to call for an appointment; walk-ins are not accepted. Appointments are readily available days, evenings, and weekends, including Sundays.

DOGGIE DAYCARE
Fowler
Peakview Animal Hospital, 1050 CR JJ, 719-263-4321. $11/day. Open 8 AM–noon and 1–5 PM, Monday to Friday.

La Junta
Krugman Small Animal Clinic, 502 E. 1st, 719-384-5050. $7.50/day. Open 8 AM–noon, 1–5:30 PM, Monday, Tuesday, Wednesday, Friday; 8 AM–noon, Thursday and Saturday.

Lamar
Eaton Veterinary Clinic, 1004 E. Maple, 719-336-5068. $6/day. Open 8:30 AM–noon and 1–5 PM, Monday to Friday; 8:30 AM–noon, Saturday.

Pueblo
Four Paw Spa, 3853 Goodnight Ave., 719-320-3074. $10/day. This is a free-run (under supervision), no-kennel facility, with indoor and outdoor play sessions for the dogs. Open 7 AM–7 PM, daily.

Johnson's Pet Motel, 6281 W. Hwy. 78, 719-561-3127. $7/day. Open 7 AM–6 PM, Monday to Friday; 8 AM–noon, Saturday; 11 AM–2 PM, Sunday.

Kamp-4-Paws, 1412 32nd Ln., 719-545-PAWS. $7/day. Open 8 AM–5 PM, Monday to Friday, 8 AM–noon, Saturday.

Mountain View Pet Lodge, 457 S. Angus Ave., 719-647-2459, www.mountainview.

petlodge.com. $11/day; $6/half-day. Kennels have floors with radiant heat, and dogs can go on a 20-minute nature walk for $4.50 extra. Open 7:30 AM–5:30 PM daily.

Paw Cottage, 270 S. Purcell Blvd., 719-647-2131, www.pawcottage.com. $11/day; $6 half-day. Open 8 AM–5 PM, Monday to Friday; 9 AM–1 PM and 5–6 PM, Saturday; 9–10 AM and 5–6 PM, Sunday.

Pueblo West Boarding Kennels, 776 E. Paseo Dorado Dr., 719-547-3815. $10/day. The owners live on the premises, and day boarding is arranged by appointment.

Wind Mountain Dog Training, 32098 Acoma Rd., 719-948-2128. $10/day. Open seven days a week.

Trinidad
Fisher's Peak Veterinary Clinic, 1617 Santa Fe Trail, 719-846-3211. $6–7/day, depending on the size of dog. Open 8 AM–5 PM, Monday to Friday; 8 AM–noon, Saturday.

Walsenburg
Rio Cucharas Veterinary Clinic, 22540 Hwy. 160, 719-738-1427. $15–$20/day, depending on the size of dog. Open 8 AM–4 PM, Monday to Thursday; 8 AM–2 PM, Friday; 8–11 AM, Saturday.

PET PROVISIONS
Pueblo
PETCO, 5843 N. Elizabeth St., 719-543-6160, www.petco.com

PetSmart, 4230 N. Freeway, 719-595-9000, www.petsmart.com

Pueblo Feed & Supply, 1811 Santa Fe Dr., 719-542-6787

Sweeny Feed Mill of Southern Colorado, Inc., 403 E. 4th, 719-544-1041

Walsenburg
Sporleder Feeds, 217 E. 4th, 719-738-1920

> **GIVE IT A REST**
> The Cuerno Verde Rest Area at the Colorado City exit off I-25 (Exit 74) has a large dog-walking area for pups on a leash.

CANINE ER
La Junta
Ark-Valley Animal Hospital, 3 Rogers Rd., 719-383-2824. Open 8 AM–5:30 PM, Monday to Friday (except closed Thursday); 8 AM–noon, Saturday.

Colorado Veterinary Clinic, 30488 Hwy. 50, 719-384-8111. Open 8 AM–noon, 1–5 PM, Monday to Friday; 8 AM–noon, Saturday.

Krugman Small Animal Clinic, 502 E. 1st, 719-384-5050. Open 8 AM–noon, 1–5:30 PM, Monday, Tuesday, Wednesday, Friday; 8 AM–noon, Thursday and Saturday.

TLC Veterinary Clinic, 511 Jackson, 719-384-7387. Open 8 AM–noon and 1–5 PM, Monday to Friday (except closed Wednesday); 8 AM–noon, Saturday.

Lamar
Eaton Veterinary Clinic, 1004 E. Maple, 719-336-5068. Open 8:30 AM–5 PM, Monday to Friday; 8:30 AM–noon, Saturday.

Lamar Veterinary Clinic, 1209 E. Olive, 719-336-8484. Open 8 AM–noon, 1–5 PM, Monday to Friday; 8 AM–noon, Saturday.

Pueblo
Animal Emergency Room, 225 E. 4th St. (at I-25), 719-595-9495, www.animalemergencyroom.com. Open 6 PM–midnight, Monday to Friday; 2 PM–midnight, Saturday and Sunday.

Springfield

Southeast Colorado Veterinary Clinic, 1500 Main St., 719-523-6828. Open 8:30 AM–5 PM, Monday to Friday; 9 AM–noon, Saturday.

Trinidad

Fisher's Peak Veterinary Clinic, 1617 Santa Fe Trail, 719-846-3211. Open 8 AM–5 PM, Monday to Friday; 8 AM–noon, Saturday.

Trinidad Animal Clinic, 1701 E. Main, 719-846-3212. Open 8 AM–5 PM, Monday to Friday; 8 AM–noon, Saturday.

Walsenburg

Rio Cucharas Veterinary Clinic, 22540 Hwy. 160, 719-738-1427. Open 8 AM–4 PM, Monday to Friday; 8–11 AM, Saturday.

RESOURCES

Carrizo Unit, Comanche National Grasslands, 27204 Hwy. 287, Springfield, 719-523-6591

Colorado Welcome Centers, 109 E. Beech, Lamar, 719-336-3483; 309 Nevada Ave. (Exit 14A off I-25), Trinidad, 719-846-9512

Forest Supervisor's Office, Pike/San Isabel National Forests, 2840 Kachina Dr., Pueblo, 719-553-1400

Greater Pueblo Chamber of Commerce, 302 N. Santa Fe Ave., Pueblo, 719-542-1704, 800-233-3446, www.pueblo chamber.org

Timpas Unit, Comanche National Grasslands, 1420 E. 3rd St., La Junta, 719-384-2181

Trinidad Tourism Board, www.historic trinidad.com

Twenty-Three

Colorado Springs and Vicinity

THE BIG SCOOP

Despite being Colorado's second-largest urban center, Colorado Springs, picturesquely situated near the base of massive Pikes Peak, is an exceedingly good place to bring your dog for a vacation. National forest hiking trails are within a 20-minute drive of downtown, and some forward-looking folks have established several off-leash areas in city and county parks. (There are leash laws within city limits as well as in areas of El Paso County.) Many of the local lodging places allow pets. And you can even bring Rover along to some of the locales to which tourists in the Springs traditionally flock (see Worth a Paws).

If your dog has a special interest in old mining towns, ghosts, or, perhaps, gambling, pay a visit to nearby Victor and Cripple Creek (though he will have to sit out any casino forays). Whatever activities you choose, your dog is likely to find something to catch his interest in or around Colorado Springs.

TAIL-RATED TRAILS

Of the state parks in the area, two—Eleven Mile and Spinney Mountain—have limited hiking trails, and the other two—Mueller and Cheyenne Mountain—don't allow dogs on them. But there are plenty of hiking opportunities in city and county parks as well as in the Pike National Forest that you can enjoy with your dog. El Paso County oversees 11 parks, and one, Bear Creek, has an off-leash dog area (see

below). To research options in addition to the ones described here, stop by the Pikes Peak Ranger District Office in Colorado Springs (see Resources).

Seven Bridges Trail
Distance: About 4.5 miles round-trip
Elevation gain: 1,500 feet
Access: From downtown Colorado Springs, take Tejon Ave. south; follow the road as it bends to the right and turns into Cheyenne Blvd. After 2.5 miles you'll come to a fork with signs pointing left for Seven Falls and right for North Cheyenne Cañon Park; stay right. Follow the road through the park. At Helen Hunt Falls, the road begins to switchback. Shortly after, you'll reach a fork where Gold Camp Rd. goes off to the right, and High Dr. is straight ahead. Park here in the dirt lot on the left.
Dogs can be off leash.

Begin your hike by walking past the wooden gate at the west side of the parking area. The first .5 mile, which leads to the actual trail, takes you and your dog along a closed section of Gold Camp Rd. The road, which was a rail line at the turn of the century, stretches all the way to Cripple Creek; because of a tunnel cave-in that's never been repaired, an approximately 8-mile section is closed to vehicle traffic. Just before you would cross North Cheyenne Creek, take an unmarked trail that heads uphill on the right side of the road; stay straight rather than continuing uphill at the first switchback, and you'll be on the Seven Bridges Trail. (An alternate access point is off Gold Camp Rd. on the other side of the creek: there's a rusted metal sign indicating the North Cheyenne Creek Trail, the name by which this hike used to be known. However, you'll merely recross the creek on a couple of planks and wind up intersecting the first trail.) You'll hike along the north side of the creek for just a short while before reaching the first bridge. The trail then follows the twists and turns of the creek, ascending up the scenic drainage via a moderate grade. In addition to the plentiful water, your dog will appreciate the shade of ponderosa pine and Douglas fir. Altogether, you'll cross six bridges, despite the trail's name (there's been some bridge reconstruction and relocation due to flooding). After the sixth bridge, the trail climbs more steeply, away from the creek. Tell your dog to take care when crossing the section of exposed, sandy slope.

The Seven Bridges Trail officially ends when it intersects the Pipeline Trail, 1.5 miles from its start off Gold Camp Rd. However, when we hiked this trail, that intersection wasn't clear. We continued along the trail as it paralleled a smaller creek, ultimately reaching a plateau and a large stand of aspen, which made a good turnaround point. On the way back, you'll get a good down-canyon vista of the eastern plains. Shoes with good traction come in handy on the return trip, as some of the downhills are a bit slippery. Your dog, with his grippy paws, should have no problem.

Bear Creek Regional Park

Access: The dog park trailhead is in the parking area west of 21st St. at the intersection with W. Rio Grande Ave.

Dog park regulations: Dogs must be under voice command and current on shots;

Max is happy to warm the bench.

owners must pick up after their pets; puppies younger than four months and females in heat are not allowed; young children must be supervised by an adult; runners, cyclists, and horseback riders are not allowed on the loop trail.

Dogs can be off leash in the dog park; they must be leashed in the rest of the park, and they are not allowed on the 2 miles of nature center trails in the park's western portion.

Not to be confused with Bear Creek Cañon Park, which is overseen by the City of Colorado Springs, this 573-acre county park in the foothills west of the Springs has about 12 miles of trails, with several access points, plus playing fields, picnic pavilions, and community gardens. The section your dog will be most interested in is the 25-acre off-leash dog park, which includes a wide trail that makes about a .5-mile loop and several shorter, informal trails that bisect the loop. The fenced park has a separate, 2-acre enclosure for small dogs. It's a great spot for an after-work hike for local dogs or a close-to-town break for travelers. Though you'll never get far from the noise of traffic on 21st St., your dog will be too excited at having an area set aside for him and his friends to notice. And he can even splash in nearby Bear Creek. Dog park amenities include poop-bag dispensers and trash cans, picnic tables and benches spread throughout, and even a tennis-ball dispenser. You can also reach the trail that leads into the park's western section as well as access the eastern section trails from the 21st St. parking area; just remember that your dog will have to leash up.

Garden of the Gods Off-Leash Dog Area

Access: From downtown Colorado Springs, drive north to Fillmore St. and make a left to head west (it turns into Fontmore once you cross Mesa Rd.). At 30th St., turn right to reach the park's visitor center. If you're coming from Hwy. 24, head north on Ridge Rd. near Old Colorado City to arrive at the park. There is no entrance fee from either access.

Dog park regulations: Dogs must have current vaccinations, license, and ID tags; spike or prong collars must be removed before dogs enter the park; females in heat are not allowed; aggressive dogs must wear a muzzle; dogs must be accompanied by someone age 16 or older; no more than three dogs per person are allowed; owners must pick up after their pets (poop bags are supplied).

Dogs can be off leash in the voice-command area; they must be leashed elsewhere.

On its own, the Garden of the Gods would only rate about one-and-a-half tail wags. However, the dog who's done his homework will know to sniff out the off-leash dog run area, which covers about 18 acres on the east side of the Foothills Trail, near Rock Ledge Ranch. To access this area, park at the visitor center and walk through the tunnel from the parking lot, which comes out at the section of the Foothills Trail south of Gateway Rd. Head south on the trail for about an eighth of a mile; you'll see signs that demarcate the dog run area, which encompasses a section of open field adjacent to the trail.

Alternate access is from the Rock Ledge Ranch parking area; look for the signs from 30th St., just south of the Garden of the Gods visitor center. The dog run area begins near the parking lot. (Note that dogs are not allowed at Rock Ledge Ranch, which is a living history site.)

The main attraction of Garden of the Gods itself, a city park, is the vivid red sandstone formations that are clustered in the area. Several short trails, some natural surface, some paved, wind around the rocks. The longest, at 2.25 miles, encircles part of the park. Though you'll likely marvel at the landscape, your dog may find the Garden less than heavenly: there are no water sources for him, and the trails can be crowded. During the summer, try to visit early in the day or late in the afternoon for cooler temperatures and less company.

Palmer Park

Access: For the dog park, in the southeast corner of the park, enter at the intersection of Academy Blvd. and Maizeland Rd. To reach the central part of the park from downtown Colorado Springs, head north on N. Nevada Ave.; turn right onto Fillmore St. and right onto Union Blvd. Turn left at the next intersection (Paseo Rd.) and drive into the park.

Dog park regulations: Dogs must have current vaccinations, license, and ID tags; spike or prong collars must be removed before dogs enter the park; females in heat are not allowed; aggressive dogs must wear a muzzle; dogs must be accompanied by someone age 16 or older; no more than three dogs per person are allowed; owners must pick up after their pets (poop bags are supplied).

Dogs can be off leash in the dog park and in the voice-command area; they must be leashed in the rest of the park.

In a *Field of Dreams*–like scenario ("If you build it, they will come") the city parks department converted a former baseball field into the Springs' first official dog park in the fall of 2000, and local canines have been visiting in scores ever since. The 1-plus-acre grassy site is contained within a chain-link fence and includes human and dog drinking fountains as well as picnic tables and benches.

The rest of 737-acre Palmer Park contains close to 26 miles of trails that meander throughout; just look for the dirt roads and parking pullouts to access them. However, your dog will first want to head to the Yucca Area, where there are 27.5 acres on which he can run off leash (as long as he stays under voice control). To reach the dog run, turn left off Paseo Rd. at the Lazy Land/Ute Crest sign, then follow signs to the Yucca Area/Ute Crest parking section. The voice-command area encompasses a 2.8-mile loop trail, which runs across the mesa top, and the land on either side of it, providing great views of Pikes Peak to the west. Just keep an eye out for the signs to make sure your dog stays within the parameters of the dog run. If you visit during June, you'll catch the beauty of flowering yucca.

Red Rock Canyon Open Space Off-Leash Dog Trails

Access: From Hwy. 24, turn south onto Ridge Rd. near Old Colorado City. Turn left onto High St. shortly after. The parking area is just ahead on the right. You can also access the park off 31st St., 1 block south of Hwy. 24, but it's about 1 mile farther to reach the off-leash dog area.

Dog trail regulations: Dogs must have current vaccinations, license, and ID tags; spike or prong collars must be removed before dogs enter the trails; females in heat are not allowed; aggressive dogs must wear a muzzle; dogs must be accompanied by someone age 16 or older; no more than three dogs per person are allowed; owners

must pick up after their pets (poop bags are supplied).

Dogs can be off leash on the dog loop trails; they must be leashed elsewhere.

This relatively new 789-acre open space property (it was purchased by the city in 2003) between Manitou Springs and Colorado Springs is a less-developed (for now) version of the Garden of the Gods, which lies just to the north. Almost 14 miles of natural surface trails wend among the red Lyons sandstone ridges, spires, and other natural sculptures, and small lakes. The trail network includes two dog loops, where canine hikers can be under voice command. To reach the .2-mile **Lower Dog Loop**, head east from the parking lot on the Mesa Trail and turn right; the dog trail is .15 mile ahead. The **Upper Dog Loop**, slightly longer at .35 mile, is another .15 mile south on the Mesa Trail after the turnoff for the lower loop. As you hike, you may spot rock climbers tackling various routes. There's also a free-ride mountain-bike skills area (with elevated boards, small teeter-totters, and drops) in the north end of the park.

Dog Park at Cheyenne Meadows Park

Access: From Cheyenne Meadows Rd. (heading east from S. Nevada Ave.), turn left on Eastmeadow Dr. Go for 11 blocks to Coolcrest Dr., then turn right and drive to the road's end at Charmwood Dr. Parking is available along the street. The dog park is west of the end of the road.

Regulations: Dogs must have current vaccinations, license, and ID tags; spike or prong collars must be removed before dogs enter the park; females in heat are not allowed; aggressive dogs must wear a muzzle; dogs must be accompanied by someone age 16 or older; no more than three dogs per person are allowed; owners must pick up after their pets (poop bags are supplied).

Tansy and her sister, Taffy, play as pups.

three dogs per person are allowed; owners must pick up after their pets (poop bags are supplied).
Dogs can be off leash.

The dog park, in the northeast corner of Rampart Park, comes courtesy of a canine-loving Boy Scout, who built it as an Eagle Scout project. Dogs have about 4.5 fenced acres to play in, with a mixed ground cover of sandy dirt and grass. Several large tree trunks have been placed around the park for dogs to jump on and over. When your dog needs a break, he can sip from the park's dog-level water fountain and take in the stellar view of Pike's Peak.

Dogs can be off leash.

Dogs can enjoy sniffing around this fenced dog park, adjacent to a neighborhood park in southwest Colorado Springs, which encompasses about an acre of native grass field. There's nothing fancy here—amenities are limited to a couple of benches, a poop-bag dispenser, and a trash can—but your dog is unlikely to care as long as he can run and socialize with other four-legged friends.

Dog Park at Rampart Park

Access: From I-25, take Exit 149 (Woodmen Rd.) and drive east on Woodmen for 2 miles to N. Union Blvd. Turn left and go for a little more than 1 mile to Lexington. Turn left again. Just past Rampart High School's track and playing fields, look for a sign for Rampart Park and a small road on the left.

Regulations: Dogs must have current vaccinations, license, and ID tags; spike or prong collars must be removed before dogs enter the park; females in heat are not allowed; aggressive dogs must wear a muzzle; dogs must be accompanied by someone age 16 or older; no more than

North Cheyenne Cañon Park

Access: From downtown Colorado Springs, take Tejon Ave. south; follow the road as it bends to the right and turns into Cheyenne Blvd. After 2.5 miles you'll come to a fork with signs pointing left for Seven Falls, right for North Cheyenne Cañon Park; stay right.

Dogs must be leashed.

This city park, with scenic North Cheyenne Cañon at its center, has several hiking trails for dogs to sniff out. The park's western end borders national forest land, where even more trails await discovery (see the Seven Bridges Trail description, for one example), and the north side is adjacent to the Stratton Open Space, which has 5 miles of trails, including three for hikers (and their dogs) only. You might begin with a stop at the well-stocked visitor center at the Starsmore Discovery Center located at the park's entrance. The **Columbine Trail** runs for about 4 miles through the park; you can access it from the lower trailhead behind Starsmore, from a midpoint trailhead off the park road, and from the upper trailhead across from Helen Hunt Falls. The 2.2-mile round-trip **Mount**

Cutler Trail begins to the left of the park road, 1.4 miles from the park entrance. It makes a gradual ascent up the flanks of Mount Cutler, providing panoramic views of Colorado Springs, including the renowned Broadmoor Hotel and grounds. Near the top, you'll also be able to see the Seven Falls in South Cheyenne Cañon. And you might hear the hourly chiming of the Will Rogers Shrine on nearby Cheyenne Mountain. Although there's no water along the trail itself, North Cheyenne Creek is across from the trailhead. Driving farther west up the canyon brings you to **Helen Hunt Falls**, where your dog can enjoy the cool spray. A short trail leads past these falls up to Silver Cascade Falls.

Fountain Creek Regional Park

Access: Located south of Colorado Springs between Widefield and Fountain. Take I-25 south to Hwy. 160 (Exit 132); turn left and drive about .5 mile, where you'll come to the exit for south Hwy. 85/87. Take this exit and make an immediate right onto Willow Springs Rd. Turn left before the parking lot onto the dirt road, then left again to reach the parking area and trail access.

Dogs must be leashed.

The **Fountain Creek Trail** runs for a level 2.5 miles through the park, allowing your dog ample sniffing opportunities among the creek's riparian habitat. The wide, flat dirt trail also makes a good jogging venue. Though you'll never really get away from the drone of highway noise in the background, the park provides a welcome refuge from the surrounding development. If you head north on the trail, you'll come to the Willow Springs Fishing Ponds and the .75-mile **"Fishing Is Fun" loop trail**, where your dog can learn all about fishing from interpretive signs (though he should refrain from jumping in the water).

Past the ponds you can also access the **Fountain Creek Regional Trail**, which extends for 8 miles from the northern end of the park to the El Pomar sports complex in Colorado Springs, where you can then pick up the 14-mile-long Pikes Peak Greenway Trail. Heading south on the Fountain Creek Trail brings you to two wildlife observation pavilions, where your dog can gaze out on a 10-acre pond and the resident waterfowl. (Note that dogs are not allowed on the nature center trails in the Cattail Marsh Wildlife Area, which lies east of the Fountain Creek Trail.) The trail continues through two open meadow areas before ending near the Hanson Nature Park in Fountain.

Monument Valley Park Trail

Distance: Runs for 2.5 miles along Monument Creek through Monument Valley Park.

Trailhead: From the downtown business district on Tejon St., head east on Bijou St. for 2 blocks to the park. If you're driving, park on W. View Pl. This brings you to the southern terminus of the trail.

Dogs must be leashed.

Monument Valley Park is where your dog can come to sniff and be sniffed by the dogs who call the Springs home. The trail makes for a nice urban stroll as it follows the creek. In the park's southern end, you may want to detour to get a closer look at the various ponds, fountains, and the Horticultural Art Society demonstration gardens. For the first 1.3 miles, the trail runs along both sides of the creek (with a slight detour at Uintah St.), providing a loop option. Another loop (.7 mile), in the park's northern end, makes up the **Monument Valley Fitness Trail**; good to know if your dog is really interested in getting a workout (though only a couple of the original exercise stations still exist).

Florissant Fossil Beds National Monument. It's best to bypass this national monument when you're with your dog: not only are dogs not allowed on any trails, they're also discouraged from being in the picnic areas. In case Fido wonders what this place is all about anyway, you can let him know that 35 million years ago, a 15-mile-long lake dominated the landscape of the present-day monument site. Over the next 700,000 years, repeated eruptions from a nearby volcano eventually buried the lake's entire ecosystem, and over the ensuing millions of years, the plant and animal remains became fossilized. Today, the monument's visitor center presents fossil displays, and hiking trails lead visitors to petrified tree stumps. The monument is about 30 miles west of Colorado Springs off Hwy. 24.

 Mueller State Park. The park, located off Hwy. 67 on the way to Cripple Creek, offers more than 85 miles of hiking trails, and your dog is not allowed on any of them. Dogs are allowed in the park's camping and picnic sites.

 Cheyenne Mountain State Park. The newest park in the Colorado State Park system, on the south side of Colorado Springs, has 20 miles of trails, but because they go through a fragile ecosystem, no dogs (or horses, for that matter) are allowed. Because the picnic areas can be reached only via the hiking trails, dogs can't enjoy those either. They can, however, overnight at the park's campground.

CYCLING FOR CANINES

The 7-mile **Waldo Canyon Trail** is one of the most popular hiking and biking routes near Colorado Springs (so plan accordingly, i.e., you probably don't want to bike here with your dog in the middle of a weekend day). It begins right off the north side of Hwy. 24, about 2 miles west of Manitou Springs. The upper part of the trail is actually a 3.5-mile loop and involves about 1 mile of steady, hard climbing. The 5.5-mile **Lovell Gulch Trail** starts at CR 22, north of Woodland Park, and features great views of Pikes Peak.

Close to downtown Colorado Springs, the 4-mile **Captain Jack's Frontside Loop** begins at the closed section of Gold Camp Rd.; follow the Seven Bridges Trail (see Tail-Rated Trails) but continue on the switchbacks up the trail after it leaves Gold Camp Rd. Take a right at the intersection with the Jones Park Trail, then another right on High Dr. to return to the parking area. It's best to do this ride between October 31 and May 1, when High Dr. is closed to vehicle traffic.

You can also bring your bike and your dog to Rampart Reservoir outside of Woodland Park (there's a $5 day-use fee for the area). The **Rampart Reservoir Trail** extends around the lake for 11.6 miles. Begin from the Dikeside Boat Ramp and ride counterclockwise; that way your dog will be ready to turn around before you ever reach the campgrounds, where he'd be treading close to leash-required territory.

POWDERHOUNDS

The 3-mile round-trip **Crags Trail** is one of the closest places to Colorado Springs with consistent snow coverage for skiing and snowshoeing. To access the trail, take Hwy. 24 west to Hwy. 67 south. Just past the entrance to Mueller State Park, look for FR 383 on the left; follow it to the Crags Campground and the trailhead. Some unmarked spur trails lead off the main trail providing more opportunities for snow travel.

The **Horsethief Park** trail system starts from Hwy. 67 a few miles south of the Crags Trail turnoff. It's about a

3-mile round-trip to Horsethief Park and back, a little over 2 miles round-trip to Horsethief Falls, and about 5 miles round-trip via the Pancake Rocks Trail. After a storm or during a good snow, the trail around **Rampart Reservoir** is skiable/snowshoeable. FR 306, which goes directly to the reservoir, is closed during the winter, so you'll need to access the Rampart Reservoir Trail via the 1.4-mile Rainbow Gulch Trail, off FR 300.

CREATURE COMFORTS

Unless otherwise stated, dogs should not be left unattended in the room or cabin.

Calhan

$$ Econo Lodge, 15 5th St., 719-347-9589, www.econolodge.com. Dogs 50 pounds and under are welcome for $20 per night, per pet. There's a limit of two dogs per room.

Cascade

$$ Lone Duck Campground and Cabins, 8855 W. Hwy. 24, 719-684-9907, 800-776-KWAK, www.loneduckcamp.com. Dogs are allowed in the five camper cabins, as well as at the campsites. The cabins have microwaves and small refrigerators, but you will need to supply your own bedding. Be sure to keep Fido leashed on the property. Open May 1 to mid-September.

Chipita Park

$$$-$$$$ Chipita Lodge, 9090 Chipita Park Rd., 719-684-8454, 877-CHIPITA, www.chipitalodge.com. Although dogs are not permitted in the historic main lodge, two nicely furnished cabins on the premises welcome canine guests with a $25 one-time fee. One cabin has two bedrooms, a bath, full kitchen, and fireplace, the other has these amenities but has one bedroom. You can leave your dog unattended inside at your discretion, though each cabin also has a small fenced yard where he might prefer to stay.

Colorado Springs

$ Amarillo Motel, 2801 W. Colorado Ave., 719-635-8539. The motel has only a couple of rooms that dogs can stay in, and the nod usually goes to smaller ones (e.g., cocker spaniel size), not "the big hairy dogs," says the owner good-naturedly.

$-$$ Crossland Economy Studios Colorado Springs Airport, 3490 Afternoon Cir., 719-638-9233, www.extendedstayhotels.com. All the studios have refrigerators, microwaves, and cooktops. One dog per room is permitted for $25 extra per night, with a maximum fee per visit of $150. You can leave your dog unattended in the room, as long as you let the front desk staff know so housekeeping service can be scheduled around that.

$-$$ Express Inn, 725 W. Cimarron St. (Hwy. 24), 719-473-5530, www.theexpressinn.com. This large hotel/conference center has standard rooms as well as a few apartment-style suites, with two bedrooms, living room, dining room, and full kitchen. Designated units are dog friendly, with a $25 one-time fee per dog. A dog can be left unattended inside.

$-$$ Garden of the Gods Motel and Cottages, 2922 W. Colorado Ave., 719-636-5271, 800-637-0703, www.gardenofthegodsmotel.pikes-peak.com. Dogs are allowed in most rooms for $15 per pet, per night. Ask about leaving your dog unattended in the room. Two two-bedroom cottages (at a higher rate), one with full kitchen, one with a kitchenette, are also available, and dogs can stay in these, too.

$-$$ Motel 6 Colorado Springs, 3228 N. Chestnut, 719-520-5400, 800-4-MOTEL6 (national number), www.motel6.com. One dog per room is allowed.

$-$$ Rodeway Inn and Suites, 1623 S. Nevada Ave., 719-623-2300, www.rode

wayinn.com. The suites have separate bedroom and living areas. Pets are allowed in any unit with a $10 one-time fee per dog as well as a $10 deposit. If your dog has a travel kennel to stay in, he can be left unattended.

$–$$ Spruce Lodge, 2724 N. Nevada Ave., 719-635-3523, www.sprucelodgecs.com. Dogs are usually relegated to smoking rooms only. Rover can be left unattended inside as long as he's in a travel crate.

$–$$$ Rainbow Lodge and Inn, 3709 W. Colorado Ave., 719-632-4551, 800-934-1102, www.rainbowlodge-inn.com. Dogs up to 25 pounds are welcome, with a $25 deposit. The motel has rooms in a variety of configurations (hence, the price range), including some with kitchens. The larger family units include two-bedroom cottages and cabins. If you leave your dog unattended inside, he should be in a travel kennel. The property includes an outdoor pool, picnic areas, and a playground; just make sure to keep Fido on his leash when outside.

$$ Airport Value Inn and Suites, 6875 Space Village Ave., 719-596-5588, www.airportvalueinn.com. About 15 rooms at the motel are pet friendly, with a $35 one-time fee and a $100 deposit. There's a limit of two dogs per room, and both of them together can't weigh more than 80 pounds total.

$$ Best Western Airport Inn, 1780 Aeroplaza Dr., 719-574-7707, 866-740-3824, www.bestwesterncolorado.com. Dogs of up to 20 pounds each, with a limit of two dogs per room, are accepted for $10 per night, per dog. They're usually put in ground-floor rooms near the exits and can be left unattended if they're in a travel kennel.

$$ Beverly Hills Motel, 6 El Paso Blvd., 719-632-0386. The motel accepts "mature dogs and mature adults." You can leave your dog in the room unattended.

$$ Buffalo Lodge, 2 El Paso Blvd., 719-634-2851, 800-235-7416, www.buffalolodge.com. This historic lodge, which is practically in Manitou Springs, dates from the early 1900s, and the exterior has that classic 1950s vacation-spot look. The rooms are large, modern, and comfortably furnished. Dogs are permitted in eight of the rooms, some of which have wood floors, for $10 per night and a $50 deposit. Your dog can be in the room unattended if he's in a travel kennel. Keep him leashed on the 4-acre property.

$$ Days Inn, 2409 E. Pikes Peak Ave., 719-471-0990, 800-DAYS-INN (national number), www.daysinn.com. The pet fee is $5 per dog, per night.

$$ Extended StayAmerica Colorado Springs West, 5855 Corporate Dr., 719-266-4206, www.extendedstayhotels.com. All rooms are studios with full kitchens. One dog under 50 pounds is allowed per room. The pet fee is $25 per night overall, with a maximum fee per visit of $150. It's okay for your dog to be unattended in the room, but the housekeepers will enter only if he's in a travel kennel.

$$ Howard Johnson, 8280 Hwy. 83, 719-598-6700, 800-I-GOHOJO (national number), www.hojo.com. There's a nightly fee of $10 per dog and a limit of two dogs per room. You can leave your dog unattended as long as he's in a travel kennel. The motel is across from the Air Force Academy south gate.

$$ Ramada Limited, 520 N. Murray, 719-596-7660, 800-272-6232 (national number), www.ramada.com. Certain rooms are pet friendly. There's a $25 one-time pet fee, and you can leave your dog unattended in the room but housekeeping won't come in to clean while he's there.

$$ Sleep Inn North Academy, 1075 Kelly Johnson Blvd., 719-260-6969, 888-875-3374, www.sleepinn.com. Dogs pay $10 extra per night each, and there's a maximum of two dogs per room.

$$ Sunflower Lodge, 3703 W. Colorado Ave., 719-520-1864, 877-850-9005, www.sunflowerlodge.com. The Sunflower allows dogs of up to five pounds in some of its rooms, with a $50 deposit, so if you're traveling with your yorkie or your Chinese crested, say, you're set. All rooms have kitchenettes.

$$ Super 8 Airport, 1790 Aeroplaza Dr., 719-570-0505, 800-800-8000 (national number), www.super8.com. Three pet rooms are available, one of which is a smoking one, for $10 extra per dog, per night. Leaving your dog unattended inside is okay as long as he's in a travel kennel.

$$ Super 8, 605 Peterson Rd. (at Hwy. 24), 719-597-4100, 800-800-8000 (national number), www.super8.com. The motel has about 20 designated pet rooms for $10 per dog, per night. You can leave your dog unattended if he is in a travel kennel.

$$ Super 8, 8135 N. Academy Blvd., 719-528-7100, 800-800-8000 (national number), www.super8.com. Dogs can stay in any of the rooms for $10 extra per night, per pet, and you can leave your dog unattended inside.

$$ Travelodge, 2625 Ore Mill Rd., 719-632-4600, 800-929-5478. Dogs are allowed for $20 extra per visit. They can be left unattended in the room, preferably in a travel kennel, but housekeeping won't enter during that time.

$$ Travelodge South Colorado Springs, 1703 S. Nevada Ave., 719-632-7077. Dogs are allowed in smoking rooms only, for $10 per night, per pet.

$$–$$$ Apollo Park Executive Suites, 805 S. Circle, 719-634-0286, 800-279-3620, www.apollopark.com. This extended-stay hotel rents out one- and two-bedroom units with kitchens on a nightly, weekly, or monthly basis. Dogs are allowed, but only in the lower-level units; it's $10 extra per night, with a $150 deposit if you're staying for a month or more. You can leave your dog unattended inside.

$$–$$$ Best Western Executive Inn and Suites, 1440 Harrison Rd., 719-576-2371, www.bestwesterncolorado.com. One big dog or two smaller dogs, up to 60 pounds total, are allowed in smoking rooms only. There's a nightly charge of $10 per dog.

$$–$$$ Best Western The Academy, 8110 N. Academy Blvd., 719-598-5770, www.bestwestern.com. The hotel offers standard rooms, minisuites, and larger suites with a Jacuzzi. If your dog is 50 pounds or under, the charge is $10 extra per night, per dog; larger dogs are charged more, usually twice that amount. There's a limit of two dogs per room, and a dog can be left unattended in the room as long as he's in a travel kennel.

$$–$$$ Candlewood Suites, 6450 N. Academy Blvd., 719-590-1111, www.candlewoodsuites.com. This extended-stay hotel accepts dog guests in any of its studio suites, with a $75 one-time fee for stays of between one and six nights, and $150 for stays of seven nights and longer. They'd prefer that your dog be in a travel kennel if you leave him unattended in the room.

$$–$$$ Comfort Inn Airport, 2115 Aerotech Dr., 719-380-9000, www.comfort inn.com. There's a $10 nightly dog fee.

$$–$$$ Comfort Inn North, 6450 Corporate Center Dr., 719-262-9000, www .comfortinn.com. The pet fee is $10 per dog, per night, with a maximum charge of $25 per dog if you stay three nights or longer. There's a two-dog limit per room. You and your dog will generally be placed on the side of the hotel that faces the highway (so if your pooch is a light sleeper, you might want to take that into consideration). It's okay to leave your dog unattended inside as long as you leave a cellphone number with the front-desk staff.

$$–$$$ Comfort Inn South, 1410 Harrison Rd., 719-579-6900, www.comfort inn.com. Dogs are permitted in first-floor rooms with a $50 deposit per dog, $25 of which is refundable at the end of your stay, assuming Rover didn't ruin anything. You can leave your dog unattended only if he's secure in a travel kennel.

$$–$$$ Days Inn, 2850 S. Circle Dr., 719-527-0800, 800-DAYS-INN (national number), www.daysinn.com. Dogs are allowed in designated rooms with a $25 one-time fee per pet. You can leave your dog unattended inside, but housekeeping won't come in to clean.

$$–$$$ Drury Inn, 8155 N. Academy Blvd., 719-598-2500, 800-DRURY-INN (national number), www.druryhotels .com. Two dogs per room are permitted. You can leave your dog unattended in the room for up to 30 minutes at a time if he's in a travel kennel.

$$–$$$ Fairfield Inn Colorado Springs South, 2725 Geyser Dr., 719-576-1717, www.fairfieldinn.com. Up to two dogs per room are permitted on the hotel's first and second floors, with a $25 one-time

fee that's charged by the week. You'll be asked to sign a pet policy that includes the stipulation that the front desk must be able to contact you if your dog is unattended in the room and acts up.

$$–$$$ Holiday Inn Express and Suites, 7110 Commerce Center Dr., 719-592-9800, www.hiexpress.com. Dogs are allowed in designated rooms for $25 per night, per pet. You can leave Fido unattended in the room.

$$–$$$ La Quinta Inn Colorado Springs Garden of the Gods, 4385 Sinton Rd., 719-528-5060, 800-753-3757 (national number), www.lq.com.

$$–$$$ La Quinta Inn and Suites Colorado Springs South Airport, 2750 Geyser Dr., 719-527-4788, 800-753-3757 (national number), www.lq.com. Dogs are allowed in all of the rooms and suites; you'll be asked to sign a pet waiver at check-in.

 $$–$$$ Mountaindale Cabins and Campground, 2000 Barrett Rd., 719-576-0619, www.mountaindalecamp ground.com. In addition to the campground, which is on 45 acres about 15 minutes southwest of downtown Colorado Springs, dogs are welcome in the seven fully furnished log cabins (these aren't camper cabins) for $5 per pet, per night. All have kitchens and sleep from four to eleven people. Dogs aren't allowed in the rental RVs, however. You can leave your dog unattended inside the cabins at your discretion. Though you should keep your dog on leash outside, a football-field-sized fenced dog park is slated for summer 2009, so Fido can stretch his legs off leash and get to know some of the other four-legged campers. The campground owners also plan on putting up some kennels so dogs will have a place to hang out if their owners are off doing something that's not canine friendly, like riding the Pikes Peak Cog Railway. Open year-round.

$$–$$$ Microtel Inn and Suites, 7265 Commerce Center Dr., 719-598-7500, www.microtelinn.com. Dogs are permitted in first-floor rooms only, with a $20 one-time fee. They can stay unattended in the room.

$$–$$$$ Antlers Hilton, 4 S. Cascade, 719-955-5600, 866-299-4602, www.antlerscoloradosprings.hilton.com. Located in downtown Colorado Springs, the full-service Hilton (with two restaurants, fitness center, and indoor pool) welcomes dogs 75 pounds and under in its second-floor rooms (though this could be expanded) for $75 extra per stay. You can leave your dog unattended in the room. The Monument Valley Trail (see Tail-Rated Trails) in Monument Valley Park is about 3 blocks away.

$$–$$$$ Doubletree Hotel World Arena, 1775 E. Cheyenne Mountain Blvd., 719-576-8900, 800-222-8733 (national number), www.doubletree.com. Dogs 40 pounds and under are welcome for $10 extra per night, per dog. On-site amenities at this full-service hotel include a restaurant and bar (with room service), workout area, hot tub, and indoor pool.

$$–$$$$ Homewood Suites Colorado Springs North, 9130 Explorer Dr., 719-265-6600, www.homewoodsuites.hilton.com. The suites here are all one bedroom, with kitchens, and there's a $25 one-time fee per pet. You can leave your dog unattended inside as long as you notify the front desk, but unless he's in a travel kennel, housekeeping won't come in during that time.

$$–$$$$ Hotel San Ayre, 3320 W. Colorado Ave., 719-632-4355, 877-726-2973, www.hotelsanayre.com. A nice change from the chain motels that dominate lodging in the Springs, this boutique lodge allows dogs on a case-by-case basis in its nine guest rooms, as well as a second-story apartment and a refurbished cottage. If your dog makes the grade, he'll pay $15 for a one-night stay and a $25 one-time fee for stays of two nights or longer. He can be unattended inside if he's in a travel kennel. The rooms in this one-time motor court motel from the late 1940s have contemporary, eclectic furnishings and hardwood floors, and all have minifridges and microwaves. The two-bedroom, two-bath mountain suite apartment is 1,100 square feet, with a full kitchen and private deck. The 1,000-square-foot cottage, adjacent to the motel, was built in 1898 and has two bedrooms, one bath, and a kitchen. Everyone is welcome to hang out on the motel's xeriscaped patio, with a fire pit.

$$–$$$$ Residence Inn Colorado Springs South, 2765 Geyser Dr., 719-576-0101, 800-331-3131 (national number). This Residence Inn charges a $75 one-time fee for a dog. You can leave Rover unattended inside your room, though housekeeping won't come in to clean, and the staffers at the front desk may even be willing to do some dog walking if you ask nicely.

$$–$$$$ TownePlace Suites by Marriott, 4760 Centennial Blvd., 719-594-4447, 800-257-3000 (national number), www.towneplacesuites.com. These studio to two-bedroom suites with full kitchens are very similar to the Marriott's Residence Inn. The fee for a dog is $100 per visit, whether you're staying a night or a month, so unless you'll be at the hotel long-term, it's certainly not an economical option (the TownePlace Suites South has a slightly lower fee of $75 per stay). Four-legged guests receive treats, a collapsible dog bowl, and a leash when they check in.

You can leave your dog unattended inside your room, but housekeeping won't come in unless he's in a travel kennel.

$$$ Homewood Suites Colorado Springs Airport, 2875 Zeppelin Rd., 719-574-2701, www.homewoodsuites.hilton.com. There's a $50 one-time fee to stay with your dog in these studio to two-bedroom suites, with kitchens. Fido can be unattended in the room if he's in a travel kennel.

$$$ Radisson Hotel Colorado Springs Airport, 1645 N. Newport Rd., 719-597-7000, 888-201-1718 (national number). There's a $25 one-time fee per dog, as well as a $100 deposit. You can leave your dog unattended in the room for a short time if you're on the hotel premises, say, at the restaurant. Rates include a breakfast buffet.

$$$ TownePlace Suites by Marriott South, 1530 N. Newport Rd., 719-638-0800, 800-257-3000 (national number), www.towneplacesuites.com. For a $75 one-time fee, dogs can stay in these studio to two-bedroom suites, with full kitchens, so it makes most sense to stay here for several nights or more (as the hotel is intended). Canine guests are usually put in first-floor units and can be left unattended if they're in a travel kennel.

$$$–$$$$ Cheyenne Mountain Resort, 3225 Broadmoor Valley Rd., 719-538-4000, 800-588-6531, www.cheyennemountain.com. This large resort and conference center at the base of Cheyenne Mountain accepts dogs 50 pounds and under in any rooms for a $35 one-time fee per dog. The 316 rooms and suites are set among eight buildings, and the adjacent Country Club of Colorado includes an 18-hole golf course, tennis courts, indoor and outdoor pools, and a fitness center. There's also an on-site lake, open to boating and fishing, as well as four restaurants.

 $$$–$$$$ Crowne Plaza, 2886 S. Circle Dr., 719-576-5900, 800-981-4012, www.cpcoloradosprings.com. This huge, full-service hotel in south Colorado Springs allows dogs in all rooms for a $50 one-time fee. The official policy is that dogs must be 35 pounds and under, but if your dog is slightly larger than that, they may well be able to accommodate him. Dog visitors receive a pooch pack on check-in that includes treats, an ID tag with the Crowne Plaza's address, and a Pet in Room sign to alert housekeepers to the presence of a four-legged guest. The hotel has also set aside a specific dog walk area on the property. You can leave your dog unattended in your room as long as he's in a travel kennel. Hotel amenities include indoor and outdoor swimming pools, a fitness center, meeting space, and a bar and two restaurants.

$$$–$$$$ Hyatt Summerfield Suites, 5805 Delmonico Dr., 719-268-9990, www.hyatt.com. Some of the Summerfield's apartment-style suites accommodate one dog per room for a $20 nightly fee for up to six nights. For a stay of seven or more nights, there's a one-time fee of $150. Your dog can be unattended in the suite, preferably in a travel kennel.

$$$–$$$$ Our Hearts Inn Bed and Breakfast, 2215 W. Colorado Ave. 719-473-8684, 800-533-7095, www.inn-colorado-springs.com. This B&B in historic Old Colorado City, an area of Colorado Springs, accepts dogs on a case-by-case basis in one of its accommodations, the Hearts Out West cottage. There's a $50 deposit for a dog that gets the nod, and the owners prefer only one dog guest at a time. Located behind the main inn (an 1895 Victorian), the vintage cottage is charmingly furnished in an Old West theme and sleeps up to three adults (or four if you have small children). A full kitchen, gas fireplace, and Jacuzzi tub round out the amenities.

$$$–$$$$ Residence Inn by Marriott Central, 3880 N. Academy Blvd., 719-574-0370, 800-331-3131 (national number), www.residenceinn.com. Dogs are allowed at this apartment-style hotel, with studio to two-bedroom suites, for a $75 one-time fee. You can leave your dog unattended inside, preferably in a travel kennel.

$$$–$$$$ Residence Inn by Marriott Colorado Springs North, 9805 W. Federal Dr., 719-388-9300, 800-331-3131 (national number), www.residenceinn.com. Rooms at this extended-stay hotel range from studios to two bedrooms, all with kitchens, and dogs under 30 pounds can join their owners for a $75 one-time fee. You can leave your dog unattended inside but unless he's in a travel crate, housekeeping won't come in during that time. The pet agreement form you'll be asked to sign requires a cell-phone or other contact number.

Clover had a smile-inducing stay at the dog-friendly Broadmoor hotel.

$$$–$$$$ Staybridge Suites, 7130 Commerce Center Dr., 719-590-7829, 800-238-8000 (national number), www.suitescolorado.com. This extended-stay hotel charges a hefty $150 one-time fee for dogs (if you're dog is really small, they might lower it a bit). Suites range from studios to two bedrooms, all with full kitchens. Your dog can be unattended in your room only if he's in a travel kennel. Rates include a breakfast buffet and an evening reception with drinks and snacks (so if you make those two of your meals each day, you might begin to recoup some of the dog fee).

 $$$$ The Broadmoor, 1 Lake Ave., 719-634-7711, 866-837-9520, www.broadmoor.com. One of Colorado's classic hotels, the immense, Italian Renaissance-influenced Broadmoor complex—700 rooms and suites, 6 luxury cottages, 18 restaurants and bars, 3 golf courses, a tennis center, a full-service spa and fitness facility, a first-run movie theater, more than two dozen shops, and a gorgeous lakeside setting adjacent to Cheyenne Mountain—is a place you almost needn't ever leave. Canine guests (up to two per room) can share in the Broadmoor's history for $35 extra per night, per pet. The hotel's pet program is known as the Pitty Pat Club, named after the beloved poodle that belonged to Julia and Spencer Penrose, who opened the Broadmoor in 1918. Upon check-in, you and your dog will receive a brochure that details pet-walking locations, both on the hotel grounds and nearby; resources for veterinary care, dog walking and grooming, and pet supplies; and the pet room-service menu, which has IAMS food and biscuits for dogs. You'll also get a Best Friend in Residence sign to hang outside your room and a Broadmoor ID tag to attach to your dog's collar, in case he's silly enough to wander away from such a lovely setting. And your dog will have use of a Broadmoor dog bed and food bowls during his stay. You can leave your well-behaved pup unattended in the room, but if he disturbs the neighbors, he'll be moved to another location in the hotel, where a petsitter will watch him for $15/hour. You should also let the front desk know so that housekeeping doesn't enter during that time.

$$$$ Cheyenne Cañon Inn, 2030 W. Cheyenne Blvd., 719-633-0625, 800-633-0625, www.cheyennecanoninn.com. Well-behaved dogs, who are considered on a case-by-case basis, can stay in the Petite Maison, an eclectic little cottage behind the main house of this historic bed-and-breakfast with an interesting past. The inn was a bordello in the 1920s, with a secret tunnel that allowed its wealthy Colorado Springs clientele to enter discreetly, and the Petite Maison was the madam's residence. During Prohibition, the bordello morphed into the Dixieland Casino. The house has operated as a B&B since the early 1990s. You can leave your dog unattended in the cottage at your discretion, but he'd likely prefer to hike on one of the trails in adjacent North Cheyenne Cañon Park; the Columbine Springs Trail starts at the bottom of the driveway.

Cripple Creek

$$ Cripple Creek/Colorado Springs W. KOA, 2576 CR 81, 719-799-6805, 800-562-9125 (national number), www.koa.com. This KOA, at 10,000 feet elevation, claims it's the world's highest. Four of the camping cabins are pet friendly (bring your own bedding and cooking supplies). Your first dog stays for free; if you have two (or more) dogs, there's

a $5–$10 nightly charge, depending on size, for each additional dog. Open May 1 to mid-November.

$$ Cripple Creek Motel, 201 N. Bison, 719-689-2491, 866-553-6805, www.cripplecreekmotel.com. The motel has a sliding nightly pet fee, based on size: dogs under 40 pounds pay $15 per night, per pet; 40- to 70-pound dogs are $25; and those over 70 pounds pay $50. Pit bulls don't pay anything—because they're not allowed. There's a limit of two large dogs per room. Your dog can be unattended inside as long as he's not a big barker.

$$–$$$ Double Eagle Hotel and Casino, 442 E. Bennett, 719-689-5000, 800-711-7234, www.decasino.com. Your dog is welcome to accompany you here on a gambling vacation if you put down a $50 deposit and pay a $50 one-time fee. You can leave Fido in the room unattended while you try your luck in the adjoining casino as long as he doesn't make a nuisance of himself.

$$–$$$ Gold King Mountain Inn, 601 Galena Ave., 719-689-2600, 800-445-3607, www.gkmi.com. Dogs are permitted in the 14 garden-level rooms for $20 nightly, per pet, with a limit of two dogs per room. You can leave your dog unattended inside as long as the front desk has your cell-phone number. The inn, which is affiliated with the Wildwood Casino, has an indoor pool and fitness center.

$$–$$$ Lost Burro Camping and Lodging, 4023 Teller Rd., #1, 719-689-2345, 877-689-2345, www.lostburro.com. In addition to campsites, there are three indoor options: a one-bedroom, fully equipped log cabin that also has a sleeping loft for four, and two two-bedroom modular cabins, which can sleep up to eight each. The 31-acre wooded property with stream is about 4 miles from Cripple Creek. You can leave your dog unattended inside only if he's in a travel crate.

Fountain

$–$$ Colorado Springs South KOA and Kamping Kabins, 8100 S. Bandley Dr., 719-382-7575, 800-KOA-8609 (national number), www.coloradospringskoa.com. Small dogs (those under 20 pounds) are allowed in three one- and two-room cabins, for $3 per pet, per night (there's no extra charge to have them at the campsites). You'll have to bring bedding and cooking supplies. There are two large fields on-site, as well as Fountain Creek, where you can exercise your dog on a leash. Open year-round.

$$ Super 8 Fountain, 6120 E. Champlain Dr., 719-382-4610, www.super8.com. It's $10 per night, per dog, and they can be left unattended inside the room.

Green Mountain Falls

$$ Falls Motel, 6990 Lake St., 719-684-9745. This 12-room motel allows dogs on a case-by-case basis and prefers one dog per room. If your dog is small and particularly quiet, you may be able to leave him unattended in the room, though the general policy is that your dog should be with you at all times.

$$ Rocky Top Motel and Campground, 10090 W. Hwy. 24, 719-684-9044, www.rockytopco.com. All of the motel's 15 rooms are dog friendly, with a charge of $2 per night or $10 per week, per pet, plus a $25 deposit. Some rooms have kitchenettes.

Lake George

$$–$$$ M Lazy C Ranch, 801 CR 453, 719-748-3398, 800-289-4868, www.mlazyc.com. On this 140-acre working cattle ranch bordered on three sides by the Pike National Forest, you can ride horses year-round, participate in cattle drives, and go for hayrides or sleigh rides. Originally built in 1906 to house the ranch's cowboys, the now-updated guest cabins are charmingly decorated with western ranch decor and most have wood-burning stoves and front porches. Three cabins allow dogs, for $5 per pet, per night, plus a $50 deposit. The cabins include microwaves and refrigerators, and one of the dog cabins, the Rustler, has a small kitchen. Breakfast is included with some cabin rentals, and you can also arrange for lunches and dinners. While on the ranch, you'll need to keep your dog leashed, but hiking trails in the national forest are a short walk away. The ranch also has RV and tent sites.

Manitou Springs

$–$$ La Fon Motel, 123 Manitou Ave., 719-685-5488, 888-598-5488. Dogs pay $5 extra per night.

$–$$ Park Row Lodge, 54 Manitou Ave., 719-685-5216. The motel accepts small to medium-sized dogs for a $5 one-time fee plus a $20 deposit if you're paying in cash. Some rooms have kitchenettes.

$–$$ Red Wing Motel, 56 El Paso Blvd., 719-685-9547, 800-733-9547, www.redwingmotel.pikes-peak.com. Dogs are allowed in several rooms for a $5 one-time fee.

$$–$$$ Best Western Sky Way Inn and Suites, 311 Manitou Ave., 719-685-5991, www.bestwesterncolorado.com. Dogs are allowed in three of the rooms, with a $50 one-time fee. They must be in a travel kennel if they're left unattended. The motel is open from March 1 to November 1.

$$–$$$ El Colorado, 23 Manitou Ave., 719-685-5485, 800-782-2246, www.elcolorado.net. Built in 1926, the lodge, on 4 acres, consists of 27 adobe cabins that sleep one to seven people. Several are pet friendly, with a $75 deposit. You can leave your dog unattended inside, but the housekeepers won't enter during that time. Inside, the cabins have been updated with southwestern-style furnishings, air-conditioning, and microwaves and minifridges. Many have wood-burning fireplaces, and a third have kitchenettes or full kitchens. Be sure to keep Fido leashed on the property and clean up after him. Outside is a pool, hot tub, volleyball court, and playground.

$$–$$$ Silver Saddle, 215 Manitou Ave., 719-685-5611, 800-772-3353, www.silver-saddle.com. Only dogs 10 pounds and under are permitted.

Monument
$$–$$$ Sundance Mountain Lodge, 1865 Woodmoor Dr., 719-623-2863, www.sundancemountainlodge.com. Dogs can stay with a $25 one-time fee. It's okay to leave your dog unattended in the room. A restaurant and conference center are on-site.

Tarryall
$$–$$$$ Ute Trail River Ranch, 21446 CR 77 (21 miles from Lake George), 719-748-3015, www.utetrailriverranch.com. This rustic fishing camp on Tarryall Creek features six turn-of-the-century log cabins charmingly outfitted with western decor. Dogs are allowed on a case-by-case basis, for $10 extra per night, and usually only one dog at a time may visit the ranch. Two of the cabins have private baths, while a central showerhouse serves the others; all have kitchen facilities. The owners ask that you keep your dog leashed on the property's 70 acres, which includes some private hiking trails, but the ranch is surrounded by Pike National Forest land, where you and Fido can hike leash free (note that you will need to leash him back up if you venture into the

nearby Lost Creek Wilderness). A small shop at the ranch sells hand-tied flies, fishing rods, and basic groceries. Open from mid-May to the end of September (one cabin is available year-round).

Victor
$$–$$$$ Victor Hotel, 4th St. and Victor Ave., 719-689-3553, 800-713-4595, www.victorhotelcolorado.com. Originally a bank, this century-plus-old property, which is on the National Register of Historic Places, now houses the Victor Hotel. The cozy, modern rooms have exposed brick walls and nice woodwork. Four of them are pet friendly for a $10 nightly fee per dog, plus a $50 deposit, and you can leave yours unattended inside as long as he's in a travel kennel. The hotel reputedly has a resident ghost, Eddie, so if your dog starts barking at seemingly nothing in the hallway, don't tell him he's just being silly.

Woodland Park
$–$$ Coachlight Motel and RV Park, 19253 Hwy. 24, 719-687-8732, www.coachlight.net. Dogs are permitted in most of the motel's rooms for $10 per night, per pet, and a $50 deposit if you're paying in cash. Tent and RV sites are also available, and a trail on the property is convenient for close-at-hand dog walking.

$$–$$$ Rusty Spur Bunk & Barn, 583 S. Forty Rd., 719-687-4260, www.rustyspurbunkandbarn.com. The house rules are absolutely no dogs on the bed. As long as he abides, your four-legged traveler is welcome to stay with you in one of the four western-themed guest rooms for $10 extra per night, per dog (bathrooms are shared). Bogey, the resident Lab, will likely be game to entertain your dog, either on the 5-acre property or in the fenced dog run. You can all enjoy the B&B's huge outdoor patio, with fire pit, barbecue grill, and hot tub. And if you have a horse, bring him along, too—four corrals are on-site.

$$–$$$ Triple B Ranch, 27460 N. Hwy. 67 (3.5 miles north of Woodland Park), 719-687-8899, 877-687-8899, www .triplebranch.com. This working horse ranch is on 80 acres and backs to the Pike National Forest, so you and your dog certainly won't be at a loss for things to do here. In addition to horseback riding, there's a full slate of activities (volleyball, archery, and games, to name a few), hay rides (and, occasionally, sleigh rides in winter), a petting zoo, and an indoor pool and a hot tub—plus an 18-hole golf course is just across the road. The owners do ask that you keep your dog leashed on the property, so as not to interfere with the working dogs on the ranch. Fifteen cabins of various sizes are available for rent—some with full kitchens, some with kitchenettes, some with fireplaces—as well as the four-bedroom original homestead house (built in the 1950s). You'll be asked to put down a $50 deposit for your dog and pay an extra $15 per night, per pet, and it is okay to leave him unattended inside.

$$–$$$ Woodland Inn Bed & Breakfast, 159 Trull Rd., 719-687-8209, 800-226-9565, www.woodlandinn.com. The B&B accepts dogs on a case-by-case basis, and only one dog at time among all eight rooms. All rooms have private baths. Outside are 2 fenced acres, where you can exercise your dog off leash as long as he's not disturbing other guests.

$$–$$$$ Eagle Fire Lodge and Conference Center, 777 E. Hwy. 24, 719-687-5700, www.eaglefirelodge.com. This small lodge offers a range of accommodations, including standard rooms, minisuites, and one-bedroom cabins, all of which are dog friendly for $10 per night, per pet (the two-bedroom condo-style suites don't allow dogs). Some units have fireplaces and kitchens; all come with a microwave and refrigerator. You can leave your dog unattended inside if he stays in a travel kennel.

$$$$ Pikes Peak Paradise Bed and Breakfast, 236 Pinecrest Rd., 719-687-6656, 800-728-8282, www.pikespeakparadise .com. At this luxury B&B—think in-room hot tubs or whirlpools, large flat-screen TVs with DVD players, high-thread-count linens, and clean-lined, contemporary style—very well-behaved dogs are welcome in any of the five suites for $20 per pet, per day. Rover will also need to show proof of his vaccinations. Your well-behaved pooch may stay unattended in the room, perhaps while you enjoy some traditional German breakfast specialties.

CAMPGROUNDS

Cheyenne Mountain State Park. Southwest of Colorado Springs off Hwy. 115 (61 sites).

Eleven Mile State Park. About 11 miles from Lake George via CR 92 (349 sites).

Mueller State Park. About 3.5 miles south of Divide on Hwy. 67 (132 sites).

National forest campgrounds: **Meadow Ridge Campground** (19 sites) and **Thunder Ridge Campground** (21 sites) are both at Rampart Reservoir, 4.2 miles east of Woodland Park via CR 22 and FR 300; **South Meadows Campground** (64 sites), **Colorado Campground** (81 sites), and **Painted Rocks Campground** (18 sites) are north of Woodland Park off Hwy. 67; **The Crags Campground,** at the end of FR 383 off Hwy. 67, is south of Divide (17 sites).

Private campgrounds: **Lone Duck Campground and Cabins** in Cascade; **Colorado Springs South KOA and Kamping Kabins** in Fountain, **Mule Creek Outfitters/M Lazy C Ranch** in Lake George, **Rocky Top Motel and Campground** in Green Mountain Falls, **Coachlight Motel and RV Park** in Woodland Park and **Cripple Creek/Colorado Springs West KOA** and **Lost Burro Campground and Lodging** in Cripple Creek.

WORTH A PAWS

US Air Force Academy. Your leashed dog is welcome to tour the grounds of the Air Force Academy with you, but he won't be able to go in any of the buildings. The **Falcon Trail** makes a 12-mile loop around and through the academy; pick up the "Visitors Map and Guide" at the academy visitor center to see the trail's route and access points. The 4-mile round-trip **Stanley Canyon Trail** begins off of the Falcon Trail and enters Pikes Peak National Forest, leading to Stanley Reservoir. The **New Santa Fe Regional Trail** begins at Ice Lake and travels through the academy's eastern side, running north for about 15 miles to Palmer Lake. On its southern end, this gravel trail connects to the Pikes Peak Greenway Trail. If you're doing the driving tour of the academy and want to let your dog stretch his gams, stop at the Environmental Overlook off Academy Dr. just south of the turnoff for the visitor center. A short trail begins at the northeast end of the parking lot (look for the signs). For a quick out-and-back, stick to the wide gravel trail that goes to the overlook. There's also a nice loop option through ponderosa pine and gambel oak: take the path leading to the right from the overlook, then stay right at the small trail intersection to return to the parking lot. You can reach the academy from Exits 156B or 150B off I-25. 719-333-2025, www.usafa.af.mil

Cripple Creek Narrow Gauge Railroad. Small- to medium-sized dogs (this includes retrievers, but not Rottweilers

or pit bulls) can accompany their owners on the 4-mile round-trip ride that goes from Cripple Creek halfway to Victor and back. The narrated tour passes by historic mines and ghost towns. Trains leave every 40 minutes from the station at Bennett Ave. in Cripple Creek, from Memorial Day weekend to early October. Call 719-689-2640 or go to www.cripplecreekrailroad.com for more information and rates.

Pikes Peak Highway. Second only to the road up Mount Evans as the quickest way to bring your dog to the top of a Colorado fourteener, the Pikes Peak Hwy. snakes 19 miles to the 14,110-foot summit of legendary Pikes Peak. Once at the top, your dog can feel his fur ripple in the breeze and enjoy a breathtaking view of the eastern plains, up and down the Front Range, and the Sawatch and Mosquito ranges to the west. The road, a combination of pavement and gravel, is open year-round, weather permitting. Access is from Hwy. 24 just outside of Cascade, and you will have to pay a toll ($10 per person). For more information, call 719-385-PEAK or 800-318-9505, or go to www.pikespeakcolorado.com.

Manitou Cliff Dwellings Museum. Leashed dogs are welcome to tour the outdoor areas of this reconstructed example of Ancestral Puebloan architecture and culture built in 1906. Genuine Ancestral Puebloan artifacts are also on display. The Cliff Dwellings, located off Hwy. 24 just west of Colorado Springs, are open year-round, unless there's a lot of snow or ice. Admission is $9.50 per person. Call 719-685-5242 or 800-354-9971 for more information, or go to www.cliffdwellings.com.

Seven Falls. You're welcome to bring Fido and his leash to this series of seven waterfalls that cascade 181 feet in South

Cheyenne Cañon, on the southwestern side of Colorado Springs. An elevator brings you to the Eagle's Nest viewing platform, or you and your dog can tackle the 224 stairs along the falls, which lead to a short trail that goes to the much smaller Midnight Falls and a 2-mile round-trip nature trail that ends at an overlook of Colorado Springs and the plains beyond. Open year-round, the falls are illuminated at night by multicolored lights from mid-May to Labor Day and during the Christmas holidays. Admission is $9 per person during the day, $10.50 at night. Call 719-632-0765 for recorded information or go to www.sevenfalls.com.

Gigi's, 728 Manitou Ave., Manitou Springs, 719-685-4772, www.gigisshop.com. Billed as the "animal lovers' gift shop," Gigi's is more than your typical pet supply store. You'll find all manner of unique collars, leashes, and other pet accessories as well as dog-themed items for humans, including Christmas ornaments and wind chimes covering all the breeds. Your dog, who is welcome to browse along with you, will want to sniff out the array of treats and toys.

Dog Washes. PETCO (all locations except Continental Hts.; see Pet Provisions) charges $12 for its self-service dog wash, which includes shampoo, towels, and dryer.

Wag N' Wash (two locations; see Pet Provisions) offers three grades of washes: basic ($13), which includes shampoo and conditioner, grooming tools, towels, and use of the dryer; deluxe ($15), which ups the shampoo to premium and adds on a leave-in coat-shine and moisturizing treatment and cologne; and ultimate ($17), which includes everything in the deluxe and uses tubs with sprayers that premix shampoo and conditioner with the water for easy one-step washing.

Colorado Springs Heart Walk. Heart-healthy dogs on leash are welcome to join their owners in this annual pledge walk sponsored by the American Heart Association each June. A 5K course and a 1-mile family course wend their way around the Grand Lawn at Cordera in northeast Colorado Springs. Participants can register either as individuals or as teams, and there are incentive prizes for raising various levels of pledges. Food, family-friendly activities, and health and wellness vendors at the start of the course round out the event. Call the Pikes Peak Division of the American Heart Association at 719-635-7688 or go to www.csheartwalk.org for more information.

Bark in the Park. Has your dog ever attended a minor-league baseball game (or even a major-league game, for that matter)? Bring Fido to howl on the Colorado Springs Sky Sox—the Colorado Rockies' AAA farm team. What started as an annual event became a regular occurrence in 2000, and now select Wednesday home games are Dog Night. The stadium has a large, grassy picnic area along the third-base line where dogs and their owners can sit during the game (bring a blanket). You might want to engage in a vigorous play session with your dog before arriving; that way, he won't be as tempted to chase down baseballs during the main event, though both dogs and kids have been seen scurrying after foul balls. The Sky Sox donate one dollar for every dog who attends to the Humane Society of the Pikes Peak Region. There's a canine-themed pregame show each time, with dog-related demos, as well as Puppie Palooza, an expo of dog-product and service booths. As if that's not enough, one lucky dog and his owner are selected to throw out the first pitch (how's your dog's curveball?). Finally, according to marketing director Rai Henniger, the usual postgame fireworks show is not held on Wednesday nights "in deference to our canine friends." Security Service Field is at 4385 Tutt Blvd. (corner of Powers Blvd. and Barnes Rd.). For more information, call the Sky Sox ticket line at 719-597-SOXX or go to www.skysox.com.

K9-5K and Pawtober Fest. Held at Nosh restaurant in Colorado Springs and in a nearby park in mid-October, this annual event includes a 5K run/walk for dogs and their owners. After the race, you and your dog can amble among the booths of pet products and information; compete in contests such as best pet tricks, doggie musical chairs, dog/owner look-alike; check out canine demonstrations; and enjoy the live music. You can also raise a glass at the beer garden on the restaurant's patio, sponsored by local beermaker Bristol Brewing (your first pint purchased includes a commemorative glass). Your registration fee of $25 (as well as pledges that you raise for the event) nets a T-shirt, a bandanna for your dog, and a goody bag for both you and Fido. All proceeds benefit the Humane Society of the Pikes Peak Region (719-473-1741; www.hsppr. org). Register at the Humane Society (610 Abbott Ln. in Colorado Springs) or on the day of the event ($5 extra).

Colorado Springs Canine Frisbee Championships. During the last Saturday in May or the first one in June, Frisbee-toting dogs gather in Bear Creek Park in the Springs to show off their leaping and catching prowess. The competition, put on by Colorado Disc Dogs, features two events: the minidistance, in which dogs receive points for catching distance and a bonus for midair catches in 60-second rounds; and the freestyle, in which they demonstrate their best tricks in 90 seconds. There's no entrance fee, and anyone and their dog is welcome, regardless of your dog's previous competitive experience. You can also bring your dog just to watch; maybe he'll get inspired to com-

pete the next year. For more information, go to www.coloradodiscdogs.com.

 Cave of the Winds. Dogs are not allowed on the cave tours of this mile-long cavern or at the nighttime laser show.

 Cheyenne Mountain Zoo and Will Rogers Shrine of the Sun. It's probably no surprise that dogs aren't allowed in the zoo, but you should be aware that they're also not allowed at the Will Rogers Shrine (Rover can ride up in the car with you, but he's not supposed to set paw outside). The zoo can accommodate your small- to medium-sized dog at the front gate, at no charge, during a visit. For more information, call 719-633-9925.

 Ghost Town Wild West Museum. Dogs are discouraged from visiting this reconstructed frontier town in Colorado Springs.

 North Pole and Santa's Workshop. Your dog won't be able to visit Santa at his mid-May through Christmas Eve residence west of Colorado Springs.

 Pikes Peak Cog Railway. You won't be able to bring your dog on the Swiss-made cog train that climbs to the summit of Pikes Peak. If you're considering bringing Fido to doggie daycare, know that the round-trip ride takes just over three hours, and trains operate year-round, leaving from the depot on Ruxton Ave. in Manitou Springs. Call 719-685-5401 for reservations and fee information.

DOGGIE DAYCARE
Colorado Springs

A Paw Above Canine Boarding Service, 1447 Woolsey Heights, Claremont Business Park, 719-386-7291, www.apawaboveboarding.com. $15/day; $10/half-day. Dogs play together in small groups or individually and get a snack and a one-on-one walk. Open 7 AM–6 PM, Monday to Friday.

Airway Boarding Kennels, 5280 E. Edison, 719-574-1886, www.airwayvethosp.com. $12/day. Proof of an internasal bordatella vaccination received every six months is required, and all vaccinations must be vet administered. The facility is part of the Airway Veterinary Hospital. Open 8 AM–5:30 PM, Monday to Friday; 8 AM–3 PM, Saturday; 8–9 AM and 2–3 PM, Sunday; closed for lunch 11–noon, Monday to Saturday.

Broadmoor Bluffs Kennel, 45 E. Old Broadmoor Rd., 719-636-3344, www.brownvet.com. $12–$15/day, depending on the size of dog. Part of the Brown Veterinary Hospital. Open 8 AM–5:30 PM, Monday to Saturday; closed for lunch 12:30–1:30 PM, all days.

Camp Bow Wow, 4295 Northpark Dr., 719-260-9247, and 1020 Ford St., 719-573-9247, www.campbowwow.com. $20/day; $15/half-day. Canine campers must go through a free interview day before being accepted. The Camp Bow Wow experience includes separate playgroups into which dogs are placed based on size and temperament; they have all-day access to indoor and outdoor play areas with dog-specific play equipment and, in warmer weather, wading pools. You can keep tabs on the great time your pooch is having via the online Camper Cam. Open 7 AM–7 PM, Monday to Friday; 8–10 AM and 6–8 PM, Saturday, Sunday, and holidays.

Canine Campus, 3116 Karen Pl., 719-448-9600, www.caninecampus.us. $20/day; $12/half-day. Dogs must pass an admissions tests to be accepted. Canine students can play with others, indoors and out, or just nap as much as they want. A school lunch is also available for $3. Open 6 AM–6 PM, Monday to Friday; 8 AM–6 PM, Saturday; 7–9 AM and 4–6 PM, Sunday.

Countryside Kennels, 7945 Maverick Rd., 719-495-3678, www.countrysidekennels3.com. $15/day. Dogs play together in a large outdoor yard, and a 15-minute nature walk is available for an extra $5. Open 7 AM–5:30 PM, Monday to Saturday; 4-5:30 PM, Sunday.

Lucky Dog Resort and Training Center, 4401 Mark Dabling Blvd., 719-599-9663, and 2801 Janitell Rd. E., 719-527-9663, www.bealuckydog.com. $17/day; $12/half-day. The lucky dogs who come here participate in at least an hour of supervised outdoor playtime with dogs of their own size, as well as indoor play sessions, broken up with several rest periods in between. They also get a Kong toy with a treat inside once a day. Add-on activities include a half-hour of one-on-one ball playing ($3), a 20- to 30-minute individual walk ($10), and swimming in the pool in summer, with a serving of doggie ice cream ($1.50 for about two hours). Web cams let you track all the fun. Open 6:30 AM–7 PM, Monday to Friday; 8–11 AM and 4–7 PM, Saturday and Sunday.

Northwest Animal Hospital and Pet Care Center, 4575 N. Chestnut St., 719-593-8582, www.nwanimalhospital.com. $18/day; $10/half-day. Dogs socialize in indoor and outdoor play yards; the latter has a swimming pool in warm weather. Open 7 AM–6 PM, Monday to Friday; 7 AM–2 PM, Saturday; 9 AM–noon, Sunday.

PetsHotel at PetSmart, 7680 N. Academy Blvd., 719-531-7870, www.petsmart .com. $16–$20/day. The store differentiates between day camp and daycare. In the former, dogs get to play with each other from 9 to 5 in one of three indoor playrooms, which have toys and play equipment, with an hour off at noon to nap in private rooms. The cost is $20 a dog, and they're divided into playgroups by size and temperament. If your dog prefers not to socialize as much, you can put him in daycare ($16); he'll get his own room to snooze in, with one hour of play breaks and two walks. Open 7 AM–9 PM, Monday to Saturday; 7 AM–7 PM, Sunday.

Polo Springs Veterinary Hospital, 5557 Austin Bluffs Pkwy., 719-264-8384, www.polosprings.com. $9.40–$14/day, depending on size of dog. Dogs get four walks a day. Open 8 AM–5 PM, Monday to Friday.

Rampart Kennels, 5977 Templeton Gap Rd., 719-591-0066. $1/hour. Open 7 AM–6 PM, Monday to Friday; 7 AM–noon, Saturday.

Sunrise Kennels, 6580 Vincent Dr., 719-598-8220, www.sunrise-woodmenpetcare .net. $15/day. A stay includes playtime off leash in an outside yard. Nature walks, on leash, are also available for $5–$10 extra. Affiliated with the Woodmen Kennels next door (see below). Open 7:30 AM–5:30 PM, Monday to Friday; 7:30 AM–3:30 PM, Saturday.

Woodmen Kennels, 6440 Vincent Dr., 719-598-4154, www.sunrise-woodmen petcare.net. $15/day. A stay includes playtime off leash in an outside yard. Nature walks, on leash, are also available for $5–$10 extra. Affiliated with the Sunrise Kennels next door (see above). Open 7:30 AM–5:30 PM, Monday to Friday; 7:30 AM–3:30 PM, Saturday.

Fountain
Land of Ahs Kennel, 12599 Jordon Rd., 719-382-1126, www.landofahskennel .com. $16–$20/day, depending on the size of dog. Various sizes of climate-controlled kennels, with an air-filtering system, and outdoor play yards are available. Open 7 AM–5 PM, Monday to Friday; 7 AM–noon, Saturday.

Monument
Camp Bow Wow, 18985 Base Camp Rd., 719-632-9247, www.campbowwow.com. $20/day; $15/half-day. Canine campers must go through a free interview day before being accepted. The Camp Bow Wow experience includes separate playgroups into which dogs are placed based on size and temperament; they have all-day access to indoor and outdoor play areas with dog-specific play equipment and, in warmer weather, wading pools. You can keep tabs on the great time your pooch is having via the online Camper Cam.

PET PROVISIONS
Colorado Springs
Canine Solutions, 2815 N. El Paso St., 719-578-8005

Circle F Ranch Supply, 115 E. Garden of the Gods Rd., 719-599-5100 and 711 N. Union Blvd., 719-578-0666

Colorado Agri-Feed, 4625 Park Vista Blvd., 719-599-5961

Countryside Kennels, 7945 Maverick Rd., 719-495-3678, www.countryside kennels3.com

Le Pooch Connection, 2360 Montebello Square Dr., 719-522-9000

Lucky Dog Resort and Training Center, 4401 Mark Dabling Blvd., 719-599-9663 and 2801 Janitell Rd. E., 719-527-9663, www.bealuckydog.com

Mike's Natural Pet Market, 3620 Jeannine Dr., 719-570-1488, www.mikesnatural petmarket.com

Moochie Poochie, 728 Village Center Dr. (Safeway Village), 719-447-1818, www .moochiepoochie.com

PETCO, 1820 W. Uintah, 719-578-1123; 5720 N. Academy Blvd., 719-536-0160; 1650 E. Cheyenne Mountain Blvd., 719-540-8090; 4515 Continental Hts., 719-495-4337; 3060 N. Powers Blvd., 719-637-8777, www.petco.com

PetSmart, 571 N. Academy Blvd., 719-570-1313; 2160 Southgate Rd., 719-447-0624; 7680 N. Academy Blvd., 719-531-7870; 2965 New Center Point, 719-637-3308, www.petsmart.com

Wag N' Wash, 1625 W. Uintah St., 719-457-9274 and 1234 E. Woodmen Rd., 719-228-9274, www.wagnwash.com

Fountain
Land of Ahs Kennel, 12599 Jordon Rd., 719-382-1126, www.landofahskennel .com

Manitou Springs
Gigi's, 728 Manitou Ave., 719-685-4772, www.gigisshop.com (see Worth a Paws)

Monument
PetSmart, 16086 Jackson Creek Pkwy., 719-484-0235, www.petsmart.com

CANINE ER
Colorado Springs
Animal Emergency Care Center North (AAHA certified), 5520 N. Nevada Ave., #150, 719-260-7141, www.animalercare .com. Open 6 PM–8 AM, Monday to Friday; 24 hours on weekends and holidays.

Animal Emergency Care Center South (AAHA certified), 3775 Airport Rd. (at Academy Blvd.), 719-578-9300, www .animalercare.com. Open 6 PM–8 AM, Monday to Friday; 24 hours on weekends and holidays.

Banfield Emergency and Critical Pet Care, 5956 Stetson Hills Blvd., 719-473-0482, www.banfield.net. Open 5:30 PM–9 AM, Monday to Friday; 24 hours on weekends.

RESOURCES
Colorado Springs Convention and Visitors Bureau, 515 S. Cascade, Ste. 104, Colorado Springs, 719-635-7506, 800-368-4748, www.experiencecoloradosprings.com

Cripple Creek Welcome Center, 5th and Bennett Ave., Cripple Creek, 719-689-3289, 877-858-4653, www.cripple-creek .co.us

Manitou Springs Chamber of Commerce, 354 Manitou Ave., Manitou Springs, 719-685-5089, 800-642-2567, www .manitousprings.org

Pikes Peak Ranger District, Pike National Forest, 601 S. Weber St., Colorado Springs, 719-636-1602

Appendix A
Fourteener Dogs

Climbing "fourteeners," or peaks with elevations 14,000 feet or above, has become an increasingly popular summertime (and occasionally wintertime) activity in Colorado. It's also somewhat controversial, as many believe that the large numbers of hikers tromping up and down the trails is causing irreparable damage to the alpine environment. You can easily deduce that many people are even less thrilled about dogs on fourteeners.

If you and your dog share most hiking outings, however, chances are you're not going to be easily dissuaded from bringing him along for the really spectacular stuff. With this in mind, I've compiled the following listing of fourteeners, grouped according to dog suitability. After turning back about half a mile from the summit of Snowmass Mountain because Clover and another dog couldn't handle the knife-edge ridge, I realized that some advance knowledge would have saved us the frustration of an incomplete trek.

Tansy, with family, on her first fourteener, Mount Shavano, at age 1½.

Athletic dogs can successfully summit many fourteeners. Clover only hung up her climbing collar at the age of twelve, after summiting twenty such peaks. Be sure to bring plenty of water. Dog booties (see the Gearhound appendix) are also an excellent accessory to take along, as tender paws can easily get worn ragged on talus or scree slopes, or other rough terrain. And if you're out to tackle peaks that require heavy-duty rock scrambling or knife-edge ridges, do both of yourselves a favor and leave Rover at home.

The categories that follow assume you'll ascend via the easiest routes. Nearly all fourteeners have alternate ascents that may or may not be suitable for dogs. For more specifics on routes, refer to *Colorado's Fourteeners: From Hikes to Climbs*, by Gerry Roach, or *Dawson's Guide to Colorado's Fourteeners*, volumes 1 and 2, by Louis Dawson.

I CAN DO THIS!
Mount Antero
Mount Belford
Mount Bierstadt
Mount Bross
Mount Columbia
Culebra Peak
Mount Democrat
Mount Elbert
Mount Evans
Grays Peak
Handies Peak
Mount Harvard
Humboldt Peak
Huron Peak
La Plata Peak
Mount Lincoln
Mount Massive

Missouri Mountain
Mount Oxford
Pikes Peak
Mount Princeton
Quandary Peak
Redcloud Peak
San Luis Peak
Mount Shavano
Mount Sherman
Sunshine Peak
Tabeguache Peak
Torreys Peak
Uncompahgre Peak
Mount Yale

GIVE ME A BOOST UP THAT ROCK, WILL YA?

Blanca Peak
Castle Peak
Challenger Point
Ellingwood Point
Mount of the Holy Cross
Mount Lindsey
Mount Sneffels
Windom Peak

PLEASE LEAVE ME BEHIND

Capitol Peak
Crestone Needle
Crestone Peak
El Diente Peak
Mount Eolus
Kit Carson Peak
Little Bear Peak
Maroon Peak
North Maroon Peak
Pyramid Peak
Snowmass Mountain
Sunlight Peak
Wetterhorn Peak
Mount Wilson
Wilson Peak

Clover, with the author, on her last fourteener, Mount Oxford, at age 12.

I COULDN'T IF I WANTED TO

Longs Peak—it's in Rocky Mountain National Park, where dogs are prohibited from all trails.

Appendix B
Gearhound

These days, as much thought is going into dog gear as into people gear; you can find an array of canine accessories that will make your dog's travels and hikes easier and more enjoyable. The well-equipped dog will want to have at least some of the following items in his travel bag. Phone numbers and websites are provided for each manufacturer; call to find out which stores near you carry the items that your dog can't wait to get his paws on.

DOG PACKS

Backpacks for dogs are a great invention: they allow Rover to schlep his own food, water, treats, or poop bags on long day hikes or multiday outings (assuming you don't overburden him, of course). And at the end of a backpacking trip, you can make your dog carry out the trash! Just as with packs for people, your dog should come in for a fitting before purchase to make sure the pack carries comfortably on his back. With the variety of packs available, your dog should be able to find at least one that suits him. Mountaineering or high-end pet specialty stores are your best bets for pack shopping. A few of the sturdier packs we've found are listed here.

Rocky Mountain K-9 Accessories, in Boulder, has developed the unique Trailblazer pack system. Rather than a pannier on each side, the system consists of a harness and one Cordura pack that sits on top of the dog's back, with an attached insulated water-bottle holder on each side. Also included are two 22- or 28-ounce water bottles, a collapsible water bowl, a nylon emergency leash, and even a small poop pouch, with a replaceable liner, that hooks on the pack's outside. The harness buckles are padded with fleece, and the pack comes in three sizes. 303-665-8533, www.rockymountaink9.com

Mountainsmith, a Colorado company well known for its human packs, offers two categories of dog packs: the streamlined Sport Line, which comes in two sizes, and the standard Dog Packs, available in three sizes, with carrying capacity keyed to the dog's weight. All of the packs have fleece-lined harnesses with mesh fabric on top for venting, reflective trim, and a D-ring on the harness for easy leash attachment. Sport Line packs have an ergonomic suspension system with slightly tear-drop-shaped panniers, an adjustable sternum strap, one large right-side pannier, and two smaller ones on the left side, one of which has a mesh bottom so wet toys or other items can dry out. Standard packs consist of two large panniers with compression straps and rain flaps over the zippers, and a mesh compartment for storing a leash. Mountainsmith also offers the Dog Trippin package, which includes everything your dog needs for a backpacking trip along with a standard dog pack: a fleece-lined blanket to sleep on, compressible food and water bowls, and a leash. 800-551-5889, www.mountainsmith.com

OllyDog, a Bay Area company founded by former employees of The North Face and Sierra Designs who have ample experience in designing packs, offers the Saddle Up dog pack in three sizes. The two large saddle bags open via two-way zippers, and a grab handle atop the harness lets you assist your dog up or over obstacles. The harness buckles are offset so that they won't chafe your dog. And the pack has reflective patches. 800-OLLYDOG, www.ollydog.com

Wolf Packs, out of southern Oregon, makes three styles of thoughtfully designed dog packs in four sizes. All packs are made out of water-repellent, urethane-coated Cordura Plus nylon; the side-release buckles are padded with Polartec 300 fleece for Fido's comfort. Panniers have slanted front edges to minimize catching on branches or brush and reduce wear on your dog's elbows. The neck area of each pack is contoured for comfort. The top-of-the-line Banzai Explorer pack has ballistic nylon side guards, horizontal compression straps, and reflective trim. The Trekker Reflector pack features reflective material for safety. The one-size-fits-all Saddle Bag is lightweight and streamlined, designed for short day hikes (and for use by assistance dogs, who may need to maneuver in tight spaces). The Wolf Packs website has helpful information on fitting your dog's pack and training him to hike with it. 541-482-7669, www.wolfpacks.com

Granite Gear, a northern Minnesota company that also produces people packs and canoe gear, manufactures the Ruff Rider dog pack. With a Cordura exterior and a fleece underside that's padded in key areas, the packs comes in three sizes and two colors. Nifty features include an adjustable harness, reflective trim, and tubular nylon webbing that won't chafe. There's also a D-ring on the pack so you can connect the leash directly to it. 800-222-8032, www.granitegear.com

Ruffwear, in Bend, Oregon, makes two canine-specific packs. Both feature harnesses with five points at which you can adjust fit and load dispersion. The premier Palisades Pack, in three sizes, has lots of bells and whistles, including removable saddle bags (handy for stream crossings), an integrated hydration system (à la Camelbak) so you can empty water directly into your dog's bowl, a webbing handle so you can lift your dog over obstacles on the trail, horizontal compression straps protected by a zippered side pocket, and a V-ring leash attachment point. The more basic Approach Pack, available in five sizes, is more streamlined and has fixed saddle bags. Both packs have fleece-padded buckles and straps as well as reflective trim. 888-783-3932, www.ruffwear.com

Kelty, a Boulder-based company known for its backpacks, sleeping bags, and tents, also manufactures the Chuckwagon dog pack, available in four sizes. Made out of sturdy ripstop nylon, the pack has two large, expandable saddle bags with reflective trim. The adjustable harness has padded buckles and a grab handle on top so you can help your dog over rocks or fallen trees, or out of streams. The pack even includes a bear bell for those trips to the wilds of Montana or Alaska—or your dog could use it to warn the neighborhood cats. 800-423-2320, www.kelty.com

Caribou, out of Alice, Texas, produces the value-priced Woofer dog pack. Made out of nylon pack cloth and Cordura Plus, the pack comes in two sizes. Quick-release buckles make for easy attachment, and a mesh yoke keeps your dog's back cool. 800-824-4153, www.caribou.com

DOG BOOTIES

The cutest thing next to infant socks may be dog booties, sturdy little shoes that slip on your dog's paws to protect them from snow and ice balls, hot desert rock, or sharp-edged talus. Clover always gets lots of compliments when she's sporting her set. The key is to find booties that will stay on. Allow your dog to get accustomed to his booties by letting him wear them around the house a few times before your first outing. And on snowy days, he'll get the snuggest fit if you put his booties on before he gets out of the car.

Ruffwear makes Grip Trex Bark 'N Boots in seven sizes. The booties have seamless mesh uppers, for breathability and drainage, and beefy Vibram nonmarking rubber soles, for great grip and traction. And like human shoes, they're built on an anatomical sole for precise fit. The cuff expands for easy on and off, and a band wraps around the dog's leg at the top of the bootie and secures with a D-ring and Velcro closure. Skyliner Bark 'N Boots, also in seven sizes, are designed more for everyday wear rather than hiking, in instances when a dog might need protection from extreme temperatures or abrasive terrain; they can also be helpful for older dogs who drag their paws or need a bit more traction. The booties have a flexible, nonmarking rubber sole and a generous cuff, with a Velcro strap to keep them on a dog's paw. And if your dog does shake off a bootie and loses it, you can purchase individual replacements from Ruffwear. 888-783-3932, www.ruffwear.com

Granite Gear offers three types of ergonomically designed dog booties in six sizes. The Endurance boot is made of abrasion-resistant Cordura nylon on the sides, laminated fleece on the top and tongue, and Hypalon synthetic rubber for the soles. A Velcro reflective strap around the cuff keeps them on. The Mush boots are almost identical in structure, except they're designed especially for grip on snow—instead of rubber, the soles are made from the same synthetic nylon plush as the climbing skins used by backcountry skiers. Dog Clogs, for urban

dogs as well as country hikers, have slightly lighter nylon uppers and soles made of ComfoTek, a lightweight yet durable closed-cell foam that cushions and absorbs impact (it's used in human footwear, too). The Endurance and Mush booties are sold in sets of two; Dog Clogs are sold in sets of four. 800-222-8032, www.granitegear.com

Ultrapaws, out of Brainerd, Minnesota, makes four styles of booties that vary in traction and durability. The Rugged dog boots, designed for use in all kinds of conditions, are made of heavy-duty, water-resistant nylon with a reinforced toe and a sturdy sole of recycled tire rubber. Two Velcro straps wrap around each leg to fasten the booties, with a bit of foam at the point of closure for cushioning and extra grip. The boots come in four sizes. The Durable dog boots, in six sizes, are similar, but the soles are made of Tough-tek, a polyester/neoprene rubber combo that's flexible, grippy in both dry and wet conditions, and abrasion resistant. The Traction boots, available in seven sizes, consist of fleece with a round patch of recycled tire rubber sewn on the bottom; they close with one Velcro strap. And the value-priced Endurance boots are simply lightweight, water-resistant nylon pouches that secure around a dog's leg with a Velcro strap; they come in four sizes. 800-355-5575, www.ultrapaws.com

TRAVEL BOWLS

A collapsible food/water bowl is an invaluable travel aid. It's lightweight and can easily be stashed in a backpack or fanny pack so your dog has something to drink out of on the trail.

Among the sturdiest we've found so far are made by **Ruffwear**. Two models of the bowls—the Quencher and the Go Between—come in 1- and 2.5-quart sizes and are made of recycled polyester pack cloth with a seamless, waterproof, nylon liner. The lighter Trail Runner model has a 24-ounce capacity. The Quencher and Go Between also come in styles with a drawstring top, so you can leave in some food without worrying about spillage. 888-783-3932, www.ruffwear.com.

OllyDog makes rectangular travel bowls that retain their shape over many days of use. The reinforced sidewalls stay upright when open, yet the bowl easily folds into a compact package with a strap and snap to hold it together. Plus, the bowls, available in three sizes, come in fun retro-pop prints and other bright patterns. 800-OLLYDOG, www.ollydog.com

Clover laps up water from her OllyDog portable bowl.

Guyot Designs, which makes innovative camping accessories, offers the Squishy Bowl Pet. A wider and flatter version of the company's popular Squishy Bowls, which are made of food-grade silicone, the dishes squash down for stuffing in a backpack or bag. Once you take them out, they immediately spring back into shape. They're also totally waterproof and easily washable, and come in three sizes. 207-348-1030, www.guyotdesigns.com

Planet Dog, an eco- and socially conscious company in Portland, Maine, makes its travel bowl in 1.5- and 2.5-quart sizes. The bowls are constructed of polyurethane-coated poly-canvas and include a small loop so you can hang them, for example, from a backpack with a carabiner. 800-381-1516, www.planetdog.com

Granite Gear has two circular packable bowls: the Grrrub Bowl, for food, has a drawstring closure; the Slurpin Bowl, for water, is open topped. Both come in three sizes and have webbing loops so you can hang them up to dry out. 800-222-8032, www.granitegear.com

LEASHES

In some cases, a leash is more than just a leash. For example, the Absorber Leash from **Granite Gear** has a stretchy base covered with accordion-pleated nylon. When Rover tugs at it, you're less likely to get your arm wrenched out of its socket, as the leash absorbs some of that force. 800-222-8032, www.granitegear.com

Ruffwear makes a variety of innovative leashes, including the Stow'n Go, handy to keep in your glove compartment. This ultralight nylon leash has an integrated collar that will fit any size dog and includes a small poop-bag dispenser attached near the handle. Likewise, the Quick Draw is useful for times when your dog is with you off leash, but you have to restrain him immediately. The length of lightweight nylon webbing clips onto your dog's collar and wraps once around it, staying put with a Velcro closure. When

Fido needs to be on a leash, pronto, pull the grab tab, and the Quick Draw speedily unfurls; voilà, instant leash. 888-783-3932, www.ruffwear.com

OTHER COOL STUFF

People have PowerBars for quick energy pick-me-ups during outings; active dogs have **Power Bones**, from Durango, Colorado–based **Zuke's**. The nutritious treats come in beef, chicken, and peanut butter flavors, and include ground oats and rice, barley, apple, carrot, beets, sweet potato, ground flax seed, vegetable glycerin, brewer's yeast, canola oil, and a complement of vitamins and minerals. Yum! Zuke's makes other goodies, too—including Hip Action, which contains glucosamine and chondroitin—and even treats for cats. 866-985-3364; www .zukes.com

Mountainsmith's system of modular totes have become popular for organizing and hauling stuff, from camping equipment to groceries. The **K-9 Cube** ensures your pooch stays organized, too. The rectangular ripstop nylon tote bag contains a vinyl-lined food container with a zip-open lid, a collapsible water bowl with a waterproof lining, a collapsible food bowl with a drawstring cinch top, and even a soft-sided Frisbee. The bag itself has two large, mesh side pockets and a top pocket that puts poop bags within quick reach; plus, one side includes a vinyl-lined panel that zips open to become a drop-down placemat, perfectly sized to hold the food and water bowls. When you're in transit, everything stows neatly inside the tote, ready for easy access at your next stop. 800-551-5889, www.mountainsmith.com

More and more people on the road with their dogs are bringing travel kennels for Rover to sleep in, especially as many hotels allow you to leave your dog unattended in your room only if he's safely crated. Collapsible lightweight crates, like the **Dog Digs** from **ABO Gear**, an Australian company with a US presence, are especially convenient. The soft-sided, steel-framed crate assembles in a flash, no tools required: just pop up the integrated poles on each side. Access the interior from the top or either side. The crate's corners are reinforced to guard against wear and tear. When you're ready to pack up, the crate easily collapses into a horizontal roll, which then fits into a handled carry bag. The crate is available in two sizes. 888-604-8249, www.abogear.com

For toting your dog's food, the **Weekender Travel Feedbag** from Planet Dog, made of water-resistant poly-canvas, holds up to 30 cups of kibble. The top-loading closure rolls down and secures with a quick-release buckle, similar to the way a paddling dry bag works. 800-381-1516, www.planetdog.com

The **Mt. Bachelor Pad**, from Ruffwear, is a roll-up blanket in two sizes that your dog can snooze on in the hotel and car. One side is lined with recycled fleece; the other is made of waterproof recycled poly-cloth. An inch of padding provides some cushioning. Attached Velcro straps secure the roll, which weighs two to three pounds, when Fido is on the go. For more cushioning, try the **Flophouse Foam Pad**. Available in three sizes, it has several layers of foam of different densities. The base layer is waterproof, and the top layer has a filterlike construction that—along with side drainage holes—empties out any water in the bed. 888-783-3932, www.ruffwear.com

Coleman, the venerable camping goods company, makes the **Hibernation Sleeping Bag** for dogs. The rectangular, flannel-lined bag comes in four sizes and has many of the same features as Coleman's human bags, including a snag-resistant zipper, construction that keeps the synthetic insulation from shifting, and a draft seal to keep heat from leaking out along the zipper. The cotton-topped bag also has a water-resistant bottom. 800-835-3278, www.coleman.com

REI's Adventure Dog Dream Bed, which comes in three sizes, has a 1.75-inch-thick self-inflating pad (like a Thermarest) made of compressible foam. (If you forget your own sleeping pad, you may be tempted to try to steal the dog's!) The nylon cover that goes over it is resistant to punctures from claws and includes thick, comfy fleece on the sleeping side. It also zips off for washing. The bed weighs about 2.5 pounds (before inflation) and comes with its own stuff sack for storage. 800-426-4840, www.rei.com

Cool Pooch, in New Mexico, makes the **Cool Pooch Sport Water Bottle**, which you can safely share with your dog. The plastic bottle has a funnel-shaped cup that attaches at the top and an attached straw. You drink from the straw, then bend it over to pour water into the cup for Fido to slurp. 877-CLPOOCH, www.coolpooch.com

Ruffwear offers the **K-9 First Aid Kits**. In addition to a complete supply of medical aids for treating on-trail injuries—including cohesive tape that sticks to itself, allowing you to create a bandage over fur—the kits come with the "Pet First Aid Quick Guide to Animal Emergencies." 888-783-3932, www.ruffwear.com

Index

A
ABO Gear, 372
accommodations. *See also* campgrounds: Arkansas River Valley area, 318–26; Aspen, 205–7; Black Canyon area, 244–46; Boulder area, 90–94; Central City-Clear Creek County area, 104–5; Colorado Springs area, 349–59; Denver area, 37–56; Durango area, 293–98; Estes Park, 137–43; Fort Collins area, 115–19; Glenwood Springs area, 215–19; Grand Junction area, 234–38; Greeley-Northeastern Plains, 127–31; Gunnison-Crested Butte-Lake City area, 254–63; Mesa Verde area, 280–86; Northwestern Colorado, 223–26; overview, 8–9; Pueblo and Southeastern Plains, 333–38; San Luis Valley area, 306–13; Steamboat Springs and North Park area, 164–68; Summit County, 177–80; Telluride-Ouray-Silverton area, 270–75; Vail-Leadville area, 191–95; Winter Park-Grand Lake-Granby area, 152–57
Action Kennel, 64
airline regulations, 4
Airway Boarding Kennels, 363
Aisik's Meadow, 21
Akron, 128
Akunow Kennel, 299
Alamosa, 305, 306, 313–14
Alamosa National Wildlife Refuge, 305
Alamosa Valley Veterinary Clinic, 313, 314
Alderfer/Three Sisters Park, 29
All About Paws, 73
Allbrick Boarding Kennels, 66
Allenspark, 137
All Pets Center, 238, 239
Almont, 254–55
Alpine Animal Hospital, 300
Alpine Dog House, The, 70
Alpine Gulch, 253
Alpine Meadows Ranch and Kennel, 209
Alpine Veterinary Hospital, 314

Alta Vista Animal Hospital, 248
American Animal Hospital Association (AAHA), 2, 10–12
Anasazi Heritage Center, 286–87
Andelt's Pet Motel, 122
Animal Care Center of Chaffee County PC, 329
Animal Critical Care and Emergency Services, 77
Animal Emergency and Critical Care at Aspen Meadow Veterinary Specialists, 101
Animal Emergency and Specialty Center, 77
Animal Emergency Care Center North, 365
Animal Emergency Care Center South, 365
Animal Emergency Room, 340
Animal ER, 77
Animal Hospital of Crested Butte, 264
Animal Hospital of the Rockies, 144
Animal Hospital Specialty Center, 77
Animal House, The, 143
Animal Lodge, 66
Animal Medical Center of Estes Park, 144
Animal Rescue of the Rockies' 5K Run and Fun Walk, 180–81
Animal Urgent Care of Arvada, 77
Animas Mountain, 291
Animas River Trail, 291
Annie Walk, 121
Antonito, 306–8
Apex, 16
Arapahoe Animal Hospital, 97, 100
Arf Walk, 327
Arfy's Mercantile for Dogs & Cats, 121
Argo Gold Mill, 105–6
Arkansas River Valley, 315–29
Arkansas Riverwalk, 317
Ark-Valley Animal Hospital, 340
Arvada, 20–21, 23–24, 60, 64, 74
Ashcroft Boarding Kennels, 122
Ashcroft Ghost Town, 203
Aspen, 198–209
Aspen Boarding Kennel, The, 208
Aspen Grove, 63
Aspen Mountain, 199

Aspen Music Festival Concerts, 208
Aspen Valley Pet Care, 219
Aurora, 24, 33–34, 37–39, 64–65, 74, 77
Avon, 191–92, 196, 197
Avon Pet Centre, 197

B
backpacks, 368–69
Bailey, 56
bakeries: Boulder area, 95; Denver area, 61; Fort Collins area, 121, 122
Banfield Emergency and Critical Pet Care, 365
Banfield 24-Hour Emergency Hospital, 78
Barbara Whipple Trail, 316
Bark! Doggie Daycare + Hotel + Spa, 66
Barking Lot, The, 64
Bark in the Park, 361–62
Barkly Manor, 66
Bark Park at David A. Lorenz Regional Park, 36
Bark Park at Pueblo City Park, 330
Barnum Dog Park, 17–18
Barr Lake State Park, 23
Bart & Yeti's Restaurant, 195
Basalt, 209, 220
Bayfield, 293, 300
B&B for D.O.G., 64
Bear Creek Animal Hospital, 227
Bear Creek National Recreation Trail, 266–67
Bear Creek Regional Park, 342, 343–44
Bear Creek Trail, 269
Beau Monde Kennels, 65
Beaver Brook Trail, 29–30
Beaver Ranch Bark Park, 26
Beds n Biscuits, 73
Bellvue, 115
Bent's Old Fort, 4
Bent's Old Fort National Historic Site, 338–39
Bergen Park Inn, 69
Berkeley Lake Park, 17
Berthoud, 122
Best Friends Forever Pet Care, 66
Best Friends Pet Care, 73
bicycling: Arkansas River Valley area, 318; Aspen, 204; Black Canyon area, 244; Boulder area, 89; Central City-Clear Creek County area, 104; Colorado Springs area, 348; Denver area, 37; Durango area, 292; Estes Park, 136–37; Fort Collins area, 114; Glenwood

Springs area, 214; Grand Junction area, 233; Gunnison-Crested Butte-Lake City area, 253; Mesa Verde area, 280; Northwestern Colorado, 223; overview, 7; San Luis Valley area, 306; Steamboat Springs-North Park area, 164; Summit County, 176; Telluride-Ouray-Silverton area, 268; Vail-Leadville area, 190; Winter Park-Grand Lake-Granby area, 151
Big Backyard, The, 66
Big Dry Creek Park, 20
Bighorn Park, 187
Big Willis Gulch, 184–85
Bill Goodspeed Happy Tails Dog Park, 21–22
Biscuit's Dog Pawlour, 122
Bishop Castle, 327
Black Canyon Area, 242–48
Black Canyon of the Gunnison National Park, 4, 243–44
Blaine Basin, 267–68
Blessing of the Animals, 263–64
Blue Hills Dog and Cat Shoppe, 95
Blue Skies Park, 86
Bluff Lake Nature Center, 25
Bohn Park, 88
Bonfils-Stanton Foundation, 150
Bongo Billy's, 324
Booth Creek Falls Trail, 189–90
booties for dogs, 7, 366, 369–70
Borrow-a-Dog, 207
Boulder, 79, 80–84, 90–92, 94–98, 99–101
Boulder Creek Path, 83–84
Boulder Emergency Pet Clinic, 101
Boulder Hiking Trails (Cushman and Cushman), 80
Boulder Lake, 174–75
Boulder's Thrift and Gift Shop, 95
Bowhaus, 98
Box Canyon Falls and Park, 276
Boyd Lake Veterinary Center, 123
Boy Scout Trail, 212–13
Breckenridge, 177, 180–81, 182
Breckenridge Barkery, The, 181
Bridal Veil Falls, 276
Brighton, 22, 39, 74

Broadmoor Bluffs Kennel, 363
Broadview Kennels, 64
Broadway Animal Hospital and Pet Center, 97
Brooks Veterinary Service, 158
Broomfield, 22–23, 39, 60, 65, 74
Broomfield County Commons Dog Park, 22–23
Brush, 128
Buckskin Joe Frontier Town and Railway, 327
Buena Vista, 315–16, 318–20, 328, 329
Buena Vista Canine Classic, 327–28
Buena Vista Veterinary Clinic, 329
Buena Vista Wildlife Trail, 316
Buffalo Bill's Grave, 58–59
Bull Canyon Wilderness Study Area, 222
Bureau of Land Management (BLM) land, 5
Burlington, 129–30, 132
Byers, 130
Byers Peak Veterinary Clinic, 158

C
Calhan, 349
Camp Bow Wow: Black Canyon area, 247; Boulder area, 97; Colorado Springs area, 363, 364; Denver area, 65, 70, 71, 72; Fort Collins area, 122–23; Greeley-Northeastern Plains area, 131
Camp Bow Wow Denver Central, 66
Camp Bow Wow Denver Southeast, 67
Camp Bow Wow DIA, 64
Camp Bow Wow LoDo, 66–67
campgrounds: Arkansas River Valley area, 326; Aspen, 207; Black Canyon area, 247; Boulder area, 94; Central City-Clear Creek County area, 105; Colorado Springs area, 359–60; Denver area, 57; Durango area, 298; Estes Park, 143; Fort Collins area, 119–20; Glenwood Springs area, 219; Grand Junction area, 238; Greeley-Northeastern Plains area, 131; Gunnison-Crested Butte-Lake City area, 263; Mesa Verde area, 286; Northwestern Colorado, 226; Pueblo and Southeastern Plains, 338; San Luis Valley area, 313; Steamboat Springs-North Park area, 168–69; Summit County, 180; Telluride-Ouray-Silverton area, 275; Vail-Leadville area,

195; Winter Park-Grand Lake-Granby area, 157
Canine Campus: Colorado Springs area, 363; Denver area, 73
Canine Classic, 96
Canine Corral Dog Park, 21
Canine Cottage, 247
Canine Fashion Show, 208
Canine Fitness and Fun Center, 62, 67
Canine 4K Feline No-Way Walk/Run, 180
Canines' Canyon, 70
Canines Unlimited, 226
Cañon City, 317, 320–21, 328, 329
Canyons of the Ancients National Monument, 278
Canyon View Dog Park, 230
Carbondale, 210–11, 215, 219–20
Caribou, 369
Carolyn Holmberg Preserve at Rock Creek Farm, 87–88
carsickness, 4
Cascade, 349
Castle Rock, 36, 39, 62, 65–66, 74, 77
Castlewood Canyon State Park, 36–37
Cause for Paws, A, 95–96
Cave of the Winds, 362
Cedaredge, 234
Cedar Hill Kennel, 220
Cedarwood Animal Clinic, 287
Centennial, 39–40, 74
Centennial Park, 31–32
Central City, 103
Central Veterinary Emergency Services, 77
Chatfield State Park, 5, 33
Chautauqua Park, 83
Cheesman Park, 19
Cherry Creek State Park, 5, 33–34
Cheyenne Mountain State Park, 5, 342, 348
Cheyenne Mountain Zoo and Will Rogers Shrine of the Sun, 362
Chihuahua Gulch, 171
Chimney Rock Archaeological Area, 299
Chipita Park, 349
Cimarron, 244
City Bark Denver, 67
City Bark LoDo, 62, 67
City Bark Parker, 72
City Bark Too-Englewood, 69
City Park, 19
Clifton, 234, 238
Club Pet, 72
Coal Creek Trail: Boulder area, 87; Grand Junction area, 228–29
Coaldale, 321–22
Cold Nose Warm Heart Pet Care, 197
Coleman, 372–73
Collbran, 234
Colorado Barkery, 324
Colorado City, 333
Colorado Disc Dog Frisbee Competitions: Denver

area, 58; Summit County, 181
Colorado Division of Wildlife, 6
Colorado Dog Academy, 65
Colorado Flyball/Team RUFF, 58
Colorado Mountain Club (CMC), 80, 137
Colorado National Monument, 233
Colorado Petfitters, 19, 63
Colorado riverfront trails, 232
Colorado's Fourteeners: From Hikes to Climbs (Roach), 366
Colorado Springs, 342–56, 359–65
Colorado Springs Canine Frisbee Championships, 362
Colorado Springs Heart Walk, 361
Colorado Trail/Junction Creek, 290
Colorado Veterinary Clinic, 340
Columbine, 164–65
Columbine Animal Hospital, 77
Columbine Lake, 149–50
Comanche National Grasslands, 330–31
Commons Park, 18–19
Confluence Park, 242
Conifer, 26, 74
Conifer Community Park, 26
Conundrum Creek Trail, 203
Cool Pooch Sport Water Bottle, 373
Copley Lake, 250
Copper Mountain, 177–78
Cortez, 278, 281–82, 287–88
Cortez Adobe Animal Hospital, 287
Cortez Animal Bed and Breakfast, 287
Cortez Centennial Park, 278
Cosmo's Retail Store and Bakery, 61
Cotopaxi, 322
Cottonwood Kennels, 98
Cottonwood Ranch and Kennel, 247
Cottonwood Veterinary Service, 329
Coulson Gulch, 134–35
Country Kennels, 328
Countryside Kennels, 363
Country Squire Pet Resort, 123
Craig, 223, 226, 227
Crawford, 244–45, 247
Crawford State Park, 242
Crazy River Dog Contest, 169
Creature Comforts Pet Retreat, 123
Creede, 308–9, 314
Creede Animal Clinic, 314
Crested Butte, 249, 250–51, 255–57, 263–64
Crested Butte Mountain, 251

Crestone, 309
Cripple Creek, 342, 356–57
Cripple Creek Narrow Gauge Railroad, 360
Critter Sitters and Outfitters, 264
Crosier Mountain, 133–34
Crown Hill Park, 23
Crown Mountain Dog Park, 200–201
Cru Vin Dogs, 59
Crystal Glen Kennel, 123
Crystal Lake, 173
Cuchara, 333
Cucumber Gulch Preserve, 176
Cuerno Verde Rest Area, 340
Cumbres and Toltec Scenic Railroad, 304
Curecanti National Recreation Area, 4–5, 251–52

D
Daily Wag, 67
Dapper Dog Day Spa, 99
Davidson Mesa Dog Run Area, 87
Dawson's Guide to Colorado's Fourteeners (Dawson), 366
daycare for dogs: Arkansas River Valley area, 328; Aspen, 208–9; Black Canyon area, 247; Boulder area, 97–99; Central City-Clear Creek County area, 106; Colorado Springs area, 363–64; Denver area, 64–74; Durango area, 299–300; Estes Park, 143; Fort Collins area, 122–23; Glenwood Springs area, 219–20; Grand Junction area, 238–39; Greeley-Northeastern Plains area, 131; Gunnison-Crested Butte-Lake City area, 264; Mesa Verde area, 287; Northwestern Colorado, 226; overview, 10; Pueblo and Southeastern Plains, 339–40; San Luis Valley area, 313–14; Steamboat Springs-North Park area, 169–70; Summit County, 181; Telluride-Ouray-Silverton area, 276; Vail-Leadville area, 196–97; Winter Park-Grand Lake-Granby area, 158
Debeque, 215–16
Deer Creek Canyon Park, 28, 31
Deleff Kennels, 247
Del Norte, 309–10
Delta, 245, 247–48
Delta Veterinary Clinic, 247
Den Doggie Daycare, The, 71
Denver, 16, 17–19, 40–49, 59–60, 61–62, 63, 66–69, 74–75, 77
Destiny's Kennel, 122
Devil's Thumb Pass, 148–49

Devon's Dog Park at Greenland Open Space, 34–35
DIA Dog Club, 64
Difficult Creek, 201
Digger's at Dad Clark Park, 32
Digstown, 67–68
Dillon, 178, 181
Dinosaur, 224
Dinosaur Hill, 233
Dinosaur National Monument, 222–23
Dirty Dog, The, 60
Divine Canine, The, 99
DnR Kennels, 181
Dog and I, The, 73
Dog Bar & Grill, 333
Dog City, 98
Dog Club, The, 123
Dog Days Inn Pet Hotel, 313–14
Dog Dayz at Scott Carpenter Pool, 96
Dog Den, The, 181
Dog Digs, 372
Dog First Aid (American National Red Cross), 11
Doggie Depot, 98
Doggie Dips and Chips, 122
Doggie Dude Ranch, 71, 73
Doggie Olympics, 120
Doggie Park, 211
Doggie Pause, 69
Dog House, The: Denver area, 69; Greeley-Northeastern Plains area, 131; Summit County, 181
Dog Park at Carter Park, 173–74
Dog Park at Cheyenne Meadows Park, 345–46
Dog Park at Glendale Farm Open Space, 35
Dog Park at Rampart Park, 346
Dog Park in Bayou Gulch Regional Park, 35
Dog Park in Fairgrounds Regional Park, 35–36
dog parks. See trails and dog parks
Dog Savvy, 63
Dog Spot, The, 98
dog tags, 4
DogTerra, 180
Dog-Topia, 6
Dogtopia of Highlands Ranch, 70
Dog Training Area at Union Reservoir, 86
Dolores, 278, 282–84, 286–87
Dolores Walking Trail, 279–80
Dominguez and Escalante Ruins Hike, 280
Door Veterinary Hospital, 247
Dotsero, 216
Double Dog Pub, 207
Double J Cross Kennel, 328
Dove Creek, 285
Downtown Dog, The, 68
Drake, 137
Duncan Park, 32
Duncan Trail, 242–43
Dundee Memorial Animal Care Center, 328, 329

Durango, 289–92, 293–95, 299, 300
Durango Animal Hospital, 300
Durango Dog Park, 290
Durango Mountain Park, 291–92
Durango & Silverton Narrow Gauge Railroad, 293

E
Eads, 333–34
Eagle, 192
Eagle-Vail Animal Hospital/Vail Animal ER, 196, 197
Earth Dog Denver, 62, 68
East Boulder Dog Park, 80
Eaton Veterinary Clinic, 339, 340
Edwards, 192, 197
Eldorado Canyon State Park, 84–85
Eldorado Springs, 84–85
Eleven Mile State Park, 342
El Jebel, 209
Elk Meadow Park/Off-Leash Dog Area, 25–26
Ella's Walk in Memory of Meredith Hope Emerson, 96
emergency care for dogs (ER): Arkansas River Valley area, 329; Aspen, 209; Black Canyon area, 247–48; Boulder area, 100–101; Central City–Clear Creek County area, 106; Colorado Springs area, 365; Denver area, 77–78; Durango area, 300; Estes Park, 144; Fort Collins area, 124; Glenwood Springs area, 220; Grand Junction area, 239; Greeley-Northeastern Plains area, 132; Gunnison-Crested Butte–Lake City area, 264; Mesa Verde area, 287–88; Northwestern Colorado, 227; overview, 10–12; Pueblo and Southeastern Plains, 340–41; San Luis Valley area, 314; Steamboat Springs–North Park area, 170; Summit County, 182; Telluride-Ouray-Silverton area, 276; Vail-Leadville area, 197; Winter Park–Grand Lake-Granby area, 158
Englewood, 31–32, 49–50, 69, 75, 77
Englewood Canine Corral, 32
Erie, 97, 98, 100
Estes Park, 133–43
Estes Park Pet Lodge, 143
Estes Valley Dog Park, 134
Evans, 127, 131, 132
events: Arkansas River Valley area, 327–28; Aspen, 208; Boulder area, 95–96; Colorado Springs area, 361–62; Denver area, 57–58; Estes Park, 143; Fort Collins area,

120–21; Greeley-Northeastern Plains area, 131; Gunnison-Crested Butte–Lake City area, 263–64; Northwestern Colorado, 226; Pueblo and Southeastern Plains, 339; Steamboat Springs-North Park area, 169; Summit County, 180–81
Evergreen, 56, 75, 77
Evergreen Animal Hospital: Central City-Clear Creek County area, 106; Denver area, 77; Vail-Leadville area, 196
Evergreen Kennel and Grooming, 69

F
Fairplay, 178
Falls Creek Meadow, 290–91
Farfel's Farm, 95
Fast and the Furriest, The, 120–21
Feet and Fur, 339
Felix and Fido, 169
Fetchers Dog Care, 68
Fido's Field at Foothills Park, 32
FIDOS (Friends Interested in Dogs and Open Space), 79
Field Guide: First Aid Emergency Care for the Hunting, Working, and Outdoor Dog (Acker), 11
Fire Hydrant Five, 120
Firestone, 21
first-aid, 11
First Aid for Dogs: What to Do When Emergencies Happen (Fogle), 11
Fish Creek Falls, 163
Fisher's Peak Veterinary Clinic, 340, 341
Flagler, 130
Flame Out Five, 120
Flatirons Vista/Doudy Draw, 83
Flat Tops Wilderness Area, 222
Flophouse Foam Pad, 372
Florence, 317, 322
Florissant Fossil Beds National Monument, 348
Foothills Community Dog Park, 80–81
Foothills to Mount Evans: West-of-Denver Trail Guide (Rathbun and Ringrose), 17, 102
Foothills Trail, 112
For Paws Bakery, 61
For Pets' Sake Thrift Shop, 181
Forsberg Iron Spring Dog Park, 25
Fort Collins, 110–11, 112–14, 115–17, 120–21, 122–24
Fort Collins Veterinary Emergency Hospital, 124
Fort Garland, 310
For the Love of Dog, 69–70
Fort Lupton, 128
Fort Morgan, 128, 132

Fort Morgan Veterinary Clinic, 132
Fossil Creek Dog Park, 111
Fountain, 357, 364, 365
Fountain Creek Regional Park, 347
Four Corners National Monument, 278
Fourmile Veterinary Clinic, 329
Four Paws & Co., 97
Four Paw Spa, 339
fourteeners (mountains), 366–67
Fowler, 334, 339
Fraser, 148, 152, 158
Frederick, 21
Fremont Veterinary Clinic, 329
Fremont Veterinary Hospital, 328, 329
French Gulch, 172–73
Frisco, 178–79, 180, 182
Frisco Animal Hospital, 182
Fruita, 228, 235, 238, 239
Fuller Dog Park, 18
Furry Friends Festival, 96
Furry Scurry, 57

G
Garden of the Dogs Off-Leash Dog Area, 344
Gateway, 235
gear for dogs, 368–73
Georgetown, 103, 104–5, 106
Georgetown Loop Railroad, 106
Ghost Town Wild West Museum, 362
giardia and drinking water, 11
Gigi's, 361
Glassier Park, 211
Glendale, 51–52, 69–70, 76
Glenwood Canyon Recreation Path, 210, 213
Glenwood Springs, 210, 211–13, 216–17, 219, 220
Golden, 26–27, 50–51, 70, 76
Golden Gate Canyon State Park, 22, 103
Golden Ponds Park and Nature Area, 86–87
Gould, 165
Granby, 148, 152–53, 158
Granby Veterinary Clinic, 158
Grand Junction, 228, 230–33, 235–37, 238–39
Grand Lake, 148, 153–55, 158
Grand Mesa, 228–30, 237
Grand Mesa Veterinary Hospital, 248
Grandview Dog Park, 24
Granite, 192
Granite Gear, 369, 370, 371
Gray Copper Gulch, 265–66
Great Bark Dog Park, 85
Great Sand Dunes National Park and Preserve, 4, 304–5
Greeley, 125, 126–27, 131, 132
Green Lake, 250–51
Green Mountain Falls, 357

Green Mountain Park, 25
Green Valley Ranch East Dog Park, 18
Greenway Park, 18
Greenwood Village, 51, 61, 76
grooming and dog washes: Boulder area, 96–97; Colorado Springs area, 361; Denver area, 59–61, 63; Fort Collins area, 122; Glenwood Springs area, 219; Pueblo and Southeastern Plains, 339
Guffey, 322
Gunbarrel Veterinary Clinic, 98
Gunnison, 249, 251–53, 257–60, 264
Gunnison Bluffs Trail, 230
Gunnison National Forest, 249
Guyot Designs, 371

H
Hallam Lake Nature Preserve, 203
Hamilton, 223–24
Hanging Lake, 214
Happy Dog Daycare, 68
Happy Hounds, 97, 99
Happy Paws Pet Spa, 299
Happy Tails Dog Park, 22
Happy Tails Dog Ranch, 122
Happy Tails Dog Wash and Pet Supply, 106
Harper Lake, 88
Hartman Rocks, 252
Harvest Challenge 5K Run/ Walk, 96
Harvey Gap State Park, 5, 214
Hawthorne Park, 234
health certificates, 4, 10
Healthy Bone, The, 97
Healthy Hounds & Fat Cats, 299
heatstroke, 11, 233
Heavenly Dog, 59
Hells Hole, 103–4
Henderson, 52
Henney (Green Mountain Reservoir), 179
Herman Gulch, 102–3
Hibernation Sleeping Bag, 372–73
High Country Kennels, 71
Highlands Ranch, 32–33, 52, 62, 70–71, 76, 77
Highline State Park, 232
High Tails Dog and Cat Outfitters, 219, 220
Hiking in Heaven: A Crested Butte Trail Guide (Hall), 249
Hiking the 'Boat (White-Crane), 160
Hiking Trails of Southwest Colorado (Pixler), 265
Hobnob, 62–63, 71
Holyoke, 128–29
Homer's Run Dog Park, 26
Honey Rock Dogs Boarding Kennel, 226
Horsetooth Mountain Open Space, 112–13
Hotchkiss, 245–46

Hot Sulphur Springs, 148, 155
Hound Hill, 32–33
Hounds on the Hill, 68
Hovensweep National Monument, 4, 287
Howard, 322–23
Howard Heuston Dog Park, 80
Howelsen Hill Trail System, 162
Humane Society of Pagosa Springs, 299
Hunter Creek/Hunter Valley Trail, 198–99
hunting season, 5–6
hypothermia, 11

I
Idaho Springs, 103–4, 105–6
Idalia, 130
Ignacio, 299–300
Independence Ghost Town, 208
Indian Peaks Wilderness Area, 133, 148
Indian Tree Pet Lodge, 64
Intermountain Humane Society Dog Walk, 57–58
International Dog Weight Pull Competition, 143

J
James L. Voss Veterinary Teaching Hospital, 124
Jason Park, 32
Jeanne Golay Trail, 212
jeep touring, 275
Jesse Weaver, 211
Jewell Dog Park, 24
Jim Creek Trail, 150
Johnny Park, 133
Johnson's Pet Motel, 339
Jud Wiebe Trail, 268
Julesburg, 129

K
Kamp-4-Paws, 339
K-9 Bed and Biscuit, 131
K-9 Castle, 71
K-9 Cube, 372
Kelty, 369
Kenline Veterinary Clinic, 328, 329
Kennedy Dog Park, 18
Keystone, 178, 180
Keystone Mountain, 175–76
Keystone River Run Gondola, 180
K-9 First Aid Kits, 373
K9-5K and Pawtober Fest, 362
KLB Boarding Kennel, 328
Kokopelli Animal Hospital, 239
Kremmling, 165–66
Krugman Small Animal Clinic, 339, 340
K-9 Uphill, 208

L
Lafayette, 85–86, 97, 98, 100
Lair o' the Bear Park, 28–29
La Junta, 334, 339, 340
Lake Christine and Toner Creek State Wildlife Areas, 203

Lake City, 249, 253, 260–62
Lake Estes Trail, 136
Lake George, 357
Lake Pueblo State Park, 331
Lakewood, 23, 25, 52–53, 61, 62–63, 71, 76, 77
Lamar, 334–35, 339, 340
Lamar Veterinary Clinic, 340
Land of Ahs Kennel, 364
La Plata County Humane Society, 299
Laporte, 117, 124
LAPS (League for Animals and People of the Summit), 171
Las Animas, 335
Lathrop State Park, 331–32
Laund-Ur-Mutt: Boulder area, 96–97; Denver area, 60; Fort Collins area, 122
La Veta, 335
Lazy Dog Ranch, 123
Leadville, 183–86, 192–93, 195–96, 197
Leadville, Colorado & Southern Railroad Company, 195–96
Leadville Veterinary Clinic, 197
leashes, 6, 371–72
Lily Mountain, 135
Limon, 130, 132
Limon Veterinary Clinic, 132
Linda's Pet Care Services, 143
Lion Gulch, 136
Lion's Den, 59
Little Doggie Daycare and Boarding, 68
Little Paws Dog Care, 276
Little Tail, The, 219–20
Littleton, 36, 53, 60, 62, 63, 71–72, 76, 77
Lizard Head Wilderness, 278
Lone Tree, 53–54
Long Lake, 254
Longmont, 86–87, 92–93, 95, 96, 97, 99, 100, 101
Lookout Mountain Nature Center and Preserve, 16
Lookout Mountain Trail, 29
Lory State Park, 113
Lost Creek Wilderness Area, 17
Lost Lake: Boulder area, 88–89; Vail-Leadville area, 188
Louisville, 87–88, 93, 96, 99, 100
Louisville Community Park, 87
Loveland, 111–12, 114, 122, 123, 124
Loveland Dog Park, 111–12
Lov-in Touch Pet Chalet and Spaw, A, 98
Lower Buckwater Draw, 222
Lowry Pueblo, 287
Lucky Dog Resort and Training Center, 363
Lyons, 88, 93–94

M
Mad Creek/Swamp Park, 160–61
Mancos, 278, 285–86, 288
Mancos State Park/Chicken Creek Trail, 278–79
Mancos Valley Veterinary Hospital, 288
Manitou Cliff Dwellings Museum, 360
Manitou Springs, 357–58, 365
Marble, 210, 217–18
Marina Mutt Contest, 181
Maroon Bells, 202–3
Marshall Mesa, 81
Matthews Winters, 16
MaxFund Lucky Mutt Strut, 57
Maxwell Falls Trail, 26–27
McDonald Creek, 231
Meadow Mountain, 186
Meeker, 224–26, 227
Meeker Classic Sheepdog Championship Trials, 226
Meredith (Ruedi Reservoir), 207
Mesa, 237
Mesa Verde National Park, 278, 280
Meyer Ranch Park, 30
Midland Trail, 183–84
Mile High Mutts, 68
Minturn, 193–94
Moffatt, 310
Monarch Pass area, 316–17, 323
Monarch Scenic Tram, 327
Monte Vista, 304, 310, 314
Monte Vista Animal Clinic, 314
Montezuma Veterinary Clinic, 287
Montrose, 242–44, 246, 247, 248
Montrose Veterinary Clinic, 248
Monument, 358, 364, 365
Monument Valley Park Trail, 347
Moore Animal Hospital Pet Camp, 123
Morningstar Veterinary Clinic, 248
Mosca, 310
Mountain Daug Outfitters, 158
Mountain Dog Biscuit and Gifts, 196
Mountain Shadows Animal Hospital, 328, 329
Mountainsmith, 368
Mountain Tails, 264
Mountain View Pet Lodge, 339–40
Mountain Village, 265
Mount Evans Rd, 105–6
Mount Falcon Park, 30
Mount Galbraith Park, 16
Mount Sanitas, 81–82
Mouthfuls, 61
Mt. Bachelor Pad, 372
Mt. Werner Veterinary Hospital, 169, 170
Muddy Paws Bath House Self-Serve Dog Wash, 59–60

Mueller State Park, 5, 342, 348
Museum of Outdoor Arts, The, 59
Mutt-Mutt Palace, 69
Mutt Puddles, 60

N

Nathrop, 323, 328
national forests and national forest wilderness areas, 5
national parks and monuments, 3–5
Naturita, 270
Nederland, 88–89, 94, 99, 100
New Castle, 218
Newlin Creek Trail, 317
Niwot, 99, 100
North Cheyenne Cañon Park, 346–47
Northglenn, 21–22, 54, 72, 76
North Park, 160, 163–64
North Pole and Santa's Workshop, 362
Northside Emergency Pet Clinic, 78
North Star Nature Preserve, 203–4
North Sterling Reservoir State Park, 125–26
North Tenmile Trail, 174
North Trail, 188–89
Northwest Animal Hospital and Pet Care Center, 363
Northwestern Colorado, 222–27
Northwest Greenbelt, 32
Norwood, 276

O

Oak Creek, 166
O'Fallon Park, 31
Oh-Be-Dogful Pet Ranch, 264
Ohio City, 262
Old Spanish Trail, 231
OllyDog, 368–69, 371
Only Natural Pet Store, 94–95
Ouray, 265–67, 270–71, 276
Ouray Hiking Guide (Kent), 265

P

packing list, 10
Pagosa Springs, 289, 292, 295–97, 300
Palisade, 237–38
Palmer Park, 344–45
Pampered Pets, 299–300
Pansy's K/9 Corral, 99
Paonia State Park, 242
Parachute, 218, 220
Parachute Veterinary Clinic, 220
Park #1 and Park #2, 86
Parker, 54, 60–61, 72–73, 76–77
Parlin, 262
Parshall, 155
Paw Above Canine Boarding Service, A, 363
Paw Cottage, 340
Pawnee Buttes, 126
Paws and Sneakers, 131

Paws Field, 65
Paw Spa, A, 60
Payton Classic, 121
P.C.'s Pantry for Dogs and Cats, 95
Peak to Peak Animal Hospital, 99
Peakview Animal Hospital, 339
Penrose, 328
Pet Emergency Treatment Services, 132
Peticular Care, 123
Pet Kare Clinic, 170
Pet Particulars, 238
PetsHotel at PetSmart: Colorado Springs area, 364; Denver area, 70, 71–72, 73; Fort Collins area, 123
Pet Spa, The, 238–39
Phippsburg, 166
Pierson Park, 133
Pike National Forest, 17, 342
Pikes Peak Cog Railway, 362
Pikes Peak Highway, 360
Pine, 27–28, 56
Pine Valley Ranch Park, 27–28
Pitkin, 262–63
Placerville, 271
Planet Dog, 371, 372
Playful Pooch, 69
Polo Springs Veterinary Hospital, 364
Poncha Springs, 323–24, 329
pooper scoopers, 6–7
Poopfest, 256
Poudre Canyon, 117–18
Poudre River Trail: Fort Collins area, 113–14; Greeley-Northeastern Plains area, 126–27
powderhounds. *See* skiing and snowshoeing
Power Bones, 372
Ptarmigan Lake, 315–16
Pueblo, 336–37, 339–40
Pueblo River Trails, 332
Pueblo West Boarding Kennels, 340
Pup N Suds, 61
Puppy Love, 299
Puppy Love Suds and Snacks, 60
Pup Stop, The, 64
Purr Y Paws, 60–61

R

Rabbit Valley Trail through Time, 232–33
Railyard Dogs, 17
Rainbow Lake, 175
Rampart Kennels, 364
Rangely, 226
Redcliff, 194
Red Creek, 289–90
Red Feather Lakes, 110, 118–19
Red Rock Canyon Open Space Off-Leash Dog Trails, 345
Red Rocks Park and Amphitheatre, 58
Red Rover Resort, 169
Redstone, 210, 218–19

REI's Adventure Dog Dream Bed, 373
Remington and Friends Neighborhood Bakery, 61
Reservoir Hill, 292
resources/information: Akansas River Valley area, 329; Aspen, 209; Black Canyon area, 248; Boulder area, 101; Central City-Clear Creek County area, 106; Colorado Springs area, 365; Denver area, 78; Durango area, 300; Estes Park, 144; Fort Collins area, 124; Glenwood Springs area, 221; Grand Junction area, 239; Greeley-Northeastern Plains area, 132; Gunnison-Crested Butte-Lake City area, 264; Mesa Verde area, 288; Northwestern Colorado, 227; Pueblo and Southeastern Plains, 341; San Luis Valley area, 314; Steamboat Springs-North Park area, 170; Summit County, 182; Telluride-Ouray-Silverton area, 277; Vail-Leadville area, 197; Winter Park-Grand Lake-Granby area, 159
restaurants, 12
(Re)Tail Therapy, 63
Rico, 286
Ridgway, 267–68, 271–72, 276
Ridgway Animal Hospital, 276
Ridgway State Park, 268
Rifle, 213–14, 219, 220
Rifle Falls State Park, 213–14
Riggs Hill, 233
Rio Cucharas Veterinary Clinic, 340, 341
Rio Grande National Forest, 304
Rio Grande Trail, 201–2
Rita Valentine Park, 161
River Run Dog Park, 211–12
River Trail, 269
Riverview Animal Hospital, 300
RK Pet Ranch, 170
Rocky Ford, 337
Rocky Mountain Dog Ranch, 158
Rocky Mountain K-9 Accessories, 368
Rocky Mountain National Park, 133, 136, 148, 150
Rocky Mountain Pet Resort, 170
Rocwind Canine Center, 64–65
Rollinsville, 99
Rough and Ready Park, 86
Rover Retreat: Boulder area, 70, 73–74; Denver area, 98
Rover Run Park, 125
Rover's Ranch, 123
Rover's Run, 33

Roxborough State Park, 5, 37
Royal Gorge Bridge and Park, 326–27
Royal Gorge Route Railroad, 328
Ruffwear, 6, 369, 370–72, 373
RUFhouse Doggy Daycare, 131

S

Sage Valley Pet Center, 70
Saguache, 310
Salida, 324–25, 328, 329
Samson Park, 59
Sand Canyon Trail, 279
San Isabel, 325–26
San Isabel National Forest, 315
San Juan National Forest, 289
San Juan Veterinary Clinic, 248
San Juan Veterinary Hospital, 300
San Luis State Park, 305
San Luis Valley, 304–14
San Miguel Veterinary Clinic, 276
Sargents, 263
Scotland Trail, 229–30
Second Chance Thrift Stores, 95
Seeley, Kate, 256
Serious Fun at West Ridge, 131
Settlers Park, 21
Seven Bridges Trail, 342–43
Seven Falls, 360–61
Shampooch Dog Wash, 60
shopping/supplies for dogs: Arkansas River Valley area, 328; Aspen, 209; Black Canyon area, 247; Boulder area, 94–95, 99–100; Central City-Clear Creek County area, 106; Colorado Springs area, 361, 364–65; Denver area, 61, 63, 74–77; Durango area, 300; Estes Park, 143; Fort Collins area, 121–22, 123–24; Glenwood Springs area, 220; Grand Junction area, 239; Greeley-Northeastern Plains area, 132; Gunnison-Crested Butte-Lake City area, 264; Mesa Verde area, 287; Northwestern Colorado, 227; Pueblo and Southeastern Plains, 340; San Luis Valley area, 314; Steamboat Springs-North Park area, 169, 170; Summit County, 181, 182; Telluride-Ouray-Silverton area, 276; Vail-Leadville area, 196, 197; Winter Park-Grand Lake-Granby area, 158
Signal Peak, 252–53
Silver Bullet Gondola, 169
Silver Cliff, 328, 329
Silver Dollar Lake, 103
Silver Queen Gondola, 208

Silverthorne, 179–80, 181
Silverton, 265, 272–73, 275
Simba Ranch, 99
Singletree Park, 24–25
skiing and snowshoeing: Arkansas River Valley area, 318; Aspen, 204–5; Boulder area, 89–90; Central City-Clear Creek County area, 104; Colorado Springs area, 348–49; Durango area, 292–93; Estes Park, 137; Fort Collins area, 114–15; Glenwood Springs area, 210–14; Grand Junction area, 233; Gunnison-Crested Butte-Lake City area, 249–53; Mesa Verde area, 280; Northwestern Colorado, 223; overview, 7; Steamboat Springs-North Park area, 160–64; Summit County, 176; Telluride-Ouray-Silverton area, 265–69; Vail-Leadville area, 183–90; Winter Park-Grand Lake-Granby area, 151–52
skijoring clinics, 157
Skyline Ranch and Kennels, 220
Smooch the Pooch, 72
Smuggler Mountain Rd., 198
snake bites, 11
Snowmass, 207
Soda Creek, 161–62
Soft Gold Dog Park, 111
Southeast Colorado Veterinary Clinic, 341
South Fork, 310–12
South Platte Ranger District, 17
South Valley Park, 30–31
Spawlash, 60
Spinney Mountain State Park, 342
Spring Canyon Dog Park, 111
Spring Creek, 162–63
Spring Creek Park, 161
Spring Creek Trail, 114
Springfield, 337, 341
St. Vrain Greenway, 87
St. Vrain Mountain, 133
Stapleton Dog Park, 18
State Forest State Park, 163–64
state parks, 5
Steamboat Lake, 166
Steamboat Ski Area/Mount Werner, 162
Steamboat Springs, 160–63, 166–68, 169–70
Steamboat Veterinary Hospital, 170
Stephen Day Park, 86
Stephens Park, 187
Sterling, 125–26, 129, 132
Strasburg, 130
Stratton, 130–31
Struttin Pup, 97
Sud Z Pup, 60–61
Summit County, 171–82
Sunnyside Trail, 200
Sunrise Kennels, 364

Superior, 97, 100
Sweitzer Lake State Park, 242
swimming pools: Boulder area, 96; Denver area, 62–63

T
Tabernash, 148, 155–56, 158
Tails Up, 65–66
Tail Waggers, 131
Tarryall, 358
Telluride, 265, 268–69, 273–75, 276
Telluride Bluegrass Festival, 276
Telluride Hiking Guide (Kees), 265
Telluride Veterinary Clinic, 276
Tenaker Pet Care Center, 65
Tenderfoot Trail, 175
Teva Mountain Games Dog Competitions, 196
Thornton, 54, 60
Three Dog Bakery, 61–62
Timberline Dog Boarding Company, 99
TLC Veterinary Clinic, 340
Tomichi Pet Care Center, 264
Tony Grampsas Dog Park, 26
Town and Country Veterinary Hospital, 220
Town & Country Animal Hospital, 264
Track Jacket, 6
Trailhead Leash Program, 79–80
trails and dog parks: Arkansas River Valley area, 315–19; Aspen, 198–204; Black Canyon area, 242–44; Boulder area, 79–89; Central City-Clear Creek County area, 102–4, 105–6; Colorado Springs area, 342–48; Denver area, 16–37; Durango area, 289–92; Estes Park, 133–36; Fort Collins area, 110–14; Glenwood Springs area, 210–14; Grand Junction area, 228–33; Greeley-Northeastern Plains area, 125–27; for guide dogs and owners, 150; Gunnison-Crested Butte-Lake City area, 249–53; land-use policies, 3–5; Mesa Verde area, 278–80; Northwest Colorado, 222–23; Ouray, 265–67; Pueblo and Southeastern Plains, 330–33; rating system, 3; San Luis Valley area, 304–5; Steamboat Springs-North Park area, 160–64; Summit County, 171–76; trail etiquette, 6–7; Vail-Leadville area, 183–90; Winter Park-Grand Lake-Granby area, 148–51
travel bags, 368

travel bowls, 370–71
travel kennels and crates, 9, 372
travel tips, 4, 10
Trinidad, 332–33, 337–38, 340, 341
Trinidad Animal Clinic, 341
Trinidad Lake State Park, 332–33
Turquoise Lake Trail, 185–86
12 Short Hikes book series (Salcedo), 17
Twin Lakes, 194
Twin Lakes Open Space, 82–83
Two Ponds National Wildlife Refuge, 24
Two Rivers Veterinary Clinic, 248

U
Ultrapaws, 370
Uncompahgre National Forest, 249
Unleashed Ultimate Dog Center, 97
Upper Piney River Trail, 189
Upper Valley Kennels, 238
US Air Force Academy, 360
U-Shampooch, 60
Ute Mountain Tribal Park, 280
Ute Trail, 202

V
vaccines, 4, 10, 11
Vail, 183, 186–90, 194–95, 196
Vail Doggie Day Spa and Lodging, 196
Vail Mountain, 190
Vallecito Lake, 289, 297–98
Valley Emergency Pet Care, 209, 220
Valmont Dog Park, 80
Van Bibber Park, 23–24
VCA Alameda East Veterinary Hospital, 77
VCA All Pets Animal Hospital Boulder, 98, 101
VCA Douglas County Animal Hospital, 77
VCA Tenaker Animal Hospital, 70–71
VCA Veterinary Specialists of Northern Colorado, 124
Veltus Park, 220
Veterinary Emergency Center, 239
Veterinary Medical Clinic, 132
Vibrant Pet Animal Hospital, 287–88
Victor, 342, 358
Villa Grove, 312–13
Vogel Canyon, 330–31
Voice and Sight Dog Tag Program, 79
Vondy and Powell Veterinarians, 132

W
Wag-N-Tails Pet Boarding and Grooming, 328
Wag 'n Trail, 57

Wag N' Wash, 361
Wag N' Wash Healthy Pet Center, 62
Wag Shop, The, 60
Wagz Colorado, 121
Walden, 168
Walkin' the Dog, 196
Walsenburg, 338, 340, 341
Waneka Lake Park, 85–86
Washington Park, 18
Waterdog Lakes, 316–17
Waterton Canyon, 37
Watkins, 73
Weehawken Trail, 267
Weekender Travel Feedbag, 372
Wellington, 119
West Arvada Dog Park, 20–21
Westcliffe, 326
West Grouse Creek, 187–88
Westminster, 19–20, 54–55, 73, 77, 78
Westminster Hills Dog Park, 19–20
West Ridge Animal Hospital, 132
Wheat Ridge, 55, 60, 73–74, 77, 78
Wheat Ridge Animal Hospital, 78
Whisker Ball, 339
Whispering Pines Pet Resort, 99
White Ranch, 16
White River National Forest, 222
Whitewater Creek Trail, 229
Whitman Park, 234
Whole Pets, 97
Wilder Gulch, 172
Willow Creek Wilderness Study Area, 222
Willow Tree Kennels, 299
Wind Mountain Dog Training, 340
Windsor, 127–28, 131, 132
Winston's Doggy Playhouse, 72–73
Winter Park, 148, 156–57
Winter Park Outdoor Center, 150
WolfPacks, 369
Woodland Park, 358–59
Woodmen Kennels, 364
Woods Walk to Peanut Lake, 251
Wray, 129
W R Veterinary Clinic, 227
Wynetka Ponds Bark Park, 36

Y
Yampa, 168, 170
Yampa Core Trail, 163
Young Gulch, 110–11
Your Best Friends Boarding Kennel & Grooming House, 239
Yuma, 129

Z
Zen Dog, 19, 63
Zuke's, 372

About the Author

Cindy Hirschfeld is a freelancer writer and editor specializing in travel, skiing, and outdoor adventure for *The New York Times* and other newspapers and magazines. She has twice received the Harold S. Hirsch Award from the North American Snowsports Journalists Association for her articles on skiing. A New Jersey native, she has spent the past twenty years hiking, biking, climbing, skiing, and running in the mountains of Colorado. She lives in Basalt with her husband, Todd Hartley; son, Griffin; and their golden retriever, Clover, Aussie shepherd mix, Tansy, and black tabby, Blue.